The American Heritage Library

# PAUL REVERE AND THE WORLD HE LIVED IN

By Esther Forbes

Houghton Mifflin Company · Boston

Copyright © 1942 by Esther Forbes
Copyright © renewed 1969 by Linwood M. Erskine, Jr.

All rights reserved.

For information about permission to reproduce selections from
this book, write to Permissions, Houghton Mifflin Company,
215 Park Avenue South, New York, New York 10003.

*Library of Congress Cataloging-in-Publication Data*

Forbes, Esther.
  Paul Revere & the world he lived in / Esther Forbes.
      p.    cm.— (American Heritage library)
  Bibliography: p.
  Includes index.
  ISBN 0-395-08370-2
  1. Revere, Paul, 1735–1818.  2. Statesmen — Massachusetts —
Biography.   3. Massachusetts — Biography.   I. Title.  II. Title:
Paul Revere and the world he lived in.  III. Series
F69.R43F67    1988
974.4'03'0924 — dc19    87-29323
[B]                              CIP

Printed in the United States of America

FFG  12  11  10  9  8  7  6

The late Esther Forbes bequeathed the royalties from the sale of her
works to the American Antiquarian Society, Worcester, Massachusetts, where for years she had done most of her historical research.

American Heritage Library and the eagle logo are registered
trademarks of Forbes Inc. Their use is pursuant to a license
agreement with Forbes Inc.

Front cover painting: "Paul Revere" by Gilbert Stuart.
Courtesy of the Museum of Fine Arts, Boston, gift of
Joseph W., William B., and Edward H. R. Revere.

# ACKNOWLEDGMENTS

THIS BOOK was written in collaboration with my mother, Harriette M. Forbes, who has done most of the work on the original papers, court records, deeds, etc., newspapers, manuscript diaries, and letters — which is the hardest part of a book like this.

Mr. William B. Revere and Mr. Edward H. R. Revere kindly allowed us to study their great-grandfather's many volumes of papers. Miss Mary C. Rogers, Mr. Joseph Warren Revere Rogers, and Mrs. Nicholas P. T. Burke (great-grandchildren of Paul Revere's), have also been most kind in making available family records and in helping in the various problems that arose.

Mr. Clarence S. Brigham, Director of the American Antiquarian Society, has spent twenty-five years studying Paul Revere's engravings and tracing down (often in European libraries) the sources from which he worked. When his book on Revere as an engraver is published, our knowledge in this field will be tremendously enlarged. In the meantime he has let me reproduce the English version of 'A Warm Place — Hell' as an example of the close resemblance between Paul Revere's work and that of some of his contemporaries. It is because of his researches into the Pelham print of 'the Massacre' I can write so confidently that such a print was made. The American Antiquarian Society has by far the largest collection of Revere engravings as well as its marvellous library of books, manuscripts and periodicals dealing with America. A large part of the work on 'Paul Revere and the World He Lived In' was done under its generous dome. To both Mr. Brigham and the American Antiquarian Society I am more indebted than I can say.

Most of Paul Revere's own papers are in the Massachusetts Historical Society (as are other manuscripts used in this book — like the Dolbear Papers). I wish to thank the Society for their kindness and interest in the book.

Mrs. Yves Henry Buhler, in charge of silver at the Museum of Fine Arts, Boston; Mr. John Marshall Phillips, Curator of the Mabel Brady Garvan Collection at the Gallery of Fine Arts, Yale; and Miss Louisa Dresser, of the Worcester Art Museum, have all been of the greatest help with their knowledge, not only of colonial silversmiths and their work, but of the way life was lived at that time and for their contagious enthusiasm for this beautiful craft.

These are my major indebtednesses, but I should also mention the Boston Athenaeum (and Mr. Charles K. Bolton), the New England Historic Genealogical Society, the Boston Public Library, and the Bostonian Society.

ESTHER FORBES

WORCESTER, *September*, 1941

R𝑈13739𝑟1784

CHICAGO PUBLIC LIBRARY
ROGERS PARK BRANCH
6907 N. CLARK ST    60626

# CONTENTS

## I

### 1715–1735

## II

### 1735–1756

## III

### 1756–1764

# IV

## 1764–1769

# V

## 1770–1773

# VI

## 1773–1775

# VII

## 1775

money. By June the battle of Bunker Hill is fought. General Washington
catches Doctor Church red-handed.

# VIII

## 1776–1779

Paul Revere gets plans for a powder mill. When Gage and the Tories
leave Boston, he returns to North Square. As a dentist he is able to identify
Joseph Warren's body. Boston is afraid of its Tories. 'Joyce Jun'r' and
his cart. Lieutenant Colonel Revere is in command of Castle Island.
He fires upon Yankee ships. Lewis Ansart teaches him the founders'
arts. Other Frenchmen arrive. The strange death of Saint-Sauveur.
Alarums and excursions. The *Somerset's* guns are salvaged.

# IX

## 1779–1792

The Penobscot campaign proves a fiasco and hard times become even
harder. Thomas Hutchinson dies before the news of Yorktown. Paul
Revere tries commercial ventures, but silver is his main support. He
fights for a court martial, re-establishes his character, and writes letters
to his cousins in Guernsey and France. Massachusetts ratifies the Constitution, and Paul Revere's part. He sets up a foundry and casts the first
bell ever cast in Boston. 'A Madman gone to Boston.'

# X

## 1792–1818

Paul Revere (no longer young) is involved in civic projects and the welfare
of children, grandchildren, and friends. He discovers the secret of rolling
copper and establishes a great industry. He sheathes the *Constitution*,
the State House dome, and many ships. In Cantondale is his abode.
He and Rachel have their portraits painted, and live happily until the
end, which comes for Paul Revere on the tenth day of May, 1818.

# ILLUSTRATIONS

Following page 250

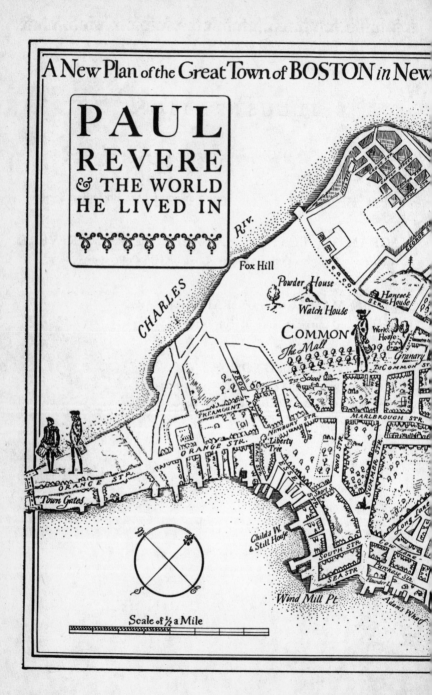

A New Plan of the Great Town of BOSTON in New

PAUL
REVERE
& THE WORLD
HE LIVED IN

Scale of ½ a Mile

England

Barton's Pt.

*from Price's Map of the Year 1769*

Spring Str.

*Charles River*

Leveret Str.

E. by N. Mill Dam

Ferry to Charles~Town *is about a half-Mile over*

Ferry

Hudson's Pt.

*Mill Cove*

Burial Place

Foundry

Lynd Str.

Stanford's Lane

Green Str.

Chambers Str.

Cambridge Str.

Maple Str.

Middlecot Str.

Salm Str.

Christ Church

Water Mill

Sudbury Str.

Back Str.

Cockrel Church

Hutchinson House

Charter St. House

Hannover Str.

Middle Str.

North Str.

Brattle Str.

Revere House

Clark House

Old North Meeting

Treamount Str.

So. Cornhill

Union Str.

Fish Str.

North Square

Ship Street

King's Chapel

Dock Sq.

Fish Str.

No. Battery

Old State House

Faneuil Hall

Cornhill

So. South Church

King Str.

Hitchbourn Wharfe

Clark's Wharf

Clark's Shipyard

7

*Old Wharfe*

6½

Kilby Str.

Oliver's Dock

Long Wharfe

Watts House

7

**HARBOUR**

Oliver Str.

Gale's Shipyard

Old Wharfe

6

Fort Hill

Fletchers Lane

Battery March

So. Battery

Rowe's Wharf

*Anchorage*

Griffin Wharf

7

Sam¹ Hanks Bryant 1941

# I

## 1715 – 1735

Apollos Rivoire comes to Boston. He serves Mr. John Coney and learns the silversmith's arts. He follows his trade, joins a church, and marries into the Hitchbourn family. On the first day of January, 1735, his eldest son is baptized Paul Revere.

*Paul Revere.*

Paul Revere's bookplate engraved by him. American Antiquarian Society.

## I

THERE had been week upon week of the cold grey fury of the North Atlantic, for it was mid-winter when the little refugee, Apollos Rivoire, made his crossing. At such a season only the hardiest of passengers ventured much above deck. Bunks were dank, bread wormy, beef tainted, and many of these small sailing ships never made port, but at least the Atlantic was crossed in great company. God brooded upon the face of these waters. His hand parted the mountainous waves. He upheld the ship. Even if one drowned, it was by the Providence of God. Apollos did not drown. He entered Massachusetts Bay either late in 1715 or early in 1716.

Land at last! The first gull, the seaweed and the changing color of the sea. The smell of the littoral — that blue cloud on the horizon, which is not a cloud but the hills of Milton. And then the wizen passengers dared crawl on deck and gaze about them.

The ship nosed its way cautiously among the icy islands. On one of them masons were building the first lighthouse to be set up in the western world. There on Nix's Mate rattled iron cages holding together bird-pecked skeletons of pirates. Apollos could hear the short happy bark of seals, the ferocious laughter of gulls. There was only one tortuous channel leading into the inner harbor. No ship could enter without almost brushing against the brass cannon of Castle Island. Above the fort floated the flag of England. Governor's Island was on the right. Next Bird Island, where gulls and terns nested. Then for the first time a boy standing upon deck could see the greatest port in all America — the famous prosperous town of Boston.

From where he stood it was apparent that Boston was almost
an island, being attached to the mainland by a flimsy mile-long
neck of mud-flats. Storm and high tide might rush over this weak
isthmus and then for a few hours Boston was an island indeed.
The promontory was made up of rough steep hills — three large
ones and a number of small ones. The valleys were covered by a
jumble of roofs. Chimneys fluttered their tatters of smoke. Bristling
steeples attested to the godliness of the inhabitants. The town
looked much like any thriving North-European port except for
one fact that must have been apparent even to a boy of thirteen.
Boston was built almost entirely of wood.

An amphibious border skirted the town; a mass of piers, shipyards, stages for drying fish, distilleries, warehouses, wharves. The
inner harbor was crowded with merchant ships, sloops and schooners, whalers, heel-tappers, ferries, lighters, fishing ketches. These
Yankee sailors and merchants 'carried' not only for all North
America, but for the West Indies and parts of Europe as well.
Madagascar, Skanderoon, South America, already knew these
smart ships. Boston, by nature some seven hundred acres and no
larger than a large farm, was already badly crowded with fifteen
thousand inhabitants. The town was beginning to bulge out over
the waterfront. But if they needed more land they would make it
(there were enough hills to cut down and throw into the sea).
If they needed more freedom for their ships (England already had
plenty of laws they disregarded), they would take that too. These
Yankees had the reputation of hard-hitting, forceful, ingenious
men. Already Boston was something more than a geographic
fact — something of a state of mind. Now the solitary French
boy was to become one of them.

Apollos Rivoire had left behind him the cruellest persecution
the world up to his time had ever seen. After generations of religious tolerance, Catholic France had decided to purge herself
of her well-to-do, well-behaved Protestant minority. This boy
was but one of four hundred thousand to leave France in the
eighteenth and latter part of the seventeenth centuries. The
exodus dragged on for almost a hundred years, which shows that,
although France was a well-organized state for that time, it lacked
the efficiency and thoroughness with which such things can be
done today.

The Huguenots went to the Lowlands, to England, Switzerland, America. France had opened her own veins and spilt her best blood when she drained herself of her Huguenots, and everywhere, in every country that would receive them, this amazing strain acted as yeast — even upon Boston. Apollos was not the first of these French refugees to arrive in the Puritan metropolis. The Faneuils, Johonnots, Sigourneys, and Bowdoins were already well-established and respected citizens. They fitted quickly into the Yankee pattern. The stories they could tell of persecution fanned the hatred the New Englanders already had for France and Catholicism. For generation after generation one of the ruling passions of the Boston people was their hatred and fear of their French Catholic neighbors — settled to their north, in Canada. And for generations the terrible French and Indian wars went on.

Apollos' father and mother, Isaac and Serenne, lived at Riaucaud, not far from Bordeaux.[1] This was the very heart of Huguenot France and here the persecutions had been the most ferocious. It is a mild and sunny land of vineyards, and to this day one great vineyard bears the name Rivoire. The family was 'ancient and respectable,' some of them living in Martet, some in Sainte Foye La Grande as well as in Riaucaud. The three villages are very close. Except for the vineyard and town records the name is now extinct there, but a massive stone house owned by the Rivoires still stands.

The Rivoires were very well off for village people. 'Apollos our son' Isaac Rivoire recorded, 'was born the thirtieth day of November 1702, about ten o'clock at night and was baptized at Riaucaud, France. Apollos Rivoire my brother was his God Father and Anne Maulnon my sister-in-law was his God Mother. He set out for Guernsey the 21st of November 1715.'

As there was no legal marriage, no baptism, no church, for the Protestants of France at the time, such a baptism would take place secretly with considerable risk of the galleys if discovered. Louis XIV died the year Apollos left home. He boasted on his deathbed that he had ended Protestantism forever in France. Many (perhaps Isaac Rivoire among them) became 'new catholics,' but practised their faith in secret. If too tired or too wedded to their comfortable stone houses and beautiful vineyards to leave themselves, they often sent their children to other countries, beyond the reach of persecution.

Many old Huguenot names died out in their own country and
their lands passed into other hands. This seems to have been the
fate of the Rivoires of the Midi. But many years later Paul Revere's
'cousin' Mathias writes him from Sainte Foye. There are only one
or two Rivoires left. There were by 1780 more Reveres in Boston
than Rivoires in the three villages.

Apollos was not the first exile from this family. His father's
younger brother Simon had been apprenticed to a surgeon and had
'fled away with his master.' The surgeon and the boy went first
to Holland, but by 1705 Simon was settled in Guernsey. It was to
this uncle Apollos was first sent. Riaucaud is not far from Rochelle,
the great port of exit for the émigrés, nor is it a long sail from
Rochelle to Guernsey. The boy could hardly have realized that
this departure was to be as final as death itself.

It was Uncle Simon who furnished the boy with money and
put him on this ship which now carried not merely one more child
refugee, but the generations that would come after him, bearing
his metamorphosed name to greater fame even as it died to extinc-
tion in its own land.

His great transatlantic ship (possibly as large as three hundred
tons) approached Long Wharf, which ran for two thousand feet
out into the harbor. It was an amazing piece of engineering. The
largest vessels in the world could come up to it at low tide. On
the north side of the wharf were warehouses, auction halls, shops,
and counting houses. The south was left open for the ships.

The crew tramped round and round the capstan, inching her
in by a dripping hawser. There was the roar of the captain's
voice, the bo'sun's pipe, the iron clang of the catch pin, and the
ship warps in. Porters in leather aprons, clerks with ledgers, come
running. Fine, fat merchants in gold lace and great wigs, attended
by black slaves, step out of their counting houses. Dogs bark, men
gee and haw to oxen. Slatternly girls, watching from housetops,
know a ship has arrived and hurry to the wharf, ready to make
the usual fool of jack ashore.

Here is the rough vitality of a thriving port. And the smell of
bread-baking and of rum, fish drying, tar, sewage, cordwainers'
shops, dye pits, and yet, unmistakable even in winter-time, a smell
of land, so sweet a smell after a month and more at sea.

It is hard at first to find one's legs on land after so long a time of heaving decks; terrifying to be alone in so alien a world. Will the captain, in all his bustle and importance, forget the least important of his passengers — only one more of these French children? Usually it was the captain who saw to the indenturing of servants and apprentices, and it had already been decided that Apollos Rivoire is to be apprenticed to a goldsmith. Thirty-two goldsmiths were earning their living in Boston at this time, Jeremiah Dummer, John Coney, the Sandersons, Winslow, Hurd, and Dixwell among them. Folk were growing rich and wanting the finest silver (for goldsmiths worked largely in silver) for their own adornment and for their churches and tables. There was no end to the opportunities open to a clever and willing boy, even if he did not yet speak English.

So he stands a moment on the great wharf, his bundle, that age-old symbol of the refugee, in his hand. He has not yet lost his sea legs nor gained his land ones. It makes a person cautious about the first step — even a little sick. He is still suspended between two worlds. Apollos Rivoire is no longer a French boy, nor is he yet an American.

## II

AMONG the Boston silversmiths none was held in greater respect as citizen and craftsman than John Coney. Mr. Coney was at this time a man of sixty. He was known as a silent man, religious and very modest. He abhorred idleness at any time and was 'diligent in God's work on Lord's day even as in his own on other days.' This sounds like a bleak household for an apprentice, but 'he had pity for the poor and was a generous housekeeper.' If he had faults, they were 'only such as are consistent with a good estate and small in comparioson of his virtues.' Apollos would not fare too badly.

Mr. Coney signed for the French boy and took him to live with him on Anne Street, close to Dock Square. Here at Dock Square was the business centre of the town and the biggest of the public markets. It was held outdoors, for Peter Faneuil had not yet built Faneuil Hall. A town drain ran down the middle of the Square. There was a lively smell of dead fish as the tides slopped in and out of the yet unfilled Town Dock. Anne Street led out of this busy square, over the Mill Creek into North Boston, hugging the waterfront. After two blocks its name changed to Fish, which in a few minutes' walk broadened into North Square, swung right, took another name, and continued.

Like so many men of his years and period, Mr. Coney was enjoying his third wife — 'Prudent Mary,' Judge Sewall calls her. Although he had married early and late and had had twelve children in all, only five small girls had survived the horrifying and often fatal experience of infancy. Now Apollos would become one of this household. He too would be as 'diligent' as his master in serving God on Lord's day at the new North Church, and work as hard on other days. Mr. Coney would clothe and feed him and teach him the ancient mysteries of the goldsmith. It would be many years before the boy would even earn his keep, but towards the end of his indenture he would be a very valuable piece of property. This would repay the master for the years he had disciplined, fed, and taught the urchin and got nothing back. For as skilled a trade as silversmith it was customary for the boy's guardian to pay a considerable sum. It was Uncle Simon who furnished this money, as his grandson tactlessly pointed out to Apollos' son many years later.

Perhaps he did not send enough, or Mr. Coney may have merely been showing those faults so consistent with a good estate, for Apollos was not to serve the seven years which had been customary since the earliest Middle Ages, but ten. For ten years he could incur no debt nor marry without his master's permission. He might seek no other employer nor set up for himself. In turn it was Mr. Coney's duty to see to it the boy not only learned his trade, but became a reputable citizen. For his good behavior he would give his bond to the town.

Now Apollos was no longer a refugee, but one more of those smart apprentices Boston was filled with, even as Nuremberg or

London, Rome or Paris, had been filled for centuries. By this system they were studying everything from law and medicine to soap-boiling and tinkering.

The Boston boys wore leather aprons and mostly leather breeches cut so full that such as followed sedentary trades could wear them turned about, hind-side before, and not go through the seat too fast. They worked hours that would supposedly kill a modern boy and had often too much energy left over. They lied, seduced their masters' daughters, fell through the ice and drowned. They left careless fires and burned down bakeshops or overheated tar in the caboose of a ship and burned up the ship. They stole great wigs and silver spoons. They ran away and were whipped publicly and privately.

A man close to the period says it seems to have been the ambition of every apprentice 'to harass their masters as much as possible without getting flogged for it.' Saturday was a good day for mischief, for no pious master would desecrate the Sabbath by beating his apprentice and on Monday his temper might cool. One Boston cordwainer whose boys all turned out scoundrels said, in self-defence, 'he had beat them till he tired of it — humanity could do no more.' But there was little teaching without a whip in those days. It began in what we would call infant schools and went on as far as Harvard, where inebriated young gentlemen might feel the president's switch. However hard the system sometimes was on boys and masters, the art, craft, mystery, or trade was well served. No other method has turned out such good workmen. John Coney himself had once been apprenticed, probably either to Hull or Dummer, and they in turn had served their masters and their masters, earlier masters, and so on back through the centuries.

If a boy did not show natural aptitude, he might be returned to his parents. This weeding-out process at an early age must account in part for the high degree of ability·in the grown workmen. Another apprentice, living close to Dock Square during Apollos' indenture, had first been tried out with a candle-maker and then with a cutler. It was not until Benjamin Franklin was apprenticed to a printer that he found his proper niche.

Apollos seems to have been docile and industrious. Doubtless he fitted into his master's family and shop happily — as did most of the boys, although the court records, newspapers, and diaries emphasize the unhappy ones. John and Mary Coney and their daughters would partly take the place of his own lost family. He would begin very humbly sweeping the shop, sifting the gold and silver dust from the débris, or feeding charcoal to the brick furnace. He might soon be allowed to stamp the tiny rabbit or cony which to this day marks his master's later period. It would be he who carried home the spurs Judge Sewall speaks of leaving for Mr. Coney to mend. His master, one of the finest craftsmen of his day, worked in a great period of the silversmiths. Many of the leading families of his time in Boston were his patrons and also many people of comparatively small means.

Fine silver was as safe an investment as a cautious man might make. There was no bank in Boston. The stock market was embryonic and shaky. Mercantile ventures (the principal source of local wealth) often cleaned out the investor; so in old stockings and mattresses silver coins were accumulated, English pounds, Spanish doubloons, Dutch rix-dollars. When there were enough, the silver was taken to the smith, beaten into cups, tankards, porringers, to form the principal reserve capital in thrifty households.

This custom was to bear bitter fruit, for specie was getting as rare as hens' teeth. The answer was to print paper money. Mr. Coney engraved the plates for the first paper currency in America. So, while with one hand he was melting up the scarce 'hard' money, with the other he was starting the New World off on unsound paper. Apollos had a chance to observe the beginning of a process which, in his manhood, nearly wrecked one of the most prosperous English colonies.

At first it would be the boxes of gold and pearl beads his master used for the jewelry he made, or the tiny rabbit with which he signed his work, that would catch a child's interest. Nor could anyone resist the snarling lions set under an inkstand, or the dragon's snout for the spout of a chocolate pot, or the women's figures used as handles of a cup; but soon he would come to understand the grace and appealing simplicity of the superb craftsman's basic design. Nothing we know of Apollos' work reflects the glories of his master. It is the son after him — Paul Revere — who seems to have served a spiritual apprenticeship to John Coney.

One thing everyone in Boston knew in those days (although not many may now) is that the Bible says that 'Paul planted and Apollos watered.' In the Rivoire-Revere family the process seems to have been reversed. It was Apollos who planted and Paul who watered, but in both Corinth and Boston 'God gave the increase.'

Before Apollos had completed his apprenticeship, Mr. Coney, after a long sickness, died in August, 1722. He was laid in his tomb in the Granary, which in the careless fashion of the time was quickly sold to someone else. The bones were often thrown in. Besides his real estate and page after page of carefully recorded tools of his trade, he left one very old-fashioned bit of property, the unexpired term of his apprentice 'Paul Rwoires Time abt Three Year & half as pr indenture ... 30.0.0.' The French boy, for some reason, was by now being called Paul, although Apollos should have been acceptable to Boston, as it also is Biblical. What to do about his last name was still a problem. Although he was twenty and a skilled artisan, unless he could raise thirty pounds he could be sold to the highest bidder, for apprenticeship was something of a short-term slavery. In some way he not only raised this sum, but ten pounds over. He paid the estate forty pounds for his release. 'Prudent Mary' may have been fond of him and made the terms easy for him. At least he did not marry one of his master's girls, as was so often done by apprentices.

There was another more enterprising apprentice right there on Anne Street and of the same age. This was Thomas Hancock. He married his master's daughter, Lydia Henchman, and thus acquired the nest egg out of which he hatched the greatest fortune in New England. Miss Lydia was a very large girl. When eighteen years of prosperity made it possible for Thomas Hancock to order a 'chariot' built for him in London, he said it must be especially high because 'you know Mrs. Hancock is none of the shortest and smallest of folks, though I'd prefer as light a one as possible to her seize,' and later the step must be uncommonly low, for 'Mrs. Hancock is ... a little weak in the knees.' But if he had not married his 'Mrs. H.,' he might never have had the wherewithal to ride in a chariot.[2]

Thomas Hancock was not the only poor apprentice in the neighborhood destined to rise. Benjamin Franklin, by the time Apollos' master died, was serving his own brother the printer.

He liked the trade, but not brother James, so broke his indenture and ran away to Philadelphia.

Apollos enjoyed neither the fame nor fortune of many of the 'leather-apron boys' of his time and town. He may not even have been sure he wished to settle permanently in Boston, for soon after Mr. Coney's death he made a visit to Uncle Simon back in Guernsey. He did not go on to Riaucaud to see his father, although in 1720 Isaac was still alive and, judging by the size of his taxes, a very well-to-do man. The briefness of his visit suggested that it was not a success.[3]

In eight years he had gone from boyhood to manhood. Now it would be French that he spoke with an accent. The sunny vineyards of the Midi would seem less real to him than the white birches and stone walls of New England. He called himself Paul and Rivoire was becoming 'Revere,' 'merely on account that the Bumpkins pronounce it easier' was his explanation. Perhaps Uncle Simon thought him too Americanized. Boston apprentices had a reputation for 'sauceboxes' and American craftsmen of being uppity and not knowing their place. Why should they know their place? What it might be was in their own hands to determine.


# III


HOW well the erstwhile French refugee fitted into the pattern of his day and town we can judge by the one purchase he is known to have made in his early twenties. He subscribed to the 'Life of the Very Reverent and Learned Cotton Mather,' written by his son Samuel. Books were not lightly bought nor are Mather books light reading.

Church-going, in spite of three-hour sermons and hour-long prayers, was probably more fun then than now. The church was the centre of intellectual life for men of the first Paul Revere's opportunities. Politics, current events, local scandals, and doctrine were all discussed. And the church produced many quarrels, with all the excitement of divided families, oaths, and cat-calls. Such a one rent the New North where Mr. Coney had attended with his apprentices. A group of secessionists built themselves 'New Brick.' This stood in the part of Hanover Street, then known as Middle Street. It was nicknamed 'The Revenge Church,' which suggests little Christian humility. Early in its turbulent career Deacon Shem Drowne hammered out of brass kettles a 172-pound cock for its weathervane. The day this was set upon its spindle 'a merry fellow' climbed the spire, straddled the cock, and crowed insolently at the mother church. Boston had not yet run out of either rum or religious fervor. 'The Cockerel,' as it was nicknamed, born of schism and revenge, started on its rough and crowing progress. Like whistling girls and crowing hens, it had a lively career and a bad end. The Reveres, father and son, attended this church.

For a while Revere may have hired himself out as a journeyman, but by the time he was twenty-eight he was on his own. An advertisement in *The Weekly News Letter* for May 21, 1730, reads: 'Paul Revere, Goldsmith is removed from Capt Pitts at the Town Dock to North End over against Col Hutchinson.'

But it was more than his annealing furnace and steel heads or a Life of Cotton Mather he moved from 'Capt Pitts.' The year before he had married Deborah Hitchbourn. The Hitchbourns had been his neighbors ever since he arrived at Mr. Coney's. His father-in-law owned Hitchbourn Wharf on Anne Street at the foot of Cross. His property included, besides the wharf, a 'mansion house' and a number of other buildings. The Hitchbourns were a large active artisan family and seem to have contributed rather more than their share to the make-up of the most famous of the many Paul Reveres.

The Hitchbourns had started out with a certain wildness. David, the first of that name in Boston, had, for some unrecorded misdemeanor, been ordered to wear an iron collar around his neck. His son, Thomas, Deborah's grandfather, was a lively, picturesque fellow. His one appearance in the records of the Supreme Judicial Court shows no lack of initiative. Back in 1683 he had taken the law into his own hands. A shoemaker, Grimstone Bowd, owed him money. As he could not get it back by fair means, he tried foul, and went to Bowd's shop and took possession of two pair of pumps — valued at two shillings the pair. And we meet him a few years later in Sewall's diary during Sir Edmund Andros' turbulent rule. Two of the soldiers brought over by this first of the royal governors of Massachusetts challenged each other for an exhibition of swordsmanship. Hitchbourn walked before them with his drum as 'one arrayed in white, the other in red, goe through the Town with naked Swords advanced.' A great crowd gathered at Mr. Wing's innyard to watch this 'stage fight.' The victor left his wounded antagonist and attended by 'seven drawn swords' rushed shouting through the streets 'in a kind of Tryumph.' Judge Sewall seems a little startled over such brawling and notes down the name of the Boston man who beat his drum to advertise the exhibition. So if Tom Hitchbourn, in a way, drummed in these first redcoats to set foot on our shores, his great-grandson, Paul Revere, did his share in drumming out the last.

But Apollos' father-in-law, the second Thomas, must have been a law-abiding citizen. He was licensed by the Town of Boston to sell strong drink from his house on Hitchbourn Wharf. Such a permit suggests that the selectmen approved of him. He is listed as a 'joiner,' but as he owned a wharf probably did some ship-building as well.

There may have been something a little exotic about Paul Revere's French father, but on his mother's side he was Yankee to the core. Back of Thomas Hitchbourn and Frances Pattishall, his wife, are rank upon rank of the hardiest type of New England mariners, privateersmen, sea captains, belligerent yeomen, and Indian fighters all ready to come to life again in Deborah's unborn and unruly son.

Take, for example, the man who, when the child finally put in his appearance, is to be his great-great-grandfather, Thomas Dexter. He was hardly off the ship before he was 'sett in the bilboes ... for speaking reproachfull and seditious words against the government here established & finding fault to dyvers with the acts of the court — saying that captious government will bring all to nought.' That was in 1632, and the same year he was fined for 'his misdeameanour and insolent carriage & speeches to S.

Bradstreet [twice governor of the colony] att his owne house, also att the Gen'l Court.' Thomas Dexter lived on the Saugus River and was a 'promoter' of the ironworks. Not content with a farm of greater acreage than the entire town of Boston, he bought Nahant from an Indian for a suit of clothes. This purchase involved the Colony of the Massachusetts Bay in lawsuits for forty years. But his most dramatic appearance is in a letter John Endicott wrote to Governor Winthrop. The irascible, autocratic Endicott had lost his temper at Thomas Dexter and slapped him. He wrote Winthrop he regretted not being in court the day the charge of assault and battery came up against him, 'because I hear I am much complained of by Goodman Dexter for striking him; understanding since it is not lawful for a Justice of the Peace to strike. But if you had seen the manner of his carriage, with such daring of me, with his arms akimbo, it would have provoked a very patient man,' which Governor Endicott never was. He was fined for his quick temper and his ignorance of the fact that a justice of the peace may not slap whom he chooses. Goodman Dexter was a thorn in the side of government, but an enterprising citizen on week days. It may have been otherwise come Sabbath. He was presented in court once 'for a common sleeper' at public worship.

Captain Woody was another appropriate ancestor for Paul Revere. Massachusetts was always at war and always short of gunpowder. During the Revolution she turned to Paul Revere for help, but a hundred years earlier, shortly before King Philip's War, to his great-grandfather Richard Woody. Captain Woody was a soap-boiler by trade. He had been admitted to the Town of Boston in 1677 'upon his promise not to be offensive by his Tryd to the Town.' Soon he was bidden 'to go at' the manufacture of saltpetre for gunpowder, and as a first and not very dignified step was allowed 'to have the liberty' to collect 'urine in the several towns.'

Richard Pattishall married Captain Woody's daughter, Martha. With his fine clothes and bold adventures he was typical of Boston Puritans of his day. It is true he prayed loud and long, but 'irreverently enough.' He was not the man to stay quietly in one village, cultivating his soul, but ranged up and down the coast from New York to Maine.[4] In Maine he owned thousands upon thousands of wild acres stretching from Salmon Falls to beyond

Pemaquid. When drums were beat calling volunteers to chase the
pirates, Veal and Graham, it was he who took charge. When he
died, it was on his own ship. The Indians boarded it at night as
it lay off Pemaquid and butchered him as he slept. It was in these
Maine waters Paul Revere was to suffer the greatest humiliation
of his life.

The Hitchbourns and their relatives had lived about Boston
so long and were so vigorous the solitary Apollos may have felt
he was being swallowed up by them. Captain Pitts at the Town
Dock was his wife's Aunt Mary's (born Pattishall) husband. All
his children bore Hitchbourn names except the boy he named
Paul for himself. None were named Isaac or Serenne for his
parents or Simon after the uncle who had befriended him. When
he married Deborah he united himself with a whole clan. They
would stand by him in adversity, but might be overwhelming on
ordinary days.

By this marriage he gave his unborn children as rough-and-
ready a maternal strain as was easily available around Boston.
These seventeenth-century forebears of Paul Revere's are very
unlike the anemic traditional Puritan of fiction. Thomas Dexter
with his arms akimbo getting slapped by crotchety old Governor
Endicott or talking back to gentle Governor Bradstreet has the
very attitude and accent of his famous descendant. Nor was blood
alone handed down in those days. With less competition from the
outside world, family stories (never losing in the telling) were
passed on from generation to generation. The children of Deborah
Hitchbourn Revere might hear over and over just how Goodman
Dexter upset three governors, or how Captain Pattishall, back in
the days of King William's War, was killed by the Indians about the
same time Great-Grandfather Hitchbourn himself got his dander
up over Grimstone Bowd's refusal to pay just debts, took the law
into his own hands, and *then* the law took him. There is one line in
a letter Paul Revere wrote as an old man referring back to these
old stories. He had often as a child gone to Great-Aunt Thomas,
daughter of Captain Pattishall, and heard how the Indians had
butchered her father. And there, doubtless, he often admired the
portraits of the Captain and of his wife and small daughter. The
little girl is thought to be Great-Aunt Thomas herself.[5]

He who had been Apollos Rivoire entered his thirtieth year

with a new name, a good trade, a church, money for the wanton luxury of a book, a house 'over against Col. Hutchinson,' a wife, and some very active in-laws. But he was to wait several years for his next blessing which obviously would be children — especially a son to carry on his fine Americanized name.

Deborah remained childless for almost three years. It would seem young Mr. Revere had not done so well marrying into the Hitchbourns, for of what use to a man is a childless wife? Nor was she for some reason a church member, although her family attended the Cockerel like so many North End artisans. On February 6 she remedied this later fault by owning covenant with the crowing Cockerel Church. She must have been far gone with child, for eleven days later her daughter was baptized with her own name — Deborah Revere.

She was still not in the expected stride, for she idled away almost three years before her next. On the first day of January, 1735, in the cold winter time, when snow and ice still lash North Boston with such fury one feels more as if on a ship at sea than on dry land, the boy Paul was carried to the Cockerel for baptism.[6] Of the Reverend Mr. Welsteed, a youngish man at the time, with a flat, unimaginative face surrounded by mathematical curls, his contemporaries could find little to say except that he was 'useful,' but he probably broke the ice in the baptismal basin and got as piercing a wail from the newborn baby as any Mather.

Then, escorted by in-laws and sponsors, the midwife carrying the baby, the father would return to his own house. Mr. Welsteed might condescend to go along too. Babies were usually baptized the day after birth, so few mothers were present at the ceremony. Deborah would still be lying abed, probably in the main living-room, proud that after almost six years she had borne her husband a son and heir to carry on his trade and name, although the Hitchbourns crowding in, taking all the best seats and boasting too loudly, may have implied that this boy was but an addition to their own clan. Tom Hitchbourn himself would not be there. Shortly before the birth of this, his most distinguished grandchild, the 'strong drink' license had been granted by the Town of Boston to his wife. It would now be his widow who doled out ale at Hitchbourn Wharf, Anne Street. Her son Thomas, a boat-builder, ran the wharf.

The day after childbirth any mother would be expected to be sitting up in bed to receive her guests and enjoy the cakes, ale, and merriment. The midwife and her obstetrical stories would be well to the fore. Mr. Welsteed and his high-born wife might wonder if they could sneak out and leave these artisans to their common amusements, but, if they left, others would crowd in to drink the caudle cup and admire the baby. It was a dark and most likely vigorous boy, for the lively good health it was to enjoy well into the next century is apt to start in the cradle.

Even the great man of the neighborhood, Colonel Hutchinson, 'over against' whom the advertisement says the first Paul set up his modest dwelling, would not be too proud to stop a moment and wish God's blessing on the newborn boy, never guessing the part he was to play in the complete, ruthless destruction of his own great family.

# II

## 1 7 3 5 – 1 7 5 6

The Revere family increases. Paul gets a sufficient education at school, in the shop, and around the wharves. He earns money as a bell-ringer at Christ's and hears the opening gun of revolution. A murder is instigated at Clark's Wharf. His father dies and he goes to fight the French. A return to Boston.

Detail from Tyrian Lodge Notification, 1795, by Paul Revere. American Antiquarian Society.

AT FIRST the boy's world would be small. His mother's kitchen and the good smells of herbs drying, a suet pudding bubbling on the hearth, ducks roasting, and the less alluring aroma of milk souring into cheese, the continual process of drying out baby flannel. In the kitchen the floor might be sanded. A child with a few bright pebbles and a shingle for a shovel could play for hours on a sanded floor. But for this child a few pebbles on his mother's floor would be that and nothing more. Young Paul faced the world factually.

An old dog (but, mind, it is not over ten inches in height — there was a town ordinance against greater dogs),[7] a cat or two, chickens, and a pig in the back yard would be part of his world. Of course the pig would sometimes wander off down the street. So did the other pigs of Boston. And in the back yard, year after year, floated those ancient banners of increase. The neighbors could read by the many diapers on the line that Mrs. Revere was making up for lost time.

In the nine years after Paul's birth, Deborah Revere produced seven children. Only once did she save labor by twinning. Of these she lost but two in infancy, which was a much better record than that of the three Mrs. Coneys. Between them they had had twelve children. Only five outlived their first year. The kitchen, which was usually the main living and sleeping room of plain families, would be dominated by Mrs. Revere and her babies.

Then there was his father's shop. This may have been a room set aside for him in the crowded little house or a separate twelve by twelve building. Here was the smell of charcoal burning in the brick furnace on which, in a crucible, silver coin and bars, outmoded tankards, were melted down. And in the furnace, silver, which when cold so quickly becomes brittle, would be annealed until malleable again. The silversmith continually passes from his anvil, planishing stakes, and hammers to the annealing furnace. In the boy's ears would ring the dullish beating — tat tat tat-a-tat — of wooden hammers or the sharper note, but the same rhythm, of the steel hammer. He would watch his father knock the cold silver blank over the crimping block, planish, and swage or peen, but stopping every few moments to anneal once more. Slowly a porringer, standing cup, tray, or spoon would begin to take form.

Being social and in no way self-conscious, the child would enjoy the men and women who came to the shop. A careless maid from the Hutchinson house across the street might run over with a cup she had melted hidden under her apron. Could the smith please put the handle on again so no one would know. A merchant, who ten years ago had been so poor a boy as had not the where-withal to buy shoes, now proudly discussed exactly how 'his arms' were to be engraved. And the talk of gadroon edges, splay feet, and what was the latest fashion of silver in London, and of politics — always and always politics.

There were enough well-to-do people in this part of Boston to support a silversmith. And plenty of poor to break in and steal. The North End was a mixture of an almost London elegance of living rubbing shoulders with poverty and vice. Here, in crooked, narrow streets, in tenements, stews, abandoned warehouses, lived outlandish jacktars, Irish shillalah boys, bullies, toughs, peddlers, and harlots. These tides of poverty washed about such islands of wealth as the Hutchinsons and their next-door neighbors the Clarks. Between these very rich and very poor was a substantial middle group like Paul's father and his uncle Thomas Hitchbourn, shipwrights, brewers, smiths of all sorts, cobblers, cordwainers, bakers, who lived extremely well by any European standard. They could buy sufficient food and clothing and apprentice their boys to the skilled trades. Many of these boys would even be sent to Harvard to train for the learned professions, but the bulk of them would remain artisans.

Here in the North End was as inflammable material for rioting as might be found in North America. Boston had long been famous for street fighting. Many of her riots seem to have arisen more from desire for excitement than any sense of grievance. The amusements of rioting, drinking, and going to church were never denied the poor. By this time many of them were tired of church, and drinking costs money. If ever these willing mobsters could be joined by the steadier master artisans and managed by a master mind, they might be used as a terrific weapon against the owners of the great houses, against anything their leaders told them was 'oppression.' The small boy playing about his father's shop would do his part in this leadership.

As for the 'master mind,' no one who knew Sam Adams (already at Harvard) guessed that this was to be his rôle. He was not especially promising. James Otis was also at Harvard — a queer, moody, charming, unsettled fellow. John Hancock, not yet adopted by Uncle Thomas Hancock (who was making money hand over fist), was a couple of years younger than Paul Revere. Two of his most likable companions in revolution, Joseph Warren and Josiah Quincy, were not even born. But John Adams was exactly Paul Revere's own age. He was learning how to drive cows to pasture out in Braintree while Paul was learning the rudiments of his craft in North Boston.

These boys, young men, and as yet unborn babies, were in time all to come together, but when Paul Revere was a small child the geographic and social gaps between them would seemingly have precluded their adult intimacy. Each was as yet by himself. Slowly the stage was being set for the great drama of Revolution, but the actors were not yet assembled.

The first of the principal performers (and the traditional villain of the piece) with whom Paul Revere came into contact seems to have been Thomas Hutchinson. Paul's boyhood and much of his manhood was passed almost in the shadow of the Hutchinson 'mansion.' When the Colonel died he left it to his eldest son, Thomas. Here, surrounded by fences and gardens, coach-houses, fruit trees, and all the state of eighteenth-century wealth, lived Boston's most distinguished citizen, young Thomas Hutchinson. William Clark, merchant, had built next door an equally impressive mansion. It was said the Clarks were determined to outshine the Hutchinsons, but money changed hands rapidly in those days. By the time Paul Revere was nine, Mr. Clark had lost forty sail of ships, died

'broken-spirited,' and left his family 'not very well off.' There
was no Clark who could afford to live in the Clark house. They
were no longer rivals of the Hutchinsons, nor was Thomas Hancock,
the new-risen gentleman who was building a great stone mansion
far out on lonely Beacon Hill. He was too obviously *nouveau riche*.

Although proud of his descent from the cataclysmic Anne,
Thomas Hutchinson was cautious and conservative. In appearance
he was 'a tall, slender, fair-complexioned, fair-spoken very good
gentleman.' He seems to have been one of those men whose self-
confidence is so great it almost becomes modesty once more. His
portrait suggests many of the qualities his contemporaries credit
him with, his grace, pride, aloofness and passion, honor and pig-
headedness, but there is nothing in the soft hazel eyes (the eyes of a
beautiful woman) nor in the delicate features which suggests that
other, tougher side. He was an expert at banking and America's
first outstanding historian. His physical courage never forsook him.

If he wished new clasps for his pocketbook, it is likely he would
turn to the Revere shop with his problem. And once there, he
would settle down as comfortably as an humbler neighbor, compliment the smith as graciously (and much more gracefully) on
his work, or on what a fine, manly fellow that little Paul was
growing into. Although so pleasing in his contacts with what he
frankly called 'the commonality' he had no belief in their wisdom
or virtue. He believed in the rule of a few well-born, well-educated
men of good will — like himself. Later his enemies were to lament
that his handsome appearance had 'captivated half the pretty
ladies in the Colony' while more than half the gentlemen had been
taken in by his courtesies. He loved New England as deeply as
ever did Sam Adams. While still in his twenties he had been sent
to England on a ticklish piece of work for Massachusetts, but had
been homesick for his own land. He loved the delicate sixteen-
year-old girl he had married the year Paul was born. John Adams,
looking back on the long years of Hutchinson's popularity, wrote
in 1760: 'Has not his merit been sounded very high by my countrymen for twenty years? Have not his countrymen loved, admired,
rewarded, nay, almost adored him? Have not ninety-nine out of a
hundred of them really thought him the greatest and best man
in America? . . . nay, often to have styled him the greatest and
best man in the world?' It was this 'very good gentleman' and

close neighbor of the Reveres who would be the villain in the drama.

But when Paul Revere was a boy around ten there was a break in this paragon's popularity. The monetary system in Massachusetts had for years been chaos. The dearth of 'hard' money (helped on by the silversmiths, but even more by the merchants, who sent it to England to pay for manufactured goods) and the frivolous printing of paper money had almost paralyzed trade. One paid in 'old,' 'middle,' and 'new tenor,' or in 'pay,' 'pay as money,' or 'trust.' Confusion was further confounded by an equally evil assortment of Rhode Island and Connecticut bills. In an honest attempt to ease the situation, 'the Land Bank' was founded in Boston. Its notes, secured by mortgages on the eight hundred members' property, would serve as one more kind of paper money.

Thomas Hutchinson had been fighting paper money and inflation for years. He called in the British Parliament to stop the Land Bank, and many small property owners were ruined. His house was attacked. Men with staves dared him to show his face. When a fire started, the mob cried, 'Let it burn!... let it burn!' and cursed him. Such treatment of their respected neighbor must have amazed a ten-year-old boy. Why were they cursing Mr. Hutchinson and what was a 'Land Bank'? In some way Thomas Hutchinson had wronged hundreds of his poor fellow townsmen.

A few men of considerable wealth had gone into the scheme and suffered ruin in its collapse. The director of the bank had been kindly Deacon Adams, a merchant who also had a wharf and profitable brewery over on Purchase Street. It must have been hard for the respectable old deacon (always very popular with the underprivileged) to see his fortune and his scheme collapse and his good name questioned. Perhaps it was even harder for his son Samuel. Sam had been living rather luxuriously at Harvard as befitted a boy who was ranked fifth in his class on the basis of family standing. He did not eat at commons with the ruck of the students, but more privately and elegantly. Overnight all this changed, but he stuck it out, worked his way through, and took his master's. After the collapse of the Land Bank, when the bell 'tolled' for meal-time he was one of the poor student-waiters who carried the victuals from the kitchen hatch to the tables of students with whom he had formerly not even eaten.

Paul Revere might wonder what a land bank was, or how banks collapse, and what Mr. Hutchinson had to dc with it, but Sam Adams knew very well. He was early set in his most characteristic pattern. He hated the Hutchinsons. That Mr. Hutchinson soon put Massachusetts currency for the first time on a sound basis made no difference in this hatred. He hated the Hutchinsons and their close kin, the Olivers. He would not forget that it was by an act of the far-distant, meddlesome British Parliament this ruin had come over his family. He hated tyranny, oligarchies, money, pomp and display. But his thinking and ambitions did not stop with hatred. Although he was not above appealing to his followers' basest instincts, religious intolerance, jealousy, and greed, although he hoodwinked and cajoled, inflamed and mistrusted the common man, yet there can be no question but he loved him.

He took his master's when he was twenty-one. That he was to fail again and again in everything he tried to do until middle-aged might already have been apparent in his personality. He had only one interest — politics. His thesis does not sound so radical in Latin, but in plain English it was, 'Whether it be lawful to resist the Supreme Magistrate if the Commonwealth cannot otherwise be preserved.' The governor himself would be present at commencement, all the clergy and prominent graduates like Thomas Hutchinson. Too much rum punch, roast geese, Madeira, and great puddings may have set these august gentlemen a-dozing. Lulled by good wine and sonorous Latin lines, they were confident that all was well.

But the Land Bank crash divided Boston into two camps. On one side was conservative capital and, we must admit, financial judgment. On the other a struggling mass of smaller folk, fearing, not without reason, to become 'but slaves and vassals of the rich.' They were swayed by catchwords, on the watch for scapegoats, and yet were fighting for some of man's noblest ideals.

The mob, crying in the streets of Boston before the Hutchinson house, 'Curse him! Let it burn!' was a first swallow, which does not make a spring, but indicates how the earth is turning.

## II

FAMILIES even less well off than
the Reveres commonly sent their children to primitive infant
schools kept by an assortment of Mother McLeods, Miss Tinkums,
and Aunt or Dame So-and-So. The charge was around a penny a
week. Not much was taught but 'manners' (on which study a
surprising amount of weight was placed) and the A B C. There
was some reading, but not much writing. Seed cakes might
reward industrious small fry. Birch and ferule certainly did the
recalcitrant. At least, as these children sat on their plank benches
and chanted the alphabet with 'quirks and quavers,' they were
not falling off wharves and drowning, nor being run down in the
sidewalk-less streets. Many Boston children stopped their education with the dame school when they were seven or eight. For
the more ambitious, Boston had five public schools, but when
Paul was a boy of six only five hundred and twenty-five children
were attending them. There were a few private schools, but for a
town of fifteen to sixteen thousand the proportion of children
receiving formal education was small. Yet Boston presumably led
the world in her public schooling.

Boys intended for Harvard and the learned professions were
sent to the Latin or grammar schools, but most of those, who (like
Paul Revere) were to be artisans, went to the writing schools.
For instance, Benjamin Franklin was started out at a grammar
school, as his father hoped to make a clergyman of him, 'but my
father, in the meantime, from a view of the expense, which having
so large a family he could not well afford, and the mean living
many so educated were afterwards able to obtain, altered his first
intention, took me from the Grammar school and sent me to a
school for writing and arithmetic.'

It is not likely that Mr. Revere had any other ambition for his
son than to make a good silversmith of him. Paul would not
have been sent to the North Latin with its sixty-five pupils, but to
North Writing. This school had more pupils than the four other

schools put together. Both of these North End schools had been
the gift of the Hutchinson family and were very famous in their
day. North Writing, on Love Lane, was a two-story, wooden
building. Reading was taught on one floor and on the other
writing. Only boys attended the school, and the Boston records
of the time show that sixty per cent of the women could only make
their mark. Grandmother Hitchbourn could do no more.

The pedagogical methods were ferocious, and the boys were not
educated in the modern sense of the word, only given the rudiments
by which they might educate themselves later on. Zachariah
Hicks was the master during Paul Revere's school days and John
Proctor, junior, the usher. John Proctor, senior, had been master
for a number of years. In 1741, just before he resigned, he was
asked to appear before the selectmen and 'discourse' with them
'upon the complaint of his refusing to take children of some families of low circumstances in the world and insisting on large demands for firing and entry money.' The old master said he charged
no entry money to any of the town inhabitants, only from 'strangers' sent in from outside for education. He had never refused a
child except 'such as could not read in the psalter.' As for 'firing,'
he charged but five shillings.

So to be acceptable to the master of North Writing, Paul Revere
would have to read in the psalter and produce five shillings to pay
for his share of heating the schoolhouse. The town paid the
master and usher. 'Johnny' Tileston, as he was called during his
long life, was a pupil of this school during Paul Revere's period.
For eighty years he was pupil, usher, or master at North Writing.
In his honor Love Lane was renamed Tileston Street. Master
Johnny had a deformed hand, drawn together like a bird's beak.
With this loathsome hand, hard as bone, he used to peck at his
pupils, and yet he was one of the most loved men in Boston. Paul
Revere has often been said to have been one of his pupils, but as
the two men were born the same year and month, this is not
likely. Master Johnny may have pecked at him as a fellow pupil,
but hardly as a master.

By thirteen a future artisan's schooling would surely be over,
for that was the age indentures of apprenticeship were usually
signed. He would have had about five years of Master Hicks' and
Usher Proctor's instruction. School kept for boys summer and

winter without vacation, only an occasional holiday for Thanksgiving or Fast Day, Training or Election Days, funerals of worthies, or during the great fires that so often devastated Boston. When the Boston ministers set out in a large black flock to inspect the schools in 1746, they found all 'in good order,' but North Writing was one of the two in 'very good order.' The education Paul Revere received was good enough to enable him later on to read 'chemical essays' and other treatises connected with his work, and he loved his books. He wrote clear letters, without a trace of the pomposity so common at the time, and no more bad grammar and spelling than many contemporary 'gentlemen.' Yet he may have felt some lack. As soon as he was able, he sent his boys to Latin schools.

North Boston, cut off by Mill Creek, was in fact (and perhaps by nature) an island — a world to itself. It was rimmed about by the sea and this littoral was the boys' playground. One of Paul Revere's Hitchbourn relatives was drowned falling off a wharf and his redoubtable contemporary, George Robert Twelves Hewes, almost drowned. Some fell from the rigging of ships and broke their necks. When Paul Revere made an engraving of the North Battery and its shoreline, he put three naked urchins diving and splashing about the wharf. So, doubtless, he had often ended his summer days after work at school or in the shop.

Hitchbourn Wharf belonged to his grandmother. Uncle Thomas not only had a shipyard, but a parcel of boys about his age. In 1742 the Reveres were also living there, for that year his grandmother Hitchbourn died; having left her one son, Thomas, among other things, 'all my part of & in my negro boy, Nulgar, and sd son paying into my estate £30 for his Diet that he owes me,' she gives 'To my daughter Reveer named Deborah 1½ years Rent for her house she now lives in.' Hitchbourn Wharf with its buildings is the only real estate Mrs. Hitchbourn owned when she died, so it must have been there Paul spent some of his childhood.[8]

When the year and a half was almost over, in February, 1743, Paul's parents and his Aunt Marrett and Aunt Douglas sold their share to Uncle Thomas. But the Reveres liked wharves. They moved a short way along the waterfront, staying on the same street which left Dock Square as Anne and soon became Fish, and rented a house or part of a house from Doctor John Clark. The Reveres were still close to the Clark and Hutchinson

houses, which stood on a slight rise a block inland. Their landlord
was the fifth Doctor John Clark in direct descent and one of the
relatives Merchant William had left 'not very well off.' He was
his brother. The Clark family was slipping slowly and inevitably
downhill, just as the Hancocks were rising. Doctor Clark lived
by the wharf himself. He kept meticulous ledgers — a page for
each house, counting up the small amounts each of his many small
and possibly ramshackle little houses 'at the head of Clark's wharf'
brought him. He could not afford to live in the Clark house. It
was sold to young Sir Harry Frankland, sent over to Boston from
England as Collector of the Port. Sir Harry never bothered the
merchants as they openly broke all the navigation acts of England
and smuggled what they pleased, but he set every tongue in town
buzzing over his infatuation with the Marblehead serving girl —
Agnes Surriage. He said he brought her to his mansion in Boston
merely to 'educate' her, a statement no one believed then or now.
Paul Revere had to go through adolescence without any novels
or screen passions to feed whatever emotional fires may have
burned in his soul, but at least he was within shouting distance of
New England's greatest romantic story — how handsome young
Sir Harry saw a barefoot New England girl scrubbing the floor
of an inn — she had to move herself and her bucket so he could
enter. She lifted her beautiful face and said nothing. But Sir
Harry had met Agnes Surriage and from his love for her he never
escaped — nor wished to. Marrying her was, however, quite a
different matter.


# III


ON SUNDAYS Mr. and Mrs.
Revere, driving, leading, and carrying a variety of well-scrubbed
small Reveres, went piously to church. The Hutchinsons also

attended the Cockerel and by their glory somewhat overshadowed
the plainer members. As a race they were apt to have the upper
hand wherever they were, beginning with the great-great-grand-
mother Ann. Thomas Hutchinson's sister had married the 'useful'
Mr. Welsteed, who was now assisted by Ellis Gray. The question
came up how the Cockerel, largely attended by North End artisans, could support their double burden of clergymen. In January,
1747, a number of the members agreed to contribute so much a
week. Mr. Hutchinson signed first, promising twenty shillings.
The other seventy-six names include that of the first Paul Revere,
who put himself down for a weekly four shillings, thus giving one-
fifth as much as one of the wealthiest men in New England. Either
he was doing much better than we have reason to believe, or his
loyalty to his church was taking him over his depth.

As the father was giving so munificently for the support of the
Cockerel, his son Paul found a way to make money for himself
out of another church. Christ was Episcopal, a denomination
which smelt a little to the Congregationalist of idolatry and brim-
stone, but even more sweetly (as other small Puritans remembered)
of Christmas greens. Christmas was carefully not observed in
such churches as the Cockerel, but the Congregational children
loved to sneak off to the Episcopal churches at Christmas-time and
smell the greens.

Christ Church did not have merely one utilitarian bell for
soberly summoning to meeting, but a 'royal peal' of eight, still called
the best and sweetest bells in America. These bells had the added
mysterious virtue of dispelling demons. The tone was so clear they
could be heard far across the water by students at Harvard. And
inside the church was an organ, beautiful wooden statues, and an
altar. In the crypt below were tombs for dead worthies who
could afford — after the English manner (but not the New England) — to lie buried within the church building.

This church still keeps the contract Paul Revere and six other
boys drew up to cover their services as bell-ringers.

We the Subscribers Do agree To the Following articles Viz that if
we can have the Liberty From the wardens of Doctor Cutler's church
we will attend there once a week on Evenings to ring the Bells for
two hours Each time from the date hereof to one year.
That we will Choose a Moderator Every three months whose

Business shall be to give out the Changes and other Business as shall be agreed by a Majority of Voices then Present.

That None shall be admitted a Member of this Society without Unanimous Vote of the Members then Present and that No Member Shall begg Money of any Person for the Tower on Penalty of being excluded the Society and that we will attend To Ring any Time when the Wardens of the Church Aforesaid shall desire it on Penalty of Paying three shillings for the good of the Society (Provided we can have the whole Care of the Bells.

That the Members of this Society shall not Exceed Eight Persons and all Differences To be decided By a Majority of Voices

> John Dyer
> Paul Revere
> Josiah Flagg
> Barth.º Flagg
> Jnº Brown jr
> Joseph Snelling.

The fact that this paper was preserved implies the boys were given the liberty to ring the bells. The two hours a week would be for practice, presumably with a skilled bell-ringer in charge. This signature, written by a boy in his middle teens, is curiously like those of his maturity and old age, which to a graphologist would suggest that his personality was formed rather early and did not change much. But small Paul Revere does put a flourish under his name that would be a credit to John Hancock himself. It grew less as he grew older, and disappeared. Hancock's increased.

Of the boys who formed this 'Society' at about the age boys so often want clubs, John Dyer, the first to sign, was five years older than Paul, who comes next. Josiah Flagg developed into a lifelong friend of Revere's adult life. Paul Revere made silver for Joseph Snelling many years later.

Christ steeple is still famous for its grave beauty and the melody of its bells. The largest weighs 1545 pounds and the smallest 620. Each is inscribed, as the young bell-ringers would know: 'We are the first ring of bells cast for the British Empire in North America. A.R. Ano 1744,' says one, and 'God preserve the Church of England,' and so on. The 'A.R.' stood for Abel Rudhall, of Gloucester, England, who 'cast us all.'

Famous as is this 'tower' with its bells, its greatest fame was to rest in the hands of the dirty, sweaty-faced, hard-pulling urchin,

Paul Revere, the goldsmith's apprentice from near-by Clark's Wharf. The scholarly rector, Mr. Timothy Cutler, the proud sea captains and fine merchants who served as vestrymen and wardens, may moulder forgotten in the brick vaults below the floor. Governor Shirley, who gave one of these bells, has become little more than a name, but those two lanterns signalling across to Charlestown that the British are coming (and by sea), and Paul Revere's actions on that night, have given Christ's its immortality.

One of the few stories of Paul's boyhood (and impossible to trace back to a contemporary source) tells how his father beat him for going over to Lynde Street to hear Mr. Jonathan Mayhew preach at the West Street Church. In a mid-Victorian version of this tale, Paul smugly expresses his gratitude for this unjust beating. It so early gave him an abhorrence of tyranny. It is also served up as proof that Mr. Revere was overstrict about the boy's church-going, yet we know that he was allowed actually to ring the demon-expelling bells of the only semi-Christian Episcopal Church. If Paul took to going over to the West Street Church in 1750, there were things being said by Mr. Mayhew which might upset a cautious father and interest a bright, fifteen-year-old boy tired of Mr. Welsteed and Mr. Gray, those tame-cats of the Hutchinsons. In January of that year young Mr. Mayhew fired what John Adams was to call 'the opening gun of the Revolution.'

Almost exactly one hundred years before, Charles the First had been beheaded by people who were the spiritual and sometimes physical ancestors of the men and women of Boston. But now the Episcopal churches and the royal governors were celebrating the anniversary of his death as a day of atonement and grief. In his three sermons Mr. Mayhew advocated chopping heads off kings — if necessary — and spoke against arbitrary rule. He scorned the supineness of people who did not resist tyranny. Boston rocked with an excitement which might well have upset the Revere household. Even in Great Britain these words were noted and by many approved. Mr. Mayhew had only stated what they believed were the ancient rights of Englishmen. Both over there and here a bitter fight against arbitrary rule was brewing. Over here it came to armed conflict. It did not in England, but the colonies were never without their sympathizers overseas. So now the University of Aberdeen sent Mr. Mayhew the degree of Doctor of Divinity. But the young clergyman 'over plied by public energies died of a nervous fever' before the Revolution actually broke.


## IV


SIR HARRY had the Clark house, but for a little longer the Clarks held on to their wharf. In size and importance it was only surpassed by Long Wharf. These two great piers were quite unlike little Hitchbourn Wharf, which lay between them. The north side of both of these semi-public wharves was built up with shops, warehouses, sail lofts, stores, and in the counting houses merchants — so bold-eyed, firm-lipped, rosy in their portraits — yelled at their clerks, swore at their captains, sent out the ships, and sold cargoes. Sometimes they made or lost a fortune from one Sabbath day to the next. All of Boston's prosperity depended upon overseas trade.

The Reveres lived 'near the head of Doctor Clark's Wharf,'[9] so they were on the dry land of Fish Street. It would be a good location for a silversmith. The merchants and sea captains spent wildly when they made a rich voyage, and the eighteenth century loved fine silver. A silversmith was almost as dependent upon sea trade as any sailmaker or wharfinger, yet this trade was, much of it, contrary to the laws of England. Massachusetts could not export directly to England. She had nothing except ships' masts the mother country wanted — no tobacco, sugar, or rice like the southern colonies. All that her lands gave were 'poor English crops,' and at this time England herself was exporting even wheat. Nor did they want her salted fishes to compete with 'true Englishmen.' Yet she must have her coffee, tea, ribbons and plush, iron wares, paper, and glass from England.

The Yankees had worked out elaborate trade habits centring on the West Indies. This included Spanish and French islands which, if she paid the customs, would be prohibitive to her. Massachusetts raised everything these tropical islands did not — pipe-staves for molasses barrels, salt fish, beef, pork, leather goods, horses, and cattle. In return she brought back raisins, limes, logwood, rice, and some iron, but her principal import from 'the Sugar Islands' was molasses for her rum. She also traded (often illegally) with South America and the Mediterranean, sometimes going as far as Madagascar, but the sum total of her ingenuity was plenty of bills of exchange to buy whatever she pleased in the London markets. As all she made was spent in England, this illicit trade was profitable to both the unruly colony and its mother. Well enough was, for a long time, let alone. The Port Collectors (like Sir Harry) took their duties very lightly, never looking into kegs marked salt to see if instead they might be carrying Madeira. Sometimes, during Paul Revere's teens, ocean-going ships were clearing the port of Boston faster than one a day. But the number of little fishing ships which came and went cannot be estimated. They were like shoals of herring.

There was plenty to see on Clark's Wharf, wonderful things and people. Here comes Mr. Thomas Hancock (Paul's father would remember how they both served their indenture at the same time down on Anne Street), and now people are saying it won't be long before he buys out the Clarks and owns this wharf himself. How fine he looks — with his double chin and portly strut and dark, confident eyes! The pretty, wistful little boy at his heels is the nephew, John Hancock, whom the merchant adopted when confident that 'Mrs. H.,' for all her generous proportions, would not give him an heir. Here is a boy who will not strip and dive off the wharf with the others. He never learned to swim until through Harvard and visiting London.

'Wonders' were often displayed upon the wharves: a 'sapient dog,' a polar bear, a doll dressed in the latest London fashion: even perhaps a pirate's head 'in pickle.' Close to the Reveres at the head of the wharf lived Mrs. Hiller, who made and displayed waxworks, figures of kings and queens, all beautifully dressed. She also ran a school where she taught such arts to young ladies, feather and quill work and fine embroidery as well. Not far away, John Dyer, who a few years before was head of the bell-ringing 'society,' had a more

striking 'waxworks.' His was a 'Lively Representation' of the unfortunate Countess of Heininburg who had three hundred and
sixty-five children at one birth.

European 'balance masters' came to perform for Boston, and by
the time Paul was old enough to appreciate such things 'the Elaborate and Matchless Pile of Art called the Microcosm, or the world
in miniature' was being displayed by Mr. Fletcher, merchant. It
was a mechanical planetarium, showing the movements of sun,
moon, and planets: the comet which Sir Isaac Newton said would
appear in 1758 and the eclipse of the sun, not due until 1764. Mr.
Fletcher had also imported from England several other mechanical
toys. Orpheus playing upon his lyre 'and beating exact time to
each Tune,' and a 'delightful Grove wherein Birds flying etc.' And
he had an entire town — a port like Boston, with tiny ships sailing
in the harbor, the wheels of coaches, carts, chaises all turning, a
minute little powder mill at work in one corner. Twelve hundred
wheels and pinions kept these marvels in motion, for man has so
often used his ingenuity first for toys. Firecrackers preceded gunpowder, electricity was a parlor game, and these wonderful, but
instructive mechanical toys came years before such things as the
spinning jenny. But Mr. Fletcher's exhibit was expensive. You
might see the Countess great with three hundred and sixty-five
children for sixpence. It took four shillings sixpence to see these
mechanical marvels.

Doctor Clark's books show that many of his tenants were sea
captains, and he had, besides Mrs. Hiller of the waxworks, a baker,
a block-maker, at least one silversmith, and other artisans. These
houses were close to his own house, barn, and apothecary shop. All
the doctors had these little shops. The darker, more mysterious, and
lethal they looked, the more faith the populace had in their efficiency. The days of witchcraft were not long over.

Doctor Clark's shop proved as lethal as it probably looked. He
had a negro slave, Robin, who is listed as a 'labourer' and seems to
have done odd jobs for his master. He had access to the shop.
Everyone about Clark's Wharf would know Robin. He wore a blue
suit lined and trimmed with yellow, and a striking black wig.

In the middle of the fifties there were some three thousand
negroes in Massachusetts, the largest proportion of them being
in and about Boston. Not only was there little place in the New

England economy for slave labor, but also strong feeling against it as an institution. As early as 1646 the General Court had ordered a 'negro stolen from Africa' to be returned. A four-pound duty was levied on every negro imported into the colony in an effort to keep the practice down. Hostile Indian prisoners were sold as slaves, and there was no feeling against that. But to be an African 'slaver' and actually catch these Ethiopians was something of a disgrace — owning slaves was not.

We have seen how Grandmother Hitchbourn owned at least a part of a black boy. Not many years later Mrs. Adams was given a slave to help her with her housework by an admirer of her husband. Sam immediately freed her. Yet even freeing slaves was costly. The erstwhile owner had to put up fifty pounds with the town treasurer as guaranty the freed man would not become a public charge. Slaves did not have the financial value in New England they did in the South, where the type of labor was so much better suited to them. There was no fear of a slave revolt, but sometimes they did rise up against individual masters, as did Mark and Phillis, with the aid of Doctor Clark's Robin.

Mark was an energetic black man who could read and write. He had hardly been bought by John Codman, sea captain and saddler of Charlestown, before he decided it was a bad berth for himself and the two negresses, Phillis and Phoebe. As Phillis said at the inquisition which finally resulted from Mark's dissatisfaction, Mark was 'uneasy and wanted to have another master & he was concerned for Phoebe and I too.' Under his leadership, the slaves first burned up his shop, hoping by embarrassing him financially to force him to sell them. But Captain Codman's credit was good. He rebuilt his shop and kept his slaves.

Next they decided to kill him. Mark read the Bible through and came to the conclusion that it was the shedding of blood that was the crime — not the murder. He decided on poison. So he went again and again to Doctor Clark's by night and persuaded Robin to steal the arsenic from his master's shop. Robin insisted that Mark only wanted it to kill three pigs. If he put the contents of the paper of powder he gave him 'in two quarts of swill it would make em swell.' But Robin knew, and an amazing number of other slaves for miles around seem to have known, that the 'pig' under discussion was Captain Codman.

Mark was married to Phillis and the two of them and Phoebe slept in the garret. Their nights were spent in whispered plotting, which went on in the daytime in 'the little house.' They never hoped more for themselves than a kinder master. Phillis had been in this house since childhood and it does not speak well for the Captain that she so hated him. As they knew their master better than anyone does today, it seems likely they had some provocation. And they also whispered of how mean a master Mr. Salmon of Boston had been until his slaves secretly poisoned him. No one ever knew and they were sold to kind people. They may have heard how, twenty years before, two slaves in Boston had put 'lumps of arsenic' in their master's chocolate. Mr. Scarlett had not died and the slaves were merely whipped.

Day after day, week after week, the two girls fed Captain Codman the poison in his 'water gruels' and his 'sagoe,' his chocolate, his 'infusions,' and his 'barley water.' He sat 'at a little round table' in the kitchen. They waited hopefully for him to begin to swell. They increased the dose and added black lead. The Captain flourished on his liquid diet and arsenic. They whispered, giggled, and laughed among themselves.

Mark went back to Robin for more arsenic. The doses had been too small, but the slaves were determined that he was not to die immediately. 'I felt ugly,' one of the girls frankly admitted. 'I want willing . . . that he should be killed so quick.'

It was not 'so quick' in the end. Captain Codman lived fifteen hours after he drank the last cup of chocolate his handmaidens mixed for him, seated at his 'little round table.' Secretly and gleefully the slaves danced in their garret, shaking themselves, 'acting as master did in Bed.'

Phoebe turned state's evidence. Robin and a host of others seemingly implicated were not tried. Mark and Phillis were the first and last people to suffer the terrible sentence which, under English law, followed 'petty treason.' The killing of a master or a husband was not merely murder, but treason as well. Massachusetts was light in her punishments compared to England, whose laws she theoretically followed, and the death penalty was rarely given in comparison to the practice in the mother country, but more freely than now.

The execution took place on Charlestown Common, now Somer-

ville. Mark was hanged and Phillis theoretically burned alive at
the stake. The evidence is that she was first strangled. It was the
most sensational murder trial ever to have taken place around
Boston and the execution was, of course, well attended. Nor was
it quickly forgotten. Mark's body was 'hung in chains' on Charlestown Common. There it hung for twenty years. The black man
shriveled up into some sort of mummy. It was one of the sights
of the neighborhood. Paul Revere knew it well. On his famous
ride to Lexington he noted when he reached the ghoulish spot
'where Mark was hung in chains.' This famous murder had come
close to his boyhood, for it was Dr. Clark's Robin who had furnished
the poison.

## V

MEN died strange deaths, ac-
cording to the newspapers and diaries of the time. We have seen
how the vehement Doctor Mayhew was soon to be carried off by
a 'nervous fevor.' And Paul's little cousin Philip, 'hearing the cry
of Fire ran out of his master's shop (a Taylor) which so chilled
his Blood that he fell into a Lethargy and expired soon after.' A
journeyman printer's death was 'occassioned by drinking cold
water.' A man drowned 'by the Providence of God.' The keeper
of the fish market, well one night and eating a hearty dinner, was
found dead in bed the next morning. 'It was supposed by the easy
position in which he lay he had no fit but an entire stagnation of
the fluids.' But whether the fifty-two-year-old silversmith drowned
by the 'Providence of God' or could not survive a stagnation of his
fluids, we do not know. The first Paul Revere died on the twenty-
second day of July, 1754. He lies buried in the Old Granary,
lying to this day as he had lived — surrounded by Hitchbourns.

He left behind him a widow of fifty, healthy enough to outlive
him by almost a quarter of a century. The oldest child, Deborah,

was a grown woman of twenty-two or three, but not yet married
to Thomas Metcalf. Paul was nineteen, Frances a year younger.
Then came Thomas, who, like his older brother, was also to be a
silversmith. John was to become a tailor. The youngest were two
small girls of thirteen and twelve — Mary and Betty. Paul's later
life, so interwoven with Hitchbourn cousins, included his two
younger brothers so little it may well be there was never great
intimacy between the three fatherless boys.

Now Paul was nominally the head of the house. For a while
there might be hard times. The first payment of rent after the
silversmith's death is by the widow, who pays Doctor Clark 'by a
silver thimble, rum and cash.' Mrs. Revere may have thriftily
saved some of the rum given her (as it often was) for her husband's
funeral feast. The next quarter is paid 'By her son's a/c for making
10 rings at 7/4 and cash.' Next it is the daughter Deborah who
pays the rent. This time with cash.

When Colonel Hutchinson died, he left two-thirds of his vast
property to his eldest son, Thomas. Foster, as younger son, had
one-third. But such primogeniture was not much practised in
Massachusetts. The first Paul Revere left no will and 'he left no
estate,' but he 'left a good name and seven children,' as his son
later wrote. Not many years before, Mr. Revere had been able
to contribute rather lavishly for the upkeep of clergymen. If in
other matters he tried to do one-fifth as well as Mr. Hutchinson,
he certainly would not have much estate to leave. Now that there
was possible calamity ahead for Mrs. Revere, her relatives would
rally around her. She had been a Hitchbourn before ever she had
taken the queer, outlandish name of Revere. Although families
seemed to have quarrelled more bitterly then than now, they at
least stood by in adversity. Paul says he continued his father's
trade. But he was only nineteen. By law, no person under twenty-
one, and no person who had not served seven years of apprenticeship, could 'open a shop.' A nineteen-year-old boy would not
have been allowed to step into his dead father's industrial shoes,
no matter how clever he was. He may have worked for Nathaniel
Hurd, for there seems to be some relationship between the two
silversmiths. He may have gone on under his mother's name,
for the widows of tradesmen or artisans were allowed to continue
their husbands' trade.

The mortality among women of child-bearing age was so high that many a man buried four wives before his fifth buried him. It would seem that both law and custom favored any woman capable of outliving her husband. Not only did wealthy men like John Hancock give them handsome benches to sit on during meeting, but the law allowed them certain rights of suffrage. More important, however, was their right to carry on their husbands' business without seven years of apprenticeship.

At this time in Boston one of Benjamin Franklin's sisters-in-law was carrying on her deceased husband's soap-boiling, and another of his dead brother's wives was the authorized printer for the Province of Rhode Island. A Mrs. Salmon, probably the widow of the man Mark and Phillis believed the slaves had secretly poisoned, was advertising in the *Boston Evening Post* for May 6, 1754, that at her shop 'gentlemen may have their Horses shod in the best Manner, as also all sorts of Blacksmith's work done with Fidelity and Dispatch.' Printing and newspaper publishing was, for some reason, the special field for widows. Before the Revolution ten newspapers were being printed and published by 'relicts' along the Atlantic seaboard. None of these women had, of course, served any apprenticeship.[10]

Although nominally Mrs. Revere might be the responsible head of the silversmith's shop in Fish Street, the work would be carried on by Paul, with young Thomas to help him. With such a clever breadwinner things would not look too black for the Reveres — if Paul kept his eye on his anvils. It was his obvious duty to stand by his mother, bring up Thomas to be a proper silversmith, see to it young John obeyed his master-tailor and the girls behaved themselves. All this was on his shoulders. Instead, he enlisted to fight the French at Lake George.

All the young men of Boston seem sooner or later to have taken their turn in fighting the French. The need for armed protection was desperate in New England. The year before one out of every eight adult men in Massachusetts had volunteered for service. Weak and divided as the little colonies were, they believed in their own form of government, the actual freedom and democracy they had established for themselves in the wilderness. Rich and poor alike, they were ready to die for these good things. Paul Revere did not like warfare. When able he would serve his country better in other ways, but at twenty-one he had not discovered these better ways. He took his turn in the army. That he himself was half-French never seems to have occurred to him. And was it not the group now in power at the French court who had purged France of his own family? So he went. Other reasons may have entered in. He may have been bored with ladies' thimbles, gentlemen's knee-buckles, and his mother's watchful eye. He longed to see more of the world than just Boston. But whatever his reason or multiplicity of reasons, in the spring of 1756 he threw down the domestic responsibilities that had come to him so early, listened to the muster captain's drum, and followed it.

## VI

LONG, long before Paul Revere was born and for thirty years afterwards, one French war followed another so fast there were few intervals of peace. All these were run together, forming one terrifying, bloody film before one's eyes. Forays of French and Indians striking down into the heart of New England, a farmer butchered as he ploughed his lonely field, women and children captured or scalped, roasted alive in their burning homes. Again and again the infuriated New Englanders (sometimes with support from the other English colonies and the mother country, sometimes without) carried the offensive against the strongholds of the French. Once they had even taken the supposedly impregnable fortress of Louisburg, only to have it returned to France next year by British diplomacy in exchange for Madras, India. England and France's titanic struggle ranged the world and the seven seas. Over here there were many names for this century of struggle — King William's War, Queen Anne's, King George's, 'the Old French War,' and the final phase Paul

Revere knew best was 'the Seven Years' War.' The sum total of them all is 'The French and Indian Wars.'

These went on over here even during periods when the parent countries were at peace. Which country would finally dominate North America was by no means decided. France had Canada and the mouth of the Mississippi. She was consolidating the intervening wilderness and claiming all but the Atlantic seaboard, where in time she hoped to pick off the struggling English colonies.

The year before Paul threw his tiny bit of humanity into this seething cauldron, General Braddock, commander-in-chief of the British and American forces over here, had been defeated and killed. The twenty-three-year-old Colonel Washington had his first chance to show the fire under his unruffled demeanor and Governor Shirley of Massachusetts was appointed to fill Braddock's place until Lord Loudoun could come over and take command. Young Washington, in full command of the Virginian forces, came to Boston to confer with Governor Shirley. It had been decided that this summer's attack should be against the French-held forts of Crown Point and Ticonderoga. Massachusetts was so exposed to massacre from Canada, it was not hard for her to raise the men.

In the spring of 1756 formal war was once more declared between England and France (although their colonies had not been keeping the previous truce). The Massachusetts General Court authorized the raising of thirty-five hundred men. Year in and year out for generations all men had been required to train in the militia. Compulsory military service for Americans is not a modern novelty. But such expeditions outside the boundaries of the colony were manned by volunteers.

So, Governor Shirley sent out his orders: 'I do hereby authorize and enjoin that [Captain So-and-So] to beat his drum anywhere within the Province for enlisting volunteers for his Magesty's service in a regement of foot to be forthwith raised for the expedition against Crown Point.' General Winslow was to command them. Under him was General Lyman. Paul Revere served in Richard Gridley's regiment. At this time there were five hundred men in a regiment, divided into ten companies. The muster captains got from two to six dollars a head for every recruit they brought in. There were certain requirements. All must be able-bodied and between seventeen and forty-five, and must measure to a certain height. George Robert Twelves Hewes could not go. He was too short, and in vain did he get a shoemaker to build up the inside of his shoes; but Paul Revere 'passed muster' and 'mounted the cockade.'

On the eighteenth of February, 1756, Governor Shirley, respectfully addressing the young artisan as 'gentleman' gave him his commission as second lieutenant in the artillery train, for he believed his 'courage, loyalty and conduct' deserved special trust. And he bids him diligently to discharge his duties 'in ordering and exercising the Great Artillery, &ca; both Inferiour Officers and Montrosses, and to keep them in good Order and Discipline; hereby comanding them to obey you as their second lieutenant'; and Paul himself is to give equal obedience to the officers above him.

The local boys stuck closely together when they went into the army and the appointment of officers usually followed the wishes of the men. This army was enlisted for not more than a year and to serve only against Crown Point. Each mess consisted of six men and was allowed 'a lamp kettle, a Bowl, and Platter and the Officers of each company two, and every Man a Spoon.' So Paul at least could have two spoons.

If a man brought a gun with him, he had a bounty, but his 'powder-horn, bullet-pouch, blanket, knapsack and wooden bottle' (for the indispensable rum) was supplied by the colony. The men had no bayonets, but carried hatchets in their belts. Their uniforms (when they had any) were blue coats with either blue or scarlet breeches. The 'wages,' as they called it, was one pound six shillings a month for a private, but an artillery lieutenant had five pounds six and eight. The Reveres, at this time, paid Doctor Clark sixteen pounds a year. Paul may have found army service was the surest way he could earn the rent money, but often the soldiers were not paid until a year or so later. There were never enough surgeons with the troops, but a disproportionate supply of chaplains, who endured spiritual suffering and disillusionment as well as the same fatigue, diseases, and dangers as the troops.

That spring Paul Revere was a part of the long, struggling line of marching men. Cannon drawn by horses or oxen, tool wagons, supply wagons, pack horses, tumbrils, men, formed one great, muddy, red-and-blue snake striking against the French.  Captain Bacon of Dedham was one of his companions.  He kept a diary. On the ninth of May the troops were as far as Natick.  Next day being Lord's day and they at Framingham, the troops first heard 'Mr. Bridgmin in the forenoon meeting in the forenoon and then between meeting march to mr Stone's meeting house and tarry there in the afternoon meeting.'  So on to 'Southbury' and 'Westbury,' the churches growing scantier as they went west and the troops less and less interested in the war as a holy crusade against the French and more and more interested in their feet, stomachs, and rum.

Their first destination was Albany, a snug, well-fortified Dutch village, the rendezvous of the other colonies' troops and base for their operations.  Each colony had its own committee for supplying and transporting and some special grievance against the other colonies.  Loudoun, who was to command the expedition, had not yet come over from England and the advantage his troops had in the earlier arrival of their spring was already lost.  When Loudoun did arrive, he did not like the provincial way of doing things, but did little himself.  'A Saint George on a [inn] sign always on horseback and never getting forward' he was called in a letter to Benjamin Franklin.  But one sympathizes with my lord when he wrote in despair to Revere's general, 'I wish to God you could persuade your people to go all one way.'

The French had the tremendous military advantage of being a totalitarian state.  There were no provincial assemblies in Canada to hamper the commanders.  'Secret' expeditions did not need to be discussed publicly for months in a series of very democratic general courts and provincial assemblies before the money for them was voted.  Although so much fewer in number than the English colonies, they were for a long time more powerful in the field.  Eight years before, a Swedish scientist, Peter Kalm, travelling our country, noticed this lack of any union between the colonies. 'It happens that in time of war things go on very slowly and irregularly here; for not only the opinion of one province is sometimes directly opposite to that of another, but frequently the views of the governor and those of the assembly of the same province are quite different; so that it is easy to see that, while the people are quarrelling about the best and cheapest manner of carrying on the war, an enemy has it in his power to take one place after another.' The little democracies showed up badly through these wars — except for the one fact that they won in the end. This summer the French had the additional advantage of Montcalm as their commander-in-chief. We only had Lord Loudoun.

From Albany, the Massachusetts men were sent to Half Moon, where the Mohawk joined the Hudson. From there they advanced to the outposts of Fort Edward and then on to Fort William Henry (at the head of Lake George). Loudoun sent an officer to see what these troops looked like after a month or so in camp. He was told at Fort William Henry, out of twenty-five hundred men 'four hundred sick, the greater part of them what they call poorly; they bury from five to eight daily....' The camp was dirty, privies, slaughter pens, kitchens, and graves all mixed up together. It was a military axiom that men may not safely be kept camped long in one place. Not even the better-disciplined French troops escaped camp diseases when left more than a week or two in one camp.

Oswego, most westerly of English forts, fell that summer to the French. It had 'changed masters,' as Doctor Williams wrote his wife, 'we may justly fear that the whole of our country will soon follow.' Neither side felt strong enough to take the offensive. Both sat and died in their forts. According to Paul Revere's fellow soldier, Captain Bacon, much time was spent 'foling tres.' Sloops were built and several hundred whaleboats to carry the army across the lake. Scouts and raiding parties were sent out from both sides. Colonel Bagley, who commanded Fort William Henry, wrote: 'I constantly keep sending out small scouting parties to the east-ward of the lake, and make no discovery — but the tracks of small parties who are plaguing us constantly; but what vexes me most, we can't catch the sons of bitches. I have sent out skulking parties some distance from the sentries in the night, to lie still in the bushes to intercept them; but the flies are so plenty — our people can't bear them.' It was only Captain Robert Rogers and his Rangers that showed any facility in the work. Otherwise the French and Indians were supreme. Almost daily the Indians could sneak up and pick off a few of the troops.

By now (the chaplains note) they are cursing and swearing and cutting divine service. The Reverend John Graham was with the Connecticut troops. He was morbid, conscientious, and superstitious, even hearing the voice of God in his own 'ventral rumblings.' August the seventeenth he 'Brakfasted this morning with the General. But a graceless meal; never a blessing asked, nor thanks given. At the evening sacrifice a more open scene of wickedness. The General and head officers ... in General Lyman's (Paul Revere's commander) tent, within four rods of the place of public prayer. None came to prayers; but they fixed a table without the door of the tent, where a head colonel was posted to make punch in the sight of all, they within drinking, talking and laughing during the whole service.'

Captain Bacon at the end of the campaign showed more interest in recording the arrival of a new supply of rum than in what 'sacrifices' attended the troops once they were settled down in the wilderness.

On the twenty-fifth of November, when food was scant, snow falling, men shivering in their light summer equipment, the Massachusetts troops were ordered on the long march home, for armies, like bears, hibernated during the winter months. The British had that summer lost one fort and gained no new ones. Colonel Gridley's regiment left many of its men in shallow graves about Lake George, marked only by the digging of fox or wolf.

And that winter as far away as on the other side of Lake Michigan, Menominie warriors could wear at their belts the fair hair of boys who but a year before had been wearing it themselves about the wharves and shops of Boston.

Paul Revere at least brought back his life and scalp with him. Now he might forget the towering forest, foaming rivers, and the Indians of the wilderness. The smells of Clark's Wharf, coffee, tar, hemp, spice, fish, were dearer to him than the clean virgin forest. Other men like Captain Rogers and his Rangers might skim the black ice of Lake George that winter, tramp the frozen mountains on snowshoes, guarding the frontier, as the young artisan settled down in his warm shop. Paul Revere did push out some frontiers for his country, but they were not so much geographic as industrial. Boston — not Albany — was to be his base.

## VII

THAT Boston Paul Revere knew is so completely gone, it is almost useless to hunt for it. The cutting-down of hills and building-out of new land has gone on for a century and a half. When in 1756 his artillery train trundled into Boston, they entered over 'The Neck.' It was the only land approach to the town. On his right was Roxbury Harbor, to his left the Back Bay, and for a mile he followed an ill-marked, ill-paved, desolate cart path over mud-flats. The first sign of civilization was the gallows and around it the graves of criminals and suicides marked with heaps of stones. Near-by in his pasture was the town bull.

Next came the town gate, where Dover Street now is. Today Boston is widest at this point. In Revere's day it was narrowest. The gate was of brick. Through one arch pedestrians entered; through the other wagons, cattle, horsemen. It was guarded night and day. Here began the town itself and 'the High Street' (now Washington). But the High Street was made up of a number of streets which changed their names every few blocks. It left the Neck as Orange, but was soon Newbury, then Marlborough. It wound up at the old State House as Cornhill. This method of renaming a street every short distance helped a stranger to find his way about at a time when there was little street numbering.

At the old State House, King Street ran brief and broad to the shoreline and was carried out to sea for half a mile as Long Wharf. Here the largest ship afloat could come to at low tide. The most conspicuous object moored there today is the Custom House Tower. North Station is in the Mill Cove, then a sheet of water as large as the Common — in it little Benjamin Franklin used to dump the offal from his father's candle-shop. Hitchbourn Wharf is lost under cement somewhere around the entrance to Sumner Tunnel. Most, if not all, of Clark's Wharf is dry land.

The top of the Bulfinch State House is only as high as Beacon Hill was then. The hill was cut down and the gravel used to fill

Mill Cove. That the western slope of Beacon Hill had a large hump on it, only the name 'Mount Vernon' now suggests. Paul Revere knew it under the more provocative name of 'Mount Whoredom.' Pemberton Hill, where the courthouse is, has long ceased to exist. It is as if the original town had been squeezed in a gigantic press, hills flattened, and the material spread out into Roxbury Harbor and Back Bay (an actual bay from which redcoats could embark from the corner of Charles and Boylston) into Mill Cove and all around the periphery. Even Castle Island, then so well out to sea, is now joined to the mainland.

Wherever the streets of Boston are well blocked out — straight and pleasing to our countrymen from other parts — the chances are you are standing on old sea bottom. Wherever the streets are snarled up, you are in the ancient town itself — a feeling often pleasing to Bostonians.

North Boston started off handsomely, but went downhill rather early. Because for a hundred years it was first an Irish, then a Jewish, and next an Italian slum, little money has been spent on modernizing it. The old streets follow their ancient channels and many of them keep their old-fashioned names, Moon Street and Sun Court, Salutation and Charter. But what Paul knew as Anne, Fish, and Ship Streets are today run together as either North Street or Atlantic Avenue, and so it goes. Yet many diminutive alleys, quick, queer turns, do suggest what it was like in his day. Only here in North Boston is part of the original shoreline still intact. Although we can imagine better what colonial Boston was like by walking about the old parts of Portsmouth, Newport, Marblehead, or Nantucket, something of the old town is left in the North End. And there is still a sparkle and freshness to the air of North Boston, which juts out so boldly to sea, that the man-made land along the Charles does not have.

The Boston of that day smelt very different. More of animals (both living and dead) and of whales, fish, and the sea, tar, soap-boiling, brewing, spice, and humanity. There might be by Paul Revere's time a slight taint of Newcastle coals, but sweet wood smoke and charcoal would predominate. A quack might come to town selling 'Seneca oil.' It had so evil a smell it surely ought to have been a powerful medicine. The Indians far off in Pennsylvania got it by dipping their blankets into 'oil springs' or 'pitch lakes' and wringing them out into bowls. You could rub it on you for rheumatism or drink it for consumption. Of course it was far too precious to burn. And the smell of burning gasoline, which now reigns supreme in our cities, was unknown.

The quack calling his oil was but one of many street cries.

'Sweep o' sweep,' chirped little negro sweeps as they peddled their services. They carried brooms and a blanket in which to take away the soot. When they reached the top of a chimney, they would pause, look about them, and sing to the town at large a sad, lost song. Nice children were afraid of dirty little sweeps.

'Fresh cod, haddock, and mackerel, come in this morning, at the head of the ferry-ways!' The fish peddlers also had tin horns.

And towards evening one heard in every month with an 'r' in it, 'Oys! Finey Oys — Buy any Oys?' The oystermen carried their wares in sacks on their backs.

There was also the voice of the town crier. How plaintively he would cry a lost child; but for martial news he could roar like a bull.

And the watch by night. 'Half past twelve o'clock and a fine, clear morning.' 'One o'clock and a severe snowstorm.' Boston was not so much quieter then than now, but its noises were different. From hundreds of shipyards and shops, from sunup to sundown, came the tapping of hammers, the thump of hand looms, the creak of wooden machinery. The hooves of horses on cobbles and the rattle of carts may have been louder than the meshing of gears and swishing of tires. But one still heard the crying of gulls and the beat of the sea upon headlands, or the croak of frogs along Frog Lane (now Boylston Street). At night the stars were as close and wonderful as they still seem to us on dark, country roads. Paul Revere would be well up in his thirties before he served on the first committee to consider street lamps for Boston.

The skyline was dominated by steeples and the whole town by bells. Everyone knew Christ's 'royal peal' and that New North's had a sour note. King's Chapel's was deep and sad. Old Brattle and Hollis had their bells. Folk would stop in the street to count the 'passing bell' tolling out the sex and age of the deceased. And they always ran to ask for whom the bell tolls.

The bells rang wildly for fires or to call out the mob, joyfully for the repeal of certain acts of Parliament or the withdrawal of an especially unpopular royal governor. They tolled over 'tyranny.'

They opened and closed the markets, and twice on Sabbath called all to church or meeting. These were the great bells — the very voice of Boston. Besides there were countless smaller ones. Hand-bells rung on the street advertising 'wonders' and sales, or that it was two o'clock and 'The Bunch of Grapes' was about to serve dinner. Schoolmasters rang for school, cowbells drowsed through the blueberry bushes and hardhack of the Common, and all day long, in hundreds of shops and houses, the tinkle, tinkle, tinkle of doorbells. In winter-time came the frosty sparkle of sleighbells as citizens rode out in their 'boobyhuts.'

The music of bells is almost forgotten by modern ears. Then it was everywhere.

Drums, too. Muffled drums for dead worthies. Drummers (such as Paul's great-grandfather, Hitchbourn) very literally 'drumming up' trade. Now only the American word 'drummer' for salesman suggests this old practice.

And how fast and sharp the drummers beat on Training Day! And off and on, and on again louder and louder through the streets of Boston in the seventeenth and eighteenth centuries, the muster captains beat their drums calling the young men to war.

# III

## 1756 – 1764

PAUL REVERE marries SARY ORNE. By joining the MASONS he meets JAMES OTIS, JOSEPH WARREN, etc. HE keeps a ledger, pays and receives rent, makes silver and fights TOM FOSDICK. Smallpox strikes the REVERES and causes horror throughout BOSTON. SAM ADAMS tells JOHN ADAMS the part HANCOCK is to play in the coming drama.

View of Boston by Paul Revere. North American Almanack, 1770.

# I

**THAT** spring the drums beat once more and again troops marched, this time to even greater disaster than the year before, but Paul Revere stuck to Clark's Wharf and his shop.

He was now a master silversmith with Thomas to serve under him as his apprentice. His mother kept the house and paid Doctor Clark the rent. John had left for his own master, who was a tailor, but the girls were unmarried and presumably at home.

At twenty-two Paul was a sturdily built young fellow, of but indifferent height. He must have seemed romantically dark to the girls of Boston, a town which, judging by portraits and descriptions, was predominately blue-eyed and fair-haired. Although he may have come back from Lake George as lean as a hawk (and there were many other times in his life that would have thinned a man down), he was, in his natural and happy state at least, stocky. The mouth had a wide, generous turn to it. Dark men today tend to give the illusion, at least, of very white teeth. That Paul's were good is proved by the long time they stayed by him. His last portrait, painted when over eighty, shows none of the prunes and prisms (as in the case of the Father of our Country) which suggest colonial dentures, nor has it the sweet, toothless smile which is the other characteristic elderly expression of the day. Dark, ruddy, stocky men are apt to laugh easily. In the portrait Copley painted of Paul when he was in his thirties, there is a quizzical lift to the eyebrow and a flick to the dark eye. He looks ready enough to laugh or answer back if his friend Copley spoke to him. There is also something of the expression one can imagine on

Thomas Dexter's face when he stood with his arms akimbo 'daring' choleric Governor Endicott himself. The dark coloring may have been French, but the expression of the face seems to personify hundreds of Boston artisans, very ready to speak back to any royal governor the Crown can send over.

'Bold' is the adjective his contemporaries used most often for him. As 'Bold Revere' he was sung on the streets and in the taverns of Boston. But to this is also added 'steady, vigorous, sensible, persevering' or 'cool in thought, ardent in action.' A nice balance between good sense and boldness characterized his whole life. It is not a rare combination, but when to it is added intelligence, fine workmanship, and a certain robustness — half physical and half spiritual — a great deal may be accomplished.

Paul Revere lived a life without serious setbacks or deep prod-dings into 'the meaning of it all.' Whatever was to be done, from fixing George Washington's teeth (if a late legend is right) to riding express for the Boston Committee of Correspondence, he did with simple dispatch. It was not for him to question whether George Washington might not be better off without any false teeth at all, or doubt the wisdom of the Committee of Correspondence.

In contrast to the men with whom his name was later to be associated, he seems to have gone ahead without great ponderings. James Otis' brilliant mind went crazy over questions of empire that never existed for Paul Revere. Paul endured none of the humiliations of repeated failure that mellowed Sam Adams, nor was he ridden with the doubts and self-questionings that John Adams, like his great-grandson Henry, was already suffering. John Hancock was proud, touchy, and given to all sorts of lying-downs and headaches, which suggest some psychic block. None of these ailments of the soul, at once so devastating and so edu-cational, as far as we know touched Paul Revere.

The leaders of revolution in Boston were a few well-educated and mostly well-born men, largely Harvard graduates. They were 'gentlemen' in the old-fashioned sense of the word, which implies lace ruffles, clean hands, and a knowledge of Greek and Latin. Such are men of ideas first and secondarily of action. They were the 'intellectuals' who often precede revolution. Paul was ad-mitted to their society because they wished the sympathy of the large artisan class with whom he was immensely popular, and he

represented an important point of view. To them he was apt to
be 'my worthy friend' or 'a man of his rank and opportunities in
life' — never quite an equal. Yet not even these high-nosed Whig
leaders could penetrate the smith's easy self-respect and confidence.
He may have had many ailments to which modern flesh is heir
(and for which he had no name), but he never suffered from an
inferiority complex, nor the overcompensation of undue pride.

But in 1757 his life had not broadened out to include this intellectual group. His friends were men like Josiah Flagg, the jeweler,
and Manasseh Marston, who lived close by him. And Captain
Cochran, the mariner, who either lived in the same house as the
Reveres or in the one adjoining. Paul had his Uncle Thomas,
building ships down on Hitchbourn Wharf, and ten Hitchbourn
cousins. He would lack neither customers for his work nor companions for his leisure.

And he had Sara Orne. He may have taken his girl rowing on
the harbor, and, after a picnic on one of the islands, lain for hours,
silent, with his head in her lap, as did other young courting men
of the period. Sara Orne may have first guessed his devotion when
she noticed how, during Sabbath Meeting, his eyes sought hers
and never the Reverend Ebenezer Pemberton's. And there
he would be afterwards, waiting to walk home with her.

A neighbor's chaise might be hired and a lovely day spent as far
out as the Blue Hills of Milton. If the young couple spent the night
with friends, no questions would be asked. Strict chaperonage
was unheard of, and young people of much more pretentious households than the Reveres and the Ornes were allowed a freedom not
to be known again in this country until the rise of the automobile.

There were plenty of frolics during which an old English rough-
ness of manner and courting customs came to the top (this phase of
Puritan life has been ignored by Thanksgiving magazine covers
and school pageants). About the time Paul went courting, another
man described the fun he was having 'when kisses and drams set
the virgins aflame,' and the party seems to have ended up in a
catch-as-catch-can.

> 'The chairs in wild order flew quite round the room,
> Some threatened with fire brands, some with a broom,
> While others, resolved to increase the uproar,
> Lay tussling the girls in wide heaps on the floor.'

But Jacob Bailey, the young schoolmaster-poet, did not like such 'scenes of vile lewdness.'

> 'Quite sick of confusion, dear Dolly and I
> Retired from the hubbub new pleasures to try.'

Paul and his dear Sara may have been equally offended — or equally anxious for greater privacy. Whether they reached their conclusion through 'kisses and drams' or by the more traditional method of exchanging glances in meeting, it is known that soon after August 17, 1757, they were married. In the family Bible Paul wrote her name down as 'Sary,' so this is what he called her.

Paul took his twenty-year-old bride home to his mother's house. Here was his shop and his father's tools. Here his means of livelihood. Young brides were not often asked whether they liked living with their mothers-in-law or not. They were adaptable, humble by modern standards, and probably happy.

On April 3 in the following spring, Sara was brought to bed of a daughter (named Deborah after Mrs. Revere). This would be quick enough to start the gossips counting on their fingers, but not quick enough to give them any scandal. And no sooner was Sara through nursing Deborah than she was pregnant with the next, and so on and on.

There were those nights when Paul (obviously a heavy sleeper) would be wakened by his bedfellow. 'Paul ... Paul ...' 'Yes, my dear ...?' — his first thought being that thieves had broken into his silver shop. 'Paul ... my time has come. The midwife.' And he'd be out of bed and into his breeches before the sleep was out of his eyes, so quick he was in action; then running down the black, cobbled streets; stopped by the watch, but hearing his errand they'd bless him, and he'd be rapping at the midwife's door. And so

> 'Old Gammer Hipple-Hopple popped out of bed,
> Opened the casement and stuck out her head ...'

Hanging on the young man's arm to steady herself over the hobbling pavement she'd boast of the nine hundred and eighty-seven babies she had delivered, and please God there would be an even thousand before she died. How many mothers and how many babies these midwives lost they never seem to have recorded. It was the quantity — not quality — of their work they boasted.

As long as she lived, Sara never had a child in an odd year and never missed an even one. So little is known about this first wife of Paul Revere, and yet that little to us seems sad. Many other women beside Sara had a child every other year and died in the middle thirties. Perhaps she was physically frail. Revere's children by Sara Orne were not very hardy. Although only three of the eight died in infancy (this may have been due to their skilful grandmother's presence in the house), only one outlived Paul himself.

Boston, in spite of its high birth rate, had grown so slowly it was but little larger than at the time of the first Paul Revere. It was not only the opening-up of the hinterland and the mortality among children and women which kept the population so stationary, but the wars. Thomas Hutchinson believed that between five and six thousand Boston boys and young men died in the first forty years of the French and Indian Wars. By the summer of 1758 the end was in sight. The elder Pitt was all-powerful in England and showing his talent for picking out obscure officers and turning them into military geniuses. During his supremacy, India was won for England at one end of the world, Canada at the other, and the power of France smashed on the continent of Europe. For the work over here, Pitt sent the young, unknown, restless, sombre Amherst, and the even younger, red-headed Wolfe. England never did greater service to her American colonies than in giving them such military leaders and the support of a considerable number of regulars and her fleet, nor was there ever a time when she was more popular in America.

Louisburg fell in '58, and this time it was not returned by diplomats to France. Amherst and his forces arrived in Boston in September. 'I had desired no ceremony,' he wrote in his journal, 'but the whole town turned out.'

Babies, inns, towns, were all named for the tall, eagle-faced Amherst. His men, camped on the Common, came in for their share of admiration. The townsmen 'would give them Liquor and make the men Drunk in Spite of all that could be done. I sent patrolles around the Town all day & night.'

Within a year under Amherst's and Wolfe's leadership Quebec fell. The horrors of the French and Indian Wars drew towards a close, although the treaty was not signed until a few more years. It was now seen to be necessary to keep a considerable force of

trained troops over here to protect the frontiers which so recently
had been the scenes of bloody fighting. Not many men — say
ten thousand. None of the colonies wished to do this police work.
All were agreed that England should furnish the men — but how
they were to be paid and maintained they did not suggest.

Peter Kalm had thought a few years before that it was 'a great
advantage to the Crown of England that the North American
colonies are near a country, under the government of the French,
like Canada. There is reason to believe that the King never was
earnest in his attempt to expel the French from their possessions
there. If once the fear of France was removed, England would
have difficulty in keeping any authority over here.'

'In the space of thirty or fifty years,' thought Kalm, the colonies
might be able to 'form a state by themselves entirely independent
of Old England.'

# II

# THE old rhyme says

'If history be no ancient Fable
Freemasons came from Tower of Babel'

— but it was not until Paul Revere's day the craft struck root in
America. The oldest 'regular' lodge in this country was founded
in Boston — two years before his birth. He was fourteen when, for
the first time, the Masons, with their regalia and aprons, paraded
the streets of Boston in honor of the Feast of Saint John. At that
time the Masons 'kept at Stones in a very grand manner.' When
Paul was twenty-five, he was accepted into the society. It was an
important step for him.[11]

The young artisan may have been fascinated by the romantic,
cloudy history of the craft. One can still read in a book of the

period how 'Master Moses often marshalled the Israelites into a regular and General Lodge, whilst in the wilderness,' or that Charles Martel was 'the Right Worshipful Grand Master of France,' and of course how Master Solomon built the Temple.

His own lodge, Saint Andrew's, was organized in 1756, but did not receive its charter from the Grand Lodge of Scotland until September 4, 1760. That day 'it was laid before the Lodge, and in the same evening work was comenced under it by receiving Paul Revere, a Goldsmith, and engraver as Entered Apprentice.'

There were not many Masons in Boston at the time. When Jeremiah Gridley, 'Grand Master of all America,' died, seven years later, the Boston brethren exerted themselves to give him a magnificent Masonic funeral. Only one hundred and sixty-one Masons marched in the procession and that was probably many more than there were in Boston when Paul Revere joined. He was entering a carefully selected group based on neither wealth nor prestige, but entirely upon character. Saint John's Lodge seems to have been slightly more elegant in its membership than Saint Andrew's, for among their brethren were James Otis, two Gridleys, three Quincys, and 'Merchant' Rowe himself, so well known in his own day and now remembered for the codfish he gave the State House, his wharf, and his diary. But the two lodges often met together at various inns. The society was a silent, but powerful influence on Boston. The brethren met on a common footing and did much to promote the idea of the brotherhood of man — and also of the American Revolution.

It was by no means entirely of 'Charges' and who built the Temple, or vague generalities of service that were discussed when the Masons met in their proverbial secrecy. By the time Paul Revere had finished his apprenticeship to the craft and could wear his apron with the full dignity of a Master Mason, Governor Bernard and the Lieutenant Governor, Thomas Hutchinson, guessed that much of the opposition to themselves and to royal government emanated from the fastnesses of the Masons. The new governor wrote home that they were meeting at 'Adjutant Trowels' *long garret*' and were spewing forth such sedition and libel they must have 'ransak'd Billingsgate and the Stews' for the language they flung at him and Hutchinson.

The victory over France had at last ended America's dependence on England's protection. If she did not like the way the mother country restricted her trade and industry, she would not now be too afraid of the French to say so. So the time Peter Kalm had foreseen had come, earlier than he had prophesied.

England emerged from her struggle punch-drunk from a victory she could hardly understand. Her taxes were tremendous, her trade dislocated. True, she had an empire such as the world had never seen before, but no machinery, not even much idea how to govern. Seemingly she had acquired this empire in an absent-minded moment and now proceeded to muddle about trying to find some method of government. Her American colonies had controlled their destinies more than any other colonies in that century. Not since the days of the Greeks had there been such freedom allowed to colonies — and the Greeks had never felt any responsibility to protect a colony. England's fleet had defended these little states. Without it they could hardly have existed.

New England had prospered greatly by England's victories and was extremely well off, although she had lost so many men. The wartime boom she enjoyed was partly due to the money England had poured in. The business of supplying the troops had made a number of new fortunes. The question now was how to get the money out of her to help pay for a war which had been very much for her benefit and to maintain from now on the army of ten thousand, at the cost of one hundred thousand pounds a year, which everyone on both sides of the Atlantic thought should be established over here. It seemed unfair that poor Yorkshire weavers should pay even heavier taxes for this army and the touchy Yankees, who had even grown rich out of the war, go scot free. The question was how to do it. There was reason enough to believe if the money was raised by the vote of provincial assemblies it would never materialize. Without some central control from England, the colonies would 'shuffle out, all together.'

Massachusetts had always been run on a loose rein compared to the more profitable colonies. 'Her wool,' it was said, 'was too short for plucking.' The southern colonies, with some cluckings and squawkings, had been laying their eggs directly into the mother country's hat. But Massachusetts had stolen a nest and was hatching a wild brood of ugly chickens — those Yankee ships which traded about as they pleased and obeyed no laws. Now, in the interest of the empire, these wild chickens were to be put back in the coop.

Sir Harry Frankland — most genial Collector of the Port of Boston — had returned to England, taking his beautiful Agnes Surriage with him. Suddenly a new type of customs official was landed upon a startled Boston. Charles Paxton, a native son, was incorruptible and efficient. This was one of the more venal periods of British parliamentary history, and where they found so many honest officials with which to bedevil Boston is hard to imagine. Paxton went to work with a relish. For the first time the Navigation Acts were to be enforced and the money due England collected. Paxton soon discovered that the sympathy with the smugglers was so universal he could not get an unbiased jury. Admiralty courts, which need no jurors, were established. But he could not collect evidence. The most conservative opposed him as bitterly as the more radical. The enforcement of these old laws, which had never been obeyed, was such an innovation and led so directly to the Revolution, Charles Francis Dana could say, with considerable accuracy on the hundredth anniversary of the Battle of Lexington, 'The King and Parliament were the revolutionists. We were the conservators of existing institutions. They were seeking to overthrow and reconstruct on a theory of Parliamentary omnipotence ... we broke no chains.'

The merchants complained that if the law was enforced, it would tie up one hundred thousand pounds' worth of shipping in Boston. Paxton and his henchmen obviously did not care. They were open to neither bribes nor pity. Being unable to collect evidence any other way, Paxton demanded 'Writs of Assistance.'

These pieces of paper allowed customs officials to break by force, if necessary, into any ship, warehouse, dwelling, or store it suited their whim. It was not made out for one emergency against one man, but could be used at any time anywhere. It was perfectly legal by English law, having been enacted, as James Otis was saying, 'at the zenith of arbitrary power, when in the reign of Charles II, Star Chamber powers were pushed to extremity by some ignorant clerk of the exchequer' and absolutely contrary to the 'rights of Englishmen' as understood then and today. Pitt himself declared these writs 'contrary to the immunity of an English home, where the wind might blow through every cranny,

but the King's writ could not enter.' Now these horrifying bits
of paper were to enter some of the richest wharves and stateliest
houses of Boston. If this was the British idea of bringing back into
the coop the wild chickens of the New England coast, they were
bad psychologists. A little well-sprinkled corn might have done it.
The Writs of Assistance were like a flapping apron.

James Otis was thirty-five and the best lawyer in Boston when
he undertook to fight the writs of assistance in the Massachusetts
courts, and it was at this time Paul Revere first became a Mason
and was thrown into personal contact with him. Otis was already
showing signs of the mental instability which was to pass from
'mad freaks' to the strait-jacket and insanity. But he had a genuinely
original mind, thought in large terms (never merely of Boston),
and was passionately attached to the British Empire, which, he
said, 'was best calculated for general happiness of any that has
yet risen to view in the World.' An independent America was a
thing no one 'but rebels, fools, madmen will contend for.' He believed the colonies should be represented in Parliament and was
ready to die fighting for their rights. Finally the Whigs would
call him a Tory and the Tories a Whig. For a brief time he was
so powerful he was called 'the mad dictator of Boston.'

Physically he was a large man — 'a great Leviathan.' He had
a short neck, bold, narrow eyes, and a big, eloquent mouth which
looks, in his portrait, capable of taking in all the liquor credited
to him and giving forth the fiery speeches. An obscure little lawyer
of the moment, John Adams, said he 'is extremely quick and
elastic, his apprehensions as quick as his temper. He springs and
twitches his muscles about in thinking.' Friends said he was
'rough, hasty, loved good cheer.' But his enemies called him
'rash, unguarded, foul-mouthed,' or even 'a rackoon' or 'filthy
scunk.' And how he could talk! The wildness and magic (sometimes boredom) of his talk must have swept the Masonic lodges
even as it swept through the diaries and letters of his contemporaries.
It varied from dreams of a perfect British Empire uniting the whole
peaceful world in bonds of love, with God over all, to dirty (and
not very funny) stories, but it never stopped.

Besides fighting the writs of assistance, he was also avowedly
out to dislodge the Hutchinson-Oliver clique. The Hutchinsons
had sprung from the cataclysmic Anne, but by the seventeen-sixties

had spent several generations respectably collecting property. Thomas Hutchinson, having all the money he wished, and a high sense of civic duty, began collecting public offices. Financially he lost rather than gained by the extraordinary number of public posts he filled. He was usually a member of the General Court, and often Speaker. He was a constant member of the Governor's Council, Judge of Probate, Justice of the Court of Common Pleas, and had recently been appointed Lieutenant Governor. The necessity of separating legislative and judicial branches of government did not bother many people at the time, but it did James Otis, who had a fine, theoretical mind. He believed such concentration of power was dangerous. What Thomas Hutchinson did not have himself, others of his own family or the closely related Olivers did.

When, the year before, Hutchinson had been appointed by the Governor as Chief Justice of the Province (although the office had been promised to Otis' own father), it seemed too much to many people. Hutchinson always said that it was personal spite over this appointment that made James Otis his bitter enemy; that at that time he swore 'that he would set the province in flames, if he perished by the fire.'

James Otis was King's Advocate, but resigned the position so he could present the case of sixty merchants petitioning against the writs. 'Jerry' Gridley, in whose office he had read law, took the side for the Crown.

In February, 1761, the case was heard, with a leading Mason on either side. In their scarlet robes and great wigs sat the five judges, with the new Chief Justice Hutchinson in the middle. Otis was too good a lawyer to attack the legality of the writs. He spoke of the rights of Englishmen and of 'natural law,' 'letting in,' as the Tories were saying, 'the Hydra of Rebellion.' For as soon as you put 'the rights' of Englishmen higher than their legal status and 'natural law' above parliamentary, you have gone a long way.

He spoke for four hours. 'I am determined, to my dying day, to oppose, with all my powers . . . all such instruments of slavery. . . . I argue in favor of British liberties. . . . I oppose that kind of power the exercise of which, in former periods of English history, cost one King of England his head and another his throne.'

That rough masculine charm that he had, his brilliance and fire, held his highly critical audience spellbound. The council room of the old State House was crowded, but no one took down his words. John Adams, looking like 'a short, thick archbishop of Canterbury,' as he said, had indeed brought pen and paper with him, but was soon too 'lost in admiration' to take notes, for he knew that then and there independence was born. But the writs went on until stopped by the guns of Lexington.

James Otis, acclaimed by all his world, went home to face his wife's stinging curtain lectures. She was a cool, proper, beautiful woman who had brought great wealth to her marriage. Seemingly she did not care much for him, but he was devoted to her. To a very bitter end she remained a high Tory, so all the acclaim he had from fellow lawyers, merchants, Masons, might well have been nullified by a bleak look in Ruth's beautiful eyes.

His unfortunate marriage may have driven him to the fraternal warmth of the Masons oftener than a happier man, for he was a devoted Mason.

If Paul Revere sat back and drank in all this new, wild, heady talk, only listening to his elders and betters, there was another 'entered apprentice' who did not. This was Joseph Warren. At twenty he was through Harvard and serving his indenture to Doctor Lloyd, mixing medicines, holding horses, helping 'make an anatomy,' tying up slight wounds, or reading Latin books of 'ars medico.' Although six years younger than Revere, in their life-long friendship he was the leader. Paul Revere was described as Joseph Warren's 'fidus Achates.' The young doctor was an elo-quent speaker — which Paul Revere was not. He wrote per-suasively for the *Boston Gazette* (signing himself 'True Patriot') while Revere was expressing his political views in crude copper plates.

Warren was as fair as Revere was dark. He had a mobile face, with very bright, light blue eyes and the 'fine color' so much admired. In his portrait his hair is powdered, but his coloring and even the shape of his face suggest he was very blond. When his contemporaries speak admiringly of Warren's 'irritability' they were using the word in a different sense from that we do now. They meant he was responsive or lively. Now the word has lost its older meaning except in biology.

His patients liked it that he was so scrupulously clean — not a
common virtue among eighteenth-century doctors. For the rather
short time that he lived and practised his profession, his reputation was high. His gaiety, kindness, enthusiasm, intelligence, and
fine appearance made him liked by many as a doctor and as a
man. Paul Revere made a good choice when he picked Joseph
Warren for a friend.

Politically, Warren soon went far beyond James Otis, following
Sam Adams instead. Neither he nor Adams cared for the British
Empire. They did not fear independence. And Paul Revere
went with Warren.

## III

THE year 1761, memorable in
Boston history as the one in which James Otis made his famous
speech, would be remembered more domestically among the
Reveres and Hitchbourns as the year Paul had a fist fight with his
cousin Frances' husband.

Paul started out the year commendably enough by buying a
ledger in which to keep a record of his business. The secret of his
methods of debit and credit seems to have died with him. Except
for the break caused by the Revolution, his books run from 1761
to 1797. Yet during this time he made many now famous pieces
of silver (like the 'Liberty Bowl') of which there is no record in
these books. He may not have been quite as 'steadfast and persevering' in bookkeeping as he was in more active work.

On the fly leaf of his first ledger he has scratched the comment,
'This is my book for me to . . .' and before he finished the sentence
he was off on something else. He never seems to have decided
just what he was to do in his book. There are in it crude sketches
of sugar tongs and spoons, a recipe to make 'Gold Sawder,' and

pages on pages enumerating the names of his customers, the amount they paid and how — whether in cape verde dollars, hard money, old silver, or rum and fish, and he wrote down the now priceless things he made for them.

On the third of January, at the top of his first page, he made a Freemason medal, the first of many such. The brethren stood by him well. He made them plain medals and medals for their watches. His first effort at copperplate engraving was a notification of their meetings. Captain Cochran, who lived in half the Revere house (if it was a double house, and adjoining if single), soon ordered tortoise-shell buttons and spoons; Deacon Thomas Hill a 'cann, pepper, gold buttons.' Sometimes the orders were very large, for he was early recognized as an outstanding craftsman, at other times merely mending the clasp on a pocketbook.

Thomas seems to have worked for him, although at twenty-one his apprentice years were over. He is regularly charged board. One of Paul's first entries was to add up how much Thomas owed him. It was fourteen weeks' board (6.01.4.) and he had lent him eighteen shillings. 'Sundrys out of the shop' came to thirteen shillings. Besides are knee-buckles, a silk handkerchief, yarn stockings, and 'a wig of Mr. Crosby's £1.08.0.' Thomas, in his second-hand wig and smart accessories, seems to have been rather dressy.

To his youngest brother, John, the tailor, he occasionally lends money or charges rent, but Thomas is mentioned much oftener than John. There is also Sam Butts who pays board. He, like other men and boys found on Revere's books, was probably a journeyman or apprentice.

Uncle Thomas Hitchbourn, whose wharf was but a short way from Clark's, gave him orders as did his cousins. There were ten young Hitchbourns — seven boys and three girls. Nathaniel and Thomas were boat-builders, like their father. Robert was a sail-maker, William a hatter. Samuel, at nineteen, would be still serving his indenture to some master silversmith — perhaps to his own cousin. But the youngest boy, Benjamin, was fifteen and going to Harvard. Like so many well-to-do artisan families, the cleverest child had been set aside for higher education and the professions. Benjamin was to be a lawyer. The three girls were Mary, Frances, and Isanna.

While Paul had been off on the expedition to Crown Point, Frances married Thomas Fosdick. This young hatter's father had been paving the streets for the selectmen of Boston for years. One of the Fosdick boys, Nathaniel, was a lifelong patron of Paul Revere's. But for some reason Paul did not like Tom Fosdick. He was not by nature a tavern-brawler. Probably he had good reason for his antipathy.

Anyway, on the eleventh day of May, 1761, the two embattled young cousins, with their witnesses, appeared before Mr. Justice Richard Dana of the Court of Common Pleas. At first Paul pleaded not guilty, but 'after a full hearing' the Judge noted down 'it appears that he is guilty.'

Mr. Justice Dana, a man of sixty-two, stately in his black robes and enormous wig, was never the one to object to a little violence if it coincided with his own ideas of justice. It was he who, a few years later, stood under 'The Liberty Tree' and before a lawless mob took Andrew Oliver's oath that he would sell no stamps. It is the taut nervousness of his hands Copley saw fit to emphasize in his portrait. He gave Paul Revere as small a fine as was consistent with any decency — six shillings, sevenpence, and costs. He also asked that two reputable citizens go bond for Paul Revere's good behavior until the next general session. Two friends were ready to risk their money.

Joshua Brackett, coppersmith, is better known today as the keeper of the 'Cromwell Head on School Street.' In 1761 his father had just died and he had not yet taken over the family business. The 'Cromwell Head' made a good deal of trouble first and last. The sign, a swinging portrait of the Lord Protector, hung so low no one could pass along the north side of School Street without inadvertently bowing low to Oliver Cromwell, which humiliated Episcopalians and Crown officers. When Joshua was its keeper, Paul engraved a likeness of Cromwell for the head of his bill of fare. The Lord Protector is shown in profile and attractively framed with grapes and vines. Already Paul had made him knee-buckles. It was at this inn that the unknown, pockmarked, very young George Washington had stopped a few years before when he had been in Boston.

Joshua Brackett put up five pounds and the other five was furnished by Nathaniel Fosdick, which suggests that he, as well as the Judge, thought Paul justified in his maltreatment of Thomas. Thomas Fosdick left his shop on the High Street, moved with Frances to Marblehead, and soon died. Her second husband was the famous, amphibious General Glover and the house they lived in still stands.

The ledgers show that the year before Paul Revere rented the house at the head of Clark's Wharf himself, he advanced the money to his mother and charged her as well for 'your excise.' But in 1762 he emerged as head of the house, from now on assuming full responsibility. On April 12, Doctor Clark notes the change, 'Paul Revere took pt House at 36 shillings per quarter.' But Paul himself waited until November before he recorded in his books, 'I hired a house of Dr. John Clark joing to Mr. Cocran.' As it was 'part of a house' to one and a house 'joing' to the other, it was probably a double house, of which there were many in Boston. It was the same house he had been living in for years.

Although his brothers came and went, Mrs. Revere evidently lived with him until her death. If the usual custom was followed, 'old' Mrs. Revere (she was about fifty-seven, but since Paul's marriage this would be her title) would know exactly, down to the least detail, what her rights were in her son's ménage. Such and such a room: so much cordwood; cooking rights in the kitchen; which gooseberry bushes she hung her dish towels on in the back yard and which were Sary's. Perhaps by working out these mundane details with such churlish nicety, friction in the end was avoided. Seemingly people lived all on top of each other in houses no larger than a fair-sized apartment, in peace and respect.

Privacy was a luxury undreamed of in that day, and you had little of it. From childbirth to deathbed one's life was shockingly open to one's family, friends, relatives, neighbors, enemies, clergymen, and the curious. It was not a matter of social position. At Buckingham the young King of England, George III, had little more privacy than a Boston artisan. Nor Louis XV at Versailles. They seemed to have had no more conception of privacy as a desirable thing than they had of electricity, and did not miss either.

Mrs. Revere also paid her son board. And if she borrowed a quarter-pound of sugar it was written down against her. The oldest sister, Deborah, had married Thomas Metcalf. The three younger girls would still be at home. The times were good in the early sixties. Paul Revere made many large pieces of silver, chafing dishes, coffee pots, porringers. For Cousin William, the hatter, 'hatt bills' and a branding iron. For Cousin Thomas, the shipbuilder, porringers and salts.

And by now he was well started on his career as a great silversmith.[12] The fashion set in London (and always followed by the American smiths) was well suited to his extraordinary talents. The William and Mary period had been followed by the Queen Anne which covered the years of his apprenticeship. By the time his father died, rococo was 'high style' and it was in this manner most of his masterpieces were done. In this, his first period, his craftsmanship was the most perfect. Rococo with its cast shells and scrolls can easily be overdone. At its best it is lively, individual, perpetually interesting, and characterized by a pleasant gaiety. Its danger is overdecoration. Many of the finest English smiths of the period were carried away by their own virtuosity. Scroll was piled on scroll, nymphs on lions' heads. Furniture and ink pots grew bow-legged and form was lost. Paul Revere always handled this dangerous fashion with restraint. He never lost sight of his basic design, took only the good, never the evil of the rococo period, and enjoyed the freedom it gave the artist. Sometimes (as in Lucretia Chandler's sugar bowl and creamer which he made in 1762) he would cover the entire surface with embossing and yet preserve the inherent purity and simplicity of form.

He made a great deal of magnificent church silver, flagons and christening bowls, cups, even at this early age. The size and importance of his orders show that his workmanship and artistic ability were thoroughly appreciated by his contemporaries.

His reputation has never grown less, but if anything risen, for he is now considered the best of all the silversmiths who worked in America during his lifetime. There is more variety to his work than to that of any other silversmith. More of it has been preserved. Probably as many as five hundred of his pieces are known to exist. A great many more are in private families and have not been listed. Much, of course, was melted as his silver went out of style and other fashions came in. During this period — roughly up to the Revolution — he marked his work with a little 'pellet' before his name. It is the 'pellet Revere' that is on the whole considered his finest silver. He was in full stride as an

artist before he was thirty. The post-war depression had not yet
set in and there was money for luxuries. The artisans in Boston
were doing well, but only because the merchants and overseas
trade were flourishing. Thomas Hancock bought Clark's Wharf,
and from now it was usually called 'Hancock's Wharf' — but not
by Paul Revere. Some loyalty to the Clarks, or mere habit, made
him go on calling it 'Clark's' in his advertisements. The houses at
the head of the wharf did not change hands.

At first the Hutchinsons and their kin, the Olivers, gave him
some trade. Mrs. Hutchinson had been dead five years when
Paul married Sara Orne. She went into 'the decline' so fashionable at the period. Old, exiled, and dying, Thomas Hutchinson
could sorrow that his 'bones' were not to lie next hers on Copp's
Hill. After her death he became that great oddity — a widower
who never married again. But he did take his sister-in-law, Miss
Grizzel Stanford, into his home to bring up his five motherless
children. The widower and the maiden lady were to share their
lives and sorrows. Paul Revere could watch the come and go
about this great mansion standing on its slope a little above Clark's
Wharf and the hurly-burly of Fish Street. That little Peggy Hutchinson would be a beauty unless she caught the consumption and
went off like her mother. Thomas and Elisha, the two older sons,
Revere would not have liked much. They were very conscious of
their wealth and breeding — not at all 'good democrats.' Those
white horses and coach, greeted by a running of servants, would
be Governor Bernard himself driving in from his country place
for tea.

By this time, if Paul Revere said, 'Bad cess to Governor Bernard
and bad cess to Lieutenant Governor Tommy-Skin-and-Bones
Hutchinson,' he would have plenty of company around Boston.
Hutchinson's popularity was over. The brief fracas over the Land
Bank had been forgotten. Otis dug it up again. Hutchinson's
destruction of paper money he referred to, with a sharper eye for
politics than for finance, as 'that fatal shock.' There was definitely
a cabal to discredit everything either the Governor or Lieutenant
Governor said or did.

Hutchinson made no effort to clear himself until it was too
late. He had the offices, the power and the friendship of such
people as he considered important. Sir Francis Bernard and he

got on well together. The Royal Governor was a well-disposed,
scholarly gentleman who memorized Shakespeare and had a gift
for architecture. He designed new wings for 'Unkity Hill,' as
Hutchinson called his country house in Milton. When fire destroyed Harvard College, he designed the present Harvard Hall.

Massachusetts had been most loyal to England during the wars.
Sir Francis expected his term of office to be a pleasant country
vacation. He was beginning to find himself up against a 'faction'
who 'spit their venom' at himself and his lieutenant governor.
Just how that faction was run and who its leaders might be was
not entirely known by those in power. James Otis, of course, and
his Masonic brethren. Sam Adams was not yet a known leader of
opposition. It did not worry the Governor much and he went
his good-natured, honest way.

On the whole, the royal governors England sent to Massachusetts were honest men. A dishonest governor, looking for fat
pickings, would never have accepted the appointment. Royal
governors in the West Indies might return to England rich as
nabobs, but Massachusetts had the reputation of giving hers little
but insults and headaches. The only governor to leave the appointment richer than he went in was the sly-boots who sold his
commission for one thousand pounds and never left England.

Bernard knew all this, but the social life (although a bit small
and provincial) was pleasant. Life was lived not too inelegantly.
There was time for Shakespeare. The rank and file of the people
in Massachusetts seemed so prosperous — even luxurious, after
the bitter poverty he had been used to in London — he could
not believe they were seriously dissatisfied or could be so unreasonable as to refuse a fair tax to England.

There may have been a certain stiffness now when a Hutchinson
stopped at Paul Revere's to order a 'baby's wistle.' Artisans' shops
were hardly as pleasant a place for 'The Oligarchy' as in the
day of this boy's father. So it was being said, was it, that this dark,
clever young smith was something of a leader among the artisans
and such common folk against the ruling classes (who certainly
knew more about ruling than they did), against the King's preroga-
tive, Writs of Assistance, laws of Parliament, and against kindly
Sir Francis Bernard? Against himself, who had given all his time,
thought, and much money to his beloved Massachusetts? It would

be a sad day for the province if ever plain folk attempted to take upon themselves affairs of empire, the problems of currency. He was quite ready to do all such things for them. Let the cobbler stick to his last and a silversmith to his planishing. Men like Hutchinson, courteous by nature and training, but fundamentally aloof, do not let themselves be drawn into argument with every tradesman that disagrees with them. They are apt to grow cooler and still more aloof — and take their trade elsewhere. Neither the Hutchinson nor Oliver names appear for long on Revere's books.

But on the whole, things went well enough for Boston and the Reveres until late in '63. In December it was discovered that smallpox was in town. There had always been sporadic outbreaks of this hideous, deadly, deforming disease, and at longer intervals it would appear as a genuine epidemic. The last devastation had been forty-one years before. Old Mrs. Revere would remember it well. She had been a girl of seventeen. In nine months one-half the entire population of Boston had come down with smallpox and one out of every six to take it had died. A vast number of her own generation could show their pitted faces as proof of the horror of those nine months.

And that was the time Doctor Zabdiel Boylston and the Reverend Cotton Mather had fought and almost died to get permission to inoculate. There had just come to Mr. Mather from England a pamphlet telling how the Turks (so Lady Mary Montagu said) inoculated for the disease. Of course it was long before Paul or Sara's day, but she'd never forget the terrific convulsions of fear and hatred that had rent Boston. Inoculation had never been practised before in America, until Doctor Boylston inoculated his own son. He had been mobbed in the streets. Bombs were thrown at Cotton Mather. One landed in his house, but not going off the reverend gentleman could read the inscription, 'Cotton Mather; You Dog; I'll inoculate you with this; With a pox to you.'

Every clergyman in Boston had favored inoculation and every doctor except Zabdiel Boylston had been against it. Doctor William Douglas, a Scotchman, and Doctor Lawrence Dalhonde, a Frenchman, had led the furious opposition. Well — now their names were all but forgotten, for the great Doctor Boylston and the good Cotton Mather had won. But the memory of Doctor Dalhonde lingered on for at least a hundred years in Boston folklore, a quaint little figure, fitter for Mother Goose than medical history. Generations of Boston children knew there had once been 'a very small French doctor who spoke very bad English. He always wore black with a long sword, that struck the ground as he walked. Sometimes he rode a small black horse and then the sword would strike the ground as he rode.' And how when the little man fell off his little horse, someone wrote a note and sent it to the parson (as was the custom):

> Doctor Delone desires one prayer
> For he falling off his little black mare
> He bruises de meat — no broken de Bone
> Please pray Sir, for poor little Doctor Delone.[13]

That was all that remained of Zabdiel Boylston's opponent. His real name was forgotten, he himself little more than a nursery rhyme. Doctor Boylston was a savior, for now no man said, at least over here, that inoculation is contrary to the will of God. Medicine had made great strides in the last forty years. Perhaps the doctors and the Lord would spare Boston another such devastation as the unforgettable year 1721. And the selectmen nowadays knew better how to control it — with their pesthouses and their flags and their guards in the street.

# IV

THE oldest newspaper in Boston was the conservative, genteel 'News-Letter.' It was published at this time by Mr. Richard Draper, who only printed such news as he thought fit to print. A large part of its columns are devoted to foreign news, dullish essays, and pious comment, for it was this paper's policy to exclude anything that was 'offensive, light or hurtful.' Mr. Draper's seventeen-year-old apprentice, John Boyle, kept a diary which, if run in his master's paper, would have made John the first of American gossip-columnists. He preserved much local news that Mr. Draper would never have thought fit to print. When published a few years ago, 'certain entries hardly suitable for publication' were omitted.

It is John who notes, when a seemingly respectable Boston citizen died, that he was 'formerly a noted Merchant, lately a noted Miser. He has left a great estate to one of his illegitimate Offspring.' Or, when a few years later Miss Sally Jackson married Mr. Henderson Inches, that 'Mr. John Hancock hath paid his addresses to Miss Jackson for about ten years past, but lately sent her a Letter of dismission.'

While other sources may tell more accurately what was going on in a larger world, John Boyle reports what people are talking about — from the death of the King or new acts of Parliament to the finding of a dead baby in a trunk, 'which the Query of Inquest immediately sat on.' Although his master was a Tory, John himself was a Whig.

According to the young diarist, 1764 begins black enough. Harvard College has burned down. A lot of costly 'apparatus' has been lost and the entire library. 'It is conjectured to have begun in a beam under the hearth, in the Library where a fire had been kept for the Use of the General Court, now setting in Cambridge on Account of the Small Pox in Boston.'

Less than a month later the industrious apprentice writes again: 'Feb 26 Many persons in Town have lately been visited with the Small Pox, some of whom have died. The Selectmen have been very viglilant in endevoring to put a stop to the distemper, but 'tis feared by Many that it will be impractible to prevent its Spreading thro' the Town. 'Tis now in 7 families. Messers Glentwood's, Flagg's, Gyler's, Dean's, Jenning's, Revere's and Hitchbournes' at the North part of the Town.'

Ten days before, Paul Revere had appeared before the selectmen (as the law required and their records show). One of his children had smallpox. Which doctor it was he had called in we do not know. Doctor Clark was his landlord and Doctor Joseph Warren his fast friend and fellow Mason. But the consternation and horror that followed the diagnosis we know.

Smallpox begins with a fever, yet children the ages of the little Reveres often run fevers. Not until the third day does the rash break out, usually on the face first. But even then it might be chickenpox. But as the characteristic pustules form, with their revolting disfigurement and odor, and the fever rises sharply, not even an eighteenth-century physician would be apt to mistake it.

The selectmen argued with Revere. They wished the child to be removed to one of the dreary pesthouses (often little more than an abandoned dwelling), away from the centre of town. Revere refused. He loved his children — 'his lambs,' as he called them. A visit to a hospital in those days was too often fatal. They could not 'prevail upon him.' So it was ordered that a flag be hung in front of his house. Moreover, a guard would be stationed. For this office any man who had had the malady would suffice. They chose Nicholas Murphy. Unlike some of the really wild Irishmen landing in Boston at the time, Mr. Murphy could read, for they gave him his instructions in writing.

Revere went back to his house by the wharf. Now the family was locked in upon itself. For the next month his ledgers show no orders. Whether the disease, probably the most contagious of all diseases, stopped with one child or went through the entire family, is not known. But none of them died. Sary, as usual, was 'expecting,' and her child was born before the quarantine period would be up. This little girl, their first (but not their last), Mary, lived about a year.

There was little chance that the Reveres could get the smallpox and their cousins escape. A Mr. Hitchbourn (which cousin we do not know), who lived next the Cockerel Church, appeared before the selectmen ten days after Paul Revere. He, too, preferred a flag and a guard to a pesthouse (although the selectmen used the fancy new name of 'hospital'). He was assigned a Scotchman, Robert McNarr. As yet the smallpox was confined to the cases in the hospital, situated in a sparsely habited part of the town called New Boston, and to the North End. The selectmen had their short-lived hopes.

By the third of March it was everywhere, and all who might were fleeing to the country. Night and day the carts rumbled out of town as 1537 people abandoned their trades and houses, struggling to get out of the infested town. John Boyle says there

will be a total stop to trade 'until the distemper has gone thro'
the Town.' The selectmen now decided to grant 'Liberty to the
inhabitants to inoculate their Families.'

Vaccination, which finally defeated this ancient terror of mankind, had not yet been discovered. The inoculation for which
Doctor Boylston and Mr. Mather had fought and nearly died
during the great epidemic of '21 and which the selectmen were
now ready to risk, was dangerous, not only to the individual, but
to the community. 'Venom' was taken from 'the best sort of smallpox,' as much as would lie on the point of a needle, and put directly
into an open wound. In this way a light case usually developed,
which was, however, real smallpox and exactly as contagious.
The patient was soon up and about with as complete immunity
as though he had taken it 'in the natural way.' The selectmen's
decision to permit wholesale inoculation was a dangerous one, but
Boston was ready for experimentation in politics, trade, or hygiene.

So John Boyle, deciding that his 'period of Life was suitable to
receive this contagious Disorder,' let Doctor Sprague inoculate
him. This was on the tenth of March. Not until the tenth of
June did he record that he was perfectly recovered from the smallpox, although he had had it 'very favorably.' He had not been
too sick to keep up his journal and noted what 'great Havok smallpox had made in France . . . people being prohibited Inoculation
on Pain of Death,' as it was in many parts of the world.

In May the overseers of the town voted their thanks to the
'gentlemen physicians' who 'in this season of difficulty & distress
have generously inoculated and carried through the Small Pox
Gratis to considerable a number of the poor inhabitants.' One
thousand and twenty-five had their inoculation free and many
people from surrounding towns had 'obtruded themselves' and in
the confusion been treated along with Boston citizens.

Doctor Sprague, who attended John Boyle, was one of these
doctors. So were two of the famous Revolutionary doctors of
Boston, Joseph Warren and Benjamin Church. It was during this
epidemic Doctor Warren inoculated John Adams, and thus started
their intimacy. Doctors Kast, Perkins, and Lloyd were later to be
run out of town as public enemies. In '64 they were among the
saviors. Doctor Clark also cared free for poor patients. There were
nineteen of these public-spirited doctors. They may have treated

their charity cases a little cavalierly, but they did the best they knew.

While Doctor Sprague was probably not paid for inoculating Mr. Draper's seventeen-year-old apprentice, Doctor Gardiner would certainly not expect a fee from George Robert Twelves Hewes — a name which startled his generation even more than it does ours. George was of very poor family. He had started out apprenticed to a shoemaker, run away to sea and fished on the Grand Banks. At the time of the great inoculation, he was of age, back in Boston, and completing his apprenticeship to a shoemaker. In spite of his diminutive size and the dignity of his name, he was mixed up in every street fight, massacre, or tea party that occurred in the Boston of his day. His escapes (as told to his ghost writer) were always close and during inoculation he characteristically almost died.

He and a friend asked Doctor Gardiner to undertake them. Hewes does not complain of the disease, nor even the doctor's astonishing bedside manner, only of starvation, 'and animal food, especially, which they most longed for, was forbidden them as they valued their lives.' One night he got up and stole a joint of roast veal from the larder of the house where he lodged, dipped it in a pot of melted butter, and ate it. The veal refusing to digest, Doctor Gardiner was sent for. The boy denied he had eaten meat. The doctor thought he was lying and warned him of sure death if he did not confess.

'"Well then!" said he, somewhat excited, "you will be cold coffee, Hewes, in twelve hours from this, and remember 'tis no fault of mine."'

Sure he must die, the boy decided to die happy and demanded a mug of flip 'sweet, hot and good.'

In the morning he felt better.

'"Why, Hewes!" the doctor greeted him, "not dead yet, you dog? Not dead yet?"'

'"No Sir," he answered, "and no thanks to you!"'

At the end of June, the epidemic was under control. The selectmen were justified in their decision and gave their figures: 4977 people had taken smallpox by inoculation, of whom 46 had died; 699 had had it 'in the natural way,' and 124 had died. The Reverend Cotton Mather and Doctor Zabdiel Boylston had not lived in vain.

The doctors with their thousands of patients had worked day and night, often without pay; now they might relax a little, and young Joseph Warren married Elizabeth Hooton, 'an accomplished lady with a handsome fortune.' The young couple set themselves up near Faneuil Hall, with a certain amount of style. The future must have looked very secure for them. Joseph's ability would assure a good practice. The bride had money and accomplishments. She seems to have been as beautiful and amiable as she was wealthy. But, like so many agreeable young women of the day, she had only one fault, an inability to withstand the shocks and strains of life. She died very young.

Paul Revere's intimacy with and lifelong affection for Joseph Warren was growing apace at this time. The two men met at the Masons', in taverns, and at the many political clubs, which were such a feature of masculine society. But it well might be that, in spite of the intimacy of the husbands, their wives would hardly know each other. The men's life centred about their taverns. The women made their friends among their female relatives. So while Revere was enjoying the 'Salutation,' the 'Green Dragon,' or 'Adjutant Trowels Long Garret,' Sara would live a much more limited life.

The children were at an age when they needed constant watching. No sooner was little Paul rescued from the fireplace than Mary was crying and refusing to suck from the silver 'teat-spoon' her father had made in his shop. And how ever could she bring up the poor little thing? Although old Mrs. Revere might speak encouragingly and Paul think her overconcerned with it, the mother may well have known that this weak child, born under the shadow of the smallpox flag, would never grow up. And Paul himself, coming in last thing at night, just in time to lock up the house and put the cat out, looking so healthy and happy, so full of his new ideas and talk of new friends (whose wives were too elegant to drop in to see his wife), Paul, with all his domestic virtues, may have been a hard husband for a fragile and ailing girl.

The pockmarks on the child or children's faces — perhaps upon her own. But it would be like Paul never to catch the contagion at all, or have so light a case it was hardly more than a few days' fever and then blessed immunity forever after. Yet during those terrible weeks when the family had been shut up together behind

Mr. Murphy's guardianship and the warning flag, Paul would have been a rock of salvation, tireless, loving, kind. If things were bad enough, his high spirits and abundant health would be worth everything. But not on those days when everything goes just a little wrong — and young mothers cry from nothing but exhaustion. The chances are Paul would be little help. Probably not even a good listener. Most likely not there at all, but out of the house and off to his clubs, his taverns, his Masons. You could not expect *him* to know that your back ached and you were so tired you'd rather be dead, unless you told him so. Paul Revere had a good mind, quick and usable, but not a subtle mind.

# V

NO SOONER had Boston recovered from the smallpox than it was shaken by another event. On the first day of August, 1764, 'the greatest merchant in New England, Thomas Hancock, Esq.,' as John Boyle wrote, was 'seized with an Apoplexy just as he was entering the Council Chamber. He was immediately carried home [to that great house he had built on Beacon Hill] and expired about 3 o'clock in the 62 year of his age. He ... came to Boston as an apprentice to Mr. Henchman, Stationer ... but having a Genius for a more extensive Commerce, turned his Views that Way, and by the Smiles of heaven ... acquired a plentiful fortune.' Then the last sentence, so fraught with meaning to the Boston Whigs and the American Revolution: 'Having no Issue, he has left the Bulk of his Estate to his nephew Mr. John Hancock.'

'A plentiful fortune' was an understatement, for Heaven had smiled so broadly on Uncle Thomas he left John Hancock seventy thousand pounds. At only twenty-seven, his nephew was the

wealthiest man in New England and the second wealthiest in
America.

Over forty years before, Thomas and Apollos had been serving
their masters down on Anne Street — both poor boys. In that
length of time certain families like the Clarks had been slipping
slowly and proudly down hill. Others had risen. Fortunes were
made in shipping ventures, land speculation, but especially by
supplying the British fleet and armies over here. The ugly charge
against New York and Pennsylvania that the merchants, at the
same time, were supplying the French, was not thrown up against
Boston. It was too close to Canada. Nevertheless, much of the
'extensive Commerce' Thomas Hancock and his fellow merchants
had 'turned their views' towards might (by a purist) be considered
smuggling.

With his 'application and dispatch,' his great house and remarkable chariot, his strong, beefy-red face, Thomas Hancock was the
typical 'new-risen gentleman' of the day. The Hancocks had
always been respectable, with a fair quota of country parsons
among their names, but not showy. Now, with that smile of approving Heaven upon them, they were showy.

Uncle Thomas lived long enough to fulfil that ambition of
every poor boy 'to ride in his own coach.' It had taken years of
correspondence with Mr. Christopher Kilby, then living in London,
before this coach, 'chariot' he called it, finally landed in Boston.
The doors are to have double slides for glass or canvas. The lining
either a light-colored or scarlet cloth, 'which ever is most fashionable.' In almost every letter his friend is begged to see to it it is
neat and in the best fashion. The Hancock and Henchman 'arms'
are to be emblazoned upon the doors. Seemingly his wife's health
would thereby be benefited — 'I hope you wont think it savours
too much of Vainty... as it is for the benefit of Mrs Hancock's
health.' 'Good Sir Harry' (Frankland) is to be consulted in any
matter of taste.

Then the harnesses are ordered ('same as Sir Harry's ). Nets for
the horses in summer and 'harness bells' for winter, when the coach
will be mounted upon runners, and a 'home cloth' to keep it
spotless in the coach house. Mr. Hancock habitually keeps three
coach horses, but if Mr. Kilby and Lord Halifax should come to
visit him that spring, 'send me harnesses for four to attend him

and you.' For three years the letters flow from the excited Boston merchant. Not only is the coach described, but inadvertently 'Mrs H.' For the coach must be high to accommodate her ('she is pretty tall'), strong enough to support her weight, and low-stepped to favor her weak knees.

At the end of three years, this elegant symbol of worldly success did 'come safe — a little rubbed, not being well packed. It is only too rich and good But it pleases Mrs. H. & all my friends. I care not for other folk.' But the chaise also sent over was disappointing. 'Its no way equal to Sir Harry's.' Nor did he need the extra horse. Lord Halifax never came over to visit him  Uncle Thomas enjoyed his wealth even without a lord to ride out with him in his coach.

Now it was all to go to his nephew, although during her lifetime Aunt Lydia had the use of the house and a settled income. When Copley drew her in pastel he suggested her great size by putting her head close against the top of his paper. He made no effort to prettify the formidable lady. The protuberant, beetle-black eyes are almost without lashes. The stern, strong eyebrows start out well at the bridge of the nose, but quickly peter out. He drew the mole over the right eye. There are no rosebuds in the virile turn to the lips. The shaking wattles under her set chir are not (one imagines) minimized. To meet Aunt Lydia only in a pastel is to meet a regal personality. Nor does one doubt but her young relative, Dolly Quincy, was right when she said she was 'as ladylike a woman as ever Boston bred.'

At the time of his uncle's death, John Hancock (according to Boyle) had been courting Miss Sally Jackson for ten vain years. Aunt Lydia may have had her ideas about Miss Jackson. She herself had her own protégée and a likely candidate in Miss Dolly Quincy. Although she never interfered (in spite of her masculine countenance) with John's politics and business, she did with his courtships. It would not have been beyond her to have dictated that letter of 'dismission' which freed Sally Jackson. It was with this formidable relic the young man would live at the Hancock house.

John Hancock was a 'very handsome,' thin, nervous young man, with a slight stoop. Although his friends, as well as his enemies, agreed that 'his natural abilities were very moderate,' he must have had considerable business sense, for he kept his uncle's great fortune afloat during years when many supposedly astuter men were forced to 'shut up.'

By modern standards there is something unlikable about John Hancock. His type of patriotism and charity is as obsolete as his brocaded dressing-gowns and jewelled buttons. He was one of those men who curiously go in and out of style. Once they are out they are hard to value. 'The golden showers of guineas' that marked his almost royal progresses, his big speeches, like 'burn Boston and make John Hancock a beggar if the public good requires it,' do not arouse in us the same genuine enthusiasm they did in his contemporaries. Such men as Paul Revere, Hutchinson, Joseph Warren, or Sam Adams never are in style or out. Their personalities exist quite independently of the accident of their birth in the first half of the eighteenth century. This is not quite true of John Hancock.

His health was always bad. He called it the 'gout' (a catch-all for many symptoms in those days), but if he had been a woman his friends would undoubtedly have called it the 'vapours.' But the touchy sensitivity that bothered friends and foes alike certainly had some basis in his physical condition. Although vain by nature and pathetically eager for the applause of the multitude, he was also sincerely eager to do great and good things with the vast fortune Heaven had smiled upon him. Sometimes he was indiscreet. He talked too much. 'Such a leaky vessel is this worthy gentleman,' John Adams lamented of him.

One day, shortly after John came into his inheritance, two men were idly strolling the Common. Seemingly their talk was of the fortunes of the Whig Party. In some way it must be strengthened to fight the taxes and customs England was determined to force upon her colonies — and without representation — which would be tyranny. The walk was casual, and the younger of the two may have been surprised to find they had gone as far as the Hancock house, were stopping before it. He was a poor country boy, easily impressed (but not always favorably) by the elegancies of life. There was the great house before him, three stories and of stone. In the coach house was its almost symbolical 'chariot' and the English coachman sent over to drive it. English gardeners (selected by 'good Sir Harry') tended the magnificent gardens.

The two men stopped and looked. Soon they were to be known as 'that Brace of Adamses.'

Sam Adams, at forty-two, already looked many years older than his age. His hair had greyed 'prematuraly.' He had a palsy which made not only his hands, but his voice sometimes shake. Seedy clothes suggested the middle-aged failure. When he left Harvard it would have seemed imperative to recoup the straitened family fortunes. Deacon Adams had little but the brewery, the wharf, and his house left, and the British Parliament still had some claims on them because of the Land Bank. Sam was first tried out in a merchant's counting house, but the merchant complained to his father he was training business men — not politicians. Sam did not suit nor last long. Then he thought to set up for himself, borrowed one thousand pounds from his father, lent it to a friend, never saw the money again and did not much care. Old Deacon Adams must have been discouraged by the boy's abysmal inability to take money seriously. So Sam went to work directly under his father's eye in the brewery, but as soon as the Deacon died Sam completely ran that into the ground. He had not an interest in the world except politics.[14]

But even in this, his chosen field, he had not by '64 made much apparent progress. While other much less gifted men were going to the General Court in their twenties, Sam had to wait until thirty-one for his first public office. Then he was only 'town scavenger.' This lack of public appreciation did not daunt him. As long as he could talk politics, influence other men's thinking and voting, he was content (as far as we know) with little position for himself; and yet how he lived and how his wife and children lived no one now knows. At this moment he was a widower.

Next he was elected tax collector for Boston. If there was ever a man less suited to such an office, it is hard to imagine him. He had a deep sympathy for the underprivileged, would listen to their hard-luck stories, and of course collect no taxes. Nor could he keep books. But his laxness made him popular and he was promptly re-elected. The business men were naturally in a frenzy over his irregular practices. There was talk about his being some fifteen hundred pounds short. Jail did not look so far away from him that day he stopped before the Hancock house, with its polished brasses and gleaming paint. Quite a contrast to the way his own house looked. That was fairly falling down about his ears, and Adams Wharf was disappearing into the sea.

Although both his house and his clothing suggested failure, certainly his face would not. Here would show that 'cheerful spirit' and 'inflexable will.' He could not honestly be said to have failed financially because he had never taken money seriously. And politically he had preferred to pull the strings, set the stage, and let someone else strut — just now it was James Otis who was strutting. All right, why not? Just so he could manage Jimmy Otis. He was the least bitter of men and had something of Socrates' love for humble people (he has been compared to both Socrates and Lincoln, as well as the Devil). He was as astute a politician as even America has ever produced and had already built up his powerful political machine, although to the world at large he was just the 'plain, decent simple citizen,' perhaps a little hipped on the 'good old days.' He wanted to re-establish in Boston a community of saints — such as the original Puritans had never been;[15] and he was by taste as well as necessity very frugal. His political thinking was far ahead of that of his associates, but he was content to move no faster than their support would take him. There is something godlike, or spider-like, in the patient way he could sit and sit for years waiting for popular thought to catch up with him, spinning his web, setting his baits. He made it his practice to watch young men rising in Boston and by his persuasive arts luring them into the web of the Whig camp. His second cousin, John Adams, was one of these bright new flies.

John was thirteen years younger than Cousin Sam, but probably looked at least twenty. He was something of a roly-poly, with a girlishly smooth, plump contour to the face and an innocent cupid's-bow mouth, in contrast to the seamed, strong-drawing, crooked eyebrows and quizzical lips of the older man's face. Of all the early Revolutionary leaders of Boston, we know John Adams best because he kept the best diary. He was keenly observant of others and ready to turn himself inside out. All his foibles and regrets, his shame at his weakness and his naïve pride in his virtues, his passionate pursuit of an education, which nevertheless always eludes him, are in his diary. John Adams' mind was trained and logical, with much of Otis' dash but none of his wildness. By temperament (hardly by background, for compared to Cousin

Sam he was a poor country mouse) he was an aristocrat, possibly an intellectual snob, who despised muddy thinking wherever he found it — especially in himself. Mob violence would be as distasteful to him as to Hutchinson. At this moment he believed as strongly in the British Empire as did Otis and, like Otis, he was ready to fight for 'the rights of Englishmen' (these being much less in fact than in the minds of the long transplanted Englishmen in America). He could write fervently of 'our British ancestors, who have defended for us the inherent rights of mankind, against kings and cruel priests, in short against the gates of earth and hell.'

John Adams was that rare, powerful thing, a logical idealist. If his cousin had definite ideas of breaking this country completely free from the British Empire, he would be clever and patient enough not to confide in John. Not now... not yet... wait... wait... he always seems to have been saying to himself. Here a little pull... there a little push.

But he did have an impressive piece of news for John as they paused in their discussion of their party and stopped before the Hancock house, for Sam Adams said:

'I have done a very good thing for our cause by enlisting the master of that house into it.'

This was extraordinary news, although everyone knew how Sam Adams continually brought under his influence and to the Whig Clubs likely young men. But Hancock... how would he affect the party?

Sam Adams insisted he had done 'a wise thing by making that young man's fortune its own.'

What did Hancock have to recommend him?

'Great riches. We can give him consequence to enjoy them.'

The idea may have at first been offensive to John Adams, who was a poor politician, brutally honest, and impatient of people who have nothing but 'great riches.' But the Whig Party already had brains, organization, man-power, enthusiasm. Up to this moment it had sadly lacked cash. Now 'the poor plucked gawky' of a John Hancock was to be 'milch cow to the faction,' as the Tories soon woke up and realized. Or 'Sam Adams writes the letters and John Hancock pays the postage.'

How had this great seduction taken place? The Tory answer was 'in the same Manner that the Devil is represented seducing Eve, by a constant whispering at his Ear.'

Being seduced, Hancock was ready to give his all. He saw to
it that Sam Adams did not go to jail. When, with the next year,
depression, unemployment, and financial panic ended the brief
post-war boom, Hancock turned his great resources into new
projects. More ships, wharves, warehouses. We have John Adams'
carefully considered words that one thousand New England families
were dependent upon this one man for their livelihood. And the
vote is apt to follow the livelihood. Sam Adams had indeed done
great things for his party. That Hancock was difficult and had
to be handled like a reigning belle, that he really contributed
little but money and a fine signature to the cause of American freedom, may be forgiven him, for what he had to give was what
they most needed. John Hancock loved to give, although he may
have been privately less generous. 'A mean contemptible pageant,'
one of his creditors, Harrison Gray, called him. Brother Ebenezer
(not adopted by Uncle Thomas and sometimes hard up) wore
John's cast-off clothes while at Harvard. 'Don't wear them shoes
of mine,' John once wrote him proudly, 'any longer, for they
look scandously.'

But to the town he gave a fire engine. To churches he gave
steeples, bells, gowns, wigs, Bibles, mahogany seats for deacons,
and plain seats for poor widows, communion tables. To the poor,
deckloads of firewood, rights to cut wood in his forests. For them,
oxen were roasted whole and casks of rum were broached on the
Common. And he always gave them a big show. He called that
young scamp, George Robert Twelves Hewes, 'my lad,' and 'put
his hand into his breeches-pocket and pulled out a crown piece,
which he placed softly in his hand.'

On one occasion he even had the bad taste (to our minds) to
stand up in his costly finery and talk about despising 'the glare of
wealth' and the advantages of being poor. Not one rotten egg
was thrown at him. He was cheered to the echo. The populace
delighted in him and gave the flattery his sensitive nature demanded. His elegant equipages were the talk of the town. His
taste in wigs, buckles, waistcoats, wine-coolers, set the fashion,
yet to certain old established families, such as the Hutchinsons
and Olivers, there was something amusing about the way he was
peacocking through the town. Having no opinion of his brains,
they never guessed he was in any way politically dangerous to
themselves.

Young Hancock delighted in his newfound glory and the rabble that ran at his chariot wheels and called him 'Squire Hancock' and 'King Hancock,' yet there were times when something backed up in him. He was fretful, unhappy, and often in bed with a headache when his sturdier companions most wanted him.

Soon Sam Adams was bringing him to the Whig Clubs, in which Paul Revere was beginning to stand out as someone worth watching — a man capable of bridging the very real gap between the thinkers and the doers. Revolution was making strange bedfellows, but none stranger than the hard-working, unadorned (he did not even powder his hair nor wear a wig) young silversmith and this finicky, overdressed young man of great prosperity.

# IV

## 1764 – 1769

Popes' days and riots. Forced by hard times Paul Revere turns to new trades. He joins sundry clubs, all revolutionary in character, tries his hand at engraving and dentistry, but excels as a silversmith. The Sons of Liberty drive the commissioners to Castle Island. And England sends troops, who make an insolent parade.

The wooden head before Lillie's shop. Richardson shooting Sneider. Middle Street and Cockerel Church. Broadside in Pennsylvania Historical Society.

I

# GUY FAWKES DAY ('Pope's Day'

it was called over here) had long been celebrated in New England. 'Powder plot is not forgot. 'Twill be observed by many a sot,' was a local almanac's comment for the fifth of November. In the smaller towns it was fairly harmless. 'In day time, companies of little boys might be seen in various parts of the town, with their little popes, dressed up in the most grotesque and fantastical manner, which they carried about some on boards and some on little carriages.' But with the coming of night the big boys and grown men took over. A huge wagon, from twenty to forty feet in length and five to six feet in width, was built. On this platform was 'a paper lantern capacious enough to hold, in addition to the lights, five or six persons. Behind that, large as life, sat the mimic Pope and several other personages, monks, friars, and so forth. Last, but not least, stood Old Nick himself with the appropriate horns, tail and pitchfork.' Boys under the platform could work these figures like marionettes, by strings.[16]

The ponderous pope's carriage started out at dusk under the command of a captain, two lieutenants, and a purser. Sometimes there were a dozen dancers and fiddlers on the platform and effigies of unpopular political figures might be added. It was followed by throngs of young men and boys. Through the evening they went from house to house, beating their popes' drums, blowing their whistles. Before the more affluent houses the procession stopped. The pope would seemingly lift his head, peer about, and

recite the hoary lines (even as they were being recited in every
village and hamlet in England on the same night):

> The Fifth of November
> As you well remember
> Was gunpowder, treason and plot,
> I know of no reason
> Why the gunpowder treason
> Should ever be forgot.

And so on for many lines. The purser collected money for food
and liquor. Sometimes the masqueraders were fed on the spot, as
an advertisement in the *Boston Gazette* (when Paul Revere was a
boy of eleven) shows: '... some of the Pope's attendances had
some Supper as well as Money given 'em at a House in Town, one
of the Company happen'd to swallow a Silver Spoon with his
Victuals, marked I H S. Whoever it was is desired to return it
when it comes to hand.'

The celebration ended in a great bonfire and everything but
the wheels of the pope's carriage and the heads of the effigies was
burned, along with stolen washtubs, tar barrels, and fences. This
is what might be called a normal Pope's Day. Obviously a nuisance
to the inhabitants (like its lineal descendant, Halloween), but,
except for its hatred of Catholicism, harmless enough. In Portsmouth, Pope's Day was celebrated down into the present century
by boys who had never heard the name Guy Fawkes. Jack-o'-
lanterns had taken the place of the old effigies and it was called
'Pork Day.'

But in Boston the celebration was much more violent. Being
so large a town, she fell into the habit of having two popes, two
popes' carriages, and two escorting mobs; one was from the North
End and one from the South. Whenever these two rival gangs,
numbering 'thousands,' met, a ferocious battle was fought for the
possession of the other side's pope and devils. People were killed
and maimed for life. Paving stones, bricks, cudgels, were fair
weapons, and great damage was done, both to human flesh and
property. All night long through Boston's unlighted, cobbled
streets, nothing was heard but 'a confused medley of the rattling
of the Carriages, the noise of the Popes Drums, and the infernal
yelling of those who are fighting for possession of the Devil.' For
twenty-four hours Boston was in the hands of a mob which custom,

if not law, had legalized. The General Court had tried to stop
these riots by law. Boston thought to cut down the carnage by
saying the celebrating must be done by daylight, but the result
was that the rival popes' carriages left their hiding place in the
morning instead of in the evening and had that many more hours
for hell-raising. There were only eight to twelve constables in
Boston and they were unable to cope with mobs.

A contemporary woodcut gives little idea of the size of these
carriages nor of the number of effigies and people that rode upon
them. By the middle of the eighteenth century there had grown
up in the English-speaking world a curious collection of semi-
mythical human monsters. In 1821 a man of seventy wrote for the
*Boston Advertiser* his memories of these carriages and the characters
represented:

> A large stage was erected on wheels. On this stage was placed a
> figure in a chair called the Pope — behind him a female figure in
> an attitude of dancing, whom they called Nancy Dawson — behind
> her Admiral Byng hanging from a gallows [in 1757 Byng had been
> court-marshalled and shot in England for refusing to fight] and
> behind him the Devil. [The pope was] dressed in gorgeous attire
> with a large white wig on, over which was an enormous gold-laced
> hat. The wigs procurred for this purpose had often adorned the
> pulpits of churches. Before his holiness was a table on which was a
> large book, playing cards scattered over it. In the extreme rear was
> a gigantic figure to represent the Devil: a hideous form with a pitch-
> fork in his hand and covered with tar and feathers. On the stage was
> music and something to drink — also boys, clad in frocks and trousers
> well covered with tar and feathers who danced about the pope, played
> with the cards and frequently climbed up and kissed the devil.
> These were called the devil's imps.

This curious Black Sabbath was lighted by the gigantic 'lanthorn
of transparent paper, capable of holding a number of men on which
were scrawled uncouth figures and rhyms.'

This gigantic contrivance was pushed and pulled through
the streets of Boston by crowds of attendants in dunce-caps.
Small boys blew horns and rang bells and the dogs barked. The
unknown seventy-year-old gentleman also reports that 'In the
day time each' (South and North End mob) 'drawing with them
their Popes . . . met and passed each other on the Mill or Draw-

bridge very civiliy, but in the evening they met at the same points and battle ensued . . . the North End Pope was never taken but once and then the Captain had been early wounded and taken from the field.'

He also mentions that in the procession 'a man used to ride an ass with immense jack boots and his face covered with a horrible mask and was called "Joyce Jr." His office was to assemble men and boys in mob style and ride in the middle of them. He called out his henchmen by a particular whistle.' He was the only one of these semi-mythical characters who was considered a hero.

For this quaint figure the folk mind had gone back for a hundred years and more, for it was Cornet Joyce who had captured Charles the First and delivered him over to the army. It was believed that Joyce had been one of the two masked men who had stood beside the block when the king's head fell. And in the popular mind (but not in history) Joyce himself had actually beheaded the king. He was a symbol of popular revolt against government — hardly a real man at all. Boston had dropped his first name (it was George) taken him to herself, and added a 'junior.'

Seemingly any man who wished might take the sinister title of 'Joyce Jr' to himself. For years this threatening anonymous name appears in newspapers, placards, broadsides. Oily and deadly 'Joyce Jr' weaves his way through the history of the town. Nothing upset his aplomb and dignity. What man or men took this odd little figure from the Pope's Day riots and turned him into a purely political one we do not know. But some master-mind evidently took a good deal from that source — the organization of the mobs, the tar and feathers, effigies, illuminated obelisks, and at least one of the leaders of the mob. This was either Andrew or Alexander Mackintosh, captain of the South End Pope. He was an extraordinarily unsavory, brutal, boastful bully and a cobbler by trade. In 1764, Swift was the North End captain. Little is known of him except that he was a friend of Sam Adams.

Early in the morning of the fifth of November, '64, the North End Pope was trundled out on its gigantic carriage, with its usual supporting train of popes' drums, tin horns, conch shells, and milling mob, and 'Capt.' Swift in command. The bully boys were all set to find out the South-Enders and give them the beating of their lives. It was a day when careful mothers were apt to keep

small fry locked up at home, but a child by the name of Brown
got too close to the carriage and fell under it. The heavy wheel
went over his head and he was instantly killed.

It was still morning, before the drinking had begun seriously,
and the sight of the mangled boy cooled the ardor of the celebrants
as well as shocking the soberer citizens. The sheriff, justices, and
military officers were ordered to put an end to the day's disorders
and destroy both the popes. The North End mob did not long
resist. Their pope was pulled to pieces by afternoon. But 'Capt.'
Mackintosh was too much for the officials.

That night the South End pope's carriage started out once
more, heading for North Boston. On the bridge that crossed Mill
Creek, near Dock Square, battle was joined, for Swift had rallied
his men, his pope had been put together again, and his juggernaut
car once more lumbered out. In the end of that homeric battle
the platoons of 'Capt.' Mackintosh won. The two gangs (leaving
their wounded comrades in the streets), as usual, joined forces
peacefully and the two popes were carried through the town gates
out to the Neck and burned close by the gallows. There was no
power in Boston that could control them.

At this time Sam Adams was turning everywhere for support
for his political beliefs. To Harvard, for the brightest of their
bright young men — and thus he got John Adams; to the medical profession — he already had Doctors Young, Church, and
Warren; to the lawyers; to the Congregational clergy, whose
anti-Episcopal feelings easily led them into his 'black regement';
to the conservative merchants who feared the innovations of
England would ruin their trade; to the artisans — from now on
he could count on such men as Revere, Crafts, and at least
two Hitchbourns. From every group he drew strength for the
Whigs. Now, how about these hundreds, perhaps thousands, of
willing mobsters? To reach the Neck they must have gone close to
Sam Adams' decaying Purchase Street house. They already had
leaders — of a sort — and some organization. They were ready,
if anything too ready, to risk broken pates and black eyes merely
for this rough game of their foolish popes, and no one could stop
them. Yet only suppose the two mobs might be welded together
and harnessed to greater purpose than they could understand?
Suppose for politics — not for rough play?

Boston had often rioted. Back in Sir Edmund Andros' day, and later, when Captain Knowles, in 1748, had tried to impress American seamen as English were impressed at that time, the mob had held possession of the town for three days and stoned the General Court. They often took punishment out of official hands. If they liked a criminal they would get him loose, or if they did not they pelted him with trash as he stood in the pillory. They had once rioted because Indian corn was being shipped out to Curaçao and they feared famine. In almost every case the mob had won. Sir Edmund had been forced to leave America. The Granary, holding twelve thousand bushels of grain under the care of town officers, was built and filled to help the poor in time of emergency.

From Purchase Street, where Adams lived (with two children and a large Newfoundland dog), he could see the orange light of the bonfire on the Neck, and hear the jubilation of the rioters who had set authority at naught. The yelling might keep Purchase Street awake all night. Sam Adams was not the man to stay awake without thinking. He may well have done some very serious scheming, drumming of his wits, for at about this time he made up his mind. Although these hardy cudgel boys, scarred veterans of many a Pope's Day, did not know it, November 5, 1764, was their last completely uninhibited old-fashioned Pope's Day in Boston.

## II

'JAN. 15, 1765: The Trade,' Merchant Rowe noted, 'has been much alarumed this day. Mr. Wheelwright stoped payment & kept his room. A great number of people will suffer by him.' 'Nat' Wheelwright was the first of many merchants to collapse that spring. During the war merchants had increased their stock and speculated. Farmers had enlarged their farms. Those boom years were over; the depression had begun, and in Boston it lasted twenty years.

'Jan 19, 1765: Very bad acc's. Mr. John Scollay shut up. Mr. John Dennie shut up & Peter Bourne at the North End. Am likely to be a large sufferer by Scollay.' Now Mr. Rowe is really apprehensive. He was a cautious gentleman, no longer young. Even the walking was dangerous that day, 'Extream bad & slippery.'

Next day was Sabbath. Mr. and Mrs. Rowe never missed services at Trinity, but 'did not go to church, my mind too much disturbed.' Just as he should have been starting, his dear friend, Joseph Scott, had come to see him, 'very disturbed.' Sure enough, next day Mr. Scott had also 'shut up' and William Hasking and Company as well.

A bank failed for £170,000. Mr. Savage fell in a fatal 'apoplectick fit' in his lawyer's office. 'Capt. Forbes shut up his shop to-day . . . am much grieve for him.'

The merchants were going down like a house of playing cards. Each big house (such as Mr. Rowe mentions) carried innumerable small ones with it. Shipwrights, sailors, and sailmakers might suffer first, but tailors and peruke-makers, button-molders or soap-boilers, silversmiths or braziers, all followed. Rents and mortgages could not be paid. The clergy began to find more copper and less silver in the alms basins. Farmers drove mutton to town, could get no decent price, and, angrily, drove them home again.

Only one-fifth of the usual number of ships cleared that year from Boston for the West Indies. Not only was the artificial wartime prosperity over, but the merchants could not pay the duties now demanded of them. They experimented in short runs along the coast or kept their ships laid up, as one after another 'shut up.'

This stagnation of trade gave everyone, from Mr. Rowe and his fellow merchants like young Mr. Hancock, dining as elegantly as ever at the Royal Coffee House, to the meanest porter in the cheapest ale house, a leisure to talk they had never enjoyed before. Boston went off into a talking jag that did not end until Lexington.

Why was there no money to be made on the fine ships which for a hundred years had been bringing wealth to Boston? Why was there no work for a willing, able-bodied man? Who was to blame? England's efforts to enforce her Navigation Acts had upset long-established trade habits, but she had not as yet actually collected enough money over here to pay for her customs officials. It seems to have been the general opinion, from the top of the social ladder to the bottom, that England was to blame. The overexpansion of the last forty years probably had as much to do with it as England. But it was the meddlesome tyranny from overseas that was the scapegoat. King George the Third was popular. Their enemy was Parliament.

Grenville, as Chancellor of the Exchequer, looked about for some other form of taxation which would actually produce the money. Controlling smuggling over so long a coast, three thousand miles away, was proving expensive, impractical, and extremely unpopular. After talking with the colonial agents in London and asking for alternate suggestions, he put the Stamp Act through Parliament. 'I am not, however,' he said, 'set upon this tax. If the Americans dislike it, and prefer any other method, I shall be content... provided the money be but raised.'

As soon as the Stamp Act went into effect (which it never did), every legal document, every newspaper or commercial paper, would need a stamp, costing from a ha'penny to twenty shillings. It would require very few officers to enforce and no breaking and entering of private property. As Grenville argued, it would fall fairly equally on all colonies and classes. But it was technically an 'internal tax,' not an 'external' like the customs duties, and its theory frightened the colonists. Whether or not England had the legal right to tax these colonies in any way she pleased does not seem to be settled yet. Probably she had — but it was the utmost folly to do so. 'This distinction between internal and external taxes seems to the inquirer today, as it did to many at that day, almost a quibble. That one should be universally accepted through generations and the other should start men to their feet shouting, "liberty or death," has never been satisfactorily explained.'

Both Governor Bernard and Lieutenant Governor Hutchinson protested the wisdom of this act, but little actual trouble was expected. Andrew Oliver, Hutchinson's brother-in-law and close friend, was given the plum of stamp collector for Boston. As Grenville had said, this tax would fall fairly equally on all colonies and all classes, but the result of this equality was to unite all colonies and classes to oppose it. The inland towns had been inclined to feel that it was no concern of theirs what laws England passed in control of shipping. The Stamp Act aroused them. But the lawyers, with their innumerable legal papers, would be hit hardest of all. The Stamp Act started the lawyers. They proved the most eloquent, the most logical, and the most articulate of any one group. James Otis was only a sample of what outraged eighteenth-century lawyers could do and say.

The colonies thus far had shown only 'a peevish reluctance' to any united effort, even while waging the long war against the French. For the first time a joint congress was inaugurated which had not been set in motion at the instigation of England. 'Taxation without representation is tyranny' all were agreed. And yet at this time large parts of England had no representation in Parliament. The Whigs over here said they merely claimed the inalien‑ able rights of Englishmen. The fact is the colonies had worked out for themselves a pretty representative form of government. England had not. While the Americans were struggling to preserve rights they actually enjoyed, in England it was to establish rights long lost or never had. It was a terrific struggle on both sides of the Atlantic.

The Stamp Act would not go into force until November. Virginia, inflamed by Patrick Henry, led with her passionate protest against it. Boston turned primarily to rioting. As Governor Hutchinson said, many of the cudgel boys never knew what a Stamp Act was. But they did know that unemployment and hard times were upon them. They were told that the local 'oligarchy' and Parliament were to blame. In the Stamp Act Congress there was talk of boycotting English manufactured goods unless the act was repealed.

At dawn of the fourteenth of August, two effigies were found hanging on one of the great elms at the corner of the present Washington and Essex Streets. One was Andrew Oliver, who had been so brash (against his knowledge, so he later claimed) as to have accepted the appointment of stamp master for Boston. The other was a gigantic boot with the Devil (probably left over from Pope's Day) peeking out. This was in dishonor of Lord Butte, who was said to have instigated the act.

Liberty Tree on that day made its professional début. It had been planted some hundred and twenty years before and was the largest of a group of elms standing in an enclosure at the corner of the present Washington and Essex Streets. The ground under these elms gave ample room for thousands to gather and was known as 'Liberty Hall.' No tree in English history — not Jack Cade's Oak nor the 'Royal Oak' that sheltered Charles the Second ever caused more trouble than this Boston tree. It was not long before 'liberty trees' were named for it in almost every town and village along the eastern coast. Its fame covered the English-speaking world. Far away in Backway, near Cambridge, England, Mr. Philip Billes left his large fortune to two friends if they would carry his body to Boston and bury it under the shadow of the Liberty Tree.

When the effigies were discovered, there was so much excitement shops were closed and work stopped. Hutchinson ordered the sheriff to take them down. The sheriff eased over, looked at the crowding thousands, and declined. Undisturbed, the dummies hung all day.

At dusk a funeral procession formed under the tree. The effigies were laid upon their bier. Everything was orderly and organized. The procession was led by forty or fifty tradesmen and artisans, among whom Paul Revere, by now, would surely be one. And the mourners included 'men of the highest reputation.' The cortége went first to the State House, where Governor Bernard and his council sat late in the council chamber. The ground floor, at that time, was an open promenade, used as an 'exchange' by the merchants. The funeral procession passed through it, chanting, 'Liberty, Property, and no Stamps.'

So far, all had been done without violence. With the coming of actual night an uglier, anonymous spirit came into control. It was the brutal 'Capt.' Mackintosh who was in command. Whatever dignified conduct may have been promised Sam Adams, as soon as the more respectable Whigs left the cudgel boys alone, they behaved more naturally. On King Street the crowd began pulling down fences in the best Pope's Day traditions. They pulled down a building it was thought Andrew Oliver was erecting for a stamp office. These planks were carried close to the Oliver house on Fort Hill and burned.

Mr. Oliver was nearly frightened out of his wits. He lived very well with his negro slaves, coach, Smibert portraits, family, and plate. The mob was out after him.

'They pulled down the Garden Fence of Mr. Oliver,' wrote John Boyle — who does not seem to have been there but sympathized — 'entered his House, drank some of his Wine, and broke some Windows. They would not have entered his House had it not been for some irratating Language from those within.'

There was no police force in Boston. The Governor, Sir Francis Bernard, was too timid to have challenged this mob. In fact he was so frightened he sought safety behind the guns on Castle Island. The Lieutenant Governor was a man of more stamina. Thomas Hutchinson appeared in the middle of it with a sheriff. He was pelted with stones and abuse. His popularity was over and the Sons of Liberty were on the march. This day, August 14, was an annual feast day for the Sons of Liberty for years. It was their 'March on Rome.'

Seemingly they had arisen overnight by the thousand. As long as they had been led by their respectable leaders, they had been well behaved. 'Property' was one of the words they had chanted. But once left to their own instincts, they degenerated into a mob and were out to destroy property. Many of their habits and faces were more than reminiscent of the Pope's Day gangs.

## III

WITHIN two weeks the mob was out again. This time they seem to have had no better leader than 'Capt.' Mackintosh. Sam Adams had not yet really organized them. The better sort of artisan, who later always went with them 'disguised in trousers and jacket' and saw to it they did not degenerate into drunken looters, was absent.

Paul and Sara were doubtless in bed when they first heard the conch shells, whistles, beating of clubs, and clump of boots which for several years caused half Boston to barricade their houses and

half to tumble out and join the 'frolic.' The mob had crossed the
Mill Creek and was pouring into North Boston. It would not take
Paul Revere a minute to get into his breeches and out on the street
to see, as he would say, 'what was acting.' The mob was milling
about the Hutchinson house, yelling for the Lieutenant Governor:
led by Mackintosh, drunk already — and God help the Hutchinsons! What Paul Revere thought of that night's carnage, we do
not know, but all the other Whig leaders of his decency who did
express themselves were bitterly offended.

Earlier in the evening an idle crowd of 'negroes and boys' had
built a bonfire in front of the old State House. This twenty-sixth
of August was a day and night of unendurable heat. It was an
odd day to select for a bonfire. The crowd grew larger and bolder.
First they ransacked Judge Storey's house, drank up his wine
cellar, then did the same to Mr. Hallowell, one of the customs commissioners. By the time they reached the Hutchinson house they
were in 'a dangerous state.'

Thomas Hutchinson had put on 'a thin camlet surtout over my
waistcoat,' which, to his propriety, was 'undressed.' With him
were his three sons. The two older boys, Thomas and Elisha, were
already through Harvard. They were arrogant, cocksure young
men, not popular with anyone but their father. Billy, his youngest,
was still a child. There were the two girls, Sallie, who was soon
to marry her cousin, Peter Oliver, and Peggy, his favorite child.
Hutchinson adored Peggy, who seems to have been a replica of
her mother — even dying the same death. She served him as
amanuensis, and many of his state papers are written in her clear,
childish hand. Presumably Miss Grizzel was there in her capacity
as chaperon to the young girls. In the house were five servants,
three women and two men. Supper was served in 'the great room
below' very late that night. Probably it had been too hot to eat
earlier. The dining-room windows would be open to catch what
sea breeze might blow up Fleet Street from Clark's Wharf, and
by August the crickets in the spacious gardens would have begun.
It was hot and the conversation probably dilatory. How dear
Uncle Andrew had been frightened nigh out of his wits by those
dreadful creatures. Miss Sallie had been disappointed in the
pomander ball she had been making, or Miss Peggy wished papa
would move out to Unkity Hill, away from 'mobbish' Boston.

A sharp knock at the door and a friend pushed in past the servant without being properly announced. The mob was 'out': talking about pulling down his house. There was not a moment to lose. Already they were crossing the bridge into North Boston. The Lieutenant Governor decided to barricade his house and not quit it. He sent the younger children to a neighbor's. None of the Hutchinson men lacked physical courage. But just as they were all set to receive their visitors, Sallie got free from Miss Grizzel and back to the doomed house. If her father was going to die, she would die with him. He could do nothing with the hysterical girl, who would not leave him, and so he himself went with her.

The boys stayed until the front door fell before axes, and they heard the mob yelling for their father, and then also left. As the mob crashed through the front door, Mr. Hutchinson slipped through the dark garden and went to his sister's, Mrs. Samuel Mather. Some of the hoodlums followed him there and began yelling for him. The Reverend Mr. Mather went to the door, told them his house was his castle and he would protect his brother-in-law. They threatened to pull the house down, but, as they argued, there was time for the Lieutenant Governor once more to escape.

There were innumerable little alleys and by-lanes in Boston at the time — well known to tom-cats and children. Little Hannah Mather went with her uncle to lead him through this maze. She knew them even in the dark. They turned up at Thomas Edes' and there spent the night. Neither man nor child tried to sleep — they sat the night out together. The yelling and howling from about the Hutchinson house could be heard all over North Boston. The little girl noted at the time, and wrote down some fifty or sixty years later, that 'he was calm through the whole, serene, & partook of Breakfast with the family.'

Sallie probably saved her father's life, for 'the hellish crew fell upon my house with the rage of devils and in a moment with axes split the doors and entered.' Everything in the house was destroyed or stolen: family portraits slashed, furniture too big to carry away broken to kindling, rugs, hangings, clocks, china. Most of Mackintosh's crew had never even seen such things before, and perhaps whoever stole his microscope or his 'Telescope razors brush etc.' never knew what he had.

The silver plate, of which Hutchinson had much, the considerable amount of cash on hand, and the women's jewelry of course went, and his wine cellar was drunk dry. Not satisfied with this gutting of the house, the mob began tearing out the wainscoting, splitting woodwork. Some men got to the roof, pried off the cupola or lanthorn, beat down the partition walls, and tore slate and boards from the roof. Of his fruit trees and garden nothing was left. The garden house was flat.

By sunrise 'one of the best finished houses in the Province had nothing remaining but the bare walls and floors.' 'Such ruin was never seen in America,' he wrote a friend a few days later. 'Besides my plate and family pictures and household furniture of every kind, my own and my children's and servants' apparel, they carried off about £900 sterling in money... not leaving a single book or paper... and having scattered or destroyed all the manuscripts and other papers I had been collecting for thirty years.'

Earlier that year, Thomas Hutchinson had published the first volume of his 'History of Massachusetts Bay,' a heavily documented, extraordinarily judicial book, especially in his treatment of those years in which he took an active part. He never had been able to work on it except in snatches, and instead of rewriting when he found new documents, naïvely admits it is easier to add footnotes. He knew his work was 'rough,' and that he had 'no talent at painting or discribing characters.' His greatest service was in getting together for the first time the source material of early Massachusetts history. The second volume, although written, was not yet printed. This, too, was flung into the gutter along with the early records of the Massachusetts Bay.

But through that night, the Reverend Andrew Eliot, of near-by New North, was picking up as many as he could find of these papers, as fast as he dared. They still show the grime and muck of the streets and the stain of wine. Mr. Eliot was a friend of Mr. Hutchinson. 'Andrew Sly who doeth draw nigh to Tommy-Skin-and-Bones' was the way a popular rhyme had it. Other well-wishers collected plate or bits of furniture, even money, and got this little back to him.

He still had Unkity Hill, out in Milton. From there one can see fifty miles west to the round, blue mass of Mount Wachusett. To the east, his fields run down to the Neponset River, and still give the most beautiful view of Boston Harbor there is. From now on his family life and deepest affection centred on Unkity Hill.

Popular opinion was outraged by this treatment of Hutchinson. And probably no one was more upset than Sam Adams. The Whigs circulated the story that letters had been found in the house which, if published, would justify the mob's action. These letters were never produced. The story sounds like more recent invasions that have been 'justified' by mysterious 'letters' found in captured capitals. The attack on Hutchinson's house by a mob which obviously was thinking largely of plunder (if it were thinking at all) frightened many of Adams' erstwhile partisans. Surely if a mob is to be used for political purposes, it must be better trained. It was. It never got out of hand again, and for this fact credit must go to those unknown men, the reliable artisans and men 'of the better sort,' who from now on went with them.

Although Sam Adams repudiated this outrage, claiming that 'only vagabound strangers' had taken part, he threatened more violence if 'Capt.' Mackintosh was not released from jail. Hutchinson always thought that it was instigated by Whig leaders who never intended it to go so far, yet were anxious to get Mackintosh and a few more of the toughs out of jail before they implicated the men higher up. After his release, Mackintosh, more swollen and unendurable than ever, was made 'capt-General' of the Liberty Tree, 'First Hanger of Effigies,' and so on. The Whig leaders made a great pet of this gorilla, which does not look as though they too heartily disapproved of the attack on Lieutenant Governor Hutchinson. At least they needed Mackintosh at the moment — and his mob.

It was once more the Fifth of November — that day so much dreaded in Boston. 'Capt.' Mackintosh had been blackmailed out of jail and the usual carnage was expected. Instead, the day started off with orderly marching of the two rival mobs. They wheeled and turned and obeyed their officers as well as any trained troops. And there was 'Capt.' Mackintosh at the head, arm and arm with Colonel Brattle of the militia, who told him his post 'was one of the highest in the government.' Mackintosh had been given a fine uniform of red and blue. He had a gold-laced hat, a cane, and a speaking trumpet. So the two rival mobs sat down to guzzle and gorge at a 'Unity Feast.' Prominent Whigs attended them, and the hatchet was publicly buried between the North and South Ends.

It was said in Boston that Sam Adams had engineered this great reconciliation and John Hancock had paid the bill. It was as if Adams had discovered how one handles mobs. You march them back and forth anywhere to anywhere in the best military order. You feed them good food and a few slogans, like 'Wilkes and Liberty,' 'Liberty or death,' 'Liberty, Property, and No stamps.' That Adams had a certain affection for humble people cannot be questioned, but he had abysmal contempt for their intelligence. He appealed only to their emotions, not to their minds. Fireworks, illuminated pyramids, flags, free feasts, and slogans were all he seems to have thought they could understand. But especially plenty of marching to build up their feeling of power and unity. He was called 'mob-master' of Boston, and he was.

On the sixteenth of November, Andrew Oliver was forced to appear before the Sons of Liberty under the Liberty Tree. He gave his oath before Mr. Justice Dana, and in the presence of two thousand, never to sell a stamp.

# IV

OPPOSITION to the Stamp Act united the Whig Party, which was so curiously made up in Boston of conservative merchants sighing for the good old days and the bully boys longing for a chance to tear down the houses of the rich. It was a supreme act of juggling to keep such an alliance together. Not even Sam Adams could have managed it if England had not helped him out.

The Whigs, as a group, were flourishing in the middle sixties, but as individuals many might fare ill enough. This was probably true of all the silversmiths. It certainly was of Paul Revere. In the fall of 1765 his estate was attached for a debt of ten pounds he owed Thomas Fletcher. Eliakim Hutchinson was the witness. Somehow the matter was settled without the unfortunate debtor being clapped in jail, as was customary.

Six months before, seeing hard times ahead (as the merchants crashed about him), he had rented 'part of my shop to Mr. Thomas Berry.' He also was renting to Joseph Webb, for whom he made a trade card, probably at this time, for he added copper-plate engraving to his usual work.

In February he and Josiah Flagg had published 'A Collection of Psalm Tunes, in two, three and four Parts from the most Celebrated Authors, fitted to all Measures and approved of by the best Masters in Boston, New England,' and so forth.

Set in Score by Josiah Flagg
Engraved by Paul Revere

The little book might be bought of either Paul Revere or Josiah Flagg in Fish Street at the North End of Boston. If only Paul could have sold one copy to a modern collector his worries for that year would have been over.

Josiah Flagg was a jeweller by trade and close neighbor of the Reveres. Paul and Josiah had been bell-ringers together. Both families had recently had smallpox and perhaps the genesis of the little book took place behind their flags and their guards, when Revere's ledgers show he had little silver work to do and there was time to sit about and sing tunes in as many parts as there were convalescents around the head of Clark's Wharf. Many years later, when Revere was making bells, William Bentley said of him, 'he has no ear.' But this would not mean he would not enjoy a lively catch or even a psalm tune.

If Josiah had only paid the amount he owed Paul Revere that year, Paul would have been able to meet his debt to Mr. Fletcher. For his ledger shows:

| | |
|---|---|
| Mr. Josiah Flagg        To Paul Revere dr. | |
| To a verabl Order from Mr. John Williams | £   6..15..0 |
| To a pr Silver Shoe Buckles 1oz and making | 5..12..6 |
| To Silver lent 2 oz pt £ 5.. to two turtle shell butt'n 10 | 5..15..0 |
| To Gold lent 3 pt £ 5..14 To Cash lent 11 | 6.. 5..0 |
| To Cash paid you on the Street | 2.. 5..0 |
| To a Silver Cream Pot Wt 5 oz £ 12..10 to making | 18..10..0 |
| To Silver lent 11 pt 27 To engraving 2 Rings | 1..12..0 |
| To gold lent 2..18 £ 5..4..6. To Cash £2..10 | 7..14..6 |
| To one half of Engraving Copper Plates for Singing Book | 150.. 9..0 |

£204.. 9..6

There is no court record that suggests Paul even thought of throwing Josiah into the poor debtor's jail even as it yawned for himself. He had not only lent silver and gold so his friend might carry on his trade as jeweller, but also 'cash in the street.' All his life he was extremely generous, but this is the only time he was sued for debt.

Five years later Josiah Flagg was part publisher of another singing book which Edes and Gill printed. For it Paul engraved a frontispiece, representing seven round little men sitting at a round table singing from their music books. They all have on fashionable wigs and curiously sour, identical expressions, which suggests Revere's lack of skill rather than any deep pessimism about the human race. The design, which is said to be superior to the execution, he may have taken from another singing book. No engraver had many scruples about using other men's works or copying the designs of artists. Paul Revere had none at all.

The art of copper-plate engraving Paul Revere taught himself and never mastered. As a silversmith he was unsurpassed in America. The engraving of arms and scrolls which he did directly upon silver is perfection, but his work on copper has little to recommend it except its humor (sometimes unintentional) and historic interest.

In Europe the eighteenth century was a great period of political and social engraving, with Goya at work in Spain and both Blake and Hogarth in England. Hogarth's pictures were often advertised in Boston papers. And in Boston both Peter Pelham and Nathaniel Hurd were far superior to Paul Revere. Politically his heart may have been in his engravings, but never his artistic integrity. It is interesting to note he first began during the only years we know he was hard up and worked extensively in this medium during a period of political unrest and usually for propaganda. After the Revolution, when money was easier for him and he had no political axe to grind, he abandoned this field, except for a possible wretched head of Washington in an almanac, a medical certificate he made for Doctor John Warren's Anatomy School, and a few trade-cards and Masonic certificates. He did not love engraving as he did his silver work and always gives the impression of slapping off his prints for some purpose, financial or political, which theoretically is removed from your genuine artist.

Whenever he might, he worked from other men's drawings, as

when in 1772 Solomon Southwick, of Newport, Rhode Island, asked him to do two 'effigies' for a new edition of 'Entertaining Passages relative to King Philip's War.' For King Philip, Revere seems to have called upon his own imagination, which he never did if he could find anything to copy. For the redoubtable Puritan warrior, Captain Benjamin Church, he copied, as well as he was able, a portrait of Charles Churchill, the English poet, as Charles Deane proved in 1882. Except for the greater skill of the English engraver, the portraits are identical: the same frame, the same air of round-eyed astonishment, the same negligent dash to the cravat. But Paul Revere did hang a small powder-horn about the poet's neck before he turned him loose over here to fight our Indians. As Mr. Deane said, Charles Churchill 'had many escapades during his short career, but he never could have dreamed of the fate destined for him across the Atlantic, or the paces he was to be put through by means of the graver of Paul Revere.' Why did Revere select this particular portrait to copy? He may have been amused by the similarity of the names. Add a powder-horn and subtract the last syllable and Churchill, the English poet, becomes Church, the Indian fighter. At the time he made this cut — so beloved of antiquarians and so detested by art critics — he was in almost daily contact with Captain Church's grandson, Doctor Benjamin Church. Henry Dexter has made the kindly suggestion that 'Dr. Church, remembering the face of his grandfather, and being struck with some decided resemblance between it and the picture of Churchill, engaged Revere to furnish a likeness of the Colonel (Captain) based upon that of the poet.' Doctor Church was a poet himself. He would have been much more apt to have a picture of Churchill in his house than Paul Revere, and Mr. Dexter's theory is plausible. He adds, 'that there is a look to this day retained by many of the Church family' similar to Revere's cut.

This was by no means the last time Paul Revere was proved to have based his work on that of other men, but the discovery came so close to the publication of Longfellow's poem as to cause a sensation.

Paul Revere could not draw, and he knew it. He makes no claims to have done more than engrave his famous plates, but because they were so long accepted as original work, he has suffered unfairly. The engravers of his period were as complacent about taking the work of other men as were the dramatists of Shake-speare's day. But few engravers were as completely dependent upon something to copy as Paul Revere.

He was a craftsman — not consciously an artist. Such subtleties he left for his friend, John Singleton Copley. From 1765 through 1767 there are many debts in Revere's ledger against Copley, like 'To a silver frame' or 'a gold case for picture,' 'To a silver picture frame,' 'Making a glass.' These were for miniatures. The tradition in old families that the wooden frames on their Copley portraits were carved by Paul Revere is not substantiated by his ledgers nor accepted by such authorities as the Boston Museum of Fine Arts.

Probably (following the custom of the day) Copley painted Revere's portrait to balance off the debit, and so it is thought to have been painted at this time. Copley was two years younger than Revere. When he had the money, he dressed elegantly. When cold, he seems to have bundled up. There is a description of him by a not too friendly friend: 'He had on one of those white French bonnets, which, turned on one side, admit of being pulled over the ears; under this was a yellow and red silk hankercheif, with a large Catharine wheel flambeued upon it. ... He wore a red-brown ... or rather cinnamon, great coat with a friars cape ... it hung near his heels. ... Joined to this dress he was very thin, pale a little pocked-mark prominent eyebrows, small eyes, which after fatigue, seemed a day's march in his head.' But this was on a day when he was coming down with a hard cold.

Copley's father came from Ireland. When he died, his mother, who kept a tobacco shop on Long Wharf, married Peter Pelham, portrait-painter, engraver, dancing master, writing master, and teacher of fine needlework. It was hard going, but Copley could not have regretted his mother's marriage, for that odd household was the most 'artistic' in Boston, and he loved his little half-brother, Henry Pelham, who was twelve years younger, with a protective, almost paternal passion. In return Harry served him as secretary, bill collector, and devoted slave. About the same time he painted Paul Revere, he immortalized this boy's face — so sensitive, sad, and turned away, forever in profile and forever thinking about something else, as his pet squirrel frisks on the table before him. He is 'The Boy with a Squirrel' which, when sent to London, won

Copley his first international fame. Henry was a beautiful miniaturist. Copley and his half-brother had different ideas about art
from those of Paul Revere.

Copley worked the tremendously long hours expected of artisans.
He also felt his sitters should do the same. When he 'took' a
portrait, one sat fifteen or sixteen times and sometimes sixteen
hours at a stretch. His small eyes must have often marched inward
from fatigue. But he was paid well — fourteen guineas for a half-
length portrait. By 1767 he could write: 'I am now in as good
business as the poverty of this place will admit. I make as much
money as if I were Raphael or Corregio, and 300 guineas a year,
my present income, is equal to 900 a year in London.' Both he
and Henry longed for Europe and a greater world, where the
portrait-painter was not classed with the sign-painter and artists
were really understood. Not that young Copley was unappreciated
in the town of his birth. He had as many orders as he could fill,
and made so much money he could buy a large part of Beacon
Hill.

It is largely due to him that the men and women of his day,
with the gold lace upon the gentlemen and the thread lace upon
the ladies, their knee-buckles and banians, their ruddy good humor
and crabbed glances, their paunches, simpering elegances and
idealism, courage and evil, exist for us now. He was a master at
grasping essential characteristics. Uncle Thomas forever struts
forth, so pleased with himself and the world which has rewarded
the industrious poor boy with a great house and a coach. Aunt
Lydia is indeed a little large, and there is that wart in her right
eyebrow, but if ever she felt shy over her imperfections, she had
risen above them before Copley painted her. Justice Dana, with
his wattles and his tense hands, appears to us today as he did
when he found Paul Revere not so very guilty of assaulting Thomas
Fosdick, or took the trembling oath of subservience from Andrew
Oliver at the Liberty Tree. That Joseph Warren was as passionate
an idealist and as blond as his contemporaries said is proved in
Copley's portrait. And hundreds of others — the proud little
face of Miss Sally Jackson, who undoubtedly received her 'dismission' from John Hancock with a shrug. The pert, sharp, prettiness of Miss Dolly Quincy, who (under pressure) did marry him;
Sam Adams, forever pointing out one's duty with his right hand,

his left grasping a petition; and no one knows what is going on behind his back.

Most of Copley's sitters wore their best clothes for so historic an occasion. The painter so delighted in showing every last furbelow on the ladies, the fine waistcoats on the gentlemen, a judge's robes or the cleric's gown, it seems sometimes as though the clothes outweighed the humanity within them.

Paul Revere's is one of his very few portraits without any of this elegant self-consciousness. He painted Paul just as he saw him when he entered his shop to dicker for a frame for a miniature. He is sitting behind his workbench, dressed in a full-sleeved linen shirt, open at the throat and partially covered by a coarse waistcoat. The delicacy of the hands and the strength of the wrists are carefully recorded. In his left he holds one of those pear-shaped tea-pots he was making during the seventeen-sixties. The nails on that hand are broken to the quick and ragged as an artisan's hands are apt to be. Before him are the tools of his trade. What Copley wished to emphasize was the animation of the dark eye, the striking coloring, and the bold turn to the lower lip. There can be no doubt but Copley reproduced the expression admirably. Nor did he disguise the fact that Paul Revere, when around thirty, had a few of those superfluous pounds that worry our contemporaries so much and his not at all.

There is a tremendous impact to this face today which was surely felt by the man who painted Revere and those who knew him. Just when it was done, we do not know, but this is the Paul Revere of the Stamp Act days, of the Sons of Liberty, the Massacre and the Tea-Party, and the many rides. It is those small, sensitive hands and strong wrists that made the beautiful silver — and the wretched engravings. It is that curved, generous mouth which could not say 'no' to poor Josiah Flagg on the street and delighted in talking back to the British soldiers who captured him. Those bold eyes, even on canvas, look able to 'watch out,' 'see what was acting' on the darkest night, or work even longer hours than John Copley's, without retreating for 'a day's march.'

# V

IN THE spring of 1766 the Stamp
Act was repealed. It had been worse than ignored by the colonists,
who had rioted and protested from stem to stern against it and
boycotted English goods. England, good-naturedly, was ready to
try 'appeasement.' The ship came in on Friday with the welcome
news. The town (which from now on is a synonym for Sam Adams)
decided to celebrate the following Monday.

An enormous transparent obelisk of oiled paper, similar to the
lanterns which illuminated the pope's carriage, was prepared for
the occasion. Its four sides, covered with symbolic pictures and
verse, were large enough to hold three hundred lighted lamps.
It was to be first set up on the Common and then carried over to
the Liberty Tree. Paul Revere probably had a hand in the prepara-
tion of this famous obelisk. His shop may have been crowded with
cronies giving advice, helping in the symbolism and the verses.
Much of the expression of Whig sentiment was more of a mass than
an individual effort. John Adams writes of 'cooking up' political
paragraphs for the newspapers with his friends, and in much the
same way Revere and his advisers probably got together and
'cooked up' what was to go on this colossal, illuminated obelisk.
Although the symbolism of devils (probably based on Pope's Day
effigies and English cartoons of the period), Indians, Chatham's
great nose, Butte in his Scotch plaid, 'The Tree of Liberty with
an eagle feeding its young in the topmost branches and an angel
advancing with an aegis' or George the Third resembling 'a Dutch
widow in a short frock,' was clear in its own day, it is now hard to
figure out.

None of Revere's political cartoons seem very inflammatory to
us now, but they were to his own generation. Like John Hancock,
they have gone out of style. Both the drawing and the verse suggest the work of a political enthusiast anxious to use all his gifts

for his cause, rather than that of an artist or a poet. The lines to
Liberty begin pretty well in the fashion of the day:

> 'Oh thou, whom next to Heav'n we most revere,
> Fair LIBERTY! thou lovely Goddess, hear!
> Have we not woo'd thee, won thee, held thee long,
> Lain in thy Lap and melted on thy Tongue?
> Thro' death and Dangers rugged paths pursu'd
> And led thee smiling to this SOLITUDE.'

Ending with the thought that it is better to die than get along
without her. Certainly that last half of that fourth line suggests
desperate haste. Lying in Liberty's lap is informal, but attractive,
but melting on the tongue of Liberty is extraordinarily infelicitous.

At one o'clock Monday morning, the nineteenth of May, the
Hollis Street Church bell began to ring. The Reverend Mather
Byles, pastor of this church, was a vigorous Tory, but as his church
was nearest to Liberty Tree it usually was the first to ring. Next,
at the far North End, Christ Church's sweet chimes answered,
and one after another all the bells of Boston. By two the cannons on
Castle Island were booming, drums beat, and musicians, while still
it was dark, went through the streets playing violins and flutes.
By dawn it was seen that Liberty Tree was hung to its topmost
branches with flags, streamers, banners. The ships in the harbor
were firing their salutes through the opalescent dawn. The steeples
were hung with flags, and everyone poured out into the soft spring
air to see the wonder of it all. This day, 'The Great Illumination,'
was long remembered for a certain, queer, innocent joy that it had.
No effigies were hung, no Tories bullied, or fences carried off.

Towards night the obelisk was set up on the Common and much
admired. All the homes in Boston were lighted, as Beacon Hill
is still lighted for Christmas Eve. James Otis and John Hancock
kept open house 'for the genteel part of town,' while 'The Commonality' had pipes of Mr. Hancock's wine broached on the
Common. Then there were fireworks. George Robert Twelves
Hewes had never seen anything like them before: 'Rockets, bee-
hives, and serpents played in every quarter and to crown all a
magnificent pyramid was erected.' But either the three hundred
lighted lamps within or an escaped rocket finished it off.

Paul Revere had already made a copper plate of it, and 'humbly'
dedicated it 'To every Lover of LIBERTY.' The description on

this plate says it was set up under the Liberty Tree, but the fact is it burned up on the Common.

It had been planned to hang lighted lanterns upon Liberty Tree, but the whole town joined in spontaneously. Men, women, and children, carrying hundreds of lighted lanterns, looking like fireflies, swarmed towards the tree, which was hung until the sailors in charge could not find another twig to bear another light.

Then people thought of the poor debtors. They passed the hat and raised enough money to open the jail doors and so led them out to marvel at this city of light, kindnesses, and love, certainly quite a change from rowdy old Boston. It was as if some Biblical prophecy had come true. Such a day had never happened before in Boston and never was known to happen again.

From beginning to end all had been quiet, all had been under control — but from whence came this control? And could it not as easily be used for violence as for innocence?

# VI

AN ARTISAN worked from sunup to sundown, but without much feeling of haste and pressure. The important thing was to have the work well done. We have seen how three years elapsed between the time Uncle Thomas ordered his chariot built him in London and he and Aunt Lydia actually rolled forth to the admiration of Boston. Paul Revere might have a political engraving to finish off in a hurry, or a customer might be extraordinarily anxious to have his 'silver squirrel chain' finished before he lost his pet, but normally his long hours would be leisurely. He had his apprentices to teach, and friends dropped in to chat. He had no Saturday afternoons off, and on Sunday he was not allowed by law to amuse himself in any way except by going to church.

Mr. Welsteed and Mr. Gray had died their strange, identical deaths. The new pastor at the Cockerel was the Reverend and learned Doctor Ebenezer Pemberton. Evidently he was Mr. Hutchinson's choice. 'Puffing Pem,' he was called, 'who doeth condem all Freedom's noble sons.' Anna Green Winslow was only ten when she saw him and wrote home to her mamma that such 'have popes in their bellys.' 'Aunt says when she saw Dr. P. roll up the pulpit stairs, the figure of Parson Trullibee, recor'd by Mr. Fielding, occur'd to her mind.' And little Hannah Mather (whose father was also a North End clergyman) reproached him that he 'set up a Chariot and lived like a Bishop — in stile.'

Paul Revere permitted his children to be baptized by this 'Parson Trullibee,' but if he did not go to hear the rumbling of the popes concealed in his generous anatomy, he had company among his fellow craftsmen. 'Puffing Pem' was liked by the wealthy Hutchinsons and disliked by the rank and file of the congregation. A day would come when, it was said, no one stayed to hear him, except only the Hutchinsons. It was he who finished off the church.

Paul Revere had some leisure after the sun went down and before it next rose. He would lock up his shop (possibly leaving an apprentice to sleep inside as a guard against thieves) and many, many a dark night turn right down Fish Street and immediately be on Ship Street. He would pass the signs of 'The Castle' and the 'Mitre,' note the lights behind the tiny, crooked panes, the smell of ale and rum, the sounds of laughter and men's talk. Over here, as in England, the social life of the men was in the taverns. From the richest merchant to the poorest porter, each man had one or two favorites where he was more apt to be found after his work was over than in his own home. Paul Revere's was the 'Salutation.' And *there* was an inn where a sound Whig, who did not believe in either Hutchinson or Parliament meddling too much with Boston, might expand and enjoy himself.

The 'Salutation,' standing on the corner of Salutation Alley and Ship Street, was already a hundred years old, probably one of those black, crabbed, scowling little old houses that were still so common in Revere's day. It had never been fashionable, depending always for its trade on the North End shipwrights, caulkers, mast-makers. Before it hung a sign which had already tickled generations of artisans — two elaborate gentlemen bowing and scraping at each other. Thus it got its nickname of 'The Two Palaverers.' In Paul Revere's day it was kept by William Campbell.

To it the young silversmith went to drink his evening dram and relax, and to see to it that Boston was being run according to the wishes of the Whig Party. Somewhere in the inn was a private room large enough to accommodate the North Caucus. Your average fellow, drinking in the warm, crowded taproom, flirting with the serving girls, was not admitted to it. It was semi-secret and part of the political machine. There were three caucuses in Boston run by the Whigs and none by the Tories, who were curiously indifferent to local politics and from beginning to end had no central leadership. Sam Adams belonged to all three of the Whig caucuses, the North, Middle, and South. Although called 'the man of the town meeting,' 'man of the caucus' would be even more accurate. His father, Deacon Adams, had first organized these clubs, and it has been said that the very name 'caucus' is a corruption of 'caulker' because of the number of North End shipbuilders who belonged in the Deacon's day. The work of these three groups interlocked and they could carry town meetings and general elections even when they did not represent the wishes of the majority.

So Paul would pass through the smoke-blackened, cheerful taproom to that inner room reserved for them. Here would be the inevitable bowl of punch with its heady fumes, the slender white pipes with their blue wreaths, a hearth-fire in winter, windows opened to sea breezes in summer, and the conniving and political jockeying which, it must be confessed, he enjoyed.

It was best that a pretense, at least, was kept up that this was honestly a North End artisan group. But of the sixty known members, many not only were by no means artisans, but lived at the extreme other end of town.

Sam Adams would be modestly withdrawn into a corner, for he was a past-master in never stealing the show, and his temper and patience never failed him. Like Socrates, he taught largely by asking questions. He would be there without fail. Some nights Revere might find honest, plump little John Adams, who often exploded with impatience at such meetings and burst out with remarks which later he much regretted in his diary (why can he not learn to keep his tongue?). He hated the mechanics of politics, much as he loved the austerities of abstract political thinking. His name is down as one of the members, but he could not have been very active.

There were also the three Revolutionary doctors. Joseph Warren, with his fair, responsive face, clear eyes, clean hands, and rousing words, would have probably been Paul's first choice among the members. Doctor Thomas Young had only recently arrived in Boston from New York. He was a man who talked much, did little, and proved more agile than brave when talk moved on to armed action. He was an avowed atheist, which would have offended Paul Revere. Paul may not have liked 'puffing Pem,' but he was devoted to his religion. The third of this medical triumvirate was Benjamin Church. It was to the greater honor of this man's grandfather Revere had recently employed his graver — and the likeness of Charles Churchill. Perhaps Mr. Dexter was right and there was on Doctor Church's own features that same look of astonishment, devil-may-care roguery which marks the face of Churchill. If so, it was amazing his associates did not see through him earlier. Doctor Church was a witty, lively fellow, who, after taking his degree at Harvard, had gone to England to 'walk' the London hospitals. Thus he had the best medical education of any man in Boston. He excelled in writing Whig poetry (if anyone can be said to excel in that doubtful art). He was high-strung, bombastic, always hard up, and it was known he was supporting a mistress. This would have offended the domestic Revere as much as Doctor Young's atheism. There was something queer about Doctor Church. Paul Revere felt it, and so did Joseph Warren.

At the North End Caucus, Revere would see another face which, like Doctor Church's, is unrecorded and unpainted. That was William Molineaux's. He was a middle-aged hardware merchant, badly broken by the depression and determined to get even with England. Molineaux was an Irishman whose father, Sir Thomas Molineaux, was an outstanding Dublin surgeon. Whatever his coloring may have been, he was 'black Irish' at heart. He stalks angrily in and out of his 'friends' letters and diaries, always in tempers and often downright insulting. Mild John Rowe, a conservative Whig, sometimes notes the 'disagreeable' evening he had

at 'The Royal Coffee House' with Molineaux. He was talking
savagely about 'destroying Josiah Quincy.' He uses people 'most
Cruelly and Barbarously' and made 'smart speeches.' Once he
threatened to cut his own throat — if he could not have his way.
He died before the outbreak of hostilities. John Rowe records
his death without regret, for he was 'First Leader in Dirty Matters.'
Another Whig diarist thinks 'his loss is not much regreted by the
more prudent & judicious part of the Committee.' The best said
of him seems to be that 'his watchfullness, labours and distresses
to promot the general interest, produced an inflamation of the
bowels of which he perished.' 'O Save my Country Heavens! he
said & died.'

But when Paul Revere knew him at the North Caucus, he was
very much alive, although perhaps already building up by his
bad tempers towards the apoplexy that is usually said to have
carried him off. Like Doctor Young, he was that new, almost
fashionable thing, a 'freethinker.'

These men and Benjamin Edes, the printer of the *Boston Gazette*,
seem to represent the outside leadership, but Edes at least was
honestly an artisan. 'Gentlemen' drew up the proposals, but 'a
mechanic for moderator' was considered good policy. The earliest
records of the North Caucus that now exists are for 1772. At that
time they are sending committees (with Paul Revere and Thomas
Hitchbourn on them) to the 'caucus in the middle part of the town
and let them know how we have proceeded.' Or, 'this body will
use our influence that William Cooper be town clerk' and John
Hancock and Sam Adams selectmen — among others. Or, 'To
choose the same representatives as we choose last year.'

The bulk of the names are bona fide North-Enders and many
of them artisans or ship captains. Landlord Campbell belonged,
as did John Pulling, who later was at least to assist in the hanging
of the lanterns in Christ's spire. Benjamin Burt lived in North
Square. He was a silversmith and now is known for his fine craftsmanship. Then he was best known for his size. On those nights
when perhaps forty or fifty men crowded together in some small
room at the 'Salutation,' it must have been a problem to know
where to put Mr. Burt. 'A very large man,' as Thomas Hutchinson's little Whig niece, Hannah, remembered, 'he weighed 380 —
a very pleasant man.'

It took all sorts and kinds to make a revolution.

There were other nights when, on leaving his house, Paul Revere turned to his left, went over the drawbridge into Boston proper, passed through dark Dock Square and by the unlighted Faneuil Hall, and there behind the old State House was Dassett Alley. It is Franklin Avenue now, but at that time a gifted man could spit across it. Here was the Edes and Gill printing office. The first floor was given over to the little hand press, the few founts of type, and the small office needed to run the greatest paper in New England, the *Boston Gazette*. Paul Revere knew this shop well. He cut crude plates now and then for Edes and Gill. It was in the *Gazette* that he advertised once in every few years.

Above the shop was a 'long room,' and here met, with a security from eavesdroppers they could not have at a tavern, that small group of men who are thought to have been the earliest of the secret clubs which brought on the Revolution. The Long Room is said to have started in 1762. Who were the members is only partially known. How they worked is not known. They were probably too close to treason to keep written record.

It was obvious that Paul Revere should belong to the North Caucus. His membership there gives no indication of either his personality or his importance. That he was possibly the only artisan selected by the exclusive Long Room Club means much. Needless to say, Sam Adams was 'the leader' in this club too. But here his authority would be badly contested. James Otis was also a member. He was still the popular idol of Boston, the bold champion of the rights of Englishmen — whether in old Sarum or Salem. By this time 'The Great Leviathan,' 'The American Hampden,' was getting badly out of hand. Hutchinson was saying that he was 'fitter for a madhouse than the house of representatives.' And Sam Adams must have often prayed that the madhouse doors would open to him and shut upon him forever and leave the leadership of the Whigs to himself and the radicals.

By 1766, Otis was an infernal nuisance, and yet he never lost his magnetism nor that rough, masculine charm that he had. Before it was known by the man in the street (who adored him), his fellow members of the Long Room Club must have guessed that something had gone radically wrong inside that broad, thick skull. He was offering to settle the entire dispute between England

and America by a duel between himself and Lord Grenville on the floor of the House of Commons. He embarrassed his friends by his fits of contrition. He would run to Hutchinson and lament that he had started so much sedition, admit that England had the right to tax her colonies in any way she chose. Or the electorate in Boston were imbeciles. It would serve the town right if the home government filled her streets with British redcoats. Cautiously, calmly, Hutchinson would let him talk. So this was the man who promised to tear down the government even if he himself perished in the flames?

Otis was tormented with an ideal of the British Empire which was very remote from the actual fact. 'If I have one ambitious wish it is to see Great Britain at the head of the World and my King, under God, the father of mankind,' and 'the good of mankind is my ultimate wish.' The British Empire and 'mankind' were more important to him than Boston — a curious misconception to the average Bostonian. And the next moment he would fall back on profanity and obscenity to explain just what he thought of the rulers of Britain.

As James Otis talked on and on, many of the members must have felt they had wasted their evening by coming to the meeting. There was no stopping him or controlling him. If he wished he would spend two hours telling a couple of trivial stories apropos of nothing. He fretted John Adams badly and was one reason why John stayed out of Boston politics as much as he was able. When Joseph Warren urged him to take part he would answer, ' "This way madness lies," thinking of Otis. Then Warren would smile, also thinking of Otis — "It is true." '

John Adams' name is not one of those of the Long Room members to be preserved. He may have dropped in now and then, for in his diary he speaks of being at Edes and Gill's. Otis came in, 'fishy, fiery-looking, acting as wildly as ever he did.'

James Otis was becoming a bore, never giving another man a chance to get a word in edgewise. Paul Revere would not suffer so acutely from this enforced silence as some of the lawyers. But Otis would sometimes jump to his feet and with a cryptic remark and no explanation dash off by himself. At such times the men gathered in Edes and Gill's upper room could get somewhere with their scheming.

John Hancock was also a member. He was worth to the Whigs his slender weight in gold. Two of the Revolutionary doctors — one as good as the other was bad — belonged, Joseph Warren and Benjamin Church. And there were two Coopers, the very handsome scholarly Reverend Samuel, pastor of the Brattle Street Church, and his merchant brother, William, who was Boston's town clerk for forty-nine years. Young Josiah Quincy was going up like a rocket for his brief spurt of fame. He was there — with his beautiful voice and wall eye, his feverish demands for liberty and justice and the prophetic, fatal cough. Royall Tyler, America's first dramatist, used to go. He was a little arrogant, intellectual, handsome, fashionable, and just out of Harvard. There were also Thomas Dawes, Samuel Phillips, Thomas Fleet, Samuel Dexter, John Winslow, and Thomas Melville.

Thomas Melville was even younger than Josiah Quincy. He was in his 'teens and early twenties during the ten or twelve years of the club's existence. He graduated first from New Jersey College (Princeton), then went on to Harvard. It may have been his radiant youth which made him memorable at his club, but it is as an old man and a grandfather he is known to us today. It was Oliver Wendell Holmes' 'grandmamma' who said that in his youth 'he had a Roman nose and his cheek was like a rose in the snow.' But in the sixties and early seventies whatever lips he may have pressed were still 'in their bloom.' Nor were the names of his friends of the Long Room Club as yet 'carved for many a year on the tomb.' He makes another brief appearance in our literary history, again as an ancient man, for he was the grandfather of Herman Melville.

Unlike the North Caucus, the Long Room Club was made up largely of Harvard graduates — at least eleven of the sixteen known names. They were primarily scholarly men or men of fairly large affairs. Paul Revere was neither, yet he had qualities which they wanted.

As these men talked through the night, made their plans, 'cooked up' their paragraphs, smoked their pipes and drank their rum in the upper chamber, below them, silent in the dark, the printing press, their servant, was waiting to pass on their thoughts, their hopes, their ideals, and their propaganda. From the articles, over many fanciful noms-de-plume, by Sam Adams or Benjamin

Church, Joseph Warren or Josiah Quincy, appearing in the *Boston Gazette*, one can get an idea of the talk that went on in the room above.

Newspaper readers had been a selected and fastidious group who preferred a neat essay of diluted Addison to anything rough, noisy, and pertinent. With the advance education was making in New England, more and more people could read. The Puritans did not wish any boy to grow up among them who could not read 'the Word of God,' and this was literally what most of them had been reading — and believing every word they found in print. No wonder, when the newspapers began to broaden out and include whole new classes of readers, many of these mistook the word of Sam Adams for that of God.

One of the most important duties of these inner clubs (of which there were several) was to direct that largest and most mysterious club of all — The Sons of Liberty. We have already seen them at their worst, drinking and sacking houses, and at their best, innocently waking citizens with their violins, hanging their lanterns on Liberty Tree, and only indulging in the wine which kind King Hancock ordered rolled out for them. It was they who established a mob rule in Boston which was stronger than any law courts. It was they who frightened the customs commissioners out of town, who bullied and threatened 'importors,' who tarred and feathered 'informers,' who paralyzed all government but their own.

Although it was mob rule, it was, as a puzzled observer wrote back to England, 'a trained mob.' With their marchings and their feasts and their secret oaths, they bear an unpleasant likeness to modern storm troopers, and yet — to their unending honor — they did not take one life in Boston nor inflict serious or permanent physical injury. Whether or not they were involved in the sack of Hutchinson's house, we shall never know. They said they were not. There is some reason to believe that they were. If so, this was their nadir. No European country, torn by its variously colored shirts, has been more bitterly divided than Boston was before the Revolution broke into warfare. To a modern newspaper reader the mildness and order of the Sons of Liberty is hard to understand — much as one may dislike mob rule, even if it is a 'trained mob.'

Like the Masons, the Sons recognized each other by a secret

language and wore medals. This medal, suspended about the neck, had on one side an arm grasping a pole on top of which was the liberty cap and the words 'Sons of Liberty.' On the reverse, the Liberty Tree. They had no special dress, like the Masonic apron, but wore cockades and (in honor of Wilkes in London) such insignia as '45' on their hats. When on public display they kept military formations and once a year sat down together to enormous feasts celebrating their 'march on Rome' — the fourteenth of August. At will they could summon thousands for their 'high frolicks,' but how many of the genuine toughs of Boston were actually members we do not know.

Two lists have been preserved from that day. One is thought to have been prepared by a Tory for some English newspaper, for the General Court is referred to as 'the House of Commons.' It names sixty-two of the leaders and gives a brief estimate of each man. Most of these are, of course, unfavorable. In it is the famous description of:

> John Hancock: a merchant, orator, milchcow to the Faction but whether public spirit or vanity has been his governing spirit is uncertain.

To select (almost at random) a few others:

> Thomas Boylston: Publican, keeper of a gaming house, very tyrannical & oppressive.
> Moses Gill: brazier, a great Puritan, but without religion.
> Newman Greenough: Sailmaker, whose house was built by unrighteousness
> Joseph Eayres: Carpenter, eminent for erecting Liberty Poles
> Benjamin Church: Physician well-versed in the art of canting, a qualification requisite for a delegate.
> Joseph Warren: Ditto

But towards many of the sixty-two the writer seems quite friendly:

> Martin Brimmer: Apothecary, civil and well-esteemed.
> Paul Revere: Silversmith, Ambassador from the Committee of Correspondence of Boston to the Congress at Philadelphia.
> Oliver Wendell: Oilman, a very worthy man.

But Benjamin Waldo is a 'surly humdrum Son of Liberty.' John Pulling, a 'bully of the Mohawk tribe.' Two are so bad the author omits their names: '—— —— is a mariner mean-spirited, swearing and silly, very amourous with the kitchen furniture'; and the other blank is a leather dresser, 'a very horney man. N.B. Horns are on his sign post.'

One (and only one) name is torn off:

'—— —— Alias Joyce Jr. chairman of the Committee for Tarring and feathering, who is now strolling the West Indies.' Seemingly whoever made out this list knew who it was that was acting at the moment under the pseudonym of 'Joyce Jr.'

It is obvious from the comments that it was made out after Paul Revere had started riding express to Philadelphia (1774) and before Joseph Warren died in 1775.

The other list is that of the three hundred and fifty 'Sons' who attended one of the famous banquets at the Liberty Tree in Dorchester, August 14, 1769. Here are about the names one would expect, including many of the North Caucus and Long Room and all leading Whigs. It includes two Hitchbourns, Josiah Flagg, Joshua Brackett, but neither Thomas nor John Revere. Paul's brothers kept out of politics, trouble, and history.

Many prominent and wealthy men felt so bitterly about England's treatment of Boston trade they honestly preferred organized mob rule for Boston to any more meddling. Perhaps an even larger group tremulously hoped that membership would ensure the safety of their own fences and windows. There are on this list a number of names such as that of Brigadier General Brattle. Although not long before he had been walking arm and arm with 'Capt.' Macintosh during the Stamp Act riots and started out a 'high son of liberty,' he ended up a Tory and an exile. Both Josiah and Sam Quincy were 'Sons' at this time, but only Josiah stuck to the Whig side to the end. His brother left Boston with General Howe's fleet in 1776.

Patterns formed and re-formed. Families were divided and united again. Men struggled desperately to keep some middle ground — until that ground was cut from under their feet by the rising tide of emotion, violence, and blood.

# VII

IN TIMES of political stress and
economic depression, there might be more people who would pay
a few shillings for an engraving than a few pounds for a silver cup.
So Paul Revere taught himself copper-plate engraving. In 1768
he branched out into another field, also related to his trade of
silversmith. This was dentistry, but he did not teach himself.

The state of teeth in the New World was so remarkably bad
travellers from Europe were constantly mentioning it. Josselyn,
writing in 1684, speaks of New England women as 'pitifully Tooth
shaken.' Abbé Robin attributed this toothlessness, which he said
began at eighteen or twenty, to hot bread and too free indulgence
in tea. Peter Kalm, Swedish scientist, and as accurate an observer
as any of our foreign visitors, wrote a long paragraph on the
shocking state of American teeth. He was over here in 1748:

> Girls not above twenty years old frequently had lost half their
> teeth, without any hopes of getting new ones. I have attempted to
> determine the causes of this early loss of the teeth, but I know not
> whether I have hit upon the true one. Many people are of the opinion
> that the air of this country hurts the teeth. So much is certain, that
> the weather can nowhere be subject to more frequent and sudden
> changes; for the end of a hot day often turns out piercing cold and
> vice versa. Yet this change of weather, cannot be looked upon as
> having any effect upon the shedding of teeth, for the Indians prove
> the contrary.... Others ascribe it to the great quantities of fruit
> and sweetmeats which are here eaten. But I have known many
> people who never eat any fruit, and still have hardly a tooth left.

Convinced that it is neither weather nor fruit which is so shaking
the American teeth, he is inclined, like Abbé Robin, to blame tea.
And yet:

> I found afterwards that the use of tea could not entirely cause the
> condition. Several young women who lived in this country but
> were born in Europe, complained that they had lost most of their
> teeth after they had come to America. I asked whether they did

not think that it arose from the frequent use of tea, as it is known
that strong tea, as it were, entered into and corroded the teeth.
But they answered that they had lost their teeth before they had
begun to drink tea.

The dispassionate investigator made further inquiries and came
to the conclusion that it was not necessarily the tea, but the tem-
perature at which it, and other foods and drinks, were swallowed
in this country that accounted for the loss of teeth. Still he is not
quite sure. He has only made his observations.

A clever artisan who could replace these lost teeth might do
very well. Paul Revere does not advertise to do more than clean
teeth and set false 'foreteeth.' He learned this art from Mr. John
Baker, 'Surgeon Dentist,' who was in Boston for at least a year
and a half, staying with Revere's old friend, Joshua Brackett, at
the 'Cromwell Head.' On the twenty-second of January, 1768,
Mr. Baker, through the pages of the *Boston Gazette*, warns his
public that he is about to leave town.

### JOHN BAKER

#### Surgeon Dentist

> Begs leave to take this method of informing the Public That he
> shall leave this Place in Twenty Days at the farthest: —
> That those who are disposed to apply to him may not be disappointed.
> He also begs Leave to express his Gratitude for the Favours he
> has received while in Boston; and hopes those who doubted of the
> Safety of his Art from its Novelty in this Country are now convinced
> of its Safety and Usefulness.

And he is staying at Mr. Brackett's. His 'dentifrice' (sealed with
his own coat of arms) may be had after he goes from Mrs. Eustis.

But Mr. Baker was still on the point of departure in April.
This time he is leaving in ten days. He thanks his public for their
favors, is 'impressed with a grateful sense of the notice taken of
him,' and hopes sometime to return to Boston.

America was behind both England and France in its knowledge
of teeth — and they were ignorant enough. A dead man's tooth
carried in the pocket was one cure for toothache, or you might
chew mastick until 'soft as Wax, then stop your teeth with it.'
The usual remedy was to call in the family physician (if you

were well-to-do) and he went to work with his 'tooth wrenches,' 'keydraughts,' or 'neat hawksbills.' Many people may have gone to barbers and blacksmiths, but the men who kept the diaries in Boston seem to have gone to as good doctors as there were in town. During the extraction, teeth, instruments, and jaws were broken. The Inquisition had no more fiendish torture. There is no time one feels sorrier for the diarists of the period than when they are getting up their courage to jump from the fires of toothache into the frying-pan of dentistry. Early in the century Judge Sewall called in 'Mr Cutler [a doctor] who pulled out a Cheek-tooth of my right upper jaw. It was loose and corrupted & hurt me.' John Rowe's tooth was either not so loose or his courage less. 'June 14, 1769 Sent to Dr Lloyd to have my tooth drawn & had not the Resolution to go thro' the Operation.'

Yet even those who had the courage to go through the operation were left with unsightly gaps and possibly a future diet of barley water and water gruel and all those other slops such as Captain Codman seems to have been reduced to before Mark and Phillis finished him off. Paul Revere now proposed to fill these gaps. He would not attempt to fill cavities, which was an almost unknown art. He did not call himself a surgeon dentist like Mr. Baker, who probably came from England — at least his reference to the 'novelty of his art in this country' suggests he was not American born and bred. Before he left, he taught Paul Revere something of the science of setting false teeth. Paul's advertisement in the *Boston Gazette* for September 19, 1768, runs as follows:

> WHEREAS many Persons are so unfortunate as to lose their Fore-Teeth by Accident, and otherways, to their great Detriment, not only in Looks, but speaking both in Public and Private: — This is to inform all such, that they may have them replaced with artificial ones, that looks as well as Natural, & answeres the End of Speaking to all Intents, by PAUL REVERE Goldsmith, near the Head of Dr Clarke's Wharf, Boston.
>
> All persons who have had false teeth fixt by Mr John Baker, Surgeon-Dentist., and they have got loose (as they will in Time) may have them fastened by the above, who learned the method of fixing them from MR BAKER.

One notices that he does not promise you can chew with these artificial teeth, only that they will answer the 'End of Speaking to all Intents.' They will also look 'as well as Natural.' He does not offer to replace anything but 'Fore-Teeth.'

Among his neighbors close to Clark's Wharf was Isaac Greenwood, instrument-maker and ivory-turner. He advertised around this time to turn everything from billiard balls to German flutes or handles for coffee and tea-pots, warming pans and walking sticks. Also wooden legs and 'Make Umbrillos.' From this neighbor Paul Revere might order the teeth to wire in, or he may have made them himself. He engraved for him an attractive trade card. Besides a number of sons, Mr. Greenwood had a young apprentice, Samuel Maverick. His mother was a widow and the boy was allowed to sleep at home over on Salt Lane. He was a 'promising youth.' What he would have been in maturity is not known, but he won immortal fame by stopping a British bullet in front of the old State House on the night of the fifth of March, 1770.

After the Revolution, when Revere dropped this trade, Greenwood went on, gaining more and more skill and is called the first American-born dentist. He would fix 'natural teeth on plates of gold or silver with gold springs if wanted.' A single tooth will only cost 21 to 61 shillings each,' and they 'do give a youthful air.' And after the Revolution teeth were filled. If with lead it was called 'plumbed'; if with gold, 'plugged.'

If Paul Revere followed the best practices of his earlier day, his teeth were 'made of teeth and tusks of the hyppotomus or sea horse.' The next best substitute was genuine animal teeth, uncarved, but 'their perculiar forms were ... a great obstacle to correct fitting.' 'Live human teeth,' for which dentists were soon ready to pay a guinea apiece, had not yet come into use, nor had china or 'chemical' ones.

One or two teeth might be fastened to their neighbors by gold or silver wires or even by silk. Even the Egyptians had known how to do that. This is perhaps as far as Revere ever ventured into dentistry. He would whittle out a tooth from hippopotamus tusk or find a sheep's tooth of not too 'perculiar' a form, and wire it in. Elephant ivory discolored too quickly.

Two years later, Paul Revere is advertising that 'he has fixed some Hundred of Teeth and he can fix them as well as any Surgeon-Dentist who ever came from London, he fixes them in such a Manner that they are not only an Ornament, but of real use in

Speaking and Eating; He cleanses the Teeth and will wait on any Gentleman or Lady at their Lodgings, he may be spoke with at his Shop opposite Dr. Clark's at the North End, where the Gold and Silver smith's Business is carried on in all its Branches.'

He spent four shillings on this advertisement in the *Boston Gazette*, but a Mr. Hamilton had lately arrived, a 'Surgeon-Dentist' from London, and was offering to 'set teeth at two dollars each.' Paul did not wish to lose his patrons.

In his second advertisement he does not limit himself merely to 'fore-teeth' and now he promises you can eat as well as speak and smile with them. His ledgers show occasional items like: 'For fasting teeth 0.4.6.' in 1771, or, 'to Cleaning your teeth & one pot Dentifrice 0.4.6.' in 1774. The 'dentifrice' that Revere sold in a pot may have contained any abrasive substance, for recipes of the time suggest various mixtures using 'broken pans' (meaning coarse crockery), cuttle-bone, coral, brown-sugar-candy, saltpetre and gunpowder, butter and crumbs of white bread. There were many secret formulas for whitening or cleaning the teeth. Doctor Zabdiel Boylston had advertised, in 1712, 'Powder to refresh the gums & whiten the Teeth.' And 'tooth sopes,' 'tooth blanches,' and 'Tooth rakes' were all sold.

There are not many items in Revere's ledgers concerned with his dental work, but as his records are known to be imperfect, he may have fixed those hundreds of teeth he claimed in his second advertisement. He seems to have gone into dentistry only for a comparatively few years. Although he must have done his work neatly enough, he added nothing to the general knowledge. His heart was not in it. This was not true of two small neighbors of his at Clark's Wharf. One was Josiah Flagg, son of Josiah the jeweller who rang bells, had smallpox, and published music with Paul Revere. Little Josiah was only six when Revere's patients first 'spoke' to him at his shop, deciding whether they would rather have a carved hippopotamus tusk or a sheep's tooth wired in. The boy's hobby was music, but he earned his immortality and his place in the Britannica for his dentistry. While still in the 'teens he served in the Revolutionary army and came into contact with Rochambeau's naval surgeon, Joseph Lemaire. The French were the best dentists in the world at the time and during the winter of 1781, while the Continental army was in winter quarters at Providence, Lemaire started the clever young private off on his life-work.

Isaac Greenwood's four sons all became dentists. John was the most famous of this great dental family and did almost as much for modern dentistry as Josiah Flagg, Jr. It was he who made George Washington that set of false teeth, with springs, still preserved at Baltimore.

It is a curious coincidence that, just at the time Paul Revere was practising his simple arts at the head of Clark's Wharf, these two small boys were his close neighbors. Neither of them practised in Boston, but both of them started from Clark's Wharf. Paul Revere's greatest service to the science may have been the good-natured way he answered their questions, let them watch him as he wired in the teeth, for they were as far ahead of him and his generation as the dentist of say 1880 was ahead of Flagg and Greenwood.

# VIII

THE same year that Paul Revere launched out as a dentist, he also made one of his most famous engravings and most memorable pieces of silver. These were both connected with the political complexion of the day. In 1768 the King demanded that the Massachusetts General Court 'recind' a circular letter sent to the other colonies. England was worried that at last her jealous and divided American possessions might unite against her, as they never had against the French.

The 'Townshend Acts' were a mild duty on tea, glass, painters' colors, and paper. The colonies hoped to fight them by a boycott on English manufactured goods. A few things which they could not live without were excepted, like salt, coal, hemp, fish hooks. These Townshend duties were frankly laid with the idea of raising money over here — not for the regulation of trade. If England could lay such a tax, why not tax New England farms, Georgia pines, Virginia tobacco plantations? One boycott on English goods had brought about the repeal of the Stamp Act and it was expected once more to save America from 'taxation without representation' by the same means.

At the King's request, seventeen members of the Massachusetts General Court did indeed 'recind.' Ninety-two refused. In their honor Paul Revere was commissioned by fifteen Sons of Liberty to make a large and handsome punchbowl. It was to hold a gallon, which would hardly dampen ninety-two belligerent non-rescinders. The strong, easy lines and the exquisite finish are all Revere's, but the innumerable thoughts engraved all over it suggest those fifteen bright Whiggish minds, all cooking up something together and, like the traditional too-many cooks, spoiling the broth. Although Revere may have been pleased politically by these noble thoughts, it must have been hard for him as a craftsman so to mar the surface of his bowl. Everything is on it. Wreaths, Liberty caps, No. 45 (referring to a pamphlet by the English John Wilkes), and 'Wilkes and Liberty.' Two standards bearing the words 'Magna Charta' and 'Bill of Rights.' One bright idea follows another, a torn document for 'general warrants,' and a long effusion to the 'glorious 92.' The names of the donors. Revere's own name appears simply on the bottom.

Far off in England members of the British Parliament were drinking toasts to 'the ninety-two patriots of Massachusetts' who had voted not to rescind. But to refuse to rescind being 'against the King's pleasure,' Governor Bernard promptly dissolved the General Court.

Having paid his respects in silver to the ninety-two who did not 'recind,' Paul Revere now turned to dishonor in copper the seventeen who did. He made a plate of these seventeen rescinders marching into the maw of hell. One devil is saying, 'A fine hawl, by Jove,' and another, addressing the leader, Timothy Ruggles, urges him on with 'Push on Tim.' The whole is called 'A Warm Place Hell.'

Clarence S. Brigham, Director of the American Antiquarian Society and the leading authority on Revere's engravings, went through thousands of English and French prints in European collections to unearth the sources from which Paul Revere worked.

Through his courtesy, a print from the 'North Britain Extraordinary' is reproduced (for the first time) on the same page as Revere's 'Warm Place Hell.'

Over the dragon's right eyebrow Paul Revere added the cupola of the Province House with its well-known Shem Drowne glass-eyed Indian on top, so anyone could know this was no dragon out of Revelation (or North Britain), but a Boston dragon. He added one devil and the two balloons. He increased the number of sinners to fit the situation in Boston. His seventeen rescinders look like innocent schoolboys, with their identical three-cornered hats, sour little faces, and juvenile proportions. None of them have clericals or a fox head, but one, Doctor John Calef of Ipswich, does have the head of a calf (as this is the way the name was pronounced and often written). Each of the seventeen faces is presented entirely, without any overlapping, and the seven tallest have obligingly formed in the back row, as groups of people are drawn by children. He did not change the title.

Paul Revere was at work on this plate when (as he remembered years afterwards) Doctor Church came into his shop, possibly rolling that bulging black eye that an unknown artist accredited to Churchill, the poet, and Revere to Church's grandfather. At least he was in some sort of poetic frenzy for on seeing the plate he seized a pen and wrote a six-line stanza at the bottom of the engraving, beginning:

> 'On Brave Recinders! To yon yawning cell
> Seventeen such miscreants will startle Hell!'

This verse pleased the engraver. He could recite it from memory when he was eighty. Doctor Church often published political poetry in the newspapers. But it was curious that no sooner did one of his effusions appear in a Whig paper than an anonymous parody came out in a Tory sheet. You looked at one and you looked at the other and for the life of you you could not help but have a suspicion that the same man had written both. Seemingly Doctor Church was the noisiest patriot in Boston, but somewhere about him was a mystery. That big summer house in Raynham, that mistress. Did he get the money for such luxuries from his practice? But he was accepted, as Revere later said, because 'the Whig party needed every strength. They feared as well as courted him.'

He was no mystery to Governor Bernard nor Thomas Hutchinson.

## IX

**BY JUNE,** 1768, there was something of a house-party out on Castle Island, which in those days was well out to sea, but now is part of the mainland. The customs commissioners, their wives and children, some fifty people in all, had been so terrorized by the Sons of Liberty they dared not stay in Boston. 'Every officer of the Crown that does his duty is become obnoxious & they must either fly or be sacrificed, the Attacks were always in the dark, several hundreds against one Man.' The commissioners were 'prohibted setting foot on the Shore again at their peril & in case any of them does, the Sexton of each Church has orders to give Notice by tolling a Bell, when all the Bells are to ring as for Fire . . . to raise the Mob to tear 'em to peices.' So writes Miss Hulton from Castle Island. Her brother, Henry, a very decent official, had come over six months before. She herself and her sister-in-law had just landed amid the 'squalling of brats.'

And yet the fifty prisoners, mostly fresh from England, found pleasure in the beauty of their island in Boston harbor. To Miss Hulton, a sprightly, genteel maiden lady of discreet years and disposition, the strange series of events that had landed her on this island 'appears romantic.' Life on it was 'rather like one of the Publik wateringplaces in England,' so she writes her dear Mrs. Lightbody back in Liverpool. She was a courageous woman under the eighteenth-century elegancies of female letter-writing. She stood by her brother and his family through what cannot be described as thick and thin, for there was little but thin in the Hultons' visit to our shores.

The Sons of Liberty had been growing ruder and ruder to the commissioners. They had broken their windows, interfered with the performance of their duty, hung them in effigy on Liberty Tree, and a few days before they had rioted.

The fracas had started at Clark's Wharf (as Revere faithfully called it, although by now its official name was Hancock's). The customs officials had seized Hancock's sloop *Liberty* for smuggling, and placed her 'under the broad arrow.' When it looked as though the crowd which quickly gathered would get ugly, they moored her under the fifty-gun British man-of-war, the *Romney*.

Captain Corner, her commander, had a few weeks before attempted to impress Yankee seamen as they were impressed in England. When the town offered to find him a substitute, he answered: 'No man shall go out of this vessel. The town is a blackguard town & ruled by mobs; they have begun with me by rescuing a man whom I pressed this morning; and by the eternal God I will make their hearts ache before I leave.' At first it was thought the *Romney* was kidnaping more seamen. Then it was known that Hancock (always so generous with his wine) had been caught smuggling Madeira. The feeling was so high against the customs, any man who smuggled was merely standing up for his rights, certainly no criminal.

Miss Hulton describes how, that night, 'These Sons of Violence after attacking Houses, breaking Windows, beating, Stoning & bruizing several gentlemen belong'g to the Customs, the Collector mortally & burning his boat,' created such panic they were obliged to fly for their lives to Castle Island. The collector, Mr. Hallowell, was actually not much hurt, but his boat was burned before John Hancock's door.

Although this occasion was referred to as 'The Liberty Riot' and had carefully assumed some of the earmarks of a mob, nothing more was done than its leaders bade. 'Whilst the boat was burning, some gentlemen who had influence over them persuaded them to depart. This was put to a vote, whereupon proclamation was made, "each man to his tent," which was a watchword among them.' By midnight there was not a disorderly person left on the Common. But it was the last straw that broke the commissioners' courage.

Besides driving them out of Boston to the pleasures of Castle Island and eventually to demanding troops for their protection, the Liberty business had another long-reaching effect. John Hancock had been caught red-handed and was threatened with penalties up to one hundred thousand pounds sterling. 'He thought fit to engage me,' wrote John Adams, 'as his counsel and advocate and a painful druggery I had of his cause. There were few days ... when I was not summoned to attend the Court of Admiralty. ... It seems they were determined to examine the whole town as witnesses. . . . They interrogated many of his near relations . . . and threatened to summon his amiable and venerable aunt, relict of his uncle. . . . I was thoroughly weary and disgusted with the court, the officers of the crown, the cause and even the tyrannical bell that dangled me out of my house every morning . . . this odious case was suspended at last only by the Battle of Lexington.'

But Miss Hulton enjoyed, as well as she was able, her romantic incarceration. Still, were it not for the fifty-gun *Romney* and the other ships and sloops-of-war which were arriving from Jamaica, she did not doubt but the mob would 'tear 'em all to pieces.'

But how pleasant were her new friends! How gallant the naval officers! She was elected 'mistress of the ceremony of the Tea table Morn'g & Even'g.' All sorts of elegant people rowed out to call upon these prisoners from Boston. 'Gov. Bernard has just now drank tea here with Us. His Excel. says, two more such years as the past and the Brit. Empire is at an end.' And yet by merely calling upon the commissioners, even 'incog' one might draw down upon oneself the 'insults and outrages' of 'the Sons of Violence,' whose Indian howlings and ferocious disguises terrified many stouter hearts than Miss Hulton's.

When fall came, Miss Hulton was a little worried. She had heard of the horrors of the New England winter. The sea breezes which had made the Castle 'a delightful & a most agreeable Summer Retreat,' would soon turn it into an iceberg. Yet until the troops which the commissioners demanded arrived, they dared not leave.

On the twenty-ninth of October, the prisoners at the Castle skipped over their ramparts for joy. There they were! They had come! Even in this wilderness England had the power to protect her faithful servants. Seven transports and ships of war followed each other Indian file. Their decks were scarlet with British regulars. The gleeful commissioners waved flags, and that night sent off fireworks. Surely the Boston toughs would never dare even show their dirty faces now.

## X

'ON FRIDAY, Sept 30, 1768,' says Paul Revere, 'the ships of war arrived schooners transports etc., came up the harbour and anchored round the Town; their cannons loaded, a spring on their cables, as for a regular seige. At noon on Saturday the fourteenth and twenty-nineth regements and a detachment from the 59th regement, and a train of artillery landed on Long Wharf; there formed and marched with insolent parade, drums beatting, fifes playing, up King Street each soldeir having recived sixteen rounds of powder and ball.' And with that love for a ship's name so characteristic of Boston at the time, he named every ship. They were: the *Beaver, Senegal, Martin, Glasgow, Mermaid, Romney, Launceston,* and *Bonetta.*

These troops from Halifax were part of that standing army for whose support there had been so much argument. Boston was stunned to see them used, not as a protection, but a police force. They were, as Governor Bernard said, 'to rescue the Government from the hands of a trained mob and to restore the activity of the Civil power.'

So Miss Hulton got off her romantic island before the first snow flew. By November her brother bought a house in Brookline which was so far out 'not one person in 50 in Boston ever saw it,' as the agreeable maiden lady writes her dear Mrs. Lightbody, confident that at last all is well in the world. The two small boys throve on country air and developed 'Contenances of Cherubs and the Constituions of Farmers.' Mr. Hulton made 'great improvements' on his property and built 'Barns, Stables, and many conveniences, amongst the rest a Green house,' and nominated his sister (who seems to have had a weakness for whimsical titles) 'Director General of the Vegitable Tribe.' She would attempt, she says, to grow artichokes and broccoli. New England was backward in such matters, everything green was lumped together as 'Sause.' And she flutters happily over the two boys and the third who is on his way. Actually there is a genteel social life in

Boston, now that a decent servant of the King is allowed off the island, a 'very good assembly' and a concert 'every other week.'

But most important of all is the fact that Henry (under the protection of British regulars) can go on with his work at the Custom House. No more do the 'Sons of Perdition' howl like Indians about one's house at night, break windows, stick their ugly soot-blackened faces into a parlor and frighten gentlewomen by demanding the blood of one's brother. She is confident that the great extremes in heat and cold are now the principal danger the family will suffer from. The mobs (which she says do not represent the actual feeling in Boston) have been put in their place by the gallant British soldiers.

The leading Sons of Liberty had met at Will Molineaux' just before the troops landed to decide whether or not to offer armed resistance. It is likely that in that stormy meeting Sam Adams' patience won out over Molineaux' ferocity. A policy of dignified non-cooperation was decided upon.

Unlike today, the civilians were about as well armed as the professionals. The fowling piece, which men like Revere used for duck-shooting, was as good a weapon as the grenadier's musket. And the American was a much better shot. A cordwainer's knife, butcher's cleaver, shipwright's adze, is not inferior to a bayonet. Many of these men, like Revere, had seen active service against the French. The rabid enthusiasts who talked about wiping out the redcoats the day they landed were not talking of an impossibility. It would be quite another thing today when the soldier has his machine guns, grenades, and aircraft and the unfortunate civilian has nothing.

Boston did nothing violent, but settled down to make things as uncomfortable as possible for the soldiers. In spite of the 'Quartering Act' she refused barracks. Some camped on the Common and others in Faneuil Hall (which must have badly rocked that cradle of liberty). Governor Bernard had given it to them. Colonel Dalrymple, the commanding officer, demanded the 'Manufactury House,' but did not use force to take it. The main guard was set up opposite the old State House. James Otis complained not only of their cannon, aimed at the General Court, but said, in his inelegant way, that the soldiers smelt.

Colonel Dalrymple did not have a good reputation even among

the Tories. Miss Hulton writes of him as 'proud, haughty, & voluptuous, devoted to self & self gratification, hated in general by those under his Comand & universally dispised.' Colonel Carr seems to have been a smaller edition. General Gage himself came up from New York to settle the matter of quartering troops. He was now commander-in-chief of the British army in America, having followed the beloved General Amherst. More than any royal governor of one colony, he represented the power of England. Thomas Gage was a good routine officer, propitiatory, obliging, kindly, and liked by Boston, although his young officers sometimes thought him a little grandmotherly by nature, and all were amazed to notice how much he looked like Sam Adams.

The regulars had not been in Boston two weeks before thirty of their men had deserted. The opportunities of the New World, as craftily advertised by the Whigs, were too much for them. If this went on long enough, the regiments would melt away and leave nothing but Colonel Dalrymple and Colonel Carr. These soldiers had no heart for police work. Many of them were exactly as whiggish as the Sons of Liberty. Recaptured deserters were shot at the foot of the Common. Lesser infringements were punished by the cruel and often fatal whippings common then in the British army. This sentence was carried out by the negro regimental drummers.

What the Fourteenth and Twenty-Ninth and their colonels might have been in actual warfare, or if not systematically badgered and insulted by the townsfolk, we do not know. In the days of William the Third the Fourteenth had fought valiantly in Flanders, and later would form one of the hollow squares at Waterloo. The Twenty-Ninth had made its name at Ramillies, under Marlborough, and was to bear a heavy part with Wellington on the Peninsula — and doubtless today these ancient regiments are still carrying on their honorable reputation. But they seem to have taken a vacation during their occupation of Boston, and serve only as unsavory examples of the 'brutal soldiery' of the time.

The colonels had their orders to keep on peaceable terms with their hosts and undoubtedly did their best. But even in small ways this was impossible. One thing that caused bad feeling was the fact that the regulars, having almost no pay and little to do, were allowed to accept private odd-jobs where they could find them. They would work for nothing more than a square meal or a drink, and this irritated the Boston workmen who had no work for themselves.

By snowfall they were quartered all over Boston, in sail lofts, sugar houses, distilleries, warehouses. Once more the commissioners went to work and the Sons of Liberty went underground a little. From now on there were few big meetings under the Liberty Tree, more sudden appearances of 'hellish crews,' men with blackened faces, or with nightcaps pulled down to disguise them, making a quick sortie on some especially unpopular opponent, a few broken windows, threats made, and completely gone before any alarm can be given. Seemingly this coming of armed order had put the fear of God and Parliament into Boston Whigs.

Yet there was one thing that must have been apparent to every thoughtful man who watched the unloading of troops and their 'insolent parade.' Eventually — it might be this hour, it might be next week, next month, next year, but surely sometime — the inhabitants who now stood watching sullenly and doing nothing would anger the soldiers and the soldiers would fire upon the inhabitants. You cannot quarter troops on a resentful town and not have fracases. A sentry, with his face cut by an oyster shell, is going to beat up the nearest urchin and hope he has caught the right one. And the urchin's screams bring his mother and hers bring the town.... Women jostled in dark alleys are going to be yelling rape. Inebriated young officers are going to ride their horses into people's parlors to get them out of the rain.

Thomas Hutchinson says of them, 'They are in general such bad fellows in that regement [referring to the especially hated Twenty-Ninth] that it seems impossible to restrain them.' There were nightly tavern brawls. Soldiers were 'accidentally' jostled off bridges and wharves into water. Soldiers were followed by small boys chanting 'bloody-backs' and 'Lobsters for sale.' This hurt their martial pride. The amazing thing is that no one was killed any sooner.

According to Sam Adams, the regulars spent most of their leisure beating up small boys, violating the Sabbath and worse yet the women of Boston. He paints a pathetic picture of an elderly patriot's emotions when he comes home to find his favorite grand-daughter in bed with a soldier. The 'lobsters' smartly answered

that female virtue was so easy in this stronghold of Puritanism
'the Yankey war contrary to all others will produce more births
than burials.'

The troops might protect the commissioners, but could not
influence the General Court. Sir Francis Bernard fluttered and
squawked about, quarrelling with the Court and being called
every evil name. Yet when he first arrived, this same General
Court had been so pleased with him they had given him Mount
Desert 'in a fit of generosity.' At Harvard, too, he had been
popular, for he did much for the college. Now someone cut the
heart out of his portrait hanging on the college walls.

He was quite as tired of the Massachusetts Bay as the Bay was
tired of him. In the summer of 1769 he left our shores in such haste
he did not even stop for his large family to pack up and go with
him. Every bell in Boston cling-clanged with joy as the sails of
his ship disappeared down Nantasket Roads.

Now his considerable authority descended upon the Lieutenant
Governor. Thomas Hutchinson would do the best he could —
which would not be enough. It is doubtful if any man could have
done very much better.

There was talk of sending the leaders of opposition to London
for a parody of a trial and certain death on Tyburn. Otis, Hancock,
and Sam Adams would be the first to go. Overseas Otis was still
looked upon as the fermenter of provincial treason, and yet it was
because one of the commissioners accused him of treason to England
he got into that worse than fatal row at the Royal Coffee House.
This tavern was the favorite rendezvous of the crown officials and
army and navy gentry. Before this influx it had been the meeting
place for the Whig Club, which by now had transferred its patronage to 'the Bunch of Grapes.' John Adams had noticed that in
the fall of '69 Otis was 'bullying, bantering, reproaching, ridicul-
ing . . . no politeness, no delicacy, no taste, no sense.' In some
such mood he charged into the Royal Coffee House, 'demanding
an apology,' because his loyalty to England had been questioned.

The officers' swords were out. Tables overturned. Candles
knocked over. From the dark room came the sounds of breaking
furniture, struggle, and blows.

James Otis owed his life to the darkness and his own strength.
He was taken home to his outraged wife and sewed up. The crack

in his skull was so deep a man could lay an entire finger in it. Soon John Rowe is writing, 'Mr. Otis got into a mad Freak tonight & broke a great many windows in the Town [State] House.' Or, 'Mr. Otis behaved very madly, firing guns out of his Windows.' And he raved against his wife.

The sad day came when he was tied up and carted out of Boston. Neither the cool and fashionable Mrs. Otis nor Sam Adams could have much regretted the sight of that chaise starting for the country — and retirement. There was not one strong voice left in New England to keep the Whig Party from demanding separation from England. And Mrs. Otis busied herself marrying off her girls to well-born young Tories. James Otis began to grow very fat and to sign himself 'Mr. Oates.'

The coming of the troops slightly altered the tempo of everybody's life, and not always for the worse. Certain trades picked up. The officers had money to spend and even the camp women would buy food and furbelows. Mr. Piemont, the French peruke-maker and barber, did a rush business. He enlarged his staff by employing a Mr. Dines (of the Twenty-Ninth) to help him when not on duty. Mr. Dines talked ferociously of how the troops would massacre everybody if they had a chance. And the officers would not pay their bills.

Paul Revere in one respect did very well by this landing of the troops upon Boston. He got the subject for one of his most famous engravings, or rather series of engravings. A friend of his, Christian Remick, was a Cape Cod pilot by trade. From there he went into map-making and then on to water-color sketching, which he did with a naïve charm. He advertised his paintings of the landing of the troops in 1769, but it was not until the next year Paul Revere got the first of his three famous engravings onto the market. In the April 16, 1770, copy of the *Boston Gazette* (and after the troops had left town) we read: 'Just published and to be Sold by Paul Revere and by the printer thereof [Edes and Gill] a Copper-Plate, containing a View of Part of the Town of Boston in New England, and the British Ships of War landing their Troops in the year 1768. Dedicated to the Earl of Hillsborough.'

He makes no slightest claim to have drawn the picture in the advertisement and on the imprint only says, as usual, 'Engraved, Printed and Sold by Paul Revere.' It is the most decorative of all his plates. There were a number of similar views of Boston's picturesque waterfront, wharves, hills, steeples, huddling houses. with ships in the harbor in the foreground. The earlier Burgis Price views are quite similar. Mr. Henry Winchester Cunningham has tentatively put forward Christian Remick as the artist He was working with Revere at this time coloring his prints with their characteristic, primitive, effective, and unfading bright blues and reds and scarce drabs and greens.

One mystery deeper than who may have drawn the picture is the contradictory quality of the two inscriptions on it. It is indeed, as advertised, dedicated 'to the Earl of Hillsborough,' which is odd enough, for he was looked upon as one of the principal enemies to American freedom. But the dedication goes on, 'His Majesty Sr'y of State for America THIS VIEW of the only well Plan'd EXPEDITION formed for supporting ye dignity of BRITIAN & chastizing Ye insolence of AMERICA is hum'y inscribed.' This dedication is placed on a shield and under a palm tree on the right-hand lower corner. Running under the picture is the familiar description of the scene — the names of the ships, how and when the troops landed, and the 'insolent parade' with which they marched up King Street. The dedication suggests a violent Tory and the description an equally violent Whig. It looks as if Paul Revere, with a shrug of his shoulders and a glint in his eye, decided to please both camps and sell as many of his views as he might.

This plate is ten by fifteen and includes only the North End and the business centre of the town. For Edes and Gill's almanac for 1770 he did a cruder, smaller, but more comprehensive view. And four years later, when working regularly for the *Royal American Magazine*, he once more makes a similar copper plate of Boston's waterfront. This time nothing is said about discharging troops, the ships in the foreground are not named, and the wharves, islands, and shipyards are. These miserable troops with their 'insolent parade' did quite a little towards supporting the Revere family.

Another pleasant aspect of their invasion was the liveliness and color the young officers of the army and navy added to the provincial social life. The assemblies were gay, the concerts military. John Rowe was Grand Master of Masons for North America and, as there were many fraternal brothers among the British troops, the two regimental bands led the procession, in which Paul Revere must have marched. 'Turtles' picnics and 'frolicks' abounded, and as is usually the case many who disapproved of the presence of the enemy found them individually kind and sympathetic men. Sam Adams, however, was horrified by their innocent amusements. He thought they and the customs officials were corrupting the natural piety of his chosen people.

The first of the young officers to surrender to the charms of the Yankee girls was Captain Ponsonby Molesworth, nephew of Lord Ponsonby, and a Mason. The day the troops landed he had been standing with his men on Queen Street, glanced up at a balcony above his head. There he saw a girl looking down. 'That girl seals my fate,' he said to the officer beside him. And so he married Suzannah Sheaffe. The Sheaffes were Tories. John Rowe was a staunch Whig, but this did not keep his dear adopted daughter, Sucky Inman, and the handsome Captain Linzee of the *Beaver* apart. John Rowe liked and admired the personnel of both the army and navy and seems to have lived in a social whirl after their arrival. He is dining with Commander Hood on a warship, sitting about the Coffee House with officers — among others a Captain Preston — and at the same time serving on committees for the town protesting their presence and signing petitions.

Yet, as he tries to show decency and respect to both sides, he is sometimes caught between the two millstones. There was that ghastly noon when Captain Dundass of the *St. Lawrence* 'most smartly accosted me' at the Coffee House, where he had gone for dinner. 'Ha John are you there — Dammy I expected to have heard of your being hanged before now, for Dammy You deserve it.' 'Surely Capt Dundass you are joking,' poor Mr. Rowe managed. 'No — Damn him if he was, for you are a Damn Incendiary & I shall see you hanged in your Shoes.' Mr. Rowe 'thought it Prudent not to take any Notice of it just then but came home to dinner.'

There was not much middle ground left for a decent, peaceful, intelligent man to stand on. The currents were running high on either side of that little reasonable island on which John Rowe attempted to keep his footing, eating away the ground from under his feet. It must have been a very thoughtful man who 'came home to dinner,' puzzled, fearful of the future.

So a year and a half passed, with street fighting and courtship, one tar-and-feathering, passive resistance, angry words, and petty insults, yet also petitions to the Crown which are still honored landmarks in man's struggle for representative government. This space of time marked the end of Otis and the end of Bernard, the rise to new power of both Thomas Hutchinson and Sam Adams. Paul Revere made silver and copper plates, cleaned teeth, and rented his 'aunt Marrets house' to a Captain Small, presumably of the occupying troops. John Rowe let two houses to them and William Molineaux tried to rent them a warehouse.

Yet this almost-normal life was only a thin crust over a molten mass of dissatisfaction, patriotic determination to win representative government, resentment, and hatred. The crust held for eighteen months. Surely that was a long time to wait between that Saturday noon on which the troops arrived and the Monday night on which the all but inevitable volley was fired.

# V

## 1770 – 1773

THE bloody work on KING STREET results in a famous engraving, a diagram, and a fair trial. The REVERES leave CLARK'S WHARF for NORTH SQUARE and illuminate their house. PAUL REVERE goes to a dance. SARA'S last child is born and she dies. HE marries RACHEL WALKER. The tea ships arrive. HIS first known ride is short. After attending the BOSTON TEA PARTY, he takes another ride — this time to PHILADELPHIA.

'5 Coffings for Massacre' by Paul Revere used in *Boston Gazette*, 1770, and broadsides. American Antiquarian Society.

# I

AND at last the day came, snowy and cold at first, but gradually clearing and warmer. On the fifth of March, 1770, Boston was padded with thick white silence. Surely a foot of snow should be enough to keep the regulars in their barracks and the inhabitants off the streets. There had been an increasing number of threats, the town boys boasting they were going to clean up the 'bloody-backs,' the soldiers swearing they would teach the 'cowardly rascals' respect for His Majesty's uniform. The fifth of March was Monday. On the previous Friday an unusually large number of pates had been broken at Gray's ropewalks, on Hutchinson Street. When the very name Hutchinson became hateful to Boston, it was renamed Pearl.

One of the ill-paid, hornet-tempered privates of the Twenty-Ninth went to the walks hoping to earn a little money. Sam Gray, a journeyman, employed there but not related to the owner, asked him if he wanted work. The soldier humbly said, yes, he did. But the work offered him (in pure Anglo-Saxon) started a fist fight between them. The soldier was defeated, ran back to his barracks, and returned with a crowd of his fellows. The 'squabble' went on, augmented by more and more soldiers and more and more workmen. It began to rise to the proportions of a Pope's Day frolic. Among the regulars was Private Kilroy, who was as bad a fellow as was to be found, even in the Twenty-Ninth. Shortly before this encounter at the ropewalks, George Robert Twelves Hewes had caught him robbing a Boston woman of most of her outside clothing. This consisted of a 'cardinal,' bonnet, muff, and tippet. Hewes forced Kilroy to give up his booty. Everyone knew that Kilroy was a scamp, even as they knew that Captain

Preston, for instance, 'bears a good character.' These six hundred men had, in a year and a half, become individuals. Finally officers and citizens ended the battle, and the soldiers, wiping bloody noses, nursing black eyes, and counting missing teeth, were forced back to their barracks. They had been defeated by the wouldering sticks and tar-pots of the ropewalk men and were swearing vengeance.

Mr. Gray promptly fired Sam Gray. The colonels, although humiliated by the trouncing their men had taken, promised to keep them under restraint. Both sides privately began to watch for a chance to go on with this interrupted battle. The soldiers, especially of the Twenty-Ninth, busily went to work preparing cudgels and sharpening cutlasses and prophesying to anyone who would listen to them the vengeance they would take on Boston.

Just how systematic the badgering of the regulars had been is now impossible to say. John Adams, who never once wavered from the principles of the Whig Party, believed that 'certain busy characters,' seeking 'to kindle immortal hatred between the inhabitants of the lower class and the soldiers,' urged them on to 'quarrels, re-encounters and combats.' And he pitied 'the poor tools' who had been 'intentionally wrought upon by designing men, who knew what they were aiming at better than the instruments employed.' To get rid of these two regiments, without whose protection civil government could not function in Boston, was the avowed ambition of the radical Whig leaders. One obvious way to do this was to goad the soldiers into firing upon the 'innocent' inhabitants. Then public opinion of all political colors would unite to demand their withdrawal. Sam Adams would have proved his statement that you cannot quarter troops on an unwilling town without bloodshed, and Boston would have some martyrs — which has never hurt any political party. There was also the possibility that a popular uprising would take vengeance into its own hands. The Boston garrison had recently been reduced, and there were left only the original Fourteenth and Twenty-Ninth. Many people thought then — and think now — that this was what Sam Adams was leading up to during the winter of '69–'70. He had certainly warned towns roundabout Boston that their help might be needed on that Monday night. Something was going to happen.

The snow, already a foot deep, stopped. The sun came out and icicles formed along the eaves. The sun set, the moon rose, and it was night. The colonels[17] did not restrain their men. More of them than usual were out 'driving the streets' in small packs. They pushed and cursed at civilians, who got in their way as much as possible and cursed back. The regulars were at their worst, and what John Adams calls 'the lower classes' (Cousin Sam had more endearing terms for them) were out in full force. But by eight o'clock that night the air was so charged with dynamite any flash-in-the-pan would blow the whole town sky high.

Captain Goldfinch, of the Fourteenth, seems to have been a well-disposed young officer, with the failing so fashionable among eighteenth-century gentlemen of not bothering to pay 'tradesmen.' He owed the French barber, Piemont, quite a bill for shaving him, and Piemont, unable to get a cent out of him, told one of his apprentices that any money he could squeeze out of Goldfinch he could have for himself.

By eight o'clock, outside Murray's Barracks on Brattle Street, a boy had been knocked down and was bawling that he was killed. Captain Goldfinch was standing there as the crowd began to gather. Some soldiers, returning from duty, tried to get down the black and narrow street to their barracks, but found their way blocked. Ensign Mall, in charge of them, lost his head, bade the men make a way for themselves with bayonets, 'he'll stand by them.' Goldfinch intervened, scolded the ensign, and got the men inside the heavy doors of the old sugar house, but a good many blows had been exchanged and both sides were ugly.

Goldfinch himself tried to slip unseen over to King Street, where the main guard was housed, and see what was afoot. So the Captain, with the 'greasy' and diminutive barber's boy bawling at his heels, emerged into the moonlit width of King Street. The child pointed at the officer, roaring out what a bad fellow he was not to pay his bills, also suggesting canine ancestry. The officer paid no heed, but it was too much for the solitary sentry stationed outside the custom house.

This man, Montgomery, had been enduring more than the usual amount of snowballs, chunks of ice, oyster shells, sea-coal, and provincial wit which was the fate of solitary sentries. For some time he had been muttering and cursing and saying what he'd do if any came within reach of his bayonet. A large crowd had gathered about him to enjoy his spleen, but he had not been attacked thus far except by missiles and adjectives. In spite of his threats he had run nobody through. Now he left his box, stepped down, demanded the saucy boy to 'show his face.' The boy smugly said he wasn't ashamed of his face and Montgomery (old enough to know better, for he was bald as an egg) hit him a glancing blow which did not even knock him down. Instantly the crowd rushed him, yelling that the blood-thirsty butcher was murdering the child.[18]

There was still a third crowd gathered in the neighborhood that night. This has always been the most mysterious. Two hundred able-bodied sailors, porters, and other likely street-fighters were lined up at this time close to Faneuil Hall, listening to an oration by a 'tall gentleman' in red cloak and white wig. This may have been Sam Adams (who was not tall), but was probably William Molineaux. It was also said that this was 'Joyce Jr.' When the oration was done, the cry went up, 'To the Main Guard!' and there were threats to kill all the 'lobsters' they could find.

What had been three separate, angry groups now all came together on King Street, milling about in the snow and the moonlight, just in front of the old State House. On its corbels strutted the lion and unicorn of England.

And now, close on nine o'clock, the bell of Old Meeting began to ring as though for fire. All over Boston doors flew open and windows went up.

'Where is the fire?'

'The regulars are cutting and slashing everyone.'

'They are cutting down Liberty Tree.'

'The regulars are massacring the people.'

And that other cry from the gates on the Neck to Copp's Hill, 'Town-born, turn out . . . town-born, turn out.'

But others were calling excitedly that the town was on fire. Many rushed into the streets carrying their fire-buckets. Boys went too. And Mrs. Maverick, a poor widow who ran a small shop, flung a cloak about her and plunged off into the snow in pursuit of her seventeen-year-old son, sure that if trouble was abroad her Samuel would be in it. He had been doing so well as Mr. Greenwood's apprentice, learning the ivory-turner's arts.

Montgomery was now hard-pressed. Besides the usual cries of 'lobster' and 'bloody-back,' there rang in his ears, 'kill him, kill him.'

'If you come near me,' he panted, 'I'll blow your brains out.'

'Fire and be damned.'

Montgomery loaded. An enormous mulatto loomed up over him. Crispus Attucks would have frightened any man. He was well over six feet, was part Indian, part negro, and part white. His master in Framingham thought highly of him. He was forty-seven at this time. Attucks had a crowd of sailors at his heels and a stick in his hand. He poked at Montgomery and said he'd 'have off one of his claws.'

The hard-pressed 'lobster' did not fire, but he called in a loud voice, 'Turn out Main Guard.' His voice carried across King Street to the guardhouse, through the hubbub of whistles, Indian yells, and jangling bells.

Instantly a corporal's guard stepped out of the main guard-house, followed by Captain Preston, the officer for the day. They had to struggle to cross King Street and reach the sentry, who stepped down and joined the semicircle of level bayonets presented to his assailants. Captain Preston's reputation was good. His colonel called him 'cool and distinct,' but the judgment that sent only seven men and himself to rescue the sentry was poor. Nine men are enough for a target, but not enough to overawe a mob. Someone yelled at Preston to keep his men in order and mind what he was about. The Captain did not answer, but ordered the soldiers to load and prime. The silence at that moment was so complete everyone heard the rattle of the iron ramrods. Preston put his body between the men and the crowd to keep them from firing. Henry Knox, a plump, likable, twenty-year-old bookseller, grabbed Preston by the arm, begged him for God's sake to take his men back; for if he fired his life must answer for it. Preston said he was 'sensible to it.'

Now the rumor spread that the guns were not loaded. But when asked, the Captain said they were 'with powder and ball.'

'Do you mean to fire upon the inhabitants?'

'By no means,' but Knox noticed that he seemed much agitated.

A number of people (Captain Goldfinch among them) were en-treating the crowd to go home, not to lose their heads. Instead

they made a sudden, blind rush at the soldiers, those behind
pushing on those in front, even jumping on their backs to see.

Crispus Attucks was still muttering about the 'claws' he was
going to get off lobsters. He hit at Preston with his stick of cordwood, grazed him, but knocked down Montgomery. The two of
them fought a moment for the soldier's musket. In the mêlée
that followed, Montgomery got it and was up on his feet. Now
'the motley mob of saucy boys, negroes, mulattoes, Irish teagues
and outlandish jacktars' (to use John Adams' words) had pushed
against the soldiers until you couldn't get a hat between them.
Among the soldiers was Private Kilroy and among the mob Sam
Gray, now out of a job. Kilroy was watching him.

Above the hubbub came the sinister word, 'Present...' The
struggle went on. And then the fatal command, 'Fire...' No one
knows who gave the order. Unbiased witnesses, close to Preston
at the moment, agreed with him and said that he did not.

Montgomery, his hat gone, his bald head shining in the moonlight, fired first at Attucks, who got two balls through the chest.

Kilroy had not forgotten Sam Gray's leadership of the ropewalk
men two days before. He took deliberate aim at him. Gray, too,
died instantly, as did James Caldwell, a mate from a coasting vessel.
Sam Maverick had been holding his master's twelve-year-old son,
Isaac Greenwood, by the hand. At this moment he threw up his
arms, crying, 'Fire away, you damned lobster-backs.' The British
bullets dropped him. He died a few hours later. But Patrick Carr,
'the Irish teague,' and the only victim who deserves our grateful
memory, lived in torture for several days. A number of others
were hit, but only these five died.

Kilroy (as unpleasant as ever) stepped forward and thrust his
bayonet into Gray's lifeless body. The crowd rushed backwards
over each other, tripping and slipping on the packed snow as they
went. The width of the street was littered with lost overcoats and
hats. It was still being said that the soldiers' guns were not loaded
with ball. And some thought all those bundles of clothing on the
snow were lost garments. A few of these bundles were struggling
and crying out. Three at least lay completely quiet. Captain
Preston, once more in front of his men, was desperately pushing
up their guns, demanding they hold their fire, and prevented a
second shot.

Now all over Boston the British drums beat to arms. Soldiers half dressed, officers with waistcoats unbuttoned, poured into King Street, forming their precise platoons, their disciplined faces stony, their bayonets fixed ready to resist the charge of the mob.

Lieutenant Governor Hutchinson, struggling through milling, infuriated masses of fellow townsmen, fought his way to the State House, under whose shadow the 'Massacre' had taken place. He was incensed through and through, loathing what seemed to him the stupid brutality of the regulars and the wilful fecklessness of the inhabitants. Although the 'lower classes' had been taught by their leaders that Thomas Hutchinson was a more dangerous enemy to their liberties than any minister in England, that night they seemed to have remembered their former confidence in him. He spoke from the balcony of the State House — and it was the last time his people listened to him. He swore that justice should be done, and they gratefully accepted his leadership. So he got the mob off the streets and the regiments locked up in their barracks.

Before sunrise, Captain Preston and his eight men were under arrest for murder. They were to be tried immediately and the feeling was so high no jury could possibly be found in Boston who would not have convicted them. Seemingly no lawyer would even dare defend them. Whoever did would be mobbed and ostracized.

## II

WHAT with diaries, reminiscences, and ninety-six affidavits, it would seem we know where everybody in Boston was that night and what he was doing and what thinking.

John Adams had been to his club in South Boston. The bells
had been mistaken for a fire alarm and the members had run out
into the snow, buckets in hand. But when the lawyer (no street-
fighter by nature) saw what was afoot, he thought first of his wife,
Abigail, alone in the 'white house' and soon to be confined. He
went to her. The streets were already lined with British soldiers.
'I had no way to proceed but along the whole front, in a narrow
space they had left for foot-passengers. Pursuing my way without
taking the least notice of them, or they of me, any more than if
they had been marble statues, I went directly home to Cole Lane.'

George Robert Twelves Hewes, of course, was in the middle of
it. He was a little fellow, but 'stood up straight... and spoke
up sharp and quick on all occasions.' Recently he had married
Sally Sumner, a young 'washerwoman.' When Captain Preston
and his men shoved their way across King Street, they had bumped
smack into Hewes. In the moonlight he recognized Kilroy's evil
face, which he especially disliked, and Kilroy 'gave him a pretty
severe recognition with his gun.' Later he saw him stick his bayonet
into Gray's lifeless body.

Nathaniel Fosdick was near Hewes. He would not move when
the soldiers yelled at him to get out of their way. 'I will move for
no man under Heaven' was what Paul Revere's erstwhile bonds-
man was saying that night.

We know Benjamin Church was examining Crispus Attucks and
finding that death had been 'immediate.'

'Black Peg' was a freed slave 'who kept much with the soldiers.'
No one in Boston was less important than 'Black Peg.' But even
she is accounted for.

Piemont, the peruque-maker, was remembering Mr. Dines'
ferocious threats, and we hope regretting that ever he had told
his industrious apprentice that any money shamed out of Captain
Goldfinch he might have for himself.

Thomas Handasyd Perkins was only five and asleep in his bed.
But next morning his father's manservant carried him to Stone's
Tavern to see the enormous carcass of Crispus Attucks. He pointed
out to the child the frozen blood in the gutter. He took him into
an apothecary shop to see the twisted body of Samuel Gray. The
nervous child never forgot the horrors of that night.

But what Paul Revere was doing we do not know. He may

have been up to no good down in the dark of Dock Square listening to the gentleman in the red cape and white wig, helping organize the one part of the performance which seems to have been organized. He may, like many others, have grabbed a bucket, rushed out to a fire, and found a massacre.

There is in the Boston Public Library[19] a pen-and-ink diagram of King Street and the massacre, which is said to have been prepared by Paul Revere for the trial of the soldiers. The handwriting on it certainly looks like his. This shows clearly where the soldiers stood and where their victims fell. The two bodies close to the hard-pressed circle of British bayonets are marked 'A' and 'G,' evidently for Attucks and Gray who, witnesses agreed, died at the soldiers' feet. The boy, Maverick, was shot while standing in Quaker Lane. In the diagram his little figure is marked with a 'G,' presumably for his master, Isaac Greenwood. James Caldwell is indicated correctly and with a 'C.' This drawing was made before Patrick Carr died, for he is not represented on it. He lived for four days. There is more animation in these struggling pen-and-ink figures than Paul Revere ever got into his more formal engravings. They suggest that he himself had stood in King Street that night and had actually seen the men dead and dying about him. This is the only representation of the Massacre that was made before Carr died.

Chronologically Revere's next artistic effort was on the ninth. That day Carr died and Edes and Gill ordered from him '5 Coffings for Massacre' as his ledgers show. These cuts were to be used in the *Boston Gazette*. The Massacre was the biggest news story ever to break in Boston, but the *Gazette* was not off the press until a week after the event.

Then Revere went to work on his very famous engraving of the Massacre. It was not designed as a frontispiece of 'The Short Narrative'[20] (a collection of affidavits, etc., hurriedly got together by the Town of Boston to be sent to England to influence public opinion there before the Lieutenant Governor and the colonels could get in their version), but merely to be sold on the street. On the twenty-sixth of March the print is thus advertised in the *Boston Gazette:*

> To be sold by Edes and Gill
> (Price Eight Pence Lawfull Money)

A Print containing a Representation
of the late horrid Massacre in King St.

All of these prints that now exist are hand-colored probably by
Christian Remick. Special emphasis is laid on the scarlet of British
uniforms and Yankee blood. Blackened by time and the soot of
country kitchens (where many of them were hung), they still have
today an elemental horror. The red of gore and 'lobster-backs'
glow in pristine fury and the darkening of the prints produces at
last a night effect. Generations of children learned to hate England
by gazing at these crude prints.

Paul Revere was primarily interested in the political aspects of
his print, not in its art nor accuracy. The pen-and-ink diagram
was done by a man who knew very well what the scenes had been
that night. But in the engraving the soldiers are standing in a
straight line, firing at an almost equally straight line of extremely
non-belligerent inhabitants. An awkward space is filled in by
exploding gunpowder and a bored mongrel dog. Captain Preston,
with an evil grin and a sword, urges on his men, instead of risking
his life to stop them. That night every man fought for himself, but
in the engraving the shooting is in a regular volley. Attucks is not
black. There is no snow. The sky is blue — only a faint moon
suggests that all this happened at night. The sign over the custom
house, 'Butcher's Hall,' is sheer propaganda. Yet Revere did do
what he wanted to do — produce as fast as possible a hair-raising
Whiggish version of the 'bloody work in King Street.' He was
so successful Josiah Quincy especially warned the jury which tried
the British soldiers against 'the prints exhibited in our houses'
which had added 'wings to fancy.'

This picture was copied many times over here and in England,
and is, undoubtedly, America's most famous engraving as well as
one of the most sought-after by collectors. The inscription on it
reads: 'Engrav'd Printed & Sold by PAUL REVERE, BOSTON.'
Although at the time it may have been well known that Paul
Revere did not make the drawing for it, subsequent generations
took it for granted (without bothering to consider the habits of
eighteenth-century engravers) that he had. But a letter from
young Harry Pelham to Paul Revere was discovered some fifty
years ago giving the first light on who made the drawing. 'The
Boy with the Squirrel' (he was twenty-one at the time) is furious.

He may have reconsidered and never sent the letter, but it reads:

Thursday morning, Boston March 27, 1770.

Sir,

When I heard that you was cutting a plate of the late Murder, I thought it impossible, as I knew you was not capable of doing it unless you copied it from mine and as I thought I had entrusted it in the hands of a person who had more regard to the dictates of Honour and Justice than to take the undue advantage you have done of the confidence and Trust I reposed in you. But I find I was mistaken and after being at the great Trouble and Expence of making a design paying for paper printing etc. find myself in the most ungenerous Manner deprived not only of any proposed Advantage but even of the expense I have been at, as truly as if You had plundered me on the Highway. If you are insensible of the Dishonour you have brought on yourself by this Act, the World will not be so. However I leave you to reflect upon and consider of one of the most dishonorable Actions you could ever be guilty of.

H. Pelham

P.S. I sent by the Bearer the prints I borrowed of you. My Mother desires you would send the hinges and part of the press, that you had from her.

Perhaps the letter did not go and no bearer arrived at Revere's, returning prints and demanding Mother's hinges and press. But the charge against Revere by Harry Pelham cannot be dismissed. Among the Copley-Pelham papers is the bill, dated March, 1770, made out to Mr. Henry Pelham from Daniel Rea, junior. Twelve quires of paper will cost him two pounds. The printing of five hundred and seventy-five prints will be three pounds nine. This is proof that Pelham's plate was engraved and printed. On March 26, the day before Pelham wrote his angry letter, Revere's print was the one advertised for sale in the *Boston Gazette*.

Not until April 9 was Pelham's print put on the market — if this is the advertisement:

To be sold by Edes & Gill
& T & J. Fleet
(Price Eight Pence)
The Fruits of Arbitrary Powers
An original Print representing the late
horrid massacre in King Street taken from
the spot.

There is little doubt that the print advertised above is the Pelham engraving, a copy of which is in the American Antiquarian Society. It is not signed. Certainly if this is the one, Paul Revere did copy it line for line. Identical soldiers fire on the same inhabitants. In both is the familiar view of King Street, 'Butcher's Hall,' the State House, and 'Old Meeting.' Here are the same 'slaughtered innocents' lying in the street. Pelham could have pointed out these resemblances to Revere. But Revere in turn (granted he did draw the diagram) might have pointed out the striking resemblance between those two famous corpses as first drawn on the diagram, then by Pelham, and last of all by himself once more. The figure marked 'C' for Caldwell in the pen-and-ink drawing, lying on his back, his right arm flung out, his right leg drawn up, has certainly been incorporated in the Pelham plate (and used again by Revere) in the lower left corner. In both prints and in the diagram appears a stout little fellow (in no way resembling the black giant Attucks, although marked 'A'). He is on his face, his bashed head turned towards one. The clouds of plagiarism hanging over the Copley-Pelham and Revere households darken. Much more was borrowed than 'Mother's hinges,' but where one artist stopped and the next began may have puzzled them and certainly does us today.

About all that can be said in defence is that such practices were common, for the engraver got his design where he could and used it as he pleased, and that in some way Revere completely satisfied Harry Pelham. Four years later the Newport print-sellers, Charles Rea and Samuel Okey, are corresponding with Pelham. The writer had been to Boston and seen a picture of Mr. Adams by Pelham, at 'Mr. Revere's ... which I admire. How unlucky for me I could neither have the Pleasure of seeing you or him ... should be glad if Mr. Revere would send us immediately one of the small ones of yours [of Mr. Adams] from which we could scrape the face.'

Seemingly by October 4, 1774, Harry Pelham and Paul Revere had not only settled matters between them, but were in some sort of business partnership. Paul Revere was handling the younger man's engraving. During the same year, Revere's ledgers show that he sold copies of his massacre print by the dozen to Isaiah Thomas and Thomas Crafts. He may have split with Pelham on these sales. At least he had satisfied the thin-skinned, sharp-

tongued young artist and they were working together. As Harry
Pelham was satisfied with Revere's conduct, the modern critic
may as well be also.

Whatever the genesis of the massacre print, it took its place in
the Whig political machine, which was well-oiled and running
beautifully. Their opponents were sluggish about such matters.
They were confident that they were right and the other side wrong,
so why talk about it? At first it seemed as though the whole 'horrid
massacre' beginning with a great public funeral had been a tremendous success. Although the colonels protested they could not
withdraw their troops from Boston without General Gage's orders
and Hutchinson claimed he had no right to do anything, Sam
Adams cleverly did get the Twenty-Ninth and Fourteenth out of
town and marooned on Castle Island. There were only some six
hundred troops. As Colonel Dalrymple wrote to Gage, the provincials could easily assemble one hundred times that number of
militiamen.

So there were only nine redcoats left in Boston. They were
confined in the new stone jail, awaiting trial for their lives — if
the inhabitants did not pull the jail down first and take justice
into their own hands.

## III

THE day after the massacre it
would seem Captain Preston had not a friend in town except his
fellow redcoats. Everywhere there was a clamor for his immediate
trial and execution — he and his eight poor devils. Through it all
he preserved a surprisingly cool demeanor. He had always been
well liked in Boston, for previously he had 'behaved himself un-
exceptionably and had the character of a sober honest man and

good officer.' Attucks had nearly broken his arm with his stick of cordwood. He was bruised all over and had been cross-examined by a justice of the peace for three hours. Luckily for him, he had a more excitable friend. This was a Mr. Forester, known by the curious nickname of 'The Irish Infant.' Mr. Forester was determined to find a lawyer for him.

He naturally went first to the well-known Tory barristers. But they feared what the Sons of Liberty (loose once more with the removal of the troops) did to Tories who dared so much as call their souls their own — much less defend 'bloody butchers.' Not even Judge Auchmuty would at first touch the case. Forester did not give up. Almost in despair he sought out Josiah Quincy. No lawyer in Boston — not even John Adams himself — had written so vehemently against England's policies, her quartering of these very troops upon Boston.

Josiah Quincy was twenty-six at this time. He was a frail, slim fellow, with rumpled, fair hair, a cast in one eye, his thin, shapely face already worn fine and refined again by sickness. Knowing he had not long to live, he was determined to get as much into a few years as most men do in threescore and ten. One of his older brothers had recently died of tuberculosis. Both he and his physician, Joseph Warren, needed no X-rays, no blood counts, no chest-tapping, to know what was the matter with him. He was one of the best public speakers in Boston. His arresting, beautiful voice seemed effortless, and yet was so clear crowds standing outside Old South could hear every word when he addressed the mass meetings within. He wrote prodigiously for the papers, signing himself 'Hyperion,' or 'Mentor,' or even 'An old Man.' If he lacked John Adams' impersonal legal mind, he made up with passion and a poetic quality which, unlike most of the poetry of his day, is still moving. Although Sam Quincy was Solicitor General for the Crown, Josiah was so distrusted by the Supreme Court, of which Hutchinson was still Chief Justice, they refused to grant him 'the long robe' of a barrister. Young Josiah attended court in his layman's clothes, but his practice was large. He was dumbfounded when the now desperate Mr. Forester sought him out and asked his help for Preston. But he consented to go to the jail and at least hear the Captain's version of the 'bloody work in King Street.'

It was still morning when 'the Infant,' now quite beside himself and in tears, burst in on John Adams, sitting quietly in his office 'near the town house steps' and, as usual, thinking. There was not a lawyer in Boston, said Forester, who would undertake the defence except Josiah Quincy, who would go into it only if Mr. Adams (who was nine years older) would act as senior counsel.

To his undying honor, John Adams consented. 'I had no hesitation in answering, that counsel ought to be the very last thing that an accused person should want in a free country; that the bar ought, in my opinion, to be independent and impartial, at all times and in every circumstance, and that persons whose lives were at stake ought to have the counsel they prefer.'

John Adams, a cautious, little, round man, had been a poor boy. To support his family decently seemed to him his first duty. And he had built up an excellent practice. Otis had 'ranted' at him that all he thought about was the state of his farm at Braintree and his clients in Boston. His diary shows he could worry about anything, the nation, the world, his wife, himself, and even his 'poor cows.' Otis accused him of 'moping about the streets of this town as hipped as Father Flynt at ninety and seemingly regardless of everything, but to get money enough to carry you smoothly through this world.'

John Adams, who had been unwilling to risk much for the Boston political machine, was now ready to throw away everything in the interest of justice. Given his temperament, he had no choice. The case 'compelled me to difer in opinion from all my friends, to set at defiance all their advice, their remonstrances, their raillery, their ridicule, their censure, their sarcasm, without acquiring one symptom of pity from my enemies.' He believed when it was known he would defend the men he would not have friend or client left. He would be forced to retire to Braintree and his cows. At first he and Josiah Quincy were insulted and ridiculed on the streets of Boston.

Quincy's oldest brother, Sam, had recently paraded the streets of Boston as a 'Son of Liberty,' but was now definitely in the Tory camp. He would represent the Crown at the trial. Their father, the colonel, was a Whig. He had been proud of his youngest boy and heard with consternation that Josiah would defend the men. 'Good God! Is it possible that you should undertake the defense

of those criminals charged with the murder of their fellow citizens?'
The young lawyer wrote back that he could, in honor, do nothing
else.

Three people emerged from what has always been known as
'The Boston Massacre' (Colonel Dalrymple called it 'a Scuffle'),
with great dignity. The two lawyers who risked friendship, fortune, and good esteem to defend them, and Patrick Carr, 'the
Irish teague.'

For Carr, shot through the abdomen, death was inevitable. He
was carried to his master's house and was tended by Doctor Jeffries.
It took him four days to die, but he refused to lay the blame for his
agonizing death upon the soldiers. Were the soldiers greatly
abused? Yes, they were. Would they have been hurt if they had
not fired? Yes. So they fired in self-defence? Yes, and he did not
blame whoever it was hit him. In Ireland he had seen mobs and
soldiers called out to quell them, but 'he had never in his life seen
them bear half so much before they fired.' And he had malice
towards no one.

This version given by the dying Carr was exactly the opposite
to the one which the political machine was busy circulating.
Carr did much to save the lives of the nine British soldiers and
Boston from the disgrace which both John Adams and Josiah
Quincy feared. Sam Adams received a blow when Carr refused
to be in fact one of those innocent victims of blood-thirsty British
tyranny, but he pointed out that the poor immigrant was a Catholic
and, of course, his word meant nothing. Sam Adams was never
above playing on the lowest motives of his followers and religious
bigotry was one.

In public Adams went on crying for vengeance on the butchers,
but what he did in private is, as usual, harder to follow. Neither
of the lawyers who undertook the defence lost his favor. At that
time and to this day many believed that there were certain things
which might come out at the trial so utterly damning to himself
and the radical Whig group he was glad to have the defence in the
hands of those who would have some interest in not washing all
the dirty Whig linen in public. Many thought there was quite a
basketful of it. A reaction set in rather quickly against the first
flaming indignation. Long before the trial, which was put off until
fall, even the staunchest Whigs were learning things about the

secret organization and control of town meetings, town office, and elections which startled them, and were shocked to find how much Boston had come under the control of a fairly small group of politicians.

Merchant Rowe struggled manfully to keep his emotional balance. 'The inhabitants are greatly enraged and not without reason.' But Captain Preston was his friend. Four days after the massacre he called on him in jail and found him 'in much better spirits than I expected.' Men like John Rowe, trying to keep a precarious balance between two violently partisan groups, do not play a romantic part in history. They are apt to be reviled and lonely in life, but after a hundred years or so may find themselves in the company of the best historians. John Rowe, a little absurd with his fussings and caution, his liking to dine well on a 'good pigy,' his passion for catching perch, his formality, which makes him refer to his wife as 'dear, dear, dear Mrs. Rowe' even in his diary, and she on the point of death, now seems an honorable observer of an impossible situation. His efforts to keep his head, judge fairly of both sides, win our respect if it did not that of his contemporaries.

On the very day of the Boston Massacre — the fifth of March, 1770 — far off in London, Parliament voted to abolish all the hated Townshend duties — except on one small item. This was enough to remind the Americans England had not abandoned her claim that she had the right to tax without representation, but was ready to try appeasement — not for the first nor last time. Surely a little tax on tea could not incommode them.

The tax was small and now the whole 'tyranny' had boiled down to little more than a theory. Can you tax, even if nothing more than on tea, without representation? Merchants were tired of non-importation, anxious to build more ships, spread more sail, get back to work again. Workmen were tired of unemployment and longed for the good old days. Everyone was ready to go. It is hard to keep the average person to fighting pitch (not, of course, such men as the Adamses) over a theory — a symbol only — of British authority. Only a tax on tea.

The Bloody Massacre was worked for all it was worth for many years. There were anniversary orations, processions, oaths of vengeance. Many who did not believe the soldiers guilty of any-

thing but self-defence took part in these celebrations.  In a way
they felt it was in truth 'a massacre' and should be remembered,
not because of what Captain Preston and his eight poor devils
did that night, but because England never should have sent the
two regiments in the first place.  It gave a rallying cry to the Boston
Whigs when they most needed it, but the whispering campaign
the massacre started (plus the *reductio ad absurdum* of the duties)
almost finished off Sam Adams.  He had so frankly accepted the
Boston Massacre as God-sent, people were suspicious it might
be Sam Adams-sent.  Little as we know now, one thing is certain.
Paul Revere knew at the time.

# IV

THE Revere family had been in
Boston for fifty-five years, but had never yet lived in their own
house.  Paul's mother had inherited parts of parcels of land in
Maine (including her share of Squirrel Island) from her great-
grandfather, Captain Pattishall.  Her father had left her a share
in Hitchbourn Wharf, which she had sold to her brother Thomas.
But the Reveres had not exactly struck root.  Even in death they
had been tucked away in the Hitchbourn lot in the Granary.

On February 15, 1770, Paul Revere bought the house on North
Square that still stands as a memorial to him.[21]  Two years before
his name disappeared from Doctor Clark's books, and the house
he had lived in was promptly rented to a Mrs. Brassier.  Although
we do not know where he himself lived during these two years,
his shop seems to have stayed consistently, for a great many years,
at the head of Clark's Wharf.  In 1768, although not down in
Clark's ledger, he is advertising his wares 'near the head of Clark's
Wharf.'  In April, after he had bought his own house, and July of

1770 he advertises 'opposite Dr. Clark.' If he had changed his place of business, he would have given his customers notice through the newspapers. This he does not seem to have done. Doctor Clark never lists him as renting a shop from him — only a dwelling. He obviously did not work and live at the same place.

So in 1770 he was done with that quarterly rent, paid sometimes with cash, sometimes with enamelled rings or wine. Sometimes it probably came easy and sometimes very hard.

But from now on he would have to keep up with his mortgage. He bought his house from Captain John Erving, one of the largest real estate dealers of his time and town. For it he paid Erving £213.6.8, and gave a mortgage for £160. Captain Erving might not be so easy to deal with as the kind old doctor. He had already foreclosed once on this same house, when Andrew Knox could not keep up his interest. Before Andrew, James Knox had owned it. Before the Knoxes, Sarah Wybourne, who had it from her father, Robert Howard. Then the Martins, and so back for almost a century to John Jeffs, who owned this land and is thought to have built this house around 1680.

In the seventeenth century it may have looked much as it does today, a two-story, peak-roofed, tiny house with a scowling medieval overhang. Seemingly there is no conceivable place to put Paul Revere himself, a wife, mother, and all those children. But the tax assessments of 1790 describe this house in that year as having three stories and seventeen windows. Paul may have added that extra story or it may have been enlarged before he bought it. As it is the only seventeenth-century house still standing in a large American city, it was wisely restored to John Jeffs' day rather than Revere's. Although not so picturesque in the eighteenth century, it was undoubtedly much more commodious.

His house was about the width of his frontage on the Square, but his land ran back all the way to the Cockerel Church, which faced on Middle Street, and it broadened out as it went back to such an extent he owned a large part of the middle of the block. He quickly sold off part of his back lot to Manasseh Marston (one of Doctor Clark's tenants). Sometime within the next few years he built himself a barn. His papers show that he owned a mare by 1773 and probably he had his barn first. After it was up he found that he had inadvertently trespassed on the land he had sold Marston. But Mr.

Marston obligingly let him 'leave it lay' — as we say in New England. The trespass was recorded on the back of the deed by Marston:

> This is to tell them that ones this a state after me that Paul Revere have Bult a Barn & Set the Barn on my Land one feet which he Is to Remove Whenever the Person that ones this Land shall Desire him or them that ones his Land after him.

Many of the blocks in Boston had been laid out deep enough for farming. The houses of the artisans and even of the gentlemen were usually close to each other or adjoining and stood flush with the street. As the town grew, more and more houses were crowded in behind in back lots and were served by an assortment of alleys. Many of these were only wide enough for pedestrians. Down some you might get a cart. Boston was honeycombed with alleys and small rights-of-way. When roofed over, they must have been very dank and rank. Doctor Clark had such an alley across his property at the Wharf, as did the Hitchbourns and now Paul Revere. These back-lot houses could not have been very desirable. Manasseh's view, for instance, was limited to the back end of the Cockerel Church and the Revere barn. Probably he did not pay much for his 'a state,' but Revere knew him, presumably liked him, and even if he did not spell like a Harvard graduate (or Revere himself), he was very obliging about the barn.

These houses stuck in behind the usually better and more elegant houses on the street accounted for more than their share of Boston's many fires and undoubtedly many of the epidemics, for the privies and wells were inextricably mixed together. 'Fevors and fluxes' were a common cause of death — especially of children. How much was typhoid (for which they had no name), how much dysentery ('bloody flux'), and how much green apples, we cannot even guess now. Probably it was just as well for the town-dweller that he had a healthy distrust of cold water. He had found by experience that cider and beer and even rum were safer than his own back-yard well.

In North Square was one of the town pumps, a public market and a guardhouse. In 1770 North Square was but a block inland from the wharves, tides, and bustle of the waterfront. Instead of being a 'square,' it is literally a long, narrow triangle. Then it was cobbled with beach pebbles, open to sea air and sunshine, and rimmed about by neat, mostly small houses, many of which adjoined their next-door neighbors, as the Revere house joined the Barnards'. There were trees, tidy fences, shop signs, shining window-panes, gleaming brass, well-scrubbed doorsteps, for the entire little square was well-to-do and 'respectable.'

On the apex of the triangle stood venerable 'Old North Meeting.' This was the 'church of the Mathers.' Samuel Mather was the fourth of his name and generation to preach in this church. Samuel, Increase, and Cotton were his predecessors. The Mather family had not grown prouder as generation followed generation, nor had they run out of brains nor accumulated much wealth. This Samuel had married one of Thomas Hutchinson's sisters, but as his daughter Hannah wrote, 'Father was a friend to the Liberty of his Country.' The house he lived in, just across Moon Street from the church, had been a present from his wealthy brother-in-law. Before he came to live in this already ancient dwelling, Mr. Mather had been a pupil in it when Mme. Knight ran an infant school, which Benjamin Franklin also attended. It was already an historic house when Hannah Mather took her first steps out of it into the sunshine of the Square, the centre of her childhood. Largely what the child and young miss saw and what she thought of her neighbors influence our opinions of North Square today. As a very old lady, she wrote down a jumble of reminiscences, chaotic, unchronological. Her vocabulary was limited ('respectable' being her favorite adjective, with 'very pleasant' for alternative), respectability and a 'considerable property' her criterion. As she writes of the people who lived about North Square in Revere's time, they seem somehow to diminish in stature. They, and the Square, become quaint toys. At Hannah's command little men pop out of little houses, hardly real people with real houses — and it is all so 'very pleasant' and everyone so 'respectable' one feels more as if looking at one of those needle-work landscapes of the period or a puppet stage.

So Hannah Mather walks about her square. Little doors open. Little people come out. She meets Benjamin Burt, the silversmith. It is from others we know that he was a member of the North Caucus, from modern connoisseurs that Burt alone rivalled Paul Revere as a silversmith; only from Hannah that he weighed three hundred and eighty pounds and was so respectable and so very, very pleasant.

And across the street, almost next to the house the Reveres have just bought, she looks at Francis Shaw, 'a respectable tailor whose family were large.' (It was upon Mr. Shaw that Major Pitcairn, in a few years' time, was billeting himself.)

Another tailor lived at the entrance of the Square at Momford Corner. 'He strutted about the town with a blue cloak, Tye Wig, gold cane in hand, placed a sign over his shop' to the effect he was 'merchant Adams.' For this piece of side he was rewarded with one of those doggerel verses that were so much a part of the humor of the day, for surely no generation ever burst more easily into rhyme and so rarely into poetry as the last half of the eighteenth century. The verse was pinned above his pretentious sign. For he had 'left his goose to pott yet more. And placed the Merchant on his door.' Hannah says 'he was a very proud man, Made many enemies, Left no decendants.'

On one side of him, Paul Revere had the Holyokes. Mr. Holyoke had been 'a respectable soap-boiler.' But his son was president of Harvard at this time.

The Barnards (whose house duplicated and adjoined the Reveres') also had a distinguished member. This was the Reverend John Barnard, of Marblehead. Once a year the elderly divine returned to this the house of his birth to sleep (or stay awake and pray) for one night, in the room and on the anniversary of his birth. He was well over eighty when Paul Revere would see the chaise stop and the reverend and venerable clergyman crawl out to pay homage to the great day on which he had first seen the light of North Square.

Near-by are respectable mast-makers with large and respectable families, respectable spinsters, respectable merchants. To vary the pattern, Hannah notes a few wretches. Captain Atkins' land adjoined Paul Revere's. This neighbor was a mason by trade and lived in 'the moonlight house,' for he did much of the work on it himself and could only work after his regular hours and on moonlight nights. With less dignity than John Rowe, he attempted to hunt with the hounds and run with the fox. (John Rowe, by the way, is approved of by Hannah as 'a rich merchant & very pleasant man.') Atkins 'adhered to the Tory party, though he had a hand in helping down Hutchinson's house & then built up his own. He assisted taking down the old N. Meeting House (during British occupation) after which he left town' (for Halifax). But even this disreputable creature left behind him 'a large family of daughters ... respectable.'

Next to Hannah's own house lived the Reverend Ebenezer Pemberton, the clergyman who had 'popes in his belly' and was theoretically the Revere pastor. 'Gov. Hutchinson,' as Hannah coolly refers to her own uncle, 'had great influence over some of the clergy. Dr. Pemberton was a warm friend to him & advocated his measures.'

Just off this attractive Square stood the Clark-Frankland and Hutchinson great mansions. Hannah knew this story well. Merchant Clark had determined to outshine his rival. There were eight hundred and sixty-five pieces of wood in the mahogany floor of the Clark house. The escutcheons were painted on the walls. But he 'was unfortunate in the French wars, lost 40 sail of shipping, died broken spirited and left his family not very rich,' as Hannah tells us. The Clark house had been sold to Sir Harry Frankland, who by 1770 had been shaken by a Portuguese earthquake into marrying his fair Agnes, died, and left the Marblehead serving girl possessor of this fine house.

Of her uncle's house Hannah says less. It was the best built house in Boston. By the time Revere moved to the Square, Thomas Hutchinson had repaired the damage done by the mob six years before — that terrifying night when Hannah had led him to safety and the two of them had sat out the rest of the night together. He was living here again, but seems to have preferred his country seat at Milton.

Hannah Mather does not damn Paul Revere with one more of her 'respectables.' He was 'a man of ingenuity & exertion ... he accumulated a handsome property' (after the Revolution). If he was not as 'respectable' nor so 'very pleasant' as the other North Square goldsmith at least he had her full approval in one respect, for he accumulated that handsome property, which in her eyes was next to godliness.

Nathaniel Hitchbourn, boat-builder, moved into the neighborhood a few years after his cousin Paul. Hannah does not mention him or his house. He bought a handsome, three-story, brick mansion two doors below the Reveres. These two houses, so close to each other, standing today in North Square, repeat in different materials the pattern of the Old Granary gravestones. Wherever there are Hitchbourn names in Boston, there were sure to be Reveres near-by. Of the houses Hannah Mather knew, so neatly bordering the Square, these two only seem to have remained to the present to indicate what all those other houses were like — some brick, some wood, some two, and some of three stories, flush on the street (which then had no sidewalk), well built, comfortable, and unpretentious.

The Square was the heart of North Boston and one of the three town markets was held there. The rules governing these markets varied from year to year, but they were always opened and closed by the ringing of church bells. Sometimes they were held daily, but closed at noon. The next year they might be only three days a week, but ran until sunset. The selectmen appointed a 'clerk' for each market. Their records show that Paul Revere sometimes served in this capacity. It would be his duty to keep the peace among the bargainers, see to it no one cheated, that stalls were set up at their accustomed places, and generally to act as referee. No sales might be made before nor after the ringing of the bells. This, too, he must watch.

Long before sunrise country people streamed towards the narrow neck. The town was awakened by a rattle of wooden wheels, the hooves of horses, the cries of drovers. The carts were mostly drawn by one horse or a tandem. The streets were so cramped and the corners so difficult, two wheels and a tandem were handier than four wheels and the horses harnessed abreast. Some of the streets were so narrow a single cart would fill the alley and pedestrians had to step inside the houses until it had passed. Loads were also carried in on the horses' backs, the market man or woman leading the horse, which hardly showed more than a nose or tail under the prodigious load of vegetables, sacks of grain, slaughtered hens, hams, firkins of butter.

Farmers who owned slaves sent them in with loads of produce. The black men were jolly, popular, and good bargainers. Crispus Attucks' master had a high regard for his ability as a salesman. In many reminiscences of the period, the poor boy (grown rich) tells how he first saw Boston, as he walked in with the basket of gingerbread his mother (usually widowed) had baked to sell on market day. Or the difficulties he had getting a flock of turkeys to market. The wary birds could only be coaxed along by a sparse scattering of grain, all the way from Chelmsford to Boston. At night they roosted in a tree and the child slept under the tree.

By the time the bells rang to open the market and the clerk had seen that all was in order, the horses were unharnessed and the wares arranged. From all over North End, men, women, and children would hurry with their baskets, intent upon that old New England sport of getting the most for one's money. The scene was identical with that of any market town in Old England, colorful, voluble, picturesque.

Some things were high in Boston — especially fuel. Miss Hulton wrote dear Mrs. Lightbody that the prices on the whole were about the same as in London. Fish very good and cheap. 'We pay for mutton and veal 2d and 2½d a pound. Beef something less. Pork more. Tub butter 6½ a pound. Plenty of wild fowl. Quails, Partridges, Pigeons and Robins.'

At a somewhat earlier period, Bennet does not think our bacon as good as English, but 'they pickle their pork so well it answers the same end.' A good turkey cost him two shillings . . . a fine goose tenpence. Lobsters sold for a halfpenny apiece. Our oysters he thought 'copperish' and inferior. Both found fruit more plentiful, but not as good as in England. There were many novelties — besides the robins Miss Hulton used to eat. Once John Rowe speaks of feasting on a 'buffalo steak.' How such an item could have been procured in New England remains a mystery. Venison and bear steak were still plentiful. The close connection between Boston and the West Indies made such exotic foods as pimentos and limes commoner than they were again until after the Civil War. Chocolate, coffee, and tea came from England or Holland. Indian and rye meal were common and cheap, but white flour was mostly imported. On the whole, the people ate well.

Neither old Mrs. Revere nor Sara Revere would have far to go for their marketing, and Paul, like many of the heads of households at the time, may have taken an especial pleasure in picking out the roasts of beef and saddles of mutton or haunches of venison himself. Here he might meet his neighbor, Thomas Hutchinson, bound on the same domestic errand. But a lieutenant governor

and a man of his social standing would be accompanied by his
butler, who carried the basket. Paul doubtless carried his own.
This market would play an important part in the Reveres' lives.

Paul and Sara had been married for thirteen years and the
children were thickening about them. There was Deborah, a big
girl of twelve and a great help to her mother and grandmother,
unless she was unusually backward. Paul, at ten, would still be
at writing school, but helping his father in his shop in spare moments and learning the ancient craft he was to follow. Sara was
eight. Then a skip of four years, representing the coming and the
going of the smallpox baby. Frances (a great Hitchbourn name
going back already for one hundred and fifty years) was four.
Mary in 1770 was two. No one knew at this time that she was the
only child of Revere's by Sara to outlive her father, for she was
to be projected far into the future, to ride in steamboats or railroads,
send telegrams. She would see Boston become a city, hear talk
of freeing slaves. Mary was still the baby at the moment, but
1770 being an even year, Elizabeth was on the way.

In those days child-bearing women quickly ran out of calcium,
and a 'tooth for every child' was an accepted law of nature. Hair
fell out and bodies became misshapen. Sara was no longer the
young girl who had caught Paul Revere's eye when he came back
from the wars, but a woman of thirty-four. If she had lost half a
dozen teeth, it was only what was expected. Women aged early.

Some women developed into patient, reproachful martyrs or
tired scolds, some into towers of strength, and their husbands could
read King Solomon's description of the virtuous woman and
truthfully say it was his own wife. The average probably took life
about as she found it. The crowding and early loss of teeth, bad
sanitation, many things we should now consider underprivileged,
she would accept as a proper and natural way to live. This average
woman loved her husband and children, did her best for all of
them, with that mixture of good and bad temper, wisdom and
pettiness which characterizes the human race. Sara Orne leaves
no impress of her own character — only a general impression of
having been one more of those women whose whole story may be
told on a slate gravestone or in a family Bible. They lived and
died. And they had so and so many children.

What with the long hours expected of an artisan, his hours at

church, his duties as master of Saint Andrew's and senior deacon
of the Grand Masons, his club memberships and activities with
the Sons of Liberty, and heavy domestic responsibilities, one
wonders when Paul Revere ever had a chance to sit back and
relax. He seems to have done as much in one day as other men
do in a week. His easy, sanguine temperament, so unblocked by
regrets or any struggle to understand more of a problem than
meets one at the moment, let him go through life with a minimum
of wasted effort. Paul Revere's energies flowed out untrammelled.

He could clean your teeth or mend your 'umbrilloo'; cut a trade
card, if you were a merchant; fix you up with spectacles and
lenses if a scholar.

He had branding irons for hatters; clock-faces for clock-makers;
for soldiers, sword hilts; for surgeons, spatulas and probes; for
babies, rattles, teat-spoons, and 'wisles'; obelisks for Sons of
Liberty; silver chains for squirrels and engraved collars for dogs;
baptismal basins and standing cups for churches.

Gold earrings for your wife and buckles for your shoes; for your
household, the best silver made in America, punchbowls, chafing
dishes, tea-pots, coffee-pots, chocolate-pots, pepper-pots.

Sugars, creamers, salts, salvers, tankards, cups. Caddies and
fine covered dishes.

He could cut you a copper plate of anything from a mouse to
John Hancock. And he was not yet, at thirty-five, in his complete
stride.

# V

ELIZABETH was born so late in
December, 1770, she nearly broke the well-established family
pattern. She was too young in March, 1771, to appreciate that
great night when the North Square house became the wonder of

all Boston. The Square was filled with thousands gazing at the beautiful and sombre illumination which her father's ingenuity had contrived in memory of the unfortunates slain by British tyranny.

A year had passed since the massacre. To the unending honor of John Adams, Josiah Quincy, and the jury (the foreman was even a 'Son of Liberty'), Captain Preston and his men received fair trial. All were acquitted except Kilroy and Montgomery, who were branded on the hand for manslaughter. Captain Preston was so glad to get out of jail he did not even stop to thank his lawyers (as John Adams sadly noted). He was pensioned off by England, retired to the country, and was 'a perfectly satisfied man, which is not to be found every day.'

For the first time John Adams was elected to the General Court. This election upset him. He did not want the office. That night, when he told his wife, Abigail burst into tears. Both lawyers were respected for the stand they had taken and both suffered in health. John Adams went off to Stafford Springs to drink the water. Josiah Quincy's disease advanced one step closer. How could he ever accomplish all the great things he had in mind before he died? His spirit waxed, but his 'constitution was yielding.'

The Sons of Liberty, with Paul Revere playing his semi-secret part among them, emerged once more after the troops were withdrawn. Such merchants as dared to import from England, like Theophilus Lilly, were bullied and ridiculed. They were none of them really injured. 'Informers' who told the customs officials who was smuggling were treated even more roughly, but none of them were killed or maimed. The commissioners were visited by howling mobs who, however, never got out of control and did no serious damage.

But 1770 had been a wild year. Shortly after the last British soldier left Boston, the Hultons were almost frightened out of their wits and completely off the mainland. It had been a dreadful experience, as Miss Hulton writes from Brookline to Mrs. Lightbody in Liverpool:

> Between 12 & 1 o'clock he [Henry] was wake'd by a knocking at the Door, he got up, enquired the person's name and business, who said he had a letter to deliver to him which came Express from New York. My Bro. puts on his Cloaths, takes his drawn Sword in

one hand, & open'd the Parlor Window with the other. The Man asked for a Lodging — said he, I'll not open my door, but give me the letter. The man then put in his hand, attempting to push up the window, upon which my brother hastily clap'd it down, instantly with a bludgeon several violent blows were struck, which broke the Sash, Glass & frame to pieces. The first blow was aimed at my Bror Head, he Providentially escaped. . . . the lower windows, all around the House (excepting two) were broke in like manner. . . . You wil beleive the whole Family was soon alarm'd, but the horrible Noises from without, & the terible shreiks within the House from Mrs. H's Servants which struck my Ears on awaking, I can't describe, & shall never forget.

I could imagine nothing less than that the House was beating down, after many violent blows on the Walls & windows, most hideous Shouting, dreadful imprecations, & threats ensuded. Struck with terror & astonishment, what to do I knew not, but got some Cloathes on & went to Mrs. H. Room, where I found the Family collected, a stone thrown in at her window.

The assailants appeared 'disghused — & their faces blacked, with white Night caps and white Stockens on, one of 'em with Ruffles on & all came with Great clubs in their hands'; and so on through a night of horror and shrieks, yet no damage was done except to windows and nerves. It was enough for the Hultons. They spent the summer on Castle Island once more. It was not until after the trial of Preston and his men and a popular revolt against mob action they dared return to Brookline. In time they understood these crowds better. Henry Hulton found that it was only himself the Sons of Liberty were after. He would trustingly leave his wife, sister, and children in their lonely house, knowing they would not be molested.

These little forays against 'governors men,' 'bastards of Liberty,' continued. Paul Revere was by his contemporaries considered one of the principal lieutenants of the Sons of Liberty. So he was undoubtedly often off on these doubtful expeditions, a nightcap askew upon his head, making terrible faces through his blackened mask at poor trembling Miss Hulton, or frightening the timid Scotch merchant MacMasters out of Boston, and yet always keeping things from going too far.

In the fall of 1770, when the merchants of Boston voted to begin importing once more, in spite of that small tax on tea, they were

not molested in their decision. The lift of the boycott was undoubtedly popular. Most people were sick to death of politics and
politicians and only wanted to forget 'tyranny.' England was
trying to readjust her Molasses Acts. Sam Adams was put to it
to keep his revolutionary kettle boiling. The publicity value of
the Boston Massacre was not to be overlooked. The part Paul
Revere played in the first anniversary of that 'dreadful day' is
described in the *Boston Gazette* for March 11, 1771.

> The Bells of the Several Congregational Meeting Houses were
> tolled from XII at noon till 1. In the evening there was a very
> Striking Exhibition at the Dwelling House of Mr. Paul Revere,
> fronting old North Square. At one of the Chamber Windows was
> the Apperance of the Ghost of the unfortunate Snyder.

Shortly before the massacre and almost in the Revere back
yard, close to the Cockerel Church, a wooden head had been
placed before the shop of Theophilus Lilly, who was one of the
eight merchants who insisted upon importing from England.
Richardson, a tidesman and a 'rough speaker,' tried to knock it
down with a team of horses, was pelted with filth, took refuge in
his own house next to Lilly's. He first threatened the crowd
gathered outside and then fired a charge of 'swan shot' into it.
The eleven-year-old German boy, Christopher Snyder, a child
servant of Mrs. Apthorp, was killed. 'The little hero' after death
was found (by the *Boston Gazette*) to have shown qualities that
'gives reason to think he had a martial genius and would have made
a clever man.' It was this child's ghost that Paul Revere produced
probably in effigy. The ghost had 'one of his Fingers in the Wound,
endeavoring to stop the Blood issuing therefrom. Near him his
Friends weeping; And at a small distance a monmental obelisk
of oiled paper with his Bust in Front. On the front of the Pedestal
were the Names of those killed.' Underneath, the following lines:

> Sneider's pale Ghost fresh bleeding stands
> And Vengance for his Death demands.

> In the next Window were represented the Soldiers drawn up,
> firing at the People assembled before them the Dead on the Ground —
> and the Wounded falling, with the Blood running in streams from
> their Wounds. Over which was wrote FOUL PLAY.
> In the third Window was the Figure of a Woman, representing

AMERICA sitting on a Stump of a Tree, with a Staff in her Hand &
the Cap of Liberty on the Top thereof — one foot on the head of a
Grenadeir lying prostrate grasping a Serpent. Her finger pointing
to the Tragedy. The whole was so well executed that the Spectators,
which amounted to many Thousands were struck with Solem Silence
& their Contenances covered with a meloncholy Gloom.

The bells tolled again at ten, 'when the exhibition was withdrawn.'

Thus the old North Square house made its theatrical début. It
must have been an exciting, proud day for the Revere family, with
so many thousands gathered in the Square to gaze at their house
and be struck silent by the head of the house's handiwork.

# VI

LIFE was not all politics and
work for Paul Revere, but his amusements were not fashionable
enough to figure in John Rowe's diary, nor of sufficient news value
for John Boyle's. For one moment he does appear at a wedding
celebration in Newburyport. In November, 1772, his friend,
Joseph Pearce Palmer, just out of Harvard, 'smart-looking,' book-
ish, social, and well-to-do, and high Son of Liberty, married one
of the 'celebrated Miss Hunts, who were known as the Watertown
beauties.' They had so many relatives around Boston they 'decided
to escape a wedding at home.' 'We went' (the bride remembered)
'in a coach and four to Hampden, New Hampshire.' But the socia-
ble groom invited a few of his intimates to meet them the day after
the wedding at Newburyport. The bride wore 'her ridding habit'
to this 'ball' which was somehow arranged. It was 'silk calmet,
light colored, trimmed with silver lace, vest of blue satin,' and she
enjoyed herself immensely, for she was a lively beauty without
any fashionable weaknesses nor vapors. She notes who of her

young husband's friends rode out all the way from Boston to dance with them that night. Coming from Watertown she probably had not met them before. And there is Paul Revere among them. With what pride she remembered that her husband 'excelled all his acquaintenances in dancing the fashionable hornpipe.' This may have been her prejudice. If Paul Revere danced with the same rhythm he rode a horse, he should have been very handy at the hornpipe.

It is not likely that Sara took the long, hard ride to Newburyport and back. The men had much social life that did not necessarily include their wives. A woman Sara's age, thirty-six, would have been considered too old to really dance. She might open the evening by treading a few stately measures, but after that would sit quietly with the women of her own age. But middle-aged men, even old men, did dance without loss of dignity. By this system the young girls were assured of plenty of partners without the necessity of sending a general call for help to the nearest male college, as is done today. Each method has its obvious drawbacks. This seeming neglect the wives took as the accepted way of the world and rarely were tempted to stir up a little amusement for themselves. Miss Hulton does report darkly of a certain Boston couple, a 'Mr. & Mrs. S.' 'He entertrained his Ladies in one Part of a great House & She her Gentlemen at the other.' Theoretically, Sara would not resent it that her husband was off dancing hornpipes to the admiration of 'mistress Bride' while she stayed at home facing her eighth confinement.

Of the first four children, all outlived infancy. Of the last four, only two. The records often show the proportion of stillborn or short-lived children increased as the women approached middle age. More and more of these children die, and so do the mothers.

On the fifteenth day of December, 1772, was once more enacted that by now familiar scene. The midwife called. The younger children sent for a night or two to relatives. Old Mrs. Revere, for she was still paying her son rent, could invite in what neighbors she especially trusted as nurses. Paul's two sisters, Mrs. Metcalf and Mrs. Baker, might turn up, and thus, in confusion, superstition, and disorder, the child would be born. The midwife would be in command, ordering hot water or warm flannels, reverting to such primitive beliefs as that a knife under the bed cuts pain, or, if the

delivery was hard, one can speed matters up by opening doors and
windows, unlocking every chest and cupboard in the house. The
only thing that can be said for those old women was the vast
amount of experience they had had. If it was the midwife's opinion
that this child would be the death of its mother, she would not
hesitate to say so. The morale of the patient was not much considered and it was thought important that the seriously sick person
be given as long as possible to 'make their peace' and prepare for
'the King of Terrors.'

Sara lived through the spring. Isanna was doubtless one of
those weakly babies, frail and complaining from birth, born without the wish to live. Sara would not need to wait long underground
before this baby would join her. It would be hard to leave the
other children motherless. Deborah, the oldest, was only fifteen.
Nor would the thought necessarily comfort her that Paul might
(like your average widower) quickly find another younger, less
worn woman to carry on the burdens she now was to relinquish.
Her place at table, her pew in church, her half of the broad bed
would be quickly filled. Another would care for the children she
had brought forth in sorrow and travail — even as the Bible said.
Sara Orne died on the third of May, 1773.

She is buried in the Old Granary at the feet of Paul Revere's
father, and surrounded by Hitchbourns. Seven of them lie about
her in marked graves. The slate stones stand shoulder to shoulder.
Here lies Paul's grandmother, Frances Pattishall Hitchbourn, who
used to sell ale from the Anne Street house after her husband died.
And poor young Philip, whose blood had been so chilled by the
cry of fire he had fallen down dead. But the unmarked graves are
more numerous than the marked, for the dead lie five deep in the
Old Granary, and but a small proportion still have their gravestones.

Paul Revere selected for his wife a type of stone at the moment
in great fashion. It has the bleak skull and crossbones in high
relief. As a design it cannot compare with the beautiful garlands of
fruits or the curly-headed cherubin or the austere winged death
symbol also in use at this time.

Paul Revere is only mentioned three times in John Rowe's diary,
for the merchant was very cautious about joining political clubs and
his fortune and fashion put him in a slightly different social group.

He did order at least one piece of silver from him. But during the May that Sara died he speaks of him twice. The first time is in connection with the committee for setting up lamps to light the streets of Boston as European cities were being lighted. Three hundred and ten were thought to suffice. The glass globes were made in England, and from now on the lamplighter with his little ladder and his can of oil would intermittently take his place in the Boston street scene. Only intermittently, however. The lamps would not be lit on moonlight nights nor in summer. The poverty and disorder of war would douse their meagre flicker for some years. Merchant Rowe mentions the men who attended the committee meeting. Paul Revere and Thomas Hitchbourn were both there, seemingly to advise where in North Boston the lamps were to be placed.

Mr. Rowe would approve of this decent Paul Revere, so obviously doing his civic duty, alert and ingenious — just the sort of fellow a busy merchant would like on his committee. But he could not approve of the man's actions a couple of weeks later: 'May 27. Two of the Commissioners were very much abused yeasterday when they came out from the Publick Dinner at Concert Hall — Mr. Hulton & Mr. Hallowell. Wm. Molineaux, Wm. Dennie, Paul Revere . . . the Principal Actors.' And obviously bad actors. Mr. Rowe had confidence that if only the colonies behaved with dignity and quiet firmness, England would in time adjust all the differences.

Whatever form of abuse Messrs. Molineaux, Dennie, and Revere were guilty of, John Rowe would not like it — not the push in a dark street nor the undignified quarrel, neither name-calling nor cat-calls nor threats.

So, even if widowed but a few weeks, Paul Revere was behaving perfectly naturally. Lamps must be devised and set up. Customs officials must be bedeviled. Life must go on. Courtship must go on — even if one's wife is barely cold in the grave.

Isanna lived through the summer. It was an accepted fact that some babies were not intended to grow up in this naughty world. It would be Paul's mother's responsibility to find a wet-nurse, to care for the ailing little thing through the often fatal summer months. To make things harder for everyone, Isanna lived long enough to give hope she might pull through and to develop a certain amount of personality.

The family tradition is that one evening that summer Paul Revere was hurrying home from his shop and met Rachel Walker. Her father was one of the several Richard Walkers in Boston at the time. Her mother was Rachel Carlile. In her girlhood two of her great-aunts lived in her great-grandfather's house (which was later called the Foster house) close to the one the Reveres rented from Doctor Clark. Probably Paul had known the old ladies and young Rachel for years. Little is known of her birth and upbringing except the fact (recorded by Paul Revere in the family Bible) that she was born in Boston. Her father was not a large property-owner (such are more easily traced by their lawsuits and their wills). We do know they gave their daughter a fairly good education for a girl of the period. All her personality suggests that she came from a good home.

Rachel was twenty-seven at the time, a smart-looking girl with dark hair, in the miniature painted of her ten years later.[22] She had the sloping Marie Antoinette forehead and oval facial contours so much admired. If it were not for the fact that Rachel looks so much like certain other women of the time who were famed for their beauty, one would be inclined to consider her a plain piece, with her long nose and the slight double chin under the soft, real chin. Clever, capable, kindly — but no beauty. However, so fashions change — she may have been considered extremely handsome. At least, she had not given a tooth apiece for eight children.

So this was the young woman Paul met that summer evening. There was a moment's pause in the Square outside the house, but in spite of Rachel's charms the man was anxious to be off, for, he said, he always tried to get home before his children were asleep — but wouldn't she go to his house with him?

Probably it was the attraction of Paul himself that made Rachel go with him, but the story is that it was pity for poor Isanna that made her stay the evening, and soon return to stay for good. She was a kind and much-loved woman. The marriage of these two seems to have been one of those perfect adjustments between two personalities. They were destined to years of mutual confidence, respect, and love. One has the feeling that Paul was too much for Sara Orne, but that Rachel could stand up to him. If she did not want the whole second floor of her house cluttered up

with a great display of ghosts of murdered children and other
innocent victims of tyranny, even America sitting on a stump, she
had her say and Paul politely (and admiringly) listened to her.
Rachel also had eight children and she did lose all her teeth, but
she did not die with her last baby and leave their upbringing to
another woman. One feels that nothing could quite defeat or
break the spirit of Rachel Walker. She was as good a stepmother
as she was a wife, but no one rode over her roughshod.

There was a certain amount of humor in their relationship —
even in their courtship, judging by a rhymed riddle Paul wrote on
the back of a bill. Much of the poetry he has been credited with
may have been 'cooked up.' This is doubtless his own. The
answers are printed in parentheses.

> Take three fourths of a Paine that makes Traitors confess
> (Rac)
> With three parts of a place which the Wicked don't Bless
> (Hell)
> Joyne four sevenths of an Exercise which shop-keepers use
> (Walk)
> And what Bad men do, when they good actions refuse
> (Er)
> These four added together with great care and Art
> Will point out the Fair One nearest my Heart.

The baby Isanna died in the middle of September. On the
tenth day of October, Rachel Walker and Paul Revere were married by the Reverend Samuel Mather. It was not their own
clergyman who read them the lines. 'Puffing Pem' was too much
under Mr. Hutchinson's influence. They preferred his brother-in-
law and Miss Hannah's father.

# VII

BY '73 any 'union between the colonies,' as Governor Hutchinson pointed out, 'is pretty well broke. I hope never to see it renewed.'

The attempted coercion of England by a non-importation agreement had been worse than a failure. It had fanned the jealousy between the colonies. Now New York was calling Boston 'the Common Sewer of America.' The *Boston Gazette* referred to 'the filthy, nasty, dirty colony of Rhode Island.'

The Whig Party was also 'pretty well broke.' The conservative wing had abandoned Sam Adams and his radical principles. They were tired of the mob rule which attempted to enforce non-importation. Prominent Sons of Liberty among the merchants were accused of secretly selling imported goods. Samuel Salisbury, a Boston merchant, wrote his brother in Worcester he had just bought English writing paper from John Hancock, that 'Son of Liberty, Son of Hell.' The whole attempt at a boycott collapsed and the radical Whig Party seemingly collapsed with it.

John Adams, with a 'farewell politics,' had withdrawn to Braintree. His irritation with those who had taken upon themselves the fine title 'patriots' is indicated by the following 'Receipt to make a Patriot' copied off in his diary and probably concocted by him: 'Take of the several species of malevolence, as revenge, malice, envy, equal quantities; of servility, fear, fury, vanity, profaneness, and ingratitude equal quantities, and infuse this composition with the brains of an ugly, surly, brutal mortal, and you have the desideratum.'

The 'Brace of Adamses' were not pulling well together.

John Hancock had almost slipped off the hook. For a few months it had looked as though he had definitely gone over to Governor Hutchinson and the Tories. He veered back and forth and finally turned up once more in Sam Adams' camp. To commemorate this reconciliation he engaged Copley to paint his and Adams' portraits and hung them together in his parlor. He was still a bachelor, but as early as 1771 Sam Salisbury had written his brother: "'Tis said Mr. Hancock courts Dolly Quincy. This is certain he visits her and has her company in private most every evening.' This was to prove a very long courtship. John Hancock had personal as well as political worries when the year 1773 began.

Governor Hutchinson, watching the dissension among his enemies, could relax a little and put a few pounds on his spare, handsome figure. 'Tommy Skin-and-Bones' wrote to his London tailor that the next suit of clothes must be a little larger around the armholes.

This lethargy in the Whig Party was true also in England, for Burke is wondering why, 'after the violent ferment in the nation, a deadness and vapidity have succeeded.'

Never had Boston Whigs known darker days. If there was any way to unite the party — so strangely made up of conservative gentlemen who only wanted England to stop her innovations, and the underprivileged who were out for a social revolution — it seemed beyond even Sam Adams' ingenuity and genius. He grasped at every straw that could be construed as tyranny. The Massachusetts judges and governors had always received their scanty salaries from the General Court. Now the King decided to pay them himself. Thus they could act independently of the wishes of local politicians. This was a serious blow to the free rights of the colonies. Sam Adams did well with this grievance, but not well enough to get the Whig Party really up on its legs once more. He was more successful in his handling of the private letters which Thomas Hutchinson had written some years before to an English friend and which were collected and sent secretly to Boston by Benjamin Franklin, who was acting as agent for the colony in London. In spite of Franklin's request that these letters be kept private, they were printed and publicized as much as possible. Hutchinson was amazed at the hatred that 'a dozen harmless letters' stirred up against him (although he had defiantly said, in one of them, 'there must be an abridgment of what is called English Liberty' over here). Sam Adams had waited year after year to ruin the Governor's reputation and at last he had succeeded, but he had not even yet united his party. Then England stepped in and helped him out.

All that was left of British tyranny was a small tax on tea, a

mere symbol that Parliament had not given up her right to tax the
colonies as she pleased. But tea was cheaper over here than in
London. Merchants were importing it and people were drinking
it. Even John Adams could sit down to tea at the Hancock house
and only hope that it was smuggled. He hardly cared any more.

People were tired of Sam Adams' dire prophecies — and his
liberty boys. They were even getting used to that small tax on
tea.

The British Government ('a nation of shopkeepers' before
Napoleon told them so) was, in '73, more disturbed over the
impending collapse of the great East India Company than over
its colonies. This company had forty million weight of tea stored
in its warehouses along the Thames, a seven years' supply, yet
was on the verge of bankruptcy. It was decided to save the company by giving it the monopoly on the American market. It would
be sold more cheaply than the smuggled-in Dutch teas and that
tax (which the finicky provincials disliked) would be paid in
London and never show.

The idea of such a monopoly terrified the merchants. If England
gave a tea monopoly, why not on Madeira, cloth, shoes? They saw
ruin ahead. The retail shopkeepers were also cut out, for the
Government had appointed 'consignees' for the tea. These men
only would sell it to the people. The consignees would make all
the profits.

The Tea Act of 1773 immediately accomplished what the Whig
leaders could not. Once more, radical and conservative elements
were united in an unholy, unnatural alliance. The thirteen colonies were ready to forget and forgive old quarrels among themselves. In Boston the situation was further aggravated by the
hoggishness of the Hutchinson clique in getting themselves appointed consignees of the expected tea. Young Thomas and Elisha,
the Governor's sons, were among them. Of course this drove other
merchants like John Hancock, William Molineaux, and John Rowe
into a frenzy. The choice of Boston consignees was one of the
Tories' crassest blunders.

By November, when the tea ships were hourly expected, the
town was in a ferment. The Sons of Liberty were back in full
stride, and once again 'Joyce Jr.' raised his threatening voice, for
although Castle Island was full of redcoats under Colonel Leslie,

and the harbor was full of Admiral Montague's ships-of-war, there was no power in Boston to check them.

Mass meetings were proclaimed by poster. The consignees were bidden to the Liberty Tree to resign their appointments. In the southern colonies they did, but not in Boston. The insolent courage of the young Hutchinsons and the fortitude of all the others won out. Not even the threats of the mob and fear of Joyce could budge them. They were forced, however, discreetly to move out to the Castle and the protection of British guns. There Miss Hulton is amazed that the Governor's sons 'sho'd be treated as fugitives & outlaws in their own country.'

The first of the tea ships to arrive was the *Dartmouth*, and next morning Boston was posted with the historic:

> Friends! Brethren! Countrymen! That worst of Plagues, the detested tea shipped for this port by the East India Company, is now arrived in the Harbour; the hour of destruction, or manly opposition to the machanitions of Tyranny, stares you in the Face; every Friend to his country, to Himself, and to Posterity, is now called upon to meet at Faneuil Hall, at nine o'clock this day, at which time the bells will ring to make united and successful resistance to this last, worst and most destructive measure of Administration. Boston. Nov. 29, 1773

This meeting (in no way a legal town meeting) ordered the *Dartmouth* to tie up at Griffin's Wharf. Mr. Rotch, the owner, was warned not to unload her 'on his peril.' Twenty-five men, hardy and discreet, were to watch that night to see she obeyed their orders. Among them (armed with musket and bayonet) was Paul Revere. So there was little sleep for Revere that night.

Next morning 'the Body' (as these mass meetings were somewhat sinisterly called) met again. It was decided that neighboring seaports should be warned that the tea ships might try to unload at their wharves. Paul Revere and five other men were chosen to ride express. So on the last day of November, 1773, we have the first record of Revere, 'booted and spurred and ready to ride.' The revolutionary Committees of Safety or of Correspondence had long before this day been keeping close contact with each other and the only quick, safe transportation of letters and news was by the mounted man on a fast horse. Revere may have 'ridden express' for them before this.

Paul Revere owned a mare at this time.  He had already 'bult'
a barn on Manasseh Marston's 'a state.'

It was late afternoon when 'the Body' broke up.  Probably
Revere went immediately to his house in North Square.  His bride
of two months (a lady of determination and the words to express
her ideas) might well have complained that it was too much for
him to go sleepless one night, guarding a tea ship, and the very
next to ride express.  Young Paul was big enough to be down at
the barn, saddling the mare, as his father and stepmother argued,
and Paul got into his surtout, boots, and buckled on his spurs.

Slowly over the cobbles, but faster once the town gates were
passed, Paul Revere started out.  But which towns he warned, and
which the other five riders, has not come to light.

# VIII

AND now that at last Paul Revere
assumes his legendary attitude and mounts a horse, it might be interesting to 'figure' (as he would have said) what sort of an animal
we find him on.  Sculptors have shown a preference for rampant
chargers, thick-bodied, arch-necked.  Such horses were not uncommonly used for noblemen's coaches in England at that time.  'The
Black horse of England' was powerful, handsome, and of ancient
lineage.  It had carried knights to battle and kings to coronations.
Peter Faneuil imported his coach horses directly from England.  He
may have owned such horses, as might the Hancocks or Olivers or
Hutchinsons.  As far as we know, the breed was not established in
New England.  Neither was any good draught-horse stock imported.
The ox was used for heavy work.  English visitors were impressed
with the lack of good, heavy horses, and delighted with the quality
of the local saddle horse.  For the horse was bred principally to

carry a rider or a light chaise rapidly over bad roads. It was for
this purpose the early New England horse was developed.

Painters are apt to give Revere a white horse for night scenes
and a black horse for daytime. But the Yankee horse tended to
sorrel and bay. Running through the newspapers of the period,
where lost horses, stolen horses, horses for sale, and the service of
stallions are advertised, one is struck by the preponderance of
sorrel, red, bay, dun, nearly all of whom have considerable white
on them, stars and blazes on their faces, white fetlocks, white
stockings on their legs, even spots. Black, mouse, and blue are not
lacking, but white and grey less common than today.

The original stock, brought over, may have been the 'Suffolk
Punch,' a long-backed, short-legged, sluggish, yellow horse commonly used in the Fen country, from which such a large proportion
of the early Puritans came. If the New England horse was descended from the old Punch, everything except the color was
quickly discarded. There is the usual story of 'an Andalusian
stallion' found swimming off the coast of Spain and brought to
Rhode Island by a shipmaster. And another progenitor of early
days called 'Old Snip' from Tripoli. These stallions, it was claimed,
gave the Narragansett pacers their fine quality. In the seventeenth
and early eighteenth centuries Narragansett led America in horse-
breeding, but there were other famous strains like 'the Clark horse'
of Plymouth, which breed was established by the first of the many
Doctor John Clarks, direct ancestors of Paul Revere's landlord.
The Narragansett pacer was as famous in its day as the Vermont
Morgan was a hundred years later.

The pure-bred horse paced naturally with none of the sidewise
swinging of the man-taught pacer. The rector of the Narragansett
church from 1721 to 1759 says these horses 'are remarkable for
fleetness and swift pacing and I have seen some of them pace a
mile in a little more than two minutes and a good deal less than
three.' The rector himself often rode as much as fifty or sixty
miles in a day over bad roads, and claimed as high as a hundred
miles a day for the best of these horses without fatigue to horse or
rider.

Rip Van Dam, of New York, in the seventeenth century bought
himself one of these pacers. The first time the horse was put on a
sloop to be freighted down to New York he jumped overboard

and swam home. When Van Dam finally got him, he writes in a letter that he was 'no beauty, although so high priced, save in his legs. He always plays and acts and never will stand still. He will take a glass of wine, beer or cyder.'

These lively saddle horses were one of New England's leading exports until after the Revolution. The West Indies was the principal market and agents came to Rhode Island with instructions to buy full-blooded mares at any price. Virginia (which turned to careful horse-breeding many years later than New England) paid high prices for the genuine Narragansett breed. There was also a demand for them in England. What Oriental blood these horses may have had, from the semi-mythical Andalusian and Old Snip, came out in courage, nimbleness, high spirits, and endurance — not in beauty. For it is praised for every virtue a horse may have except that. A few years later, when a farmer is selling Revere a horse, he describes him in a letter as a 'large, homely horse, six years old this spring and perfectly broke to any kind of harness and very very sound. I believe you will find him as good as he is homely.' It is probable that the farmer used 'homely' in the oldest sense of that word, and meant that his horse was a gentle, friendly beast.

The usual horse, up to the Revolution, was a little fellow by modern standards. The newspapers hardly mention any horse higher than fourteen hands. 'The Yankee Hero,' a famous sire, was only thirteen. Today these would be classed as ponies. During the Revolution an English colonel's horse was captured by the Americans and offered for sale. He was a gigantic creature of sixteen hands. So when Revere buckled on his spurs and mounted his horse, he was probably riding a plain, lively, surefooted little creature, who paced naturally, was as enduring as the Arab, sorrel in color, and would get him to wherever he was going as efficiently as any means of transportation then evolved, and he was a cheerful and gay companion, capable of swimming rivers or taking his glass of cider.

In 1773, Revere owned a horse of his own, a mare, for he makes a note that he has sent her to Groton, perhaps for her lying-in, for it was common for a man of moderate means to keep a mare so her increase would somewhat pay for her upkeep.

Paul Revere did not need a horse for his business. No town-dwelling silversmith did. So it would seem he was keeping one merely for pleasure and because he liked horses. He did not even have the excuse for this extravagance that his family must be carried to meeting. The Cockerel was in his own back yard.

He may have acquired his first horse in one of those New England dickers — so many teaspoons and hollow ware against the horse, and one side throwing in fire tongs and the other a broken saddle. But a love of horses must have gone back to childhood: perhaps as he hung about the Hutchinson stable and coach house, and earned a penny leading a horse up and down on a cold morning before the mounting block waiting for the master to finish breakfast, or helping the groom with his currying.

On Clark's Wharf he had seen country horses being loaded on board the ships which would take them to the West Indies. These rambunctious, small beasts would need skilful handling to get them up any gangplank and a boy who was clever at managing them could both earn money and enjoy himself. Horse-races were fairly common. Pieces of silver were often given as prizes and, oddly enough, the beach now known as Revere was a favorite course to run over at low tide. Paul Revere could have spent many a happy afternoon watching better horses than he probably owned himself racing for silver he had made, over the dark, wet, half-moon of sand that would be named for him. Anyway, by the time he was in his thirties he was ready to make some pecuniary sacrifices to own an utterly unnecessary horse. It is the only extravagance we can accuse him of except lending friends money 'on the street.'

On fine days he could drive with Rachel out to the Blue Hills of Milton, over to Cambridge, to Roxbury, to Watertown. Or he could ride out with the other men to some country tavern where the food and drink tasted so much better than in Boston. There was always fishing and duck-shooting. Paul Revere enjoyed gunning so much in his declining years, he doubtless always had a taste for it. But best of all was the country food, the air, and the conversation. The talk would swing from duck-shooting to politics; from the Reverend Samuel Cooper's inflammatory sermon to politics. These country jaunts sometimes included women, but mostly only men, and were one of the social habits of the day. William Molineaux — a somewhat sporting character, would have

a good horse, as would of course the three doctors, for a lively
horse was the most dignified way a doctor could advertise the
successful urgency of his career. John Adams was devoted to
'his little mare,' but wonders, as he writes of her in his diary, who
in future time will be interested in her or himself. Sam Adams, at
this time, could 'never be persuaded to mount a horse.'

The Reverend Mr. Cooper's diary during his travels shows more
interest in his horse than in his wife. He is always noting down
where his horse slept. Rarely his wife. Among all these Whig
leaders, it was probably well known that Revere was a good horseman, with the easy seat, the light hands, the subtle coordination
of his muscles and will with the horse's muscles and will, until the
two almost literally become one and both are happy and confident
in the relationship. Paul Revere rode thousands of miles as 'express'
for the Boston Whigs. There were plenty of men to choose from.
It would not be too hard to get both a discreet man and a good
rider, but he was their first choice for their hardest work.

## IX

TWO more ships, the *Beaver* and
the *Eleanor*, joined the *Dartmouth* at Griffin's Wharf. On board they
had three hundred and forty-two chests of tea, valued at eighteen
thousand pounds. 'The Body' meetings continued at Old South,
for Faneuil Hall was too small. They were attended by thousands,
many of whom were not legal voters. Manhood suffrage was
undreamed of. To vote, one must own property. But now the
underprivileged were saying that even if they had no property
themselves, God willing, their children should have, and in the
meantime they intended to vote. Sam Adams' henchmen from
neighboring towns crowded in. They too voted. Women went.

Patriotic schoolmasters dismissed school and took their boys over
*en masse.* Voting was by ayes and nays and anyone's shout was as
good as the next man's. Many of the law-abiding citizens, Whig
and Tory alike, stayed home. John Rowe was shocked by these
'Body — as 'tis call'd' meetings which were taking over the authority of the town meetings. But Sam Adams did not dare trust
the authorized town voters for his schemes and had set up 'the
Body' instead. It was this wild mob that decided the tea ships
must return to England.

But by Massachusetts law they could not be cleared until they
had unloaded. And they must unload within twenty days or be
liable to seizure. The *Dartmouth* had already been in for eighteen.
Time was short. Governor Hutchinson discreetly stayed out in
Milton. He had given Colonel Leslie, on Castle Island with some
British troops, orders to fire on these ships unless they could present
a passport signed by himself. The harbor was under the guns of
the British fleet. The Governor had stubbornly refused to permit
the peaceful (but illegal) return of the tea ships to England with
the cargoes.

On the sixteenth of December, a dull and rainy day, seven
thousand people were gathered in Old South, or were crowded in
the streets outside. They were waiting for Mr. Rotch, the owner of
the *Dartmouth,* to return from Milton. He had been sent to beg
permission for his ship to leave. It is fourteen miles to Milton and
back. As they waited the people were regaled by their favorite
entertainment — speeches. Wild, inflammatory, big-mouthed,
eloquent speeches. The leaders took turns addressing them.
Young Josiah Quincy stood up in the east gallery. Earlier in the
year he had gone to South Carolina in one of Mr. Rowe's ships,
hoping the milder climate might stop his coughing, his fevers, pain
and lassitude. In the South he found 'such a multitude of shadows
and ghosts here, that I make not so bad a figure in comparison.'
But he had spent his days with southern patriots instead of the
consumptives. Now he was back in Boston, his disease and his
patriotism both burning higher than ever. But his impassioned
words were interrupted by Harrison Gray, who warned him against
such intemperate language. 'If the old gentleman on the floor
intends by his warning to the "young gentleman in the gallery"
to utter only a friendly voice in the spirit of paternal advice,'

young Quincy burst out, 'I thank him. If his object is to terrify
and intimidate, I dispise him. Personally perhaps I have less
concern than anyone present in the crisis approaching. The seeds
of dissolution are thickly planted in my constitution. . . . I feel how
short is the day alloted to me'; and then, 'I see the clouds which
now rise thick and fast upon our horizon, the thunder roll, and
the lightning play, and to that God who rides the whirlwind and
directs the storm I commit my country.'

The people were kept well amused while waiting. The December
sun set early and the patter of rain on the roof stopped. A few
candles were lighted, and then Rotch came back. It was quarter
of six. The Governor had still refused. Sam Adams was on his
feet seemingly accepting defeat. 'This meeting can do nothing
more to save the country.'

Evidently this was a prearranged signal, for there were war-
whoops from the dark galleries, yells:

'To Griffin Wharf!' and

'Boston harbour a tea-pot tonight!'

Shouts and running feet below. One of the last things George
Robert Twelves Hewes remembered, as he tore out of the building, was John Hancock's voice crying above the hubbub:

'Let every man do what is right in his own eyes!'

Hewes scurried about hunting for a blanket, blackened his face,
and joined in. A great many other boys and men who had not
been invited to this most celebrated of Boston parties went anyway
and seem to have behaved as well as the original guests. The leadership was complete and accepted. It had been well organized before
Sam Adams gave the signal from the pulpit of Old South.

Two of Paul Revere's clubs, the North Caucus and Saint
Andrew's Lodge, are known to have had a hand in it. The Masons
had met the night the ships arrived, but their records read, 'Lodge
adjourned on account of few Brothers present. N.B. Consignees of
Tea took the Brethern's time.' This night the record is even briefer:
'Lodge closed on account of few members present.' Saint Andrew's
had by this time bought the old 'Green Dragon.' This was a large,
brick tavern standing on Union Street. Before it, on an iron
branch, hung a dragon hammered out of copper. It was already
green with verdigris and time. More Revolutionary eggs were
hatched in this dragon's nest than in any other spot in Boston.

Other lodges and radical clubs were beginning to meet there, sheltered by the inviolable secrecy of the Masons. It was at the Green Dragon the plan to destroy the tea was perfected and either there or at Benjamin Edes' house Paul Revere and others put on their disguises.[23]

It was decided that the work was to be done 'by young men, not much known in town and not liable to be easily recognized.' Yet so anxious were the powers to keep the party from running off into looting, a certain number of the boldest and most discreet went along as lieutenants. They ran considerable risk, for if their names were known they might have to stand trial for destruction of the East India Company's property. We may be sure they blackened and painted their faces well and uttered as few grunts as possible.

Young Lendall Pitts (son of a wealthy merchant) was the commander-in-chief. He recklessly made no effort to conceal his identity. William Molineaux and Doctor Young were both there that night. Paul Revere's dark face would be well known in Boston. He went, although by doing so he risked his little house in North Square, his horse, his liberty. Certain delicate ruffles were noted that night peeking out from under the disguise. Were they attached to Hancock? Probably not. But Hewes says he recognized him, not only by ruffles, but by his figure and gait. Also his voice, 'for he exchanged with him an Indian grunt and the expression "*me know you*," which was used a good deal... for a countersign.' He also believed Sam Adams was present. Thomas Melville, with his Roman nose and cheek 'like the rose,' was in the thick of it.

Under these men were journeymen, apprentices, and strangers who had been let in on the secret and were ready to join in. They were to wear 'ragged clothes and disfigure ourselves... smeared our faces with grease and soot or lampblack... and we surely resembled devils from the bottomless pit rather than men.' The majority seem to have simply gone along, on their own initiative.

No one invited George Robert Twelves Hewes, but no one could have kept him home. On the other hand, Peter Slater, although only thirteen, knew what was up. So did his master, the Tory ropemaker, William Gray. He locked the boy in his chamber, but Peter slid to freedom and brief fame by knotting his bedding together, and joined in.

Amos Lincoln's master was Thomas Crafts, whose son, Thomas Crafts, Jr., was an intimate of Paul Revere's. The Whig master sat up praying that night 'for the young men out on a perilous errand,' as his son and apprentice hurried to Griffin's Wharf. Amos was to be Paul Revere's son-in-law twice over, for he married first the oldest girl, Debby. When she died, he married Elizabeth. These two children were but fifteen and three at this time, and Amos was still serving his apprenticeship. Joseph Eayres (the carpenter who specialized in rigging up 'liberty poles'), whose most unfortunate son, Thomas, later married Paul Revere's almost equally unfortunate Frances, was another of the Indians.

Hewes says there were one hundred to a hundred and fifty 'indians' (and very little attempt at any Indian disguise). At the wharf these men and boys were silently divided into three groups. Hewes' group (commanded by Lendall Pitts) went aboard one of the brigs. Pitts sent to the mate demanding lights and keys. The mate said nothing to them, only gave over the keys and sent the cabin boy for lights. The chests were hoisted on deck, broken open, and the tea thrown into the harbor. The tide was low. When it rose there was a windrow of tea from Boston all the way to Dorchester. Sometimes a man would be suspected of saving a bit for himself. He was quickly and silently dealt with. And so on all three ships.

Thousands watched from the dock, in absolute but approving silence. Joshua Wyeth, fifteen at the time, remembered that he 'never worked harder in my life. Although it was late in the evening when we began we had discharged the whole three cargoes before the dawn of day.'

When done, the 'mohawks' shouldered their 'tommyhawks,' fell into marching order, and proceeded, to the music of a fife, to march back to the State House. They were amazed that they had met no opposition. The British squadron rode at anchor less than a quarter-mile away. They did not know that Admiral Montague himself happened to be spending the night with a Tory friend at the head of Griffin's Wharf, watching the whole thing. The Admiral kept a discreet silence until the marchers were under his window. Then a window flew up and out popped the Admiral's head.

'Well, boys,' he said, 'you have had a fine, pleasant evening for your Indian caper — haven't you? But mind, you have got to pay the fiddler yet.'

'Oh, never mind!' shouted Lendall Pitts, 'never mind, Squire, just come out here, if you please, and we'll settle the bill in two minutes.'

The Admiral snapped down the window.

Children were frightened that night — or early morning — when fathers, whose faces still showed red paint and black soot, returned tired to their houses. Or did not recognize them and cried with fear, but lived to tell their grandchildren how well they remembered that night and great-grandpa said 'ugh-ugh' at them, and they did not know him.

Betsy Hunt Palmer, at whose wedding celebration Paul Revere had been dancing hornpipes only a year before, was 'sitting rocking the baby when I heard the gate and door open. I supposed my husband was just returning from his club and so I opened the parlor door and there stood three stout indians. I screamed out and would have fainted out of very fright, had I not recognized my husband's voice. "Don't be frightened, Betsy, it is I. We have only been making a little salt water tea."' Foster Candy and Stephen Bruce were the other Indians.

Hewes may have been provoked with his wife, Sally, for when he told her what he had been doing she said, 'Well, George, did you bring me home a lot of it?' She was 'more of a tea-drinker than a Whig.'

When Thomas Melville took off his shoes, he found they were full of tea. He put it in a glass bottle, with a label. It is still in existence.

Paul Revere was probably as well disguised and as tired and as pleased with himself as were all the others. But he did not get much sleep.

That same day (for it was dawn when the men got home) an account of what had been done in Boston was drawn up by the Committee of Correspondence. It must go immediately to Philadelphia and New York. A number of men volunteered to do the riding, but Paul Revere was chosen. He started instantly. Sleep was always a thing he could do without.

Now there appeared in the taverns and about the wharves

and shops a new song honoring Joseph Warren, Paul Revere, and the Green Dragon:

> Rally Mohawks! bring out your axes,
> And tell King George we'll pay no taxes
>     On his foreign tea;
> His threats are vain, and vain to think
> To force our girls and wives to drink
>     His vile Bohea!
> Then rally boys, and hasten on
> To meet our chiefs at the Green Dragon.
>
> Our Warren's there and bold Revere
> With hands to do, and words to cheer
>     For Liberty and laws;
> Our Country's 'braves' and firm defenders
> Shall ne'er be left by true North-Enders
>     Fighting Freedom's call!
> Then rally boys, and hasten on
> To meet our chiefs at the Green Dragon.

What the tune may have been for this 'Rallying Song of the Tea Party' we do not know, nor who this anonymous poet who first realized that Revere is as easy a name to rhyme as any you could find in all Boston.

# VI

## 1773 – 1775

BACK from PHILADELPHIA, PAUL REVERE finds BOSTON in confusion. HE makes silver and engravings, but is always ready to ride. GOVERNOR HUTCHINSON turns BOSTON over to GENERAL GAGE, and leaves for LONDON. BRITISH soldiers once more possess the town, but PAUL REVERE carries word of their plans. HE spends SABBATH on CASTLE ISLAND as COLONEL LESLIE retreats. A MASSACRE oration. BRITISH and REBEL spies infest each other's camps. The time has come.

Device used by *Boston Post Boy* during middle of eighteenth century. American Antiquarian Society.

**I**

IF PAUL REVERE read the letters sent by him to the Sons of Liberty in New York and Philadelphia, he would only follow the precedent set by the post-riders. For the post-riders not only perused the letters, but gossiped from village to village about the contents. Politicians often used code.

'We are in a perfect jubillee,' the letter to New York ran in part. 'Not a Tory in the whole comunity can find the least fault with our proceedings. . . . The spirit of the people throughout the country is to be described by no terms in my power. Their conduct last night supprised the admiral and English gentlemen, who observed that these were not a mob of disorderly rabble (as they have been reported) but men of sense, coolness and intrepity.'

It is likely a man riding express would follow the post-riders' route, going from Boston to Cambridge, Watertown, Marlborough, to Worcester, then on through Brookfield to Springfield. At Springfield they turned south along the Connecticut to Hartford, southwest to Meriden, Wallingford, New Haven, and so into New York by King's Bridge.

For a hundred years there had been a postal service in America, and since Queen Anne's day it had been under the Crown. Benjamin Franklin had been postmaster general until very recently and had done an excellent job. When Sam Adams publicized the Hutchinson letters Franklin had sent him secretly, he had lost this appointment.

It took six to nine days for a letter to get from Boston to New York, which was an easy enough schedule to permit at least one of the post-riders to knit as he rode. They also did errands. Mr.

Hurd of Connecticut undertook to deliver a yoke of oxen along with the mail. During the next year Paul Revere rode to Philadelphia and back four times. On this, his first trip, he was gone but eleven days in all. If one estimates the mileage from Boston to Philadelphia as three hundred and fifty at that time, his rate was about sixty-three miles a day, which was a good deal to ask, even of a tough little Narragansett. Probably he changed horses often, but it was a fair test of his own physical endurance.[24]

A little over a year later, John and Sam Adams took the same trip, part of the way by coach and only partly on horseback. John decided that as a statesman it behooved Sam (in spite of protests) to learn to ride. It was all right for John, who was a country boy and, as a lawyer, used to following the judge's circuit, but Sam suffered, although he did have a 'very genteel, easy little creature' to ride. John finally bought some linen and that night got the innkeeper's wife to make a 'pair of Drawers.' This padding healed up 'the little Breeches which had begun' in Sam. Paul Revere would not need to stop for 'little Breeches' nor wait for a kind woman to make him any drawers. He was obviously already hardened to the saddle.

But how good the inns must have looked to him at nightfall. Bowls of hot punch, tankards of flip. Legs of lamb and country bread and butter, roasted apples, and a great fire blazing on the hearth. And a warming pan in the broad bed waiting for him. But he must be called before sunrise.

So at dawn, on through the short December days which give an austere and lonely beauty to the New England landscape. Bare elms etched against a pale sky. Slender white birches huddling close to the fir trees as though for warmth. And a white spire, first seen from a far hill, with its brass cock all a-glitter in the sparse sunlight, indicates the next village. And here it is. Meetinghouse and common, smithy, gristmill by the stream, a huddle of houses, and the sweet smell of wood smoke. The tavern sign rocking on its iron branch — a red, white, or black horse; lions or lambs; General Wolfe or King George himself. Here for a moment a man might stop, have his horse rubbed down and watered or a fresh horse saddled, himself sit by the fire. Then on again.

It was seventeen years ago Revere had last made so long a journey. Then, with the artillery train, when he reached Spring-

field he had kept west to Albany. And he had seen Lake George
and the wilderness. Now he was to see those two great seaports
which within his lifetime had surpassed Boston in size. Judging
by comments of other provincial Bostonians, neither city probably made a very favorable impression. From John Adams to
George Apley, Bostonians are smugly apt to like their own town
best. For instance, John Adams (but it might almost as well be
George Apley), when he first got to New York, thought they all
talked 'very loud, very fast, and all together.' He confides to his
diary that he had 'not seen one real gentleman in that town.'
But he had to admit that Boston, in comparison to Philadelphia,
seemed but a village. 'Still,' he bolsters up his sinking morale,
'Philadelphia with all its trade and wealth and regularity is not
Boston,' for 'our own language is better, our taste is better, our
persons are handsomer' (he must have been thinking of his charming Abigail — not of himself), 'our laws wiser...' and so on. It
certainly was bad taste of the Philadelphians, after a hundred
years, to throw up against John Adams 'our hanging of the
Quakers.'

Paul Revere was less sensitive and critical by nature. For John
Lamb, with whom he put up when in New York, he developed a
great liking. The number of things mentioned in subsequent
letters suggest that the men must have sat up all night. They discussed starting a new postal system in rivalry to the Crown's.
Revere gave Lamb such a dramatic account of the Tea Party,
John Lamb (who was an engraver as well as a wine merchant)
immediately set to work to commemorate the event with a copper
plate.

By dawn Revere was in the saddle once more. The ferry carried
him to New Jersey and so on into Trenton, once more waiting for
the ferry to take him over the Delaware into the Province of Pennsylvania. At Bristol, where John Adams found 'the scenes of nature
are delightful,' was the good 'Red Lion,' and at last Frankfort,
which was only five miles out of Philadelphia.

Revere brought good news back to Boston. The Sons of Liberty
and the radical Whigs in both New York and Philadelphia would
back Boston to the hilt. She had done right in destroying the tea.
They'd see to it none of this 'worst of plagues' landed in their
ports.

On the twenty-seventh day of December, John Boyle writes
in his diary:

> Mr. Paul Revere returned from New York and Philadelphia, per-
> forming his journey in a much shorter time then could be expected
> at this Season of the year. The inhabitants of these Cities were highly
> pleased with the Conduct of the People here in destroying the Tea
> and they were determined that when the Tea Ships expected there
> arrive, they should be immediately returned to the Place from whence
> they came.

This approval was not, however, true everywhere in Whig circles.
Although John Adams called it 'the grandest Event which has
ever yet happened since the controversy with Britain opened,' he
foresaw 'the terrors' that England might devise in reprisal, but
'they had better be suffered, than the Great Principle of Parli-
mentarian Taxation given up.' Franklin, in London, was shocked.
He thought it a lawless act and Boston must pay for the tea. As it
could not be discovered who threw it over, the town itself must
raise the eighteen thousand pounds for the East India Company.

But Sam Adams said that 'Franklin may be a good philosopher,
but he is a bungling politician.' Both Adamses seemed to have
looked forward eagerly to the British Government's retaliation,
knowing that the punishment meted out to the Town of Boston
might be so severe as to unite public opinion and bring on a crisis.
And it was.

## II

ONCE more back in Boston,
boots and spurs laid aside, Paul Revere would try to catch up
with his work. But the excitements of the day impinged upon
everybody. He had not been back at his workbench for a month
before the most famous of Boston's four tar-and-featherings took

place within shouting distance of his house and shop. If he went on minding his business on the twenty-fifth of January, 1774, he was perhaps the only person in Boston who did. He may have been one of the respectable gentlemen who tried to stop it, or the very man who produced the feathers for the purpose, but it is unlikely that he cut much copper or shaped much silver that day.

Although John Rowe refers to tar-and-feathering as 'the modern tast' in punishment — a coat of tar and feathers was worn for amusement by 'the devils' imps' on Pope's Day — it was not invented by American mobsters. As far back as Richard the First's day it was an allowed (but unusual) legal punishment. In 1623 it was ordered in England for 'a party of incontinent friars and nuns.' Nor was it as common in Boston in fact as in fiction.

The first man to be tarred-and-feathered against his will in Boston seems to have been George Greyer, in October, 1769. He had been caught giving information to the customs officials. He was stripped, painted with tar, covered with feathers, carted about town for a few hours, and then let go. This happened while the Twenty-Ninth and Fourteenth Regiments were supposedly keeping the King's peace on the streets of Boston.

After the soldiers were gone, in the following May, Owen Richards, also an 'informer,' was treated the same way. Samuel Salisbury, a young merchant, had 'by the care of Providence' returned to Boston that evening:

> I perceived candles in a number of windows, what, thinks I, is there an illumination tonight? Getting home I was informed that an Informer had been carted through the streets, Tarred and feathered. After I had been to the Barber's my Curiosity led me to the point at New Boston [the section about modern North Station] where I found the Informer in a Cart before Capt Homer's door surrounded with a great number of People he had his shirt taken off & his bare skin tarred & Feathered. Sometimes they would make him say one thing sometimes another. Sometimes he must hold the Lanthorn this way, sometimes that, then he must hold up a glass Bottle & Swear he would never do so again & let the bottle fall down & break & then Huzzah — from thence they carried him into King Street Let him get out of the Cart made a lane down the street where 3 or 4 carried him off from the multitude in safety, being about nine o'clock.

Over three years passed before the next victim was treated by the Boston mobs to this particular humiliation. There had recently moved into Revere's neighborhood 'such an oddity as naturally excites the curiosity and ridicule of the lowest class of people, wherever he went.' This was John Malcolm, commonly called 'Johnny.' Miss Hulton refers to him as 'a Poor Old Man... reckond creasy.' He was fifty at the time, violently loyalist in his feelings, and undoubtedly touched.

Malcolm was known to have been one of the 'murderers' who had taken Governor Tryon's part against the 'Regulators' and that governor had recently sent him a purse. When the Carolinas became too hot for him, he had gone to Maine. There he had been tarred-and-feathered over his clothes by the inhabitants of Pownalborough. No sooner had he got the tar off than he was back in Boston, in the employ of the custom house and once more in trouble, for he chattered and grimaced constantly, 'baiting the lowest class of the people' with his impudent and provocative gibes, daring them to do their worst. On the night of January 25, 1774, they did.

It started in the morning. George Robert Twelves Hewes came to the aid of a small boy who accused Malcolm of having knocked over the sled on which he was collecting chips for kindling. Malcolm, with a big cudgel, seemed on the point of braining the child. Hewes stepped in and 'the oddity' hit the thick-skulled Hewes such a blow Doctor Warren insisted anyone else would have been killed. Warren urged Hewes to get a warrant for his arrest.

By the time the constable and Hewes got back to Malcolm's house, which was almost at North Square, they found it barricaded. Johnny was hanging out a second-story window haranguing the crowd gathered below. The constable, not liking the looks of things, immediately went home. Malcolm by now had armed himself with a 'naked sword,' loaded pistols, and a broadaxe. He was boasting that he would 'split down the Yankees by the dozen and receive twenty shillings sterling a head.' The people reminded him that he had been recently tarred-and-feathered. 'You say I was tarred and feathered,' he chattered on, 'and that it was not done in a proper manner, damn you, let me see the man that dares do it better.'

Finally they took him up on this. Ladders were put up. He was disarmed and passed down to a cart waiting below. He was taken to a wharf, stripped to the waist, and painted with tar. The contents of two feather pillows were stuck to the tar. By now over a thousand people had gathered. For four hours the poor creature was carted all over Boston. To King Street, the Liberty Tree, out to the gallows on the Neck (where he was forced to drink the health of all eleven members of the royal family in tea, and nearly burst). Back to the Tree and King Street again, then to Copp's Hill. At every stopping place he was flogged. After four hours of this torture, half frozen and seemingly half dead, he 'was rolled out of the cart like a log.' His skin came off with pieces of the tar and feathers still sticking to it. Both Whigs and Tories were indignant at this treatment of Malcolm and both sides had tried vainly at the time to stop the mob — showing more courage than the twelve constables. John Rowe writes in his diary, 'sober people thought it was an act of outrageous violence.'

Even 'Joyce Jun'r' felt this deed was beneath his dignity. On January 30 this placard was posted up on the most conspicuous buildings in Boston,

Brethern and Fellow Citizens

This is to Certify, That the modern Punishment Lately

Inflicted on the ignoble John Malcolm was not done

by our Order. We reserve that Method for Bringing Villains

Of greater Consequence to a Sense of Guilt and Infamy.

Joyce Jun'r.

*Chairman of the Committee* of Tarring *and*

Feathering.

☞ If any Person be so hardy as to tear this down, they may expect my severest Resentment

J. jun'r

This is typical 'Joyce Jun'r' literature. His character is mild, lofty, unctuous. He rarely threatens more than 'resentment,' yet there is something definitely unpleasant in his studied courtesy.

Although the Tories said Malcolm's life was despaired of and Miss Hulton writes Mrs. Lightbody 'that his flesh came off in stakes,' Johnny Malcolm, as 'creasy' as ever, is soon mincing about the streets of Boston once more. He sent a box of his tar, feathers, and hide to England which got him a two hundred pound pension from the Government. John Adams thought his tarring-and-feathering the luckiest event in his whole miserable life.

These seem to be the only tarring-and-featherings that can be thrown up against the Sons of Liberty or mobs in Boston. The brutality of such mob action is impossible to defend, but it is equally hard to understand now, living in a period of so much greater ferocity, how revolution finally broke over this country without even greater cruelty. Compared to either the Russian, the French, or the Nazi revolutions, the temperance on both sides is amazing. In no place in America was feeling higher nor the growing hatred between the two groups more bitter, yet no man lost his life or was seriously injured by Boston mobs. There were no firing squads, no concentration camps, no parodies of legal trials, no retaliation on a man's family.

The fourth of Boston's tar-and-featherings happened a year later. Then it was the British soldiers who tarred-and-feathered Thomas Ditson of Billerica. The young countryman was either trying to persuade a grenadier to desert or to sell him his musket. Colonel Nesbit ordered him stripped, coated from head to foot with tar and feathers. 'He was paraded by a regiment through the streets ... with the colonel at its head, halted before the Spy office, the music playing the Rogues March; some of the soldiers vociferating, "the printer of the Spy shall be the next to receive this punishment." '

Nor did tar-and-featherings entirely drop out of the folk-mind for years. During Shays' Rebellion two horses, who were unfortunate enough to belong to the wrong political party, were partially tarred-and-feathered. After 1790, Mr. Giles Alexander, living in Governor Shirley's magnificent 'seat' in Roxbury, was suspected of maltreating his wife. A group of young men, very well disguised, came down on him one night, broke the heads off some stone lions Alexander had in his garden, and tarred-and-feathered him.

In passing, we have noticed how young Captain Ponsonby Molesworth saw Sukey Sheaffe on her balcony as he stood with his men in Queen Street. He married her and by 1784 the two of them were living in Dublin. The erstwhile Boston girl wrote in a letter, 'Anyone who wears anything but Irish manufacture, is immediately tar'd & feathered ... this Day a pretty Milliner was strip't down to her waist, tar'd & feathered and were they not prevented in time wou'd set fire to or hung the poor creater.'

It was not until 1808 that old 'Flud Oirson, fur his horrd horrt,' was 'Tarr'd an' futherr'd and corr'd in a corrt, By the women o' Morble'ead.' The ladies, however, have indignantly denied that they did it themselves.

This humiliating punishment was not limited to one political party, one decade or one country.

# III

IN 1774, Paul Revere cut more copper plates than in any other year. These were, on the whole, less picturesque, less political, less memorable, and the most careful of any of his engravings, except the beautiful bookplates. For James Rivington of New York he copied the old illustrations in 'Captain Cook's voyage' for the new edition and engraved a map. Revere's reputation as an engraver was fairly limited. He probably picked up this commission for himself during his flying trip to New York in December.

That Isaiah Thomas should turn to him for embellishments of his *Royal American Magazine* seems inevitable. Both men were Bostonians, both Masons, both Sons of Liberty. They were lifelong friends in spite of the fact Paul Revere was fourteen years older. Isaiah Thomas was only twenty-five at this time, but he had been publishing the wildly radical *Massachusetts Spy* for three years. It was in honor of this service to the Whigs Colonel Nesbit stopped his men before his office and threatened to tar-and-feather him next. The *Spy* was as frank a bid for the patronage of the semi-literate as the tabloids are today. It was rabid, yellow, and very successful. In comparison, Edes and Gill's *Boston Gazette* was a Tory sheet. Now Isaiah Thomas, that infant prodigy of the Ameri-

can press, was ready to branch out. The *Royal American Magazine*
was to be as refined and as high-brow as the *Spy* was the opposite.
The word 'royal' in the title suggests the conservative market the
publisher hoped for it. This was not designed for 'mechanics and
other classes of people who had not much time to spare from business,' as he said of the *Spy*, but was addressed unctuously to 'the
Literatti of America.' That young Thomas would be America's
first great printer, great publisher, might easily have been guessed
even by this time. He had a sure publisher's instinct for the time
and the place and the reading matter.

Personally he does not seem to have been very attractive, with
his ugly, smart, one-sided face, eyes bright as glass buttons under
rough, black brows, and a heavy, full mouth, brought by determination into something resembling the Puritan pattern. He had endless ambition, a certain pugnacity, and a Bermudian wife who was
a scandal. Printing presses and books were his absorbing passion.
To them he gave his life.

When Paul Revere met this extraordinary young man, it may
have been the first and last time he found anyone with an energy
equal to his own. But there is a gentle, loving quality in Paul
Revere that nothing in Isaiah Thomas' triumphant business career
and unfortunate private life suggests. Sometimes one may even
feel a sneaking sympathy towards that wretched slut he married,
Mary Dill, even if she did prefer British officers to her husband.
Once she swore she would go off on a jaunt 'even if to her Eternal
Ruin' — which it was. But no personal worry or disgrace could
have stopped Isaiah from printing, for he had ink in his blood.
It was in the middle of Mary's antics that he conceived and brought
forth this ambitious magazine. He was undoubtedly worrying
about his first number more than his young wife's jaunt.

The *Royal American Magazine* was a costly venture to try out on
the troubled waters of 1774. Isaiah Thomas sold it, after six
copies, to Joseph Greenleaf. Next year armed revolution ended
its brief career forever. Paul Revere often made two engravings
for one copy. He was paid about three pounds a plate. For it he
did his third view of Boston and some unflattering likenesses of
John Hancock and Sam Adams, a portrait of a jumping mouse
common to Russia, among other things. At least two of his prints
are based on work of Benjamin West.

'Mlle Clarion,' a French actress, is obviously copied from a French print. The work in this plate, as in some of the others in this magazine, shows that by 1774 Revere was gaining a mastery over copper-plate engraving. The plates are a long way ahead of his first attempts, but the work did not interest him and he did but very little more.

One of the plates thought to be by him is a diagram showing how saltpetre is made. War clouds were looming and one thing America would quickly run short of was gunpowder and saltpetre. There are two political cartoons: 'America in Distress' and 'The Able Doctor.' In the latter a female form of unlikely anatomy representing America (for which we trust Rachel did not pose) is held hand and foot by a crowd of bullies as the doctor pours tea down her gullet. From his pocket a paper marked 'Boston Port Bill' protrudes. A soldier stands at the woman's head with a drawn sword, inscribed 'Military Law.' In the background Boston is indicated.

And what this cartoon represents had really happened. Boston was to be strangled, beaten, coerced into paying for that tea. Admiral Montague had not been so wrong when he told Lendall Pitts that the fiddler had not yet been paid.

## IV

ON THE tenth of May, His Majesty's ship *The Lively* arrived in Boston with order for her punishment. On the first day of June the port of Boston was to be completely closed to all seaborne traffic until the town agreed to pay for the tea. Governor Hutchinson was to go to England to report and during his absence General Gage was to be governor. Order was to be kept by British regiments, the first of which were momentarily expected. From henceforth Salem was to be the capital of the colony and Plymouth the seat of the customs. Boston, utterly dependent upon her shipping for her life, was to be starved into submission. As John Boyle wrote, 'thousands of our inhabitants will be involved in one undistinguishable ruin.'

Now that Parliament had taken this severe disciplinary step, there was little more talk about paying for the tea. If she could treat Boston so high-handedly, why not Philadelphia, or Charleston, or New York? The Whig Party was united, and many men who had honestly tried to keep their heads and remain neutral (seeing so much evil on both sides — and so much good) now swung towards the more violent wing. The question was how far would the other towns and colonies stand by Boston in her predicament?

By the fourteenth of May an indignation meeting was held, resolves and committees drawn up, and Paul Revere was once more in the saddle. The nearer towns would be notified by other expresses, but Revere was given the long, hard ride to New York and Philadelphia. In choosing such a messenger, it would also be important to have a man who would say the right thing when cross-questioned, as he always was. The Tories referred to him as 'an ambassador' from Massachusetts to the Continental Congress. This is as much of an overstatement as to call him only an 'express' is under. In a P.S. on one of John Adams' letters he says, 'Mr. Revere will give you all the news.' He felt he could trust his judgment and accuracy.

On this trip Revere also carried broadsides of the Boston Port Bill, grimly decorated with mourning bands, a crowned skull and cross-bones resting under the cap of Liberty. Probably this was his own work. He dealt them out as he went along. He noted the fact that he hired a horse from David Wood to take him as far as King's Bridge, and paid £4.0.3.

Another ship had brought the news to New York on the same day as the *Lively* had entered Boston. An almost equal amount of indignation had flared up there. John Ludlow was sent as an express to carry to Boston New York's sympathy and determination to stand by. In an account, hard to trace back to any contemporary source and very possibly legend, we find Ludlow on his black horse swiftly approaching a wood near Providence. There, by a cool

spring, he finds Paul Revere, 'on a large grey horse' stopping a
moment for lunch. 'The wood is just receiving its summer foliage.'
So these two couriers eat together. Revere shows him his broadsides and tells of the cries of 'Barbarous, cruel, bloody and inhuman
murder!' that greeted his news and his engraving. Then the two
men set out again in opposite directions on 'their holy missions.'

The story has a legendary flavor to it, especially the dramatic
sense that puts one courier on a black horse and one on a large
grey horse. But Paul Revere is as much a part of American legend
as history, so he may as well continue his holy mission on the large
grey horse. This horse (property of David Wood), he left at King's
Bridge, which was then considered fifteen miles out of New York.
The Uncas River ran in front of Cock's, the tavern which John
Adams admired very much.

When he reached New York, it was to find a meeting of the
'51' already in session. John Lamb hurried him over. They had
voted their 'detestation of the execrable port Bill' and Boston
could count on New York's support. Then, with a fresh horse,
he would take the ferry to New Jersey, ride on to the ferry across
the Delaware, and at last reach Philadelphia.

Here, also, mass meetings and indignation met him. The cautious Philadelphians seemed ready to cast discretion to the winds,
and stand by Boston to 'the last extremety,' although they did
recommend 'prudence and moderation' to the Bostonians, whom
they always considered a town or a state of mind quite antipathetic
to law, order, and Quakers. But it was the Philadelphians who set
in motion the machinery for a Continental Congress to discuss the
plight of the colonies in general and Massachusetts in particular.
Paul Revere was in the midst of all this excitement.

In New York he saw his friend, John Lamb, and delivered to
him Doctor Young's letter in which the doctor refers to Revere
as 'my worthy friend Revere ... no man of his rank and opportunities in life deserves better of the community, Steady, vigorous,
sensible and perserving.' A thin-skinned man might have resented
the patronizing tone of this letter. To Revere such words probably
seemed about the truth. Neither his rank nor opportunities were
dazzling. He knew himself to be steady and all the rest.

Revere was back again in Boston in twelve days. But how much
can happen in twelve days!

Seemingly the clumsy British colossus could move fast when it
had a mind to it. General Gage himself had already landed and
Thomas Hutchinson was on the point of departure. Certain men,
one hundred and twenty in all, had sent Hutchinson a farewell
letter thanking him for his care. Among the signers were the
Harrison Grays, father and son, John Singleton Copley, Theophilus
Lilly, Martin Gay, the coppersmith, father-in-law of young
John Boyle, but not many of the famous Tory names. As late as
1773 seemingly the vast majority of people still did not know which
side they belonged on. A broadside of the period printed not only
their names, but their trades. Of the one hundred and twenty,
only twenty-seven are put down as merchants. Most of them are
artisans. There are hucksters, powder monkeys, bookbinders,
mariners, among them. It would long be remembered against
these signers, rich and poor alike.

General Gage had been respectfully greeted by the town authorities and wined and dined at Faneuil Hall. He was well known
and liked. He was fifty-two, cautious and peaceable by nature,
probably not very alert, but kindly and well-meaning towards
everyone. He was almost an American himself, having lived here
so long and being married to an American wife. The Bostonians
had high hopes of his leniency and sense of fair play.

Although he was deferential in his treatment of the civil authorities and never a sabre-rattler, he set to work with complete
impartiality and thoroughness to carry out Parliament's commands, and closed the port of Boston. To do this there were sufficient of His Majesty's fleet already in Boston Harbor. These
frigates, armed schooners, and ships-of-war began taking up
strategic stations. Not even ferries would be allowed to cross to
Charlestown. Frantically (for there were only two more days before the Port Bill went into effect on the first of June), merchants
were getting goods into Boston and their ships moved to Salem or
Marblehead. Barges brought fuel and grain. Many families moved
out to their country places, fearing famine and rioting. Already
the transports, bringing in the first of General Gage's regiments,
had been sighted. Revere came back to a Boston wild with excitement, making what preparations she might for a very black future.

General Gage, coolly, almost gently, went on with his preparations. If 'grass did grow in the streets of Boston' and all the in-

habitants starved to death together, it was no concern of his. He had come for one purpose — to close the port of Boston. And he closed it.

# V

GOVERNOR HUTCHINSON never thought, when it was decided he was to go to England to report to King George the Third and Lord North, he was leaving his country forever. After a brief period of semi-martial law under General Gage, he would return and once more be governor. His belief that a soldier would now take over problems, which he, as a civilian, had been unable to cope with, gave him confidence in the final outcome. He was in a sanguine mood. His neighbors in Milton long remembered (and told their grandchildren) how the last royal governor passed his last hours on New England soil.

They said he appeared cheerful, walking about his estate, smiling to his neighbors, 'Whig and Tory alike,' for he was 'good friends with all.' It was a fair day, this first day of June. His apple trees would be through blossoming. He would see how the fruit was setting; and the butternuts he had planted and cared for with his own hands — how were they making out. In June in New England bluebirds, brown thrashers, and bluejays flash through new foliage. Far away (if you are lucky) comes the unearthly nostalgic call of the hermit thrush. And the crows slouch along the furrows of sprouting corn and help themselves. There was the ha-ha wall he had built to keep the cattle out of his garden. That, too, should have been worthy a farewell glance, for although his butternuts outlived him by over a hundred years, this quaint wall, half lost in tangle, still stands.

To the west he might see where, fifty miles away, rises the blue mass of Mount Wachusett; to the east his fields rolled away in

gradual descent to the Neponset River, meandering as it meets
Boston Harbor. Across these waters, if the wind was to the northeast, he might have heard the faint tolling of the bells. For today
is June 1, 1774, and the Boston Port Bill has just gone into effect.
Old Meeting's sombre note and Christ's lovely peal, the harsh
Cockerel, King's Chapel, Hollis, at such a distance melt into one
voice as the town mourns its captivity. Not one sail in that harbor
which had been so crowded with fine vessels, except the ships-of-
war and the transports carrying the first of many regiments.

The stately house, for which Governor Bernard had so kindly
designed new wings many years before, had been packed up,
shuttered, and left in charge of the gardener. Sallie, Peggy, and
Elisha were ready for the journey. Billy, the youngest, was already
in England. Thomas stayed a little longer. Now Miss Grizzel
must get the young ladies off — in the usual flurry of hatboxes,
lapdogs, excited chattering, mob-capped maidservants of the
period. Were not these girls headed for court? And is not London
as much greater than Unkity Hill as the Thames is greater than the
Neponset? London fairer than this wicked provincial Boston?

It must have seemed odd that Papa preferred to walk down to
the Lower Falls by himself. For it was not until then he entered
the coach which, in about a year's time, was to be given to Washington. The coach took them to Dorchester Heights and there the
*Minerva* lay waiting for them. But first the old governor wished
to be rowed to Castle Island for a final conference with General
Gage. Now the tolling of the Boston bells was very clear as for
several hours he talked with Gage. Then he was rowed to the
*Minerva*, waiting for ebb to drop down past the headland of Hull.

No man ever loved Massachusetts with greater intensity than
did Thomas Hutchinson. He had written her history, fought for
her boundaries, re-established her currency, seen to it that her
courts and judicial system were kept to a high standard. He had
honestly believed in the centralization of power, and that the
centre should be in London. The side which won did not, and yet
their grandchildren (two of Paul Revere's among them) were to
be dying within a century for the centralization of power in the
Federal Government. Hutchinson lost everything by backing the
wrong system at the wrong time. His houses, wharves, horses,
coaches, great estates, even the tomb of his wife on Copp's Hill,

were confiscated. His name was to become for years anathema. Hutchinson Street would be renamed Pearl. A new town close by Wachusett had thought to take his name, thought better of it, and named itself for Colonel Barre of the House of Commons. Yet if the other side had won, Thomas Hutchinson would undoubtedly be regarded as one of our great patriots.

## VI

THE wharves of Boston were entirely deserted, 'not a top-sail vessel to be seen either there or in the harbour, save ships of war and transports.' There was no work, and 'we have reason to believe that this devoted capital will be reduced to the utmost distress. God send us speedy releif. . . .'

And now once more Boston streets echoed to the heavy clumping of army boots and the rolling rub-a-dub-dub of drums. The inhabitants had plenty of time on their hands to stand about and watch their coming. The Fourth (the 'King's Own') and the Forty-Third landed from Ireland the day the Port Bill went into effect. The Fifth and Thirty-Eighth soon after. Three transports from New York brought the Royal Welsh Fusiliers. And a royal train of artillery camped on the Common. The Marines landed. In all, Gage brought in eleven regiments that summer, many of them famous and finely officered. He did not intend to make the mistake of six years ago and expect two regiments to keep order in Boston.

Either these new soldiers behaved better, or their very numbers frightened the agitators from playing up their peccadilloes.

The British hoped that the still free ports along the Massachusetts coast would seize the opportunity to make fortunes at the ex-

pense of Boston. They did not. Salem and Marblehead offered
the use of their wharves and porters to the Boston merchants.
The passage of goods from these ports to the beleaguered town
was made by carts called 'Lord North's Coasters,' for the carters
alternately whipped their animals and cursed Lord North all the
way.

In Boston the redcoats drilled and marched all day. There were
about five thousand of them — almost a third of Boston's normal
population. General Gage was determined that no one could
criticise the conduct of his troops. His officers complained of him
in their diaries and letters. Lieutenant John Barker (a very critical young man), of the King's Own, writes:

> Yesterday in compliance with the request of the Select Men Gen'l
> Gage order'd that no soldier in future should appear in the streets
> with his side Arms — Quaere, Is this not encouraging the Inhabitants
> in their licentious and riotous disposition? Also orders are issued for
> the guards to seize all military men found engaged in any disturbance,
> whether aggressors or not. . . . Tommy [Gage] feels no affection for
> his army.

That summer the Fifth Regiment, under Lord Percy, camped on
the Common. The young earl was ambitious to do well in the
profession so many of his ancestors had followed. 'That Percy . . .
who as a younger son, fought for King George at Lexington. A
Major of Dragoons,' as the poem has it. He was in fact a colonel.

Aunt Lydia, John Hancock, and their perennial house guest,
Dolly Quincy, were charmed by this very charming British earl,
thus camping out in their own front yard. Percy came to the
Hancock house, where magnificent meals were served every few
hours, on the most informal, friendly basis. This intimacy started
gossip in both camps.

Will Molineaux lived next door. The young voice of Lord
Percy, drilling his men on Boston Common at break-o'-day delighted Miss Dolly Quincy (she never forgot it), but it may have
been the last straw for the irascible Irishman, for it was at this
time he suffered his final shock.

Aunt Lydia had moved her candidate for her nephew's hand
into the Hancock house. She knew John was pretty busy and
she was ready to make his courtship as easy for him as possible.

Likewise she did not trust Miss Dolly out of her sight. The young lady was a relative of hers and, since her mother's death, her informal ward. Squire Edmund Quincy of Braintree had five daughters, all beauties, all gay, all amusing. Miss Dolly was the youngest, the prettiest, the gayest, and most amusing of them all. She was a mere sprig of a woman — short nose, pointed chin, pointed fingers — all ruffles, flounces, bows, but sharp as a little switch under her flower-like prettiness. Living at the height of the 'La — Sir!' school of female conversation, she often came out with remarks as definite as the kick of a mule. She may have been spoilt and capricious, but she was no fool.

John Hancock had been courting her for three years. The year before he had almost married her. Her father had hopefully redecorated the family parlor with paper sent express from Paris for the great event (there were appropriate Venuses and Cupids in blue, wreathed with red flowers on it), but the wedding had not come off. John had already wasted ten years courting Miss Sally Jackson, who had married Henderson Inches and promptly died. It was certainly time for him to marry. He was thirty-seven. Obviously he would wish an heir to carry on his name and inherit his fortune, as Aunt Lydia would certainly remind him. But first Miss Dolly would — and then she wouldn't. She was ten years younger than he — but no young maid. If she kept on being so pernickety, she might find herself hanging upon the Quincy tree — a spinster. But if she would not settle down and marry John Hancock, neither would she let him slip through her fingers. He was the most eligible bachelor in New England. Through it all Aunt Lydia grimly kept her head and trusted to propinquity. Eventually the girl would see reason.

But that summer, as Dolly woke, it was to hear the voice of a belted earl, to see through the twilight of dawn the slender young nobleman galloping his horse across the Common. Seemingly Miss Dolly often woke early that summer. She at least got some pleasure out of the Boston Port Bill, even if it was ruining her fiancé's (if he was her fiancé) health and fortune, for it is not often one can look out of a house on Beacon Hill and see an earl skirting the Frog Pond. Then almost the next moment he would be running up the stone steps of the Hancock house, flushed, happy, and hungry from his exercise, hardly waiting for the servant to open the door — Yes, this morning he will breakfast with the family. He was not a handsome man, his face was too narrow, but he was graceful, alert, and always ready with his sidelong glances and quick smiles. Probably, when John Hancock, his aunt, his tentative fiancée, and Lord Percy sat down to that feast which was called breakfast at this most hospitable house, the young colonel was the only one who never thought whether he was an earl or not. All he wished was to be a good soldier and a pleasant guest — not only in the sight of Hancocks but of rebellious Boston.

The incarceration of Boston roused a storm of protest from one end of the thirteen colonies to the other. For if Boston could be thus bullied, why not the rest of them? Now any evil was believed possible of the clique in whose hands lay the power of the British Empire. Farmers were sure their lands would be taken away from them or that they would be taxed to support an Episcopal Church. They saw themselves reduced by tyranny to the status of Ireland.

Provisions for the town began to pour in over the Neck. Charleston, South Carolina, sent rice; Maryland, meal and flour; Philadelphia (and strange as it seems, London) sent money. (There was great indignation in England.) Marblehead, quintals of codfish; Baltimore, rye and bread; Alexandria, flour and money.

The Massachusetts towns did what they could: Chelmsford, forty bushels of rye and sheep and cattle; Groton, Pepperell, Wrentham, and so on, to such an effect 'that even our poorest people have not yet suffered for want of bread.'

On an August day the 'renowned Col Putnam' himself arrived from Connecticut, driving a flock of sheep. 'Old Put' 'was so much caressed' by the Bostonians he had difficulty in leaving.

The selectmen started projects. Docks were cleaned; wharves repaired; streets paved. They saw to it that every man worked for his share of the food sent in by these sympathetic towns. Some of the workmen did not like this. Boston was angry, despairing, gloomy, and all her trades and industries paralyzed.

To add further to her distress were the hundreds of Tories, perhaps most of them simple farmers and artisans, but a large number of doctors, lawyers, merchants, and large landowners, who began seeking refuge in Boston from the rough handling they had experienced in their own towns. Epes Sargent fled from Cape Ann; Brigadier Ruggles, from Hardwick; Colonel John Murray, from Rutland.

So Boston, already the headquarters of the Whigs, now in a way became the headquarters of the Tories. That this did not always work out well is less surprising than that there was no worse violence. Mrs. Sam Adams wrote her husband 'that the once happy town' has become 'a cage for every unclean Bird. Consignees, Commissioners and every denomination have made this town their ark of safety.'

Henry Hulton himself dared not stay out in Brookline, but his wife, small boys, and sister did, and were in no way molested. Today they would have fared differently. The stories of brutal treatment the Tory refugees told when they finally escaped to Boston inflamed all the other Tories to white fury. The high-handedness of Parliament (which proceeded during the summer to pass more and more destructive acts) infuriated the Whigs until they honestly believed, with much reason, that all Tories were enemies and traitors to their own country.

Parliament had abolished town meeting — that very rock and symbol of freedom as the New Englanders understood it. Leading rebels could be sent to England for trial — especial emphasis being laid upon the seizure of Sam Adams and John Hancock. Jurors were to be chosen by governmental machinery — not by town meeting. Troops might be quartered on the people. And so on. The acts were certainly 'oppresive.' Barre warned the Government that it had been 'goading and teasing the Americans for ten years' into rebellion. Mr. Fuller, leader of the Opposition in Commons, said, 'if ever there was a nation running headlong to its ruin it is this.' The Earl of Chatham opposed these measures in the House of Peers. Such voices were unheeded, and many Englishmen, who sympathized wholeheartedly with the provincials' fight for 'the rights of Englishmen,' waited, half in dread, half in hope, for that shot which was not to be fired until the following April.

Sometime that summer Paul Revere seems to have taken an unofficial jaunt to New York. For on the fourth of September he is writing John Lamb expressing his pleasure in his visit. If he was referring to his visit of last May he was shockingly late with his bread-and-butter letter, which runs:

Boston Septr 4 1774

Dear Sr, I embrace this oppertunity to inform you, that we are in Spirits, tho' in a Garrison; the Spirit of Liberty never was higher than at present; the troops have the horrors amazingly by reason of some late movements of our friends in the country the week past.

This refers to a seizure of powder made by the British soldiers three days before. Two hundred and sixty redcoats had gone up the Mystic by boat, seized stores at Charlestown, and been off before it was even known they had left Boston. But such thousands of angry, armed provincials arrived at the scene too late, Gage might guess the fighting temper of the country people, and no wonder his poor soldiers had 'the horrors.' And Revere writes about the closing down of the courts because the justices 'cannot git a Jury' (not mentioning the fact that he himself was one of the many jurors who refused to serve under judges who from now on were to accept their salaries directly from England). He sends affectionate greetings to Lamb's wife, father, sister, and a host of friends 'particularly to Capt Sears, for his kind care of my Horse & Sulky.'

It is this last sentence which suggests a trip not otherwise recorded. He sends thanks for care of his 'sulky,' so he was not riding express. The sulky (so named because it carried but one) was not what it is today, but no more romantic. Gentlemen would take whatever easy-chair pleased them most and their wives could spare from the parlor and have a coach-maker mount it upon wheels. Paul Revere has been pictured so much galloping through darkness and danger, it is almost with pleasure one can contemplate him seated in the old chair which he had loved for years, but which Rachel thought outmoded, jogging peacefully through fine summer days to New York and back. Like the post-riders he would even have time to knit if he wished. And in New York he had plenty of time to make a vast number of liberty-minded new friends. He sent his bread-and-butter letter by John Marston. But a week later he himself was suddenly called upon to ride all-haste to Philadelphia, where the first Continental Congress was then sitting. Coming events were casting longer and blacker shadows.

Although town meetings had been prohibited, nothing had been said about county meetings (a thing England did not think to forbid because they had never been even heard of). Representatives of Suffolk County gathered at Milton and passed the famous 'Suffolk Resolves,' which Joseph Warren had drawn up. They proved a springboard from which it was easy to plunge into the bloody whirlpool of civil war. Revere's affection and admiration for Warren was so great there is little he would have refused him, and it was Warren who wished Paul Revere to ride express to the

Continental Congress in Philadelphia with those resolves. For the principles stated in them, Warren himself was to die.

The first Continental Congress was in session at Carpenters' Hall. At last the brace of Adamses were pulling together, but Boston's radical reputation was so feared they sat quietly in a corner and were 'very modest.' Some of the southern representatives were so frightened by Boston's 'leveling' principles and highhandedness they thought New England quite as dangerous as Old England and said Sam Adams wanted Massachusetts to be the head of America, Boston the head of Massachusetts, and Sam himself dictator of Boston. Adams was a man of no property and looked it, in spite of the handsome suit of clothes that had been given him for this great occasion. He was too mistrusted to do much in public, but as usual won over almost everyone who had a private word with him, and marked down for destruction those he could not win — like Joseph Galloway.

When Paul Revere appeared with his inflammatory 'Suffolk Resolves,' it seemed incredible that such an out-and-out statement of potential revolution could have passed the Congress. John Adams said 'tears gushed from the eyes of old, grave pacific Quakers,' for it was almost a declaration of war. Congress endorsed it, and also agreed that if the British troops in Boston should take the offensive, the other colonies would go to her help with armed force.

Once again it was decided to try 'non-importation.' Revere went back with letters and fine promises. But the Tories were saying that this Congress, instead of fairly representing American opinion, 'gave such a blast from the trumpet of sedition as makes half of America shudder.' Probably it was nearer three-fourths of America that shuddered as they saw revolution and the horrors of civil war gathering momentum. It would seem inevitable now that sooner or later a shot would be fired. And it would be in Boston or near-by. And a shot heard round the world. Any hour, any day, this week or next, next month, next spring, civil war would begin.

When Paul Revere returned to Boston, he would once again see changes, even in so brief an absence. General Gage was fortifying the Neck. The number of armed men who had risen up so suddenly (and too late) when he had seized the powder at Charlestown had given him 'the horrors' as well as his soldiers. What if they should decide to sweep in from the country? He said the reason he was putting up this fortification was to keep his men from deserting. No one believed that. And on every village green that fall minute men were drilling. They said they feared another war with France. General Gage did not believe that either.

But these fortifications which Revere saw going up in his absence did not impress old veterans of French and Indian wars like Revere himself. They called them 'beaver dams' and said they could kick them down. Gage's own informants brought back some very amusing stories to him about the quality of the local troops, drilling so hard in fear of the French. Just country bumpkins. Would run at the smell of powder. No uniforms, no uniformity. No fine martial ardor. The veriest peasantry. Gage, luckily for himself, did not believe such stories. He had fought side by side against the French with exactly such unpromising-looking militiamen, farmers and frontiersmen, and had a wholesome respect for the queer-looking squirrel guns they carried. He wrote to England saying his mere five thousand troops were not safe. He must have at least ten thousand.

General Gage was having trouble getting supplies for his men from the country. Wagonloads of straw tipped over. Boats carrying bricks for his fortifications mysteriously sank. Idle laborers stood about gibing at his fortifications and refused to work. He had to send to Nova Scotia for workmen. Through it all Gage was good-tempered, ponderous, and anxious in no way to play the tyrant. The Whig press continued to print scathing denunciations of him. Whig orators spoke publicly and treasonably. He now had the right, at discretion, to send any leaders of rebellion against the Crown to London for trial and certain execution. He was loath to use this right.

## VII

GOVERNOR GAGE refused to convene the General Court at the new capital at Salem, but the representatives met anyway, calling themselves 'a provincial congress.' John Hancock was the chairman of this semi-legal legislature which now carried on the duties of the old General Court.

Hancock was anxious to know what was happening in the larger Continental Congress now sitting in Philadelphia. In the middle of October he sent Paul Revere down to find out and carry letters.

That fall another man was dispatched from the Boston Whig camp carrying even more important messages and to a far greater distance. Josiah Quincy took ship secretly at Salem for England. He was to talk with Lord North, Benjamin Franklin, and others of both parties over there, try to explain the American point of view. There was consternation when it was found he was gone. The Tories were afraid his persuasiveness might win the ministerial ear; his friends that he would be hanged on sight as a rebel.

When November came, the regiments were moved into winter quarters. The Quartering Act gave them the right to be put up in any man's house. The Revere house was probably rather crowded to tuck in even a couple of soldiers. The artillery went into the warehouses on Griffin's Wharf. The King's Own into a distilling house in West Boston.

The Sixty-Fourth, under Colonel Leslie, stayed on at Castle Island. The Royal Irish and the Forty-Third were on Back Street, not far from North Square, but the Marines were landed down almost on top of the Reveres. Major Pitcairn[25] himself, with a Lieutenant Wragg, took up his residence almost next door to the Reveres, with the Shaws, who were violently anti-British. But when the Lieutenant disparaged the rebels at the family table and the sons grew angry, the Major would interfere and keep the peace.

Everyone liked the Major, a pious man who dutifully attended service at Christ Church on Sundays, and whose weekday profanity was a Boston legend. He was a tough, honest old soldier and his

death was regretted by the men who killed him. Major Pitcairn's
face, as handed down to us, is impossible to reconcile with the
reputation he left behind. In his miniature (at the Hancock-Clark
house, Lexington) he has a look of innocent wonder. That girlish
mouth could hardly have uttered all those oaths nor those round,
soft eyes strike such terror and respect. Both Pitcairn and Revere
have left pleasant reputations for getting on well with men who
did not share their political views, approving of the man even
as they hated the politics. If Revere did not like and admire Shaw's
curious house-guest, he was in a minority. Revere got on so well
with the Tories after the Revolution, it suggests that he behaved
decently towards them during those cruel months when feeling
ran so high and such black hatred was built up. Paul Revere
seems to have been a man of no spite, envy, or vindictiveness.
There is something very attractive about this quality which is hard
to dramatize.

On the seventh day of December, Rachel Walker bore her first
child. Revere already had five daughters and only one son, so
Joshua must have been a welcome addition to his house, although
where they had room to put him is a mystery. Letters still exist
between the high-spirited Rachel and her husband, reflecting the
affection, camaraderie, humor, that existed between them. As
far as we know, he was never away from Sary long enough to
justify a correspondence. If he had been, it might have shown an
equally attractive relationship, but whatever he may have thought
of the shadowy Sary, there can be no question but he liked Rachel.
It would be hard to leave 'his dear girl,' as he called her, only a
week after her confinement. December is a dark month to try
out new routes, but the Sons of Liberty had discovered that General
Gage intended to send soldiers from Boston by sea to Portsmouth,
to so strengthen Fort William and Mary that the local militia
could not seize it. Someone must go immediately to warn of the
plan, forestall it. This was by far the most ticklish ride Revere
had as yet undertaken.

And now a man might not get on his horse at North Square, jog
down Fish and Anne Streets, cross the drawbridge into Boston
proper, and so out over the High Street, pass through the gates,
and where he went from there was nobody's business but his own.
Unless you were a Tory, given a permit for your conspicuous loyalty

to the Crown, you must first go to military headquarters at the
Province House and get a pass. And sit about cooling your heels
for some time, waiting your turn to see 'I. Small Major of Brigade.'
Watching the short, smart pacing of the sentries, see orderlies come
and go and young officers, gorgeous in their scarlet, white, and
gold, at their endless gaming which so amazed the citizens of
Boston. And at last Major Small himself was ready to attend to
you. Your name? Paul Revere. Trade? Silversmith. And, Mr.
Revere, why is it necessary for you to leave the Town of Boston?

Almost any excuse would be good enough — except the right one.
He could not say, I ride to Portsmouth to urge certain men there to
seize a fort before you can send reinforcements . . . Oh yes, . . . I've
thought it out. I know this is armed insurrection. I know that,
although we have put treason on paper and into speeches, we have
not as yet taken so serious a step, to seize His Majesty's fort, and
munitions. Are we ready for civil war? Revolution? Yes.

He would have to say something about a sick grandmother, a
hope to sell silver in Newport — any excuse he might think of, so
he did not betray his true destination. The Major satisfied, the
pass granted, he would loiter out past the sentries before the
Province House, careful in no way to suggest his haste, mount the
nimble little horse tied to a hitching-post, very careful that his
own excitement would not start his horse to capering, slowly, as
slowly as he was able, he would reach the town gates, show his pass.
Time enough to make speed out of sight of British eyes. He had
sixty wintry miles to ride.

The next afternoon, December 13, Paul Revere drew up before
John Sullivan's door in Durham, New Hampshire. The broad,
white Sullivan house still stands beside the Oyster River, a few
miles inland from Portsmouth. For over a year this able, second-
generation Irishman had been drilling the local boys. He was sure
there would be fighting before long. Sullivan was prodigiously
strong and a natural leader of men. If anyone would undertake an
attack upon a King's fort flying the flag of England, garrisoned
by loyal troops, it would be John Sullivan.

Paul Revere's horse was 'nearly done,' as an eyewitness remembered. He may have been done-in himself. There were snow
and ice on the roads. John Rowe had found the road to Salem
'very bad traveling.' The sixty miles had been covered at top

speed. John Sullivan heard his news. Two regiments were to be sent out from Boston immediately to reinforce the fort in Portsmouth Harbor and garrison the town itself. The thing to do was to get the fort first. Sullivan sent his hired man to collect a handful of choice young men ready for such a lawless venture.

After dark they started down the river in one of those clumsy lateen-rigged vessels called 'gundalows.' It was a moonlight night, cold and clear. The men reached Portsmouth Harbor and pushed their awkward craft as close to Fort William and Mary as they could, waded ashore, and demanded the surrender. Captain Corcoran refused, fired three times, hit no one, and surrendered. He had only a few men and was completely surprised. For several hours the provincials waded back and forth, waist-deep in icy brine, carrying ninety-seven kegs of powder and some hundred small arms from the fort to their gundalow. It was a tremendous haul. The men did not dare put on their shoes again lest the iron hobs might strike a spark and the whole thing blow up. They got back to Durham, very frozen, very triumphant, and hid the stores in a pit under the pulpit of the meeting house. The next day John Boyle in Boston has had word of the expedition, so it looks as though Paul Revere only waited for one night's sleep and to learn what had happened, then started back. The names of the young men who took part in this first direct attack on a British fort over here are pretty well known. As Paul Revere is not one, the chances are he was sleeping his well-earned sleep at the Sullivan house, only waking at the return of the gundalow with its booty, then starting over the icy road back to Boston.

Nothing the Yankees had done thus far so enraged George the Third personally as this seizure of his fort and his supplies. When he heard of it he demanded the punishment of every man concerned and the immediate seizure of all rebel supplies. The result of this policy was Lexington.

Yet there was still a certain amount of pleasant give-and-take between the troops and the inhabitants. A few days after his return, Paul Revere would have had a chance to show his good-will toward a sergeant of the Forty-Seventh and a fellow Mason. '152 Brethern [of Boston] followed the corps & the whole 47th Regem't.'

After this ride, Paul Revere was something of a marked man. It would be hard for him to get a pass and he says he kept a boat hidden in North Boston. He seems to have taken but one more ride before Lexington. Late in January the Provincial Congress of New Hampshire was (against the will of its Tory Governor Wentworth) meeting at Exeter. 'Paul Revere went express thither.' The Governor reported sourly, 'it portends a storm rather than peace.'

But there were plenty of ways a man could get in and out of Boston without a pass. One was to dress up as a countryman and pretend to be bringing in fuel and food for the troops. The other was by merely going fishing — and promising to sell your fish to the British commissary, or going by boat on a dark night. It is very unlikely that, after Portsmouth, Paul Revere would come and go on a pass through the town gates. He was known as a storm warning.

## VIII

THAT winter of '74–'75 was 'the warmest in memory of man.' This freak of nature was a blessing to Boston; five thousand of whose inhabitants (and many of these Tory refugees) were 'poverty struck.' And it was a load off the British officers' minds. They had feared that when ice formed over the Charles, as it always does, uniting Boston with Charlestown and Cambridge, 'the country' would rush in. General Gage, with all his shortcomings, never, like so many British ministers and generals, underestimated the fighting value of the odd-looking local militia. They might be all sizes, ages, conditions in life, and carry a curious arsenal of weapons, but they were dangerous opponents if roused.

That winter the Charles never froze.

Gage's forces were being steadily increased by new troops. And steadily decreased by desertion. Many of these deserters were

openly for the Yankees. It was the secret business of such men as
Paul Revere to get in touch with them, help them out of their
red coats and into farmers' smocks. It was for some such reason
Ditson was tarred-and-feathered by Colonel Nesbit that spring.
Some deserters were caught and shot at the foot of the Common.
Some not only got away, but even helped drill the minute men.
In Freetown, Rhode Island, one such British drillmaster was taken
up by the Tories to be returned to Gage and the firing squad. He
was rescued and presumably went on drilling. John Adams speaks
of another.

Paul Revere might well have been grateful for the abnormal
warmth of that winter. Not only was fuel very scarce, but he was
out much at night. Some years later he wrote:

> In the fall of '74 and the winter of '75, I was one of upwards of
> thirty, chiefly mechanics, who formed ourselves into a committee
> for the purpose of watching the movements of the British soldiers,
> and gaining every intelligence of the movements of the Tories. We
> held our meetings at the Green Dragon. We were so careful that
> our meetings should be kept secret, that every time we met, every
> person swore upon the Bible that he would not discover any of our
> transactions but to Messrs. Hancock, Adams, Doctors Warren,
> Church, and one or two more. In the winter, towards spring, we
> frequently took turns, two and two, to watch the soldiers, by patrol-
> ling the streets all night.

Very late in December occurred an event too small for any
history book, unmentioned in diary or letter. Paul Revere had a
birthday — a memorable birthday, for he left behind him the
semi-youthful thirties and entered the sober forties. No matter
how ardent his heart, thick his hair, untiring his body, he was now
definitely a man in his middle years. Even if he could forget it,
there were his children to remind him. His 'Debby' (as he called
his oldest) was seventeen. Young Paul, at fifteen, learning his
father's trade, would be taking upon himself the manner and responsibilities of manhood. No children stay young very long, but
childhood in the eighteenth century was far briefer than in the
twentieth.

Revere's self-appointed committee were conscious that in spite
of the Masonic secrecy of the Green Dragon, Bible oaths, and pre-
cautions, General Gage was always well informed of what they

were about. There was a leak somewhere. ' . . . when things began to grow serious, a gentleman who had connections with the Tory party, but was a Whig at heart, acquainted me,' he wrote, 'that our meetings were discovered, and mentioned the identical words that were spoken among us the night before. We did not then distrust Dr. Church, but supposed it must be some one among us. We removed to another place, which we thought was more secure; but here we found that all our transactions were communicated to Governor Gage. (This came to me through the then Secretary Flucker; he told it to the gentleman mentioned above.) It was then a common opinion, that there was a traitor in the Provincial Congress, and that Gage was possessed of all their secrets.' (Church was a member of that Congress for Boston.)

At this very time Doctor Church 'kept company with a Captain Price, a half-pay British officer,' and Revere noticed 'he frequently dined with him and Robinson, one of the commissioners. I knew that one of his intimate acquaintances asked him why he was so often with Robinson and Price. His answer was, that he kept company with them on purpose to find out their plans.' Church, like the other doctors of his period, had his apprentices or students. One of them, who 'lived with him and took care of his business and books,' noticed 'he had no money by him, and was much drove for money; that all at once, he had several hundred new British guineas; and . . . he thought at the time, where they came from.' But said nothing of his master's treachery.

So while Secretary Flucker, whose daughter, Lucy, had recently married the promising young bookseller, Henry Knox (who well may have been 'the gentleman mentioned above'), was inadvertently giving Revere the information of Gage's plans, Doctor Church was handing over the Whig secrets to Gage.

General Gage was holding recalcitrant Boston in his mailed fist, but had no power beyond his own fortifications. He attempted a few sorties, always by boat, not only to seize powder and arms, but cautiously to try out the temper of the people. His expedition to Portsmouth had miscarried through Paul Revere's efforts. In January he sent out a sloopful of soldiers to Marshfield to protect loyalists there from the local mobs. They seized no powder and were not molested. In February he planned a slightly more war-like manoeuvre. He had word from the Tories in Salem that materials of war were being collected there, obviously to be used in armed insurrection. If his men were to take possession, they must move secretly and quickly. He had only one regiment, the Sixty-Fourth out on Castle Island, which he could expect to use without the knowledge of the townspeople. The General was using the old Province House for his headquarters. Here Secretary Flucker would learn of the intended excursion to Salem.

Only a few doors from the Province House was his Whig son-in-law's bookshop. 'It was a store of great display and attraction for young and old, and a fashionable lounging place.' Harrison Gray Otis says of it, 'I passed it every day and have often seen Knox at the counter. This was just before the siege.' Henry Knox was twenty-five at this time, 'very fat, but very active and of a gay and amiable character.' His shop was much patronized by the British officers, who liked him. For them (and himself) he had laid in a stock of books on the arts of war — especially artillery. He read his books, talked with the officers, and by this unusual method became a good artillery officer — far better than the young red-coats who inadvertently served as his instructors. The most active service he had seen thus far was a disastrous duck-hunt, which had resulted in the maiming of one of his plump hands, and the Boston Massacre, when he had called to Captain Preston that his life must answer for it if his men fired. That was five years before. Henry Knox was a stout Whig, but in the interests of trade and his own education, he was not saying much about his politics. Mr. Flucker may not have intended to pass on General Gage's plans to the extent that he did. Henry Knox, in spite of his bulk, had a quick mind. What he got from Mr. Flucker and passed on to Paul Revere was as important as what Benjamin Church was telling Messrs. Price and Robinson and they carrying to General Gage.

Word came to the waiting mechanics that the Sixty-Fourth, under Colonel Leslie, might embark for Cape Ann. Castle Island was a difficult spot for them to watch, but they made the attempt. They rowed over on Saturday afternoon and 'were detained there till 10 o'clock Monday . . . lest we should send an express to our brethren at Marblehead and Salem.'

It would have been hard for Paul Revere to enjoy the sea breezes of Castle Island and the hospitality of the garrison as he watched from behind bars the transport carrying the Sixty-Fourth towards Salem. For once the redoubtable courier, who had already ridden before several 'storms,' was under lock and key. There was no way now he might mount, ride, and warn Marblehead and Salem that the British were 'coming out.'

By Tuesday a self-appointed Boston committee is writing the Sons of Liberty in New York giving an account of 'Leslie's Retreat' and explaining why it was no word reached Salem in time. It is signed by six men, presumably the leaders of the 'thirty and upward, mostly mechanics.' Joshua Brackett, keeper of the Cromwell Head, signed first; next is Paul Revere, then Benjamin Edes, the printer, Joseph Ward, distiller, Thomas Crafts, painter, and Thomas Chase, distiller. The P.S. refers to 'these persons' being locked up on Castle Island when the Sixty-Fourth embarked.

Colonel Leslie went with his men. Miss Hulton knew him pretty well and liked him. 'An Amiable & good man, the Father of his Choir & the soldiers who all look up to him with respect & affection, he's of a Noble Scotch family, but distinghused more by his humanity and affability.'

By three o'clock this amiable gentleman and one hundred and fifty men reached Marblehead. The people were all in church when the transport arrived and began discharging its scarlet cargo. They stopped for no closing hymn that day, but sent word immediately to Salem that the regulars, with fixed bayonets and loaded muskets, 'were out' and had taken the Salem road. Probably they intended to seize war stores. This cache could only be reached by a drawbridge over the North River.

Of course by the time Colonel Leslie arrived the draw was up. Why was the King's highway thus obstructed?

It wasn't the King's highway, but the property of the inhabitants.

Now drums were beating alarm, the bells of Salem summoned the militiamen. As far away as Amesbury, minute men were soon on the march. And mounted expresses were riding furiously, 'the regulars are out!'

The argument about putting down the draw went on towards two hours and every moment the crowd grew greater, tempers shorter, and provincial wit more piercing. They joked about the number of lice in the soldiers' heads and other simple matters that occurred to them. At last the Colonel promised that if the draw was dropped and he and his men allowed to pass over it, they would immediately turn around, go back to Marblehead, and embark. This evolution (so suggestive of the King of France in the nursery rhyme) was solemnly carried out.

Sarah Tarrant leaned out of her window to yell, 'Go home and tell your master he sent you on a fool's errand and has broken the peace of our Sabbath. What! Do you think we were born in the woods to be frightened by owls?' She had the last word.

One man, Joseph Whicher, had been pricked by a British bayonet. Thus Salem has put in a claim for the first blood shed in the Revolution. Certainly, if it had not been for either the amiability and humanity Miss Hulton credits Colonel Leslie with, or his wise fears of the ever-increasing number of armed citizens, the battle of Lexington would have taken place almost two months earlier and in Salem instead of Lexington. Paul Revere would not have been out riding the moonlight roads, but locked up at Castle Island.

# IX

THE Queen's Birthday had been celebrated on the eighteenth of January. All the British regiments and the fleet put on a great display and their officers drank healths and feasted with the loyal Tories.

On the fifth of March the opposition had their big day. This was the fifth annual anniversary of the Boston Massacre. Once again an orator would stand before the yelling crowds at Old South and remind them of the reckless tyranny of England that had quartered troops upon a peaceful town, with the inevitable resulting bloodshed. But now Boston was suffering much more tyranny of the same sort. Would Gage permit such a celebration? Would Joseph Warren, who was to be the orator that year as he

had been two years before, be allowed to speak? Exaggerated talk
was going around. Some said that Gage intended to let his most
avowed enemies gather in one place and then arrest them *en
masse*. But people began to crowd into the meeting house early.
'Each man felt the palpitations of his own heart' and their faces
were 'very pale.'

The British officers began to arrive early too. When Sam Adams,
who was moderator, noticed this infiltration of scarlet coats, he
politely invited them to the best seats in the house. 'I took care
to have them treated with civility,' he said, 'so they might have no
pretence to behave ill; for it is a good maxim in politics... to
put and keep the enemy in the wrong.' The officers accepted their
reserved seats, but some preferred to sit on the steps leading up
to the pulpit, while the selectmen, Sam Adams, John Hancock,
Doctor Church, and others all sat about in the deacons' seats.

It seems to have been agreed among the soldiers that if the
orator went too far in denouncing the King or British tyranny,
they would seize John Hancock, Sam Adams, and Joseph Warren.
The signal was to be an egg thrown at Warren's head by an ensign.
But on his way over, the young fellow had fallen down, dislocated
his knee, and broken his egg. The hall was so packed that when
Warren did arrive at last, he could not enter except by a ladder
put up to a window behind the pulpit.

For this occasion he had put on 'a Ciceronian toga, etc....
He then put himself into a Demosthenian posture, with a white
handkerchief in his right hand and his left in his breeches,' spoke
with dignity and to great applause. It was noticed that he did not
once refer to the massacre as 'bloody.' He had some heckling from
the soldiers. Captain Chapman, sitting on the steps, held up a
handful of bullets, but Warren neatly dropped his handkerchief
over the Captain's hand and went on talking.

When done, Sam Adams voted that plans be made for the next
year's celebration of the '*bloody* massacre' and a shout of 'fie, fie'
went up from the redcoats. It was thought to be a cry of fire. 'The
gallerians, apprehending fire, crowded out of the windows and
swarmed down gutters like rats.' At the same time, Colonel Nesbit
(who had tarred-and-feathered Ditson) was marching his men past
with drummers and fifers going full blast. This caused further confusion. Whether or not things would have worked out differently

if the ensign and his egg had arrived, we do not know. Certainly
the affair went off with remarkably good behavior on both sides,
although one matron did tell an Irish officer she'd 'like to ring his
nose.' There is perhaps not a country in the world today where a
corresponding scene could be enacted.

John Hancock and Sam Adams showed plenty of courage by
appearing at such a meeting. They knew that at any moment
Gage might seize them and either hang them over here or send
them to London to stand trial for high treason. It depended only
upon the General's discretion.

It was said that Sam Adams was scared. He turned pale at the
sight or mention of hemp. Politicians seemed to have been fond
of accusing their opponents of 'turning pale' and 'blanching.'
Either our modern counterparts are less sensitive or this particular
gibe has lost its savor. Scared Adams may have been, but he stayed
as long as he could. John Hancock was nervous too. There was a
rhyme abroad hardly designed to quiet the nerves of either of them:

> As for their King, John Hancock
> And Adams, if they're taken
> Their heads for signs shall hang on high
> Upon that hill called 'Beacon.'

Joseph Warren, too, was to a lesser degree a marked man. He
was continually reminded of his likely fate. Once, as he was going
along the Neck where the executions were commonly held, he
passed a group of three officers. One of them called after him,
'Go ahead, Warren; you'll soon come to the gallows.' He turned
about and went back to them. Which one had spoken to him?
They did not answer.

Early that spring of '75 one after another of the Boston rebel
leaders found it expedient to leave under the threat of the British
army. Only Joseph Warren remained to the very end. He was
tense and keyed up, and the quality which his friends admired as his
'irratability' was apparent. His medical students begged him not
to make night visits to patients, fearing he would be ambushed.
He showed them the pistols he carried. A sick woman on Cornhill
had sent for him. He would go. And once at least he broke out
fiercely, 'These fellows say we won't fight: By heavens I hope I
shall die up to my knees in blood.'

The most determined debunker would have difficulty in finding

any self-seeking motive, any personal vanity or spite, or any small-
ness of action in this young physician. He believed passionately in
his cause and was willing to die for it.

He had some small vanity, not that he cared whether or not he
was handsome, but he insisted, in an age when hot water did not
come out of a faucet, on always being extremely clean. It would
have bothered him more than most of his friends when he lost,
either by accident or by toothache, two teeth. One of them was
an eye tooth.

For him Paul Revere, that spring, carefully contrived two
artificial ones cut from one piece of ivory and wired them in.
Warren would hardly expect to eat with these makeshifts, but they
would stop any whistling noises and fill an ugly gap.

# X

ARMIES have always tended to
lie inert in winter and to move in spring. And now it was April.
No one could expect the sluggish scarlet dragon not to wake from
hibernation in its Boston den, uncoil and meander a little through
the spring-drenched countryside. Gage knew that the ministry
at home was impatient with his inaction. They were even sending
over three showier generals — Howe, Clinton, and Burgoyne — to
start something. His high-spirited young officers sneered at him.
The regulars, bored with close barrack life, were deserting and quarrelling. And everywhere it was spring. The time to act was close
at hand — but in which direction?

Gage knew that powder and arms had been collected to a formidable degree in both Worcester and Concord and the King had
especially commanded all such stores to be seized. He sent out
spies to look over both places, to advise him on the state of the

roads, the temper of the people, and the type and number of troops
he should employ.

On the fifth of April Lieutenant Colonel Francis Smith, who
makes a more sensational appearance exactly two weeks later as
commander at Lexington and Concord, set out with Private John
Howe [26] to spy out the way. They planned to walk from Boston to
Worcester and back to Boston by way of Concord. Colonel Smith
has always been remembered as a very fat, slow man, but his
willingness to undertake such a ramble suggests that his overweight
has been exaggerated. He may have been a little ponderous.
Private Howe was twenty-two and as nimble-footed and quick-
witted as his commanding officer was sluggish.

They disguised themselves as Yankee workmen by wearing grey
greatcoats, leather breeches, blue mixed stockings, and silk 'flag
hankercheifs' about their necks. Gage had given them letters to
inland Tories and they carried notebooks, a few personal effects
done up in checked kerchiefs, and walking sticks. Supposedly they
were day laborers looking for hire.

The Colonel, according to John Howe (who later wrote up his
experiences), only lasted as far as Watertown and his first breakfast. The two spies had gone to a tavern and as they ordered their
food conversed with the black girl who served them. The Colonel,
probably looking very stiff and military in his rustic garb and
speaking the best King's English, asked the maiden 'where we two
could find employment.'

The girl looked him in the face and said:

' "Smith, you will find employment enough for you and all
Gage's men in a few months." This conversation about wound up
our breakfast.'

Colonel Smith was flabbergasted. He complained to the landlord of the 'saucy wench.' The landlord told him that she had but
recently come from Boston and while there had been much with
the soldiers. She knew their faces.

The spies got out of there as fast as they could. 'Smith' decided
to cut for home. 'He told me if I pursued the route and got through,
he would assure me a commission,' and swore that if 'he came out
with his regiment on that road he would kill that wench. The last
I saw of Smith he was running through barbary bushes to keep
out of sight of the road.' As the officer scuttled off through the

bushes, the much more resourceful private continued on his way to Worcester. He asked a farmer if he knew of work to be done. Although he would take a job as a farm hand, 'I should rather work at Gun Smithing for that was my trade. . . . He told me I could get employment at Springfield, for they were in want of hands to work at that business, and said that I had better get there as soon as possible, for they were in want of guns, for they expected the regulars out of Boston, and they meant to be ready for them.'

Once, while poking about in a swamp beside a causeway to see if artillery and supply wagons could get through if the bridge was up, a black fisherman demanded to know what he was after. He said 'sweet flag root for the stomache ache.' Private Howe was never at a loss, and aroused little suspicion. But two teamsters a little farther down the road, who stood about 'tackling their team,' answered his usual question of 'did anyone want to hire?' with they 'did not know of anybody that wanted to hire an Englishman. I asked them what reason they had for thinking so; they said I looked like them rascals they see in Boston.' He began to hurry a little.

Although John Howe went secretly by night to the Tories, on the road he claimed to be a gunsmith eager to fix Yankee guns for the fight soon to come. By talking loudly about liberty he was able to learn the few simple secrets of the somewhat naïve minute men. But the rumor of spies abroad was always catching up with him and he moved fast.

He did (under the guidance of a Tory) see the stores at Worcester and near-by were two wells into which they might be dumped. He got out of Worcester, found Marlborough too hot to hold him, and took back roads to Concord. As a liberty-loving gunsmith he was immediately introduced to Major Buttrick, who set him to work repairing guns. He had found out everything Gage wished to know and so, saying that he must return to Maine to get his own tools, he left Concord.

At Lexington he stopped at a small house to buy food of the old couple who lived there — 'the old man was cleaning his gun. I asked him what he was going to kill, as he was so old I should not think he could take sight at any game. He said there was a flock of redcoats at Boston . . . he expected they would make very good marks. . . . I asked the old man how he expected to fight.

He said, open field fighting or any other way to kill them redcoats. I asked him how old he was. He said seventy-seven.' The young redcoat thought the Americans were wonderful.

Once more in Boston, he put off his 'Yankee dress' and put on his uniform. The first man he met on King Street was Colonel Smith, who hurried him to General Gage, although Howe protested he would rather have some breakfast. At the Province House the senior officers were gathered, making plans for the spring campaign. Private Howe was received with enthusiasm.

'I thought they had all been taking their bumpers rather too freely,' John said afterwards, a little smugly for a man who drank so many brandies, molasses-and-rums (which he called 'the Yankee drink'), hot slings, and what-not on his travels.

The group of officers gave him a drink.

'Take that John... you are not half drunk enough for officers company.'

They all made much of the clever young private. He handed in his written report, then General Gage asked him his opinion. How many men would it take to destroy the stores in Worcester and return safe? Private Howe says he realized that 'by answering that question I must stand or fall, but I was determined to give my opinion in full — turn as it would. I said if they should march 10,000 regulars and a train of artillery to Worcester which is 48 miles from this place, the roads very crooked and hilly, the inhabitants generally determined to be free or die that not one of them would get back alive.'

Colonel Smith told him he had been scared by the stories of old women. Major Pitcairn twitted the Colonel about his own flight from a black wench. John Howe reported that Concord would be a very different matter. General Gage praised him. His judgment, he said, was 'very good for a beardless boy of twenty-two.' He was 'a good soldier and a lucky and expert spy,' and he handed him a generous purse.

So Gage decided upon Concord. The route would be partly by water, with only a few miles to march. Howe had told him exactly where the stores were hidden. Gage also may have thought the time had at last come to pick up John Hancock and Sam Adams. Everyone knew they had left Boston for the Provincial Congress and were somewhere about Lexington. The British Government

could not understand why Gage delayed in their arrest. In vain
he had explained that if he attempted any such thing it would
be the last letter they would receive from him, for he would be
knocked on the head.

He had given the rebellion plenty of time to cool — almost a
year. And it was daily getting hotter and hotter. He had maintained as gentle a military rule in Boston as was humanly possible,
but things could not go on forever like this. This time he would
send out a sizable number of men (no ten thousand, for he did not
have so many) and keep the closest secrecy as to his goal. No one
would know until the troops were actually marching that any
sortie was planned. The men were to leave Boston on the eighteenth
of April.

By the fifteenth of April, which fell on Saturday, Paul Revere
and his associates knew something was up: 'about 12 o'clock at
night, the boats belonging to the transports were all launched, and
carried under the sterns of the men-of-war (They had been previously hawled up and repaired) We likewise found that the grenadier and light infantry were all taken off duty.'

North Square was filled with marines who were billeted on
everyone with a spare bed — which the Reveres do not seem to
have had. Paul Revere himself could keep an eye on them. The
light companies were preparing for a march. The heavily built
Scotch Major Pitcairn, quartered almost next door at the Shaws',
may have shown by his rising spirits that something was afoot.
He loved a good fight. It would be hard for him if men marched
and he was left behind.

Paul Revere had rented part of his shop to Isaac Clemens, who
was an engraver, thought to have come but recently from England,
and a staunch supporter of the English Crown. Clemens may have
given him information. He himself seems to have been little at
his shop these last few months before the storm broke. He makes few
entries and his handwriting, usually quick and clear, grows worse
and worse. He had much on his mind — and lucky he was if he
could turn an honest penny letting Isaac Clemens use his shop,
no matter what his politics were.

To reach Joseph Warren's house, which was the Whig headquarters as much as the Province House was of the officers and
Tories, he would almost pass the shop and dwelling of his friend,

Isaiah Thomas. Here that night he would find the impassioned young printer hurriedly, secretly packing his little press, his few founts of type, the precious, scarce paper, preparing for flight. He had already sent two children (whose paternity he never could be sure of) and his worthless wife to Watertown. There was no more time to lose, for he had it on good authority that General Gage was going to seize his press, and hold him for high treason. Some way, the next night, he would smuggle out his equipment and himself and go on printing until he died. Doctor Young had long ago left Boston. Doctor Church had, as we know now, nothing to fear. Both Adamses were out of town, as was John Hancock. Josiah Quincy was in England. Will Molineaux dead. James Otis crazy. Of the principal leaders only Joseph Warren, risking life itself, stuck it out to the very end in Boston. It was to him and to his house Paul Revere would turn with news and schemes.

That Saturday night it was decided between them that Paul Revere should next day warn Sam Adams and John Hancock (whom they knew — but the British did not — to be stopping at Hancock's relatives, the Clarks, at Lexington) that a sortie was expected and it was likely they would be picked up. Also the stores at Concord were a probable object. These must now be hidden.

On Sunday, probably starting before light, Paul Revere made this trip seemingly without undue haste or incident. He found the statesmen pleasantly ensconced at the parsonage close by Lexington Green. The Provincial Congress, which had been sitting at Concord, had adjourned the day before, not to meet until the middle of May. It was impossible for the Boston delegates to return to Boston, and very shortly they must start to Philadelphia for the Second Continental Congress, where they and John Adams represented Massachusetts. The Clark house was practically another home to John Hancock. It had been built by his grandfather, the Reverend John Hancock. Uncle Thomas, after he had made money, had added the new part as a present to his father and mother. Mrs. Clark was John's cousin. The Reverend Jonas Clark was a heavy man in his middle fifties. He had a bulldog jaw and looks in his silhouette to have been able to hold his own even with the imposing collection of week-end guests which the uncertainty of the time and kinship had landed down upon him.

Aunt Lydia, who looks much more like a major of Marines than

Pitcairn, had, the day before, driven out in the chariot her husband
had so thoughtfully ordered to meet her requirements. She always kept a protuberant eye on John's love life, keeping him firmly
in one hand and Miss Dolly in the other. Probably she did not
dare leave Miss Dolly behind her — listening to Lord Percy's
arresting voice as he drilled his men at dawn. She was going to
make this match if it killed her — as it seems to have done. John
Hancock was harassed enough with his public life without Aunt
Lydia bringing out Miss Dolly to torment him in private, but there
they both were.

So he had an aunt, a sweetheart, horses, chaise, chariot, a clerk
named John Lowell, and a large trunk. This trunk had been made
to fit the chaise in which he and Sam Adams would soon be driving
in state to Philadelphia. It contained papers so treasonable they
must not fall into the British hands, and as it was large enough
to need two men to carry, it probably contained a number of
choice items from the famous Hancock wardrobe. Seemingly the
trunk and the clerk were both put up at near-by Buckman's Tavern.
John Hancock was never the man to travel light.

Sam Adams, who was as underattended as his companion was
overattended, never needed anything but a pen, ink, and paper.
As crisis followed crisis, his spirits, always good, rose. His hands
might shake from palsy, but not from fear. He faced the gathering
storm clouds without qualms, without doubts. America should be
entirely free. To this end he had devoted his life, he had made
mountains from molehills. He had used every trick known to
politicians and written magnificently. He firmly believed the great
end he saw in sight justified any means. For himself he asked
nothing, only the public good. Once free of English rule, he believed a state of Spartan simplicity, virtue, and honor would arise.
Automatically the virtues of 'the old Puritans' would come to the
top. He was to be bitterly disillusioned. Year after year he had
waited very patiently. If blood must be shed, very well, let it be
shed. A great nation was struggling to birth.

So the statesmen got their warning and Paul Revere may have
had a very good chance to watch that three-cornered courtship or
Sam Adams' mounting confidence. He may have ridden over to
Concord himself, for the town was warned that day. Ox wagons
and carts and all the men and boys in the village went to work re-

moving the stores, hiding cannon, disguising flour, carrying sacks
of bullets into the swamps. For miles about word went to the
minute men to keep their guns in their hands and be ready to
march at a moment's notice.

Paul Revere came back to Boston by way of Charlestown, so he
seems to have started and returned from this trip by the boat he
kept hidden in North Boston. At Charlestown he hunted up
William Conant, a prominent citizen, high in military circles, and
a Son of Liberty. From here, over the broad mouth of the Charles,
Boston and its steeples are plainly visible. Highest of all is the
spire of Christ. That evening Revere told Colonel Conant 'that
if the British went out by water we would show two lanterns in the
North Church steeple — and if by land one as a signal, for we were
apprehensive it would be difficult to cross the Charles or get over
Boston Neck.'

He would himself attempt to reach Charlestown and give more
detailed account of the British plans if — or rather when — the
troops marched. It might be impossible. Watch, then, for the
lanterns in the spire.

So once more he returned to Boston.

# VII

## 1 7 7 5

As ROBERT NEWMAN hangs the lanterns, PAUL REVERE crosses to CHARLESTOWN. HE carries the alarum to LEXINGTON. The BRITISH capture him, set him free, and he returns to JOHN HANCOCK and SAM ADAMS. HE saves HANCOCK's trunk for him and goes into CAMBRIDGE. He risks a trip into BOSTON. His family finally succeed in getting a pass. By MAY he is printing money. By JUNE the battle of BUNKER HILL is fought. GENERAL WASHINGTON catches DOCTOR CHURCH red-handed.

Colonel Smith and Major Pitcairn at Concord. Drawn by Ralph Earl. Engraved by Amos Doolittle, 1775. American Antiquarian Society.

Clark's Wharf was second only to Long Wharf in the eighteenth century. This enlarged detail from the Burgis-Price view of Boston does not show the warehouses, sail lofts, etc., that covered the wharf. The Reveres, father and son, rented a house at the head of Clark's Wharf for at least sixteen years and Paul Revere had his goldsmith's shop here even after he moved a block inland to North Square. Doctor Clark's ledgers show that sometimes Paul paid his rent with enamelled rings, sometimes with rum and fish. The Clarks sold this wharf to the Hancocks. It was here John Hancock's *Liberty* was seized for smuggling.

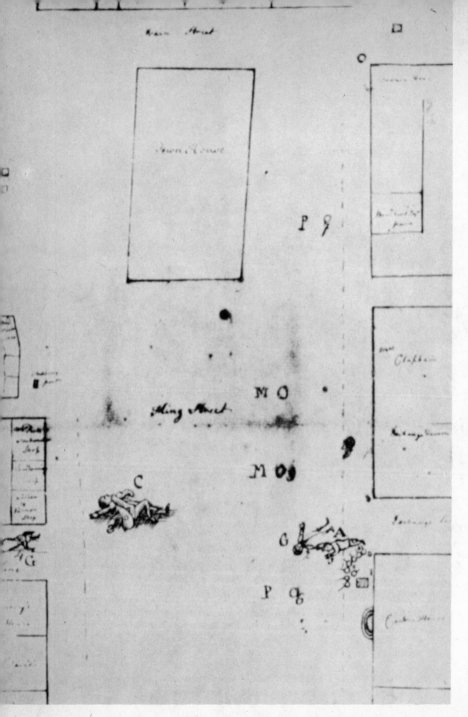

This pen-and-ink diagram of the Boston Massacre was drawn by Revere to be used in the trial of the British soldiers. It is very accurate.

Revere's famous print of the Massacre (based on an engraving by Henry Pelham) shows not what happened on that night of the fifth of March, 1770, but what the Whig political machine wished people to believe. It was good propaganda.

Just before the Battle of Lexington, shown here, Revere was in an upper chamber of Buckman's Tavern (6) rescuing Hancock's trunk. He saw the British approach from 'behinde the Meeting House.'(5)

# I

MONDAY came taut and overstrung. At the Province House General Gage was constantly in conference with his officers. Colonel Smith was to command the eight hundred men. Pitcairn himself was to go as second in command, serving as a volunteer. Lord Percy was to bring up reserves if necessary. General Gage 'did not think the damned rebels would ... take up arms against his Majesty's Troops.' He was confident the sortie could be made, the stores destroyed, and his men brought back to Boston before any alarm roused the 'countrymen' to action. Only two people were told the destination of the regulars — Lord Percy and Gage's own wife.

Tuesday was even tenser. The grenadiers and light infantry companies of the various regiments were ordered to prepare to march that night. Some of these men were billeted in private houses, or their women worked as servants. It was impossible to keep it a secret that they were to report for active duty. For instance, a Mrs. Stedman had hired as a housemaid the wife of one of the soldiers. As the sergeant went about rounding up his men, he could not find the husband, Gibson. He went to Mrs. Stedman and asked her to tell the man, if he turned up at her house, 'he was to report himself at eight o'clock at the bottom of the Common, equipped for an expedition.' Mrs. Stedman immediately sent word to Doctor Church. When Gibson arrived, she told him to prepare for the march, and 'Oh, Gibson,' she said, 'what are you going to do?'

'Ah, Madam, I know as little as you do. I only know that I must go.'

So in one way or another it might be guessed that the British were about to march. But where? Somehow Gage's secret was betrayed.

On Tuesday afternoon Gage sent out a group of picked officers. It was for them to block the roads leading towards Concord so no rebel express could ride through and warn the town. They were to pretend to be merely a pleasure party riding out to Cambridge for a dinner in the country. Their arms would be hidden by their cloaks. If questioned closely, they could admit that they were out after their own deserters. At Cambridge some of these men would turn towards Charlestown and after dark hide in the bushes to waylay any messenger who might cross the river and try to reach Concord by that route. The other officers were to do their intercepting closer to Concord. This latter is the most famous of the two groups. They were under Major Edward Mitchell. With him were Captain Lumm, Captain Cochrane, Lieutenant Grant, and one other officer — or perhaps the 'sarjant' that Revere noticed. The British accounts say that all these men were officers, the Yankees call them sometimes officers and sometimes officers and their servants. These men knew Paul Revere's name, but not his face. Of these two nets spread out to catch him or any other man who attempted to go through that night, Paul Revere knew nothing. Of the third precaution all Boston knew. The man-of-war *Somerset* was moved into the very mouth of the Charles River, commanding the expanse of water any boat headed for Charlestown must cross.

The officers must have known before they left Tuesday afternoon what was their destination. Hanging about the stable, making sure for themselves that their horses were properly saddled and in top condition, talking happily about 'the hell to pay tomorrow,' it is likely they are the ones who let slip Gage's plans. For a groom at the Province House is said to have overheard the officers' talk. He confided in a friend of his, a fellow hostler at a near-by stable. This second boy (who had pretended to be a supporter of the Crown) then ran to Paul Revere. There was hell to pay on Wednesday and Concord was the objective.

'You are the third person who has brought me the same information,' Paul Revere said, and he cautioned the boy not to say anything to anyone else. But even as the web of Paul Revere's and

Joseph Warren's spy system closed about Gage's secret, the British officers were, with a pretence at nonchalance, but causing much excitement wherever they went, preparing to take their stations along the country roads to ensnare Paul Revere.

At dusk, Lord Percy left General Gage at the Province House and went quietly to the Common, where the boats were drawn up and already troops lined up waiting to embark. The townspeople stood about watching these preparations. The Earl was not recognized and listened to their comments. He heard a voice say: 'The British troops have marched, but will miss their aim.'

'What aim?' asked Percy.

'Why, the cannon at Concord.'

Percy went back to Gage. In some way their secret was known. The story is that Gage believed it was his American wife who had betrayed him, she being, as an early historian has it, 'unequally yoked in point of politics' to her famous husband. This version seems to be gossip started by Gage's own officers, who did not like him and wanted to throw suspicion upon him and his wife.

At Joseph Warren's, the plans were perfected. As soon as it was definitely known whether the British went by land or sea, Robert Newman would be notified and the lanterns in Christ's[27] hung. This he had already agreed to do. He was twenty-three at the time. His older brother was organist at Christ's and he was sexton. He did not like the work, but had taken the job 'because,' as he said, 'times are so hard.' Not only did he have the keys to the church, but lived just across the street from it. The only drawback was that his mother's house was full of British officers billeted on the family.

These lanterns would give the warning, but no detail, of the expedition. Farther up stream the British boats would be ferrying over the troops. There was a chance Paul Revere could get past the *Somerset* — but only a chance. He was ready to take it.

William Dawes, the young cordwainer, would attempt to ride out through the British sentries on the Neck. He lived near North Square and his father was a silversmith. Undoubtedly Revere knew him well. He had played no conspicuous part in the brewing revolution, as had Revere, and was not a marked man, although he had recently knocked down a soldier for insulting his pretty wife. In previous years he had carried letters for the Salisbury

family. 'Billy' Dawes was a born actor. Later, during the siege of
Boston, he used to go in and out almost at will, disguised as a
drunken farmer, thoroughly enjoying himself and the risks he took.
In the portrait painted of him in middle age, when he could write
Major in front of his name and the proud word 'merchant' after
it, he is still a comical-looking fellow, with his close-set eyes, long
nose, and humorous mouth. If anyone could allay suspicion of
the sentries, act the part of an inebriated farmer or a half-witted
bumpkin, it would be Billy Dawes. Paul Revere looked as clever
as he was. Billy Dawes did not. He would have farther to go than
Revere and about an equally poor chance of getting through.
He passed the gates by pretending great innocence and with the
connivance of a British soldier.

Now that the troops were actually at the bottom of the Common,
Joseph Warren started Billy Dawes over the Neck and sent for
Paul Revere. The time had come.

'About ten o'clock Dr Warren sent in great haste for me, and
begged that I would immediately set off for Lexington, where
Messre. Hancock and Adams were, and acquaint them of the
movement, and that it was thought they were the objects. When
I got to Dr Warren's house, I found he had sent an express by
land to Lexington, — a Mr William Dawes.' As is often pointed
out, Paul Revere never got to Concord, it is noteworthy that it
was only Lexington he originally started out to warn. Yet he
definitely had Concord in mind as well.[28]

The two friends parted. When, if ever, they would meet
again they could not know. Joseph Warren would chance staying
inside the lines a little longer for the sake of the information he
might pick up. But any moment he might hear the rap on his door
and see a corporal's guard, an officer with the warrant for his
arrest in his hand — wanted in London for treason. Paul Revere
also risked all he had and life as well. General Gage had handled
the insurrection thus far with kid gloves, but no country has ever
hesitated to drop with a bullet, if necessary, a man caught exciting
to armed revolt.

First Paul sought out Robert Newman, who, knowing that it
might be awkward for a prominent Son of Liberty and express
rider to rap at his mother's door and call him out, had pretended to go to bed early, leaving the officers in the living-rooms,

then slipped out an upper window, over a roof, and was already in the dark street waiting for any orders. One of the vestrymen at Christ's, John Pulling,[29] went with Newman, as probably did Revere's neighbor, Thomas Barnard. The door was locked after him and the guard stood in the street as the young fellow took the lanterns from the closet and softly mounted the wooden stairs Paul Revere's feet had once known so well. Higher and higher, feeling his way in the darkness, he climbed, past the eight great bells, silent in the bell loft, until he came to the highest window of the belfry. To the north he could see, over the shoulder of Copp's Hill, the mouth of the Charles, the black hull of the *Somerset*, the glimmer of her riding lights. Beyond was Charlestown, and there he knew men were waiting, watching for his signal. He lit the lanterns, hung them, and felt his way back to the floor of the church. Probably Newman displayed his lanterns for a moment only. He certainly could not wish to warn the *Somerset*. They were out by the time Paul Revere had crossed into Charlestown. In spite of the poem, they were not a signal to Paul Revere, but from him. The Sunday before he had told Colonel Conant to watch for them. When the men in Charlestown saw 'a glimmer and then a gleam of light,' Paul Revere was still in Boston.

Something must have happened in the street while Newman was inside, for he dared not leave by the way he had come. Instead he climbed out of a window at the rear of the church, circled about, and entered his mother's house by the roofs and the upper window. Lying awake, he might hear below him the laughter of the officers over their cards. That much of the deed was done.

Having started Robert Newman on his ascent to fame, Paul Revere went to his own house in North Square. In all directions, marching in full battle gear, small groups of redcoats were leaving their barracks and billets, heading for the Common. Troops were lined up in North Square. No one was allowed to enter it or leave. Somehow Paul Revere got through them. He put on his short surtout and heavy riding boots. Perhaps Rachel tried to argue him out of this dangerous ride, for he seems to have been curiously absent-minded for so competent a man. He forgot two things. His spurs and some cloth with which to muffle the oars of his row-boat. So he left the house, and his dog followed him.

Joshua Bentley, a boatbuilder, and Thomas Richardson were

ready to row him across. He picked them up at some prearranged place and the three started for the part of North Boston where that winter Paul Revere had kept his boat·hidden. Then the matter of muffling the oars came up. None of them wished to return to his own house, but one of them had a girl friend. He gave a peculiar whistle outside her window, at the corner of North and North Centre Streets. The window went up. There was a whispered conversation and a flannel petticoat was tossed down. Revere told his children that it was still warm when they got it. Then Revere remembered his spurs. He wrote a note to Rachel, tied it to his dog's collar. Soon the dog was back again with the spurs. This story he also told his children, but perhaps only to amuse them. So at last he was booted and spurred, but a long way yet from being ready to ride.[30]

The *Somerset* blocked the shortest route, forcing them to keep rather well out to sea. She was a great frigate of sixty-four guns and was stationed there for but one purpose — to keep men like Paul Revere in Boston. A cry to heave to or even a spatter of shot was expected. Beyond her, upstream, the British boats were going back and forth already, carrying the regulars to Cambridge.

All winter it had been abnormally warm and spring had come almost a month ahead of itself. Fruit trees were in blossom; the fields already ploughed. That night, however, was chill, and 'it was young flood, the ship was winding and the moon was rising,' as Paul Revere noticed. The muffled oars softly eased his little rowboat closer and closer to the Charlestown side. There had been neither hail nor shot from the *Somerset*. So he leaped to dry land close to the old Battery. Richardson and Bentley had done their work. Revere went on alone.

At Colonel Conant's he found a group waiting for him. Had they seen his signals? They had. He told them 'what was acting' and learned to his surprise that the roads towards Cambridge and on to Concord were already patrolled by British officers who had left Boston in the afternoon.

Richard Devens, of the Committee of Safety, said he had left Menotomy in his chaise around sunset. And he had seen 'a great number of B.O. [British officers] and their servants on horseback.' As they were behaving in a suspiciously nonchalant manner and had asked where 'Clark's tavern was,' Devens had sent word to the Clark parsonage. It might be they were out to arrest the two rebel chiefs housed there. He knew this messenger might be picked up, as he was. Paul Revere himself might have better luck. He would need a good horse to slip through the cordon. Probably he had as fine a mount as the luxurious town of Charlestown could produce. John Larkin was one of the wealthiest citizens. It was his best horse that was now turned over to Revere. Twenty-three years later, he gratefully remembered how good, how 'very good,' was this Larkin horse. It would be slender and nervous in the Yankee manner, small by modern standards, surefooted, tireless. Now for the remainder of the night Revere's success, perhaps his life and the lives of others, would depend upon this horse. He would adjust the stirrups carefully to his own length, test with a forefinger the snugness of the girths. They must be tight, but not binding. The bit must hang exactly right. In that unhurried moment before mounting, he could measure the courage and stamina of his companion, catch the flash of white in the wild, soft eye, note the impatient stamp of the small hooves, feel under his hand the swelling of muscle along the neck, the strength in withers and loin, his touch and voice assuring the sensitive animal that he was his friend.

And now it was eleven o'clock. Only an hour before, he had stood in Joseph Warren's parlor knowing that the time had come. Then, by the bright cold moonlight everyone noticed that night, he swung to the saddle. Colonel Conant, Richard Devens, the light from the open door, were left behind. He eventually rode about twelve miles to get to Lexington and Concord was six miles farther on. Probably he would set a pace which he believed would last him through. With the hundreds of miles he had ridden the last few years, he would be able to judge well. Nor would he wish to fling himself headlong into any trap set for him by that advance guard of officers Devens had warned him of, with a jaded mount. For such an emergency his horse must have an extra spurt of speed left in him. That he rode the Larkin horse with more care than he does on sugar boxes, American Legion posters, copper advertisements, and all known pictures and statues is proved by the excellent condition the animal was in five hours later.

So away, down the moonlit road, goes Paul Revere and the Larkin horse, galloping into history, art, editorials, folklore, poetry;

the beat of those hooves never to be forgotten. The man, his bold, dark face bent, his hands light on the reins, his body giving to the flowing rhythm beneath him, becoming, as it were, something greater than himself — not merely one man riding one horse on a certain lonely night of long ago, but a symbol to which his countrymen can yet turn.

Paul Revere had started on a ride which, in a way, has never ended.


## II


CHARLESTOWN like Boston was a promontory attached to the mainland by a slender neck. Paul Revere rode over this neck. The Charles River was on his left and the Mystic upon his right. He was now in a sparsely settled, desolate stretch of salt marsh, moors, clay-pits, and scrub. In his day this was the 'common' of Charlestown and now is Somerville. Of the two roads traversing this dreary expanse, he took the one to his left which led directly into Cambridge and was the shortest way to Lexington. Only two days before he had travelled this road and knew it well.

So he rode on through the moonlight and the delicate shadows of spring trees and came to the gibbet where for twenty years Mark had hung in chains, as a horrifying warning to any other slaves who might plan insurrection against their masters. For some reason, that caused comment at the time, Mark had kept surprisingly well, but surely by now little could have been left of him but a few old bones rattling about at the bottom of his iron cage. Paul Revere noted and remembered that he reached the spot 'where Mark was hung in chains.' The memory of Mark may have quickened his blood, taken his thoughts back to Clark's Wharf, the apothecary shop, black Robin in his blue coat and wig. And Phillis, too.

They had burned her. These two had died for petty treason. He himself rode upon high treason — armed insurrection against the King. The penalties which England could then legally inflict for high treason included the barbarous drawing and quartering. Mark's lonely gibbet might well pull his thoughts back into his youth — or forward into an unpredictable future. Luckily for him it did not make him absent-minded.

'The moon shone bright,' he remembered. 'I had got almost over Charlestown Common towards Cambridge when I saw two Officers on Horseback, standing under the shade of a Tree, in a narrow part of the roade. I was near enough to see their Holsters & cockades. One of them started his horse towards me and the other up the road, as I supposed to head me should I escape the first. I turned my horse short about, and rid upon a full gallop for Mistick Road.' In this brief, slippery, cross-country race the heavier British charger (handsome enough for parade) was no match for the light-footed Yankee horse. Out of the tail of his eye Paul Revere could see how he was outdistancing his pursuer in three hundred yards. And next the clumsy animal had 'got into a clay-pond.' No shots were fired and, if any words were spoken, Paul Revere did not record them.

As the road to Cambridge was blocked, he quickly came down on that other road (now Broadway), followed the Mystic River, which he crossed, and entered Medford over a plank bridge. Here 'I awaked the Captain of the minute men: and after that I alarumed almost every house till I got to Lexington.'

Bells rang, drums beat — 'The regulars are out!' Women gathered children and silver and fled to swamps. Men seized muskets and powder-horns. Other men mounted and rode off to other towns to carry the warning — 'The regulars are out.' 'The horror of that midnight cry' was not quickly forgotten in Middlesex County.

Paul Revere recrossed the Mystic, went through Menotomy (as Arlington was called at that time — Lieutenant Sutherland calls it 'Anatomy'), and so was back on the route he had planned to take before the officers forced him to détour. Cambridge, now behind him, did not need any express rider to tell them the British had marched. Colonel Smith had already landed his men at Phipps' farm in East Cambridge. With that curious disregard for the

privates' comfort and health so many of the British officers showed,
he left his men drawn up and shivering until two o'clock. They
had waded up to their middles in salt water to get ashore. If only
they had marched immediately, they would have been in Lexington
and Concord before any sizable force could have been raised to
oppose them.

With these troops General Gage had sent his favorite spy, John
Howe. The young fellow crossed with the troops to Cambridge,
changed into his 'Yankee dress,' was given a 'country horse,' and
told to deliver letters to certain Tories in Malden, Lynn, Salem,
and Marblehead.

Close upon midnight Paul Revere came into Lexington. And
here was the meeting house casting its moonstruck shadow across
the Green where so soon men were to die. Close by it was Buckman
Tavern from which he might have heard the voices of men, laughter
even, or the clink of tankards. Captain Parker had called out the
local minute men that afternoon when word first came that a
handful of unexplainable British officers were abroad and might
be after Adams and Hancock. It does not seem to have been
known in Lexington that a considerable force of the regulars were
coming until Revere arrived. As it was cold standing about outdoors, the militiamen had retired to Buckman's. The Yankee
soldier had as strong a regard for his own comfort as the British
officers had disregard for their men. Colonel Smith's forces freezing
in their disciplined ranks in the salt marshes of East Cambridge,
and Captain Parker's men so cozy and undisciplined at the same
moment at Buckman's, make a characteristic contrast.

Paul Revere went straight to the Clark parsonage. There he
found Sergeant Munroe and seven men guarding the house.
Revere demanded to be admitted, in so loud a voice the sergeant
reproved him. The ladies and gentlemen had gone to bed and had
'requested not to be disturbed by any noise that night' (this sounds
more like Hancock than Adams).

'Noise,' shouted Revere. 'You'll have noise enough before long!
The Regulars are out.'

He knocked loudly on the door.

The Reverend Mr. Clark opened a window and thrust out his
granite head. Paul Revere demanded to see John Hancock. But
the clergyman, 'ever deliberate and watchful,' not recognizing the

man in the dark, said he could not be admitting strangers at that
time of night without knowing who they were and what they
wanted. John Hancock had 'retired to rest, but not to sleep.'
He recognized Revere's voice.

'Come in, Revere, we are not afraid of *you*.'

So he went in and told his story. It was not merely a patrol of
British officers that was out this night, but probably 'over a thousand
light troops.' He had seen them crossing the Charles at ten. They
might be here any moment now. There was no doubt but their
destination was Lexington to pick up the rebel leaders, and Concord
for the stores. This was thundering news and all was commotion.
John Hancock would have on the finest of silk banians, moroccan
slippers — elegant even when thus rudely summoned. Aunt Lydia
would look even grimmer than ever with her nightclothes showing
below the hastily thrown cloak. There was the minister and his
wife. We can count on Miss Dolly to be pert and enchanting even
if in bare feet. Sam Adams would be cheerful, self-contained,
quick-witted, although reduced to a night rail.

Paul Revere asked for William Dawes, but he had not yet arrived. Although Dawes had four miles farther to ride, he had
started earlier, nor had his departure been delayed by seeing about
lanterns and the slow rowboat ride across the Charles River, nor
did he have the cordon of British officers to penetrate.

John Hancock was demanding his sword and gun. He was
determined to take his place with the minute men if they opposed
the march of the British. Sam Adams tried to persuade him against
such foolishness. These two men had just been elected Massachusetts delegates to the Second Continental Congress in Philadelphia. They argued about the matter, and then, half an hour
after Revere, Dawes came in.

The two expresses ate and drank, and once more mounted. The
countryside as well as Hancock and Adams had been warned.
Three days before, Revere had got word to Concord that the British
might seize the stores there and by now they were pretty well
hidden. However, the two men decided to go over to Concord,
alarming the minute men as they went.

As they moved out of Lexington, they were joined by Samuel
Prescott, a young doctor from Concord, who had been over to
Lexington courting a Miss Millikan. As it was now after one

o'clock, he was hardly keeping the early hours credited to our forebears. When he heard what was happening, he offered to ride
with them, for being a local man and a high Son of Liberty, he
pointed out that people would 'give more credit' to what he said
than to strangers. Paul Revere says:

> ... when we had got about half way from Lexington to Concord,
> the other two, stopped at a House to awake the man. I kept along.
> when I had got about 200 yards ahead of them, I saw two officers
> under a tree as before, [not far from Hartwell Farm, North Lincoln.]
> I immediately called to my company to come up, saying here was
> two of them. (for I had told them what Mr. Devens told me, and of
> my being stopped) in an instant I saw four officers, who rode up to
> me, with their pistols in their hands & said G — D d — m you stop,
> if you go an inch further you are a dead Man. Immeditly Mr. Pres-
> cot came up he turned the butt of his whipp we attempted to git thro
> them, but they kept before us, and swore if we did not turn into that
> pasture, they would blow our brains out. They had placed them-
> selves opposite a pair of Barrs, and had taken the Barrs down. They
> forced us in. The Doctor jumped his horse over a low stone wall, and
> got to Concord. I observed a wood at a small distance and made
> for that intending when I gained that to jump my Horse & run afoot,
> just as I reached it out started six officers, siesed my bridle, put their
> pistols to my Breast, ordered me to dismount, which I did. One of
> them, who appeared to have command there, and much of a Gentle-
> man. asked where I came from; I told him. he asked what time I
> left it; I told him, he seemed much supprised, He said Sir may I
> crave your name? I answered my name is Revere. What said he
> Paul Revere? I answered yes; the others abused me much; but he
> told me not to be afraid, no one should hurt me. I told him they
> would miss their Aim. [This seems to have been a common catch-
> phrase that night.] He said they should not, they were only after
> some Deserters they expected down the Road. I told them I knew
> better, I knew what they were after; that I had alarumed the country
> all the way up, that their Boats had catch'd aground, and I should
> have 500 men there soon; one of them said they had 1500 coming.
> ... Major Mitchel of the 5th Reg't clap'd a pistol to my head and
> said if I did not tell the truth, he would blow my brains out. ...
> I gave him much the same answers; after he and two more had spoke
> together in a low voice he then ordered me to mount, and the Major
> rode up to me and took the reins. G — d sir you are not to ride with
> reins I assure you; and gave them to the officer on my right to lead me.

I asked him to let me have the reins & I would not run from him, he said he would not trust me. He then Ordered 4 men out of the Bushes, and to mount their horses they were country men which they had stopped who were going home; they ordered us to march. He came up to me and said 'We are now going towards your friends, and if you attempt to run, or we are insulted, we will blow your Brains out.' I told him he might do as he pleased.

Major Mitchell had reason to worry. They must join Colonel Smith's columns before the country was aroused and they themselves were cut off. He also wished to warn Colonel Smith that, in spite of General Gage's confidence that the 'damned rebels' would not fight, it looked to him as though they would. He would now ride as fast as he could go to join the British marching out. There was no more time to bother with prisoners.

Although he had caught one of the three riders headed for Lexington, two had escaped him.

William Dawes (always the actor) made his dash for freedom, flapping his leather breeches and yelling, 'Haloo, boys, I've got two of 'em.' But he pulled up his horse so short, he not only fell off, but lost his watch, and presumably his horse as well. A few days later, he retraced his steps and found the watch. It was only Doctor Prescott who got through to Concord that night.

The British officers formed a circle about Paul Revere and the four countrymen. The little cavalcade 'rid down towards Lexington, a pretty smart pace. I was often insulted by the officers calling me dammed Rebel, etc. etc. The officer who led me said I was in a d—m—d critical situation. I told him I was sensable of it. After we had got about a mile. I was given to the Sarjant to lead, who was Ordered to take out his pistol and if I should run to execute the Major's sentance.'

There was the soft thudding of horses' hooves, the clink of bits, spur-chains, military accoutrement. So they rode through the chilly silence of those darkest hours before the dawn. Sometimes at such an hour a cock will crow, a watchdog bark. And now there came another sound, for 'when we got within about half a mile of Lexington Meeting house we heard a gun fired. The Major asked me what that was for. I told him to alarm the country.'

There was no time to lose. Major Mitchell ordered the girths and bridles on the four countrymen's horses to be cut and the

horses to be driven off. These men might now go home as best
they might on foot. Paul asked the Major to dismiss him too. At
first he would not, but admitted he could not 'carry me let the
consequence be what it will.' More alarm guns were heard from
Lexington. 'The Major ordered us to a halt he asked me how far
it was to Cambridge and many more questions which I answered.
He then asked the Sarjant, if his horse was tired, he said yes;'
Paul Revere noticed in the dark it was a small horse. 'he Ordered
him to take my horse. I dismounted, the Sarjant mounted my
horse, they cutt the Bridle and Saddle off the Sarjant's horse &
they told me they should make use of my horse for the night and
rode off down the road.'

Paul Revere saw the last of the 'good' Larkin horse with a
British grenadier sergeant on top of him. Although the Major
promised to make use of it for only the one night, it disappeared
completely into the British army and that was the end of him.

## III

THE mounted patrol drifted away.
The four countrymen had already departed. Revere was alone.
Either Billy Dawes or Doctor Prescott would surely get through to
Concord. As he was less than a mile from Lexington, he decided
to look in on Hancock and Adams and find out, as he would say,
'what was acting.' Fearing to be picked up again, he left the road
and made his way cross-lots over stone walls and pastures. The
riding boots of the period were amazingly heavy once you were
dismounted, with spurs making it almost impossible to walk over
rough ground without tripping. He did not know the environs of
Lexington, but when he found himself in a graveyard, stumbling
over the stones, he knew the parsonage was close at hand.

At the Jonas Clarks' the same argument was going on that he

had left perhaps an hour before. Hancock was still anxious to take
his place with the armed farmers who would challenge the movements of the regulars. 'Mr. H. was all night cleaning his gun and
sword, and putting his accoutrements in order, and was determined
to go out to the plain by the meeting-house where the battle was,
to fight with the men who had collected,' but who (Miss Dolly
remembered) 'were but partially provided with arms, and those
they had were in most miserable order'; and it was with very great
difficulty that he was dissuaded from it by Mr. Clark and Mr.
Adams. The latter, clapping him on the shoulder, said to him
'that it is not our business; we belong to the cabinet; It was not
till break of day that Mr. H. could be persuaded that it was im-
proper for him to expose himself against such a powerful force.'

And here, in the confusion of that argument, the question rises,
Why did the minute men form their lines that morning on Lexington Green? They were too few to stop the advance of the regulars.
Captain Parker himself said that they had met together merely
'to consult what to do, and concluded not to be discovered nor
meddle, nor make with regular troops unless they should insult or
molest us.' If they had not wished to be discovered, they would
have stayed in Buckman's Tavern — well out of view of the marching British. Once lined up in belligerent attitudes on the Green,
they could not have expected to escape insult or molestation.
Captain Parker was an experienced soldier. But 'the blood shed
by Preston's men in King Street had been ably used by Adams to
solidify the popular cause; and did he feel that the time had come
to draw once more the British fire?' as Harold Murdock asks.
Was it indeed Sam Adams' wish to have a few more innocent victims? It is a pity that Miss Dolly did not give a fuller account of
the long wrangle that went on between these two members of 'the
cabinet,' as every moment the British drew nearer. Paul Revere
does not mention it.

But at last a chaise was brought round. Miss Dolly and Aunt
Lydia decided to stay where they were. Perhaps even now John
Hancock was arguing with his girl. She remembered (when an
old woman) that she was determined that night to go to her father
in Boston and her fiancé said:

' "No Madam you shall not return as long as there is a British
bayonet left in Boston." '

' "Recollect Mr. Hancock, I am not under your control yet. I shall go to my father tomorrow" '; and so on and so forth, for 'at that time I should have been very glad to have got rid of him.'

Paul Revere says that Hancock and Adams 'concluded to go from that house towards Woburn. I went with them.' This house where they first sought shelter was then in Woburn but later in Burlington. It was owned by Madam Jones — the widow of a clergyman. But soon Revere's curiosity, restlessness, or patriotism got the better of him. He and Hancock's clerk, John Lowell, returned to Lexington. Reports were coming in fast: The British had not marched. The British are almost here. The British even this moment are 'coming up the rocks.' Lowell asked Revere to go with him to Buckman's Tavern and help him carry away the trunk containing Hancock's papers. He did not wish them to fall into British hands. Revere went.[31]

And now the night was over. The strange, unearthly, grey, and dewy hour of dawn. The belfry bell still tolling, the rub-a-dub of William Diamond's drum called the minute men to take their historic places. Revere crossed the Green, where in the unreal light of dawn some fifty or sixty men, farmers mostly and dressed as such, were forming ranks. Women and children and others stood at open doors and windows to gaze. Was it true? Was it these men, their sons, fathers, husbands, brothers, friends, who would oppose the march of the British? The King had forbidden all such military organizations as these. Any moment now the King's regulars would be upon them. This handful could not give battle — only serve as martyrs. Some of the minute men preferred to live and fight another day, but even as these 'poltroons' dropped out of the ranks, more and more men took their places, lining up between the meeting house and Buckman's Tavern. Revere silently passed through them.

He and Lowell found Hancock's trunk in an upper chamber at the tavern. And from that window Revere looked down 'and saw the British very near upon a full march.' Here were the orderly scarlet ranks of the marching grenadiers, the glitter of the just-risen sun glowing on pipeclayed baldrics, brass buttons, gold lace, and satin coats of horses, steel bayonets. All as fine and orderly as a pack of playing cards — at least from the waist up. They may have been a bit bedraggled from there down, after their struggles in the salt marsh of East Cambridge. The officer in command was Revere's North Square neighbor of the last year — 'firery and profane,' 'aminable and galant,' Major Pitcairn himself. That round and wide-eyed face of his, the way he sat his horse, a trick of turning his head, addressing his men, would all be very familiar to Revere. He must have been amazed to see this Major of Marines. It seems the Major had gone as a volunteer. Near him was Major Mitchell and his officers — perhaps one of them on the Larkin horse.

Colonel Smith had landed his men as quietly as he could, but kept them standing around until two in the morning, which was about the time Paul Revere was captured. They moved rapidly into Cambridge proper without drums, ensigns or breakfast.

When Major Mitchell had joined the main body of troops, the soldiers gathered about him to hear his story. It was 'between 3 & 4 in the morning,' Lieutenant Sutherland says, 'he told us the whole country was Alarmed & had Galloped for their lives, or words to that purpose, that they had taken Paul Revierre but was obliged to lett him go after having cutt his girths and Stirrups.' Richard Pope, who seems to have been a non-commissioned officer, also stood about listening to Major Mitchell's account, 'They took three prisoners, one the noted Paul Revere, who assured them that the country was alarmed; that he saw the embarkation, which was then publick. This information was soon after confirmed by Firing of alarum guns, the bells rang, and drums beat to Arms in concord, and were answered by all the villages Round.'

Colonel Smith on Mitchell's advice immediately sent back to General Gage for Percy and the eight hundred men held as reinforcements, for it looked like bloody work ahead. He also ordered Major Pitcairn to go ahead quickly with six light companies and seize the two bridges at Concord. The patrolling officers went back over the road they had just galloped down 'for their lives', probably acting as guides.

So it was Pitcairn, the British officers, and these six companies Paul Revere now saw from the upper window of Buckman's Tavern. What would happen when this orderly flood of scarlet and steel met the frail lines on the Green was not his business. His was to rescue John Hancock's trunk.

He and John Lowell carried it through the militiamen, who waited for they hardly knew what, stonily staring at the approaching redcoats. At one hundred and fifty feet the regulars came to a smart halt. Pitcairn himself and at least two officers galloped towards the provincials to disband them with words — if possible.

In this pause Revere passed close to Captain Parker, a good man already close to his fatal sickness. He heard him say, 'Let the troops pass by and don't molest them without they begin first,' and then Revere was off the Green. 'A gun was fired. I heard the report and turned my head,' but by then some shed or shrub cut off his view of the minute men. He could only see the regulars: 'and saw smoke in front of the troops, they immediately gave a great shout, ran a few paces and then the whole fired.' But he went on with Hancock's trunk, towards the Clark parsonage, with that simple absorption in what was to be done at the moment which characterizes the whole man. Embattled farmers might stand and shots fired that would be heard round the world. He gave them one glance and went on with his job. How it began, who fired the first shot, he does not pretend to know. Nor did he hear Major Pitcairn's famous 'Disperse ye rebels, ye villians, disperse . . . Lay down your arms. Why dont ye lay down your arms?' Seventy-seven men were still on the Green, Captain Parker's words ringing in their ears:

'Don't fire unless fired on, but if they mean to have a war let it begin here.'

Major Pitcairn also had commanded his men not to fire — yet someone did. The evidence seems to be that it was one of the provincials, not in the ranks upon the Green, but well hidden behind a stone wall or (as Lieutenant Sutherland swears), someone from an upper window in Buckman's Tavern did take that first shot and the British immediately answered with a volley. Sutherland did not stay to see much of the battle, for he was mounted on a Yankee horse that he had picked up since starting out. The animal bolted with him across the Green, heading for the Clark parsonage — even as was Paul Revere himself. With difficulty he got the runaway horse under control and back to the rest of the troops. One would like to believe that this was the last appearance of the Larkin horse. The British would hardly have stolen an animal from any except a mounted rider. Revere's is the only one we know that they took possession of, and certainly Revere's horse would have headed for the Jonas Clark parsonage — it was the last place that he had been fed.

Parker ordered his men to withdraw. One British private and Pitcairn's horse had been wounded. The regulars broke ranks to pursue the flying militia, killing a few more of them. They had been shut up in Boston for almost a year and were wild to get out and after this enemy. Their officers could hardly make themselves heard above the huzzahing of the exultant troops, and had difficulty in re-forming them again upon the Green. In the middle of all this, Colonel Smith arrived with the rest of the soldiers. Eight of the provincials had been killed and ten wounded. The engagement was quickly over and the British on their march to Concord.[32]

Aunt Lydia had been hanging out of an upper window to watch. A bullet whizzed by her head and hit the barn. 'What's that?' They told her a bullet and she'd best take care of herself. And Jonathan Harrington, shot through the chest, was able to crawl the few yards to his own door and die there. Jonas Parker, brought to his knees by the British fire, had been finished off by a bayonet. So it went. When only eight men have been killed, each one is a tragedy, and ten wounded men are heroes — although ten thousand may be primarily a sanitation problem. Two of the wounded were carried to the Clarks'. Miss Dolly remembered that the one who had been grazed insisted that he was killed and the one who had been really wounded 'behaved better.' It seems that John Lowell, Paul Revere, and the trunk were by now at the parsonage.

Sam Adams and John Hancock were back once more in their carriage, moving still farther away to safety than Woburn, where Revere had left them. They, too, heard the rattle of musketry. 'Adams felt his soul swell with uncontrollable joy as he contemplated the mighty future, and with prophetic utterance of his country's dawning independence he exclaimed:

'"O! What a glorious morning is this!"'

But Hancock (probably upset over Miss Dolly's starchy answers) mistook the prophecy for a mere comment upon the weather. The nineteenth of April was (in one sense of the word) a very nice day.

# IV

THE men of Concord had been warned by Revere's Sunday ride that their stores would be a likely object of British attack. By early Wednesday morning, when Doctor Prescott arrived, the alarm was sounded. It was said the first man to appear with his musket was William Emerson, the minister. Most of their arsenal had already been moved to safety. Only a couple of cannon, some bullets, and flour remained to be hidden. A farmer was in his field ploughing furrows over the hastily buried cannon when the regulars came in sight and a woman was dropping the church silver into a barrel of soft soap. Concord was fully alarmed. Minute men from neighbor towns were on the march or already there. They were ready for anything, peace or war, and probably had had no word as yet that these invaders had already killed eight of their fellow countrymen at Lexington, a little more than an hour ago.

A group of provincials waited on the highroad to Lexington until they saw the approaching flash and glitter of Colonel Smith and his columns. But instead of standing their ground, they had good-naturedly turned about. Their drums and fifes struck up as they marched in front of the regulars escorting them into Concord. The British, not to be outdone, also began to play. 'We had grand musik,' a provincial soldier remembered.

Unmolested, the British inundated the village like a scarlet tidal wave, and the taverns as well. They had marched fifteen miles without breakfast and demanded food and drink for which they punctiliously paid. And chairs were set out on green lawns, under blossoming cherry trees for officers to rest in. Colonel Smith sent out small detachments to find what munitions they might. The sacks of flour and bullets were thrown into the creek and later rescued. And he sent Captain Laurie to North Bridge and Captain Pole to South Bridge with orders to destroy them. Now that the British were here, they did not seem to have much to do. Major Pitcairn's genial good deportment was noted and remembered here, as it was in Boston. It is quite another Major Pitcairn who in the old stories made his tragic appearance at Lexington Green. That one was a ferocious, blood-thirsty bully firing the first shot himself. Colonel Smith has been remembered for his unwieldy bulk, which, however, is hard to reconcile with his willingness to go spying. And in Amos Doolittle's sketch of him and Pitcairn watching the movement of the troops that day, he is as thin as a grasshopper.

But Pitcairn (as he idles at Wright's Tavern) made one joke (according to tradition) which might have been considered poor taste. He ordered a brandy-and-water. This he stirred with his finger, saying, 'I hope I shall stir the damned Yankee blood so before night.'

Word came to Colonel Smith that quite a number of the provincials had gathered on the far side of North Bridge. He himself decided to bring reinforcements to Captain Laurie. And slowly, very, very slowly, he walked off at the head of his men. His subordinates thought if Colonel Smith could only have walked a little faster they might have got to the bridge in time.

Major Pitcairn, left in charge at the Square, could enjoy his brandy and his joke. Before him were rank upon rank of redcoats. Every man in his place. Every button sewed on. Perfection (at least from the waist up). He may have thought of those poor devils on Lexington Green: all sizes, ages, conditions of dress and life. Too bad it had been necessary to shoot a few of them, but on the whole doubtless a good lesson. How could provincials think to stand up to the British army? Yet it was just as well Smith had sent back for Percy. The country was certainly aroused. Bells ringing from town to faraway towns. Percy should be here before long. Then from the direction of North Bridge a scattering of shots, followed by a volley. It was after nine o'clock, and the provincials had won the skirmish at Concord Bridge.

All the British were now drawn back into the Square. Captain Laurie at the North Bridge had been badly outnumbered. And one thing was noticeable, half of the British officers had been picked off. Among the wounded was young Lieutenant Sutherland. The militia were much better marksmen than their opponents. For some time Colonel Smith kept his men in the centre of Concord. He marched them to and fro, obviously waiting for Percy, and Percy did not come. As long as he was in Concord, he might burn the town if attacked, and so was fairly safe.

Now in ever-widening circles the cry to arms spread over New England. Concord's bell was heard by Lincoln, Lincoln's by Carlisle, Carlisle's by Chelmsford, and there a woman tries to keep her boy at home. But, 'Mother, I hear the shoots; I'm going' — and he went.

Bedford, Acton, Westford. At Watertown, Joseph Palmer runs to the barn, throws himself on 'Rising Sun,' his wife's beautiful saddle horse, and is off. Fifty years later, Betsey Palmer remembered that this horse, her father's wedding present to her, was ruined that day.

Two young men in Weston were building a barn. They jumped off the scaffolding, seized their guns, and left. The barn could wait. It waited for some years.

In Worcester, Portsmouth, Marblehead, bells and drums called out the men. As far away as Pomfret, Connecticut, 'Old Put' left his plough in the furrow, rounded up his command, and started to march.

Ministers laid down their Bibles to take up their muskets.

Schoolmasters dismissed their scholars forever. 'Deponite libros,' they remarked as the urchins tore out of schoolhouses.

Old Indian fighters filled the powder-horns engraved with the once loved faces of Wolfe and Amherst and seized antiquated flintlocks. In defence of their homes no one was too old or too young to go.

Wives tied up 'notions' in pillowcases — a loaf of bread, a pie, a hunk of salt beef, an extra pair of stockings, just enough to carry a man through a day's fighting. The fight was to last for six years.

Thousands of men were hurrying towards Concord as fast as legs or horses would carry them. By now innumerable men had mounted and were riding to spread the alarm. Among them was Private Howe.

He had heard the news of bloodshed while at breakfast and decided the safest place for him was with Colonel Smith and the easiest way to avoid seizure was to pretend to be a Yankee express. Where are the redcoats? At Concord; so he made for Concord. He had been yelling 'To arms' and 'The regulars are out,' although he was the only 'regular' within fifty miles, until he was hoarse, and had whipped up his horse until it could hardly stand, but he reached Concord and reported to Pitcairn. He was still in his 'Yankee dress.' Of all the men who rode that night Private Howe is the least sung and (according to his own account) the smartest. Pitcairn gave him a fresh horse and bade him ride back to Boston and tell Gage Percy must hurry.

Still Percy did not come. Gage had received Colonel Smith's first cry for help and ordered the reinforcements to march out. Among these troops would be Pitcairn's Marines. It was forgotten that the Major himself had already gone and an order was sent to him to march with his men. This extraordinary stupidity held up the relief column for over an hour. At last Percy, with about six hundred men (but possibly eight hundred), a baggage train, and two cannon, trundled out of town. His band played 'Yankee Doodle.' As they pushed through Roxbury, a schoolboy followed, shouting in derision the famous old ballad of 'Chevy Chase' telling of the defeat of that earlier Percy. The Earl did not like this, but did nothing to stop the boy.

At noon, fearing the ever-increasing number of militiamen, Colonel Smith decided to march his men back by way of Lexington. And the slaughter began. No one opposed the British openly — in the honorable traditions of European warfare. From farmhouse windows, from behind stone walls and barns, an enemy they rarely saw fired and took a terrific toll. So the ever-decreasing column of redcoats ran a bloody gantlet. Colonel Smith was hit. Pitcairn unhorsed. For a long time the soldiers took this butchery very well. As their comrades fell, they closed up the ranks and went on. But it was said Colonel Smith would have surrendered if only he could have found 'somebody of sufficient rank to whom he could offer his sword.' There was little thought of rank that day among his enemies. Each man fought for himself.

At last panic seized the regulars and, completely demoralized, they struggled into Lexington. They passed that Green where the first blood had been shed at daybreak and pushed on for half a mile towards Boston where they met Percy and the fresh men and two cannon. Colonel Smith's men lay panting on the ground like spent hounds.

It was not until after nightfall that these men got to Charlestown and camped on Bunker Hill. The destruction had been terrific, and they had been able to do little but burn farmhouses that sheltered snipers and kill an amazingly small number of their skilfully hidden enemies. Colonel Smith's men had been on the march and much of the time under fire for twenty-four hours. The 'promenade' to Concord had been a ghastly failure. Gage had lost one in nine of the number he had sent out.

## V

THE last we saw of Paul Revere on the memorable nineteenth of April, he and Mr. Lowell were carrying Hancock's trunk across Lexington Green. It was dawn only. A shot had been fired and he had turned his head, seen the ranks of regulars dash forward, heard their shouts — but gone on with his trunk. He does not reappear in anyone's reminiscences (nor his own) until the following day. As it was Hancock's trunk, he may have stuck by it until he had delivered it to its owner.

After the British passed on towards Concord, a messenger (who may have been Revere himself) arrived at the parsonage with a letter for the ladies from Hancock, telling them where he and Adams were hidden and asking them to get a carriage and join him. Also they were to bring along a very fine salmon which had been planned for that day's dinner: '. . . this they carried over in a carriage, and had got it nicely cooked and were just sitting down to it, when in came a man from Lexington, whose house was upon the main road and who cleared out, leaving his wife and family at home, as soon as he saw the British bayonets glistening as they descended the hills on their return from Concord. Half frightened to death he exclaimed "the British are coming! My wife's in eternity now." Mr. H. and Mr. Adams, supposing the British troops were at hand, went into a swamp and stayed there 'till the alarum was over.'

John Hancock intended to drive to the second Continental Con-

gress in Philadelphia. Aunt Lydia and Miss Dolly had come out
from Boston in the family chariot. In spite of Dolly's protest that
she would return to her papa, she did not. The chariot Thomas
Hancock had ordered so long before would roll her south in John
Hancock's train. She would have a little fling with Aaron Burr,
struggle a little longer, but before the summer was out she would
marry John Hancock and Aunt Lydia could die happy in the
village of Fairfield, Connecticut.

We do not know who finally ate that salmon, for when Hancock
and Adams got out of the swamp, 'they were glad enough to dine
off cold roast pork and potatoes served in a wooden tray,' or where
Revere slept that night, but we do know that the next day he was
in Cambridge. And there already ahead of him was Joseph Warren.
Word had come to him before it had to Gage that the shooting
had begun. He first arranged with one of his students, Doctor
Eustis, to care for his patients, then got out of town by boat. He
was in time to take part in the worrying of the British as they retreated to Charlestown, and to have been grazed by a British
bullet. Revere could see that a lock of the heavy fair hair had
been shot away. Another of the three revolutionary doctors had
also arrived in Cambridge. Doctor Benjamin Church's battle
scars were even less impressive than Doctor Warren's. Paul Revere
met him and noticed his bloody stockings. The physician said he
also had been in yesterday's battle. The man next to him had been
killed and his blood had spurted on him. This might well have
humbled Revere, who does not seem to have been anywhere near
the fighting — and possibly was eating salmon instead. 'I argued
with myself, if a man will risk his life in a cause, he must be a
friend to that cause; and I never suspected him after, 'till he was
charged with being a traitor.'

Doctor Warren was president of the Boston Committee of Safety,
most of whose members had by this time escaped Boston. In Cambridge they set up their headquarters. Paul Revere joined them
at the Hastings house. He was ready to serve in any way he might.
Warren 'engaged me as a messanger to do the outdoor work for the
committee.' He was to stand ready to ride at a moment's notice
and 'two of the colony horses' were turned over to him.

He would naturally be worried about his family left behind in
the enemy's hands, but compared to a man in similar situation

today he would have little cause. It was not the custom of the British to punish a man's family for the treason of the head of the house, nor did they hold them as hostages against his good behavior. And Miss Hulton, out in Brookline, was equally at the mercy of the rebels. Her brother had sought safety for himself, but his sister, wife, and small boys stayed behind. Miss Hulton was deeply shocked by her country's troops' defeat by 'what they call Minute companys' who had had 'a signal its supposed by a light from one of the Steeples in Town.' She scorned the tactics of the provincials who 'never would face 'em in an open field, but always skulked & fired from behind Walls,' yet of her own safety she had not the slightest fear. Both Hulton's and Revere's women and children were in the hands of their enemies, but they lived in a world of greater decency and humanity than the one we know now. Why this was so, who can say? Men had in those days a greater pride in themselves than we have today. Many of the punishments dealt out to criminals in colonial Massachusetts hurt a man's body and pocketbook but little — only his pride. The standing for an hour upon the gallows, even the stock and the pillory, the iron collars and the sewed-on letters struck our ancestors in their most vulnerable spot — their self-respect. Even the rough Sons of Liberty hurt people's feelings more than their persons. It is one of the qualities which differentiates the old-fashioned American from the modern most sharply. There is something aristocratic, undemocratic in such pride. Where it came from, whither it went, we do not know. Both sides were proud of their English blood. 'Brittons famed for humanity and tenderness' is the way John Boyle puts it. Something left over from the days of chivalry. Or a deep conviction that whatever a man did, he did in the sight of God. And in the end each man would stand alone before that God, answerable only to him — not to führers, commissars, new orders.

Of the march to Concord and the appalling retreat to Charlestown, both sides told atrocity stories — doubtless old when Caesar entered Gaul and recurring in every war since. The British claimed two of their men had been scalped and mutilated,[33] the Yankees that aged gentlemen had had 'their heads mauled, skulls broke.' A woman in childbed had been forced to take shelter in a barn. These are old stories likely to reappear again. What may not come again is the safety and confidence in which Miss Hulton wrote her letter to Mrs. Lightbody just after Lexington and Rachel Revere minded her household and wrote her letters to Paul.

## VI

THE ferocious one-day skirmishes from Lexington to Concord, from Concord back to Lexington to Charlestown, which have been abbreviated to 'The Battle of Lexington,' took place upon Wednesday. Thursday, Paul Revere himself says, he was in Cambridge talking with Joseph Warren and admiring the blood-stains on Benjamin Church's stockings. It is unlikely he went back into Boston Wednesday night, for all night long Gage's boats were ferrying his troops to Boston. The river was filled with armed sloops and schooners. By Thursday, Gage had withdrawn all of his men from Charlestown, things had quieted down a little. If Paul Revere wished to take a desperate chance in order to see his family, he might have done so. It would be a dangerous trip, for now that blood had been shed, General Gage was not so lenient in his treatment of rebels. Robert Newman, only suspected of hanging lanterns, was clapped into jail. John Pulling was forced to hide in his grandmother's wine-butt to escape the searching party sent out to get him. Major Mitchell had made his report at headquarters, and it was well known that Paul Revere had carried the warning of the British march. It is obvious that 'the noted Paul Revere' (as the British soldier, Richard Pope, called him) was the one express they knew by name and had been watching for. Jail was the best he could hope for if caught, but he could not rest without talking to his family, making what plans he might for their safety. Also, he needed money. By Friday he was riding express for the Committee of Safety (who agreed to pay him five shillings a day for his work), so the chances

are he went to Boston Thursday by boat, and by night saw Rachel
and told her to collect what money she could for him.

Friday evening, the Committee of Safety was sitting in Cambridge. As Paul Revere was engaged to do its 'out door business,'
he was present. Joseph Warren was chairman. Reports were
coming in from all directions. More and more minute men were
arriving from the surrounding countryside. There were now
thousands of them, anxious to finish off the redcoats, but without
organization, camps, food, tents. They were perfectly ready to
stay and fight — and perfectly ready to go home and plant corn;
hardly as yet an army, only a milling mass of individuals — and
what in Heaven's name to do with them! The Provincial Congress
was not sitting. What authority there was at this desperate moment
rested upon Joseph Warren and his fellows, now sitting in their
room at the Hastings house in Cambridge. In time these men —
tired out and a little edgy from the strain they had been through —
became the 'harmless ghosts' which Oliver Wendell Holmes remembered as haunting this, the house of his birth and childhood.

As the conversation pulled this way and that, Doctor Church
suddenly jumped to his feet and threw a bombshell.

'Doctor Warren, I am determined to go to Boston tomorrow.'

Not a man in the room could go openly to Boston without risking
death. Paul Revere says that Church's sudden statement 'set them
all a-staring.' He knew at this time that 'Dr. Warren had not the
greatest affection for him . . .,' and 'I was a constant and critical
observer of him, and I must say, I never thought him a man of
principle,' but he recollected the blood upon his stockings. Doctor
Church had risked his life for the cause. He must be a friend to it.

'Dr. Warren replied "Are you serious Dr. Church? they will
hang you if they catch you in Boston."

'He replied "I am serious, and am determined to go at all
adventures." After a considerable conversation Dr. Warren said —

' "If you are determined, let us make some business for you."
They agreed that he should go to get medicine for their and our
wounded officers.'

Paul Revere was anxious to get the money that Rachel was to
collect for him and now saw how it might be done through Doctor
Church. Having made this arrangement, he started off on some
brief, unknown ride for the Committee, and Saturday morning,

Doctor Church got into his chaise and drove to Boston. By the following Sunday both were back once more at the Hastings house.

> After he had told the committee how things were [Revere says], I took him aside and inquired particularly how they treated him. He said, that as soon as he got to their lines, on Boston Neck, they made him a prisoner, and carried him to General Gage, where he was examined, and then he was sent to Gould's barracks, and was not suffered to go home but once. After he was taken up, for holding a correspondence with the British, I came across Deacon Caleb Davis; — we entered into conversation about him; — he told me, that the morning Church went to Boston, he (Davis) received a billet for General Gage — (he then did not know that Church was in town) — when he got to the General's house, he was told, the general could not be spoke with, that he was in private with a gentleman; that he waited near half an hour, when General Gage and Dr. Church came out of a room, discoursing together, like persons who had been long acquainted. He appeared quite surprised at seeing Deacon Davis there; that he (Church) went where he pleased, while in Boston, only a Major Caine, one of Gage's aides, went with him. I was told by another person, whom I could depend upon, that he saw Church go into General Gage's house, at the above time; that he got out of the chaise and went up the steps more like a man that was acquainted than a prisoner.

But that Sunday after Lexington, Doctor Church told Paul Revere about what he pleased and Revere believed him — even if he did not like him. How could the doctor possibly have gone around to Paul Revere's house, seen Rachel and got the money, if he had not been allowed to go to his own house except once? He had been treated as a prisoner the whole time, so he said. He did not tell Paul Revere that Rachel had written him a hurried letter and sent him the great sum of one hundred and twenty-five pounds. Her letter did not turn up until over a hundred and fifty years later, when Gage's official papers (twelve pine chests full) were discovered at his old home, Firle Place, Lewes, Sussex, bought and shipped over here, adding immeasurably to our knowledge of the times. The letter reads:

> My dear, by Doct'r Church I send a hundred & twenty-five pounds & beg you will take the best care of yourself & not attempt coming into this towne again & if I have an opportunity of coming or sending

out anything or any of the Children I shall do it. pray keep up your
spirits & trust yourself & us in the Hands of a good God who will
take care of us. Tis all my dependance for vain is the help of man
adieu my Love

> from your
> Affectionate
> R. Revere.

So it seems that Doctor Church turned both the letter and the
money over to Gage. If the General acted characteristically the
money was returned to Rachel. The letter, with the warning not
to 'attempt coming into this towne again,' he kept. But Paul
Revere, talking aside with Doctor Church, must have been utterly
disappointed. He needed the money. He needed reassurance that
Rachel was well. He had been so depressed that time he had stolen
into Boston to see her, he probably even needed her advice to keep
up his spirits. His secret visit had not reassured her much, for
'vain is the help of man' (such as her husband). Only God will
now save the Revere family. All Paul got from Doctor Church
was a cock-and-bull story, which he believed.

General Gage now organized Boston to withstand a regular
siege. On the very day of Lexington, a corps of loyal Tories
offered him their services. At last the General began to round up
his known adversaries. Most of the more active Whigs had already left town. The Reverend Samuel Cooper, political firebrand,
counted on his cloth to protect him, which it did. On the nineteenth of April he merely 'rose, and set off with Mrs. Cooper,'
heading for Framingham.

Isaiah Thomas left for Worcester two days before Lexington.
Benjamin Edes got out the last moment, but his nineteen-year-old
son, Peter, was put in jail and had the leisure to keep a diary. In
it Captain Linzee, who is so attractive a figure in John Rowe's
diary, appears as a minor monster. Paul's cousin, Benjamin
Hitchbourn, was arrested. Although only out of Harvard for
three years, the Tories were already complimenting him by saying
he 'stood a fair chance for the gallows.' He was locked up on
board the *Preston*, one of the hated prison ships in Boston Harbor.
Prisoners of war on both sides suffered from the sanitary ignorance
of the time. There was no way known by which a man could be
kept locked up and in health.

James Bowdoin alone of the old leaders still stayed on in Boston and was not jailed, but 'he, poor gentleman, is so low that I apprehend he is hastening to a house not made with hands, he looks a mere skeleton, speaks faint and low, is racked with a violent cough, and I think far advanced in consumption,' as Abigail Adams wrote to John. It was this sick and courageous man who presided over the town meetings which sent petition after petition and one committee on the heels of the last to Gage, demanding that the inhabitants might be allowed to leave the town before the siege began. General Gage at first agreed to this, provided Joseph Warren would give safe-conduct to any Tories who might wish to move into Boston. Both sides restricted what the other might or might not take in or out of Boston.

Gage demanded all weapons to be turned over to the selectmen before anyone could leave the town. It resulted in 1778 firearms, 973 bayonets, 634 pistols, and 38 blunderbusses, which gives an idea how heavily armed the average citizen was in those days. Although the selectmen promised to return this arsenal to their owners at some later date, care was taken that few of these weapons would be serviceable if they fell into British hands. Among the many citizens whose names are recorded as turning in their weapons is 'Paul Revere, two muskets.' This was, of course, young Paul. His name is so close to Thomas Hitchbourn's, it is likely he went over with his cousin. So by the twenty-fifth, anyone who wished theoretically might get a pass and leave Boston. These passes were, however, very hard to get. But neither food nor merchandise could go with them. If they went, they could never return as long as the British held the city.

Merchant Rowe was much upset. He wished to leave the town — but not his 'effects' — and at last decided to stay where he was. It was said in Boston that 'the soldiers, they have liberty to plunder everyones house and store who leaves town.' This was hardly true, for Gage did not hesitate even to hang soldiers found stealing, but he could not control them. The Whig houses, many of them very large, most of them no bigger than the Reveres', were, during the next year, generally reduced to little more than four walls.

As the Whig refugees streamed out of Boston, the Tories streamed in. They, too, were leaving almost everything they had behind them to be plundered by their enemies. It was hard for many people on both sides to decide whether to stand by their political beliefs and see the last of their 'effects' or stay with their property and keep their mouths shut.

Among those to return to Boston was Agnes Surriage, now at last Lady Frankland. Sir Harry died soon after marrying her and she had returned to Massachusetts to enjoy her hard-earned title and wealth at Frankland Hall, Hopkinton. She was no longer the fair child who had captured a baronet with a glance, but a middle-aged widow. She thought she would feel safer in the great town house near North Square and begged the Provincial Congress at Watertown to grant a pass for herself and 'six trunks, one chest, three beds and bedding, six wethers, two pigs, one small keg of pickled tongues some hay and three bags of corn.' The Congress rose gallantly to beauty in distress. '*Resolved*, that Lady Frankland be permitted to go to Boston with the following articles, — viz., seven trunks; all the beds and furniture to them, all the boxes and crates; a basket of chickens, and a bag of corn; two barrels and a hamper; two horses, two chaises and all the articles in the chaises, excepting arms and amunition: one phaeton; some tongues, ham and veal; and sundry small bundles.' Benjamin Church signed the permit and she was furnished with an escort of six soldiers to protect her and her effects over the road from Hopkinton to the British guard on the Neck.

That May 'you see parents with bundles in one hand and a string of children in the other, wandering out of town, not knowing whither they go.' And an almost equally large number of these pathetic people — rich and poor alike — were arriving in Boston, not knowing 'whither they go.'

War had begun in grim earnest, with its hordes of refugees upon the roads — a bundle in one hand and a string of children in the other. Not many, like Lady Frankland, had a great house waiting, and arrived at their destination with baskets of chickens and some tongues. Each side tried to look out for their refugees, but there was plenty of hunger, cold, and heartbreak. Among those leaving Boston that May was the Revere family, but they were luckier than most. The head of their house would find means of supporting them. He seems to have begun charging for his express riding only after Lexington, when he had no access to his tools and did not see where the money was coming from. The hundred and twenty-five pounds Rachel had attempted to send him had miscarried. For a short time he stayed in Charlestown waiting impatiently for Rachel and his children to join him. Likewise his mother and his two sisters, Deborah Metcalf and Betty (who does not seem to have been married at this time) 'if they think to come away.'

Late in April he wrote Rachel this letter:

My Dear Girl

I receiv'd your favor yesterday. I am glad you have got your self ready. If you find that you cannot easily get a pass for the Boat, I would have you get a pass for yourself and children and effects. Send the most valuable first. I mean that you should send Beds enough for yourself and Children, my chest, your trunk, with Books Cloaths &c to the ferry tell the ferryman they are mine. I will provide a house where to put them & will be here to receive them. after Beds are come over, come with the Children, except Paul. pray order him by all means to keep at home that he may help bring the things to the ferry tell him not to come till I send for him. You must hire somebody to help you. You may get brother Thomas. lett Isaac Clemmens if he is a mind to take care of the shop and maintain himself there. he may, or do as he has a mind. put some sugar in a Rasin cask or some such thing & such necessarys as we shall want. Tell Betty, My Mother, Mrs. Metcalf if they think to stay, as we talked at first, tell them I will supply them with all the cash & other things in my power but if they think to come away, I will do all in my power to provide for them, perhaps before this week is out there will be liberty for Boats to go to Notomy [Arlington] that we can take them all. If you send the things to the ferry send enough to fill a cart, them that are most wanted. Give Mrs. Metcalf [torn] in, their part of the money I dont remember the sums, but perhaps they can. I want some linen and stockings very much. Tell Paul I expect he'l behave himself well and attend to my business, and not be out of the way. My kind love to our parents & our Children Brothers & Sisters & all our friends

Young Paul was fifteen and practically a grown man. He was now to act the part and look out for his father's property in Boston. Isaac Clemens, the English engraver,[34] and a Tory, would, by his presence, safeguard the shop at Clark's Wharf, but the responsi-

bility was on the son's shoulders. His father added this note to his
letter to Rachel:

My Son.
    It is now in your power to be serviceable to me, your Mother and
yourself. I beg you will keep yourself at home or where your Mother
sends you. Dont you come away till I send you word. When you
bring anything to the ferry tell them its mine & mark it with my
name.

Your loving Father
P. R.

By the second of May, only two weeks after Lexington, Rachel
had the situation in hand. She does not like asking 'Capt Irvin'
for a pass. One can sympathize with poor John Revere, who 'did
not incline' to make his brother a coat, as we know that he had
but a few months more to live.

Boston, 2, May, 5 o'clock afternoon 75

Dear Paul
    I am very glad to hear you say you are easy for I thought you
were very impatient but I cannot say I was pleased at hearing you
aplyed to Capt Irvin for a pass as I should rather confer 50 obliga-
tions on them to receive one from them. I am almost sure of one as
soon as they are given out I was at Mr. Scolay's yesterday and his
son has been here today and told me he went to the room and gave
mine and Deacon Jeffers name to his Father when no other person
was admitted I hope things will be settled on easier terms soon I
have not received a line from you till this moment Why have you
altered your mind in regard to Pauls coming with us? this Capt
Irvin says he has not received any letter and I send by this 2 bottles
beer 1 wine for his servant. do take care of yourself. O I forgot I
have not received but 3 £ L.M. of Parkman and that was not enough
to pay our friends  Mr. S. [torn] promised to pay you shou'd be glad
to know that your coat is not made [torn] John did not incline to
do it and I spoke to Mr Boit he engaged to make it if he could not
get a pass but as he has that prospect he cannot I have got a woman
to make Pauls in the House and if you choose I will ask John to
cut it and get her to make it she is a very good work woman and
works for Doct Mount [torn] Rand.

Yours with affection
R. Revere

The next day, Ezra Collins, a Clark's Wharf neighbor, wrote Paul Revere asking him to look out for his sister who was leaving that day, as was Mrs. Revere. Also preserved is a letter to Paul Revere from 'Jas Singer Segt' writing 'By Desire of Capt Irving': 'Mrs. Rievere Informed Capt Irving this morning (by me) that you had some Veal & Beef to send over which will be very acceptable. . . . There is a pass ready for Mrs Rievere, Family & Effects.'

Very likely the veal and beef followed Mrs. Revere's '2 bottles beer 1 wine' down the gullet of the hungry sergeant, but the trick was turned and the Reveres left town.

A family tradition, going back far enough to be worthy of respect, has it that the final exodus was not accomplished by bribing a pass out of Captain Irvin's gluttonous servant, but by one bought from a chimney sweeper, and they did not go by ferry to Charlestown, but over the Neck and in a cart overflowing with children, grandmother and goods.

And in May, another old acquaintance decided to leave Boston. This was Private Howe. On the tenth, 'I put on my Yankee dress again, I called on Col Smith and I told him I had a notion to make a trip to Rhode Island and Conneticut and see what preparations the Rebels were making. Smith answered "John the devil's in you, you'll get hanged before youre done, but if you have a mind to try again you shall have some money." ' The colonel gave him fifteen pounds. He walked over to Roxbury, kept moving until he got to Albany, enlisted in the American army, and when the war was over settled on the Ohio River.

There was little to eat in Boston but salt meat and fish. The British allowed no food to go out with the exiles. There was considerable smuggling. The sister of Paul's friend, Thomas Crafts, sewed two legs of ham and some sugar in a feather bed. This was not discovered. But another woman was less successful. She tried to keep her children quiet during the inspection of their cart by the sentry at the gate and gave each child a piece of gingerbread. The sentry — a truly horrifying British ogre — took it all away from them. He said, 'gingerbread was too good for rebels,' and ate it himself.

Whatever their difficulties, the Revere family did get out. How soon they would see their North Square house, no one could guess. If the side Paul Revere backed failed, it might be never.

## VII

UP TO the seventh of May, Paul Revere was charging the Colony of Massachusetts five shillings a day for riding express. This would hardly support a wife, a mother, and seven children, or do much towards supplying two sisters left behind in Boston 'with cash and other things.' But, being a versatile man with more arts than mere horsemanship by which to make a living, Revere was quickly on his feet again. In May, the Provincial Congress at Watertown engaged him to cut copper plates and print money for the colony. He went to Watertown and immediately settled down to work.[35]

Watertown is seven miles up the Charles from Boston. It was a farming community, set upon the blackest, fattest, finest loam in eastern Massachusetts. There were only about one hundred houses at the time and these normally sheltered seven people to a house. The day after Lexington, it began to fill up, for Watertown was to be the capital of Massachusetts for over a year. Here the Provincial Congress met, summoned hastily by express riders like Paul Revere. Not until the British evacuated Boston did they return to the old State House and assume their ancient title of 'Great and General Court.'

Most of the prominent Boston Whigs settled in Watertown. Not the two Adamses nor John Hancock, for they were on their way to the greater congress at Philadelphia. But Samuel Cooper was soon regaling his congregation with much the same sermons they had been listening to at the Brattle Street Church, Boston. Benjamin Edes arrived by rowboat, carrying his press with him. His best founts of type were left behind and the *Boston Gazette* in its Watertown period is almost unreadable. He, like Paul Revere, was put up at the Cook house, as was Henry Knox (Revere called him 'Hennery' if he pronounced the name as he spelled it) and his wife, Lucy, whose full petticoats had hidden her husband's sword. Joseph and Betsey Palmer, whose wedding celebration Paul had attended not many years before, were already living in the new capital. After the Tea Party, Palmer had been told he was on the British 'black-list.' His wife was a 'Watertown Beauty' and they decided to move out to her father's house. At this, the Hunt house, Joseph Warren stayed. Watertown was full of Revere's Boston friends.

Edes left the Cook house about the time Paul Revere's sizable family must have arrived, but the Knoxes stayed on. If the house was crowded, it was probably not much more than they were accustomed to. The whole town was crowded, busy and important.

The Provincial Congress not only had to establish a makeshift civil government, but also care for the army which was now besieging Boston. It had sprung up, like the dragons' teeth Jason sowed, from the very furrows of the New England fields. Now that they were gathered, they hardly knew what to do. Should they fight? Should they go home? There were not enough guns, munitions, tents, clothing, for them. A great many went home. Some thousands stayed. And while the machinery was being evolved for their care and command, they were very ragged, very dirty, and a little quarrelsome. A few months before, it was the tidy provincials who had been twitting Colonel Leslie's men about their lice. Now it was the Tories who returned the compliment. Lousy, dirty, ill-fed, unpaid, sick and hungry, they stuck it out and established the siege of Boston, as Joseph Warren struggled heroically to bring order out of chaos.

At this time it was not even known if the other colonies would back New England. They had said they would — if she was attacked. It might turn out that this war, which had started at Lexington, would be a private matter between Massachusetts and the entire British Empire. Much might depend upon the eloquence of those delegates riding for Philadelphia. Through it all Joseph Warren kept his head, his contagious enthusiasm, a certain unaffected but very moving nobility that he had. He was quickly emerging as one of the very great leaders Boston had produced. Josiah Quincy, who had promised so much, had died when in sight of Gloucester Harbor the week after Lexington. He had performed his mission in England successfully. He brought back news so important he dared not, even as he lay dying in his wretched bunk, commit certain facts to writing. It was a lonely and terrifying death. He, like Joseph Warren, had all the elements of true greatness — except the ability to keep alive.

There was nothing Massachusetts needed more for her disorderly army than money. Worthless paper money was better than none. In some way Paul Revere got his old copper plates out of Boston. Copper was always imported and the lack of it was to be felt all through the Revolution. Probably he brought out his own tools and his tiny press as well. It may have been Billy Dawes who made the trip in and out. Revere's young co-rider had gone to Worcester, but made weekly visits into Boston. 'Every Saturday his sister [in Boston] would cover his gold peices with cloth and sew them on [his coat] while as regularly in Worcester his wife would remove the cloth and put button molds in their place.' 'On these journeys he disguished himself in different ways, usually as a countryman selling produce' or by 'feigning drunkenness and following the officers on guard wherever they went, even passing his fathers house, from the windows of which a young sister recognized him and annoyed him very much by her loud cries of "Brother Billy."'

The British had to admit country carts and countrymen into Boston to bring in food. It would not be too difficult for one of these to bring out Paul Revere's tools, press, and copper.

So Paul Revere set up his workshop at the Cook house, with the Knoxes as fellow guests and young John Cook to help him. He printed everything from six-shilling to four-pound notes — in all many thousands of pounds. He was cautioned 'not to leave his press exposed when absent from it' and a military guard was assigned to him, night and day.

His 'Sword in Hand' money he printed on the reverse of his 'View of Boston.' For another he used a rather fine plate he had cut a few years before of Harvard College. Because the Boston Massacre plate was used for colony money, it is now preserved at the State House in Boston.

In Philadelphia the Continental Congress felt the same desperate need for currency. John Adams and Benjamin Franklin were on the committee which engaged Paul Revere to cut the plates, but, far more important, this Congress decided emphatically to back the northeast colonies in the struggle against England.

Paul Revere had his difficulties with his plate-making and printing, which went on until the following December. Not only was copper hard to get, but paper as well. The notes were so thick the British called them, scornfully, 'pasteboard currency.'

Even this poor paper was scarce and costly. Paul Revere was writing, 'The Paper for the last, cost me Six dollars a Rheam, when I did not expect to give but four . . . the Committee of the House orderd the paper to be made & did not agree for the price. & I was obliged to pay the paper maker his demand.' It soon became apparent that the paper was hardly worth more after it had been printed than before, although now the money he printed has considerable value among collectors.

## VIII

EXCEPT for the fact Paul Revere would be paid for his services with his own pasteboard money, everything was going well for him. He had shelter for himself and his family. Watertown was filled up with his best friends. The news which came in was good. The British dared no more than make sorties on the various harbor islands, carrying off livestock and hay, and the provincials did the same.

On the fifteenth of May, Colonel Easton arrived in Watertown with the great news of Ticonderoga's fall. There had been a slight skirmish, but soon enough (so Easton was telling them, according to John Boyle) he and Colonel Allen had won and he was clapping the commanding British officer on the shoulder, telling him he was a prisoner, and 'The officer was in great Confusion and expressed himself to this Effect — Damn you — what — what — does this mean?' But he surrendered his fort, his men, and some hundred pieces of artillery. If only it were possible to move these heavy guns the hundreds of miles to Boston, Gage would be forced to leave the town. But how could it be done? In many places there was not even a cart path through the wilderness. This was accomplished by young Henry Knox, who had acquired all his knowledge of

military affairs out of the books he had read in his shop. He was
something of a correspondence-course officer.

Then it was June, and General Gage offered pardon to all those
who would lay down their arms, except John Hancock and Sam
Adams only. His proclamation was ridiculed and answered a few
days later by entrenchments thrown up on the promontory of
Charlestown. On the fourteenth day of June, Joseph Warren was
made a major general of the Massachusetts troops and a few days
before George Washington (although it was not known until after
the battle of Bunker Hill) had been chosen commander-in-chief
of all the Continental troops by the Congress sitting in Philadelphia.

Joseph Warren had been appointed a major general, but as
yet had no commission. He had no command, nothing but the
title, the confidence of all who knew him, and his desperate determination. By the evening of the sixteenth, it was known at
Watertown that 'Old Put' and his men were throwing up earthworks on Breed's, or, as it was miscalled then as now, Bunker Hill
in Charlestown. The British would certainly move across the
river to dislodge them. Joseph Warren was restless and talkative.
He asked the women of the Hunt household to prepare lint and
linen for the poor fellows who would be wounded on the next day.
In some way, he hardly knew how, he would himself take his
place in the engagement, keep his rendezvous with death.

Betsey Hunt Palmer wrote, years later: 'I am sure I liked him
better than anybody . . . he was a handsome man and wore a tie
wig. He had a fine color in his face and light blue eyes. He dined
with us [the night before Bunker Hill] and while at dinner said
"Come my little girl, drink a glass of wine with me for the last
time for I am going on the Hill tomorrow and I shall never come
off." '

So he had his glass of wine. He was a highly organized, imaginative man. One thought followed another. He tried, but he could
not sleep. The night was hot and very still. At daybreak he got
on his horse and by five was in Cambridge. In June it is broad
daylight by five in the morning. He went to the Hastings house
where for days after Lexington he and his companions had struggled night and day to bring order out of chaos. Elbridge Gerry
let him in. The young doctor was sick and feverish. The two men
talked together and were agreed that occupying Charlestown was

folly — and yet, folly or not, Warren had to go. 'It would be madness for you to expose yourself,' Gerry said, 'as surely as you go there you will be slain.' Warren knew that. His head was aching badly, but 'Dulce et decorum est pro patria mori,' he said. He had not slept all night and now in broad daylight he went upstairs to lie down.

'Dulce et decorum...' — but is it? He was young, healthy, alive, and very anxious to stay alive. Half of him could say (and mean it), 'I hope I shall die up to my knees in blood.' But the body (with its will to life) could fight against such idealistic desires. From its point of view it is not sweet to die for anything. First it produced that raging headache. Surely that ought to be enough to keep the most passionate soul safe in bed? There was no real reason why Warren should go to 'the hill.' Let him stay at home and nurse his head. There was one more thing the body could do to clip the wings of the soaring soul. Warren had had no sleep. Flung down in the hot upper chamber at last he slept. He slept for hours. If the body can keep this up long enough, Joseph Warren will sleep through the Battle of Bunker Hill. Joseph Warren will not keep his rendezvous with death.

He woke at noon. The battle between his two desires was over and the Battle of Bunker Hill not yet commenced. But by the time he reached Charlestown, the British had landed and had engaged the provincial troops. Already a number of Americans had decided that it was too stiff a fight for them. Warren had no arms — only a book of poetry in his pocket. He got a musket and a cartouche box from a retreating sergeant.

Colonel Prescott offered him the command. (The cannons had already begun to boom.) No, no. He was not ready to assume his rank as general.

'I did not come to take command, but to act as a volunteer.'

'Do you mean to stay, General?'

(The bullets were coming fast.)

'I mean to stay.'

So Joseph Warren went to the hill and he never did come off.

Those waiting at Watertown could hear the rumble of cannon and see the smoke of burning Charlestown. Joseph Warren's negro servant paced back and forth before the Hunt house — 'Ah Missie, Missie, The Devils ha killed ma master.'

The day grew hotter and hotter. There was not wind enough to stir a leaf, hardly enough to breathe. The moaning negro got on Betsey Palmer's nerves. Watertown could not, like Boston, watch the progress of this battle, only wait and pray. But Paul Revere, who could coolly carry his end of a trunk full of papers through the battle of Lexington and merely turn his head, would need more than the battle of Bunker Hill, several miles away, to upset his work. No matter the suspense, dread, heat of the seventeenth of June, 1775, he was quite capable of going on printing more and more paper money. He is like the 'spritely tailor' in the fairy story — ' "I see that but I'll sew this," and he kept on stitching on the trews.'

Rumors were plentiful. The battle had been won — no, lost. The British were in possession of Charlestown. Joseph Warren was killed, wounded, missing. Seems he had gone to 'the Hill' dressed in his best clothes, 'a light colored coat with a sprig on the buttons' a tie wig and a white-fringed waistcoat. Although by far the highest ranking officer, he had fought as a private. He was alive — and he was dead. Then word came from Boston that his clothes had been hawked for sale by a British soldier. Doctor Jeffries had seen his body lying close to the redoubt, with bloody hands. He had been buried by the British, then dug up to exhibit to the curious. And buried again in the grave with a countryman in a farmer's frock. General Howe said his death was worth five hundred men to him.

At Bunker Hill, Major Pitcairn uttered his last oath. He was shot through the chest. His son carried him from the field on his back, kissed him, left him to die, and returned to the engagement, to be wounded himself. The dying major had been carried to Boston and his body buried in a vault under Christ's Church, where it still lies.

The battle of Bunker Hill had been fought and, although the British remained in possession of Charlestown, they could not claim a victory, so appalling had been their losses. As long as the American munitions had held out, they had been supreme. The first time Prescott found all his powder gone, those many kegs which Paul Revere's ride to Portsmouth had saved for the provincials began to arrive. Old John Demeritt had carried it sixty miles in his ox cart. It was this powder which enabled the rebels to hold out to the very last and make an orderly retreat. Such slaughter had never been known before in British military history. They had over eleven hundred casualties, almost one-third of the troops engaged. It is estimated that every musket in American hands accounted for one man.

It is easy enough to point out now that both sides were stupid. The Americans might have chosen better positions. The British expected their precise and beautiful soldiers to keep their artificial lines even when climbing New England stone walls and in the face of deadly gunfire. Each regular started out with one hundred and twenty-five pounds of equipment. But no one has denied that both sides fought with unparalleled courage — wildcats against bulldogs. As stupidity is a much commoner characteristic of the human race than heroism, it is perhaps as well to do, as did our first historians — remember the heart-breaking, desperate courage — the rail fence and the redoubt — the three successive scarlet waves of British soldiers, 'Old Put' on his horse, the cool fury of Prescott, and 'Don't fire till you see the whites of their eyes': General Howe himself leading his men, keeping his promise that he would not ask them to go one step farther than he himself was ready to go, and the tears in his eyes as he saw his soldiers mowed down: Joseph Warren's smile of recognition when he heard his name called by Major Small, a friend of his among the British officers, and the next moment dead in his tie wig and fringed waistcoat: Pitcairn, the bold old soldier, bleeding to death in the high salt grass and hot sun — and forget the considerable number of not-so gallant minute men who, when they got to 'the Hill,' decided they did not care much about fighting and very quickly 'got off'; the reserves that never arrived; the British folly in deciding upon a frontal attack.

This battle did much to hearten the Americans. It proved to them that their men and methods were equal or superior to those of the British. It was a lesson to the British. They never again behaved with such arrogance. General Gage, no longer commander-in-chief, had never underestimated the provincial soldier. He had proof for his old contention that 'the rebels are not the despicable rabble too many have supposed.'

# IX

EVEN if life was not easy for the Reveres, Watertown was a better place to be that summer than Boston. The Americans not only could keep food from coming in over the Neck, but boldly held up supply ships. Food quickly grew scarce. A song of the time asks General Gage what he now had but

> A town without dinner,
> To sit down and dine in.

Before he left for England, carrying with him a damaged reputation and those pine trunks of letters, the General counted up the number of mouths to be fed: 13,600 troops and camp followers. But only 6573 inhabitants, including all the Tories who had fled to him for protection. Almost fourteen thousand Bostonians had left the town. Many of these settled in the western part of the state and never returned.

Disease made inroads on the beleaguered town. Although Gage had promised freedom of departure to all who wished to leave, he was forced by the Tories to go back on his word. They believed that as soon as the last rebel left, the besieging army would destroy the town. If Gage would not hold the remaining Whigs as hostages, they would lay down the arms they had taken up and leave town themselves. Still, by one trick and another, people were leaving for as long as the siege lasted.

George Robert Twelves Hewes fished nine weeks for the British fleet until he saw his chance and took it. Landing in Lynn, he was immediately taken to Washington at Cambridge. The General enjoyed the story of his escape — 'he didn't laugh to be sure but looked amazing good natured, you may depend.' He asked him to dine with him, and Hewes says that 'Madam Washington waited upon them at table at dinner-time and was remarkably social.' Hewes was one of the many Boston refugees who never went back there to live. Having served as a privateersman and soldier during the war, he settled outside of the state.

In July an energetic barber 'swam from Boston to Dorchester, says that it was very sickly in Boston, that provisions was very scarce in Boston and the people in great distress.'

So those waiting outside the beleaguered city often had word from those within, the bad food, bad health, and many deaths. Among those who died that August was Paul's brother, John. Paul had never named a son John; perhaps now that his brother was dead he felt fonder of him than he realized. His next child he named John, and he tried the name twice again until at last it stuck.

Although many things of greater importance happened as that summer wore away into fall, nothing probably affected Paul Revere more personally than the arrest of Benjamin Church. The old Sons of Liberty, Long Room, North Caucus, and Masonic crowd were paralyzed with amazement. The showy doctor had been made Surgeon General of the American army. He was said to be the best surgeon in New England. He set up his headquarters in one Vassal house in Cambridge, while General Washington was setting up his in another Vassal house almost across the street.

On October 3, General Washington wrote to John Hancock in Philadelphia this letter:

> I have a painful, though necessary duty to perform, respecting Dr. Church, director-general of the hospital, almost a week ago, Mr. Secretary Ward of Providence, sent up to me one Wainwood an inhabitant of Newport, with a letter directed to Major Cane [the aide whom Gage assigned to Church that day he went in to town for medical supplies] in Boston, in characters; which he said had been left with Wainwood sometime ago, by a woman who was kept by Dr Church. She had before pressed Wainwood to take her to [certain loyal customs officials etc. in Newport]. She then gave him a letter with a strict charge to deliver it to either of those gentlmen. He, suspecting some improper correspondence, kept the letter, and after some time opened it; but not being able to read it, laid it up, where it remained until he received an obscure letter from the woman, expressing an anxiety after the original letter. He then communicated with me. I immediately secured the woman, but for a long time she was proof against every threat and persuasion to discover the author. However at length she was brought to a confession and named Dr Church. I then immediately secured him, and all his papers. Upon his first examination, he readily acknowleged the letter; said it was designed for his brother Fleming and

when deciphered would be found to contain nothing criminal. He
acknowledged his never having comunicated the correspondence to
any person here, but the girl, and made many protestations of the
purity of his intentions. Having found a person capable of decipher-
ing the letter, I, in the mean time, had all his papers searched, but
found nothing criminal among them. But it appeared, on inquiry
that a confidant had been among the papers before my messanger
arrived.

This letter was written two days after the court martial at which
George Washington himself presided. Church was found guilty
'of holding criminal correspondence with the enimy.' But what his
punishment was to be was left to the Provincial Congress sitting at
Watertown, of which he was a member. Not even the day in July
when Washington had stopped in Watertown on his way to take
command of the troops, nor when Mrs. Washington, cosy and
domestic, had trundled along after him — winning the heart of
every Watertown housewife — had there been such an excitement
as the day Benjamin Church went on trial in the old meeting house
where the Congress sat. The galleries were packed. He defended
himself pretty well, but seems to have been guilty beyond any
reasonable doubt. In vain now his rolling eye and poetic fancies,
his 'the warmest bosom here does not flame with a brighter zeal
for the security, happiness, liberty of America,' and so on. Abigail
Adams, writing to John, describes what most of his old friends like
Paul Revere were thinking, 'You may as well hope to bind up a
hungry tiger with a cobweb as to hold such debauched patriots
in the visonary chains of decency.' And now at last Paul and
Rachel might put two and two together and guess exactly what
had happened to that letter she had written last April.

With the shedding of blood it would seem the time had passed
when a man could (as poor Merchant Rowe was still trying to do
in Boston) understand both sides and steer a middle course. Doctor
Church had been caught at last in his treachery, which we know,
although his contemporaries did not, had been going on for almost
ten years. He was found guilty of actually spying for a British general while holding his high office in the American army. Surely
the firing squad was the best he might hope for? Or the gallows,
on which the much more worthy Major André was later to die,
will now be erected on Watertown Common? He was only sent

to Norwich jail in Connecticut and there 'debarred the use of pen, ink and paper.' On nice days he might ride out with a 'trusty guard.' Only very, very slowly did the country work itself up to a martial pitch where one hangs one's neighbors because they are caught spying. A year later Doctor Church would have had no such lenient treatment. The American people were not only unprepared for the 'horrors of civil war,' as John Rowe calls it, in munitions and military organization, but they were not even psychologically prepared.

# VIII

## 1776 – 1779

PAUL REVERE gets plans for a powder mill. When GAGE and the TORIES leave BOSTON, he returns to NORTH SQUARE. As a dentist he is able to identify JOSEPH WAR-REN's body. BOSTON is afraid of its TORIES. 'JOYCE JUN'R' and his cart. LIEUTENANT COLONEL REVERE is in command of CASTLE ISLAND. He fires upon YANKEE ships. LEWIS ANSART teaches him the founders' arts. Other FRENCHMEN arrive. The strange death of SAINT-SAUVEUR. Alarums and excursions. The *Somerset's* guns are salvaged.

Tory ships leaving Boston, Boston Light and Castle Island. Broadside of 1776. American Antiquarian Society.

I

BY NOVEMBER Paul Revere had
a new task assigned to him. The Americans were in desperate
need of powder. If only their powder had not given out at Bunker
Hill the June before, they might yet be in possession of Charlestown.
During the French and Indian Wars England had furnished them
with most of their gunpowder. That source was now naturally
cut off. They had tried again and again during the earlier period
to manufacture it themselves (Revere's ancestor, Captain Woody,
among them), but without much success.

In August, General Washington had written from Cambridge,
'Our situation in the article of powder is much more alarming than
I had the most distant idea of. We have but 32 barrels.'

Left over from the old wars was a scattering of abandoned
powder mills and a few people who understood its manufacture.
Pamphlets were printed telling how powder is made or giving instructions for its most difficult ingredient, which is saltpetre or
nitre. In a copy of the *Royal American Magazine* for August, 1774,
there is a plate, undoubtedly engraved by Paul Revere although
not signed, and an article on the making of saltpetre. In it one
learns that most of the saltpetre used in Europe at the time came
from Persia or the East Indies, 'where it is found embodied in the
ground as metals in their ore and separated from the earthy parti-
cles by water as metals are from their ores by fire.' In Europe,
France only was independent of saltpetre imported from the East.
It is an 'effluvia of animal bodies. Pigeon houses, stable, and barns
but especially old walls were full of it.' And as the French were
clever enough to collect it in this form, they were independent of

Persia and the East Indies. It now behooved the Americans to be equally ingenious. The article, so obviously written with revolution in mind, ends by mildly extolling the merits of saltpetre as a medicine and the fine flavor it gives to brandy. Gunpowder, and how to produce it almost overnight, was as great a problem to the American army of that time as the production of planes today.

In Massachusetts it was decided to set up powder mills at Andover, and what is now Canton. These towns were inland and could not be easily reached by the British fleet. Canton had the added advantage of having had powder mills for towards a hundred years. The Everendon or Everton family had been handing down their knowledge from father to son for generations. Sometimes their tiny, one-room mill would blow up and they would go out of production. In 1775, they knew the way to make powder, but had no mill. Before he died, Joseph Warren received this letter, signed merely 'True Son of Liberty':

> There is now living or rather pining in poverty, one Everton of Stoughton [Canton includes part of old Stoughton] that by proper encouragement might at this day become a most useful member of society. He perfectly understands the making of Gun-powder, and ... he is the only one in the Province that has the practical skill. What pity that the Art should die with him.

The Provincial Congress at Watertown may have been influenced by this letter to select Canton, but did not evidently believe that Everton knew all there was to his art. Philadelphia was far ahead of New England in powder-making. They asked Paul Revere to go there and find out how things were being done in the best and most modern manner. For 'in Philadelphia powder mills are Erected and the manufacturing of powder is carried on with Considerable dispatch and advantage, you are desired to make the following Enquiries, and possess yourself as far as you Can of the Knowledge of making powder. VIZ Obtain an Exact plan of making powder, powder mill, the Quantity of powder that may be made in One day in said mill, the Expence of the powder mill.'

He was also told to get in touch with the Massachusetts delegates to the Continental Congress, who would make him the necessary contacts with the powder-masters. James Otis, whose wits were by now pretty much befuddled, but whose name still carried great weight, gave Paul Revere a letter asking 'all persons upon the road' to assist him 'with Horses or any other thing he may stand in the need of.'

The road from New York entered Philadelphia by way of Frankford and it was there Oswell Eve had his fine modern powder plant, but Paul Revere went first into Philadelphia, was introduced to Robert Morris by the Massachusetts men, and then back to Frankford. Morris recommended 'the bearer of this letter Mr. Paul Revere, He is just arrived from New England where it is discovered they can Manufacture a good deal of Salt Peter in consequence they desire to erect a Powder Mill & Mr. Revere has been pitched upon to gain instruction & knowledge in this branch. A Powder Mill in New England cannot in the least degree affect your manufacture nor be of any disadvantage to you.' And Mr. Morris hopes 'you will cheerfully and from Public Spirited motive give Mr. Revere such information as will enable him to conduct the business on his return home.'

Oswell Eve was a ship captain and prominent merchant who came from South Carolina. He was a man well on in years, but not stricken by them. He had a number of ingenious or poetic sons, several of whom made considerable name for themselves. His girl, Sally, had been engaged to Doctor Benjamin Rush, but died before marriage. It was to this household Paul Revere now presented himself and Robert Morris' letter.

The story is that Captain Eve did not have the public spirit Morris rather doubtfully hoped he had. He did not wish any ingenious Yankee setting up in competition with himself, even in times of war. Let him make his powder in the good old-fashioned way — collecting urine like Captain Woody. Although he dared not refuse to show his powder mill at Robert Morris' request, he walked Revere through rapidly and did not let him study the machinery nor question the workmen. This brief walk was enough for Paul Revere, although it must have been a bitter disappointment. His knowledge of chemistry and mechanics would have been limited at that time, but he was observant, and he also turned to exactly the right man among the Massachusetts delegates for help — to Sam Adams. Next month he had a letter from Adams enclosing a plan of one of the Philadelphia powder mills — probably Captain Eve's. By hook or by crook he had found a fellow patriot,

a 'Mr. Wisner,' who had access to the mill and had 'drafted it.' Sam
Adams had always been able to get needed but withheld information.

At Canton the work on the mill began in January and by May it
was in production. Paul Revere is credited by an almost contemporary source with having overseen the building and the setting-
up of the simple machinery, but Major Thomas Crane was the man
who actually made the powder — with armed guards stationed
around the little building. By September he had on hand 37,962
pounds of powder and 34,155 of saltpetre. For the first three years
of the war he furnished most of the powder used by the Massachusetts troops. Among the many trades Paul Revere followed,
powder-making is always part of the tradition, but there does not
seem to be any proof that he actually did the work. Considering
how poor much of this amateur gunpowder was, it does not seem
in any way to clip a laurel from his brow to let the powder be manufactured without more help from him than the general design of
the mill.

A year later, General Heath was writing to Washington that
'the powder made and belonging to this state was found to be bad.'
The commander-in-chief was alarmed. 'There must be roguery
or gross ignorance in your powder-makers,' he wrote back. The
little mill in Canton continued to serve its country in its own,
perhaps ignorant, but surely not roguish manner, until 1779, when,
after the manner of its kind, it blew up.


# II


ONE more winter was over and
the time of the singing of birds and moving of armies was at hand.
There was no fear now that the British would attempt a sortie.
They would either stay in Boston or evacuate by sea.

While Isaiah Thomas was getting his press to Worcester and
Benjamin Edes was setting up his at Watertown, John Boyle fled
to Hingham. He was having rather a hard time personally. He
had been fond of his in-laws and they were Tories, and his young
wife was sick and soon to die. But in spite of these domestic sorrows,
his diary is principally concerned that spring with the great question of what General Howe will do next. On the fifth of March
he knew, for the Continental troops commanded by the Virginian
general, George Washington, had taken possession of 'two large
Hills in Dorchester, about a Mile from the South Part of Boston —
these Hills the Enemy must dispose us of, or quit the Town';
and on Sunday, the seventeenth of March, they quit.

Before the British fleet had even cleared the harbor, Washington's
army was marching in. On their heels came a horde of exultant
Boston Whigs, John Boyle, the Reverend Samuel Cooper, and
probably Paul Revere. All of these exiles were in what they
would call 'a state' to find out how friends, family, and property
had survived eleven months of British domination.

On the twentieth, General Washington himself entered, and
with him was Henry Knox. The last time Boston had seen Henry
he was only a fashionable bookseller, now he was a colonel of artillery. It was this stout city boy who had accomplished the almost
incredible feat of moving the howitzers, cannon and mortars, captured at Ticonderoga and Crown Point, to Dorchester. Yoke upon
yoke of oxen had hauled them through the wilderness and deep
snows of winter. These guns had forced the evacuation of Boston
upon the British. Perhaps he did strut a little, and a stout boy strutting is always an invitation to wit. Unfortunately for Henry's
complacence, he passed close to the most celebrated wit in Boston.

Doctor Mather Byles was the only Congregational minister in
New England to side with the Crown against the colonies. Even
'Puffing Pem,' whose Tory sympathies had finished off the Cockerel
Church, had at the end come out for the Whigs. Byles had been a
handsome man in a long-past youth. Some fifty years of acid re-
torts, quips, and bad puns had pulled his face awry. In his later
portraits one eyelid drops in an almost perpetual wink and his lip
curls up to meet it — yet it is a tough, amusing old face. His intelligence and sour charm made him many friends as well as enemies.
Certain of his remarks handed down to the present make pretty

good sense. 'They call me a brainless Tory,' the famous Doctor Byles once said as he watched three thousand Sons of Liberty parading the streets of Boston, 'but tell me, my young friend, which is better, to be ruled by one tyrant three thousand miles away or three thousand tyrants not a mile away?'

He loved large wigs, elegant clothes, high society, Hogarth prints, books, and good living. The more sophisticated of the British officers had been delighted with him. No one would regret their departure more than he, yet he did not hesitate to turn out to see the American army now move in — nor to make a pun. The hard physical work Henry Knox had been through that winter had in no way upset his natural metabolism. Doctor Byles peered at the young hero.

'I never saw an ox fatter in my life,' he said clearly.

This pun upset Henry. He said Doctor Byles was a damned fool.

Perhaps he was. At the very moment over a thousand less foolish Tories were 'pigging it' on board the overcrowded transports, fishing smacks, coastal sloops, which made up the vast makeshift flotilla still hanging about Boston. Doctor Byles' own son was on one of those ships — but not he himself. His daughters, Miss Polly, twenty-five, and Miss Kitty, twenty-two, stayed with him. What stories they had to tell of the siege! Those summer afternoons when they had promenaded the Common, the one on Lord Percy's arm, the other on General Howe's! That night Lord Percy had ordered a regimental band to serenade them! No wonder after such attentions they never married and remained loyal to the British Throne for over half a century. Doctor Byles had been pastor of the Hollis Street Church for forty-three years. He intended to stay where he was — and keep on punning.

So Doctor Byles, in his neat little cassock and large frizzy wig, trotted home to his daughters, well pleased with himself and the effect of his joke upon Henry Knox, if not with the state of the world.

The Boston refugees, returning in the wake of the army, gazed about them in amazement. Everywhere there were signs of the occupation: British earthworks on the Common, Copp's Hill, the Neck. In out-of-the-way places these trenches and gun emplacements would last longer than Paul Revere himself. Fuel had been so scarce most of the trees were gone. Liberty Tree was but a stump.

The famous row of sycamores before Doctor Cooper's church —
also stumps. And the town had been cleaned out of fences, old
wooden houses, tumbled-down wharves and warehouses. For over
a hundred years Governor Winthrop's ancient black house had
stood in the very heart of the town. It had gone for the soldiers'
mess fires.

North Square would look strange to Paul Revere without Old
North Meeting, but the church had been pulled down, partly to
give more room for drilling troops, partly for firewood. Captain
Atkins, the mason, who lived next to the Reveres in the 'moonlight'
house, had helped destroy it, as formerly he had helped pull the
insides out of the Hutchinson house. He now seems to have known
which side he was on. He was 'pigging it' out in the harbor. The
steeple of West Street Church, where Paul had heard Jonathan
Mayhew fire the sunrise gun twenty-five years before, was gone.
Old South had been cleared out of its pews and, after loads of gravel
had been carted in, used for a riding ring for General Burgoyne's
favorite regiment, the Queen's Light Dragoons. One pew had been
preserved for a pigsty. The Episcopal churches, where the invading
hosts had worshipped, fared better. Although King's Chapel was
uninjured, the rector had left with Howe and taken the church
records, vestments, and plate with him.

The food situation had been desperate and disease everywhere.
Not even his venerable twenty years had saved the town bull from
the butcher.

In spite of martial law, the abandoned houses of the Whigs had
been looted by the bored, hungry, cold British troops. The more
important mansions had been protected by assigning them to
generals. General Clinton had been living in the Hancock house
and he seems to have been a neat housekeeper, although John
Lowell is reporting to his employer that a backgammon board is
missing and the fences are broken.

Paul Revere seems to have left his son to sit out the siege within
the British lines and care for his property. His house would therefore be in good shape. His shop was let to Isaac Clemens, the
Englishman, who at this time took ship for New York, where he is
soon advertising his engravings as being especially attractive to
military and naval men, and then drops out of sight. A shop occupied by so good a supporter of the Crown would not be robbed.

But many houses were completely cleaned out, inside woodwork and staircases having gone for fuel: furniture, beds, linen, and of course all food and valuables. But now it is the Tory houses that are vacant. The Tories are the refugees.

Doctor Samuel Cooper returned the Tuesday after the evacuation to 'a melancholy Scene. Many Houses pull'd down by the British soldeiry, — the shops shut. Marks of Rapine and Plunder everywhere ... found all my Beds Bedsteeds Sheets Blankets Quilts etc etc plundered.' It was impossible for him to move in. He and his horse (and this time he remembered to mention his wife as well) spent the first night with Doctor Bulfinch. 'Wednesday; went with Mrs. C. to our house procur'd an order f'm Gen Green to take Furniture f'm desrted Houses ... to supply my desolate empty House with Furniture f'm Dwellings left by the Enemies to our country. removed more Things from Paxton and Richard Smith's house.' Three days later he was 'still employed in removing Things to my House.' The Reverend Mr. Cooper kept a careful list. He only 'removed' things in the presence of witnesses. He had his order from the General, but the sack of the Tory houses had begun.

All this time the British fleet hung about the harbor. It landed men on Castle Island and blew up the fortifications. And it did not leave the waters about Boston for several weeks.

When General Howe knew he must evacuate Boston, he had no idea of abandoning the faithful Tories 'to the rage and insults of rebels.' He left military equipment behind, General Gage's handsome chariot, blankets and clothing, but not one single Tory who wished to go with him. In all, some eleven hundred 'well affected inhabitants' left with him. Although some nine hundred more were to go from Massachusetts, this first great migration in General Howe's makeshift, unseaworthy fleet is the most unforgettable.

Many of these refugees had already left most of their property behind them when they had fled from inland towns to the safety of the British in Boston. They had been confident that a quick victory would soon re-establish them in their homes. Very few of them would ever see those homes again. For them the trip to Halifax was a second removal.

For the Boston Tories it was the first. General Howe gave them

ten days in which to pack up. In the end, a large proportion —
but by no means all — of the wealthiest Boston merchants had preferred the innovations of England to those of Sam Adams. Now they
faced the problem — what do you take from a great house if all
you can carry is a few cartloads? Are sheets or family portraits the
most important? Your scarlet robes as judge of the King's Court —
or warm underdrawers? One's best wig — or a wig-rest for the
one you wear? A silver punchbowl, or another feather bed? What
to do with the old dog — too sot in its ways to move — too much
loved to be abandoned? Families were broken up. Some men
thriftily left their wives behind to hold on to their property. Lady
Frankland turned hers over to a brother. It was ten days of
anguish and confusion. General Washington said, 'One or two
of them have done what a great number ought to have done long
ago, committed suicide.'

Boston lost so many of her best citizens, this exodus can only
be compared with that of the Huguenots which sixty years before
had landed Apollos Rivoire upon our shores. Great merchants,
distinguished lawyers, doctors, judges, were on those ships crowding
Boston Harbor. Old names, famous since the founding of the
colony, like Saltonstall, Oliver, Sewall, Clark, Mather, or Hutchinson; Huguenot names, Cazeneau, Faneuil, Johonnot — were represented in this exodus, although many of the same names took the
opposite side.

Of the men who left with Howe, one hundred have been classed
as 'officials,' eighteen as 'clergymen' (all Episcopalian), one
hundred and five 'from the country,' two hundred and fifteen
'merchants' and 'other residents of Boston,' but by far the largest
and unsung group is the four hundred 'yokels, mechanics, tradesmen.' The parties did not divide as closely along economic and
social lines in fact as in legend. Legend had always tended to make
the losing side in such a struggle wealthier, more genteel, more
romantic, than they were. Many a poor man fought against Oliver
Cromwell, but is forgotten for the more glamorous 'cavalier.' It is
true of our own Civil War. The bulk of the rebels did not live in
Tara Halls. To the winning side goes the glory of victory — and a
chance to make a mess of things. To the losing side, a sad, nostalgic
beauty. On those ships were many a simple mariner, peruque-
maker, runaway slave, yeoman; for over half of Howe's passengers

were such plain men who will eventually be forgotten for the traditional great gentleman and proud lady — or in the course of time become metamorphosed into such by their descendants.

Josiah Quincy's brother Sam was on one of those boats. His country was to need lawyers of his calibre, as they were to need such men as the Chandlers and Paines of Worcester, the Winslows of Plymouth — for there were no better men. And we needed Thomas Hutchinson's financial wizardry. Brigadier General Ruggles, of Hardwick, was as good an army officer as New England had. He had proved his ability in the French and Indian Wars. His neighbor in Worcester County, Colonel John Murray, would not easily be replaced. Colonel Murray had been mobbed out of Rutland a year before. His wife (née Lucretia Chandler) carried with her into exile much of the magnificent silver which had been given her at the time of her marriage to the hearty, handsome, coarse-grained, self-made Murray. Her sugar bowl never got to Halifax. It fell into the hands of one of the Yankee privateersmen which quickly gathered to waylay Howe's fleet. The cream pot did, but was later sold, for many a refugee family supported themselves for years selling off the family plate. It was only a short time ago that these two small companions and witnesses of such misery were reunited at the Boston Museum of Fine Arts, where they represent Paul Revere's work at its highest artistry. His books show that he made much silver for these families now flying the wrath to come. So the ships now leaving are carrying many of Massachusetts' best citizens and some of Paul Revere's most famous silver with them.

Chief Justice Peter Oliver was thrice-over united to the Hutchinsons by marriage. For generations these families had intermarried to an amazing extent. He had been a faithful and just man, according to his own lights — which were not brilliant. General Howe had put him on the *Pacific*, a fine Indiaman. For several weeks the ship lay at anchor, first in King's Road and then in Nantasket Roads. The judge had plenty of leisure to write in his diary. 'Here I took my leave of that once happy country where peace and plenty reigned uncontrolled. Until that infernal Hydra Rebellion with its hundred Heads, had devoured its happiness, spread desolation over its fertile feilds and ravaged the peacefull mansions of its inhabitants, to whom late, very late if ever, will return that security and repose that once surrounded them. . . .

Here I drop the filial tear into the Urn of my Country.... And here I bid A Dieu to that shore which I never wish to tread again till that greatest of Social blessings, a *firm established British Government*, precedes or accompanies me hither.' So the old judge wrote, dropping his tears for his country — but none for himself.

If young Harry Pelham was indeed (as he claimed) the creator of Paul Revere's most inflammatory, most frankly anti-British propaganda engraving, he had in the last five years completely changed sides. He went with Howe. A young country could spare many men more easily than this artist, map-maker, engineer. His half-brother, Copley, would never care to return to the New World hurly-burly, for he was already convinced that for him Europe was the place to paint; nor was he ever, in a greater world, to equal the painting he did in his youth, stifled by the provincial town of Boston. Perhaps he had better sitters there. Surely the kings or queens he painted in England have none of the dash and verity of, say, Uncle Thomas and Aunt Lydia Hancock. His own country lost when he left and seemingly he lost as well.

The Paxtons, Hallowells, and the Hultons were off. Miss Hulton would not soon forget the horrors of Boston, those blackened faces leering at her through the windows of the Brookline house; our tent caterpillars, mantua-makers dancing with admirals' sons, the ferocity of our weather, and politics.

A few — a very few — of these people would return. Doctor John Jeffries would go on with his medical studies in London and with Blanchard fly in the first balloon ever to cross the English Channel (in a leopard-skin cap and wristlets — a pixie smile upon his face, if the old picture does not belie him). So bold a man naturally came back when he pleased. He lived long enough to overlap Oliver Wendell Holmes, who admired him.

First and last, this was the saddest day ever to come to Boston.

But there were enough Tories left behind to create that unsolved problem — what to do with minorities in times of war? No war, and especially no revolution, has ever solved this problem decently. What does one do, for instance, with a man like the 'famous Doctor Byles'? Was he to continue to 'strut' the streets? Now he had no congregation to preach to, no way to support himself and the almost equally famous 'Byles Girls,' but nothing could stop his puns.

If one compares the treatment such men got with an ideal of

human conduct, they fared badly enough, but if contrasted to the fate of similar groups in the French or Russian or Nazi revolutions, or to what they might expect in any country today, they were extremely fortunate. Not without reason, the party now in power feared the Tories among them. It was believed the British would attempt to seize Boston again. The Tories might (and possibly did) send intelligence, burn military stores, spike cannon. Most of them were frank in expressing opinions which now would be considered enemy propaganda.

There was an even larger group who attempted to remain neutral. Every person who had stayed in Boston during the siege was suspected of being a lukewarm supporter of the enemy. Among these was Merchant Rowe.

On the night of Lexington he had written in his diary, 'this Unhappy affair is a Shocking Introduction to all the Miseries of Civil War.' For the fact that the American Revolution was 'the first American Civil War' was quite apparent to the generation who fought it, and no modern discovery. During the siege of Boston, Rowe's diary is ill-kept, scanty, and some of it stolen 'out of My Store,' possibly by a British secret-service man. He is not dining well on 'good pigys' nor getting himself 'pretty mellow,' at Mrs. Clapham's, nor catching yellow perch at Flax Pond. His ships do not sail nor his warehouse 'fall in with fish' so full it is of this Boston currency. He writes down the coming and going of the British men-of-war and sells some of his ships to the English. He lets his two maids go. Captain Linzee, the young British naval officer who had so recently married that apple of his eye, his adopted daughter, Sukey Inman, 'behav'd very cruelly to me. I shall not forget it.' But he does forget and forgive. He loves young Linzee, although he regrets his politics. Toward the end of the siege he has more to say. Early in March, 'God send me Comfort in my Old Age. I try to do what Business I can but am Disappointed & nothing but Cruelty & Ingratitude falls to My Lot.'

As the British prepare to leave, Crean Brush and other rascals attached to the British go off with goods of his valued at twenty-two hundred pounds. 'This party behaved very Insolently & with Great Rapacity & I am very well Convinced, exceeding their orders to a Great Degree. They stole many things and plundered my Store. Words cannot describe it. . . . I remained all day in the

Store but could not hinder their Destruction of my Goods. This day I got a peice of Bread and one Draft of Flip. They are making the utmost Speed to get away & carrying . . . everything they can away, taking all things they meet with, never asking who is Owner or whose Property — making havock in every house & Destruction of all kinds of Furniture.' Among the people whose houses he mentions as being plundered is 'the Widow Newmans.' This was on the eleventh of March.

By the thirteenth, 'the Confusion still continues & Plundering of Houses Increasing . . . the sailors from the Ships have Broke open my stores on my wharff.' Even Sam Quincy's house was 'broke & great destruction' and so was the Reverend Mr. Caner's, rector of King's Chapel. Both of these men were Tories fleeing to Halifax with General Howe.

By the fifteenth, the British soldiers were smashing what they could not take with them, but on 'March 17 St Patrick's . . . this morning the Troops evacuated the Town & went abord the Transports at & about Long Wharf. they sailed and got most part of them into King's Road. About noon Gen'l Putnam & some troops came into Town to the Great Joy of the Inhabitants that Remained behind' — and obviously to his own.

This was the treatment he had had from the Tories. The American forces moved in and with them General Washington himself who 'Rec'd us [some merchants who had sat it out in Boston] very Politley.' John Rowe did not realize that he himself would now be a suspect among the patriots.

## III

THERE had been rumors a-plenty just where Joseph Warren had died, and how. It was said that Major Small, who not long before had been issuing passes

from his office in the Province House, had called upon him, 'For
God's sake to stop,' as the retreat from the redoubt had begun.
He liked him and hoped he would surrender. Warren had turned
his head, recognized him, but not surrendered. A bullet had gone
through his face and he had died instantly. Those long dying
speeches of Warren's, credited to him by his contemporaries, like
'I am a dead man, fight on, my brave fellows, for the salvation of
your country,' etc., were never said by a man shot through
the head. And the story was told how the wounded General
Howe had slept that night on a pile of mouldering hay on the
battlefield. In the morning he was told that Joseph Warren had
been identified among the dead. He had been buried and dug up
again and buried again. Even General Burgoyne had rowed over to
see the body. There seemed little hope now that his remains would
ever be identified. The British had held Charlestown ever since
Bunker Hill, but now they were gone and the time was come to
give Joseph Warren a proper burial, if they could find him.

Doctor John Jeffries had served as an army surgeon with the
British troops at Bunker Hill. He had seen and recognized his fellow
physician's body, but as he was at the moment on one of those ships
heading for Halifax, he could hardly help in the identification.

Harry Pelham had also known, for he had written to his mother
soon after Bunker Hill, 'I have often passed Doct Warren's Grave
I felt a disagreabl[e] Sensation, thus to see a Townsman and an
old Acquaintance led by unbounded Ambition to an untimely
death — and thus early to realize that Ruin which a Lust of Power
and Dominion has brought upon himself and partly through his
means upon this unhappy country.' But Pelham, like Jeffries,
was now far away. Someone in Boston, however, had been told
by Jeffries where he lay and promised to lead Joseph Warren's
brothers straight to the spot. It was known that he had been
buried in a grave with 'a person with a frock on.'

The two young brothers, a sexton, and some friends, among
whom seems to have been Paul Revere, as he figured in the identification, rowed over to Charlestown and started on what must
have been the dreariest day of their lives. The sexton began to
dig 'and a corpse soon began to appear. The brothers, unable to
remain longer, retired.'

The story that Warren had been stripped of his clothes seems to have been true, for it was not the beautiful fringed waistcoat that gave the first clue, but the farmer's frock. The body which 'our savage enimies scarce privledged with earth enough to hide it from the birds of prey,' had lain there for some ten months and was 'disfigured.' It was said that Warren had been shot through the face, as was this skull lying with the skeleton farmer and his frock. The brothers believed that this was Joseph, but Paul Revere settled the question once and for all. He had fastened in for his friend shortly before Lexington two artificial teeth. Not many of the hundreds buried there on Bunker Hill would have such luxuries. This skull had two. And one was an eye tooth. If further proof was necessary, the silversmith recognized his own silver wire. Perhaps Revere was not the first American dentist to say 'yes, this is he. I recognize my own work,' but he seems to be the first of whom we have record.[36]

This shocking mass of corruption was indeed all that remained of the fresh-faced, 'very clean' young doctor. He was thirty-four when he died. Revere had known him intimately for at least fourteen years. And the two of them had, almost a year ago to the day, been watching the movement of the British troops together, planning signals, sending out messengers. The head of Warren, the sight of his own work, must have haunted him all his life.

Although Warren had never assumed his rank, he had been a major general when he died. He was President of the Provincial Congress and also Grand Master of the Masons. He now would have a worthy funeral. This would, of course, be Masonic. General Washington and his lady had left Boston by the fourth of April, so he — the most distinguished of American Masons — could not attend. The funeral was to be upon the eighth. Among the many things Merchant Rowe had gone without during the siege was the fraternal warmth of his beloved Masons. Here at last was the time for him to reassume his way of life. Almost joyfully he 'went accordingly to the Council Chamber with a Design to Attend & Walk in Procession with the Lodges under my Jurisdiction with our Proper Jewells & Cloathing but to my great mortification was very much Insulted by some furious & hot persons with'o the Least Provocation one Brethern thought it most Prudent for me to Retire. I accordingly did so — this has caused some Uneasy Reflections in my mind as I am not Conscious to myself of doing anything Prejudicial to the Cause of America either by will or deed. The Corps of Dr

Warren was Carried into Chapell. Dr Cooper prayed & Mr
Provoz Morton delivered an Oration on the Occassion. There was
a handsome Procession of the Craft with Two Companies of Soldiers.' For Doctor Cooper life had returned almost to normal. His
entry for that day shows that having prayed over Doctor Warren's
corpse at King's Chapel he 'slept at home' but 'horse at D. Storer's.'

After the interment, the Masons (but not John Rowe) went back
to the council chamber and voted that 'our Brothers Paul Revere,
Edward Proctor, and Stephen Bruce [who married one of the
Hitchbourn cousins], be a committee to wait upon our brother
Perez Morton, Esq. and present our cordial thanks for his oration
delivered this afternoon, and request a copy thereof for the press.'

But in spite of his 'Uneasy Reflections,' Merchant Rowe's entry
for April 8 ends on a note of cheer: 'There is Confirmation of Crean
Brush & Wm. Jackson being taken also my Negro Fellow Adam.'
The ship they had attempted to make Halifax in had been picked
up by a Yankee privateersman and brought into Boston laden with
loot from the plundered houses and stores. Adam may not have
been one of those aristocratic Tory refugees one hears so much
about, but his master was doubtless glad to get the black fellow
back once more.

John Rowe notes that seven Tories are to be 'exiled':

> Richard Green set out this morning for Brookfield for 4 months
> Exile
> James Perkins for 4 months to Medfield
> Nat Cary      "    "      "    " Dedham
> John Timmins "   2    "    " Waltham
> Tho's Amory   "   2    "    "    "
> Wm. Perry     "   4    "    " Medfield
> Nat Brickley  "    "      "    " Framingham
> [but] Dr. Whitworth & Son Committed to Close Gaol.

That spring we see the last of another of the three Revolutionary
Boston doctors, but Mr. Rowe was too concerned over his own
predicament to do more than mention the fact. Doctor Church
arrived in Boston on June 2. His brief and comfortable imprisonment was over. He was now to be exchanged for a captured
American doctor. The boat which took him to the West Indies
never arrived at any port. Many pious patriots thought God
had been more just in his treatment of the traitor than had

man. Rowe makes no further reference to him. He was too busy trying to adjust his peacetime shipping to the needs of war and clearing his own character. A special court had been set up winnowing the patriot grain from the Tory chaff. Gossip was rampant.

June 15, John Rowe was 'very busy all this morning in finding out some Persons that have wickedly & Maliciously spread a false Report about me & have had them before Justice Hill & have got the first of them to Acknowledge it to be a lye & she hath signed a Declaration which I hope will Satisfy and Clear my Innocence.' Next time the Brethren marched, he could go with them.

# IV

THAT the British forces had left Boston forever and would not attempt its recapture was not guessed in spring of '76. In fact, we now know this was General Howe's original plan. Washington was in Boston only a few days after the evacuation, but the tradition is that he himself asked Paul Revere to go out to Castle Island and repair the damage the British had done to the cannon. Paul Revere found the guns by no means past repair and invented a new type of gun-carriage. This work he must have done as an artisan — not as a soldier. During Washington's brief visit he had no commission. When the commander-in-chief left, he took the bulk of the Massachusetts troops with him to New York. Soon he sent back for more. It was up to Boston to defend herself as best she was able. By the tenth of April — two days after Joseph Warren's funeral — Paul Revere was commissioned as a major in the regiment of militia raised for the defence of Boston. General Ward and then General Heath commanded the section.

The colonel of this Boston regiment was Revere's old friend and

associate, Thomas Crafts. He had been an active Son of Liberty
from the beginning. He had gone on the 'Tea Party' and was one
of the watchful mechanics who seem to have been locked up on
Castle Island while Colonel Leslie invaded Cape Ann. Although
usually referred to as a 'painter,' he did japanning and some
carpentry. Unlike Paul Revere, he had seen recent military
service, for, when Henry Knox brought the heavy guns through
the snows of the preceding winter, Thomas Crafts had served him
as a major. Physically he was enormous and strong as a bull.
This great strength he supported, to the amazement of his contemporaries, by a diet 'entirely of vegetable products & milk.'
Like so many of his fellow townsmen, he was very blond. A nephew
wrote a poem about him which begins:

> Dear Justice Crafts, fair, factious, partizan,
> I like thee much, thou fiery-visaged man,
> I love to hear thee charm the listening throng
> Thy head and wig still moving with thy tongue.

And —

> The mind of Justice Crafts no subject balks
> Of King-craft, priest-craft, craftily he talks.
> Oft have we heard his crafty tales and laughed
> But never knew him mention justice-crafts.

John Adams thought so highly of him he once wrote that he
had 'more merit than half the Generals in the Army.'

Boston was so open to attack, Colonel Crafts, as the highest
ranking officer, had a position of great importance. Civil law did
not give way to martial, but it broke down badly. When this home
guard finally took shape, Crafts as colonel could expect (and
whistle for) twenty pounds a month, Lieutenant Colonel Paul
Revere, eighteen pounds, and Major Thomas Melville, fifteen
pounds. This regiment and its deeds (and lack of them), its quickly
apparent weaknesses and its extremely democratic spirit dominated
Paul Revere's life for the next three years. It is not certain he
dominated theirs. Most of the soldiers lived at home and came
out to drill about when they felt like it. If the colonels wanted the
men, an alarm was 'beat round the town,' then theoretically the
men 'shall immediately repair to the parade with their arms &
accoutriments, and not leave it till discharg'd by the Command'g
Officers.' The number of times the men were ordered to turn up

'clean' does not suggest the traditional military dandyism. As time went on and no one attacked Boston, they grew fewer and lazier and less and less interested. They started out with great spirit — the old spirit of Lexington or Bunker Hill.

Mrs. Adams wrote her husband on the ninth of May how briskly the work was going forward fortifying the port of Boston. 'Six hundred inhabitants of the town meet every morning in the town house [old State House], from whence they march with fife and drum, with Mr. Gordon Mr. Stillman and Mr Lothrop [three clergymen] at their head to Long Wharf where they embark for the island.' This picture is much more reminiscent of the Sons of Liberty and their way of doing things than it is of an army. Those who felt like going out to the islands and throwing up gun emplacements went. Those who did not stayed at home.

Paul Revere seems to have had every quality to make an extremely good army officer. He was intelligent, resourceful, tireless. His robustness was both physical and mental and he had plenty of courage. Among the semi-secret Sons of Liberty and the Masons he quickly went to the top. He could learn a new trade as fast as most men turn around, yet his military record is undistinguished. He certainly had no liking for army life. If he had, he would have belonged to one of the well-known Boston regiments before the Revolution, like Hancock's Cadets or the Ancient and Honorable Artillery. He does not seem to have done so. He would (as the law required) turn up every so often for 'training day,' but he does not figure as an officer until he was over forty, except for that one youthful trip to Lake George. This may have cured his martial ardor.

If he had been a real fire-eater, he would have dropped John Hancock's trunk in the middle of Lexington Green and figured in that historic battle, but he went on doing his duty by the trunk. He did not leave Watertown (as far as we know) when word went about on the sixteenth of June that on the next day there would be 'fighting upon the Hill.' Joseph Warren got himself into both these battles. Henry Knox also seems to have been a born soldier. Paul Revere was born a good many things, but not a soldier. He may have been too much of an individualist — psychically as well as traditionally something of the lone horseman. Or he may have had bad luck. If Boston had been attacked and successfully de-

fended the summer of 1776, he might now be remembered primarily
for his military skill. For years the defence of Boston was in his and
Colonel Crafts' hands. How good was their system was never
tested — the chances are it was worse at the end of a few years
than at the beginning.

By fall, Paul Revere was a lieutenant colonel and commander at
Castle Island. Rachel had borne the first of her three Johns, and
the baby had died. General Heath (as kind and unmilitary a
general as even the American Revolution produced) commanded
Paul Revere on the first day of September 'to repair to and take
Comand of Castle Island.' This position he held most of the years
of the war. His rank never went higher. Henry Knox was going
up like a kite or a balloon — a general while in his twenties. Joseph
Warren and the gentle, brilliant Rhode Island Quaker, Nathanael
Greene (it was he who had given Doctor Cooper permission to
furnish his desolate house from the Tories' houses), were both
generals at thirty-four, but Paul Revere never rose to higher rank
than he had at the end of the first six months. But if he did not
prove a distinguished army officer, there were other things he
could do of possibly greater value.

The need for cannon was almost as desperate as for gunpowder.
In Boston 'old things' that had been stuck in the ground to keep
wagons from bumping house-fronts, were taken up and put back
into service. America was backward industrially. The laws which
England passed (but without much machinery for enforcement) for-
bade her to manufacture steel, set up slitting mills or triphammers,
weave cloth, make hats and other things, had not hampered her
seriously. We have seen how Paul Revere made a branding iron
for Cousin William Hitchbourn. Obviously this hatter practised
his trade with the greatest frankness, branded the felt so anyone
could see who made it, and probably sold such hats· to the best
loyalists in Boston. The same was true of the ironworks, such as
Paul's great-great-grandfather, Tom Dexter, had on the Saugus
River. The theory that the colonies should produce raw material
and England the finished goods had not seriously hampered a
people who were mainly agricultural and nautical.

During the Revolution, however, they were forced to produce
such things as powder and cannon or fight the British with their
bare hands. Probably Paul Revere had never cast anything in

his life larger than a handle for a cup or in a heavier metal than silver, but he was an ingenious man with a liking for skill, and the letter he received from the Massachusetts War Council in February, 1777, would have been pleasing to him, for he was ordered to 'proceed to Titicut [part of Bridgewater] make Enquiry how they go on in casting Brass and Iron Cannon at the State Furnace under Direction of Mess're Marguguelle & Orr. If practicable attend the proveing of the Iron & Brass Cannon finished, & desire all effective Cannon that are proved to be sent to Boston immedaitly.' He is also to see about five tons of eighteen-pound 'shott' and to 'apply to the proper Forges for a Qty of Tyre Iron.'

He sent this letter to Hugh Orr with the postcript in lead pencil.

> Friend Orr
>     I send this that you may see what my Business is.
>                         Paul Revere

The man referred to in the letter as 'Marguguelle' was Louis de Maresquelle, the French foundryman, who finally (having married several American girls and established his business at Dracut) lies buried on our soil as Lewis Ansart. He had come to Boston, 'glowing with ardor' for the Revolution, almost a year before Lafayette arrived, and boasted that he could make all the cannon they could use — 'one every twenty four hours' if but given the material and a place to work. He was satisfied with the wretched bog iron our ancestors were in the habit of fishing out of shallow ponds with oyster rakes, for he had 'a peculiar method of softening the Iron by a mixture of Ores & Minerals.' He could also bore the cannon after they were cast, which was a great improvement on the usual method. There was little this remarkable thirty-four-year-old Frenchman could not do — according to his own account  The strangest part of Ansart's claims is the fact he really was as able a man as he said he was. He describes himself as 'an old Infantry Captain' and says he was 'brought up in the forge of France.' This was true. His family (most of them titled) had been casting the French kings' cannon for generations. The French were as clever at such work as any people in the world.

From Massachusetts he asked three hundred dollars in cash, a commission as a colonel (but no command), one thousand dollars a year for duration of the war and a life annuity of six hundred and sixty-six dollars. His services were so much appreciated by the Commonwealth that when currency depreciated and six hundred and sixty-six dollars would not support him, they gave him the equivalent in purchasing power. Although now his name is almost forgotten, he played an important part in New England's industrial history. He also offered to teach his revolutionary methods to 'such persons as the state selects.' Paul Revere was selected to watch and learn how he did his work. He would undoubtedly delight in the ingenuity, precision, novelty, of the young engineer's skill and in his robust good-humor. Ansart was a gigantic fellow weighing two hundred pounds. His portrait shows him with a cherubic face, surrounded by curls and ruffles; but even so, he looks capable of casting a cannon a day. New England needed his cannon, needed his knowledge of the foundryman's arts. He taught his secrets gladly. Paul Revere was to be one of his most capable pupils — for he himself was the founder of a great modern industry.

Caught as he was in a back-water from the main stream of the fighting, Paul Revere was probably bored. He often lacked equipment, money, and good men, and must have been discouraged, but he did his best. In April, 1777 — after almost a year in the army, most of the time on Castle Island — he wrote the following letter to John Lamb, in New York, with whom he had stayed while riding back and forth to Philadelphia. It seems to be the only fretful letter he ever wrote (but many people were discouraged and writing fretful letters at this time — even George Washington). His old friend was now a colonel. He had been wounded and taken prisoner in the attack on Quebec a year and a half before, but was now exchanged and back in the army.

Dear Sr.

It is with pleasure I imbrace the opportunity of acknowledging the recipt of your letter. It always gives me pleasure to break your seals — much more so now after your long imprisonment. I congratulate you on your return to your family. I hope they are well. pray give my regards to your good lady & father. I long to see the old gentleman, but as matters are now I do not expect it. I did expect before this to have been in the Continental Army, but do assure you, I have never been taken notice off, by those whom I thought my friends, am obliged to be contented in this States service. I do not write you any news, as Capt Mansfield can relate all that

passes here. I shall be very glad to hear from you often, and when
any thing turns up will write to you or Col Arnold. remember me
to him and lady. I would have wrote but had not time. pray tel¹
good Mr Holt it is not in my power to procure him a journeyman.
Friend SEARS is here — a very merchant; in short I find but few of
the Sons of Liberty in the army. I wish you a Successful Campaign.
Victory & Laurels to you — that you may long remain the scourge
of Tyrants is the Sincere wish of your Friend & Humble Ser't.

> Paul Revere.

Benedict Arnold had been in Boston a few weeks before. He
had asked Paul Revere to do some shopping for him — a sword
knot and sash, 'Two best Appalets' and 'one doz silk hose.' As he
also sent his compliments to Mrs. Revere, they must have had some
social meetings. But on the whole, life was dreary enough — he
living most of the time on Castle Island and Rachel and the children
and his mother, who was now sick and poorly, at North Square.
All he had out there with him was the boy Paul, who served under
him as lieutenant. Although the British commanders of the Castle
often had their families with them, and Miss Hulton found life as
pleasant in Boston Harbor as at a watering place, Paul Revere does
not seem to have moved his family out. Joseph Warren Revere
was born the spring of 1777, and he always said that at this time
his father 'was off to the wars' — but seemingly no further off
than the Castle.

## V

THAT spring — the spring of
'77 — John Eliot wrote to his friend, Jeremy Belknap, ' ... the
people in Boston are buying places in the country ... we are much
alarumed and expect another attack.'

The British not only had taken possession of New York, but also
of Newport, Rhode Island. It was from Rhode Island and the

sea Boston expected a sortie. The town was fortified as well as it
was able. The home guard, made up largely of artisans, were not
impressive troops, and the proportion of officers to men is amazing.
They were probably as good as most towns today could assemble
under similar circumstances.

Boston not only feared attack from without, but treachery from
the Tories within her gates. The year before, the state had required
all adult males to say 'they believed the war, resistence and opposition in which the United American Colonies are now engaged
against the fleets and armies of Great Britain, is, on the part of the
said colonies, just and necessary,' and to swear 'they would do
nothing to help the British forces.'

Men who refused to take this rather mild oath must give up
their arms — for which Massachusetts agreed to pay them! A few
were exiled to the environs of Boston for a month or so. A doctor
and his son were kept in jail. But when the war went into its third
year, another act was passed. Tories who constituted an actual
danger might be tried and turned over to 'the honourable, the
Board of War.' If guilty they were to be banished to the West
Indies. Their estates were not yet confiscated, but that was soon
to come.

On the seventeenth of April there was a stormy town meeting.
A few weeks before, Danbury, in Connecticut, had been sacked by
a British raiding party. It was said the local Tories had a hand in
directing this manoeuvre, for the houses of the patriots were burned
and the Tories' were not. There were two obvious conclusions to
draw from this savage attack on Danbury. First, that the same
thing might very well happen to Boston if the possible inside agents
of the British were not got out of town, and the second conclusion
was (as John Eliot wrote Belknap), 'Because a knot of villians have
done much mischief in the State of Connecticut, it is not right the
people should suffer in Boston. Nevertheless the poor Tories of
Boston must do penance for what is done by their nominal brethern
in Conneticut.'

John Eliot probably represented a very small, very intelligent,
dispassionate point of view. He was physically a little fellow and so
frail his family believed 'it was only by the favor of Providence the
tender plant was not cut down.' His father, Andrew Eliot (who had
saved Hutchinson's papers from the mob that sacked the house),

lived near North Square. Everyone around that section of town
knew this tender plant, held their breath over whether it would
live or die, and watched with pleasure its blossoming into a promising young divine. Just out of Harvard when the war broke, he
had served his country as a chaplain for a few weeks. At this time
overwork had caused 'his health to flag and spirits fail . . . in a
word made me a hippochondriac.'

He was as gentle a creature as ever lived and Jeremy Belknap
was also very gentle. Once he reproved a friend who was killing
spiders in his garden. Eliot had no sympathy with the two militia
officers on whom was the responsibility of defending Boston —
Thomas Crafts and Paul Revere. Neither of them was a 'hippochondriac.' It is doubtful if they would let spiders multiply in their
back yards — nor Tories in the town. Feeling was running high
against these possible Trojan horses. It was said fire engines 'have
been stopped and rendered useless and that dark lanthorns were
seen near the powder magazine . . . fourteen Tories have been taken
in the act of burning the town.' Thus the rumor. The Colonel and
the Lieutenant Colonel were anxious at least to keep track of who
the Tories were and where they went. If the innocent among them
suffered with the guilty, it would not bother them as much as it
would the supersensitive young clergyman. It is largely what John
Eliot wrote about the town meeting and his sharp gibes at the
militia officers that have been preserved. He evidently did not
consider Paul Revere much of a public speaker.

'O Tempora, O Mores,' he wrote as one divine to another, 'is at
present the universal cant. Paul Revere haranguing in town meeting, the commandant of every particular company, the gentleman
in his domestic circle, & every drabbling dishclout politician, however various their opinions, have all some kind of observation to
make upon the times . . . If the Tories are to be destroyed who is to
draw the line between Whig and Tory? In this town the most
respectable triumverate, Thomas Crafts, Paul Revere, Harbottle
Dorr. The like jewels are not so precious, I suppose, but they may
be found all over the Province.'

Both Colonel Crafts (who, with his great size, 'fiery-visage,' and
nodding wig) must have been an impressive speaker, and Paul
Revere believed that the General Court was not strict enough in
dealing with the danger in their midst. Benjamin Hitchbourn op-

posed his own cousin — which may be the reason John Eliot refers
to Revere's 'domestic circle.' This youngest of the many Hitchbourn boys had a year before been a prisoner of the British. This
spring he had been selected by the Town of Boston to give the annual Massacre oration. He was brilliant, talkative, full of oaths,
and an extremely able lawyer. Major Dawes was also opposed to
going to any extent in dealing with the Trojan horses not sanctioned
by law. John Eliot (who does not seem to have said anything, although so ready to criticize others) summed the matter up, 'Have
these men done amiss, the law is open. If there is not power eno'
lodged in our General Court to take hold of the enimies of the
country, it is a pity the Court has a being. If we are in a state of
anarchy, let us not have the credit nor the expense of maintaining
a Legislature.'

But obviously he was not talking in terms of the British arriving
that night — and that was the way most of Boston was thinking.
But the meeting could not even decide who the Tories might be.
They were sure of four doctors, Lloyd (under whom Warren had
studied), Danforth, Rand, and Kast, as well as the Reverend
Doctor Byles.

'Thomas Crafts, Esq., Colonel Reveire, Deacon Caleb Davis,
Colonel Isaac Sears,' were voted 'to wait upon One of the Hon'ble
Council of this State & Desire that the Persons voted by the Town
to be inimical persons to these States be immediately apprehended
& confined.' Colonel Sears was the New York Son of Liberty
Revere had mentioned (sarcastically) in his letter to John Lamb, as
'a very merchant.' He had left his own town because the British
now held it.

But young John Eliot, brooding over the scene, thought, 'It got
to be just as the affair of the witches at Salem, every man naming
his neighbour & the moderator put an end to the meeting.' It was
probably about time.

Two days later, on the second anniversary of the battle of Lexington, the sinister, mysterious 'Joyce Jun'r' took matters into his own
delicate hands. He seems to have been the personification of
anonymous threat.

On the nineteenth of April in '77, Joyce moved into action against
the Tories, and Abigail Adams wrote John about it, and John Eliot
wrote Jeremy Belknap.

I hate to tell a story [says Abigail], unless I am informed in every particular. As it happened yesterday and today is Sunday I have not been so fully informed as I could wish. About eleven o'clock yesterday William Jackson, Dick Green, Harry Perkins and Sargent of Cape Ann and A Carry of Charlestown, were carted out of Boston under the direction of Joice junior, who was mounted on horseback, with a red coat, a white wig and a drawn sword, with drum and fife following. A concourse of people to the amount of five hundred followed. They proceeded as far as Roxbury, where he ordered the cart to be tipped up, then told them if they were ever caught in town again it should be at the expense of their lives. He ordered his gang to return, which they did immediately without any disturbance.

Next day she added a postscript.

It seems they have refused to take paper money, and offered their goods lower for silver than paper: bought up articles at a dear rate and would not part with them for paper.

Abigail Adams says nothing about the donkey, the boots or the whistle, which characterized the Joyce Jun'r of the Pope's Day celebrations, nor does she throw any light on who was personifying 'Joyce Jun'r' at the moment. Neither does John Eliot:

The first affair that has happened since I wrote my last was the exhibition of Josie Jun'r at the head of a mob carting a number of Tories out of town. I believe this was not mentioned in the paper, tho' he often puts in his blustering threats & you doubtless have heard strange & large accounts about the matter.

He thought that 'most of the people in the cart were justly obnoxious. Mr. Sargent in particular, by his affectation of Toryism, has alternately filled the minds of the people with indignation and contempt,' but 'old Mr. Perkins' inoffensive carriage raised up a spirit of tenderness & compassion.'

Abigail Adams' postscript, accusing these men of hoarding and refusing to accept the provincial paper money (such as Paul Revere had turned off his press), seems to have given the correct reason why this particular five were selected from Boston's enormous crop of Tories.

Epes Sargent of Gloucester was a proud and fiery little man. When the people of his own town had refused to sell him food, he had taken refuge in Boston behind the British fortifications. He had intended to sail with Howe to Halifax, but at the last moment could not bear to part with his family. Once he was very rich and a most appreciative patron of Paul Revere's, ordering a large amount of church silver which still exists. Twelve years before, Paul Revere had engraved his arms for a bookplate. Lacking the delicacy of Nathaniel Hurd's bookplates, there is an attractive ruggedness to Revere's work. Epes Sargent's represents Revere at his best in this particular field. It was this munificent patron and erstwhile great shipowner who was now being carted out of town.

William Jackson had done his best to leave with Howe, but was picked up by a privateersman along with Crean Brush. He advertised his shop on Cornhill as a 'variety store' and seems to have been the first person to use the phrase.

Nathaniel Cary, James Perkins, and 'Dick' Green had all been picked up as suspects and banished for a few months the year before. They now were back in Boston and, such was the liberty granted to minorities at the time, even during a war, they were saying about what they pleased and selling illegally.

'Joyce Jun'r,' having rid the town of this selection of Tories for a week or so at least, sent out the following typical explanation of his conduct and threats for other hoarding shopkeepers.

Mr. Edes                                    Boston April 19, 1777
                                                 5 o'clock. P.M.
Omit publishing the following at your Peril

## A NOTIFICATION

Whereas, by my express Command, this Day five Tory Villains were carted over the Line in BOSTON NECK, VIZ [and he names them] Persons whose Characters have been so uniform for some Time past, as not to be marked even with a Shadow of a Virtue: —

AND whereas there are many more of the same Stamp in this Town, and others daily coming in from the Country because the Towns they resided in could no longer bear their Unparallelled Wickedness, lest they make others as bad as themselves: — AND whereas I have certain Information of a Gang of Tories, who have weekly Meetings at Particular Houses in the Town, under Cover of Night, then and there, consulting and wickedly contriving to ruin, if possible this once Happy Land: — AND whereas there are several Merchants Shop-keepers and others in this Town, who have a large quantity of Dry Goods and West-India Produce, which they have secreted, and still refuse to sell, altho' the good people of this State, and the Army are in immediate Want of such Articles; and others that do sell are guilty of many wicked and evil Practices in adulterating certain of their Goods and others refusing Paper Currency: — AND whereas, not withstanding the many good and wholesome Laws of this State, Villains of each foregoing Denominations, either by Evasion, or by having their Cause supported by Persons of a Certain Class, called Moderate Men, alias Hyprocrites, escape condign Punishment I have therefore thought fit to issue this NOTIFICA-TION strictly charging and commanding all.

Joyce goes on for some length as he takes upon himself enforcement of the laws the General Court had passed. An attempt had been made to nail prices and stop inflation, for the price of living had already doubled, but to enforce such laws there was not the least shadow of authority. The town was practically without a police force. The Whig merchants might (but probably did not always) feel a sense of honor in regarding these laws. The Tory merchants obviously could feel none.

Joyce goes on with his notification, touching upon that other group of Tories — the ones who might be sending military intelligence — seemingly the group which Paul Revere and Thomas Crafts were the most worried over.

> ... I do further comand and require all Meetings of Tories to cease from this time, or else I shall take an Opportunity of breaking up their future gossippings at the Widow's and I do Caution the said Widow for permitting her Son going with any more Letters to Reading and Concord. I most affectionately return my Thanks to those free Sons who gave me their Assisstance this day. I shall notify when I would be glad to see them again.

### JOYCE JUN'R

The Tories were clamped down on that spring. A few were tried, locked up, exiled, but it was a curiously half-hearted, ineffectual, and decent treatment they got compared to what the same men living today might expect.

Doctor Byles was among those tried and judged to be dangerous. He was ordered to keep to his own house and an armed guard was stationed before it. A friend asked him who the uniformed man was in front of his door. 'Ah,' said the Doctor, always relishing his pun, 'that's my observe-a-tory.' One day he wished cold water from a near-by well. He was old and frail and his daughters (who should have been his granddaughters) were not hewers of wood and drawers of water by nature. By now they surely had no servant, so he asked the sentry to fetch him a bucket of water. The fellow at first refused. His officer had told him to take a gun and walk up and down in front of this house. Those were orders. But the clergyman said that if he would go for the water, he himself would guard the house in his absence. Boston was delighted to see the courageous and tricky old fellow, dressed in his black clerical and enormous wig, a musket on his shoulder, pacing back and forth before his own house. The farce of keeping him under guard was soon given up and he was back in circulation again. 'The Doctor,' John Eliot noted, 'struts about the town in the luxuriance of his self sufficiency, looking as if he despised all mankind. How he doth for a maintenance, nobody knows besides him, and the only account he can give is "That he doubles and trebles his money." He is a virulent Tory, and destitute of all prudence. . . .'

Now he was definitely growing shabby — and he had always been so elegant. The Hollis Church had thrown him out. Nobody knew how he supported himself and his two maiden daughters. They were shut in more and more upon themselves in the stuffy, book-filled, dusty little house. He had a fine library, a remarkable collection of Hogarth prints, a famous collection of 'curiosities,' and friends did come to see him and enjoy or squirm over his wit. But Miss Polly and Miss Kitty already had little to live for but memories. Their faces began to set early into the sharpness of traditional New England spinsterhood.

# VI

**IN MAY,** Paul Revere put this notice in the *Boston Gazette*:

> May 26
> Last Saturday died after a tedious Confinement, Mrs. Deborah Revere, aged 73. Her funeral will be on Tuesday when her Relations and Friends are desired to attend.

He had lived with his mother or she with him all his life. Paul Revere was passionately attached to his family. For him there were never too many children, too many relations, or too many mouths to fill. For them he was ready to work the incredibly long hours of the eighteenth-century artisan. There is reason to believe that even while commander of Castle Island he sneaked back to his own shop now and then and produced a pepper-pot or two and a few small pieces of silver. This was the work he loved. How good the shop on Clark's Wharf must have seemed to him after the inertia and disappointments of army service! Here about him were those hundreds of tools which a silversmith even today makes each man for himself. Today, as one touches his silver, one is conscious of its sensuous, mushroom smoothness. His short, curiously delicate hand was the first to delight in its cool perfection. He may not have known that he was the finest master craftsman in America, but he may well have guessed it. This fact would not have impressed him unduly. It would not have turned his head. He knew other men's work and his own. His neighbor, portly Benjamin Burt's, would command his respect, as it commands connoisseurs' today. There was the marvellous but sometimes overdecorated silver brought in from England. Paul Revere never sacrificed the purity of design for elaboration. The little creamer and sugar pail Lucretia Chandler Murray tried to save from the great house in Rutland is as elaborately embossed as any English silver, but loses none of Revere's characteristic simplicity of line.

As a lieutenant colonel, the regulations required him to powder his hair. His hat would be laced and cocked. His blue uniform and white breeches stiff. At his side swung a useless sword — and his pay was almost non-existent. One cannot grudge him the happy hours in his shop, the sword laid aside for gravers, the uniform for the coarse linen shirt, his throat bare, and hair reverting to its natural blackness.

At home, at the time of his mother's death, he had five girls ranging from Elizabeth, who was seven, to Debby, who was nineteen. These girls were all children of Sary's. Her one son, Paul, was at the Castle with his father. Rachel thus far had had three sons — Joshua was three, the first John dead, and the very remarkable Joseph Warren less than a month old.

Besides Revere's devotion to his craft and to his family was his equally passionate attachment to the cause of American freedom. For it he was not only ready to die himself, but (often the harder choice) ready to sacrifice the good of his own family. As a silversmith he could provide well for them. Money was already being made by a few (only a very few) privateersmen who could pay well for their silver, not in the worthless paper money, but in goods taken at sea. But Paul Revere stuck to his country's service (except for an occasional pepper-pot). His devotion is the more poignant because he had no reward — none of those 'Victory and Laurels' he is generously wishing his friend John Lamb.

This year, for the first time, the Fourth of July was celebrated in Boston, for it was a year ago that the Declaration of Independence had been signed. Paul Revere was ordered to get out his flags and the guns of Castle Island were to salute the great day. A detachment of his artillerymen were ordered into town to fire 'a grand salute' and the militia were to parade. By this time the company of 'Independents' under his cousin, Major Benjamin Hitchbourn, had been organized. They had smart uniforms, black, faced with scarlet, and evidently spent more time drilling than did Colonel Crafts' men. John Boyle had joined the 'Independents.'

'The Day being the anniversary of American Independence,' wrote Boyle smugly after he got home that night, 'the Regt of Militia . . . and the Company of Independents under Major Hitchborn were mustered and performed their Firings in Congress Street [only a short time before it had been Quaker Lane] The Independent Company performed *admirably*; but nothing can be said in

praise of the Militia, who Perfom'd *worse* than *ever*.' As Revere
seems to have contributed only a few of his artillerymen to this
humiliating exhibition of the Boston regiments, we can hope he
passed the day at the Castle, flying his flags and firing his salutes.

Soon Boyle writes of a message from the Governor of Rhode
Island. Forty sail of transports were seen off Newport 'which news
threw the inhabitants [of Boston] into open consternation.' This
proved untrue. But Boston, hungry, badly organized, and jittery,
was fertile soil for any rumor or rioting. Boyle tells of 'a Female
Riot.' 'About one hundred women of the *North*-Part (always prone
to rioting), getting information of a Quantity of Coffee being in
the Store of Thom. Boylston, Esqu. which he refused to sell at the
regulation Price; attacked him in King-street, and demanded the
Keys to his Store, which he refusing to deliver, they immediately
placed him in a Cart and threatened to Cart him out of Town';
and so on.

On the first of August another rumor, this time from Cape Ann.
More transports, and Lord Howe himself had been seen heading
for Boston. 'Many families moved into the Country with their
Effects,' but by six o'clock the rumor was known to be false.

Although Boston was from now on to be in a back-water, rumors
were so thick and times so hard no one could forget there was a
war going on. Once more (as in the old days of the British occupation) deserters were being shot at the foot of the Common. But on
the twenty-second of August an express came with good news and
true:

'General Stark and his New Hampshire militia had totally routed
the Enemy near Bennington.' Some six hundred to seven hundred
prisoners had been taken, Hessians and Canadians, Tories, 'fields
peices and a baron.'

General Burgoyne had detached from his great army, pushing
south from Canada, Colonel Baum and over a thousand picked
men. He had told Baum 'to seize Benington, try the affections of
the country, meet me, a fortnight hence at Albany.' But the
affections of the country had been violently anti-British and Baum
had met Stark and his furious fighters at Bennington instead of
Burgoyne at Albany. Almost the entire collection of sharpshooters,
Germans, regulars, well-organized Tories, had been captured or
killed. Colonel Baum had been killed. It was a tremendous victory

for the colonials, for it showed them they could stop the steam roller Burgoyne was driving from north to south across the country.

General Heath ordered Paul Revere, on the twenty-seventh of August, to go to Worcester and pick up these prisoners of war. He was to take 'five Drums & five fifes, one hundred & twenty Sergants, Coporals, Bombadiers, Gunners, Matrosses.' The day they left was appointed one of 'Humiliation and Prayer.' The whole regiment was ordered to attend services 'dressed in their Uniforms, Clean and Powdered' and listen to the Reverend Mr. Thatcher. After the service, Paul Revere and his one hundred and thirty men started for Worcester.

They left Boston at six in the afternoon, got to Watertown by nine, and spent the night. The next morning they ate breakfast at Weston. The officers went to the Jones Tavern. Mrs. Jones was an avowed Tory. She probably liked these militiamen as little as they liked her.

At Sudbury, Revere found his one wagon could not keep up even with the marching men. He hired another horse and Mrs. Jones' messenger and letter caught up with him. She said his men had been stealing her sugar. 'I have all their Packs searched, find nothing,' their commander notes. 'Suspect they stole the Sugar themselves out of pretence charge our people.' It is humiliating to be charged with petty thievery, but at least Revere could comfort himself that there had been a theft on the other side. Captain Todd said his servant had hung his coat on the hook in Jones' kitchen and his pocket had been picked. Revere disliked Captain William Todd, for he was 'so very Eminical to the Corps of Artillery,' and Todd disliked Revere. Not long afterwards Todd transferred to a different service, and his erstwhile commander could believe himself well rid of him. But he was not, and in his new position he was able to revenge himself on Revere, who thought him a trouble-maker and a liar. But as Mrs. Jones' servant watched the searching of the one hundred and thirty packs and Captain Todd tells his story of the pocket picked in her kitchen the night before, Revere must have had some affection for the fellow — even if he did not believe everything he said.

So they went on to Marlborough for their second night, and, starting at six the next morning, came into Worcester at five in the afternoon.

The men put up at the 'Town House,' as their colonel called the county courthouse. Next door to this was the house and printing shop of Paul Revere's old friend and fellow Mason, Isaiah Thomas. No man in America loved good paper, fine print, more than this amazing young publisher, but the *Spy*, 'owing to unskilled workmen, bad ink, wretched paper and woren down type,' as he himself said of this period, 'appered in wretched deshaille.' This professional shame probably weighed upon his spirits more than his private, for not long before he had divorced his wild Bermudian wife. Every bit of dirty Thomas linen had been washed in public. Divorces were not common.

In the *Spy* he notes the arrival of Lieutenant Colonel Paul Revere, the 'strong guard' he had brought with him, and the four days the men waited for the arrival of the prisoners. At last they came, tired, sick, discouraged, four hundred defeated and ailing men, Tories, British, and Germans. All Worcester had seen Tories before. These they hated as traitors to their own country. Most of the people had seen British regulars. A regular was not necessarily a bad fellow. There was considerable fraternizing between the provincials and the regulars. But the great novelty was the 'Hessians,' as they called all the Germans, although these men happened to be from Brunswick. People gaped at them in amazement. Certain classical scholars, seeing these big, stolid men, thought of the old line, 'fierce Germania's blue-eyed sons.' The average Yankee despised these peasants who had so docilely permitted their rulers to sell them at so much a head to fight another country's wars. They were the very personification of tyranny. Had *they* never heard that 'Taxation without representation is tyranny,' or, 'Give me liberty or give me death'? They never had.

General Burgoyne's young lieutenant, Anburey, was also amazed at the conduct of the German troops. They were so incredibly and fatally homesick. 'Thus it is that men, who have faced the dangers of battle and shipwreck without fear (for they are certainly as brave as any soldiers in the world) are taken off a score at a time by a mere phantom of their own brain.'

As they could not speak English and had not known enough to revolt against their rulers, they were considered by the provincials to be half-witted — so like dumb cattle they lined up, accepting a Massachusetts militia officer's orders as gratefully as their own.

Tell them what to do and they would do it. The British soldiers captured from Burgoyne made endless trouble for the colony (at this very county seat, in a short time two would be hanged for murder and one for rape); the 'Hessians' might die of 'heimweh,' but rarely took to crime. In time most of these German prisoners became American citizens.

This first contingent of German soldiers had been under the command of Baron von Riedesel, but the Baron and the rest of his troops, his Baroness, and three little daughters were not captured until Saratoga. Some two months later they were making this same journey to Boston. The Baroness could not get used to so homespun an army. In her husband's command most of the officers could write 'von' before their names and the privates were mere lumps of humanity — hardly men at all. Here was democracy really at work. The highly born, pretty little aristocrat is surprised, but not especially displeased. 'Some of the officers who accompanied us, had been shoemakers, and on our halts, made boots for our officers, and sometimes even mended the soldiers shoes. . . . One of our officers, whose boots were much worn said in jest to an American of military rank, who had a good pair, he would pay a guinea for his in exchange. He immediately alighted from his horse, took the guinea, gave up his boots, and putting on the old ones of the officer, again mounted his steed.'

She found the people who came out to stare at the captives naïvely curious, but 'I must say in justice the Americans were civil.' The militia colonels did not impress their prisoners by their military smartness, but they were considerate, kindly, and very democratic. Actually they had not the slightest idea of the great chasm which separates a baron from a common man. Probably Lieutenant Colonel Paul Revere was no exception.

But this victory at Bennington, with its few hundreds of prisoners, was as nothing compared to the capture of Burgoyne and his thousands at Saratoga a couple of months later. It had come none too soon, for now at last France was ready to come in on the American side. Shortly before this 'decisive battle of the world,' John Adams had been in despair at the state of his nation. 'O Heaven! grant us one great soul! One leading mind could extricate the best cause from that ruin which seems to await it for the want of it. We have as good a cause as ever was fought for; we have great resources; the people are well-tempered; one active, masterly capacity, would bring order out of this confusion, and save this country'; for not even Washington himself had by the fall of '77 emerged out of the confusion as the hoped-for, prayed-for great leader.

The British possession of Newport was a continual threat to Massachusetts. Paul Revere took part in both the futile expeditions organized to dislodge them. The first time was in the fall of 1777. The troops marched to Rhode Island and home again. Colone. Crafts, on the return of his regiment to Boston, complimented them on their 'extraordinary military and soldier-like behavior on the Rhode to & from Camp' and 'the polite treatment the Inhabitants rec'd from them.'

Of the success of this expedition he can say little except to praise his men's courtesy. John Boyle is less reticent: 'Nov 1 The 9000 Men lately raised to go upon a Secret Expedition returned home without effecting any Thing. The public Expence attending this Manoevure has been computed at 35000 dollars pr day.'

So in spite of the great victory at Saratoga, the third winter of the war settled down upon Boston black enough. There was only one rift in the sombre clouds. This was the sudden return of their beloved 'King' Hancock. He had resigned as President of the Continental Congress (saying that the Philadelphia air did not agree with his delicate health) as soon as he had heard that Massachusetts was ready to set up a state government. He intended to get himself well entrenched before Sam Adams could get home and seize control. Ever since that time, two years before, John Adams had nominated George Washington as commander-in-chief and Sam Adams had seconded the motion, Hancock had been the open enemy of his erstwhile confederate, Sam Adams. It was thought he had expected the appointment for himself. Although John Adams had shown himself a genuine statesman at Philadelphia (and soon was leaving for France), neither Hancock nor Sam Adams had added anything to their reputations. The elder man was too provincial and had had too much practice in backstairs politics, the younger was too provincial and too small-minded for the really great work that lay ahead.

So 'King' Hancock's chariot rolled into Boston escorted by mounted soldiers (sometimes he would have two dozen in front of him with drawn swords and two dozen behind — he liked to do things nicely). Here he was idolized. There was no public office he would seek that the voters would not give him. He was cheered on the streets, and grubby people ran at his chariot wheels, gratefully picking up the coins he tossed and taking a vicarious, unresentful pleasure in his wealth — much as they would follow a movie star today, greedily admiring the mink coat, the costly car, but not exactly envying. The time had not yet come when a 'plain man' could be a hero to the Americans. They wanted to look up to some royal family leading a life far above their own. Franklin could at the same time dazzle the French court by his simplicity. But it took John Hancock to dazzle republican Boston.

Once more the Hancock mansion on Beacon Hill was flung wide open for entertainment. Those who did not rate an invitation could stand outside and stare at the fashion and feasting within. Seemingly they enjoyed this privilege as much as a modern audience can enjoy luxury upon the screen. Smart little Mrs. Hancock was a great improvement as a hostess upon Aunt Lydia. She had recently borne a son — John George Washington Hancock — to serve as a little Prince of Wales.

But for your average citizen food was scarce. Wheat flour, rice, and coffee out of the market or at prices no one could pay. The General Court had attempted to control prices, prevent inflation, profiteering and hoarding, but with slight success.

There was a rage for carting people — in September five shopkeepers guilty of 'monopolizing and Extortion' were taken on this short but ignominious ride.

War had upset everything. Violence and crime became common, and John Boyle notes the extraordinary fact that 'High way Robbery now is practised in the Streets of Boston almost every night.'

## VII

GLOOMY as the winter of '77–'78
seemed to the citizens of Boston, it was even blacker for Washington
and the pitiful remnants of his Continental Army at Valley Forge.
But with the spring came news to hearten all Americans. France,
who had been a non-belligerent ally of the colonies from the beginning, was ready to throw away all pretence of neutrality and
once more go on with her old war with England.

A large proportion of the men of Revere's age and of his father's
and grandfather's had fought the French. It had been a very long,
very cruel war, and not long over. Many of the best American
officers from George Washington down had gained their first
experience and fame fighting the hated French. And in those days
the British had been the ally. Although many Bostonians, like
Revere himself, had French blood, it was the blood of exiles. The
stories of parents and grandparents flying from the terrors of the
Huguenot persecution still echoed in the memory of their sons and
grandsons. Few Americans had ever seen a Frenchman except at
the other end of a musket. They were called the 'Mounseers' and
a whole folklore had grown up about them — their morals, their
cruelty, their religion, their scrawniness, and their eating habits.

The first French vessel to arrive in Boston was the frigate *Nymphile*. In a month or two she would be followed by a magnificent
fleet under Count d'Estaing.

On the thirteenth of March, Paul Revere was ordered to 'fire
the Heavy Cannon on Castle Island when the French Frigate
passes by the Castle Provided she Salutes the same.' The very
wording of this order shows the suspicion these new allies were
under in Boston.

The *Nymphile* came and went without incident. There could
have been no question about her willingness to salute the American
flag, for the Frenchmen, during this trying period of readjustment
with their old enemies, showed all their traditional tact.

In September, Count d'Estaing sailed into Boston Harbor with his beautiful fleet. His flagship was the ninety-gun *Languedoc*. With her came the *César*, the *Marseillaise*, *Protecteur*, the *Hector*, the *Zélé* — twelve ships of the line and fifteen frigates. The French at that time built the finest fighting ships afloat. The people of Boston jammed the wharves to look over these foreigners who by the curious workings of diplomacy had now come as their allies. The first thing they noticed was they had been misinformed about the physique of the Frenchmen. 'They beheld plump, portly officers and strong vigorous sailors,' and had been expecting a 'soup maigre crew.' One of their preconceived notions tottered, but it was noticed the Frenchmen were hanging around the Frog Pond on the Common, eyeing the frogs. At least they had been right about their favorite diet.

Even before Hancock gave his famous breakfast for the officers, an ugly incident did happen which might have completely ended this new alliance. The Admiral kept his head.

A bakery was set up in Boston by the French to supply their own men with bread. Flour was no longer to be had in Boston and the wonderful smell of that good French bread drew a crowd. Hardly a person in Boston could speak French, so when the baker refused to sell his crusty long loaves to the citizens, the people (probably thinking he was holding out for a higher price) became angry. There was a row. Street fighting. Neither side knew what the other was talking about.

Two French officers tried to interfere. Pléville Le Peley, commander of the *Zélé*, had already lost a leg fighting for France. He was wounded. But the very highly born lieutenant, the Chevalier de Saint-Sauveur, was killed. He was buried in the vaults under King's Chapel (*'dite chapelle du roy'*). A Franciscan monk, his servant, and a mere handful of his companions attended the young Chevalier to his grave. It was all done as quietly as possible — but very decently. And the Frenchmen appreciated the fact that someone had considerately lighted candles in the vaults where the burial took place. This sad, semi-secret service was probably the first Catholic Mass ever said in Boston. From now on the old Pope's Days were curtailed in fear of hurting the allies' feelings.

In a few days D'Estaing and his fellow officers of the fleet were enjoying Hancock's famous hospitality as though nothing had happened. As long as there were some British prisoners of war on

ships in the harbor, it was agreed between them that of course it
was the British who had, in some mysterious way, killed the young
Saint-Sauveur. Not the Americans! The French politely said that
'our common enemies will stop at nothing,' and went on drinking
toasts. Once it was seventeen toasts 'at the interval of five minutes
and accompanied with a discharge of Cannon.' Were not the
Americans and Frenchmen comrades in arms, friends at last, after
a hundred years of fighting? The affair was hushed up even in the
newspapers, but the clerk of the French fleet tells the story, which
the Americans would have been glad to forget. The tact and
modesty of these French officers, with their fine titles and great
names, is one of the most striking things to have come out of the
Saint-Sauveur affair. But another is worth pointing out. By the
fall of 1778, the people of Boston were ready to riot for good bread.

The French immediately went to work fortifying Boston, although they had to dismount naval guns from their ships to do it.
Paul Revere must have seen much of them and this contact cured
him of a dislike which he admits, in a letter, he used to have. 'I
can easily account for your prejudice; before this War, I was as
much prejudiced against them as you are. . . . They are a brave,
humane, generous and polite Nation,' which sounds as if the
French engineers carried out their work in a manner satisfactory
to the commander of the Castle, whose professional feelings might
have been hurt if they had been arrogant or he thin-skinned. The
French selected Hull for their principal fort. Cannon shot farther
than they used to. Castle Island was somewhat superseded by
this new fort; from now on it was little more than a place from
which to fire salutes and show flags.

Governor Hancock and a small group of still wealthy men did
heroic work in entertaining these strangers and making them feel
appreciated. Some of the parties must have been dreary enough,
for the Frenchmen spoke French and the Americans English.
They often fell back on Latin. Doctor Cooper spoke it so readily,
he was in great demand as a guest. They misunderstood each
other in other ways. Mr. Tracy, of Cambridge, had a large house
and plenty of plate. It was his duty to entertain the officers, but
the only thing he knew about Frenchmen was that they ate frogs.
Samuel Breck, a very small boy at the time, remembered the story
of Mr. Tracy's party as told at the time.

'Tracy filled a plate with soup which was passed to the Admiral, the next was handed to the Consul. As soon as L'Etombe put his spoon in his plate he dished up a large frog, just as green and perfect as if he had hopped from the pond into the tureen. Not knowing at first what it was, he seized it by one of its hind legs. . . . "Ah! Mon Dieu! Un grenouille" . . . then bowing to the gentleman next to him gave him the frog. He received it, and passed it round the table. Thus the poor crapaud made the tour from hand to hand until it reached the Admiral. Mr. Tracy, not understanding what the laughter was about, concentrated on ladling out his frogs.

'"What's the matter?" he asked, and raising his head surveyed the frogs dangling by a leg in all directions. "Why don't they eat them? . . . If they knew the confounded trouble I had to catch them in order to treat them to a dish of their own country they would find that with me, at least, it was no joking matter."'

Hancock, of course, kept open house. It was at this time that Dolly was so put to it, serving one elaborate meal after another to the counts, chevaliers, and plain Mounseers, she ordered her servants to milk every cow on the Common — no matter whom they belonged to. People on the whole approved of this theft, but in back alleys and along the waterfront sailors of all three nations (for there were a great many paroled English prisoners of war) fought a number of bloody battles. The British and the Yankees often ganged up on the poor Frenchmen.

One of the most tactful things the Frenchmen did was to fill Paymaster Ebenezer Hancock's parlor with sacks of French silver. Not paper. The war was in its third year. Supplies were needed, men needed, and hard money. Now Revere could pay his men and pay himself. The sight of all this genuine money, the weight of it in one's pocket, cheered the troops. Their new allies were wonderful fellows. Ebenezer Hancock was a younger brother of John. He had never been adopted, however, by Uncle Thomas.

Encouraged by the promised aid of the Frenchmen, a second 'secret' expedition was fitted up to drive the British from Newport. The French fleet would attack by sea and, if necessary, could land a strong force. Washington sent men to join the militia of Rhode Island, Connecticut, and Massachusetts. Major Hitchbourn would lead his Independent Cadets. Colonel Revere commanded the Boston artillery train, which was very much reduced. John Hancock was the major general of the Massachusetts militia, three thousand of them in all. Sullivan was commander-in-chief. Generals Glover and Lovell were also present. And so was Lafayette himself. The French fleet sailed. The men marched. The heavy artillery bumped over the bad roads, all converging upon the Rhode Island, as the island on which Newport is situated is called.

The attack began with success, and Paul Revere could write hopefully to Rachel:

Rhode Island August 1778

My dear Girl,

Your very agreeable letter came safe to hand, since which I have wrote, but received no answere. I beleive you are better; what a *pleasure* to hear! Pray take care of yourself & my little ones. I hoped ere this to have been in Newport; my next I hope will be dated there. We have had the most severe N. East Storm I ever knew, but thank Heaven, after 48 hours it is over. I am in high health and spirits, & [so is] our Army. The Enemy dare not show their heads. We have had about 50 who have deserted to us; Hessians and others. They say more will desert & only wait for opportunity. I am told by the inhabitants that before we came on, they burned 6 of their Frigates; they have destroyed many houses between them & us. I hope we shall make them pay for all. The French Fleet are not returned but I just heard they were off Point Judith with 3 frigates, prizes; this, I am told, comes from Head Quarters. I donot assert it for fact, but hope it is true. You have heard this Island is the Garden of America indeed it used to appear so, but those British Savages have so abused and destroyed the Trees (the greater part of which was Fruit Trees) that it does not look like the same Island; some of the inhabitants who left it hardly know where to find there homes. Col Crafts is obliged to act under Col. Crane which is a severe Mortification to him. I have but little to do with him having a seperate command. It is very irkesome to be seperated from *her* whom I so tenderly love, and from my little Lambs; but were I at home I should want to be here. It seems as if half Boston was here. I hope the affair will soon be settled; I think it will not be long first. I trust that Allwise Being who has protected me will still protect me, and send me safely to the Arms of her whom it is my greatest happiness to call my own. Paul is well; send Duty & love to all. I am suprised Capt. Marett has not rote me. My duty to my Aunts, my love to Brothers & Sisters, my most affectionate love to my children. It would be a pleasure to have a line from Deby. Lawson desires to be remebered to you. My best

> regards to Mrs Bennet, Mr Burt, Capt Talling, & all enquiring
> friends. Col. Marescall, who is [one] of Gen'l Sullivans Adi Camps,
> tells me this minute that the French have took a Transport with
> British Grenadiers, but could not tell particulars.
>
> > Your Own
> >
> > Paul Revere

But the 'French fleet are not returned. . . .' Just before this wild
storm of August 12 and 13, 1778, which was remembered in Rhode
Island for almost a hundred years as 'the great storm,' the British
fleet, under Lord Howe, had put in its appearance. D'Estaing
went out to meet him. The storm Revere mentions swept them
apart and broke up both fleets. But this Revere, writing in his camp
on the Rhode Island, did not know. He only knew 'It is very
irksome' to be away from home. Once more he is in contact with
Lewis Ansart, or, as he calls him, 'Col Marescall.'

With the French fleet and its four thousand land forces out of
the way, the besieged British troops dared to take the offensive and
won the engagement in spite of the fine beginning the Americans
had made. It had been impossible for the Frenchmen to stand by
and give the help they had promised. The seafaring New Englanders knew it, but even so the name 'Frog-eaters' was the least
scandalous of the reproaches they threw up against their allies.

When the French fleet left, General Hancock decided to go
home too. 'He complained of the length and tiresomness of the
campaign, He heard that his child was sick and dying — he fancied
that the fleet had gone to Boston, and could not re-fit in his absence,
but more than this he imagined that the British were round and he
could not believe it safe or prudent for the man of the people to
remain any longer.'

His little Princeling was well, the French ships able to refit,
Boston was not attacked. He had not proved himself a very capable
general, but as a soother of French feelings he was admirable.
Without him we might have lost our allies before they had even
begun to fight.

On the fifth of November, 'The Count D'Estaing sailed yesterday,' John Rowe noted. 'A Good Deal of Snow fell this day. This
Evening came news that the Somerset Man of Warr was cast away
on the back of Cape Cod.'

The British, in spite of the losses they had sustained during 'the

great storm,' had attempted to block D'Estaing in Boston Harbor.
Another storm had blown their fleet out of position and the *Somerset*,
whose name is so inseparably linked with Paul Revere's by both
fact and poetry, was wrecked upon the Clay Pounds.


## VIII


A PROCESS which had been going
on from the beginning of the war was now accelerated. The most
warlike of Boston's citizens were going into the Continental Army
and the most adventurous and ambitious into privateering. Colonel
Crafts' regiment was disbanded. Fifteen of its battalions had gone
into the Continental Army. Three companies of artillery remained,
and this was called 'the artillery regiment.' Paul Revere was in
command of them. Command is a rather strong word to use. He
was having trouble with two of his captains — Winthrop Gray
and William Todd. They had been disgruntled over the reorgan-
ization of the troops. And his own men were running away to get
aboard the privateers.

In privateering, fortunes might be made. Its inherent reckless-
ness, almost lawlessness, appealed to the seafaring traditions of
the New Englanders. Sitting out at Castle Island, showing flags
and firing salutes, with never enough to eat or wear, did not. You
could have more fun and chance of fortune on the ships than in
the forts.

Both the privateer captains and the officers of our few warships
did all they could to get recruits. Boston resounded with the
'scream of fife and the tuck of drum' as recruits were raised by
'artifice or liquor.'

'Our coast was lined with British cruisers, which had almost
annihilated our commerce,' as one young man remembered. 'All

means were resorted to, which ingenuity could devise, to induce
men to enlist [on the ships]. A recruiting officer bearing a flag and
attended by a band of martial music, paraded the streets, to excite
a thirst for glory and a spirit of military ambition.

'The recruiting officer possessed the qualifications required to
make the service appear alluring, especially to the young. He was
a jovial good natured fellow, of ready wit and much broad humor
... when he espied any large boys among the idle crowd around
him, he would attract their attention by singing in a comical
manner the following doggerel.

> "All you that have bad masters
> And cannot get your due
> Come, come my brave boys,
> And join with our ships crew."'

Some of those who followed this enticing performer were already
enlisted as artillerymen under Paul Revere.

He knew he had deserters on three vessels at that moment in
Boston Harbor. The frigate *Providence* and the sloop *Providence*
and the *Boston*. One of these *Providences* was part of the Massachusetts Navy, one of the Continental. The *Boston* was a privateersman. So Paul Revere had deserters on all three of the armed naval
services of his period, and none of them would hesitate to enlist
men from each other's ships. It was hard for both navy and army
to get good gunners and the ship captains refused to give up their
men merely because they had an unexpired term of enlistment
elsewhere. None of these ships could leave the harbor without
sailing within musket-shot of the fort. Revere asked advice from
the War Council and was told to fire upon them if they tried to
get past with his men on board. He next asked that 'one large
speaking trumpet for hailing' be sent to him on the island, and
settled down to wait for the ships.

Early in April he saw the frigate *Providence* brazenly approaching
through the tortuous channel. Seemingly 'the one large speaking
\rumpet' did its work. She stopped and unloaded ten of Revere's
men. But the colonel knew there were five more aboard. After
some parley, and probably bad language and feeling on both sides,
the frigate started on. At last Revere gave the order to his fort to fire
upon her. This brought her to in a hurry, and she disgorged five more.

So Revere got his scamps back and presumably off the other two ships as well, for the word would go around fast that the commander of the fort was ready to fire upon American ships in his determination to have his own men. It could hardly have made Paul Revere very popular with the sea forces.

There was reason why the soldiers did not want to stay in the Boston Artillery Regiment, although their colonel seems to have done all he could for their comfort. His letters in the State Archives show the situation: 'Most of their blankets are woren out; some lost their blankets on the retreat from Rhode Island, many have been without all winter. They have received no pay ... many have no shoes, and but one shirt.' He begs the Council also to ease his men's minds, 'they have not the advantage of Continental Soldiers; the Towns they be to will not supply their Familys,' and he says the families are starving. He wishes to be rid of some forty non-commissioned officers (including drummers and fifers), 'the Bread they draw will be wanted.'

Never in the old days when the Sons of Liberty had chased royal governors and their families, tea-assignees, customs officials (and poor Miss Hulton), out of Boston to this same fort, had anyone been hungry or cold. Now that the rebels had the fort, they were both.

As Paul Revere struggled with this impossible situation in which he found himself, his young cousin, Benjamin Hitchbourn, was serving as colonel of the really fashionable 'Independents' and moving into the curious 'high society' which centred about 'King' Hancock. He was a very clever lawyer, and the general upheaval of social life, business, and politics could use such a man. Although already thirty-three, he had not married. He was in fact the very Benjamin of the Hitchbourn family. The youngest and smartest, and figuratively had worn the coat of many colors ever since it had been decided to send him to Harvard. His brothers, shipwrights, hatters, silversmiths, must have been proud of the young man who was now carrying their family name to new distinction. Of course, they may not have liked him.

Early in '79 he was sitting in the Andrews' fashionable parlor polishing the rust off a pair of 'elegant' pistols his friend, Benjamin Andrews, a merchant, wished to take with him on his travels. Times were so violent — what with deserters from all three armies on the road — no one dared venture beyond the Neck unarmed. Mr. Andrews sat at his desk writing a letter. Mrs. Andrews, a dashing, handsome woman, was the only witness to what happened next. Mr. Hitchbourn handed the pistol to his friend, who 'brought his thumb down upon the trigger,' or the gun 'exploded,' or 'Mr. Benjamin Andrews, a worthy Good Man, shot himself by mere accident' — if it was an accident.

Anyway, there he died with the bullet through his temple, leaving behind him a number of children and a widow young and pleasing enough to seem to furnish a motive for what was known for years as 'The Hitchbourn Murder.' The young lawyer was crushed by this undoubtedly accidental killing. The widow was lamenting wildly that she had lost her breadwinner. Her first thought was how she and her children would live. There seemed to Benjamin Hitchbourn but one way he could make amends. He married the lady, and thus supplied a motive for 'The murder.' Legally acquitted at the time, he and his wife never lived down the suspicion. Longer than either of them lived, speculation and gossip did their work. So for love of the wife Ben Hitchbourn had shot the husband and Hannah Gardner Andrews Hitchbourn had aided and abetted? If Hitchbourn had just cleaned the pistol (as he said), why did he not know it was loaded? How did a chance shot happen to kill a man so instantly? Were they as sorry as they said they were, or were they Boston's version of the old Aegisthus-Clytemnestra story? So they went through life under a pall of gossip, the lawyer growing more and more successful and the lady more and more fashionable.

## IX

THE *Somerset* had been cast away against the 'Clay Pounds' of Cape Cod. Thoreau calls it a 'voracious beach.' As you stand on this steep and clayey cliff (counting the swallows if you are Thoreau), there is no land between you and

Spain. The full force of the Atlantic expends itself at your feet.
And at your feet lie buried the lost ships of generations. It is one
of America's most ancient and dignified graveyards. In the eighteenth century, before Highland Light was built, these wrecks furnished the scarce population with firewood, treasure-trove, and
a chance to practise the Christian virtue of charity upon survivors.
When the *Somerset* came ashore in a wild night of November, the
inhabitants were startled to find themselves accepting the surrender of four hundred and eighty British seamen and naval officers. You did not often see that many people in one place in
those days along the tip of the Cape. The heavy breakers rolled
up a hundred more for the fishermen to bury. The carcass of the
ship was picked over by the industrious inhabitants who then attempted to burn her.

The wreck lay unmolested, except for the beating of the waves
and the pilfering of the Cape-Codders, from November to March,
when Paul Revere was put in charge of mounting her cannon for
the further defence of Boston. He may have personally taken
charge of the salvaging, for he writes that he will try to get off more
of her guns in a way that suggests he will try in person.

In the spring of 1779, the shattered monster would show none
of her paint, quick-work, and gilding. Paul Revere, gazing at
her pride thus brought low, could not help but think of that
night when Joshua Bentley and Thomas Richardson had rowed
him under the very shadow of this ship. 'It was then young flood,
the ship was winding, and the moon was rising' — and she the
very personification of British power. Now she was less potent
to hurt him than the gulls flying over his head or a crab scuttling
up the beach. In all, he got twenty-one of her big guns — and
hoped to get more. Considering how scarce brass was since the
fighting had begun, and the reputation the Cape-Codders had for
picking up just such inconsiderable trifles (with which the Lord
often provided them), he was lucky to find so many of the original
sixty-four.

Among the privates serving under Paul Revere was John Thoreau.
When certain of the Reveres had fled France for the English island
of Guernsey, certain Thoreaus had taken refuge on Jersey. Young
John left Jersey and had not been over long when he went into
Revere's 'regiment.' He was a powerfully built young man, ad-

venturous and cautious in the best Huguenot tradition. He spoke French more readily than English and was to prosper in Boston and die young of tuberculosis.

Seventy years later, a gaunt, grey-eyed, downward-glancing young man ('as if he had dropped or expected to find something') undertook to explore Cape Cod. This was Private Thoreau's grandson, Henry, who also would die of tuberculosis. He found a strange, wild land, permeated by sea and wind. Sometimes as many as a dozen wrecks could be counted along the Clay Pounds. Thoreau himself found an old silver coin, heard how a silver watch picked up after the wreck of the *Somerset*, still ticked in a fisherman's pocket. Somewhere under these sands her bones still lay. As far as he knew, her loss was not recorded in any history. He was quickly more interested in devils'-needles, dorr bugs, beach plums, geology, and plovers. His philosophical mind pondered on the curious way the sea takes possession of man's works and then arbitrarily returns them again. So on he walked with his companion.

In 1886, the ghostly hulk of the *Somerset* did again rise from the graveyard of the Clay Pounds. Tradition had not forgotten how she had struck on the Peaked Hill Bar, then been cast up on this beach a hundred years before. Now it was souvenirs the Cape-Codders wanted from her. They went to work with wedges and dynamite to get off what wood they could before the sand covered her again, as it quickly did. She may rise again from the dead.[37]

# IX

## 1779 – 1792

THE PENOBSCOT campaign proves a fiasco and hard times become even harder. THOMAS HUTCHINSON dies before the news of YORKTOWN. PAUL REVERE tries commercial ventures, but silver is his main support. He fights for a court martial, re-establishes his character, and writes letters to his cousins in GUERNSEY and FRANCE. MASSACHUSETTS ratifies the CONSTITUTION, and PAUL REVERE'S part. He sets up a foundry and casts the first bell ever cast in BOSTON. 'A Madman gone to BOSTON.'

### The YANKEY's return from CAMP.

Broadside of Yankee Doodle printed around 1775. American Antiquarian Society.

I

THE American Revolution had begun as a flame of rebellion in Massachusetts, spread like a grass fire to all the other thirteen colonies, and by 1779 involved much of the world. As long as England held the sea power and could supply her own forces and cut off the rebels, she was sure of ultimate victory, but the entry of France into the war upset her control of the sea. She was without an ally in the world and at war with the principal marine powers of the day, France and Spain, as well as her own colonies. She was fighting desperately in the Orient, Europe, and America. At home, for the first time since the days of the Spanish Armada, she was in momentary danger of invasion. The French had fifty thousand troops concentrated at Havre and St. Malo, waiting the spring and summer of 1779 for an opportunity to jump the Channel and land at Falmouth. The fleet with which they could carry out this manoeuvre was almost twice as strong as the British.

In the face of the threat hanging over her at home, the wonder is she bothered as much as she did with that mere appendix to this fight for her life — the rebellion in America. But that June she landed a small garrison at Castine, Maine. General McLein had only parts of two regiments and three armed sloops. It was his duty to hold on, establish a naval base from which British ships could harass American privateersmen and French warships and merchantmen.

Maine was at this time part of Massachusetts and the threat was primarily against Massachusetts shipping. Nine days after McLein seized Castine, Massachusetts was organizing a large expedition to dislodge him. Colonel Revere was ordered 'to hold himself and one hundred of the Matrosses under his comand, including proper officers, in readiness at one hours notice to embark for the Defence of this State, and attack the Enemy at Penobscot.'

General Lovell, who had done extremely well on the Rhode Island expedition the year before, was to command the twelve hundred militiamen. Dudley Saltonstall, of the Continental Navy, was in charge of the very mixed fleet. There were three Continental ships taking part in the expedition (among them the sloop *Providence*, Captain Hacker, with whom Revere had recently been quarrelling over gunners) and Massachusetts' entire navy of three ships. In all there were nineteen armed ships and twenty-one transports, mostly privateersmen who were extremely loath for the service. It was only by threats and bribes that they were forced to go along at all. Their heart was not in it. Washington referred once to 'our rascally privateersmen.' They were accustomed to hunting alone and by their own methods. Organizing them into a regular expedition was about like harnessing so many seagulls. Incredibly brave, ferocious as wild hawks on occasion; on others they simply made sail and left. Commander Saltonstall probably had no control over them whatsoever. He belonged to the Connecticut branch of the already distinguished family. Before Penobscot and after he was an extremely good man, but rightly or not he has always been blamed for the failure of the expedition.

There was considerable delay in getting this flotilla to sea. They needed nine tons of flour, ten of rice and salt beef, twelve hundred gallons of rum, and an equal amount of molasses. These twelve hundred militiamen had but '500 stand of arms' among them. The three nine-pounders and four field pieces — not a very impressive 'artillery train' — were under Paul Revere. Besides these militiamen the ships had some eight hundred marines.

So they at last sailed from Boston and were as far as Towsend (Boothbay), Maine, on the twenty-first day of July. By this time, of course, the British had heard of the plan and sent to New York and Halifax for help, which they had no idea would arrive in time. At Townsend the Americans waited for four days. The Reverend Mr. Murray entertained the General and his officers ('family' as it was called) in a 'much Genteeler seat than was by most persons expected in that part of the country,' for the coast of Maine was indeed wild enough in those days. Only at Townsend did General Lovell call for a review of his troops and there came off the ships (which were smart enough) and lined up on shore such a collection of 'scare crows' as even the American Revolution in its fourth year rarely brought together.

Massachusetts had already furnished more than her share of troops and boys of sixteen were referred to as 'seasoned continentals.' This year Abigail wrote to John Adams that in Braintree half of all the men between sixteen and fifty were already in the army. To get up such an expedition as the Penobscot campaign one was forced to rely somewhat on the sweepings. Adjutant General Hill said of them, 'if they belonged to the Train Band or Alarum list they were soldiers, whether they could carry a gun, walk a mile without crutches or only *compos mentis* sufficient to keep them out of fire and water ... most of them had arms but many were out of repair.' To General Wadsworth, second in command, 'one-fourth ... part appeared ... to be small boys and old men unfit for service.'

Three days later the fleet and transports entered Penobscot Bay with all the majesty of the old sailing flotilla. The British expected to fight — that being the tradition of their race, and also expected to be beaten. Their earthworks were so low 'a soldier with a musket in each hand could jump over them.' Their three armed sloops seem to have been reduced to two. Two of the men in this fort at Castine kept diaries. Sergeant Laurence of the Eighty-Second had already fought at Lexington, having been sent along at the last moment on the nineteenth of April to instruct the soldiers in throwing hand grenades. He wrote his account as did Doctor John Calef, the Tory, who had already been living at Castine for a year and had built him a house. He acted as surgeon for McLein's forces. As a young man he had served through two campaigns of the French and Indian Wars. It was he whom Paul Revere represented in his cartoon with a calf's head and thus gave to him his nickname of 'the rescinding calf.' Driven from Ipswich to London by the rebels, he had been driven back to his own country by homesickness. Castine was so far from Boston and so lonely, he had hoped to live there unmolested. He was no longer a young man.

For a few days the 'small boys and old men' fought with the

same courage other similar groups had fought at Lexington and
Bunker Hill. They stormed a height, got their guns in place, and
looked to be in a position to demand the surrender of the fort.

Paul Revere may have felt this expedition was to be his great
bid to fame, for he kept a diary,[38] as men do when they know they
are about great business. It is as impersonal a diary as well can
be — merely what guns he got on and off what islands and how
many councils of war were called on board the *Warren*, which was
the flagship. That the Americans were quarrelling among themselves before the second week was out, he does not suggest.

The troops were extremely raw, 'there was great want of discipline,' as another officer reported, 'and subordination. Many of
the officers are being so exceedingly slack in their duty, the soldiers
so adverse to service and the woods in which we are encamped so
very thick that on an alarum . . . nearly one fourth part of the army
are scuttled out of the way and concealed.' Paul Revere said that
he and his 'matrosses' did as well as anyone. He admitted he did
not like taking orders from William Todd (a major now serving
under General Lovell). He had disliked Todd when he had been
a captain under himself, had been glad to be rid of him, and
probably was disgusted to see him popping up again into his life.

But it was not the untrained militiamen, whose understandable
instinct for self-preservation had not yet been drilled out of them,
who seem to have ruined the expedition as much as the naval force.
By the fifth of August there was much bad feeling between these
two groups. Roughly, the soldiers wanted the warships to move in
and finish off the two armed sloops in the river. Then the militiamen would attack. Saltonstall did not wish to. A colonel tried to
persuade him, claiming 'that as the wind breezed up he might go
in with his shipping, silence the two vessels, and in half a hour
make everything his own. In reply he hove up his long chin and
said, "You seem to be dam knowing about the matter! I am not
going to risk my shipping in that dam hole!" '

He did not. While the naval forces sat and waited Lieutenant
Colonel Revere and his men were busy doing what they could.
There was that morning which Lieutenant McIntyre remembered
that his colonel was so busy sawing off 'fuzes' he could not stop to
drink a cup of coffee and how once, after a conference of the officers,
he came back to his own men — 'they must prepare some Field

pecis, for it was determined to attack the Enemies Shipping. I
observed,' says McIntyre, 'he looked very chearful. I could not
help remarking it. I said I thought something was going to be
done the Colo looks so chearful.' If he was so 'chearful' in front
of his subordinate he could hardly have felt that way at heart.
The argument between the naval and land forces went on until the
fourteenth — and the arrival of four British warships from New
York. They did not hesitate to attack the much bigger American
force, which proceeded to run themselves aground, blow up
stores, burn ships, and make for the bushes. That day General
Lovell wrote in his journal:

> To attempt to give a description of this terrible Day is out of my
> Power. It would be a fit subject for some masterly hand to describe
> it in its true colors, to see four ships pursuing seventeen sail of Armed
> Vessels, nine of which were stout Ships, Transports on fire, Men of
> War blowing up every kind of Stores on Shore, throwing about, and
> as much confusion as can possibly be conceived.

The eighteen hundred militiamen were left to get home as best
they could. Paul Revere wrote on this ghastly day:

> Our armed Ships had got abreast of the Point [Fort Point]; they
> soon overtook the Transports who had got under way, (the Enemy
> pursuing) when the Transports found that the Armed Vessels all
> went ahead of them they ran on shore and landed their men, in
> the utmost confusion. The Ordinace Brig, in which was most of
> my men, was the last who came on shore. I got most of my men to-
> gether in the Edge of a Wood, but while my Boat was getting some
> men from a Schooner, who had lost their Boat, I was seperated from
> them (all but two officers and eight men) they taking into the woods,
> I supposing they were gone up the River. I followed in my Boat (it
> being Sun down) expecting to overtake them; after serching till
> 12 o'clock for them, I went on board a Transport which had got up
> the River and stayed till Day light.

His cousin, Philip Marrett, was lieutenant on board the *Sky
Rocket*. He saw 'Colo Revere who always appear'd as he all ways
did . . . as an Active & Deligent officer on the retreat up the Penob-
scot River, Colo Revere pass'd the Ship Sky Rocket a little after
Sundown Capt Bush Ask'd him to Come on bourd & Drink some
Grog he told him he could not stop for he was trying to Collect

his men. I told him he had better stop & I would hand some in
the Boat he told me could not.'

Earlier in the campaign he had been too busy to stop for coffee
and now was too 'deligent' to stop for grog. So he rowed upstream
past the *Sky Rocket*. In his diary he goes on:

> 15th — Then sent an Officer in the Boat down the River, to seek
> my men; and if he found them, to Order them up to me. As I was
> going up the River, I saw General Lovell coming down; he told me
> he was agoing to bring up his men to make a stand. I went as far as
> Grants Mill, where I found considerable body of men; there I landed
> to wait for my Boat; She returned about 12 oClock and could find
> nothing of them. I staid there all that day; towards night I went on
> board the Vengence, Capt Thomas, to enquire what news; he told
> me he should burn his Vessel in the morning; he had landed some
> of his men and was delivering out provision to some Soldiers who
> had none. I went on shore, and went about a mile into the woods
> with my men, two officers & eight men & there encamped.
>
> 16th — Next morning I sett off with a party and came thro the
> wood to Kennebec River.
>
> 19th — I got to Fort Western [Augusta] where I found most of
> my officers and men; after supplying them with what Money I could
> spare I ordered them to Boston by the nearest route.

But even by the nearest route it would be a long hot walk for
the stocky forty-four-year-old town-dwelling lieutenant colonel.
And discouraging — heartbreaking. He had started out with
high hopes and a diary in which to record his own feats and that
of his light-footed command, and it had ended up with this mad
scramble through the bushes. There are points of similarity between this campaign and the one the year before into Rhode
Island. In neither case did the land forces have a chance without
the support of a fleet. It was not Revere's fault the expedition had
failed — but he would have to bear his share in the shame of it.

The only thing that can be said of the Penobscot expedition is
that very few lives were lost.

A fourteen-year-old drummer boy of the British had been killed
by a chance shot and he bothered the inhabitants of Castine by
various midnight drumming for some years, but it was mostly
reputations and money that were gone. The Massachusetts Board
of War estimated the trip had cost £1,139,175. And nothing to

show for it but sore feet, bad temper, mosquito bites, where one had hoped for glory.

Less than six months before, Paul Revere had been waging a one-man war against the local sea forces. He himself, when called upon to defend his conduct, said the reason 'why stories have been propagated against me' was 'because ... I did all in my power, to hinder men from deserting.' The sea captains were ready to get back at him when and how they could. The humiliation and confusion of the retreat gave opportunity for many old scores to be settled. Captain Saltonstall's reputation suffered the most. He was court-martialed, and people said then and are still saying he should have been shot. Committees of investigation were set up in Boston. All the militia officers were ready to put the blame on the fleet (where it is still usually put) and all the sea captains upon the militia officers.

Captain Thomas Jenness Carnes, who commanded the marines on the *General Putnam*, was out to get Revere. He brought charges of disobedience, unsoldier-like behavior, cowardice, and so on. General Wadsworth also made some bitter criticism of his conduct. Revere was relieved of his command at Castle Island on the sixth of September and told to 'repair to his dwelling house in Boston and there continue till the matter complained of can be duly enquired into.'

Paul Revere, who certainly had given all his time, energy, and intelligence to this perhaps uncongenial job war had dumped down upon him, may have been relieved to be off the fort and back home. But he was determined to clear his name. He wrote a number of letters to the 'Hon'ble Committee to investigate the Failure of the Expedition to Penobscot etc.' General Artemas Ward was this committee's president. He wrote confidently, sure that this committee believed in him.

> Had your Honors have shown as little regard for my character as my Enemies have done, Life would have been unsupportable. Were I consiouse that I had ommitted one thing to reduce the Enemy either thro' fear, or by willful opposition, I would not wish for a single advocate.
>
> I beg Your Honors, that in a proper time there may be a strict enquiry into my conduct where I may meet my accusers face to face.

His seafaring accusers were hard witnesses to catch. Captain

Todd also brought formal accusations against him, which, like Carnes', never seem to have amounted to much.

What Revere wanted was a court martial, but he could get nothing started. His 'character' was more dear to him than life itself, but until the trial it would be under a shadow. Yet in the meantime he could get back to his silver work. He was no longer a colonel. Young Paul, who had been his lieutenant for five years, was now ready to enter the shop. His apprenticeship to his father had been interrupted by the war. This may be the reason why this, the third Paul Revere, never became a great silversmith, being listed as 'a spoon and buckle-maker.' His father did the more skilful hollow ware. Many artisans considered twenty over-old for a boy to learn a skilled trade. There is nothing in Revere's books to suggest that either of them made much silver these hard years, although he wrote to his second cousin, Mathias Rivoire, that at this time 'I thought it best to go to my business again.'

Paul Revere was not so embittered against the 'rascally privateersmen' he was unwilling to risk a little money on one of these wild ships himself. He bought shares on the *Minerva*. This may have been the same *Minerva* a cousin of Dudley Saltonstall armed and turned over to the unfortunate commodore of the Penobscot Expedition ... 'that you might regain your character with the world ... you never lost it with me, and this I believe you never doubted.' Confident the charges against himself were unfounded, Paul Revere may have felt a certain sympathy for the much more maligned naval commander and, like the cousin, wished to show his belief in him.

As captain of the *Minerva*, Saltonstall proved himself a bold and successful privateersman. Paul Revere certainly made some money if this was the same *Minerva*, and if he went on backing her through the next few years he made quite a lot. It was the *Minerva* who captured the English *Hannah* after a hard fight. The *Hannah's* cargo was valued at eighty thousand pounds. Her loss was said to have enraged the British into their attack on New London, for this was Saltonstall's home. So the Commodore regained his character.

In May, 1780, the Reveres left the North Square house, for it was rented to George De France for twenty Spanish milled dollars. De France is not a Boston name, and presumably the tenant was one

of the many transient Frenchmen who came and went through
Boston during the last years of the Revolution. Among Revere's
odds and ends of papers, and somewhat temperamental ledgers,
there is no mention of taking another house for several years. If
he was as hard-pressed as most of his fellow citizens, he may have
doubled up with some of his many relatives.

Young John Eliot was writing that winter to Jeremy Belknap:
'the miseries of famine are now mixed with the horrors of war. The
poor people of Boston in the alms house have been destitute of
grain and other necessities these many days. Many reputable families are almost starving. Good Lord Deliver us!'

Judge Curwen, one of the exiled Tories, who, although living in
London, kept close track of affairs over here, wrote in '79: 'those
who five years ago were among the meaner people are now by a
strange revolution become almost the only men of power, riches
and influence. The Cabots of Beverely, who you know, had but
five years ago, a very moderate share of property are now said to
be the most wealthy in New England. Hasket Derby claims the
second place on the list.' And shortly afterwards he points out that
'a dollar is worth only 2⅔ of an English half-penny.'

## II

OUTSIDE London, close to Croy-
don, Thomas Hutchinson lived at Brampton. It must have been
a fair-sized house, for not only did his entire family live with him,
but enough other dependents to bring the number up to twenty-
five. The British Government did its best for the several thousand
Tories who had lost everything they had through their loyalty to
England. In all it is said to have spent some six million pounds on
pensions and in efforts to re-establish them in Canada or England.

But they were unhappy folk. At first they clung closely together. There was the New England Coffee House on Threadneedle Street where the northern exiles met. At the Old Jewry Meeting House a Massachusetts man could count on finding Thomas Hutchinson and his family. Judge Curwen, at the beginning of his stay in London, wrote happily, 'There is an army of New Englanders here.' Soon they became homesick and captious. They did not like England, and characteristically thought it badly heated. 'The fires here [are] not to be compared to our large American ones of oak and walnut, nor near so comfortable; would that I were away!'

Governor Hutchinson, now distinctly an old man, although still slender and handsome, was the centre of the New England exiles' lives. The Crown supported him and he in turn helped many of his fellow refugees. He knew the English people were a little tired of the exiles. 'We Americans are plentiful and very cheap,' and 'I assure you I had rather die in a little country farm in New England than in the best nobleman's seat in Old England and therefore have given no ear to any proposal of settling here'; and again, 'New England is wrote upon my heart in as strong characters as Calais was upon Queen Mary's.' He brooded upon 'poor Boston, what have those men to answer for who have brought on this destructive war.'

He worried over the British Empire at war with both France and Spain as well as her own colonies; Ireland on the point of revolt, and torn at home with civil strife that might any moment break into civil war. The mobs in London were much more violent than Boston's carefully 'trained mob.'

Most of all he worried because 'the prospect of returning to America & laying my bones in the land of my forefathers for four generations . . . is less than it has ever been. God grant me a composed mind.' First and last, it seems to have been 'his bones' that disturbed him most. That tomb on Copp's Hill, where his dear wife had been laid some forty years before, had been seized along with the rest of his property. He had tried to have her body sneaked out to Unkity Hill, but without success. He thought much of Unkity Hill. When he had left it six years before, he had never doubted but in a few months or a year or two he would be back there once more.

His children stood by him. Thomas, the oldest boy, had joined him in England. Peggy, who had never married in spite of offers from peers, died of consumption after only three years of exile. The Hutchinsons did not transplant easily to foreign soil. On the second anniversary of her death, 'Stopped at Croydon, went into the church and looked upon the grave of my dear child; inquired whether there was room for me; and was informed there was.' So by the fall of '79, he had definitely given up hope of ever getting his poor bones back to Boston.

Early in 1780, his youngest child, Billy (always something of a ne'er-do-well), died, and the rioting in London increased.

June came, so fair a month in rural England. The 'Governor,' as he was always called, had slept 'tolerably.' As usual, he got up at eight and his son Elisha and his son-in-law, young Doctor Peter Oliver, sat in his chamber as he shaved and ate his breakfast. They told him of the terrible rioting of the day before. His servant, Ryley, offered him a shirt. It was not fresh enough to suit him. The young men were amazed that he told his servant he wished another, for he would 'die clean.' Nothing seemed much wrong with him. He was only discouraged and a little tired.

As usual, the coach had been ordered, for he always 'drove out' after breakfast. He walked unaided down the stairs into the sunlight of the June day, but before he could enter his coach he fainted. He was carried into the servants' hall and there died.

That day London was at the mercy of the Gordon rioters. The murderous mob surged back and forth from Saint George's Fields to the Houses of Parliament, from Westminster to Newgate, and the rioting went on the next day and the next. Four hundred and fifty people were killed or wounded in the streets of London during the Gordon riots. London was burning in many places. Through the howling of this mob and under the pall of this smoke, those bones Thomas Hutchinson had worried so much about were carried to the grave. Here he was soon joined by the rest of his family. A grandchild and his daughter, Sallie Oliver, both died before that June was over.

His Milton house is long gone, but some of the venerable trees that he planted and cared for still stand. The once elegant gardens, overgrown and forlorn, show here and there their English box. The ha-ha wall, by which he protected the privacy of his family life from the proverbial curiosity of his cows, is intact.

The fields before his house, sweeping down to the Neponset

River and Boston Harbor, are publicly owned and still kept —
not as a park — but 'Governor Hutchinson's Fields.' So that wonderful view he loved is preserved, although everywhere else his
name has been obliterated.

If any ghost walks a New England field, haunts a deserted garden, it must be the slender wraith of Thomas Hutchinson. Sad and
aloof, he would, alive or dead, be too much the gentleman to pop
out at one, but still he would be seeking to lay his bones in his native soil.

## III

ALL through the spring and sum-
mer of 1781, word came to Boston of the fighting to the south: the
battle of Cowpens, the battle of Guilford, Hobkirk's Hill, Eutaw
Springs, the battle of the Capes (and by now it was September).
October found Lord Cornwallis bottled up at Yorktown. On the
nineteenth he surrendered. So the six and a half years of fighting
were over, although no peace was signed for a couple more years.

And at last, when probably no one cared whether Paul Revere
went up or down a river and in what or whose boat; whether on a
certain night he slept on shore or on a transport, he had the court
martial he had six times petitioned for. In 1780, the 'Hon'rble
Council' had gone as far as to appoint a court — which never
seems to have met. Revere never stopped trying, but it was not
until February, 1782, he was given a trial.

Twelve captains and one general considered the charges brought
against him, which had in three years boiled down to only two —
'For his refusal to deliver a certain Boat to the order of General
Wadsworth when upon the Retreat up Penobscot River, from
Major Bagwaduce,' and 'For his leaving Penobscot River without
Orders from his Commanding Officer.'

The decision was:

> The Court finds the first charge against Liu't Col Paul Revere
> to be supported (to wit) his refusing to deliver a certain Boat to the
> Order of General Wadsworth when upon the Retreat up Penobscot
> River from Major Bagwaduce: but the Court taking into considera-
> tion the suddenness of the refusal, and more especially that the same
> Boat was in fact employed by Lieu't Colo Paul Revere to effect the
> Purpose ordered by the General as appears by the General's Deposi-
> tion, are of the Opinion that Lieu't Colo Paul Revere be acquitted
> of this Charge.
>
> On the second charge, the Court considers that the whole army
> was in great Confusion and so scattered and dispersed, that no regular
> Orders were or could be given, are of the Opinion, that Lieu't Colo
> Paul Revere, be acquitted with equal Honor as the other Officers
> in the same Expedition.

Paul Revere had persevered and been rewarded with the re-
establishment of his character. It is doubtful if he took the affair
too hard. He had a certain practical outlook on life and knew very
well that when expeditions go wrong there is always name-calling
and bad feeling.

## IV

THEY had been lean years—those
war years. In Boston the population was far below its pre-war
figure. Her trade was ruined. For a hundred years her wealth had
come largely from commerce with the West Indies. These islands
were now closed to her by England. One great maritime period of
her history was over and she had not yet begun her second and
greatest. Most of her shipping had been lost in privateering. Her
wharves were falling down.

As the Continental Army disbanded (ending up eventually with only eighty-four men in our regular army) and the men returned eagerly to peacetime pursuits, it was to find no place for themselves. They wandered about, sick, idle, hungry, sometimes desperate, but usually pathetically patient. It is thought that at this time the word 'soldiering' came into our language as an expression of contempt. Less than a year after the great victory at Yorktown there was armed rioting in the western part of the state. There was now no danger England would impose taxes. The people might be free, but they were unhappy. Peace and plenty had not come back hand in hand.

To make the situation more bitter, there were a number of people who had made money out of the war. The heroic Revolutionary officers might be dying in poor-debtor jails, but there were those others who had kept out of the army and, by speculation, profiteering, and sometimes by privateering, had made fortunes. Boston socially had always been flexible in contrast to anything known in England, but there had never been so complete a turnover as in the years after the Revolution. Boston was flooded with a new gentry, ready and anxious to take the place of the old aristocracy which had gone. A surprising number of new names came from Essex County. The big, sad houses of the Tories were no longer empty. James Warren noted bitterly that 'fellows who would have cleaned my shoes five years ago now rode in chariots.'

The connecting link between the old aristocracy and 'the mushroom gentry' was, of course, John Hancock. Although the Hutchinsons had smiled at him a little, as something a bit new from the mint, there was no one left in Boston who could lift an eyebrow at him now. He was the great gentleman *par excellence* of this strange new world.

The palsy which had always shaken Sam Adams increased. Some days he could hardly write his own name. Needless to say, he was as poor as ever. It was never for such a republic as he saw burgeoning about him that he had toiled throughout his life. He had honestly believed that if the old royal governors, the British customs officials, and the old 'oligarchy' were removed, Boston's natural virtue and austerity would come into its own. But the six bay horses on the governor's coach, the balls, extravagant clothing and houses of the new 'oligarchy' made the little 'routes,' 'frolicks,' 'turtles,' and concerts, such as Miss Hulton used to attend, seem very modest. Sam Adams wrote: 'I love the people of Boston. I once thought that city could be a *Christian Sparta*. But alas! will men be free? . . . there are times when people are not worth saving, when they have lost their virtue. I pray God this may never be said of my beloved Boston.'

Characteristically, he thought it was still England who was ruining his beloved town. England was sending over her fripperies and tempting the citizens to buy things they could not afford.

'The artful and insidious Cabinet of Britain,' he wrote in the fall of 1782, '. . . have, in excess of their folly and lust for domination adopted the absurd idea of subjegating America by throwing in upon us a flood of their manufactures, and encouraging a commercial intercourse between us and them. . . . By this trade they expect . . . to revive that foolish prediliction which we once had for British Manufactures and British manners.' And he fears a plot, for the British intend to 'drain us of our money, the sinews of war. Having drawn from us our medium in this way, having made their arrangements, posted their emissaries, and secured their partisans, they expect, by a violent run on our national bank, to annihilate at one blow our national credit, and deprive us of all future means of defense. Such are clearly their views, and these are the mean arts which haughty, though fallen Britain is compelled to make use of.'

He hoped once more to start another 'non-importation' agreement among the merchants — enforced as of old by organized mobs. That time had passed. Sam Adams was a man in his sixties. He had always been admired for his 'inflexible will,' but he was utterly and pathetically unable to shape himself to the new republic he had been so active in creating. Nor could he shape the republic to his own ideas of what it should be. From now on he was to know little but heartbreak. He was still much admired by visiting statesmen, although often sneered at by his own bailiwick.

One of the more interesting foreign observers arrived in Boston in the fall of 1784. This was the young soldier and revolutionist from Venezuela, Francisco de Miranda. He was to give his life fighting to free his own country from the rule of Spain — to fail, and to die in Cadiz jail. He looked over the young republican life in Boston and did not think highly of it:

> Luxury, ostentation and a little vainity are the predominate figures in the character of those who now are called rich. Ten years ago a

young man who wore silk stockings, breeches made of plain satin, and powdered his hair, had not need of anything else to forfeit his 'character' forever. Today, they all have this, and also when going bootlegged and on horse-back, they wear their silk stockings, satin breeches etc. The women aim to wear silk goods, girdles, and embroidered muslins, and use pomades and perfumes every day; so that living in a country where not even one manufactory of the above mentioned things, has been established, and being obliged to pay for all abroad, it necessarily follows that ruin will be inevitable; and if they take into consideration that the products with which the country may pay its debts are ashes, tar and codfish, we will not be supprised when the merchant remarks that all wealth which at present exists in this capital, could hardly pay the half of its actual debts to Europe, mainly England. And if this has happened within so short a space of time, what will it be twenty years from now? Trade will always be the principal cause of ruin of the Democratic virtue, from the simplicity and the equality of the people. . . . I have had the pleasure to meet the famous republican, Mr Samuel Adams. . . . He is a talented person with great knowledge of legislation. We had prolonged discussions upon the constitution of this republic, and the two objections set forth by me on the subject, he finally agreed to after having chewed well the points. The first was as to how it is that in a democracy, the foundation of which is virtue, no importance whatever is given to it, and on the contrary all dignity and power is given to property which is poisonous in a republic like this one. The other point was as to the contradiction I observed in admitting, as one of the rights of humanity, the attributing cult to the Supreme, in present manner and form, without according predominance to any one sect; that it excluded from any legislative or representative office one who would not upon his oath declare himself to be of the christian religion.

Few visitors came to Boston in those years with a clearer head than this young ex-colonel of the Spanish army, but his comments are usually unflattering and his temperament seems a little gloomy. He found our social life boring — especially our ladies. Poor Miss Dalton was 'the fattest creature I ever have seen of her age.' Mrs. Morton had 'read somewhat and therefore she is presumptuous.' He recounts with pleasure that it was well known that Mr. Hitchbourn had 'been infatuated with his lady' before he shot her husband. Mrs. Bulfinch was 'a presumptuous and ridiculous woman.' Miss B. de Blois and Miss Temple 'both are regarded as beauties' — but he will not say so himself.

He was amazed at the strictness of Sabbath-keeping, and the trustfulness of the Bostonians. One day, when about to cross a stream, a stranger with a woman on his pillion, whose horse seems to have been unmanageable, asked 'whether I was willing to take the woman over on my saddle, for she was afraid. I answered "yes," and she dismounted immediately and sat herself on my saddle, and I carried her about two miles to where she asked to be allowed to dismount. She then stopped at a house, and waited for her husband who was some distance behind us. Now, who in Europe would favorably judge that human heart, that delivered in such a manner, his young and pretty wife to a stranger? Nor were there one that held the silly belief it were a sin to cross a river on Sunday?'

Of the men, he liked Sam Adams and Henry Knox as well as any — especially Knox, 'the best instructed soldier . . . of all the chiefs I had known in this continent, including the Idol Washington.' But one feels he praises Knox partly because it gives him a chance to belittle a greater man.

Architecturally Boston did not fare much better than socially, although Long Wharf (already a very old story to the Bostonians) amazed him — 'it exceeds all other works of the kind that might exist on this continent.' The old State House 'was without charm.' He found the 'figure of a cod-fish of natural size made of wood in bad taste.' (The 'sacred cod' was brand-new that day Miranda passed judgment upon it. Only the spring before, Merchant Rowe had 'moved the House that leave be given to hang up the representation of a Codfish in the room where the House sits, as a memorial of the importance of the Cod-Fishery to the welfare of the Commonwealth.')

So Francisco Miranda gloomily eyed the Boston of 1784. One may doubt if Miss Dalton was so fat or our ladies (especially those who read somewhat) were so presumptuous; disagree with his estimate of our old State House and its codfish; but no one has seriously questioned two of his statements. Boston was ravenous for English luxuries and buying heavily on credit. And 'luxury and ostentation' was a hall-mark of the era. Yet it was in this era that Paul Revere must live, work, and use his best ability to survive. Very few people ever live their middle years in the same world in which they grow up as children. None whose lives have been broken in two by a great war ever do, and none of Paul Revere's generation did. They could fall to rioting, as they did in the western part of the state. They could slump into an embittered old age, as did Sam Adams. Or they could take things about as they found them and go ahead. Paul Revere did the last.

The basic change was complete upset in trade. A London paper for March 9, 1784, says, 'Two ships arrived in our river from Boston New England, both in ballast, not having been able to procure cargoes of any kind'; and it goes on to recall those pre-war years when the New England states 'were to America what Holland has been to Europe — the carriers for all the other colonies.'

The ledgers which Paul Revere was once more keeping of his silver work indicate the departure of the old names (with whom he had done so much business before the war) and the rise of the new ones. But Revere could watch the chariots roll by without wondering whether or not five years before the occupants would or would not have been glad to clean his shoes. There had always been people richer than himself — and poorer. He would not suffer over the higgledy-piggledy, often flashy (and often painfully proper) new life. Although Sam Adams might fear it would ruin Boston and make her no longer worth saving, — if the new people paid their bills, this is probably all Paul Revere asked of them. He does not seem to have mixed much with this new social life, but his cousin, Benjamin Hitchbourn, did. The handsome wife, whether acquired by remorse or murder, was something of a social leader. Ben Hitchbourn bought first the Josiah Quincy house in Boston and then Andrew Oliver's famous 'seat' in Dorchester. A man might buy these great Tory houses for a song. Undoubtedly it was a good investment — and undoubtedly the new occupants were often cleverer, gayer, and fully as able as the old.

It was sadly said, however, that these new men were not of the same cut as the old. This was true enough. Take this new occupant of the Oliver house and compare him with the old lieutenant governor. One was as unconcerned with his dignity as the other was overconcerned. Sometimes efforts were made to give greater sobriety to the young republic's activities. Most of the Boston lawyers had at the end sided with the Tories. The new crop hoped to carry on the great traditions of the Massachusetts Bar with equal austerity. They voted to assume once more the stately black aca-

demic gowns of their predecessors — such gowns as the Olivers and
Hutchinsons had worn with imposing dignity. Clever, even brilliant, as many of these newcomers were, they were men of a different cut. The lawyers wore their gowns so badly they had to give
them up. It was Ben Hitchbourn who forced them to back down
on their gowns. A countryman came to town and saw what he
thought was a clergyman in his black clericals and white wig
happily bargaining for a load of wood. Such rolling oaths and
sulphurous profanity issuing from a clergyman shocked him. It
was really Ben Hitchbourn, but the countryman was saying everywhere 'how these Boston parsons would swear.' The 'long robe'
was given up forever. It did not suit with the post-war tempo.

Unlike the merchants whom Sam Adams felt the most bitterly
about, Paul did not smuggle in goods from England before the
Treaty of Paris officially ended the war, but he had made arrangements with Frederick William Geyer, a Boston Tory exiled to England, to ship him goods the second this became a legal possibility.
The treaty was signed on the third of September, 1783. Two weeks
later the *Rosemond* left London with five hundred pounds of English
manufactured goods for Paul Revere to sell in Boston. He habitually used old friends among the London Tories as his agents: John
Joy, Gilbert and Lewis de Blois, John Clark, as well as Geyer. The
letters back and forth show how quickly the hatchet was buried.
Often there are references to old days together, or a genuine expression of affection, as when John Joy wrote him not to be too much
bothered because he is unable to pay the eighteen pounds he owes
him, and goes on to say, 'yet my dear Paul, if you can make me
one Doz of Desert Spoons, very neat & of proper seize, of silver up
to the standard, which cannot cost you much as its in your line, this
done I will fully discharge you.' Sam Adams believed these exiles
were the tools of the British Cabinet intent upon draining America
of her money. Paul Revere looked upon them as his old
friends.

In 1783, with the arrival of the *Rosemond*, Paul Revere opened
a shop opposite the spot where once the Liberty Tree had flourished. A Liberty Pole had been set up in its memory.

His invoices show what sort of goods Boston had lacked most
during the long dearth. The bulk of his imports were hardware,
but also fine cloth like 'coatings' of 'claret,' 'mixed,' 'striped,'

or plain brown. German serges — all sorts of things to wear —
even toupees. Sandpaper, blotting paper, foolscap writing paper,
'superfine folio post,' 'fine red sealing wax,' and 'superfine red
sealing wax.' Inkhorns, 'two gross Mogul playing cards,' packs
of 'messanger cards.' Boston was badly in need of paper. None of
his items does he describe with quite the same loving words as
his wallpaper. It shows the nice eye he had for color. Some of
his paper is 'tan orange on apple green,' or 'wheat blue on stone';
'gold stone on blue white.' It did not come in rolls, but 'in pieces.'
The '20 pieces of rose blue on olive, 2 borders,' would be enough
for a large room. These (and the playing cards) were exactly the
sort of unnecessary gewgaws which broke Sam Adams' heart — and
John Hancock and his wealthy friends were revelling in.

He also imported pencils, fish lines, pumice stones, and large
quantities of plated silver. Sheffield plate was a fairly new invention. Paul Revere does not ever seem to have made any himself,
but he must have sold a large amount of it at his shop. Boston had
also been short of eyeglasses. Revere set himself up with spectacles
and 'visuals.'

He paid for his goods in Spanish milled dollars or by ingots
he 'made up of metals the sweep of a goldsmith's shop,' or 'gold
lace burned and melted,' as well as in more usual currency. Paul,
Jr., was in this business with him. As the father was making a great
deal of silver at the same time, the young man may have had much
to do with the actual running of the shop. It never engaged all of
Paul Revere's time, nor did he ever refer to himself as a 'merchant,'
but invariably as a goldsmith. For 'my chief dependence is on my
goldsmith's business for the expense of my Family.'

Paul Revere had never lost track of his European connections.[39]
He had a first cousin, John Rivoire, in Guernsey, to whom he wrote
now and then (with a long pause representing the years of Revolution), and a more distant cousin, Mathias, near Bordeaux.

Soon after Yorktown, Mathias wrote Paul Revere asking him of
himself. He answers saying he is carrying on his trade of goldsmith and, 'I trade some to Holland. I did intend to have gone
wholly into trade but the principal part of my interest I lent to
Government which I have not been able to draw out; so must content myself until I can do better. I am in middling circumstances,
and very well off for a tradesman. I am forty-seven years old. I

have a wife and eight children alive; my eldest daughter is married [Debby had married Amos Lincoln in 1780]; my eldest son has learned my trade since we left the army, and now is in business for himself. I have one brother [Thomas, the silversmith] and two sisters alive.'

This letter is unsigned and undated — probably the one he gave to some French friend to translate for him. Mathias knew only French, John and Paul only English. These men never seem to have met, but they carried on quite a spirited correspondence. Paul Revere was naturally curious to learn more of his genealogy. Thus it was he learned his grandparents' names, Isaac Rivoire and Serenne Lambert (one of his children named her child Serenne Lambert), and how 'Apollos, our son, was born the thirtieth of November, 1702 about ten o'clock at night and was baptised at Riaucaud.' His great-grandfather Rivoire had been called Jean and he had married Magdelaine Malaperge. Now definitely in his middle years he was discovering the pleasures of genealogy.

Mathias, the Frenchman, writes quite affectionate letters. He is a 'kinsman sincerely attached to you by affection and friendship proof against every accident.' And likewise these two cousins had been on one side in the recent war and John on the other — and losing side. John has a less expansive, more British nature. He hates the French and wishes 'Americans would see their error before it is too late and that England and America were so firmly cemented nothing would break their Union. We might laugh at the whole world.' As for the Frenchmen, 'They seem at first like turtle doves, polite and humble till they get their ends; but after they are masters there is none in the world for such tyranny and oppression . . . the French court is very glad to see us destroying one another and with joy give their assistance to our mutual destruction, instead of us being hand in hand, united together to destroy the vermine and scum oft the earth.' In a postscript he says America and England ought to get together and 'attack the Gold and Silver mines of the Spanish Dominions in South America. As it is certain there is a revolt in those parts between the Spanish and the natives.'

This letter, which John Rivoire wrote in January, 1782, drew Revere into a long reply. He does not agree with his cousin in politics. But his letter starts courteously with a little joke about

John's unmarried state, and then opens up on the political situation. 'I am very sorry my dear Cousin, that you have such despicable sentiments of the French Nation — I can easily account for your prejudice.' He had felt that way himself but now Americans see with 'more impartial eyes, and find the French Nation to be quite the reverse of what you suppose them and of what we used to think them — they are a brave, humane, generous, and polite Nation. You tell me that the alliance we have entered into with that Nation is a dangerous one; we do not conceive that to be the case — So much is a fact.' That if France turns out to be a tyrant like Britain they will 'drive them from our Country.'

He also gives the reasons for the quarrel between America and England as they probably appeared to the average, intelligent, but uncomplicated American of his day. 'You say we have entered into a war with Brittain against all laws human & divine. You do not use all the candour which I am sure you are master of, else you have not looked into the merits of the quarrel. They covenanted with the first settlers of this country, that we should enjoy all the Libertys of free natural born subjects of Great Britian. They were not contented to have all the benefits of our trade, in short to have all our earnings, but they wanted to make us hewers of wood and drawers of water. Their Parliament have declared that they will have a right to tax us & Legislate for us, in all cases whatever — now certainly if they have a right to take one shilling from us without our consent, they have a right to all we possess; for it is the birthright of an Englishman, not to be taxed without consent of himself, or Representatives.'

At the end he cools off and tells his cousin how things are going with him personally, the first day of July, 1782. 'I now follow my business again of Goldsmith & trade a little.' And he begs his dear cousin to come to him in Boston, 'that you may injoy all the liberty here, which the human mind so ernestly craves after. I am not rich, but am in good circumstances & if you will come here you shall not want; while I have a shilling, you shall have part.'

Reading these letters from cousin to cousin during the decade, one wonders what they looked like. Of Paul himself we can have some conception — the heavy dark hair streaked a bit with grey, the compact, strong body taking on that look of prosperous eighteenth-century middle-age portliness. Evidently he suffered from some curiosity about his cousins and asked them both to send him their pictures.

John of Guernsey did his best, but he evidently felt the portrait hardly flattered him, but he sent it over.

> You'll observe it is Coarse Paint the Painter has drawn the features very near — but the Colour is much drawn on the Brown & the Hair Red or near it. My hair are of the Inclosed colour which I have cut from my head. You may observe it was not drawn by a Master hand of that business. If I go to London I intend to Spare 5 Guineas on that purpose.

Paul sent both cousins small presents of silver seals or buttons, and he wrote Mathias that his 'kind acceptance of them [the buttons] & your saying that you would wear them for my sake is all I wish for so trifling a compliment, tho I must say should your Picture reach me which you mention in a former letter it would give me exquisite pleasure.' But Mathias' picture did not come. Not even a lock of his hair. He had once sent Mathias, not his own portrait, but 'a small engraving' of George Washington. '. . . it is said to be a good likeness and it is my engraving.' Ever since this letter, written early in the eighties, came to light, collectors have been hunting for this 'good likeness' of Washington by Paul Revere, but without success unless an extraordinarily unpleasant, lopsided little face of the father of our country in the *Weatherwise Almanac* for 1781 is indeed the one referred to. But Mathias rose courteously to the engraving. It was 'a kind present' and represented 'a gallant warrior.'[40]

In the spring of 1786, Revere is still writing his long friendly letters to Cousin John. A Paul Rivoire turned up near Philadelphia, died almost immediately, and the French Consul can tell nothing about him. Does John know who he is? As usual, his last paragraph sums up his family situation. 'Since my last letter I have lost one of the finest little boys that ever was born, two years and three months old, named John, for you. I have now begun to think,' he goes on sadly, 'I shall have no more children. I have had fifteen children and six grandchildren.'

Paul was fifty-one when he wrote this letter. Like so many men of his period, the grandchildren that both Paul, junior, and Debby were producing at a great rate were the same age as his own younger children. After Joseph Warren Revere's birth in 1777, he had had the short-lived Lucy, next Harriet, then this little John he referred to in his letter, and Maria, who was only a year old. Rachel was ten years younger than himself. He might (and did) hope for another child, and the last of his three Johns was born the following year. Whether he named it for his brother or his cousin might be argued. Probably for both.

In time he limited his store more and more to hardware, much of which would be made in this country, and left the English 'frippiers' to other men. After three years opposite the Liberty Pole, he put the following advertisement in the *Boston American Herald* for February 3, 1786:

> Paul Revere, would respectfully inform his Customers & the Publick that he had *Removed* from the South Part of the Town opposite Liberty Pole to Dock-Square, in the store adjoining Mr. Joseph Burt, near the Market
>
> Where he has for sale
>
> A General Assortment of Hard *Goods* consisting of Pewter, Brass, Copper, Ironmongery, Plated, Jappaned, and Cutlery Wares; Files, Tools etc for Goldsmiths, Jewellers, Clock and Watch Makers, Chapes and Tongnes blue Melting pots from No 1 to 20 Crucibles, very neat Scales Beams 32 inches long with box Ends, Willards Patent Jacks, Looking Glasses etc etc.
>
> ☞ The *Goldsmiths Business* is there carried on in all its Branches; all kinds of Plate made in the newest taste, and finished in the neatest manner
>
> Constant Attendance given, and the smallest Favours gratefully acknowledged.

It is this store and goldsmith's shop which the city of Boston has remembered with a bronze tablet, at 175 Washington Street (50 Cornhill in his day). Although he says he is at Dock Square, he was actually closer to the old State House than to Faneuil Hall. From his front door he could see both buildings. It was an admirable location. The store seems to have done well enough, but he became more interested in other projects and gave it up after about six years.

In 1789, the year Paul Revere left, Ebenezer Larkin rented this store and obligingly had its picture engraved for the head of his trade card.[41] It would have looked much the same when Paul

Revere occupied it the year before. The unknown advertising artist has done his best to give an imposing front to 50 Cornhill, for the Suffolk deeds show the lot of land on which the shop stood was less than thirty feet in width. It was two stories high and stood in front of a wood-and-brick dwelling house. The 'kitchen' referred to in the records may have been attached to the shop, or may have been a minute separate building. Paul Revere doubtless used it as a workshop. In the store itself he would have had his ironmongery on display rather than Mr. Larkin's neat rows of books. And surely he would have had a shelf or so of his own silver 'made in the newest taste.' There had been a radical change in the fashion of silver since he had first started out, as there had been a radical change in everything else.

# V

PAUL REVERE was no hermit living and working in a vacuum. Everything he did, from riding express before the war to importing English wallpaper immediately after it, was in response to changing needs and modes of his own day. Even in the satin surfaces of his silver one can see reflected the Boston in which he lived.

Up to 1785, like his contemporary silversmiths, he had worked in the rococo. With the rise of the republic came a new fashion in architecture, furniture, and silver, with emphasis on classic purity. In silver it is characterized by the delicacy of the engraving, an insistence on stately urns, straight-spouted tea-pots, usually oval in shape. The danger of this new style is that it may seem a little dry, unimaginative, too pure. The earlier is more convivial, less concerned with its own respectability. One is suited more for the hand and the other for the sideboard. Paul Revere followed this drift in taste as faithfully as did the cabinet-makers and architects. He was a superb artist, and was not likely to fall into the pitfalls of the new 'tast' any more than he had into the dangers of the suddenly outmoded rococo.

Much of the silver he made after the Revolution and in this Federal period was for men who not long before had been boarding 'prizes' with a bloody cutlass in one hand and a smoking pistol in the other, or for those amazing merchant adventurers who found a new gold mine for Boston in the China trade. When they had money to spend on silver, they fancied a style which (oddly enough) is characterized by, perhaps, too much 'good taste.'

Probably more of Revere's designs from this Federal period have been reproduced than of the earlier. The Federal's lack of personality makes it more suited to everybody's taste. Its light strength and grace are impossible to dislike — although some may find it harder to feel personally attached to it. Its perfect gentility suits oddly with the new aristocracy, who, however, liked it and bought it. Nothing could smack less of the self-made, bold sea adventurers than the delicate Federal — which was soon to run off into Empire.

Why it was that both America and France, rising out of the hurly-burly of revolution, fancied such delicate elegance is hard to say. Perhaps it is because both countries had thought and talked much about republican Greece and Rome. (Back in 1775 Joseph Warren had delivered his Massacre Oration in a 'Ciceronian toga.') Or it may have been a natural swing of the pendulum away from the contortions into which rococo often fell. Could it have been that in both countries the new aristocracy wished to advertise its respectability — as well as its wealth? There is no teetotaller like your reformed drunkard — no matron as respectable as the hussy who has settled down. The little grotesque masks, the dragon snouts, bold scrolls of the earlier period, might seem (to a very unsure newcomer) just a touch vulgar. The last trace of medieval or Renaissance gaiety was wiped away.

Soon young girls were to be chaperoned for the first time in America, and carefully brought-up young girls, like Anna Green Winslow, would not be quoting Fielding or saying that an unpopular clergyman had 'popes in his belly.' The English language had been wide open to our Puritan ancestors, but by the end of the eighteenth century (and before Victoria was even born), it began to be sicklied o'er with a pale cast of respectability. Horace Walpole was already using 'gothic' as a reproach. People would begin to wonder if perhaps they did not drink too much, and spouts and covers transformed Revere's convivial 'canns' and tankards into ice-water pitchers.

Although Emerson has pathetically pointed out that 'from 1780 to 1820 there was not a book, a speech, a conversation, or a thought in the state,'[42] there were such ships and such sailors as even Boston had never seen before. For the ingenuity of her merchants had discovered a profitable new trade route. In 1786, Elias Hasket Derby's *The Grand Turk* came back from Canton. She was the first Yankee ship to have made the fabulous voyage. Only one American ship had preceded her, and that was the *Empress of China*, from New York the year before, whose commercial success was due to Samuel Shaw, her supercargo. This young man Paul Revere knew well, for he was one of those Shaw boys who used to quarrel with Lieutenant Wragg when Major Pitcairn was quartered upon the family at North Square. He was only a fair sample of the type of young man Boston had by the dozen, ready and eager to venture anything — everything. It seems captious of Emerson to complain that they also did not write books, make speeches, and that their conversation and thoughts were perhaps on a lower level than that of Concord in its heyday.

Within six years of the arrival of the *Grand Turk*, the merchants had established a new trade route — from Boston to the northwest coast. The ships — usually very small — there picked up from the Indians otter skins to trade with the mandarins of China, for Massachusetts was woefully deficient in acceptable exports — not much more than the ashes, tar, and codfish that Miranda viewed with contempt — and so the ships returned to Boston carrying the exotic riches of the East. From Revere's store on 50 Cornhill he could smell cinnamon and sandalwood drifting up from Long Wharf. Nankeens, Chinese silks, blue Canton ware, Java sparrows, mangoes and coconuts, monkeys, Malacca canes, became the common luxuries of Boston life. Men rounded the Horn as nonchalantly as Cape Cod. Any American was known in the Far East as a 'Bostonian.' Ships and fortunes were lost in this bold commerce — but more ships and more and more were always rising, and more and even greater fortunes were made. This was the age in which Paul Revere was to live his middle years, and these the men for whom he made his later silver.

For Elias Hasket Derby (a Salem man), Paul Revere made a great deal of silver, among it one of his most beautiful pieces — whether from the earlier or later period. This is a silver 'waiter.' One of its minor charms is the fact one can see upon the reverse the blurred shape of the silver coins (doubtless Spanish doubloons, picked up by a 'King Darby' ship) from which it was hammered. The design is not in the cautious Federal manner, but very bold and handsome. On Derby's *Grand Turk* was imported the first of the beautiful Chinese porcelain to come directly to Boston. Paul Revere was evidently delighted with the grace and simplicity of these Chinese bowls, and complimented them by using them as models for some of his silver. Within a year after the landing of the *Grand Turk*, he made such a bowl to be presented to General Shepard 'for his Ability and Zeal in quelling Shays' Rebellion.'

How closely Paul Revere's silver ties in with the doings of his days is exemplified by this bowl. The design for it he got from the first cargo of the *Grand Turk*. He made it for one of the generals who put down that very sad incident in Massachusetts history called 'Shays' Rebellion,' which was but one of a number of symptoms of the unhealthy condition of the young state.

The Federal Government was almost non-existent (there was not as yet even a Constitution in 1786, and the states were wrangling so it did not look as if there ever would be one). The state government was bankrupt and weak. Berkshire County completely refused obedience to what little power there was in Boston and the western part of the state (entirely agricultural) refused to pay taxes and debts. Forty per cent of the state's income was raised by poll tax, which was too heavy a burden for the western and central farmers to bear.[43] Seemingly everyone was in debt to everyone else. The foreclosure of mortgages forced men off farms their families had owned for generations. With a spirit not so far removed from the spirit of '76, they decided that they would not permit courts to open and insisted upon a moratorium for debts.

So once more men marched through snow on bloody feet with the word 'liberty' upon their lips. Many of these men, like Captain Shays himself, had fought for the establishment of this republic

in which now they could not make a living and their farms were
taken from them. They were ready 'to water the Tree of Liberty
with their blood.' The militia was called out to disperse them.
They would move on and the militia would move on. Neither side
wished the blood of the other on its hands. Shays kept a little army
in the field for six months. The whole thing was a protest rather
than a rebellion. In all each side lost two men, and to an extraordinary degree both sides, during the six months of insurrection,
kept their heads and their tempers. Whatever it was our ancestors
had (and we have not) was never more conspicuous than during the
dreary months of Shays' Rebellion. There was a great deal of
sympathy with the rebels, even in Boston, although the uprising
represented inland agrarian interests versus the seaboard commercial. Surely Sam Adams would understand the predicament these
men, mostly poor, were in. He, if anyone, should have been sympathetic. But the old Revolutionary leader wanted no revolution
except his own. When the leaders were captured and tried, he
was bitter in his demands for their blood. To revolt against a
monarchy was, he said, understandable and to be forgiven, but
'the man who dares to rebel against the laws of a republic ought to
suffer death.' Such sudden conservatism from Sam Adams must
have made Thomas Hutchinson laugh in his English grave.

Luckily for Massachusetts' good name, it was John Hancock —
not Adams — who was governor. Prematurely old, sick, pressed
for debt himself (but putting up as good a front as ever), John
Hancock pardoned everyone concerned with the revolt — 'go and
sin no more.' He was weary, ready to die — 'I feel the seeds of
my mortality growing within me'; and so towards the end of his
life he rose above his wine coolers and flowered satin waistcoats,
his gold buttons, vanity, and enormous dinners, and by his humanity and wisdom silenced the critics who have always taken pleasure
in pointing out his obvious shortcomings. As he signed this general
pardon, he was worthy of his signature.

That bowl, for which Paul Revere followed the design of the
potter rather than the English silversmith who habitually set the
fashion in New England, was not the only time he turned to ceram-
ics for a pleasing form. Towards the .end of the eighteenth century, 'Liverpool pitchers' (characterized by landscapes or ships
on their sides) were imported into Boston from England. In porce-

lain the shape is attractive, but Revere's version of it in silver is so extremely satisfactory it has become a classic. Replicas of it in various metals can be bought in department stores for a few dollars. This, the 'Revere pitcher,' is quite independent of the silver fashions of his day. Neither in this nor in the bowls of Chinese shape did he slavishly copy. He looked at them, was pleased, and translated their basic forms into silver — regardless of the Federal fashion of the moment.

But even when he worked closely in the post-war delicate manner, he gave his work strength and character. A beautiful example is the Hartt tea-set, made by Revere to be presented to his neighbor, Edmund Hartt, and it is one of the last pieces of silver he is known to have made. Hartt's fellow citizens gave it to him in 1799 in honor of his 'completion of that Ornament of the American Navy,' the frigate *Boston*. Six years before, he had built that even greater ornament, the *Constitution*. It is hard to imagine how the Federal taste could be raised to a higher perfection than in these three pieces.

One is not surprised to note, however, that in this later period Paul Revere's workmanship is not quite so perfect as in the earlier. The silver is not always hammered to exactly the same gauge. Sometimes covers do not fit so meticulously. Either he was depending more and more upon his apprentices or working in greater haste. Perhaps he found more sameness in the new designs and was less interested. Possibly his new patrons had not quite so high a standard — they themselves were in a hurry in this new age. Uncle Thomas had waited for years for his chariot. Such patience was out of date.

The great ships were spreading more and more sail — hurry or you will not be first to Canton. Some other merchant will get there first this season and your tea will fetch but half the price when you get back to Boston. Hurry to buy the sea-otter skins from the west coast Indians, hurry for Bombay, even for the Cannibal Isles. The big, square, brick houses (Bulfinch, McIntyre) were going up fast. There must be a great display of silver on the sideboard to impress the people who can remember when you were a poor sailor before the mast and your lady had only one petticoat — and that patched. There had been long lean years in Boston. Now everyone was rushing into new ventures, hoping to make a 'good property.' So

Paul Revere may have hurried a little too. He certainly tried new ventures himself during those expansive, heady, unthoughtful years, and he did make a 'good property.'

## VI

EARLY in 1788, the Federal Constitution came up for ratification before the Massachusetts Convention. The Boston artisans were strong Federalists, but they were afraid their old leader, Sam Adams, was about to vote against the Constitution. He had not as yet expressed an opinion.

A mass meeting of mechanics was held at that old hotbed of revolution, the 'Green Dragon.' They voted unanimously for adoption and sent an enormous delegation to call on Sam Adams and to tell him how they had voted. The delegation, headed by Paul Revere, marched through the streets of Boston, to Sam Adams' house (he was now living on Winter Street).

'"How many," asked Adams, "were gathered together when this resolution was past?"

'"More, sir, than the Green Dragon could hold."

'"And where were the rest, Mr. Revere?"

'"In the streets, sir."

'"And how many in the streets?"

'"More, sir, than there are stars in the sky."'

Sam Adams voted to ratify.

Thus the story was told by Daniel Webster some fifty years later. That last sentence, 'More, sir, than there are stars in the sky,' sounds much more like Daniel Webster than Paul Revere. Revere did not go in for big flourishes, whether in silver or conversation.

Paul Revere had been for years the acknowledged leader of the Boston artisans — who were calling themselves 'mechanics,'

a word which seemed more fashionable to them (although less so
to us).

As in pre-Revolutionary Boston, the artisan's or mechanic's
livelihood depended upon the success of the ships. Paul Revere's
first venture into shopkeeping was as an importer of English goods,
but by 1788 his stock in trade was largely hardware. Such strides
were being made in New England industry, much of this hardware
was of local manufacture. He decided to go into this work himself
— produce the goods, not merely retail them.

Up to this year he does not seem to have ever cast anything of
baser metal than silver. By November he had set up his little works
on the tip of North Boston (corner of Lynn and Foster Streets).
'We have got are furnass agoing,' he wrote jubilantly, 'and find
it answers our expectations. I have no doubt the business will do
exceedingly well in Boston.' He wants Brown & Benson, of Providence, to send him 'a constant & regular supply of Piggs from your
furnass.' Other letters show that he is visiting foundries and reading 'chemical essays.' His shop was set up amid the shipyards
and many of his castings were various gadgets used by shipbuilders.
He also made stoves, chimney backs, hearths, anvils, and forge
hammers.

There is a wretched little engraving of Boston in 1788 showing
bursts of black smoke rising from Revere's 'furnass.' If the wind
veered about, he would be drenching all that end of town with his
soot. The housewives of North Boston may have been amazed to
find linen, spread upon the grass to whiten, was soiled by the
foundry. It was a new experience. Boston streets might be dirty,
but the air had always been clean. As they were human, they
would complain bitterly among themselves. What sort of neighbor
would a foundry be? Paul Revere himself liked it so well he rented
a house from Samuel Savage on Charter Street, and then another
house on Charter Street, so he could be as near it as possible.
Within a year he also built an air furnace.

Joseph Warren Revere was only twelve when his father branched
out into something which is recognizable to us as a modern industry. He must have revelled in the excitement of the foundry, for
he loved such things all his life. And he lived to be very old — to
wear side-whiskers, and to be remembered by people, still living,
to become the head of an industry still one of the greatest in Amer-

ica. But his father saw to it the boy did not spend all his time hanging about the foundry. He also was trained as a silversmith. Paul Revere had now a silversmith shop on Anne Street. The experiments going on at the furnace were still so unproven, one could not be sure they could be counted on for a livelihood. There always have been silversmiths, and none of them seem to have starved.

It was characteristic of Paul Revere that he did not work long in simple iron castings. Any number of men could do that, and he preferred more difficult arts. Although he made a great many brass cannon, his reputation as a foundryman (he called himself a 'founder') was in the extremely tricky art of bell-casting. His first effort was for his own church.

'Puffing Pem' and the war had about finished off the old Cockerel. It had even during the hard year of 1779 been driven to exchanging 'a red velvet pulpit-cuchion and case' with the church at Hingham for six cords of wood. (Thomas Hitchbourn had arranged this barter.) Next, it joined with the Old North congregation who had no church building, and from now on these two churches were known as the Second Church. Old North's bell had not been destroyed by the British when they took the church down for firewood and was hung in the familiar cock-crowned steeple. In 1792, this bell cracked and was forbidden to ring except in case of fire. But to our ancestors a church without a bell was like a bird without song. The metal must be recast. Should it be sent to England?

Thirty-five prominent members of the church met to consider the problem of where it was to be recast — and how paid for. Each man agreed to give so much. Paul Revere was among them, as were his cousins, Samuel Hitchbourn, the silversmith, and Thomas, the shipbuilder. Such meetings were never run off without a few bottles of Madeira or a bowl of hot punch to mellow the donors, so one is not surprised to read that the meeting ended with a small joke. It was voted that if any man failed to make good his promised subscription, he was not to be allowed to hear the bell.

So thirty-four members of the Second Church had their joke and went home to sleep, but hardly Paul Revere, for he had offered to recast the bell. He did not know one thing about bell-casting. Nothing more musical than a cowbell had ever been cast in Boston. Characteristically, he was neither afraid to make the attempt

nor lacking in the knowledge of how to get help. He knew that in
Abington, shortly before the Revolution, Aaron Hobart had set up
a bell foundry. Although isolated bells had been cast before in
America (especially noted being the Liberty Bell), Hobart is
thought to be the first regular bell-caster. His instructor was a
man called Gillimore — one of those many British soldiers to desert
from the army before the Boston Massacre and become ardent
Americans. By trade Gillimore had been a bell founder. The few
bells the deserter and Hobart managed to make before the Revolution were sold in Boston by Revere's friend, Joseph Webb. In
'75, Hobart was called upon to produce cannon. The state gave
him material and he went to work. All his cannon burst as they
were being proved. Hobart was in despair, but luckily a French
engineer (obviously Lewis Ansart himself) happened to stop at the
Abington Inn. He heard of the bursting cannon and Hobart's sad
story, and told him it was all a matter of the size of the flue in proportion to the chimney, and other technical tricks.

When Paul Revere decided to cast his first bell, he went to
Abington and brought back to Boston with him one of Hobart's
sons and a foundryman who knew something about making bells.
This may have been Gillimore himself. Part of his bill to the church
is for trips to Abington 'to get men and implements to aid preparing the molds for casting.'

From the old bell he had five hundred pounds of metal, but it
was to be enlarged to nine hundred and twelve pounds. He would
need both copper and tin. Probably zinc and lead as well. None
of those things grow on trees in New England. Although he had
worked in metal all his life, the bellmakers' arts are very individual
and had always been surrounded with the deepest secrecy, almost
magic. How to construct the core and cope for a mold was a delicate art, far removed from stoves and anvils. The mold must be
very accurate and the bell of varying thickness. Large bells cannot
be cast in the same shape as small ones. Even the ores that go into
the make-up of bell metal varied constantly in those days and played
a large part in the final beauty and strength of the bell. The length
of time the amalgam stays in the furnace, the speed with which
the mold is run, also affect the success or failure of the bell. For an
amateur at this trade, what the bell sounded like was largely a
matter of luck.

At last the great pit having been dug, the molten mass poured, there was the long wait for the bell to cool before it could be taken out and sounded. This, Paul Revere's first bell, was 'panny, harsh and shrill.' Its most impassionate admirers could say little for it except that it excelled in calling people out for fires. Probably some of the thirty-five church worthies who had financed it wished they had not paid the subscriptions and literally could not hear it. But Boston was inordinately proud of this shrieking bell — and so was Paul Revere.

For hundreds of years bells had been inscribed with pious sentiments and the names of donors. But Paul Revere was a modern man. He put on his bell, 'The first bell cast in Boston 1792 P. Revere.' Not for him the 'Man made me to show forth the Glory of God,' or (like the bells of Christ), 'Since Generosity has opened our mouths, our tongues shall ring aloud its praise.' Such sentimentality belonged to pre-war days and was being thrown over-board for cruder facts. This was indeed the first bell cast in Boston. It might have a heavy sound, but 'P. Revere' had done it. It has always been a good strong bell but its voice has been silent for years. Saint James's Church in Cambridge finally bought it, but, having no bell tower, never hung it. It is today in the nave of that church.

Now Paul Revere was prepared to go on with this new, half-mastered craft and in the end to excel in it. He was ready to make a bell for every steeple in New England, for Savannah, Havana, Quebec, or Kentucky, and this is almost what he and Joseph Warren Revere eventually did.

In 1911, Doctor Arthur H. Nichols estimated that the number of bells these two Reveres made from 1792 to 1826 could not have been less than three hundred and ninety-eight. Seventy-eight were still in use (but mostly badly hung and the tone injured), forty-seven had cracked (in some cases by careless sextons hitting them with sledgehammers). Fire had taken thirty-nine of Paul Revere's bells, and lightning, two. Five at that time were in museums. The fate of the rest was unknown.[44]

A great many of Paul Revere's letters about his bells have been preserved. He took pride in his workmanship, and 'we know we can cast as good bells as can be cast in the world, both for goodness & for sound. Since the year 1793 we have cast upwards of 100 Church bells we have never heard that any one has been broken or received any complaint of the sound.  On the contrary we have frequently been complimented by the purchasers for their good and pleasing sound.'

He always insisted that before a bell was purchased, a committee come to Boston and approve the sound.  If he is recasting (as was often the case) an old broken bell, he stands ready to buy up the old metal at the going rate if they are not satisfied with the way the bell has turned out.  The bells were carted from the foundry to the Reveres' own back yard on Charter Street, where, in the presence of church deacons, vestrymen, selectmen, or donor, the bell was sounded.  Naturally the small boys of the North End crowded in and in their anxiety to miss nothing got too close to the bell for their own safety or the convenience of the sale.  Years after (and they men in their seventies and eighties) they remembered the scene, the committee, the back-yard garden, the bell, and Mr. Revere himself.  When they really got in the way, he would good-naturedly push them aside with his cane.

'Take care, boys!  If that hammer should hit your head you'd ring louder than these bells do.'

But he had a certain amount of trouble with his customers (as well as from the admiring small boys).  There was that bell he cast for Providence: 'the Bell was got into place & rung for the first time. It is gratifying to be able to state to you that the *tone* is very much admired but there is a difficulty & that a very important one, the Sound is so feeble that persons within a quater of a mile' can hardly hear it.  This was probably the fault of the hanging rather than the fault of the bell itself.

Business was done in a curiously trustful and unbusinesslike way, by our standards (and it was by the same method the China trade was carried on), as Paul Revere's long and troubled correspondence over the Farmington (Maine) bell shows.  He had obviously delivered a bell to a young man whose name he did not bother to take down, had not asked for a receipt for the bell, and it was not until over six months later that he began to worry a little about where his pay was coming from.  On the first of July, 1809, he wrote this letter to an acquaintance in Farmington, telling the situation:

> The 24 of November last we delivered a bell to a young Gentleman who said he was implaced to purchase a bell for the said Academy

(by the Trustees of Farmington Academy) of about 500 lbs. The one we delivered weighed 495 £ at 42 cts came to $207.90. He did not leave his name but engaged to call again for a bill. He said the Trustees would send the pay early in the spring. As we have not seen him since nor heard from the Trustees we will thank you to require them to write us whether they received the Bell or that they gave any person order to purchase the Bell.

He also wrote the trustees, who kept a dignified, sinister silence. He is at last angry enough to write another letter to his acquaintance in Farmington (Mr. Supply Belcher). 'Are any of the Trustees Gentlemen, or are they Persons who care little or nothing for Character?'

Seemingly they are just persons — not gentlemen. Their silence remains abysmal, but Revere knows by now that they have received and hung his bell and he knows their names. They even are 'gentlemen.' The following letter (written almost two years after he saw the mysterious young gentleman go off with his bell, headed for Farmington) shows Paul Revere with his dander up:

> We think it extrordinary that Gentlemen of your Respectability will not so far respect your own Credit as not to notice in anyway our letters to you: You know you have a Bell, you know who it was purchased of, who purchased it & the terms it was purchased upon & hear that Bell every Sabbath call you to the house of God & you all know it is not paid for. What are we to think of the Gentlemen who composed the Trustees of Farmington Academy?

What indeed — except they did not have any money. Probably their flesh did creep as Paul Revere's unpaid-for bell solemnly called them out to worship God. But they eventually did pay.

Difficulties in collecting payment were very rare. People were still (by our more cynical standard) morbidly afraid of being classed as merely 'persons,' not 'gentlemen.' The old aristocratic virtue of 'honor' was by no means dead in the young republic.

Revere was often troubled by finding his bells hung and rung improperly (as Mr. Nichols says most of them still were in 1911). Joseph Warren Revere once wrote: 'Bells made here and in England are intended to be rung by a wheel: by which method the Bell strikes the tongue and frees itself at once. Bells used in the Spanish dominions [for which the Reveres made many] ought to be made much heavier of the same dimensions or they ought not to be struck on the inside by the same weight of tongue.' An English or a Revere bell breaks if improperly rung. So delicate is the bell that the young man says, 'with a yard of twine I would undertake to break every Church bell in Boston.'

In one respect Paul Revere was unable to make bells as fine as the old English bells, such as Christ's. Doctor Nichols says, 'mines no longer produced such elastic copper.' The quality of the bell depends much upon the quality of the copper which is such a large part of bell metal. To get sufficient elasticity, Paul Revere was forced to use more copper of the type he could get in his amalgam than the bell founders who had preceded him. The length of his vibration (by which a bell is partly judged) is not as long as in the older bells, although longer than any except a very few modern ones. On the whole, they are beautiful bells, 'powerful and mellow.'

His contemporaries (like William Bentley) compared his work with the most famous of the early English bells — made from a no-longer available vein of copper. Most of them thought his work exactly as good. William Bentley did not. He was a Salem clergyman, a good and intelligent man and a wonderful diarist. It was his father who had rowed Paul Revere across the Charles and started him off on his famous ride. Two of Paul Revere's bells were hung in Salem and the clergyman had a good opportunity to listen to them. He thought 'Mr. Revere has not yet learned to give sweetness and clearness to the tones of his bells. He has no ear & perhaps knows nothing of the laws of sound and his excess of copper to ensure the strength of his bells depreciates their value.' He did not think Paul Revere entirely deserved the extravagant praise he was getting for his bells. People 'venture to prefer it to any imported bell & so did we, but from patriotism.' But Mr. Bentley obviously did not know that Paul Revere had to use more copper than he probably would have chosen. As a man, Bentley admired his father's old friend. He was such 'an enterprizing mechanic.' One morning, when the clergyman was spending the night in Boston, he rose early and walked about the town. Before breakfast he found Paul Revere already up and happily at work at his foundry on Lynn Street.

Luckily for Paul Revere's reputation, the largest and most famous of all his bells still hangs in the stone tower of King's Chapel. This is considered a 'brilliant bell' with a 'unique and charming sequence of harmonic effects.' For over a hundred years Bostonians have known and loved this bell. Its sound is so individual it can easily be recognized even when heard from far away. This is the largest bell Paul and Joseph Warren Revere ever cast. It weighs 2437 pounds and much of the metal came from the older bell. The tradition is that silver too was added to ensure an especially beautiful tone. When the bell was hung, it was celebrated by a few anonymous (presumably non-Episcopal) verses:

> The Chapel Church
> Left in the lurch
> Must surely fall;
> For Church and people
> And bell and steeple
> Are crazy all.

> The Church still lives,
> The priest survives,
> With mind the same.
> Revere refounds,
> A bell resounds,
> And all is well again.

Considering the comparatively few bells of his that yet can be heard today, it is fortunate that this, his masterpiece, is not only still in service, but has always (as Doctor Nichols points out) received the most scrupulous and loving care. Still today its rich voice from the heart of the city answers the silvery singing of Christ in North End. Boston has not entirely lost its voice.

# VII

PAUL REVERE'S foundry was surrounded by shipyards. Although he cast so many bells for inland churches, his primary interest as manufacturer was in furnishing the ships. His bells still ring in memory of his skill, but 'the bolts, spikes, cogs, braces, pintles, sheaves, pumps etc' he made for the ships (of infinitely greater practical importance to the young country) are little more now than a series of words. Such ship gear had to be made from copper or brass and was largely imported. There were certain secrets about how the amalgam was made up (for pure copper would not serve). He went to work to discover for himself how it was done. Soon he can write, 'what is more no man but myself in the four New England States can melt Copper & draw it into Spikes'; and soon he realizes 'there are no persons in either Philadelphia or New York, that can make Copper so maleable that it can be drawn in Bolts, Spikes, &c under the hammer.' He does not at first seem to realize how rare a secret he had discovered, but soon, 'I farther found it was a Secret, that lay in very few Breasts in England. I determined if possible to find the Secret & have the pleasure to say, after a great many trials and considerable expense I gained it.' Paul Revere was not the only man in America who was hunting for these scientific 'secrets' — Harvard at the same time engaged Doctor Benjamin Waterhouse (Yankeeborn but educated at Oxford and Leyden) to teach mineralogy. Such a subject had never before been taught in this country. It was not among his learned fellow professors Doctor Waterhouse encountered the most knowledge of his own field. Later he said he 'found Mr. Revere the only man (in America) in 1794 who appeared to know anything of the discrimination between ores and the seven metals.' What Doctor Waterhouse and Paul Revere knew between them would hardly impress a technological freshman today. Then they were blazing trails into an unknown world. What Paul Revere discovered he immediately applied to the business at hand — copper for ships. Especially for warships.

The young republic had not a friend in the world. England looked upon her with an understandably jaundiced eye. France (metamorphosed by her revolution) began an undeclared war upon her in 1794. This was fought on the high seas for some six years. Our war with the Algerian pirates began in 1785, when the Dey captured the trading schooner *Maria* in the Mediterranean and held American seamen for slaves. Ten years later the United States Government agreed to pay the Dey a million dollars in cash and presents and an annual tribute of twenty thousand dollars if he would let our ships alone.  A popular demand for 'Millions for defence, not a penny for tribute,' was the answer to that humiliating treaty.  It was not until then the Government believed the country would support an American navy.  Up to 1795 the peace party and the isolationists were so strong we did not have a single warship nor naval yard.  The belief that if we bothered no one, no one would bother us, had not worked.  The French would charge in and seize our ships within sight of our shores.  The Dey of Algiers had to be bribed to let our ships sail, yet, without some sort of 'freedom of the seas,' the country could hardly exist.  The usual reaction against war had set in after the Revolution, but never has the reaction gone so far in this country nor resulted in such danger.

The start of the American navy, in 1795, was modest.  Three frigates of forty-four guns and three of thirty-six guns were ordered built.  These, of course, had to be constructed in private yards, for there were no others.  The most famous of these ships, the *Constitution*, was built at Hartt's yard, so close to Revere's house and shop he could have seen the men at work on her from an upper window in Charter Street and heard the shipwrights hammering as he labored in his foundry on Lynn Street.  The smaller *Essex* was also built soon afterwards in Boston.  Paul Revere was determined to make the copper and brass for these ships himself.  Before the keels were laid, he wrote,

> I understand that there are to be two Ships built in this State, for the General government, and that they are to be Coppered, if so, they will want *Composition bolts, Rudder braces* &c &c
>
> I can purchase several tons of Copper here, and my works are fitted for such business; Should those things be wanted, and I understand by General Jackson, that it is in your department, if you would be kind enough to give me the refusal, you will much oblige me.
>
> I will do them as cheap as any one and as well.

Two things are noticeable in this letter—Paul Revere's vagueness about whom he should write to (there was no Secretary of the Navy when he wrote this letter) and his reference to the 'General government.'  Even as well informed and patriotic a citizen as Revere hardly knew what to call whatever it was that was running the country.

He did furnish the metal for both the frigates.  His bill for the

*Constitution* was for $3820.33. Some of the large copper blocks and sheaves he made for her were still used a hundred years after her launching by a rigging company around Boston. Paul Revere made things to last.

By the time the *Essex* was being completed, there was a Secretary of the Navy to whom Paul Revere wrote:

> I understand that you have advised the Committee for building the Frigate in Boston not to send abroad for anything they can get manufactured in this Country; those Sentiments have induced me to trouble you with this letter. I can manufacture old or new Coper, into bolts, Spikes, Staples Nails &c. or anything that is wanted in Shipbuilding.... I supplyed the Constitution with Dove-tails, Staples Nails &c &c. The Frigate building here has upwards of 5000 lbs of my bolts & Spikes already in her, of my manufacture; and I have supplyed Jacob Sheafe Esq. Naval Agent at Portsmouth with 600 lbs of spikes for the Frigate building there. My greatest difficulty is to get old Copper, Could I get a sufficient supply of Copper, I would undertake to roll Sheet Copper for Sheathing Ships &c.

Although the *Constitution* (like some of her sister frigates) had been bolted together by Revere's bolts, and although he had cast for her a bell (which was carried away many years later during her fight with the *Guerrière*), there was one thing he had not been able to do for her and that was roll the sheet copper for her sheathing. She was sheathed with British copper. Warships and merchantmen were both absolutely dependent upon England for sheet copper. Without it (so important was this rather new invention) a ship was greatly handicapped. When the *Albatross* tried to go about the Horn to the northwest fur coast without a copper bottom, she found that her collection of tropical barnacles and seaweed had reduced her speed to two knots an hour. There was no greater service a man could do for his country at the moment than to find a practical way to roll copper. We were still at war with France and the pirates, England did not look too friendly. The bulk of our wealth was in shipping, yet any moment we might be cut off from the British supply of copper sheathing.

Undoubtedly Paul Revere saw a chance to make money by being the first man in America to fill this great need, and he also saw a patriotic duty and an intense personal satisfaction. One always feels, as he writes of his various crafts, that he is principally interested in making fine things and not so much in the money. That is probably why he started a number of ventures he quickly dropped. Obviously false teeth did not interest him — although there might not have been much money in it. Neither did engraving — he did not excel in it and this he would have been the first to know. He liked to excel. Shopkeeping had been but a stop-gap. The army, a sober obligation, and no joy. But to make silver, to cast bells, and now to furnish the sheathing for the American ships — these were the three trades he excelled in and which in turn delighted and supported him.

One can feel his excitement in the letters he writes as he makes his plans for his rolling mill and gets his financial backing from the Government. Give him the wherewithal and he can do it. He felt himself upon the threshold of great things. This was his most daring venture, for he put every cent he had into his new works, and even borrowed money. The vitality in the man flowed out to meet the opportunity. The tide of life runs high. Yet in 1800, when he decided to go into this new work (which links him so closely to our own day), he was already sixty-five.

## VIII

PAUL REVERE had early been looked upon as a leader of that powerful group that formerly had called themselves 'artisans.' He had been scarcely out of his twenties when the intelligentsia of the Revolution had turned to him, partly because of his own innate ability, and partly in the hope that he would carry along with him the North End artisans. Although the merchants had from the beginning of time had their clubs and organizations, the men who made things did not. By

1794, they first decided to form the organization which in time became the Massachusetts Charitable Mechanic Association. The story is that Henry Purkitt, cooper (but he also 'was inspector of pickled fish, the duties of which he performed with distinguished ability'), put an advertisement in the newspaper suggesting such an association. Paul Revere was surprised it had been done without consulting him. For over twenty years everyone had known he was the acknowledged leader in such matters.

The first notice in the *Columbian Centinel*, December 31, 1794, reads:

> The Tradesmen, Mechanics and Manufacturers of this Town and vicinity, who keep apprentices, are desired to meet at the Green Dragon, on Tuesday evening next, at 6 o'clock, for the purpose of consulting on measures for petitioning the General Court, to revise and amend the Law respecting Apprentices.

The master craftsmen had always had a hard time with their apprentices, but now, with the many new trades, new opportunities, and greater ease in travelling about, the old system was badly shaken up. Paul Revere himself had had trouble with some of his boys. He had only got David Mosely back by suing the shipmaster who had seduced him away from his goldsmith shop (and considering that Mosely then turned around, married his master's sister, Betsey, although she was much older than himself, drank too much, and was a spendthrift and a thorn in Revere's side forever after, he may have wished he had let the boy go). This problem of how to hold on to one's apprentices was but one of the many which confronted the ingenious men when they finally got themselves organized, and one of the first points they agreed upon was never to hire a boy who had run away from his master. They referred to themselves at first as 'The Association of Mechanics.' The 'Charitable' came later. It was an employers' organization open only to 'mechanics and manufacturors,' who were twenty-one, and 'if a mechanic he shall be a master-workman; — if a manufacturor, he shall be a proprietor of a manufactory, or supretendent thereof.' But they stood ready to help the apprentices by 'encouraging the ingenious' and 'rewarding the faithful.' They were soon giving prizes for good work, certificates of approval, and helping boys financially with books, advice, and opportunities, as well as helping their own distressed members, usually by a free funeral.

The merchants and other citizens were at first badly frightened. They feared that once all the mechanics got together prices would go up. As a matter of fact, the society gave a great boost to 'Yankee ingenuity' and the enthusiasm which these men felt for new inventions and labor-saving devices did much for the prosperity of New England. People began to joke about the curious machines the very mechanically minded New Englanders could think up. The *Columbian Centinel* said that 'a curious machine has lately been advertized which will *churn, scrape potatoes, rock a cradle* and *darn stockings.*' Paul Revere was the president of this powerful organization for its first few years.

It seems obvious that these men themselves knew what a 'mechanic' was, yet studying the list of the first eighty-three charter members one can get no idea. They were certainly not using the word as Shakespeare did when he referred to 'the poor mechanic porters crouding in' that is 'comon, vulgar, mean' (according to *Century*), nor in the common usage of the word today. Among the eighty-three were bakers, hairdressers, book- and paint-sellers, six tailors, a painter. Paul Revere puts himself down as a goldsmith — although his work as a foundryman, casting bells, would in our eyes be the mechanic side of his life. The 'engine-builder' and the 'pump and block maker' would be expected, as would the blacksmiths, copper or white smiths, or Edmund Hartt, the shipbuilder.

The association became very prosperous (as were many of the members) and of tremendous influence in Boston, growing in strength throughout the next century. The meetings were quite convivial. Not only were all the extraordinary new steps in manufacture discussed, but dinners were eaten, toasts drunk, and songs sung. James Phillips, the ropemaker, seems to have had the sweetest voice. It was not soon forgotten how he could render the 'Parson and the Barrel of Beer,' or 'Why should we at our lot repine?' Peter Smink, the silk-dyer, furnished the comedy of those earliest days. He had come over as a 'Hessian,' his figure was 'orbicular,' and he played profoundly on the bassoon. They compared him to Falstaff. One of the menus for a dinner is so startling and so excessively 'mechanical,' one wonders if this method of determining courses was often practised.

Starting with soup, they went on to — '*Boiled* — Turkeys (with oyster sauce), Fowls, and Legs Pork — Beef alamode.'

Second course — 'Roasted — Beef, Turkeys, Chickens, Pigs, Ducks, Geese &c.'

Third course — 'Baked — Chicken pies with Oysters in them — Beefsteak pies — Plum puddings, Pies, Tarts, &c.'

'Roots, vegetables and celery, &c.'

Sometimes in those early days they had 'festivals' and paraded the streets. By 1800, forty-five different trades were recognized (much in the manner of modern Rotary) and a delegate from each carried a banner emblematic of his trade, Burt represented the Goldsmith; and yet even then it is impossible to figure out just what they had in mind when they called themselves 'mechanics.'

Paul Revere was very active in the society as long as he lived. His son, Paul, was also a charter member — but dropped out. Joseph Warren joined and so did at least two of Paul Revere's sons-in-law, Amos and Jedediah Lincoln. The young Lincolns were house-wrights and Amos was the master builder of Bulfinch's State House.

When the cornerstone was laid on the Fourth of July, 1795, Paul Revere, as Grand Master of the Grand Lodge of Massachusetts, led the Masons to the scene and assisted as Governor Sam Adams laid the cornerstone. It was drawn into place by fifteen white horses (representing the fifteen united states) and decked with ribbons. The new State House was built on 'governor's pasture' next to the old Hancock house, where Mrs. Hancock had been living for two years as a widow — but she would not be alone for long. Captain Scott would soon marry the widow and move into his old employer's mansion. Sam Adams himself was very feeble. He had tried to walk in Hancock's funeral procession, but had not been physically able.

He made the first speech at the dedication of the cornerstone. May the building which will rise above it 'remain, permanent as the enduring mountains'; 'May the principals of our excellent Constitution, founded in nature and in the Rights of Man, be ably defended here.'

Paul Revere then addressed the assembled Masons. This is the only time we have record of his making a formal speech. Probably he struggled over it and appreciated the many allusions he got in about Masonry, for he preserved it among his papers.

Worshipfull Brethern. I congratulate you on this auspicious day; — When the Arts and Sciences are establishing themselves among us in our happy country, a Country distinguished from the rest of the World by being a government of Laws, where Liberty has found a safe and secure abode, and where her sons are determined to support and protect her.

He ended with the hope:

May we, my Brethern, so square our actions thro life as to show to the World of Mankind, that we mean to live within the compass of Good Citizens, that we wish to stand upon a level with them, that when we part we may be admitted into the Temple where Reigns Silence and Peace.

Under the cornerstone was placed a silver plate inscribed with the doings of that day and giving the names of those who took part. So the cannons boomed and the ceremony was over.

Yet even while engaged in this solemn occasion, one thought might have persisted in playing about in Revere's mind. He surely had seen the plans young Bulfinch had drawn up for this stately edifice, as his son-in-law was to be the builder. There was the problem of the dome. Obviously it must be protected — and obviously with sheet copper. It would not be only the ships that needed sheet copper. Someone must make it — why not he? The *Constitution* was on the ways over at Hartt's yard, and here was the State House, its cornerstone already laid, both crying out for sheet copper. There was no reason (as he used so often to write of his bells and his copper) why he could not 'do it as well as anybody.'

## IX

REVERE had, through the years, given many a hostage to fortune. He had had eight children by Sary and eight more by Rachel. Not one child seems to have disappointed the father in any way except by dying, which almost a

third did in infancy. But surely a man with eleven children growing to maturity, learning trades, helping him with his expanding
industrial ventures, having children of their own, could not be
accused of carrying all his eggs in one basket. Not like John Hancock, for instance. He and Dolly had had a little girl, who died
early, and one son, John George Washington Hancock. One night
this small prodigy of nine had been dancing a stately minuet at
Portsmouth and almost the next dying of a fall on the ice. Hancock's heart was broken.

Paul Revere suffered with his children, but no matter what
happened to them the supply never quite ran out. His sons-in-law
replaced in his warm affection the lost sons, chief among whom was
Captain Amos Lincoln. As a boy, Amos had taken part in the Tea
Party with Revere. He had served under his future father-in-law
all through the Revolution. He was now to build the new State
House. Amos and Deborah had nine children, and when she died,
at thirty-nine, he married, three months later, her younger sister,
Betty, and had four more. His younger brother, Jedediah, also
married one of Revere's girls — Mary. A man could hardly have
better sons-in-law than these Lincolns. It was a good family, tough,
plain, and intelligent. At the same time Amos and Jedediah were
doing so very well in Boston as carpenters, and the oldest brother,
Levi, was making a name for himself as a lawyer in Worcester, their
fourth cousin, Thomas Lincoln, was not doing quite so well in
Virginia. Like his Boston cousins, he also was a carpenter, but was
living a shiftless, wandering life. He had not yet married Nancy
Hanks. Both of these Lincoln strains had a preference for the
names 'Abraham,' 'Enoch,' and 'Levi.'

Revere's oldest boy, Paul, had early married Sally Edwards and
before he could support a wife, for Revere paid the rent on his house.
He had seven children. In 1788, Sarah Revere had married John
Bradford and that same spring Frances (or Fanny as she was always called) married an apprentice of her father's, Thomas Stevens
Eayres. The young goldsmith, with his love of music, his personal
charm and instability, may have been more appealing than the
hardy, capable Lincolns. Paul Revere had great affection for this
boy. His father, Joseph Eayres, was an old crony of Revere's
(fellow Son of Liberty, member of the artillery train, and Tea
Party Indian).

When the young couple had been married for three years, they decided to try their fortunes in one of the inland towns which were growing more and more prosperous as the farmers turned towards industry.

Soon Thomas arrived in Worcester to consult with Isaiah Thomas, carrying a letter of introduction.

'The bearer,' his father-in-law had written, 'is a son of mine has a mind to carry on his business, which is a Goldsmith, in the Town of Worcester, provided there appears any tolerable encouragement. . . . I can recommend him as an Industrious and Ingenious Tradesman, and of good morals, and I dare say, he will be an acquisition to the artisans of any town he may settle in.' This was in May, 1791.

Eayres and Fanny came to Worcester. He made a good start. Levi Lincoln was Fanny's brother-in-law twice over. Isaiah Thomas immediately gave Eayres an order. In turn, he advertised in the *Spy* with the smug pride of the artisan of his day — nothing flamboyant, but surely no understatements. His silver work is large and fashionable. He can do anything from steel-topped thimbles to gold necklaces. He is there to serve the community.

Although his work and morals were both undoubtedly good, he did not prove, as his father-in-law had prophesied, an acquisition to Worcester. He had been there but two years when the town recorded they would abate his taxes, for he was 'A Madman gone to Boston.'

His contemporaries say he was always 'harmless and inoffensive.' His mania took the rather delicate form of flute-playing (sometimes without making any sound) and a passion for wiping off everything with his handkerchief before he could bear to use it. He was terrified of dirt and poor Fanny was terrified of him. She and her three small children went home to her father. The young wife had not long to live. A woman was engaged to nurse her. It took her towards a year to die. Eayres was boarded with various farmers outside Boston. He was still to his father-in-law 'a very promising young man,' but 'he is now so bad that we have sent him to the country. His wife is in a very bad state of health. He frequently gits home in the night, it being so near Boston, which disturbs her much & the people where he is, are only coman farmers.' Eayres was getting the same treatment as James Otis had

had — boarded in the country. The other alternative was the alms-
house. Here the insane were beaten if unreasonable and often died
of neglect. But humane people already were trying to work out
better methods. When Uncle Thomas Hancock died, he had not
left all his great fortune to his favorite nephew. One thousand
pounds had gone for the care of the lunatics of Boston. The treatment of the insane was rising from the superstition and horror with
which it had so long been regarded. Doctors rather than clergymen were being called in. There was not the same talk now about
people being 'possessed of devils' as when Apollos Rivoire had
landed in Boston.

In the morning of the ninth of June, 1799, Fanny Revere Eayres
died. Thus she 'ended a life of Trouble, anxiety & pain,' as her
father wrote to the Eayres brothers and sisters the same day. 'I
am told that your Brother not long since (when he was in his right
mind) wrote to you that she could not live a great while, but as no
answer was received I suppose you did not receive the letter.' In
one respect this letter which he wrote the day of his daughter's
death does not follow the customs of his day. There is no expression
of belief that his poor Fanny is now enjoying a better life without
trouble, anxiety, and pain. But the quick way he gets down to
business in the midst of personal sorrow is typical. He promises to
bring up the three Eayres children and he accepts the considerable
expense he has been to in boarding Eayres, but from now on he
thinks the crazy man's own brothers and sisters should support him.
At the moment Thomas, 'poor man,' is confused and at a house in
Dorchester, 'quite distracted.' One of Eayres' sisters had married
into the Livingston family of New York. All seem to have been well
off. He hopes they will set aside the rent of a house they all own
together in Boston for the support of their unfortunate brother. His
request does not seem unreasonable. If the Eayres family will not
pay for their brother, Revere threatens to let him 'come upon the
town.' The brothers and sisters seemed quite willing to let this
happen, but Revere himself was never able to carry out his threat.
A few years later he wrote: 'Had your brother received no more
Friendly action from me than he has from his Sisters & Brothers
he must have been confined in one of the cells of the Alms House
[philanthropy only professed is too much like our modern patriots]
where he now walks about at large, tho' seldom so much himself as

to be agreeable, yet so that he eats with the Doctors Family & visits the Neighbours.' For Revere did find a doctor for him.

Unlike so many people of his day, Revere always regarded his 'son's' peccadilloes as sickness — not malice. He scolds over the expense he is at to maintain him with little help from his relatives. He beats the doctor down on the amount charged, but he sends him clothing, the tools of his craft, pays his bills, and never blames him that he probably shortened Fanny's life.

All records of Paul Revere's human contacts show him a man of generosity, warmth, and imagination. There are many letters preserved thanking him for money, for favors. Paul Revere made a tidy fortune while many of his contemporaries, with seemingly less brains and industry, were making great ones. But he was very generous. If, during the siege of Boston, his sisters wished to join him in Watertown, 'I will do all in my power to provide for them.' If they stay in Boston, 'all cash & other things in my power.' If his cousin, John Rivoire, wishes to leave Guernsey for America, 'while I have a shilling you shall have part.' And his letters show that he believed it is better to pay workmen good wages — even if you can get them for less. His sons were given the best educations, European travel (for the younger ones, born into greater affluence). If they were hard up, he paid their house rent. If his daughter's husband went crazy, he did more than his share. People with such tendencies rarely accumulate great fortunes. There are too many holes in their pockets. He and his cousin, Robert Hitchbourn,[45] had an estrangement over a lawsuit involving a small sum. It is Paul who writes the letter wanting to make up. 'You left me in a *pet*,' he wrote Robert, sounding more like a modern schoolgirl than an eighteenth-century industrialist. 'An old saying is "There are no Friendships in Trade"' — but he hopes with them it may be different — and also hopes for the money due him.

He went to church 'as regular as comes Sabbath' and yet without any of the Sunday piety and weekday intolerance the stage, screen, and novels associate in our minds with such old-fashioned piety. About this time his letters show he took into his house the unfortunate Catherine Shreve. She had run away from her clergyman husband in Nova Scotia with another man. Where this other man went to or what his name was is lost, but she bore her illegitimate child while staying with the Reveres. Paul Revere could

hardly have approved of such goings-on, but Catherine was not
shot out into a snowstorm. Virtue or no virtue, she was treated as
a human being. So was Thomas Eayres. After Fanny's death,
Revere hoped to rid himself of the expense. He never did for long
—nor did his sons after him.

In the same year that the selectmen of Worcester were describing
Thomas Stevens Eayres as a 'Madman gone to Boston,' Esquirol
reported on the condition of the insane in Europe as 'treated worse
than criminals . . . naked, covered with rags . . . stones to lie on . . .
deprived of air, of water . . . filthy cells, fastened with chains.' All
over the civilized world compassion for the insane and scientific
interest in their care were rising. Luckily for Eayres, one of these
pioneers was a relative of his father-in-law (through the Town-
sends). He was Doctor Samuel Willard. In the pretty Blackstone
Valley village of Uxbridge he ran an establishment for the insane.
It could hardly be described as an asylum or hospital, boarding
house or medical school, but was something of all of them. Revere
wrote to him for help soon after Fanny's death.

Doctor Willard was a dozen years younger than Paul Revere, a
man of 'quaint thought' and rash action, outspoken and obstinate.
He had enough eccentricities of his own to have some understanding of those who had gone one jump beyond him. During the Revolution he had been a Tory. During Shays' uprising, a rebel. Sometimes he drank too much. He loved hospitality and his fellow-man,
among whom he included his lunatics. His approach to his chosen
field was typically modern, being based on experimentation. The
September after Fanny's death, Paul Revere drove Thomas
Stevens Eayres down to this extraordinary 'cousin.' Thomas was
never violent and often had, at first, long stretches of rationality.
One of these would have been chosen for the trip. Perhaps Thomas
did dust off his chairs before he sat in them, yet to the casual diner
there would be nothing extraordinary in the appearance of the
young and middle-aged goldsmiths sitting down at the inn somewhere between Boston and Uxbridge.

Here they were joined by a similar couple — a patient for Doctor
Willard and his attending relative. The patient was Thomas Hancock, who recently had also been a 'promising young man.' He
was the son of John Hancock's younger brother, Ebenezer, whom
Revere would know well from the days they had been Sons of

Liberty together, and while he was the Massachusetts paymaster.
So these four ate their dinner together and started a friendship between the two 'non compos mentis' which was to last for forty
years. Young Hancock had started out at Harvard with all the
flourish one would expect from a nephew of the Governor. He was
a good classical scholar and a poet. His form was 'fine.' His
manner 'dignified.' When his uncle found himself in difficulties
with the overseers (he was treasurer and his books did not balance),
Thomas had been withdrawn. This disappointment started him
off on his insanity.

Paul Revere left Eayres and it was probably Ebenezer Hancock
who left his son in the care of Doctor Willard. It was this pioneer's
theory to treat his amazing collection of 'n.c.'s' as the Boston
record calls them, as much like other people as possible. His wit
and magnetism made him a popular guest everywhere, but he
might arrive with a hair-raising assortment of patients, often on
horseback, for the doctor loved a good horse, and he and his patients
rode out in cavalcade. He was soon writing to Revere that Eayres
'has rode my horses hundreds of Miles, & been introduced to the
best Company.' But he finds him expensive to keep, at the prearranged price. 'Wou'd I have tho't that he would have eaten
more than two labourers?' There was an argument as to how
much the father-in-law was to pay for his keep. This ran from
two dollars and fifty cents to five dollars a week, but if Colonel
Revere does not like the charge the doctor tells him to make out
the bill himself. For Doctor Willard is in this work 'from a love to
my fellow man and with the hope that inspires every Artizan to
act. ... I hope to serve my fellow men in restoration of reason,
which I have tho't of more consequence than from death to life . . .
The means to obtain it has been sought by me with the zeal of
an alchemist.' Eayres' reason 'I twice supposed I had obtained,
the last time he appeared Genteel and inteligent far beyond the
coman citizens of your town . . . but unfortunate for him, the fibres
of the Brain, like a high toned instrument, the strings of which,
when in health are ever in unison & like them, they are the Sport
of every rude touch, the seasons & even of the air itself.'

Leaving out the seasons and the air, Doctor Willard was treating
his patients in a surprisingly modern manner. Eayres was given his
tools to work with and made spoons in Uxbridge for people who

were kind to him. This was an expensive form of occupational therapy. He rode horseback and visited the 'best society' of the region. Uxbridge was glad to have the doctor settled among them. Many of his patients were very rich and it brought money to the town. He also ran a medical school. Under his influence the towns-people had no fear of his poor lunatics.

Part of the doctor's once large house still stands close by the old church on the green. He had a large hall for social hours, but cells in the attic, with heavily barred doors. He also had perforated wooden boxes. Out of the largest hole stuck an unruly patient's head. The box was placed in near-by Shuttle Brook and left there. He found this treatment worked.

Sometimes his habit of going about with an escort of patients had startling results. There was the time when he decided he would like to join the church and was told to present himself for question-ing before the pastor, the standing committee, and the entire con-gregation. The doctor, who was at this time drinking too much, fortified himself for this ordeal and took his Comus crew with him. He quibbled over every point of doctrine, and 'to complete the farce Hancock was called in to speak pieces and Ayres and others to play tunes on the flute and violin.' The doctor was turned down for church membership.

Sometimes things went wrong. There was Cotton Tufts. He was also driven crazy by Harvard (class of '69). His relatives said he had worked too hard. One day he saw a girl riding slowly past Doctor Willard's. He jumped out of the window, grabbed the horse by the tail, pulled himself aboard, and began kissing the girl. After that Uxbridge ladies were wary of Cotton Tufts. And there was William Gray of the great New England family. He had been sent to France on business and his nature was 'proud and haughty.' Although clever enough at times, he had black fits. In one of them he bit off a piece of his kind doctor's thumb. In another he hanged himself in the barn.

But nothing seemed to have disturbed the doctor's aplomb, kindness, and scientific curiosity. Nor were he and his madmen quickly forgotten in Uxbridge. In 1869, an old judge read a paper telling of his boyhood in Uxbridge fifty years before, of the tiny mills that were becoming world-famous industries, the old academy, and those good old days 'when Eayres the lunatic used to dress in uniform, brandish his sword, or play the flute without making a noise; and when the portly Hancock used to indulge his voracious appetite at every house where people would give him anything to eat, and wrote acrostics upon the name of every man, woman and child who requested him to do so.'

Paul Revere had done as well for Thomas Stevens Eayres as was possible at that time.

# X

## 1792 – 1818

PAUL REVERE (no longer young) is involved in civic projects and the welfare of children, grandchildren, and friends. He discovers the secret of rolling copper and establishes a great industry. He sheathes the *Constitution*, the STATE HOUSE dome, and many ships. In CANTONDALE is his abode. He and RACHEL have their portraits painted, and live happily until the end, which comes for PAUL REVERE on the tenth day of MAY, 1818.

By Horace Doolittle, aged twelve. Sold wholesale by Amos Doolittle, New Haven. American Antiquarian Society.⁴⁶

I

LETTERS of condolence are always hard to write. Early in 1800 Paul Revere, as one of the Past Grand Masters of the Grand Lodge, was asked, with two other 'R. W. Brothers,' to write to Mrs. Washington. The General had died on December 14, 1799.

The letter follows the formalities of the day. It is hard to see, through such heavy foliage, the sorrow these men actually felt.

It was a melancholy occasion. They have wept. They presume not to offer consolation, only wish to mingle their Masonic tears with Madam's. And so on. At the end is a burst of originality. 'The Grand Lodge have subjoined an order that a *Golden Urn* be prepared as a deposit for a lock of hair, an *invaluable* relique of the Hero and Patriot,' to be preserved 'with the jewels and regalia of the Society. Should this favor be granted, Madam, it will be cherished as the most precious jewel in the cabinet of the Lodge.' And so it was — and is.

For it Paul Revere made an exquisite little urn, smaller than a pepper-shaker, about the same shape, and all of gold. The top unfastens and, under glass, is the lock of hair. He is thought to have made the wooden case it is kept in and which also serves as a pedestal.

The Masons held one of their most magnificent processions on the eleventh of January, in mourning for Washington's death. Funerals — even mock ones — had always been a popular entertainment from the founding of the Bay Colony. And so also were processions, whether composed of the local train-band or Gage's lobster-backs, and led to the dedication of a new church, the turning off of a pirate, or to the grave. The Masons, with their jewels, regalia, and mystery, always drew a crowd.

The procession was conceived of in black and white — white horses, black weeds. Masons from all parts of the state came to Boston to take part. Among them was Isaiah Thomas, of Worcester, who when he got home again wrote for his paper the best account. First came 'Two grand Pursevants, clad in sable robes and weeds, mounted on elegant white horses, properly caparisoned bearing an eliptical Arch' with a sacred text on it in silver. Beside them walked 'two continental veterans in uniform with their badges of merit.' Then followed on and on (starting from the old State House) a deputy marshal, nine stewards of the lodges, 'suitable shrouded' tylers, entered apprentices. Fellow crafts, master Masons. Another deputy marshal, more stewards — with mourning staves and deacons with 'mourning wands.' 'An elderly mason bearing an elegant figure of Minerva on a banner — she being an emblem of wisdom.' 'Three times three sons of masons about 11 years of age bearing Sprigs of Cassia,' and nine daughters of Masons with baskets of flowers. These children were also dressed in black. The 'reverent clergy of the Fraternity'; and so on until at last a large symbolic urn. This was three feet high, made of 'artificial white marble composition.' In it was a relic of the deceased (probably the lock of hair). Weeping over this urn was 'the genius of masonry.' The whole thing was shrouded with a pall and six pallbearers marched three on a side — one of whom was Paul Revere, who, like the rest, was 'drest in full mourning with white scarves.' A band played appropriate music. Everyone (except the small daughters of Masons) carried sprigs of what they called 'cassia.' As this magic herb does not grow wild in New England, they may have contented themselves with twigs of local hemlock. The procession left the old State House at ten, but it was not until five o'clock when at last 'The brethren returned to the old state house, unclothed and seperated.'

It was the Reverend William Bentley who had preached the funeral sermon. As he came from Salem, he could not get home that night. Seven hours of aprons, funeral music, jewels, regalia, banners, and mourning weeds would leave any man hungry. He accepted Paul Revere's invitation to supper and wrote down in his diary the pleasure he took in this impromptu party.

Born in Boston's North End, he would have known Paul Revere
for years and doubtless could remember very well that night (and
he a boy — twenty-five years ago) when his father, a boatman, had
rowed Paul Revere across the Charles, under the very shadow of
the *Somerset*. The bonds of Masonry had kept up the acquaintance.
Bentley had already noticed at another Masonic occasion how
'Col Revere enters into the Spirit of it and enjoys it.'

William Bentley was a broad-minded clergyman, caring little
for race, color, or creed. He was one of our first Unitarians and an
early defender of the rights of the Catholic Church in New England.
He had gone a long way from the tight, intolerant theocracy of the
early days of the Bay Colony. Thomas Jefferson was his friend —
but so also was John Adams. Every shipmaster who sailed from
Salem knew that wonders, curiosities, or manuscripts picked up on
his voyage should be given to Mr. Bentley. Although a good
clergyman, it was as a student of natural history and a linguist
that he excelled. During our troubles with the North African
pirates, it was only Bentley in America who could translate the state
papers written in Arabic, and they were always sent to him from
Washington. Arabic was but one of the twenty languages he could
read. His library was full of rare Chinese, Arabic, and Persian
manuscripts, and yet his diary shows he was exactly as interested
in ingenuity of all varieties, all arts (especially music), all trades,
and human nature.

Personally he was good-tempered, unmarried, fond of teaching
young lady parishioners how to sing, or taking them on nature
rambles along the beach to pick up seashells (giving rise to exactly
the gossip one would expect). He was physically active and men-
tally a dynamo. His round head soon became bald, but he did not
take to a wig. His long upper lip suggests a caricature of an Irishman. He was keenly intelligent, but (by the old standards) not very
religious. It was this agreeable companion Paul Revere selected for
a supper guest. Milling about the old State House — unclothing
and separating — were any number of men from whom he might
make his choice. He chose William Bentley, Jacob Perkins, Isaiah
Thomas, and a more mysterious Mr. Reynolds.[47]

It is not likely that he landed this party down on Rachel. Probably he took them to the upper chamber of one of the famous inns
close by in King Street, which now was called State. There would

be a blazing fire upon the hearth (for it was January), the flicker of candlelight, and the come-and-go of the smart inn servants with their mugs of hot flip, crackling roast geese, rosy hams, apples baked to bursting, quivering jellies, towering puddings with flags on top — or even a mourning ribbon. When the last cloth was drawn, a bowl of fragrant punch, smelling so sweetly of cinnamon and clove, rum, Madeira, lemons and oranges, would be set before them to help the gentlemen through the evening, and of course tobacco, either the slender white pipes or, by now, cigars.

William Bentley, a critical man, found this was a 'select company.' At the table, across the punchbowl, through the wreaths of tobacco smoke, he could see the ugly, clever, one-sided face of Isaiah Thomas, no longer the publishing prodigy who had startled Boston thirty years before, but, as Bentley wrote down, 'the father of the Press in New England ... who has aided its improvement & carried the Extent of the business beyond any man in America, who also is high in Masonic honours.'

By 1800, Isaiah Thomas was running a paper mill, a bookbindery, a chain of newspapers, presses, and bookstores. He was the largest book publisher in America. In all, towards a thousand books bear his imprint, with Benjamin Franklin's eight hundred odd volumes coming second, and Hugh Gaines a poor third with four hundred. Although a rival, Franklin generously referred to Thomas as 'the Baskerville of America.' Thomas' books range from folio Bibles to 'Goody Two Shoes.' From 'Fanny Hill' (printed secretly) to 'Sacred Dirges.' Lullabies of 'the Good Old Nurses, calculated to amuse children and excite them to sleep,' and his great two-volume 'History of Printing,' 'Robinson Crusoe,' and 'Tom Jones,' the 'Vicar of Wakefield,' Handel's 'Messiah,' books for 'improving the mind,' dictionaries, the best English poetry, textbooks, and of course endless almanacs. He was a beautiful printer, a collector of historical papers, founder of the American Antiquarian Society, and an amazing man.

'And also present,' wrote the approving clergyman, 'was Mr. Perkins of Newburyport — so eminent for his mechanic genius, & on this occasion so well known by his excellent medals ... of our General Washington.'

Like Isaiah Thomas, Jacob Perkins had shown his unusual gifts at twenty-one, for at this early age he had invented a machine which could cut and head nails 'instantly.' This revolutionized the industry. Like many of the ingenious men of his day, he had been trained as a silversmith. He had also invented a 'sterotype steel plate' first used for engraving paper money. It was said to be proof against counterfeiting and was the beginning of steel engraving. He was so celebrated in his own day that in England he was referred to as 'The American Inventor.' At this time he was thirty-four.

'In addition to our company, we had the ingenious Mr. Reynolds, who formed the admirable Urn & the weeping inocent which was displayed with so great success by the Brethern for the public admiration. He exhibited for our entertainment several busts in artificial stone which had great effect & were honourable to his talents.'

Of Mr. Reynolds and his success in artificial stone we now know nothing. Probably, unlike the work of Paul Revere, Jacob Perkins, and Isaiah Thomas, the materials in which he worked out his ingenuity were too frail to last long. He kept no diary as did William Bentley.

So Mr. Perkins showed his medals, Mr. Reynolds his heads. Surely Isaiah Thomas had some proof of his skill in his pocket — he loved books so much he could hardly have felt dressed without one — and Paul Revere a sample of his malleable copper. One thing is certain, the conversation was good, the mood merry, and Revere's supper-party a success. But it is noticeable that the clergyman is something of an observer. The four mechanics and their practical gifts are already outweighing the man of the soul and of the spirit. The time had passed when a minister was automatically the lion at any social occasion in New England. If he had been an old-fashioned divine, he would not have even been invited. He may have blessed the meat and returned thanks. If Thomas had a copy of his wretched 'Fanny Hill' in his pocket, he would not insult the gentleman's black cloth by producing it. Great respect would be shown to him, but ingenuity — rather than piety or even scholarship — was in demand.

Messrs. Revere, Thomas, Perkins, and Reynolds had the floor and the Reverend Mr. Bentley admired them. The new — the great industrial — nineteenth century had begun.

## II

IT IS unlikely that the Reveres lived in their famous, crabbed, crooked, crowded little North Square house very much after the Revolution, although it was not sold until 1800. It had been rented first to George De France and later, in 1784, to Joseph Dunkerly,[48] the miniaturist. In 1789, Boston published her first directory. In it one finds that John Revere, a nephew, is a tailor on Anne Street. Brother Thomas is a silversmith on Newbury (now part of Washington) Street. The year before, the selectmen of Boston had 'approved Mr. Thos Rivorie being liscenced to retail spirituous liquors at his shop on Holyoke St. and recommended him as a person of high life and conversation suitably qualified & provided for the exercise as being a firm friend to the Constitution & of such an employment & having a lame arm which unfits him for his trade & will be hereby greatly served.'

Paul Revere's papers show that he helped a number of young Reveres (as well as various Hitchbourns) whose names are not those of his own children, so must be sons of the dead John and the lame-armed Thomas. These two brothers, living their lost and unrecorded lives, represent the average artisan of the day, as Paul does the extraordinary one.

That same directory of 1789 puts Paul Revere down as having a goldsmith's shop at 50 Cornhill, a house at North Square, and a foundry on Lynn Street. It was in May of that year he advertises as leaving Cornhill for 8 Union Street, where 'Paul Revere & Son' will carry on the 'Gold and Silversmith's Business.' He seems to have completely dropped the hardware, except for what he sold at his foundry. By 1796 his goldsmith's shop is (according to the next directory) on Anne Street — where his father had first learned his trade of John Coney — and his house in North Square, but for several years before and after this time he was paying rent for various houses on Charter Street. He may have gone back to North Square now and then for a year.

After 1800 there is no difficulty in placing him. He sold the

North Square house to John Hunting and bought the Newman Greenough house on the corner of Charter and the present Hanover Street. This was the southwest corner. His frontage was sixty-four feet, but his land ran back for one hundred and forty. This was the very house which that unknown summer-up of leading Sons of Liberty had referred to as 'Newman Greenough, Sail maker, whose house was built by unrighteousness'; but it was a good house and much loved by its new owner. After his death it passed its last years as a refuge for 'Penitent Females' (which would have suited the man who took in Catherine Shreve well enough). So whatever unrighteousness may have gone into its building, it ended its days in a fair odor of sanctity, penitence, and illegitimate children, for in those simpler days females had but one thing to be penitent about. It was taken down in 1843.

It was a handsome house, three stories and of brick, not unlike the house the Hitchbourns had bought close to his North Square house. The narrow end was flush with the street, and one entered, through a fence of swinging iron chains, to the front door on the side. There were many houses of this general type in Boston at the time, and a few still stand. Elderly citizens of the last century who remembered it well say it was painted a pale yellow; always pleasant with green grass, blue sky, gardens and trees, of which the Reveres at last had plenty.

Rachel must have loved it: these broad halls, spacious square rooms, large windows, and three full stories, after all those years of living all on top of each other at North Square. And those years of renting — here one year and somewhere else the next; and everyone knows that three moves are as bad as a fire! It was hand-somely furnished: two 'lolling chairs' — one apiece — and 'Squabs' on the window-seats; the 'Washington Urn' to admire, for Paul Revere had taken home with him this particular expression of national sorrow and Mr. Reynolds' ingenuity. Surely this stately ornament, with its weeping innocent and black streamers, would be kept in the best parlor. Now and then through the years the Masons voted to visit the urn at Brother Revere's. They always reported they had 'found it had been given the most scrupulous care.' Rachel was not the sort of housewife that lets even three feet of artificial marble collect dust. Houses were decorated by mourn-ing pieces and hands by death rings. The Reveres doubtless thought nothing added greater tone to their parlor than the urn. From their 'lolling chairs' they could read the inscription — 'Sacred to the Memory of Brother GEORGE WASHINGTON, Raised to the ALL PERFECT LODGE Dec. 14, 5799 — Ripe in Years and Full of Glory.'

There was a backgammon board so the congenial elderly couple could play backgammon, card tables for whist. In the dining-room was a 'sett' of mahogany tables, the silver which Paul Revere made for his own use, and a great store of china. Some of the china and silver and beautiful furniture, as well as Rachel's embroidered fire-screen, still exist. But the seven feather beds, the hair mattresses and quilts, which added so much to their comfort, are but words in an inventory, as are the handsome 'suits of curtains' for the windows, the hearthrugs and carpets. They lived very well on Charter Street. In the stable was an expensive horse (at this moment a somewhat fractious beast, for he dislocated his owner's shoulder early in 1800), but undoubtedly handsome and fast. For winter-time was a 'booby hut.' No mention is made of any more unsocial sulkies. Plenty of books.

It often happens that when the head of the house is financially able to live on a larger scale, his children have moved on. This was not true of Paul Revere. Although all of his children by Sara had gone on either to houses of their own or to the grave, five by his second marriage lived with him on Charter Street. Joshua was the eldest. The father would not be apt to forget how he had left Rachel in bed with this boy as he started out to warn of Gage's intention to seize the gunpowder at Portsmouth, and how it had arrived at Bunker Hill; but not in time to save his friend, Joseph Warren's life. But Joshua had, by 1800, 'a pain in the chest.' So many people with pains in their chests did not outlive the twenties — nor did Joshua. He died within the year.

Joseph Warren Revere was three years younger. He was a tall, muscular young man; his face broad, handsome, short-nosed, with something of his father's bold turn to the mouth. And he inherited his father's ability and energy. Although trained as a silversmith, he preferred rolling mills, foundries, and furnaces. At twenty-three he was closely connected with his father in business and soon to become his partner. Much of the success of Revere copper was due to this son. As he lived to be over ninety, his actual personality is still remembered — an erect, powerful, handsome old man. But there is no one today who can remember the young man in his early twenties — happy, confident, full of new ideas, striding back and forth from the sunny house on Charter Street to the little foundry on Lynn, entering so enthusiastically into the industrial century in which he lived his mature years.

John, the other boy, was at this time thirteen. Physically he resembled his older brother. Both of them have the generous width between the eyes, short, strong nose; and the whole family seems to have been dark. He would have been working hard at the Latin School, for he was to go to Harvard and become a doctor, especially famous as a professor of medicine at New York University.

Harriet was seventeen and Maria fifteen. Painted in their young ladyhood, these two contrasted personalities still face each other the long length of the charming living-room of the grandchildren of Joseph Warren Revere. Both are dark and handsome girls, with heavy black hair. But Maria (as anyone who has read the family letters would guess) is the prettiest, probably the most courted. She has the furbelows and trinkets, the softer contours to the face. Harriet is unadorned. Structurally hers is a finer face than Maria's, but not so beguiling. Harriet has a look of idealism, old-fashioned New England integrity, and yet it is a generous face. Such girls often find no man to measure up to the high standards they set. Or their family needs them. It would be selfish to marry this year . . . perhaps the next. But the next, in turn, becomes the next, and they, like Harriet Revere, never marry. The Marias always do.

Then there were the three little Eayres. Their grandfather wrote hopefully of them. Sally is 'a fine little girl.' Thomas and Joseph are going to make 'fine' and capable men. But little Sally died of whooping cough. Thomas struggled manfully to take on some responsibility for supporting his crazy father, and died young. Joseph committed suicide in New Orleans. The well-balanced Reveres could not imagine why he did such a thing. His uncle, Joseph Warren, had given him money and letters of introduction. He had gone to New Orleans because he wished to get away from Boston, but (as is often the case) it was from himself he wished to escape — not merely Boston. Only Thomas Stevens Eayres lived on and on at Doctor Willard's, with the portly poet Hancock for a friend, playing his flute, dressing up in an old uniform, brandishing his sword, and making his now treasured silver spoons with their roses on the handle for people whom he especially liked. He was happy and quite unconscious of the tragedy which had come into the world with his birth.

So in all Paul and Rachel Revere had five children and three grandchildren to share the large house with them. And there was plenty of room for everyone. The ailing Joshua could sit in the sun of the large yard. The sea breezes would come to him from three sides, for Charter Street is still well out to sea. He could watch the gulls float above him — or the soot of his father's foundry. It may have been hard for him to see his father and younger brother starting off every morning before breakfast, so healthy and happy — excited even, as they planned soon to set up a rolling mill. What part could he have in such a world? But — 'the pain in the chest,' the coughing, weakness and despair, the irrational bursts of hope, the first time he spit blood; and the last. All we know of Joshua is that he was born, had a pain in his chest, and died 'suddenly' when he was twenty-seven. That is all that is known of many of his generation.

Harriet, like her mother, would spend considerable part of her time in household tasks — all the preserve-making and pickling, smoking of meat, drying of herbs, mince pies enough to last through winter; such things the ladies themselves did or closely superintended. By now there would certainly be a hired girl or two (probably a farmer's daughter who would be practically a member of the family). If you wanted a real 'servant,' you could not get it in Boston. Like Uncle Thomas Hancock, it was safer to send to England. If you wanted 'help,' it was easy. There was no opening for women in industry, and the servant problem did not exist except for the really fashionable. The Reveres' hired girl would eat with the family, go to church with them, and it was only luck if she did not marry one of the sons of the house. Paul Revere employed a good many apprentices and journeymen. His maid-servants probably contented themselves with such.

Harriet would have a leisure her mother had never known. She might practise the spinet — if that was where her talents lay — embroider fire-screens, make hair portraits — if she inherited her father's manual dexterity. She could read her Bible, keep one of those pathetic records of her 'sins' if she was pious, but Harriet could always be depended upon. She was that sort of girl. One cannot be so sure of Maria. She may have burned the preserves, had giggling fits in church, flirted with her father's young men, but she was kind, gentle, loving, and much loved.

There were the same problems in family life then as we should find today, only translated into different terms. Joseph Warren was just as fond of good horses as was his father. Transportation can always furnish family disputes — whether it consists of four wheels or four legs. Mrs. Revere would not worry that the miller had taken all the vitamins out of her flour, but she might often find, to her horror, that worms had been left in. There could be sand in the sugar in those days, dead mice in the cider barrel, sawdust in coffee. She would not be called to the phone in the midst of a hot bath, for she had neither commodity. Friends would not wire at the last moment they were not coming to dinner, but when they came they might stay all summer, like her Carlile relatives. The radio was no problem, but some people hated the continual street cries. Some were even getting bored with the long sermons. As a mother, she would have the unending problem of the younger generation.[49] The influence of the French Revolution was thought to be to blame. 'Chaos has come again.'

It was seven years before that Boston had celebrated the burgeoning of liberty across the seas with an enormous and rowdy banquet. Word had not yet come of the execution of the King and Queen, which soon sobered Boston's first enthusiasm. Later, enthusiasm turned to enmity. 'Citizen S. Adams' was one of those who led in the approval of the Frenchmen's bursts for freedom. Although it was January, the feast was held out-of-doors in front of the old State House. A thousand-pound ox, with gilded horns, was roasted whole. Two hogsheads of punch (each drawn by six horses) quenched the thirst, and bread was served by the cartload. While the multitudes feasted, according to the *Centinel*, 'the streets, houses, yea, even the chimney tops-were covered with male spectators, the balconies and middle stories exhibited bevies of our aminable and beautiful women, who by their smiles and approbation cast a pleasing lustre over the festive scene,' but so imbued were the *canaille* feasting in the street, with their new ideas of liberty, that they ended up by throwing pieces of the ox at the bevies of

smiling ladies. A balloon, inscribed 'Liberty and Equality,' refused
to sail, and the feast became what was called (euphemistically) an
uproar. It may have been Parisian in spirit, but not Bostonian.
It was not long before the United States was fighting its undeclared
war against these revolutionists. But in the early days of the
century, French fashion (even if not French revolutions) were
heartily approved. Joseph Warren could have had his hair cut
(if, as is not likely, he was a 'dapper beau') 'à la Brutus,' for
Alexandre Lavigne had just arrived from France. Harriet could
have gone to him to be dressed 'à la liberté' or 'in the manner of
the greek Flora or Virginia.' Pantaloons were in and small clothes
and long stockings were out. (But Paul Revere himself always
followed the fashion of his youth.) The ladies' stately hoops suddenly fell away to a few yards of muslin, and dancing became the
rage. 'The dancing disease having gradually ascended until it
reached middle-aged, now begins to descend on to the other side
of the hill and attacks the old.' There were even dancing schools
for the black folk. Everybody danced. Music was played by
'Turkish bands' in costume. Italian songs were sung. Life was
gay, carefree, disapproved of, and fashionable. But 'ladies were
some of them too much caricatured in their dress, and the beaux
were not so gallant as those of the old school.' Stage-acting and
card-playing were in high fashion. There had always been lot-
teries — even in the sternest colonial days.

If Paul Revere was one of the gentlemen who still clung to dancing, even when 'on the other side of the hill,' we have no record.
Young Joseph Warren was certainly invited to some elegant balls.
We do know what Paul Revere's attitude was towards the theatre.
Although there was never a law in Boston against dancing, there
always had been one against the professional stage. In 1750, a law
reads that plays 'not only occasion great and unnecessary expense,
and discourage industry and frugality, but likewise tend generally
to increase immorality, impiety and a contempt for religion.' If
the audience exceeded twenty people, actors and the owner of the
premises might be fined. This limitation of the size of the audience
made amateur dramatics possible, but not professional. In defiance
of this law, in 1792 a playhouse was set up in an old barn. The
sheriff arrived just as Richard III (played by Harper) was en-
countering the ghosts of Bosworth Field, and hunchback and all

were hustled to jail. The audience was furious. The time had certainly come when the old law must be repealed.

In a town meeting shortly afterwards a 'remonstrance' was drawn up demanding that the General Court change the laws as 'made antecedent to the establishment of our present free and happy form of government.' The old laws were 'unconstitutional, inexpedient and absurd.' A committee was appointed to go to the Governor and present the resolutions. Among these men were Joseph Russell, the town treasurer, John Adams' son — John Quincy Adams — Harrison Gray Otis, and Paul Revere. The laws were changed, and Bulfinch was engaged to build a proper playhouse. Within a year it was open to its admiring public.

As for card-playing, this, too, Paul Revere enjoyed, although brought up in a world which believed a playing-card a temptation from the Devil. (Could not Paul Revere remember the old pope's carriages with 'devils imps' fingering the cards on the table before the Pope?) But he had not only imported 'mogul playing cards,' but owned card-tables, and he seems to have taken his whist seriously. When one of his young Hitchbourn cousins married, Paul made for the bride a handsome silver tea-pot — and invited the young couple to his house for a game of cards. The bride, 'young and shy,' had the Colonel for her partner, which so rattled her 'she naturally made some mistakes, which irritated the old gentleman so that she never dared play with him again.' One's sympathies are about equally divided between nervous brides and old gentlemen who do not like to have their partners trump their aces.

Although Paul Revere clung to his breeches and cocked hat when others were taking to French pantaloons, 'hats about the size of Aunt Tabby's snuff-box,' he was flexible enough when it came to changes like play-acting and card-playing. He was not one of those men who set early in a mould and never get out of it. He could go along very comfortably with the nineteenth century — socially, politically, and especially industrially. He did not think the world about him necessarily worse than the world of his youth. A number of letters he wrote his children have been saved. In none of them does he preach to them — although that was a common form of amusement for parents of his day.

## III

COMFORTABLE as was the
Reveres' life on Charter Street, supported by the profitable little
foundry and the goldsmith's shop, Paul Revere, at sixty-five, was
as ready to risk a present good for a future better as he had been
in his youth. To set up a rolling mill for sheet copper [50] was an expensive gamble. He took it. Late in December, 1800, he was con-
tracting for the materials, and this was his situation:

> I have engaged to build me a Mill for Rolling Copper into sheets
> which for me is a great undertaking, and will require every farthing
> which I can rake or scrape.
> For the Houses which I must necessarily build, I shall want fifteen
> thousand of Boards & about 25 Casks of Lime. If you can supply me
> with those articles I shall be much obliged to you & wish you to be
> so kind as to inform me by Post.

The mill was to be set up on the east branch of the Neponset
River in Canton, for from now on he would need water-power.
He bought the old powder-mill property where Major Crane had
made gunpowder during the Revolution. The little powder mill
had blown up long ago, and by 1800 Leonard and Kinsley owned
the land. On it was a frame dwelling house, a triphammer shop
(or 'slitting mill'), and a 'cole' house. Paul Revere paid six thousand
for the property, which he immediately began to improve. Leonard
and Kinsley still had enough land and water-power for their own
ironworks. The usual lawsuits followed. Revere was fined sixty-
four dollars for a dam and he sued Leonard and Kinsley for 'with-
holding the water' from him. The same sort of lawsuit was going
on in every New England village at this time, for it was suddenly
realized what tremendous wealth water-power represented.

In the old days it had been used for little but grinding corn and
sawing wood, but now it was taking over more and more of the old
hand processes. It would work metal, spin thread, weave cloth,
make nails, paper, and even simple tools. Soon — very soon —
the farmers' daughters would not be working out as 'help' in such

kitchens as the Reveres', but minding spindles and bobbins, delight-
ing in their new freedom — never guessing how soon they would be
pitied as industrial white slaves. No wonder such an age — with
its ships leaving the coastal harbors, bound for unknown lands
and a mechanical genius rising on almost every New England
millstream — did not do much that Emerson could recognize as
'thinking.' Even as the merchants risked every cent they had on
their ships, ready to 'try all ports,' the manufacturers were ready to
take any chance and try any experiments in their own line.

Paul Revere had to send to Maidstone, England, for his rolls.
There were plenty of foundries in New England (including his own),
but he could not get over here rolls 'in such perfection as the English
ones.' He risked twenty-five thousand dollars of his own money,
the United States Government lent him ten thousand, and nineteen
thousand pounds of copper, and he started out. If he failed, he
would be completely ruined.

Less than a year after he had first engaged to build him a mill,
he could write to our Secretary of the Navy, Robert Smith, 'I have
erected my Works & have Rolled Sheet Copper which is approved
of by the best judges as being equal to the best Cold Rolled Copper.'
This was a thing no other man could do in America, and naturally
the navy was very anxious for his success. The French war was over,
but the North African pirates not only were injuring our shipping,
but our national pride. In 1800, when the *George Washington* (Captain Bainbridge) had arrived at Algiers with the annual tribute, he
and his ship had been commandeered to do errands for the Dey,
for, as he said, 'if you pay me tribute you are my slave.' Public feeling was ready to support a larger navy, and for this navy (as well as
for merchants' ships) Paul Revere would roll the copper. But his
first large order was six thousand feet of sheathing for the dome of
the now-completed State House. Not for sixty years was it gilded.
He also furnished the copper for the roof of the New York city hall,
and many other public buildings. The contract for our national
capitol's dome went to the Baltimore Copper Mill (set up several
years after his and now a part of Revere Copper), but his principal
customers were the shipbuilders, merchants such as Thomas
Handasyd Perkins, or naval contractors.

The *Constitution*, for which he had already made such a collection
of bolts, spikes, blocks, dove tails, etc., was drydocked at Boston,

overhauled and recoppered with Revere copper, preparing to start out after the Algerian pirates. On June 26, 1803, her log reads, 'The carpenters gave nine cheers, which was answered by the seamen and calkers, because they had in fourteen days completed coppering the ship with copper made in the United States.'

So the *Constitution* sailed away, flagship of the fleet which was to fight it out with the Algerians, and to earn for herself the proud name of 'Old Ironsides.'

As she left the shipyard in 1803, she was the very symbol of the young republic. First there had been such trouble in getting her launched, but now, with her great spread of sail — all woven in Boston — her decks of the best Carolina pitch pine, her live oak and red cedar from Savannah and Charleston, her Yankee crew, 'keen as mustard' (Captain Edward Preble, of Maine, to command her), from her flag of stripes and as yet only fifteen stars, to her home-manufactured copper bottom, she was typical — even to the fact the copper work was unpaid for and poor Revere & Son were 'now distressed for money; and if you will be so kind as to put the means ... to supply us you will lay us under very great obligation.' The Reveres were furnishing enough copper for several warships and the Government owed them twenty-five thousand dollars — which in time they got.

'Old Ironsides' herself was a wonderful ship. At first it was feared she might be unlucky — but she proved very lucky. In all, she successfully fought the French, the Algerians, and the English, and when she was old and doomed to be broken up, a twenty-one-year-old Harvard boy wrote a poem about her and saved her.

The Reveres always had considerable difficulty in getting the materials out of which to work. Paul Revere urges the Government to bring copper home from Smyrna on the warships, as ballast. There was no American mine that could supply them. From Sweden and Turkey they got their copper in plate; from South America in pigs; from Russia in bars. It was considered a big industry, and Isaiah Thomas refers to it in his *Spy* with great pride, but at the most Paul Revere probably never employed more than about fifty men. A good workman, 'a journeyman — not a master' — got two dollars a day. This pay Paul Revere admits in a letter is higher than it is necessary to pay. You could get men for less, but it is important that they should be contented. Both he and Joseph Warren worked with the men with their own hands, even as the master silversmith had always worked with his apprentices and journeymen. There were few, if any, white collars in our early industries.

There is a letter that Paul Revere wrote to his friend, Captain Thomas Ramsden, in London, in August, 1804.

> My good friend, I am yet among the living, thanks to the first Cause. I have enjoyed as much health since I last saw you as most people.; I have not lost 4 days at any time by sickness since. I have spent the last three years most of my time in the country, where I have Mills for Rolling sheets and bolts, making spikes & every kind of copper fastening for ships. It has got to be a tolerable advantageous business. I have my son in partnership with me. He takes care of the business in Boston. I take the care at Canton about 16 miles from Boston.

This suggests that Joseph Warren was running the bell foundry in town and his father the rolling mill in Canton. Although Revere has no complaints as to health and business, he has to the political situation and 'the present administration' (Jefferson's).

> My sentiments differ very widely from theirs in politics. My friend, you know I was always a warm *Republican* I always depreciated Democracy as much as I did *Aristocracy*. Our Government is now completely Democratic; they turn every person out of office, who is not or will not be in their way of thinking and acting. Col Hitchbourn was of their Party & it was said he had great influence, but that influence is now of little consequence, 18 months ago he had a paralytic stroke, when they found he could do but little for them they turned his nephew, Nath'l Fosdick out from being Collector for the Port of Portsmouth for no other reason but because he was not a democrat.

But still, through the Lincolns, he may have a little influence at Washington with 'the Atty General of the U.S. 2 of his brothers married my daughters.'

Soon after his letter was written, 'the great gale' of October 9, 1804, blew the roof off his Lynn Street foundry (as well as wrecking ships, smashing buildings, felling church steeples and trees the length of New England), and he moved the bell foundry out to Canton too. And in that year he sent Joseph Warren to Europe for the first time. He was to study bell-casting and copper work.

During this trip, and a later one, he went from England to France, Holland, Denmark, and Sweden, keeping a notebook and sketching machinery and methods. He also (like almost all travelling young men of his period) bought hats for his ladies — 'please inform my mother and the girls that Mrs. Miller has selected for me a Bonnet for each.' He has seen many of his father's old friends in London and feels at home in England. 'I cannot find a face but I know perfectly well and every person I see I think I have seen before.' He was evidently very fond of Harriet and Maria, not only sending them bonnets, but wishing he was home with them, 'if it was only for the pleasure of scolding them a little.' A few years later John went over with Joseph Warren. One studied medicine and the other industry, but the French captured the English ship they sailed on, and for a while no one knew where they were or how soon they would get out of France.

Before he was thirty, Joseph Warren, his natural aptitude reinforced by his European travels, was a large factor at the Revere bell foundry and copper mill. Paul Revere, with such a tower of strength beside him, need not worry much, but the work interested him immensely. There were those years of working closely with Robert Fulton, making the copper for the boilers of a curious contraption which might or might not work — a steamship. Much of its success would certainly depend upon its copper boilers.

## IV

THAT house which Paul Revere bought with his mill site was a plain, two-story frame house, differing little from the usual farmer's home. It was as good and unpretentious as country bread. There was now no business reason to keep the family in Boston. The work was all in Canton. In winter they went back to Charter Street, but they spent their summers at 'Canton Dale' as they called their property. On the large ell was a little bell tower (probably for summoning and dismissing the workmen). On the bell tower was a quaint wooden fish weathervane, studded with nails. This fish is said to be the work of Paul Revere, and for years there were a number of small objects about Canton Dale which he made with his own hands. Nor were his pleasant flower gardens soon forgotten.

From in front of his house started the slow, creaking wagons, carrying bells to churches and copper to shipyards. Once he sent a load all the way to Philadelphia by oxen. These new industrialists were in a hurry, compared to the old artisans, but measured their speed by ox cart and (in spite of Mr. Fulton's experiments) by wind. Sometimes his wagons only went the sixteen miles to Boston and his goods were then loaded upon sailing ships. Little could happen at the furnace and the mill that was not instantly known at the house. In those days the master of an enterprise usually lived in the middle of it — as the farmer still does today. A foundry, rolling mill, and a mill wheel were considered quite as pleasant neighbors as a barn full of cows. The 'cole' house Paul Revere bought with his property suggests, however, that mills would not for long be as clean and companionable as they had been formerly.

Canton had just been set off as a separate town. Its odd name was selected because a local geographer had decided it was 'exactly antipodal to Canton China' — not a very convincing reason, but an indication of the excitement felt even in an inland town over the China trade. Paul Revere was not the first man to use the Neponset's mild power for metalwork. Among his contemporary manufacturers in Canton was Jonathan or 'Quaker' Leonard. It was from him and Adam Kinsley he had bought his property. These two men rolled iron and made saws and scythes at a rate which amazed their contemporaries.

Over a hundred and fifty years before, when Paul Revere's ancestor, wild Tom Dexter, had been a proprietor of the Saugus Ironworks in Lynn, two young English workmen had been imported from Pontypool, England, to help with the forge. These were Henry and James Leonard. For generations before them Leonards had been ironworkers in Old England, and for generations their descendants, like 'Quaker' Leonard, were ironworkers in New England. It was a saying that 'where you find ironworks, there you find a Leonard.' Their name was bound up with the idea of iron as the name Revere is today with copper.

This particular Leonard finally ruined himself through his obsession that there was a rich lead mine in Easton, Massachusetts. All that he made on his saws and scythes he sank into this non-existent mine. At least he was a man of imagination. Adam Kinsley was more level-headed. Such men (in spite of an occasional law-suit) would doubtless be very congenial to Paul Revere in his last phase — an industrialist.

He himself speaks of the parson and the doctor as choice friends of his Canton years. Zachariah Howard was the parson at Canton up to 1806, and after him William Ritchie. Mr. Howard had served as a private during the Revolution, then had gone to Harvard. He 'was, in his way, a dry joker.' His religion was 'cheerful,' for it was not Mr. Bentley alone who was turning away from the gloomy hell-fire of Calvinism. Mrs. Howard was so fond of cats she had 'a small staircase made in order that her favorite cats might have access at all times to the upper story of her house.' If she had any method by which she kept the less favored from coming along with the pets, it is not recorded. Mr. Howard, however, fined his parishioners fifty cents apiece for the dogs they brought to meeting with them. The doctor was Moses Baker, who also taught school. He was a Federalist.

Major Crane, who had been powder-master during the Revolution (Paul Revere had bought powder from him while he was in command of Castle Island), was an old acquaintance. Revere's books show that the Major (one of Canton's most distinguished citizens) was sometimes engaged as a superintendent of Revere's copperworks. Peter Crane (grandfather of Margaret Fuller) also seems to have worked for Revere, but the money put down as paid to him may represent the rent of a house. Paul Revere does not always write down why he is paying out money.

The town of Canton had plenty of congenial neighbors, as the Reveres soon found out. And there was a vast amount of wild land over which a man might shoot. 'Fowl Meadow' was good for ducks. Deer were not uncommon. The hunting and fishing attracted many sportsmen out from Boston. Part of the Blue Hills are in Canton. In those days they were still infested with rattlesnakes.

Ezekiel Price took two young ladies walking in the Blue Hills and casually notes that 'Miss Betsey killed two snakes.' If Miss Betsey killed the right sort of snakes and carried their rattles to the selectmen of Canton, she would have earned two dollars by her afternoon ramble with the notary.

Paul Revere was now living fairly close to Unkity Hill. He had started his life under the shadow of Thomas Hutchinson's great house and was ending it close to the country seat Hutchinson had loved so much. Already the feeling against Hutchinson was dying down. Perhaps even now Joseph Warren Revere was courting the girl he later married — Mary Robbins (the old governor's grandniece), for soon the Hutchinson and Revere blood came together. In the houses of descendants of Joseph Warren equal care is given to magnificent Hutchinson furniture and brocades and to Paul Revere's silver and engravings. A great deal of water had already run down the Neponset's channel since the days of Paul Revere's youth. In the letter already quoted he says once he fought the aristocracy and is now ready to fight democracy. One did not look much worse to him than the other by the time he was passing on into the seventies.

If Paul Revere chose to ride into Boston by way of Quincy, he might stop for a glass of wine and a little chat with his old companion of the Long Room Club and the North Caucus, ex-President John Adams. He would find a healthy, peppery little round man of exactly his own age, able for many more years to rise at four or five, make his own fire, and start out on those long, thoughtful walks which were becoming famous. He was enjoying his retired life as a country gentleman as he surely could not have enjoyed the party battles that had marked his years as President. These two men would agree on the wicked 'democrats' who were now in power. They might well agree in their estimate of Thomas Hutchinson. It was about this time John Adams wrote of him, 'If I were the witch of Endor I would wake the ghost of Hutchinson, and give him absolute power over the currency of the U.S. . . . I will acknowledge that he understood the subject of coin and commerce better than any man I ever knew in this country.' This is choice praise from an old enemy.

Or, on his way to Boston, he could stop at Dorchester to see poor Ben Hitchbourn. He had had such a successful and (compared to his cousin or brothers) such a fashionable life. Now he was paralyzed and dying. So this was Andrew Oliver's old house, and Paul Revere could well remember the cartoon he made of Oliver hanging by his neck from Boston's Liberty Tree. Surely times and passions change. Thomas Jefferson, in his rundown slippers, was as much a danger to the country (so Revere would think) as ever had been the Olivers and Hutchinsons, in their gold lace and great wigs. But Ben Hitchbourn (if he still could think) would not have agreed.

In the other direction from Canton, Paul Revere did make a curious and picturesque friend. This was Deborah Gannett, née Sampson, the one woman to fight in the ranks during the American Revolution — the 'famous female soldier.' At twenty she had run away from home, disguised as a boy, and enlisted in the Continental Army. She was quick and courageous, 'fleet as a gazell, bounding through swamps many rods ahead of her companions.' She was a tall girl for her period, being five feet and seven and a half inches. Although it was noticed that she had a 'smock face,' many of the other Revolutionary soldiers were too young to shave much. For over a year and a half, as Robert Shurtleff, she made a good record as a 'faithful and gallant soldier and at the same time preserved the virtue and chastity of her sex unsuspected and unblemished.' When she was wounded, she pried the bullet out herself rather than fall into a doctor's hands, but malignant fever was too much for her, and her sex was discovered. Nevertheless, she was given an honorable discharge by General Knox himself, who, being an unconventional soldier, was not too affronted to find that one of the gunners who had fought at White Plains and Yorktown was indeed a girl.

After the war, Deborah married a Sharon man and was always hard up. In 1797, she attempted to make a little money by writing a story of her escapades (for she is thought to be the author of 'Female Review'), throwing in considerably more love-interest than there probably was. She had a suitor (in the narrative) whom she wished to escape, as well as a rather Freudian dream about snakes. A beautiful girl in Baltimore had fallen in love with her, etc. By the time Paul Revere became interested in her, she was a woman of forty-four and the mother of three children. He hoped to persuade Congress to give her a pension. So he wrote to —

Wm. Eustis, Esq.                              Canton
Member of Congress                         Feb'y 20, 1804
Washington
Sir —

   Mrs. Deborah Gannet of Sharon informs me, that she has endorsed
to your care application To Congress in favor of Her.  My works for
manufacturing copper, being at Canton, but a short distance from
the neighborhood where she lives, I have been induced to inquire
her situation & character, since she quitted the Male habit & soldier's
uniform: for the more decent apparel of her own sex, & since she
has been married and become a mother.  Humanity and Justice
obliges me to say, that every person with whom I have conversed
about Her, & it is not a few, speak of her as a woman of handsome
talents, good morals, a dutiful wife, and an affectionate parent.  She
is now much out of health.  She has several children, her husband
is a good sort of man, though of small force in business, They have
a few acres of poor land, which they cultivate, but they are really
poor.
   She has told me that she has no doubt that her ill health is in
consequence of her being exposed when she did a soldier's duty &
that while in the army she was wounded.
   We commonly form our ideas of a person whom we hear spoken of.
whom we have never seen, according as their actions are discribed.
When I heard her spoken of as a Soldier, I formed the idea of a tall,
masculine female, who had a small share of understanding, without
education & one of the meanest of her sex — When I saw her & dis-
coursed with her I was agreeably surprised to find a small affeminate
conversable Woman, whose education entitled her to a better situation in life.
   I have no doubt your humanity will prompt you to do all in your
power to git her some relief.  I think her case much more deserving
than hundreds to whom Congress has been generous.

She did receive her pension and went on a lecture tour, but her
financial difficulties did not end.  In 1806 she wrote to Paul Revere.
'Honored Sir:' then goes on to tell him that she and her son
were ill and solicits 'your Goodness in our favor, though I with
Gratitude Confess it rouses every tender feeling & I blush at the
thought that after receiving ninety & nine good turns as it were —
my circumstances require that I should ask the Hundreth — the
favour that I aske is the loan of 10 dollars for a short time.'
So once again the good old colonel would have to saddle his

horse (or send the colored servant, Henry, who his papers show
was by this time part of his family, to fetch the animal for him) and
jog down country lanes to Sharon. The house still stands where he
stopped his horse to chat with this 'conversable' woman whose
gumption and 'handsome talents' would certainly appeal to him
much more than Benjamin Gannett's 'small force in business,' and
slip her yet one more (and the 'hundreth') favor. Then back again
to Canton Dale — his good deed done; yet one gathers that he will
probably have another and another call upon his generosity.
Deborah seems to have been firmly fastened upon his pocketbook,
but her pension was small, her husband shiftless, her health bad.
She was lucky to have so kind a neighbor as the colonel, who could
forgive her (as some of her contemporaries could not) the months
she passed fighting in our army.

In appreciation of the simple pleasures of Canton Dale, Paul
Revere was moved to write a poem. It is not a great poem, but it
praises great and good things. First, the pleasant house, kind wife
(who one is glad to note has time to sit 'lolling' in her chair):

> Not distant far from *Taunton road*
> In *Canton Dale* is my abode.
> My Cot 'tho small, my mind's at ease,
> My Better Half, takes pains to please,
> Content sitts lolling in her chair,
> And all my friends find welcome there
> When they git home they never fail,
> To praise the charms of *Canton Dale*.

But there is more than lolling chairs in the old gentleman's life:

> There's *Business* with his chearing face,
> And Labours-Arm, by nerves well brac'd,
> The Interest seek, of all concern'd;
> They strive to have their wages earn'd.
> *Labour*, and *Health* go hand in hand;
> *Industry*, claims the cheif comand;
> *Prudence*, attends with early care;
> And *Discontent's* but seldom there.

> In my last *Stage*, how blest am I,
> To find *Content*, and *Plenty* by?
> Just *work* enough to keep in *health*
> I *exercise* prefer to *wealth*

Within my *Cot*, I sit reclin'd;
I sooth to Peace my thoughtfull mind,
Receive my Friends with kind embrace
Give them the best with Chearfull face.

Next he sings his honorable hymn of hate and praises the generous men whom only he wished for his friends (a generosity which had marked his own life from that day in '65 when he was lending money 'in the street' to Josiah Flagg, down to his last visit to Deborah Gannett).

The double dealing *Hyprocite*,
I try to shun, with all my might,
The *Knave*, I hate; the *Cheat* dispise;
The *Flatterer* fly; but court the *Wise*.
The poor *Man's* hope, the *Widow's* friend;
The Orphan's guide; who often lend,
Within my Cot, I'm pleas'd to find;
Such *men* congenial to my mind.

Having stated in four stanzas what might be called his philosophy of life, he goes on to describe a typical day at Canton Dale:

Around my *Cot*, at break of day,
The *robin* pipe's his artless lay;
The *yellow-Bird*, with pleasing note,
Sings sweet, and trills his little throat.
Near to my Couch, congenial guest,
The *Wren* has wove Her mosey Nest,
Her hopes in safe repose to dwell,
Nor ought suspects the silvian dell.

At early morn I take my round,
Invited first by *hammer's* sound;
The *Furnace* next; then *Roleing-Mill;*
'Till Breakfast's call'd, my time doth fill;
Then round my Acres (few) I trot,
To see what's done and what is not.
Give orders what ought to be done.
Then sometimes take my *Dog* and *Gun.*

Under an aged spreading *Oak.*
At noon I take a favorite *Book*
To shun the heat and feed the Mind,
In elbow chair I sit reclined.
[This seems to be the third reference to his 'lolling chairs']

When dinner's call'd, I feel prepar'd
For to refresh from fruagal board;
When Table's cleared, and dinner ends
With Chearfull *Glass drink absent* Friends.

In afternoon, when weather's fair;
And business *suits*, on *Horse* or *Chair;*
For *exercise*, or see a *Friend*,
My *Better Half*, and I attend,
Or ere the Sun sinks in the West
Or tunefull birds skim to their Nests
To walk thro *Groves*, and *grass'y Fields*
Contemplating what *Nature yealds*.

At eve' within my peacefull *Cot*,
Sometimes I meet, and sometimes not,
The *Parson*, Docter; or some Friend,
Or neighbour kind, one hour to spend;
In social chat, our time we pass;
Drink all our Friends, in parting Glass
The Parson, Docter; neighbour gone,
We prepare for Bed, and so trudge on.

These were the things he loved — house, wife, friends. The birds who wake him, the beat of hammer at the forge, the turgid roll of the mill. The book read under a tree, horse, dog, and gun. A frugal meal, a 'Chearing glass,' the absent friends (many of whom for him were dead) — contentment above all things — and so to bed.

As he writes his poem (if it can be called a poem), he joins great company, for such simple things have always been loved long before and long after him. A man might make a spurt now and then (like that ride to Lexington), and that would be remembered, but most of life (and he knew it) is the unromantic courage and quiet heart that can still 'trudge on.'

But even here at Canton Dale the peaceful music of hammer and bird and the voices of friends were interrupted. On the eighteenth of June, 1812, war was declared between the United States and Great Britain. Once more Massachusetts was assigned her quota, ten thousand men. And so during the lovely June weather every day Lieutenant Wellington put on 'full uniform' and, attended by his drummer, marched through the streets of Canton. First he went to the western limits of the village, as far as Sharon, and

Deborah Gannett might pause to listen and to think, and then back again, and the rattle of his drum came closer and closer to the peace of Canton Dale as the recruiting officer strutted up Taunton Road, past the Reveres' house and works. There came the rub-a-dub, rub-a-dub, of his drum, calling, as it had always called, to the young men to follow. Lieutenant Wellington would stop now and then, 'urging all suitable mercenary, or patriotic persons to enlist.' Then the two-man parade, followed by its usual throng of curious men and boys, turned back to end its tour at 'The Corner.'

Paul Revere was seventy-seven. He had known almost as many years of fighting as of peace and the beat of the muster drum had always been louder than even church bells, triphammer, or birds. It was with a heavy heart such men as Paul Revere heard this latest call to arms. The war against England, as senseless a war as America ever fought, was bitterly unpopular among New England Federalists.

# V

NAPOLEON was probably more hated in Boston than anywhere else except London. The War of 1812 was thought by the Federalists of New England (who seem to have represented a majority opinion) to have been brought on by French contrivance, hatred of Old and New England and Western land-hunger. Although it was their ships which had been seized and searched by England in her blockade of Napoleon, and largely Yankee seamen who had been impressed, they did not think the war was fought to protect free trade and the rights of American seamen. The Boston Federal press joyfully announced every defeat of Napoleon and sympathized with the acts of England. England, to them, was the one bulwark, the last obstacle, the Corsican must overcome in his ambition to dominate the world. It was only that

little island which he dared not invade (although he had sworn
he would) and England's supremacy at sea that was holding him
back. Today it would seem that stopping Napoleon was more important than the battle of New Orleans, but in words, at least, the
New England Federalists were very close to treason — and even
talked of seceding entirely from the other so-called United States.
Yet Massachusetts sent more men into this war than any other
state except New York, and she took great pride in the brilliant
daring of the American navy — so largely manned and officered
by New England men.

Napoleon, having conquered most of Europe (forming out of the
captive governments a new order — called 'the Continental System'), had been unable to invade England and finish off her sea
power. So he turned east and attacked his erstwhile confederate,
Russia, although it had not been long before that he had been
promising Alexander his share in the new order. As we were in
this war against England, the news of Napoleon's disasters in
Russia should have been heavy news in Boston. It was not. The
*Columbian Centinel* for March 27, 1813, gives a glowing account of the
thanksgiving service held in King's Chapel and the great banquet
which followed it at the Exchange Coffee House. Paul Revere
may well have taken his seat among these leading citizens and
drunk his share of the toasts.

As each toast was drunk, appropriate music was played and often
illuminations or transparencies were unveiled for the gentlemen to
applaud. The first toast was to 'Alexandre the Great, Emperor of
all the Russias. He weeps not for the conquest of a new world, but
rejoyces in the Salvation of the old.' A Russian march was played.
'Alexandre' himself appeared, 'a transparent likeness' in full uniform with this motto — 'Alexandre — the Deliverer of Europe.'

The second toast was 'Our National Rulers: May the people see
in them now what history must say of them hereafter.'

Washington himself was remembered: he was 'rendered more
precious by the errors and follies of the present times.' (A dirge
was played while the people thought that over.)

Even the French people were toasted — for as usual an attempt
was made to differentiate between the people and the wickedness
of an ambitious leader. 'May they be delivered from oppression,
and be too happy in their own to visit other countries.' Moscow

was the tenth toast: 'Its flames illuminated the path of oppressed nations to freedom and that of their oppressors to destruction.' Moscow in flames appeared in a transparency. Rising above the fire and smoke was the Russian eagle 'bearing in his beak a scroll "Moscow is not Russia."'

Only one toast had a strongly patriotic note (as one must admit with a certain amount of embarrassment) and that was to 'Our Navy: The brilliant star of glory, shedding its beams on the disastrous night of this once favored land.'

Likely as it was that Paul Revere attended this wholehearted demonstration of hatred of France and devotion to Great Britain, it is even more likely that he was among the Cantonese in the following June who went to the top of the Blue Hills to watch the battle fought in Boston waters between the *Chesapeake* and the *Shannon*. The American ship was defeated, and 'Don't give up the ship,' said Captain Lawrence, dying on his bloody deck.

Paul Revere was certainly among the men and boys who volunteered to build more forts in Boston Harbor in September, 1814. The Federal Government had been so piqued (and certainly not without reason) at Boston, they had taken all the soldiers from these fortifications and left the town to defend herself as best she was able. No matter how strong the feeling might be against 'Boney,' Boston must defend herself. The British were so completely masters of the sea they were not only able to blockade the continent of Europe, but send ships over here and invade us almost at will. That summer of 1814, Washington was burned. Nearer at home, the Massachusetts shore was ravaged at Falmouth, Wareham, Scituate, Orleans.

There was that Sunday at Salem. The Reverend Doctor Bentley was in the middle of his sermon when someone stuck his head in the window, yelling, 'The British fleet is chasing the Constitution into Marblehead.' He seized his hat and ran out of church to join the men struggling to get cannon pulled into position. But 'being a short, thick-set man, and the mercury at eighty-five, the good doctor soon gave out, when he was lifted astride one of the cannon, and in this way proceeded to the beach.'

In September, the British landed on Cape Ann. But the coast of Maine was the most heavily attacked and invaded. In some towns the people were rounded up and forced to swear allegiance to the

British King. The small American navy fought with a valor and
skill which is still a great legend. Seemingly never had there been
such a combination of great captains, great crewmen, and great
ships. But they could not prevent landing parties.

Stephen Longfellow, the Portland, Maine, lawyer, had a very
beautiful and dreamy son. Henry was seven or eight at this time
when he heard, and later remembered and put into words —

> the sea fight far away
> How it thundered o'er the tide.
> And the dead captains as they lay
> In their graves o'erlooking the tranquil bay
> Where they in battle died.

Sure that Boston would be attacked any moment, volunteers
were called for to work upon the forts.

There still exists the small notebook, resembling a safe-deposit
book, with the names of one hundred and fifty-odd 'Mechanics of
the Town of Boston' who formally tendered their services to help
'by manual labor in measures for the Defence of the Town and
Naval Arsenal.' Paul Revere, already in his eightieth year, was the
first to sign and is thought to have started the whole thing.

These men were put to work building Fort Strong on Noddle's
Island (East Boston). Each man was asked to bring his own shovel
or wheelbarrow. Schools were dismissed and all boys large enough
to be useful were rowed over to help with the digging. For a
moment there were no political parties. Paul Revere, thanks to the
'exercise' which he praised twice over in his poem, and his naturally
robust constitution, would still be able to handle a shovel. Surely
he would have recalled that other hurried, desperate, amateur
fortifying of Boston: the spring of 1776. General Washington had
taken the Boston troops with him to New York and left the town to
do as good a makeshift job as she was able. Forty years would not
seem as far away to him as it would to the schoolboys digging beside him. In those earlier days three Protestant clergymen had led
the workmen to their labors. Today it was the first Catholic bishop
of Boston, John Cheverus, a refugee from the French Revolution,
a man as beloved by Protestants as Catholics, who wrote thanking for the services. Boston had gone a long way in religious tolerance since Revere's youth.

Bishop Cheverus presents his compliments to Mess P. Revere & Son & thanks them for having permitted the men in their employ to work yesterday with him at the fortifications & for generously allowing them their usuall wages as if they had been working for him.

But the end of this most short-sighted war ('Mr. Madison's War') was in sight. By February a Boston miss wrote in her diary:

Monday Feb. 13, 1815 — After breakfast all the bells began to ring. I asked Mamma what it meant and she said she supposed it must be a town meeting. A friend burst into the room exclaiming, 'Do you know what the bells are ringing for? Peace Peace Peace!' We thought her out of her senses, and papa went out to learn the truth. He soon returned and told us that it was indeed true, and that the whole town was in an uproar about it. We felt that we could not stay at home; so we ordered the sleigh and set forth. First we went through Cornhill, then past the Common, and through the main street down to the North End. The streets were crowded: In State Street you might have walked upon the peoples heads. Almost every house had a flag on it, and in some places they were strung across the streets. We rode again all over town, and met several companies of soldiers. In the main street we met a company followed by three sleds, each drawn by fifteen horses. A man was in the front of each, with the word *peace* printed in large capitols on his hat. These sleds were full of sailors who, just as they came up gave a most tremendous huzza, which was echoed by the immense crowd about us. The ladies were running about the streets as if they did not know what they were doing; the gentlemen were shaking hands and wishing each other joy. All this time bells were ringing, cannon firing, and drums beating.

Ten days later, this young lady (dressed in 'sheer dotted muslin, trimmed with three rows of plaited white satin ribbon,' her hair 'arranged in braids, bandeau and curls,' attended the Peace Ball at the Concert Hall. Her comments on all the guests are amusing, but the oddest among them seems to have been 'several British officers in full uniform were actively employed in flirting and dancing . . . they seemed favorite partners among the young ladies.'

It could not be called a 'victory ball,' for the young republic had been trounced by her erstwhile mamma. But no one seemed to care. 'Peace' was good enough. To many thoughtful people the most important thing for the world and for the United States was the defeat of Napoleon.

## VI

THE manner of man Paul Revere was in his later years, his letters, actions, and even his poem record. What he and Rachel looked like as they received their guests at Canton Dale with 'kind embrace, give them the best with chearfull face,' has been preserved by Gilbert Stuart.[51] It was the devoted son, Joseph Warren, who ordered these portraits painted. The acknowledgment of payment reads:

> Rec'd of J. W. Revere two hundred dollars in full for painting two portraits.
> Boston 3 June 1813.

Here is Paul Revere's familiar face, as known to every reader of America's history. A dark and still ruddy face, framed by thick white hair. It is not only some forty years older than the one Copley painted, but gentler. There is still the bold, quick turn to the dark eye and lower lip, the quizzical lift to the eyebrow. But the kindness which he had shown the world (and got much back in return) has given a new quality. 'The hundreth' favor to Deborah Gannett, those workmen paid a little more than the going price, a shelter for Catherine Shreve, and the comfortable life he was able to give Thomas Stevens Eayres, the many charitable organizations in which he interested himself, have left their mark.[52] It had been a gay, clever, bold face in his youth when Copley painted it. Now it was taking on lines of compassion and human dignity. He had (probably many years before) added a double chin — a double chin which suggests that lower down he had also added a substantial paunch. A paunch, to our ancestors, suggested wealth, dignity, importance in the community. It set off in Revere's case a gold watch chain and a fine topaz watch pendant. It upheld one's snowy ruffles, displayed a fine waistcoat to advantage. It was not a handicap against which a man must fight with golf, bending exercises, diet, and wifely sarcasm. It was very dignified.

Rachel is also a freshly colored old person. She faced Gilbert

Stuart and the world brightly, confidently, surely never guessing as she sat for that portrait she had only months, perhaps but weeks, more to live. She has on a short-waisted, ruffled-neck, grey Empire dress. If her husband wished to go about in three-cornered hats, breeches, and 'all that,' he might, but she herself is dressed in the very latest Parisian fashion. Her little frilled cap sits modishly on her chestnut-colored hair. She has a sprightly eye that looks as if she could still decipher a love-riddle, if such was sent her. And the expression — a mixture of the benign and the humorous — promises she was as good a 'better half' to Paul Revere as he himself believed. Also one can guess why it was that even her step-children delighted to name their children after her. The nose, surely long enough in her young womanhood, has lengthened, as noses will. Under it is tucked one of those sweet, toothless little mouths of the period, which still proclaims to our generation, as it certainly did to her own, that she took no stock in anybody's skill in setting false teeth.

They look a comfortable and well-wedded old couple.

As the new century advances, small boys begin to appear — all eyes, all ears, they watch 'old Mr. Revere' in church, on the street, at his foundry. Some sixty or seventy years later, when asked, they remember him well. There was Rowland Ellis, born in 1807; he did not die until 1893. He knew every house and street in the old North End, and 'the history of every family that had made its permanent home there during the century' (his family had bought the Clark-Frankland House). 'When a boy he attended the same church as Paul Revere' and could accurately describe him 'as he used to stride up the Church aisle.' When Elbridge H. Goss wrote his Life of Paul Revere (published in 1891), he reported that Mr. Ellis, 'now living in Newton Center,' was formerly a North-Ender, residing in Garden Court Street but a short distance from Revere. He distinctly remembers him as 'a thick-set round faced not very tall person who always wore small clothes.' The Ellis family pew in the 'New Brick Church' was directly behind that of Revere, and there Mr. Ellis says, 'I used to see him as regularly as the Sabbath came.'

That oddity of small clothes alone would be remembered by a small boy. The old elegance of knee-breeches, ruffled shirts, long stockings, and cocked hats had passed out of fashion years before.

Others besides Paul Revere clung to the picturesque costume of their youth. There were a number of these 'last leaves' about Boston besides Paul Revere's old companion of the Long Room Club, the Tea Party, and the Artillery Regiment, Major Thomas Melville, who aroused Oliver Wendell Holmes' compassionate amusement. It may have been a sin for small boys 'to sit and grin . . . but the old three-cornered hat, And the breeches and all that, Are so queer. . . .' [53]

Of Paul Revere we only know that he 'always wore small clothes.' Seemingly (and judging by the Stuart portrait), from the waist up there was nothing very quaint about his appearance to tickle the small fry of the Boston streets — not like Major Melville nor the old schoolmaster Tileston nor the Byles girls. Often on leaving his Charter Street house, Paul Revere must have encountered 'Master Johnny' Tileston, who attended (probably with Revere) or taught old North Writing for eighty years. His odd little round figure was embellished with a great powdered wig and a cocked hat. His coat was broad-skirted, his vest very long and 'cut away at the bottom.' He clung to knee-breeches and large shoe buckles to the very end. Although Tileston lived longer than Revere, his health does not seem to have been so good. The small boys, watching him behind his teacher's desk or on the street, remembered how loudly he puffed. And once a day (puffing as he went), he would walk over to Old South Church to check his watch by the clock in the steeple. Several generations of Boston merchants, bankers, registers, wrote the beautiful, unadorned, legible hand that 'Master Johnny' had taught them — with the aid of a ferule and that deformed hand which could strike blows (as Edward Everett remembered) that 'would have done credit to the bill of an albatross.'

But the very last of the last leaves to hang upon the tree 'in the spring' were 'The Byles Girls.' Their father had died years before (with a pun upon his lips — he could not get to his feet to greet guests. They must excuse him, but 'he did not belong to the rising generation'). His spinster daughters, one broad and smiling, one sharp both as to face and figure, lived on and on, lonely relics of the past. They had had their great day when, during the siege of Boston, they had walked out, the one on Earl Percy's arm, the other on General Gage's. 'They gloried, they triumphed, in the firm adherence of their father and his family to the royalty of England,

and scorned the idea of even now being classed among the *citoyennes* of a republic, a republic, which, they said, they had never acknowledged and never would; regarding themselves still as faithful subjects to His Majesty of Britain, who ever that majesty might be,' as they told a young visitor of the period. But it must have puzzled King William the Fourth, when he ascended his throne, to have a letter from a Boston Byles girl assuring him that the family of Doctor Byles had never renounced their loyalty to the British Crown. This was well over fifty years after the guns of Lexington. More ferocious revolutionists than the Americans had sent cartloads of thus-minded ladies to their deaths, but Boston enjoyed them for the picturesque qualities they lent the republican life, and boasted about them to strangers. Neither their principles nor their manner of dress changed, for they wore the costume of their heyday — clothes 'of exceptional antiquity.' These two 'old Esther Dudleys' and their story were more legend than fact before they died. The actualities of the older generation were becoming the romance of the next. Hawthorne, Longfellow, Whittier, and Holmes were all born before these last leaves fell from the Revolutionary tree.

Paul Revere and his generation were becoming the grandparents of the next. That powerful young Frenchman who had served under Paul Revere during the days of the Boston artillery train — there had not been so many soldiers in that train nor so many people in Boston but the colonel could remember him well. So he was dead, was he? But his name and strain were being continued in New England. Henry Thoreau, his grandson, was born before Paul Revere died. It would have astounded the very handsome, proud Major Melville if he had known that he would be remembered only as the grandfather of Herman Melville and by a few stanzas that a little boy over in Cambridge would grow up and write. Paul Revere would himself have been amazed at the debt he would owe to a super-sensitive, almost super-beautiful little Portland boy whom he had never seen or heard of. The boy's grandfather, General Wadsworth, he had known well enough. He had been second in command of that fiasco, 'the Penobscot Expedition,' and had at the time (when seemingly every pot was calling the kettle black) made some scathing criticisms of Lieutenant Colonel Revere and the artillery train. Luckily his grandchild, when he grew up and wrote poems, was more attracted by the midnight ride than that most wretched excursion, although his grandfather probably told him about it, cursing the artillery train and Paul Revere.

People understood that the scenes their elder citizens had gone through were history, romance, poetry. 'Eb. Stiles' seems to have been the first to realize the unending charm of Paul Revere's most famous exploit.  His poem is called:

Story of the Battle of Concord and Lexington and Revears
ride Twenty years ago

> He spared neither Horse nor whip nor spur
> As he galloped through mud and mire
> He thought of nought but 'Liberty'
> And the lanterns that hung from the Spire.
> He raced his Steed through field and wood
> Nor turned to ford the river
> But faced his horse to the foaming flood
> They swam across together.
>
> He madly dashed o'er mountain and moor
> Never slackened spur nor rein
> Until with a shout he stood by the door
> Of the Church by Concord green
> 'They come They come.' he loudly cried
> 'They are marching their Legions this way
> Prepar to meet them ye true and tried
> They'l be hear by Break of day'

— were the two stanzas that would have interested Paul Revere the most.  He may have been surprised at the mountains which lay across his path, and the way he and his horse swam floods, or to read that he got all the way through to Concord.  Knowing how carefully he had ridden his horse that night, he may have been offended by such a foolish use of whip and spur, but if he ever saw it he probably thought this was pretty good poetry — never guessing how much better General Wadsworth's little grandson would do with the same material when he reached his full stature.

The Massachusetts Historical Society was founded largely through the heroic efforts of Jeremy Belknap and John Eliot.  It was John Eliot who had written so critically of 'the Great Revere' back in 1777 and had thought the town meetings called to discuss the treatment of the Tories too reminiscent of the witch-hunting days. Jeremy Belknap (who was too kindly to kill a spider) had been the receiver of young Eliot's outpourings. These two divines were still very close friends. Their infant society had modest rooms in the Tontine Crescent and went passionately to work to collect everything of importance to early Massachusetts history, portraits of early governors, King Philip's samp bowl, and books and manuscripts (among them those papers John Eliot's father had picked up in the wet gutters outside the Hutchinson house the night it was sacked). There is no possible way now to value such a collection in dollars and cents.

As secretary, Jeremy Belknap kept after Paul Revere to write out an account of his ride and other doings just before and after Lexington. Paul Revere did so as early as 1798.

He had already written an account for his own family. In this he refers to himself as living in 'the Colony of the Massachusetts Bay,' which suggests that the Revolution was not over and won at the time of the writing. With this account, his rough draft is also preserved. So there exist today three accounts in Paul Revere's own hand. The rough draft is the most colloquial and shows best how he actually spoke, and his fondness for 'gitting' to wherever he was going. When he copied it over, he cut a few redundancies and slightly corrected the grammar, but the rough draft and the neat copy are practically the same.

The narrative he wrote out for the embryonic Massachusetts Historical Society is much longer. As would be expected, he gives more general information. In it he goes into Doctor Church's treachery (not mentioned in the family version). He explains how the 'upwards of thirty, chiefly mechanics' had been watching the movements and plans of the British that winter and spring, how he had already gone over the road he was to ride that night on the Sunday before and had made his arrangements with Colonel Conant 'that if the British went out by water we would show two lanthorns in the North Church steeple; and if by land, one as a signal.' None of these things does he mention in the family account. But for his family he writes out at length the conversation between himself and the British officers who captured him, preserving the 'By Gods' and 'damns' which sprinkled the back-chat of that historic night. For the Reverend Mr. Eliot and the Reverend Mr. Belknap there is not one 'damn' recorded.

Also for his family he has more to say about the commencement of the fight at Lexington. But in both versions it is noticeable that Paul Revere (who was almost in the middle of the shooting, carrying his half of John Hancock's trunk) does not commit himself on that greatly argued point — who fired first. If he could conceivably have said the British had, he would certainly have done so. In his account for the Historical Society he goes as far as 'I saw and heard a gun fired, which appeared to be a pistol.' This suggests a British officer, for they commonly carried pistols. The minute men did not. In the earlier version he had written, 'a gun was fired I heard the report, turned my head, and saw smoake in front of the [British] Troops.' Seemingly this is as far as he was ever ready to go in whitewashing his fellow countrymen; he did not commit himself at all, probably for the good reason he did not know. In this respect he showed himself a more honorable man than the Reverend Jonas Clark, of the Lexington parsonage, whose narrative of that day's bloody butcheries during the British retreat to Charlestown were accepted as gospel truth for years, wormed their way into history books, but much of which is now dismissed as sheer propaganda — not even subtle, for it can be so easily disproved at a number of points.

Revere's rough draft has certain charms pruned away on second thought and lost in the formal Historical Society account, as:

'We rid down towards Lexington a pretty smart pace,' which becomes 'We rid towards Lexington on a quick pace.' Already a certain amount of speed is lost, but the third version, in which they 'all turned towards Lexington' is completely static. But only in the formal account is the beautiful line describing the crossing of the Charles. 'It was young flood, the ship was winding and the moon rising,' which is a great improvement over his earlier, 'the moon shone bright.' It is the Massachusetts Historical Society's account that is usually printed.

Paul Revere had plenty of grandchildren who (having no radios, comic strips, or movies, and being in other ways equally underprivileged) would hang upon the told story — and never forget. These family stories have one very pleasant quality — a complete lack of bombast and the narrator's emphasis on his own stupidity, not his cleverness. From the Revere family comes the legend that great-grandfather forgot that he would need cloth with

which to muffle the oars of the rowboat which would carry himself across to Charlestown. Lincoln descendants preserved the
equally absent-minded story about their illustrious grandfather
forgetting his spurs that night. This story sounds a little as
though made up to amuse small children, who would be much
more delighted by grandpa's absent-mindedness and the dog's
cleverness than anything John Hancock and Sam Adams might be
doing. Certainly in this version the dog was the hero — which
speaks very well for Paul Revere as an autobiographical story-
teller.

Once when he was in his eighties a friend showed him an impression of his most famous caricature — 'A Warm Place Hell.' 'He
had not seen it for years — was pleased to know that one was still
in existence — and offered to buy it. He said he was a young man,
zealous in the cause of liberty, when he sketched it, and had forgotten many of the circumstances; but *this* he did remember, that
while he was doing it, the famous (?) Doctor Church came into his
shop, and seeing what he was about, took a pen and wrote the following lines,' which the old gentleman could still repeat from memory, although he was no longer interested in the details of the political passions which had driven him to thus lampoon the 'Seventeen
Rescinders.'

Of the Tea Party, Paul Revere seems to have kept his oath
of secrecy to the very end. George Robert Twelves Hewes was
holding young listeners spellbound out in Oswego County, New
York, and even farther west in Ohio, Joshua Wyeth was telling of
his part. In fact these famous 'Mohawks' produced a number of
extraordinarily long-lived and talkative individuals, but Paul Revere did not join in. An oath was an oath and he would not go back
on it even for the sake of a good bedtime story. The only tradition
of tea to be handed down in the family seems to have come from
Rachel. She had made a pot of tea just before the embargo went
on and, as she poured it, said, 'Children, this is the last cup of tea
you will get for a long time'; which it was.

# VII

RACHEL REVERE, although almost ten years the younger, was the first to go. On the first of July of 1813 this notice appeared in the *Boston Chronicle:* 'In this town on Saturday, after a short, but distressing illness Mrs. Rachel, wife of Paul Revere, Esq. aged 68.' This places her death on the twenty-sixth of June, as do the records of the Granary. So Paul Revere was to 'trudge on' without her — his 'dear girl.'

People were less self-conscious about death — talked about it more, but took it more in their stride. While our undertakers do all they can to disguise death, theirs seem to have taken a professional pride in rubbing it in. The 'Sexton of the Old School,' writing in the middle of the last century, tells how things were done in his own boyhood. 'It filled me with the most delightful horror when the clergyman and sexton got together for their grand finale, "Earth to earth," and Grossman, who did his duty marvellously when he was sober, rattled on the coffin a whole shovelful of coarse gravel, "ashes to ashes" — another shovelful of gravel — "dust to dust" — another: it seemed as if shovel and all were cast upon the coffin lid.'

The milliners, haberdashers, glovemakers, jewellers, and tailors furnished their clientèle with mourning of terrifying sobriety. Mourning wreaths and pieces decorated all the best parlors. The Reveres even had the Washington urn. Death was not a thing one was supposed ever to forget. They were well hardened to the thought of it. Then, too, most of them believed confidently in a better life. Paul Revere, standing bareheaded in the Old Granary, could look forward resolutely to the day of doom when the last trump would sound — and what a flight of Hitchbourns and Reveres would rise up about him! — all saved, no longer to fight the weakness of their flesh, but radiant with their immortality. Such thoughts, at least, should have been Revere's comfort as he stopped in now and then on summer days to assure himself that all was right and decent at the new tomb, which held as yet only Rachel herself. There was hardly a spot in Boston where he could have found gathered together so many old friends as in the Granary. Often during the next few years, on the anniversary of her death, he must have come to this graveyard and pondered upon the past.

From the new Revere tomb it was a walk (but a brief walk) to the old lot where for so long Reveres and Hitchbourns had lain side by side. There was Sary's grave. Was it indeed true that in the glories of the risen life all hurts and jealousies would be left behind? Would not Sary feel a little slighted that as the last trump sounded she would see her husband stepping out of a fashionable tomb with Rachel Walker and realize that she had been left alone with her dead babies and in-laws? Paul Revere had had no choice. By the time his second wife died, no more graves were allowed to be dug in the Granary. The dead — mostly in unmarked graves — were four deep. A sexton could not get in his spade without throwing up pieces of old coffins, bones. It was full, and judging by selectmen's reports it was overfull. Only the owners of tombs could, for a little longer, still bury their dead here. So Paul Revere bought a tomb. He had not deliberately left his first wife so far away. It was the best he could do. Close to her was his father's grave. By 1816, it would be just a hundred years before that this boy — doubtless a forlorn boy — had been landed down upon Boston. Apollos Rivoire had looked about him. The town he saw, the way of life, even the color of the thinking were not in any very striking way different from those of centuries of European civilization. True, this was a frontier and the frontier has always fostered democracy. There were opportunities for a smart apprentice one could hardly have found in the Old World. There was not, for instance, even the ghost of the feudal system which Napoleon had by 1816 wiped from the face of Europe. But there had been no religious freedom, no manhood suffrage. And a boy might still meet a devil any dark night out behind the woodpile. It was well known that devils caused insanity. Probably half the citizens of Boston believed in witchcraft, although the terrible scandal of the Salem witches (some twenty years before) had resulted in Massachusetts being the first state in the world legally to deny it.

The tools the boy had used, the terms of his indenture to Mr. Coney, were in no way different from those of the medieval craftsman. Smallpox, uncontrolled, scourged Boston as it had always the European towns and no better treatment of it had been discovered than prayer. God was very close — and often angry. If offended, He let loose the Indians (who the more ignorant thought were actual demons from hell), or He shook the earth and half the steeples of Boston fell down. Or (if His anger was more personal) He sent the toothache. He was indeed a jealous God — not much like the kind Father men like William Bentley were talking about a hundred years later. Paul Revere could have much to think about in comparing the dates 1716 and 1816 as he looked at his father's headstone.

Friends, as well, lay in the Granary. Joseph Warren, forever young, forever heroic, cut down just as he was showing himself a really great leader, was at the moment resting here. His was a most migratory corpse. The digging up and reburial of Joseph Warren had been going on ever since Bunker Hill — and he had not yet found his final resting place. Whenever there was any doubt of the identity, those two teeth Paul Revere had wired in for him settled the matter. What would his name now mean to his old friend? The tightening shock of pain he had felt when first he heard that he was dead (and how hot that June had been when Joseph Warren had gone to the hill and never came off). Would he think of the 'very clean' face of his friend — or of the skull? Probably he would now first think of his own son. He might well have wondered (as many others have done) whether or not Warren and Josiah Quincy would indeed have fulfilled their early promise if they had lived on into the Revolution.

Not far away lay Will Molineaux — and his bad tempers.

A larch tree rose over the mound under which rested Crispus Attucks, Sam Gray, James Caldwell, Sam Maverick, and Patrick Carr. March 5, 1770 . . . lobster-backs driving snowy streets, cudgel-boys with cudgels . . . all the bells of Boston clanging and jangling. 'Fire, fire . . . where's the fire?' Men running, dogs barking . . . mothers chasing small boys . . . the shooting . . . 'they are butchering the inhabitants . . . Town-born turn out,' and Sam Adams sitting and waiting like God Himself — or like a spider; for which did he most resemble? And *that* was long ago.

Boston had not yet absent-mindedly mislaid the bodies of Sam Adams and James Otis and lost forever the overdressed remains of 'King' Hancock. Paul Revere could have gone straight to the Cunningham tomb where James Otis lay, remember James Otis at the Long Room Club, the Masons. How that fellow could talk! Some-

times too much. It was appropriate that his flashing, disordered
life had been ended by a bolt of lightning. And it was appropriate
(although Paul Revere would not know it) that the roots of a great
elm had already broken through the walls of the proper Cunning-
hams' tomb — and through the coffin, and wrapped their fibres
about his skull. You could not hold James Otis and his 'natural
rights of man' in earth. His passionate words had pointed to the
new world which Paul Revere could see about him. His voice had
flowed up and spread out as the great elm itself flowed up out of
his tomb feeding secretly upon his body.

And here the grave of Sam Adams. Those dear, long-past secret
days of the Sons of Liberty! Little meetings in back garrets, printing offices, ale shops. The blowing of a conch shell — a certain
whistle and the boys come running. What is it to be tonight? An
importer lugged before the Liberty Tree? A vast procession of
solemnly marching men? A quick sortie out to Brookline to put
the fear of God — and Boston mobs — into the Hultons? Grimac-
ing at poor Miss Hulton through one's mask of soot? Boston had
been a bit lawless in those furious years, but they could have been
much worse.

Kitty-corner across the Granary — almost as far away from Sam
Adams as it was possible for a body to get — lay John Hancock.
At the end Hancock could not have been too far away from Sam
Adams to suit him. Yet once they had been so close together. That
night when Paul Revere had ridden up to Jonas Clark's parsonage
in Lexington to warn them that the British were coming. 'Noise?
You'll have noise enough before long! The regulars are out'; and
Hancock's voice calling to him, 'Come in, Revere, we are not
afraid of *you*.' Sometimes one remembers a voice longer than a
face — longer even than all that 'pageant' which won John Hancock his most enduring fame.

Across the street in King's Chapel Billy Dawes had slept for
many a year.

What men they had been! It was easy for their contemporaries
to remember Sam Adams' political trickery, King Hancock's
vanities, James Otis' craziness. Even Joseph Warren had been a
little febrile himself. But should they not be judged (even as the
artist is judged), not by personal shortcomings, but 'by their works
ye shall know them'? Paul Revere, almost the last left of the old

guard, standing in the full sunshine of the new republic, would hardly have criticized them that they were not all as great as their own handiwork. Few great men are. Was not what they had accomplished enough? Should they be overblamed that each man of them worked within the limitations of his own humanity? The generation closest to them were not hero-worshippers, not romanticists. It would doubtless have puzzled and pained Paul Revere that a generation would arise which would be disappointed that he himself was no gallant young sprig when he took his ride to Lexington, but a man turned forty. That he had never been slender and never got all the way to Concord. That he had sixteen children and that his greatest service to his country was probably the prosaic manufacturing of copper for ships when it was desperately needed.

The generation which had started and organized the Revolutionary movement in Boston were mostly gone by 1816. Of the old leaders only John Adams and Paul Revere still lived. John Adams' little short legs could still carry him all over Quincy and neither did Paul Revere's legs give out early. If he wished to take a turn about Beacon Hill and see 'what was acting' after leaving the Granary, he could do so.

When a hundred years before, Apollos Rivoire had come into Boston Harbor, he would have noticed that the town was a conglomeration of hills, dominated by one large one, on top of which was a beacon. Now, in a frenzy of filling in, building up, making new land, Beacon Hill and all the others of Boston were being shovelled into dump carts. That 'leveling principal,' which Hutchinson had so feared as characteristic of Boston thinking, was being carried out in very fact. Considering the simplicity of the mechanical equipment, Boston was levelled off very fast when once these men put their minds upon it.

Paul Revere would have been delighted with the ingenuity of the engineer in charge of cutting down Beacon Hill to little more than half its original bold height. He had fixed up dump carts to run downhill on little iron tracks. It was a 'railroad.' Nothing like it had ever been seen before in America. The loads of gravel were dumped into the Charles (and Charles Street resulted), then the carts were pulled back up the hill by horses.

A charter had already been given to build a dam across the broad tidal waters of the Charles, all the way over to 'The Punch Bowl' in Brookline. In 1816, no one looking down on the Back Bay from the top of Beacon Hill could have guessed how soon solid land would follow this first dam and that the expression 'Back Bay' would, in the course of time, mean a residential district — not water.

It was not only down the railroad the dump carts were moving from the great gravel pit on Beacon Hill. In the other direction the Mill Cove was being filled. Where there had been seventy acres of the dirtiest water in Boston, there would be seventy acres of land to accommodate the great growth of the town in the last twenty years.

The Neck, whose narrowness was so long regarded as a great safety to Boston, was broadening in a goitrous fashion. In time it would be the widest part of the entire town. People were saying that in the old days Boston had been like a clenched hand — now it was opening and spreading out. The bridges which connected the town with Charlestown and Cambridge were compared to outstretched fingers. All this Paul Revere could see from the summit of Beacon Hill.

Beside the new State House (its dome encased in Revere copper) stood the old Hancock house. So far out of town when Uncle Thomas Hancock had built it, it was now at the very centre of this wild, new energy. Miss Dolly (now Madam Scott) lived there enjoying her second husband, Captain Scott, perhaps no more than her first, but surely in a different way. She was lamenting the evil days that had befallen her hill. They were cutting down all the trees. She was still slim, gay, brisk, and her conversation had lost none of its edge through time. Young men like General Sumner hung upon her words. The old lady was vastly amusing. She told him about that night at the Clark parsonage. What a night it had been! — with messengers arriving and the British were coming. 'Mr. H.' had insisted that he would join the minute men on the Green, but Mr. Adams said no — they belonged to the cabinet. Her quarrel with John Hancock — 'at the time I should have been very glad to have got rid of him.' Did Mr. Sumner know that Aunt Lydia nearly got shot the next morning? And there was that salmon. And the trip to Fairfield, Connecticut. Aaron Burr's courtship. He had been 'a handsome young man, of a very pretty fortune,' but of course Aunt Lydia had made up her mind and . . . so Miss Dolly chatted on and on. The good Captain Scott (who had been employed by John Hancock) never stole the show from her. True, as she said, 'what were dimples once are now wrinkles,' but Miss Dolly enjoyed herself from the beginning to the end of her long life — with John Hancock or without.

From Beacon Hill Paul Revere could, in a few minutes' walk, come to State Street (as King Street had long been called). Here and along the wharves he would see less change. In spite of the copper he had been making for Robert Fulton's experiments with steam, the ships moved with the old, clean, silent, white majesty of wind and sail. Hereabout the streets still followed the ancient channels his father had known a hundred years before. But the names were changing all over Boston. First it had been necessary to blot out any suggestion of British domination, and next, people grew a little sensitive about living on Beer Lanes and Paddy's Alleys. Frog Lane had already become Boylston Street; Cobbler's Court, Harvard Place; and so on all over town. But Turnagain Alley had not yet become Winter Street. May Street was not re-named Revere for forty years.

Anne Street still led out of Dock Square over into North Boston. It was definitely going downhill. 'Brothels and low dram-shops,' sailors' boarding houses, lined the street which had been so respectable in John Coney's day. It did not reform until it was widened and rechristened North Street.

At North Square itself Revere would find little change. Hannah Crocker had recently looked it over and pronounced it as still 'respectable.' So had Colonel Henry Lee, but already he was finding it quaint. Both the old lady and the young man had stopped to ponder on the Clark-Frankland and Hutchinson houses, now beginning on their second century, as Paul Revere himself must have done on passing them. The Ellises owned the Clark house, which was still decorated by the arms of the builder. The Clark family were utterly gone . . . and almost the memory of them. ' . . . there's honour for you,' thought Hannah Mather, gazing at their old mansion 'with the family up in the North Burial Ground.' Agnes Surriage survived at least as a legend and an object lesson.

> The old old story — fair and young
>     And fond — not over wise
> That matrons tell, with sharpened tongue
>     To maids with down cast eyes.

Rachel Revere may well have told that story herself to her growing girls — how wicked and unprincipled Agnes had been and the best people of Boston had snubbed her. But she should have stopped there, for the fact seems to be that Agnes gained everything from her liaison with Sir Harry except the approval of the best people in Boston.

Although well kept, these two great houses, monuments of past grandeur, already seemed a little haunted. Side by side the two rivals had some fifteen years more to stand. Across their fronts. hung unkempt bangs of Virginia creeper. Paul Revere might pause to glance at Christ Church, still dominating his end of town, might remember how his hands blistered as he rang the bells, or that night he had trusted this lofty spire to carry the news of the British march. Major Pitcairn. He had lain in his vault beneath the floor for forty years. Sometimes Paul Revere attended services at this church himself. All of his children by Rachel were Episcopalians.

And so, Charter Street, at last, and home. It would still, after three years, seem strange with Rachel gone — no longer sitting content in her 'lolling chair.' And there in the parlor was Mr. Reynolds' artificial marble urn to George Washington and on it the black streamers insisting upon it that all men must die.

# VIII

**I T** was in November of 1816 that Paul Revere set himself the sober task of making his will.

'In the name of God, Amen,' he wrote, 'I, Paul Revere, of Boston in the County of Suffolk and Commonwealth of Massachusetts, Esquire, being in good health and of sound memory, but knowing that all men must die do make and declare this to be my last will and testament.'

That 'handsome property' which his contemporaries mention amounted to some thirty thousand dollars, which was indeed handsome for its day. Now how to divide it. He had five children living and four of the dead children had lived long enough to leave children behind. After giving the usual orders that his just debts and funeral charges be paid, he started first with Mary, the only one of Sary Orne's brood to outlive him. She was a woman of forty-eight and lived with her husband, the housewright, Jedediah Lincoln, not far from Old North Square. The gap of almost ten years between her and Joseph Warren represented four children — among them the short-lived Isanna whose motherless state is said to have aroused Rachel Walker's maternal instincts, and Joshua with the pain in the chest. Next after Joseph Warren he mentioned his other son and youngest child, Doctor John Revere, finished now with his studies at home and abroad and practising his profession just around the corner on Middle Street. By now Paul Revere could not have worried how his boys would turn out. A man could have hardly had better sons. The handsome Harriet was thirty-three and unmarried. The pretty Maria had married Joseph Balestier, but in 1816 was also living with her father — as was her husband and his younger brother, John. Paul Revere had always liked a full house and he had always had one. To each of these five he left four thousand dollars. This left him ten to divide up between his dead children's children. Half of them were Lincolns. It would come to about five hundred dollars apiece.

First, there were those six children of Debby and Amos Lincoln. The youngest of these, Frederick Walker Lincoln, he had taken into his own house and brought up himself. He was twenty now, a cheerful and busy young fellow, already hard at work at the copper mill and highly approved of by his grandfather. Frederick Walker not only got his five hundred, but also the five hundred which his older brother Frank did not. Frank was cut off with a dollar: 'my grandson Frank (who now calls himself Francis)' is the way the old gentleman refers to him. Sometimes Frank Lincoln ran a crockery store and sometimes he was an undertaker. He seems to have been a decent citizen. What Paul Revere did not like about him we now do not know — but probably both of them knew at the time. It is unlikely that Revere would cut him off merely because he did not like young men who are baptized 'Frank' calling themselves by the more elegant 'Francis.' Paul Revere had had a grandmother, an aunt, sister, daughter, and granddaughters all called Frances — it may have struck him rather sissy of the young man to prefer the name Francis.

Then there were Paul, Jr.'s, seven children to consider. The two young Eayres and the four children Amos Lincoln had by Betty Revere after Debby had died and before he himself moved on to a third wife. 'To each and every of them five hundred dollars,' but young Joseph Eayres (who killed himself soon after his grandfather's death) got two hundred and fifty dollars extra.

There was one thing more he was anxious to do: give Joseph Warren due recognition for the success of the copper works, which was indeed the child of Paul Revere's old age. ' . . . as I have at great pains and expense with the assistance of my said son Joseph Warren, brought the copper business to the state in which it now is, and in order to bring it to perfection of which it is capable, I am desirous of giving it every encouragement in my power, consistently with my duty to my other children.' Joseph Warren is given the chance to buy out his brother and sisters within the next four years. He is also to be the residuary legatee, John the executor. Harriet is left all the household furniture.

So having decided how his property was to be divided, he called in his lawyers, William Minot and Andrew Ritchie. They witnessed his will for him, as did Sam Hitchbourn, the silversmith, and last of all the ten Hitchbourn cousins.

On the fifteenth of November, 1816, the lawyers, cousin, and testator gathered for the brief ceremony of signing the will — an occasion that would surely call for a bottle of brandy or hot toddy, perhaps even a bowl of punch and 'Your health Cousin Paul' or 'May you live to be as old as Methuselah, Mr. Revere,' to which he may have answered as John Adams was answering to a similar wish, 'My friend, you could not wish me a greater curse.'

A year and a half later he added a codicil to his will. On that fourteenth day of March, in the year of our Lord one thousand eight hundred and eighteen, he had not long to live and he may have known it. There is nothing in the strong, easy handwriting to suggest ill-health. The codicil only suggests his growing confidence in Joseph Warren. He wishes him to look out for the girls' property.

Early that year the largest of all of the Revere bells had been hung in the stone tower of King's Chapel. The excitement over its casting (and how wealthy vestrymen had thrown silver into the molten metal to ensure its beauty) had not yet died down. It was a magnificent bell and a certain sadness which it has was appropriate enough, for King's Chapel was 'the passing bell,' rung to tell the town that someone had died, and it tolled out the age and sex as well. That spring, as Paul Revere woke in the night to count its strokes, his feelings must have been mixed. Truly it was a bell any bell founder might take pride in — and how soon would it ring for him?

## IX

WHEN 'Joyce Jun'r' and his henchmen had, in the spring of 1777, carted Tories out of town and lists of suspected enemies of the people were being drawn up daily and town meetings broke up with every man calling his neighbors names, there had been among the questionable citizens an extraordinary proportion of doctors. Doctor Lloyd (with whom Joseph Warren had studied) was among the temporarily persecuted. The good old gentleman had survived almost unruffled and lived to be one of Boston's most respected citizens. Doctor Thomas Kast had been a young fellow in his twenties. It was he who had tried vainly to stop the great flow of blood from Major Pitcairn's shattered chest. Every committee to name potential enemies were satisfied that Thomas Kast was dangerous, but at the end he was remembered only as having established in Boston a scientific attitude towards that long-neglected, despised branch of medicine — obstetrics. That Paul Revere's granddaughters would not die off at the rate of the women young in his own youth was due, in part at least, to

Doctor Kast. Doctor John Jeffries had (having recognized Joseph Warren's body on Bunker Hill) left with the British. He had established a brilliant, titled practice in London, been the first scientific observer to go up in a balloon — and in the first contrivance to fly the English Channel. But when peace came and passion died down, he had returned to Boston. He lived long enough to be remembered by Oliver Wendell Holmes 'when he came probably to administer the professional *coup de grâce* to an aged relation of mine . . . it was he who helped deprovincialize the medical science in Boston.'

Doctor Samuel Danforth was also one of the Boston Tories who had stuck it out in spite of anything 'Joyce Jun'r' could do. And he too lived long enough to overlap Holmes, who says he was 'Danfurt as the common speech would have it, who died ten years after the time I looked upon Dr. Jeffries. I used often to hear him spoken of as being in "consultation," as the extreme unction of the healing art is called.' 'If "old Dr Danfurt" or "old Dr Jeffers" was seen entering a sick man's door, it was very likely to mean nothing more or less than *nunc dimittis*. Dr. Danforth's handsome features are well known to us in the fine portrait by Stuart. . . . He was very positive, somewhat passionate; swore like our army in Flanders, and did not care much for other people's beliefs. Of course he was an interesting personage; but he has special claims to professional remembrance by giving up blood-letting. His *materia medica* was very limited, having as its leading articles "mercury, antimony, opium, Peruvian bark," but to these he added "rubbing, blistering and the warm bath." He quarrelled with his medical associates, but he was a great favorite with his patients, and commanded their entire confidence.'

Doctor Danforth was Paul Revere's doctor. The bill he handed in to the estate was for seventy-seven dollars. Not so very long before, the Boston doctors had agreed to charge fifty cents for a visit, but a dollar for consultation, with double pay for night work — eight dollars for an obstetrical case, a guinea for a fracture, and fifty cents for pulling a tooth. The highest charge suggested by the Boston doctors was five guineas for a capital operation. Later, 'the medical fees were made more adequate to the services rendered,' but were still very low. Paul Revere's workmen, with their two dollars a day, were not as underpaid in buying power as they might seem at first glance.  In less than two weeks they could pay for the most expensive operation the city of Boston could offer them; for a new baby in four days.  Have all their teeth pulled for sixteen days' wages (which seems high in comparison to other medical services).  That bill of seventy-seven dollars suggests a long illness, but bills were often allowed to run for years.  It may have included Rachel's death in '13, or Doctor Danforth (being so at odds with the rest of the Boston medical men) may have charged more than the recommended fee.  One notes optimistically that Paul Revere's estate was also charged by Mr. Thomas Peabody forty-six dollars for shoeing horses.  One hopes that up to the end Paul Revere was personally able to account for a large part of this prodigious number of horseshoes.  He died possessed of a very good horse.  The obituary notices speak of his extraordinary good health and nothing is said, as often was, about the patience shown during a long illness.

It is pleasant to know that 'Dr Danfurt' did not bleed him to death as Doctor Craik is said to have bled Washington.  But mercury, antimony, opium, and Peruvian bark, given in the doses popular at the time, can be equally lethal.  These old doctors, on their 'rhubarb colored horses,' their saddle bags stuffed with drugs, or walking the street so pompously with gold-headed canes (as Oliver Wendell Holmes remembered), did kill a good many patients.  No wonder the more enlightened among them, like Doctor Danforth, were turning to rubbings and hot baths.  Doctor Danforth and Paul Revere were men of the same generation.  Although they had been so bitterly opposed to each other back in the days when 'Joyce Jun'r' was out with his cart, by now (between a hot bath and a rubbing) they could talk even affectionately of the good old ferocious days — although the doctor still might swear with all the eloquence of our army in Flanders.

It was on the tenth day of May, 1818, that Paul Revere died.  He had had thirteen more years than the psalmist promised us, nor was this extension of time filled with 'labour and sorrow.'

When the Reverend Doctor Mather Byles had died, Jeremy Belknap was amused to find in his inventory '5 or 6 dozen pair of spectacles . . . of all powers and fashion,' and an almost equal collection of 'hearing tubes,' showing how the poor old Tory in his later years had struggled to keep his contact with the world about

him.  Also such a collection of rat traps!  Evidently his house had
been overrun with rats.  Paul Revere left no such contrivances
behind him, and his inventory proves how extremely comfortable
his Charter Street house was.

The news of his death would spread from the sick chamber
throughout the house.  Next the neighbors would know.  If they
had seen 'old Dr Danfurt' entering the house, they might have been
expecting the '*nunc dimittis*.'  Soon the news would spread all over
Boston.  Paul Revere was dead.

'The Sexton of the Old School' says that around this time King's
Chapel bell was the 'passing bell.'  'I should have known it among a
thousand. . . . I counted the strokes — one-two-three — an adult
male, of course — and then the age . . . the strokes of that good old
bell, corresponding with the years of his pilgrimage — and then
the pause.  I almost expected another — so doubtless did he, poor
man — but it did not come.'

It was on a Sunday that Paul Revere died — when the bells of
the Christian world were ringing and among them hundreds of his
own casting.  A charming clamor, a golden bubble of sound, as bell
answered bell.  That day, all over New England, bells rang out
to the glory of God — and their maker, Paul Revere — from Lexington to Castine, Maine, Newport, Nantucket, Worcester, up and
down Cape Cod.  But even farther away his bells were ringing —
Savannah, Kentucky, the West Indies.  And on the ships at sea.
Under the strange shadow of Java Head or in the cruel Straits of
Sunda — far away at the other ends of earth, along the Baltic or
the North African coast — his bells might sound the change of
watch.  For this country was at peace the year he died — the
Yankee ships were everywhere.

About Boston in a number of newspaper offices, journalists inked
their pens.  A prominent citizen and a very worthy man had died.
They all knew 'old Mr. Revere,' something of his story and character.  'Cool in thought, ardent in action,' wrote the *Boston Intelligencer*, 'he was well adapted to form plans, and to carry them into
execution — both for the benefit of himself & the service of others.
In the early scenes of our revolutionary drama, which were laid in
this metropolis [Boston was still technically a town but the word
"metropolis" was rather new and elegant] as well as at a later period of its progress, his country found him one of the most zealous

and active of her sons'; or, 'He was one of the earliest and most indefatigable Patriots and Soldiers of the Revolution.'

They knew he had an 'ample property, which his industry and perseverance had enabled him to amass.'

His health also aroused the admiration of the obituary writers. All through his life 'the vigour of his mind, and the strength of his constitution were unabated' was the way the *New England Galaxy* put it. The *Boston Intelligencer* was more specific. 'A long life, free from the frequent afflictions of diseases, was the consequence of constant bodily exercise & regular habits.'

All agreed that his outstanding characteristics were his generosity and integrity, and had much to say about his willingness to help both publicly and privately. 'Seldom has the tomb closed upon a life so honourable and useful.'

That the tomb had also closed on one of America's most legendary heroes they could have had no idea, for the legend had not as yet risen up to swallow the actual man.[54] They, who had so recently seen the stocky, benevolent old gentleman, walking the streets of Boston, could hardly have guessed that he was destined forever to ride a foaming charger, his face enveloped in the blackness of a famous night of almost half a century before, to become in time hardly a man at all — only a hurry of hooves in a village street, a voice in the dark, a knock on a door, a disembodied spirit crying the alarm.

Notes
Genealogical Data
Bibliography
Index

# NOTES

## I

1. In 1875, Paul Revere's grandson, General Joseph Warren Revere, being in France, looked around for the genesis of the Rivoire family. He went first to Vienne, near Lyons, as this was the headquarters for the noble Rivoires of Dauphiny. This was 'a militant Catholic house without one record of a schismatic shoot.' The General found no proof that would link Apollos to this house, but thought there was a relationship. In 1923, Paul F. Cadman took up the hunt, basing his researches on the letters Cousin Mathias Rivoire wrote Revere in the 1780's. Sainte Foye (written by Mathias as 'St Foy') was described as being fourteen or fifteen leagues from Bordeaux, and he mentioned the villages of Riaucaud and Martet (read 'Riancaud' and 'Martel' by Goss). In these three villages, Mr. Cadman found records of Apollos' father and other members of the family, long established in the Midi. He saw no reason why, however, these Rivoires might not originally have been related to the Dauphiny house. The arms which both the first and second Revere used on their bookplates are those of this house, but one notices that when Paul sent Mathias (living where the family had always lived) a silver seal cut with these arms, Mathias writes back: 'I cannot give you any light on the question of whether these Arms are the same as mine. On the contrary, may I beg that you will let me know how you and our relatives in Guernsey came to make use of them.' Evidently the arms were news to him. Mr. Cadman believes that Paul Revere's father got them from the Guernsey uncle.

2. Thomas Hancock wrote his letters describing his chariot (and inadvertently his wife) to Christopher Kilby, who was Massachusetts' agent at the time in London. They are unpublished and copies are owned by the American Antiquarian Society. This marvellous chariot — so symbolic of success in this world — not only added to the glory of Thomas and Lydia Hancock as long as they lived, but to their nephew, John Hancock, after them.

3. Apollos' brief return to Uncle Simon and Guernsey is not supported by any contemporary evidence that I know of. A trans-Atlantic passage was extremely expensive, representing in labor around three years of a workingman's life. How the apprentice got the money to pay off his indenture and then cross the ocean twice has not been solved. Perhaps he did not go. Goss merely makes the statement that he did take such a trip and, except where he is proved wrong (nothing of very great importance — a few dates, details of where he lived, etc.), I have tended to accept him, although a little warily. He was not an imaginative writer. I do not think he would have sent Apollos on this trip without what

seemed to him good and sufficient reason — perhaps verbal tradition. Goss was working on Paul Revere some sixty years ago. At that time people who actually remembered him were still alive.

4. In 1680, Jasper Dankers, a diary-keeping Dutchman who naturally hated all New Englanders, sailed from New York to Boston with 'Paddechal,' Paul Revere's great-grandfather. 'First it was announced we were to leave on Wednesday, then the following Saturday, afterwards on Tuesday and again Thursday without fail. Finally we spoke to the skipper or supercargo Paddechal, who told us he could not leave before the govenour returned who had some letters of importance to send by him'; but 'June 1680. We embarked at noon in the yatch of Mr Padeschal ... the crew consisted of three men and a boy besides the captain. ... Many persons came to escort the captain, & also a woman who was going with us; and as soon as they were gone we hastened to leave.' 'Friday the 21, Our Captain had prayers every evening, performed in this way. The people were called together, & then, without anything being spoken previously, he read a chapter, then a psalm, after that they all turned their backs to each other half kneeling, when a common formulary of prayer was said which was long enough, nut irreverent enough delivered.' 'Sunday June 23, We arrived at the entrance of the harbour (at Boston) where we found a considerable rolling sea caused by ebb tide and wind being aginst each other. There are about thirty islands here, not large ones, through which we sailed; reached Boston at four o'clock in the afternoon, our captain running his yatch quite up to his house in the Milk-ditch.' 'The skipper received us politely at his house, & so did his wife, but as it was Sunday, which it seems is somewhat strictly observed by the people, there was not much for us to do today. Our captain however took us to his sisters where we were welcome, & from there to his fathers, an old competent man, where there was a repetition of the worship which took place while they were in the kitchen turning the spit & busy preparing a good supper. We arrived while they were engaged in the Service but he did not look up. When he had finished, they turned round their backs, & kneeled on chairs or benches. The prayer was said loud enough, if that makes it good. This done he wished his son welcome and insisted on our supping with him.' Captain Pattishall invited them to spend the night with him. 'We were taken to a fine large chamber, but we were hardly in bed before we were shockingly bitten. I did not know the cause, but not being able to sleep I became aware it was bed bugs, in such great numbers as was inconceivable. My comrade, who was very sleepy, fell asleep at first. He tumbled about very much; but I did not sleep any the whole night. In the morning we saw how it was, & were astonished we should find such a room with such a lady.'

5. The Pattishall portraits seem to be companion pictures, painted in the last half of the seventeenth century by an unknown artist. Mr. Francis R. Stoddard, who owns the 'Captain,' has tentatively put forward Courturier, who was painting in New York at the time, as the painter. When 'Mrs Pattishall and Child' was shown in the Worcester Art Museum's 1934 Exhibition of seventeenth-century painting in New England, the scholarly committee for the exhibition pointed out the similarities between it and a group of portraits painted around Boston between 1675 and 1695, artist unknown, but possibly Smith. In this group are Captain Smith's own portrait and his wife, Captain George Curwin, and Major Thomas Savage. The committee thought this Mrs. Pattishall was the Captain's second wife, Martha Woody, and her daughter Anne (Paul Revere's

great-grandmother and the Great-Aunt Thomas he speaks of visiting as a boy
and who at that time owned these portraits). Mr. Charles K. Bolton ('Portraits
of Founders') also believes this is the second wife. Miss Isabella Curtis, who owns
this picture, points out, however, 'that it is not authenticated whether she is the
first . . . or second wife.' The two portraits hung together in Plymouth until 1850.

6. By the records of the New Brick (or 'Cockerel') Church, Paul Revere's
baptism is written down as December 22, 1734. This was during the trying years
of adjusting the calendar from 'old style' to 'new style.' By the 'new style' his
baptism was on the first day of January, 1735; for to 'old style' dates falling during
the winter months one adds ten days.

# II

7. In 1728, the butchers were so annoyed by the dogs worrying their animals
before they were slaughtered (often in the streets) and making off with the meat
after it was hung up, the town restricted the height of dogs to ten inches. This
brings up the question how thoroughly our ancestors enforced such laws. Seemingly they usually let well enough alone. If you had a twelve-inch dog and he
behaved himself, you were not brought into court. Sam Adams himself had an
enormous Newfoundland called 'Queque,' who, being continually badgered by the
British troops in Boston, would attack a redcoat whenever he saw one. He was
no ten-inch dog.

8. Benjamin Bangs, of Eastham, Cape Cod (Manuscript diary, Massachusetts
Historical Society), indicates the type of work done at this wharf: 'Sept 10, 1747
Wind & rain. Came in to Mrs Hichbon's Wharf' — and sold wood, unloaded
mackerel. Four days later, 'moved our sloop to Hichbon's yard to grave.' Next
year he 'lay at Hichbon's graving yard,' but in two days 'we finished graving &
moved to Long Wharf.' That summer 'Capt. young Christ. Remick' (so closely
associated with Paul Revere's pictures twenty years later) went back to the Cape
with him as a passenger, and in the fall of 1748 he is back once more 'graving the
sloop at Hichbon.'

9. Doctor Clark was born in 1698. His daughter was the wife of Jonathan
Mayhew. His ledgers (at the Massachusetts Historical Society) deal only with
his real estate. Among his many houses 'at the head of Clark's Wharf' there were
two of considerable importance — the very ancient family house which Paul
Revere's uncle, Philip Marrett, and Mrs. Hiller sometimes rented, and the brick
house where he himself lived with his family. The names one finds on the Doctor's
ledgers reappear again and again in Paul Revere's life, like his cousin, Thomas
Hitchbourn, his Uncle Marrett (to whom he was at one time selling 'white, pink,
and blew hose' by the dozen, and whose son, Lieutenant Marrett, during the
confusion of the retreat up the Penobscot, tried to make him stop for a glass of
grog — but Paul Revere was too busy). Other tenants were his friends and associates, like Manasseh Marston, Ezra Collins, the Webbs, and the Cochrans.
The picture of the Wharf is an enlarged detail from the Burgis-Price view of

Boston which was reissued several times (with slight changes) during the first half of the eighteenth century. It gives an impression of the environment in which Paul Revere lived for at least sixteen years of his life and where he still had his goldsmith's shop even after he moved his family to North Square in 1770. It is not very accurate. We know there were sail-lofts, counting- and ware-houses down the length of it (in his three views of Boston Paul Revere indicates them), but they are not shown on this engraving.

The Foster house and goldsmith's shop adjoined Doctor Clark's property. When Paul Revere (although no longer paying Doctor Clark rent) advertises as 'opposite Dr. Clark,' it may have been this very shop he was using. It is at least the type of shop he probably had and the house similar to those Doctor Clark owned. He knew it well, and there in his young manhood he might often have seen Rachel Walker, whom he eventually married. It had belonged first to her great-grandfather, Captain Thomas Moore. (According to Sewall, Mrs. Moore had one of those fine funerals the Judge loved so dearly — with himself and Elisha Hutchinson walking first among the mourners with black gloves and scarves. 'She was a very loving familiar friend of ours,' says Sewall, and quotes Increase Mather himself as saying her 'death was like a Translation.') Up to the time Rachel was fifteen, two of her great-aunts lived in the two halves of this house. It was bought in 1760 by Abraham Foster. His son, Joseph, the silversmith, lived in it until well into the next century. Henry Lee, writing in 1881 of the North Boston of his boyhood, speaks of 'Honest Foster, the silversmith, who in his long coat, knee-breeches and shoe buckles, dwelt with his spinster sister in an impractically low-jettied house on Anne Street, one step below the narrow sidewalk.' The sketch is said to have been made by a 'French drawing master.' By comparing the inscription on it and Boston records, it was drawn between 1825 (when Fish Street was renamed Anne) and 1839, when John McGinty moved from this address.

10. 'Colonial Women of Affairs' gives many curious examples of the work engaged in by women before 1776. Those mentioned in the text are mostly from this book. The contemporary records (like John Boyle's diary — he could not get on with his old master's widow) give many indications of the number of women who were by no means limiting their lives to the four walls of their homes, but Mrs. Dexter has gathered together in one book a great many colonial 'business women.'

# III

11. Paul Revere's association with the Masons continued throughout his long life. His memory is high among them today. See Goss, chapter XVII, for the best account I know of Revere as a Mason. John Rowe's diary has many interesting items about the Masons at this time.

12. Although much of Paul Revere's silver is in private ownership, there are notable collections in the following public museums.

The Museum of Fine Arts, Boston, has the principal collection of his silver. Its 'Paul Revere Room' has the four family portraits, Revere furniture, china, prints, given by the descendants of Paul Revere, and 'the silver bequeathed by Mrs. Thayer is without doubt the largest and most representative collection of her great-grandfather's work in this metal which will ever be assembled.'

The Mabel Brady Garvan Collection at the Gallery of Fine Arts, Yale University, is a magnificent collection of colonial silver, in which Paul Revere is very well represented.

At the Worcester Art Museum is the beautiful Paine silver and other Revere silver, as well as a sample of the father's work.

The Metropolitan Museum of Art has a number of Paul Revere's pieces.

The Cleveland Museum has the Hollis French Collection of colonial silver. Among the Revere silver are the spurs he made for himself.

The Addison Gallery at Andover, Massachusetts, has some notable silver by Paul Revere.

13. This story was written down almost a hundred years later by Hannah Mather, the daughter of Samuel and Hannah (Hutchinson) Mather, born June 27, 1752. She married Joseph Crocker April 13, 1779, and died July 11, 1829. Her jumbled, unchronological reminiscences are in the New England Historic Genealogical Society and have never been printed. The American Antiquarian Society has other manuscripts of hers, a play among them.

14. In writing of Sam Adams I have had two books constantly before me, 'The Life and Public Services of Samuel Adams' (1865), by William V. Wells, and John C. Miller's 'Sam Adams, Pioneer in Propaganda.' Wells tells his story in three stately, slow-moving volumes, very laudatory and sometimes bombastic. (The quotation on page 269 is typical of Wells.) The Miller book is a very brilliant study of politicians and political clubs centring about Adams. I am especially indebted to Mr. Miller. To a curious extent the books vary little in the facts they present — but considerably in their interpretation.

15. It is obvious to anyone who studies the portraits of Puritans, or reads contemporary accounts of New England Puritan life, that they little resembled in dress, manner, or speech the traditional 'Puritan.' How were these honorable but very human Englishmen metamorphosed into the legendary Puritan? My theory is that it began with Sam Adams, who wished to point out the way Boston should go by creating an ideal past for his people. We have no reason to believe Adams ever studied the past. He merely said that all the civic and domestic virtues he most admired had existed then.

# IV

16. Henry Winchester Cunningham edited the Reverend Samuel Checkley's diary. As Doctor Checkley mentions Pope's Day, Mr. Cunningham explains the custom, giving the most information about it I have seen in print. Another source is the unsigned reminiscences in the *Boston Advertiser* for November 9, 1821. The writer says he is seventy at the time, so he should have been able to remember the pre-

Revolutionary Popes' Days (after the French came in as our allies they were much modified and finally given up). This is by far the most detailed account by a possible eye-witness. The tarred and feathered devil's imps and the presence of 'Joyce Jr.' link the Pope's Day mobs even more closely to the later Sons of Liberty, who also, obviously, took over the effigies, devils, illuminated lanterns — as well as 'Capt.' Mackintosh.

Albert Matthews seems to have successfully traced Boston's 'Joyce Jr' back to Cornet Joyce of England. Although letters written during the Revolution (John Eliot and Abigail Adams) mention him as 'Joice Jr' or 'Josie Jr,' etc., no one attempts to explain him.

# V

17. The British Headquarters papers from 1763 to 1775 were not turned in to the War Office by General Gage. Professor Clarence E. Carter discovered them in the old Gage mansion in 1930, when they were bought *en bloc* for the William L. Clements Library at the University of Michigan. In the Proceedings of the American Antiquarian Society for 1937 are printed in full the letters which Colonels Dalrymple and Carr, Captain Preston, and Lieutenant-Governor Hutchinson wrote to General Gage in New York, giving their account of the Massacre. The colonels seem to have been primarily concerned with the care of their own men and how they were going to get the money to pay for the barracks.

18. Peleg Chandler's 'American Criminal Trials,' 1841, gives what seems to me the most careful analysis of the Massacre and I have used this book as my primary source, adding to it various contemporary accounts, especially George Robert Twelves Hewes', who has more to say about 'the greasy barber's boy' than anyone else. I have dismissed much of Boston's 'Short Narrative' as propaganda. The truth of this fracas seems to have been settled for all time at the trial of the soldiers.

19. As far as I know, this diagram was first reproduced (but without the handwriting) in Mellen Chamberlain's chapter, 'Revolution Impending,' in 'The Critical and Narrative History' (1887). Mr. Chamberlain was librarian of the Boston Public Library. His reputation for historical accuracy is very high. He says it 'was used in the trial ... and was made by Paul Revere.' He owned it at the time. I do not know how he got it or why he attributed it to Paul Revere. The handwriting (which he did not reproduce), when carefully compared to Revere's ledgers, etc., does seem like proof. Strangely enough, Pelham and Revere wrote rather similar hands, but with the three photostats before one, certain mannerisms (especially in the script capitals) seem to give the diagram definitely to Revere.

Although the capital letters close to the dead men seem to indicate who they were, the unattached capitals present a deeper problem. The 'P' (lower left) suggests Edward Paine, who was standing in his doorway (the inscription says this is his house) when wounded. Other casualties were Patrick Carr, Robert Patterson, David Parker, John Clark, John Green, and Christopher Monk.

20. A copy of 'The Short Narrative' has for a frontispiece a folded engraving of the Massacre (later than Revere's) bound up in it. It is this copy which started the often-repeated story that Paul Revere made his plate as an illustration. This copy, 'The Brinley Short Narrative,' was bought by the American Antiquarian Society.

21. November 2, 1681, Daniel Turell, Sr., of Boston, and Thomas Walker deeded to Robert Howard, merchant, land with a dwelling house upon it 'near the New Meeting house.' It was bounded east by the street, west by Matthew Barnard. (Suffolk Deeds, 13–86.)

Robert Howard seems to have lived here for nearly forty years. When he died in 1717, he left it to his daughter, Sarah Wyborne, who, after living in it about twenty years longer, deeded it to James Knox in 1741. (Suffolk Deeds, 61–216.)

The money matters of the Knox family did not go smoothly, and although it was in the family for fifteen years, Andrew Knox, the son of James, was forced to mortgage it to John Ervine. Probably Ervine allowed the Knoxes to stay on long after they had ceased to pay their interest, but after thirty years his patience became exhausted. He foreclosed the mortgage and sold the house and land to Paul Revere. Neighbors had come and gone — the house still bounded east on the street and west on the Barnard house it so much resembled. It still is near the New Meeting House.

As far as we know, the house when in the Reveres' ownership was always a three-story 'mansion.' There is nothing to suggest that Revere ever made such a radical change as to add a third story to a smaller house. In the census of 1790, it is described as 'a wooden dwelling... 630 sq. feet — 3 stories, 17 windows,' which, with the land and barn, were valued at $2000.

22. A reliable family tradition says that Rachel's miniature was painted by Paul Revere's friend, Copley. It is unsigned. But (quoting from the Boston Museum of Fine Arts Gallery Book for the Revere Room, where it now is), 'Authorities on miniature painting, however, attribute it stylistically to Joseph Dunkerly, and we have found, from the ledgers, that this artist was renting from Paul Revere his house in North Square.' Rachel was then thirty-nine. She has on a lavender dress.

23. No papers of the secret doings of Boston's many secret pre-Revolution Whig societies have ever come to light. Seemingly they were systematically destroyed even years afterward. Peter Edes (son of Benjamin, the printer) thus wrote: 'My father was the only person who had a list of them [Tea-Party Indians] and he always kept it locked up in his desk while living. After his death [1803] Benjamin Austin called upon my mother, and told her there was in his possession, when living, some very important papers belonging to the Whig Party, which he wished not to be publically known, and asked her to let him have the keys of the desk to examine it, which she delivered to him; he examined it, and took out several papers, among which it was supposed he took away the list of the names of the tea-party, and they have not been known since.' But through reminiscences, etc., many are now known. Austin's action (so long after the events) does suggest the Tories were right in thinking quite a little went on in the Whig Party that they would not wish 'to be publically known.'

# VI

24. The distance today (by my Shell map) from Boston to Philadelphia is three hundred and six miles. It was longer in Revere's day of winding country roads, so I have added forty-four miles for the three hundred and fifty, but probably I have not added enough. John Howe said it was forty-eight miles from Boston to Worcester. We now call it thirty-nine.

25. There is a charming water-color of Major Pitcairn on horseback, said to be by Paul Revere (see article by F. F. Sherman, *Art in America*, 1923). The face of this little mounted man, strong, coarse, genial, and middle-aged, is the Major Pitcairn of the contemporary accounts, as the innocent miniature is not; but as I cannot feel this water-color (and a View of South Bridge, also credited to Paul Revere) have been completely verified, I have passed them by.

26. 'The Journal Kept by John Howe, as a British Spy,' was published at Concord, New Hampshire, in 1827. It is extremely rare. His account, written so long after the events, cannot be compared in historical accuracy with some of the other British soldiers' letters and diaries. There is no reason to believe all Howe said, but his amusement value is high.

# VII

27. Paul Revere, in the account he wrote for the Massachusetts Historical Society (1798), says the lanterns were hung in 'North Church Steeple,' and yet, in 1775, Christ Church was popularly Christ and the church at North Square 'Old North.' After the latter was pulled down in 1776, the nickname of 'North' and 'Old North' was transferred to the oldest church in North Boston, which was Christ. Although the North Square Church has been put forward as a candidate for the lanterns, it could not have been so used. Its spire was so 'stumpy,' lights hung in it would not have been seen in Charlestown. Copp's Hill lay between. Paul Revere, in calling Christ 'North Church,' was using the nomenclature common at the time in which he wrote, instead of when he rode.

28. In Chapter X, I have gone into Paul Revere's own three accounts of his activities just before the nineteenth of April, the Battle of Lexington and a few days later. The present chapter is based on these accounts, but sometimes I quote from one and sometimes from another — depending on which gives the most detail. I also have arranged his material chronologically. In no way do his three versions contradict each other, nor the testimony of the most reliable eyewitnesses.

29. A rather weak case for John Pulling as the actual hanger of the lanterns was put forward some seventy years ago by J. L. Watson and answered most convincingly by William W. Wheildon, who goes as far towards proving Newman was the man as would be apt to be possible one hundred years after the event. The City of Boston and Christ's Church have both, after careful research, ac-

cepted Newman and left Pulling in the street guarding the tower. What Revere's nextdoor neighbor, Barnard, was doing is even vaguer, but tradition says he did something.

30. The idea that Paul Revere was the only rider out that night was so picturesquely implanted in the American mind by Longfellow in 1863 there was a natural reaction when it was learned he was by no means out alone. Although Joseph Warren officially sent out from Boston but two men — William Dawes and Paul Revere — at least three others noticed something was afoot that day in town and in a mild way did spread the alarm. These are Ebenezer Dorr, Joseph Hall, and Solomon Brown. Brown lived in Lexington, and on his way home from market noticed the little advance guard of British officers. His news resulted in the guard stationed that night about the Clark parsonage, and he and Sanderson and Loring were asked to go on to Concord and tell them there what he had seen — not that the British were marching by the hundreds, but that officers were abroad. All three of these men were picked up by Major Mitchell and were among the 'countrymen' Revere mentioned as having been collected in the pasture before he himself was caught. Richard Devens had tried to get word through to Lexington as soon as the lanterns had been shown on Christ's spire. This man also seems to have been picked up, for no word of an actual expedition had come to Lexington until Paul Revere arrived. Although Longfellow made several historical mistakes, in one thing he was right. If there was room for but one man in the limits of his poem, Revere was the one to choose. He had already ridden thousands of miles as an official express. His reputation and name were well known to his friends and even enemies — like Governor Wentworth, Major Mitchell, and the two other British soldiers, Sutherland and Pope. It was he who had arranged about the signals from the spire and had already (the Sunday before) warned Concord they might be attacked and it was time to begin hiding supplies.

His part was much more active than Dawes', and (what with slipping past the *Somerset* and getting through the officers on 'Charlestown Common') much more adventurous. Neither man got to Concord. Revere was captured and Dawes fell off his horse, but by then the alarm was so general someone else would be sure to get word in time. This happened to be Doctor Prescott, for riders were setting off in all directions as soon as they heard Paul Revere's warning, at first, second, or third hand, that the British had marched. By breakfast (one notes) Private Howe found so many men on this errand that claiming to be a patriot express was the best alibi a British spy could offer. Paul Revere was well known as the principal express long before Longfellow immortalized him (see notes on Chapter X). Dawes, who certainly did his share that night, seemed for a while to be destined for oblivion. At present the opposite is the danger. Realizing that he never got his dues from Longfellow, people are now saying that he really did all the work, that he got to Concord, and Revere did not, etc. Since I have begun on this book I have been asked several times if it is true that Paul Revere never took that ride at all.

31. This trunk (large and very heavy) was given by Mrs. Dorothy Quincy Gardner White to the American Antiquarian Society and in 1865 by this society to the Museum of the Worcester Historical Society, where it now is. Mrs. White was a favorite grand-niece of Dorothy Quincy Hancock. She states the trunk was made by Bell, whose shop was in Star Lane (now Summer Street), Boston. John Hancock ordered it for the trip (May, 1775) he took to Philadelphia, where he was

President of the Continental Congress. It was made to fit exactly the Hancock chaise and was held in place by heavy leather straps. No chaise could have carried more than one such trunk, and there seems no reasonable doubt but this was the, one left at Buckman's Tavern and carried through the Battle of Lexington by Paul Revere and John Lowell. Mrs. White says she remembered it in the attic of the Hancock Mansion, full of letters of the Revolutionary period. Her grandmother, Sarah Quincy Greenleaf (one of Miss Dolly's sisters), married into a Worcester family and Mrs. White lived in Leominster, so it was natural that the trunk should have been given to the American Antiquarian Society.

The John Lowell, who was at that time Hancock's clerk, was also the brother of Ebenezer Hancock's wife and a great-uncle of James Russell Lowell.

32. The Connecticut militia arrived to take part in the siege of Boston a few weeks after the Battle of Lexington. Among these troops were Ralph Earl, an embryonic portrait painter, and Amos Doolittle, silversmith and would-be engraver. Both were twenty-one. Sometime that summer they were allowed to go to Lexington and Concord to attempt a record of the events of the nineteenth of April. The result was a series of four engravings (six shillings the set, plain, eight shillings, colored, and now among the most highly priced of American prints). Earl did the drawing on the spot and Doolittle posed for him. In their engravings both militiamen and British regulars look more like crickets than men, or, as Harold Murdock says, 'birds of prey.' He believes the chief difficulty 'is all traceable to Doolittle's faulty conception of the cut of a military coat, from which we may infer that if Doolittle was a bad engraver, he would have been a greater failure as a tailor.' The picture of the Battle of Lexington is a later version of the identical scene as redrawn and engraved by Doolittle in 1832. The original view as done by the two young soldiers is so extremely ludicrous I preferred a later attempt. But the figures of Pitcairn and Smith at Concord are from one of their original plates. These two figures seem to be the most carefully drawn of any in the series. Evidently some effort was made at a portrait of Pitcairn, who was a round-eyed, round-faced man, but the portly Smith is reduced to the merest grasshopper. Their little bird-like legs and tiny feet were shared (according to Earl and Doolittle) with all the other combatants of that famous day.

33. It was said at the time (and has been whispered ever since) that the two British privates left behind at North Bridge were scalped and mutilated. When Hawthorne took up his residence at the 'Old Manse' he says that 'Lowell, the poet,' told him this story: 'A youth in the service of the clergyman had been chopping wood at the manse. When he heard the shooting he ran across the field, his axe in his hand. The British had by this time retreated, the Americans were in pursuit; and the late scene of strife was thus deserted by both parties. Two soldiers lay on the ground — one was a corpse; but as the young New Englander drew nigh, the other Briton raised himself painfully upon his hands and knees and gave a ghastly stare into his face. The boy — it must have been a nervous impulse, without purpose, without thought, and betokening a sensitive and impressible nature, rather than a hardened one — uplifted his axe and dealt the wounded soldier a fierce and fatal blow on the head.' Later, another British party passed by and saw the mutilated head of their comrade and claimed he had been scalped. Of this story Hawthorne says: 'It comes home to me like truth. Oftentimes ... I have sought to follow that poor youth ... observe how his soul was tortured. ... This one circumstance has borne more fruit for me than all that history tells us of the fight.'

The boy (according to Stark) was Ammi White. He married Mary Minot in 1788. In 1807, he was still 'tortured' by the memory of this curious tropism on his part. 'It worried him very much.'

The British 'atrocities' were mostly concerned with burning houses and shooting innocent bystanders when upon the retreat. See Murdock's 'The Nineteenth of April' for ample proof that the houses were full of snipers and the innocent victims militiamen. They did some plundering (much to the anger of their officers).

34. Isaac Clemens is referred to by good authorities as probably English. However, there was a Clemens family in Boston — Paul Revere's brother, John, married an Anna (daughter of Jeremiah) Clemens in 1764. E. Alfred Jones follows his career to New York where he 'distressed, harassed and perplexed the rebels by counterfeiting their bills of currency' — presumably Paul Revere's among them.

35. Goss has the fullest account of Paul Revere's paper money that I know. At the same time Revere cut a seal for Massachusetts. It was used from 1775 to 1780, and his bill of August 17, 1775 reads:

| To Engraving a Colony Seal | 3.0 |
| To Silver for the Seal | 1.14.10 |

This had a little soldier on it with a sword in one hand and Magna Charta in the other — similar to his cut on his 'Sword-in-Hand' money.

In 1780 he engraved the seal still used by Massachusetts, with its familiar Indian. Inflation had gone so far in five years he charged £900, but was paid '£600 or £8 hard money.' He cut other seals like the one for the short-lived 'Rising States Lodge,' and the seal of Phillips Andover Academy, ordered in 1782 by John Lowell, as Revere's ledgers show. It was presented to the new school by Lowell and Oliver Wendell.

# VIII

36. The *New England Chronicle* for April, 1776, mentions the artificial teeth by which Warren's skeleton was recognized, as do other contemporary sources. Sometimes it is referred to as one tooth, sometimes as two, or an eyetooth and the one next to it. Sometimes it is one tooth and a missing fingernail. General Sumner, in his reminiscences says, 'If stronger identity were wanting, that afforded by Col Revere, who set the artificial tooth, and who recollected the wire he used in fastening it in, would afford it.' The body of Warren was moved from the Granary in 1824 to the vaults under Saint Paul's. In 1855 it was moved again out to Forest Hills. At that time a photograph of it was taken. The two teeth Paul Revere wired in for his friend seem to have been carved out of one piece of ivory and have outlasted most of the natural teeth. The bullet which killed Warren entered a few inches above them and came out the back of the skull. He made no dying speeches.

37. The *New York World*, May, 1886, carried a story about the *Somerset's* reappearance and the stir which swept the country. 'Above her charred and crushed timbers old ocean had piled a cairn of sand thirty feet high. The wirey beach grass

grew rank above it. The gulls made their nimble track across it; the men of the life-saving service trudged over it daily,' etc., but now 'the amateur wreckers and relic-hunters are swarming the beach.' Since that time she is said to have risen from the sand several times. Isaac M. Small ('Shipwrecks on Cape Cod,' 1925), whose professional interest in wrecks makes him a valuable authority, says, 'since that day (in 1886) no part of the old Man of War has shown on the surface.' Seemingly, however, other wrecks have been pointed out to tourists as bona-fide *Somersets*. In spite of the dynamiting her hulk received from the relic-seekers, much of her heavy oak vertebrae was still intact when she was covered again by the sand over fifty years ago.

# IX

38. This diary is printed in full by Goss. It runs from July 21st to the 19th of August. Paul Revere sent it to the Committee of Inquiry as vindication of his conduct. In the 'Documentary History of the State of Maine' the papers concerning the trial of Colonel Revere and others have been published.

39. There is no better indication of the educational and social position of the Rivoire family than the long time the Reveres of Boston kept in touch with their European relatives. They did not belong to the illiterate class of immigrant who so quickly loses contact with the relatives left behind. The first letter among the Revere papers is dated in January, 1775. It is from John Rivoire, grandson of the Uncle Simon who helped Apollos. He was the harbor-master and receiver-general of customs for Guernsey as well as captain of the island's militia company. His statement that 'several years have elapsed since I had the pleasure of receiving any of your favours' suggests that there were many earlier letters. He remembers that Paul Revere has written him that 'your Father made this alteration (in the family name) merely on account the Bumpkins could pronounce it easier.' In a London paper, a couple of months before, he noticed that Paul Revere had been sent express to Philadelphia, so, 'it seems, Dr Cousin, you are a person in good circumstances.' Then he goes on to suggest that a cargo of rum can be imported duty-free into Guernsey and 'a vast Trade is carried on by the Smugglers from here to the Coast of England.' The Yankees were not the only respectable smugglers in those days. He himself is a bachelor of forty — the only male Rivoire on the island. In a later letter it comes out that there are 'five ladies of the name who were my first Cousins.' He mentions 'Our Cousin Mathias Rivoire of Martet near St Foy 14 or 15 Leagues from Bordeaux' and that 'we have other relations at a place called Riaucaud and very rich.' So Paul begins to write Mathias too, who had his notary's office at Sainte Foye. Mathias was his second cousin and, living where the family had been living for some four or five generations, was in a position to furnish Revere with genealogical data. In Guernsey the name Rivoire was almost extinct, as it was also in the three villages of the Midi. The Riaucaud property had recently been inherited from Paul's Cousin Simon (who had died at eighty) by a son of one of his sisters, Mons Mervillaux. At the same time, hunting about for information, he went to the oldest notary's office in Sainte Foye and

told the young clerk what his problem was. 'Mathias Rivoire,' he said, and a strange smile came over his face, 'why, you are standing in the very office which was once owned by Mathias Rivoire, Notary, and which was sold years ago by his descendants.'

40. Charles Henry Hart, in the Massachusetts Historical Society Proceedings for December, 1903, thinks that this portrait of Washington referred to in Paul Revere's letter appeared in John McDougall and Company's *Weatherwise Town and Country Almanac* for 1781. This is the year Paul Revere wrote his cousin (judging by his reference to Yorktown). Mr. Hart points out that the ornamental border is similar to those Revere used in bookplates. It is cut in type-metal, is small and unskilful. It is surprising that Paul Revere could have done such a miserable likeness (and be so pleased with it), especially as he was able the very next year to do a really beautiful copper plate for Doctor John Warren. This is for a medical certificate for students attending Doctor Warren's classes in anatomy. It is framed with skeletons, and at the bottom is a doctor 'making an anatomy.' Like many people of sanguine temperament, Paul Revere seems to have had a healthy enjoyment of the morbid — he fairly revels in the ghoulish scene on his medical certificate.

41. The text below the picture of this shop of Ebenezer Larkin (nephew of Deacon John Larkin whose horse is so integral a part of the Revere legend) reads:

Ebenezar Larkin, Junr.
At his Book & Stationery Store
No 50 Cornhill
Boston
Keeps constantly for sale
A large & general assortment of
Books & Stationery

42. Samuel Eliot Morison's 'Maritime History of Massachusetts' is the classic in this field, and I am indebted to him throughout this book. The quotation from Emerson, for instance, was quoted first by him. He also quoted Timothy Dwight, of New Haven, who thought the Bostonians of the Federal period 'distinguished by a lively imagination ... their enterprises are sudden, bold and sometimes rash. A general spirit of adventure prevails here.' In my estimate of the temper of Boston during the War of 1812, I am also indebted to Mr. Morison's 'Life and Letters of Harrison Gray Otis.'

43. This advertisement from the *Columbian Centinel*, December 16, 1795, is an example of how delicately taxes were collected at this period around Boston (but not in the interior of the state).

'The Town Treasurer presents his most respectful compliments to those citizens who have tax-bills unpaid, and requests the favor of them to pay the same to the collectors immediately, as he has large drafts from the Selectmen and Overseers of the Poor in favor of mechanics, schoolmasters, and others, to whom, especially at the present season, money would be very acceptable.'

44. Doctor Nichols, 'Bells of Paul and Joseph Revere,' says Revere bells are usually marked 'Paul Revere,' 'Paul Revere & Son,' or 'Revere & Co.' Young Paul started out working with his father and half-brother, but in 1801 was making bells by himself. His are marked 'Revere' and rarely carry a date.

45. Robert Hitchbourn's life and education was quite a contrast to his younger brother, Benjamin's. He was a sailmaker and Paul Revere helped towards the education of his son, Henry, and bought the boy a pair of overalls. In 1799 he wrote the following sad and illiterate, yet vaguely poetic, letter to his 'brother,' Paul Revere, after his girls had been drowned between Cape Ann and Cape Cod. It was a tragedy that could have been duplicated in innumerable New England homes.

I received your very obliging letter which gave a degree of pleasure at this time it being a Time and Day of Trobel.

My dear friends the news whose so sudden and unexpected that my mind teuk ets flitz and never returned till it had ransacked the bottom of the Oshon from Cape Ann to Cape Cod and back down the Oshon Shor and over the face of the Great Waters after my dear daughters till it portadged my old body in such a manner that I was ardly abel to sleep about but live in hopes that the great Orther in dew time will now string the harp and cause me to partake of mercy as well as judgment that you and your dear friends and families may enjoy pece of mind is the wish of your friend and Brother

Robert Hichborn

P.S. My respects to all friends my mind whont admit of polliticke. Let me hear from you as soon as poshebel.

# X

46. Except for this delicate little copper plate, nothing is known about Horace Doolittle. In 1798, Amos Doolittle wrote a friend, 'however, I have a little son that has just begun the business in the copper plate way very well.' Presumably this was Horace, who hopefully marked 'My dog and gun,' 'I,' but does not seem to have lived to make another copper plate in his intended series.

47. The mysterious Mr. Reynolds may have been John Reynolds, a Boston man whose estate was settled in 1824. He had a pew in the Roman Catholic Church, two Bibles, twenty-six small chimney ornaments, and a silver medal (appraised at fifty cents).

In the Boston Directory he is described as a 'Labourer living at the rear of 27 Ann St.'

48. Joseph Dunkerly (he signed a letter to Revere as 'Dunckerly') is a little-known, much-admired miniaturist. During the few years he was in Boston he advertised twice in the papers, once as a miniature painter and once as running a drawing school (with John Hazlitt, brother of William Hazlitt, the essayist). Then (according to Wehle) he left Boston and drops completely from sight. Among the Revere papers, however, is a letter he wrote Paul in 1787. He is in Cape François, paying the stupendous price of forty dollars a month for 'convenient lodgings... but if business should answer I shall not care.' He asks Revere 'if you have as yet turned my effects into cash should be glad if you'll be so kind as to send me the bill of sale if any remains should be glad if you'll pay Mr Pons

$13.00. . . . Mrs Dunkerly joins with me in our warmest acknowledgements of your generous Friendship, & beg you'll present our tenderest respects to Mrs Revere & all your family.' 'The next vessel which sails for Boston Sophia intends to send Harriet a cask of Oranges & begs you'll shake a cloc for her. Mrs. D. expects a little stranger to Town any day.' What this 'cloc' Revere was to shake for his four-year-old daughter was, I do not know.

49. But this worry over the rising generation was nothing new in Boston, for back in 1722 Jeremiah Bumstead had noted in his diary: 'On ye 8 a fast at ye New Brick on ye acount of ye Rising Generation.' This was during the time Apollos was attending the New Brick Church with his master, John Coney.

50. Joseph Warren Revere died in 1868. Associated with him in the copper business was his son, John Revere, who next ran the business and who in turn had his son, Edward H. R. Revere, in partnership with him. In 1900, Paul Revere and Son merged with the Taunton Copper Manufacturing Company and the New Bedford Copper Company. In 1927, Mr. E. H. R. Revere became president of this company, which was known as the Taunton New Bedford Copper Company.

When in 1928 this company merged with the Baltimore Copper Mills, the Rome Brass and Copper Company, the Michigan Copper and Brass Company, and the Higgins Brass and Manufacturing Company and Dallas Brass and Copper Company (widely scattered over the country), they decided to carry on their work under the name of Revere Copper and Brass, Inc. Mr. E. H. R. Revere was and is on the board of directors.

Although Paul Revere had but one or two small buildings on the Neponset, Revere Copper has seven plants in different parts of the country. He probably never employed more than twenty men. His weekly pay-roll (which he carried out from Boston with him in his saddle-bags) ran around fifty dollars. Revere Copper's pay-roll is now toward fifteen million dollars per year and they employ ten thousand men. He struggled alone to find the 'secret' of making copper so malleable as to 'hammer hot.' Now there is a research staff of twelve experts discovering new alloys.

The Revere Copper Company, under its various names, has served this country in peace and war for around a hundred and fifty years. It is the largest and most famous of such industries in America.

In times of war one is most conscious of how basic is its service. Without Paul Revere's copper the warships of his later period could hardly have been built and today Revere copper alloys are used on all naval ships.

He cast a few cannon at his foundry, but now every bullet and cartridge made in this country require metals made by the Revere Copper and Brass Company, as do the shells and torpedoes. The company furnishes thousands of tons of metal for tanks, armored cars, trucks, airplanes, and field kitchens, as well as more domestic radios, telephones, plumbing, insulation, or washing machines.

Paul Revere probably never manufactured more than a few hundred tons of metal a year, in contrast to an average of six hundred tons a day made by the great company which he founded.

51. There is a profile portrait of Paul Revere, done when he was about sixty-five, by the Frenchman, Saint-Memin. 'His method in portraiture was unique' (says Dunlap). 'He first made a profile head, life size, in crayon on pink paper, then by a device of his own called a pantograph he made a mechanical reduction

of his drawing to the size he wished to engrave it. After the plate was engraved, the life size crayon was framed and delivered with the copper plate and twelve proofs for thirty-three dollars.' But Paul Revere seems to have paid one hundred and twenty dollars for his and to have sat to the 'Physiognotrace' while in Philadelphia in 1800.

52. Paul Revere, among his civic activities, served as coroner in 1796; in 1798 he started the Massachusetts Mutual Fire Insurance Company — the first successful organization of this type in Boston; in 1806 he was foreman of the jury which found Thomas O. Selfridge 'not guilty' of the murder of Charles Austin. He also served as health officer for Boston in 1799.

53. The honor of being 'The last of the Cocked hats' certainly belongs by tradition to Thomas Melville, who lived until September 16, 1832. Other candidates are Master 'Johnny' Tileston (died 1827), Joseph Foster, the goldsmith (in the 1830's). Benjamin Austin also wore the Revolutionary costume until his death. The last 'Byles girl' did not die until 1837. Although George Robert Twelves Hewes lived (he thought) to be one hundred, he did not wear the old costume. Having left Boston during the Revolution, he did not return until 1821. His anonymous biographer thus wrote of this visit:

'What emotions must have filled the old man's bosom, at the age of eighty years, on the vast variety of scenes around him, — most familiar and strange together; . . . what changes have taken place in Boston during the interval of his absence. The very hills were cut down, — the valleys and ponds filled up, — streets built over "made land," — the names altered of the few scattered relics which remained as they were of old. The shop he had worked in — nobody alive had heard of it. The house where he was born — not the ground it stood on even could be found. If he asked for *Griffin's Wharf* itself, it was but a sorry chance that one of a thousand of those he encountered in the streets could inform him of so much as where it had been. The city was a solitude — a vast solitude — a wilderness of men. . . . He stood in the market one morning in a crowd when an aged man slowly approached (perhaps Melville), looked at his face a few moments, as if dreaming, and then approached and studied his features again. It turned out to be a member of the Tea-Party; and they stepped aside and talked over old times by themselves for half an hour, and parted to meet no more!'

54. Most American heroes of the Revolutionary period are by now two men, the actual man and the romantic image. Some are even three men — the actual man, the image, and the de-bunked remains. For a very brilliant analysis of these fates see Dixon Wecter's 'Hero in America.' Paul Revere has not suffered so much from the de-bunkers (but see Stark's 'Loyalists in Massachusetts' for a good try. He is even represented in that book with a full beard and a leer). Although it has been rumored that he never took his ride and it is now well known that he engraved (but did not draw his pictures), about the worst that has been said of him is that he was really a 'middle-aged goldsmith on a stout plough horse' — which is not very bitter. His reputation divides into pre- and post-Longfellow periods. The 'Tales of the Wayside Inn' was published in 1863 — when the pressure of the Civil War had created a demand for popular heroes. The story of his gallant ride filled a need. How much was known about it before that time? The earliest biographical sketch I have found of him (except the obituary notices) is in the *New England Magazine* (1832) — fourteen years after his death. The unknown

author seems to have known him personally. Here is the first account of his running away to the West Street Church, Doctor Church adding the poem to the 'Recinders' caricature, etc. He speaks of him as a 'messanger' and quotes almost completely his own account of the nineteenth of April as it had already been published by the Massachusetts Historical Society. Twenty years later, 'The Massachusetts Charitable Mechanics Association' published their 'Annals.' Its frontispiece is a steel engraving of Revere and he has by far the longest of the biographies. He is accepted as the outstanding mechanic of his day and place, and 'he was several times sent by the Provincial Congress to the Continental Congress on confidential business.' For his most famous ride the reader is referred to the Massachusetts Historical Society Proceedings. In 1855, May Street was renamed Revere in his honor. He was not forgotten in Boston, although already dead for over thirty years.

But in Snow's 'History of Boston' (1825) he is not mentioned. In S. G. Drake's 'History and Antiquities of Boston' (1856) he is mentioned many times — but not his ride. Yet it had already caught the popular imagination. In the text I have quoted the first known attempt to put this ride into romantic form, by 'Eb. Stiles,' written in 1795. In 1835, Joseph Warren's sister wrote a child's life of General Warren. It is a dialogue between a mother, 'Mrs. M.,' and her two children, whose well-timed questions help Mama tell her story. Mrs. M. says, 'Col Revere was one of his messangers. I think he was sent to Lexington'; and she describes his escape from the British officers on Charlestown Neck. 'I think he was a brave man, do not you, Mama?' says the priggish little William. 'I fear I should have turned back when I saw the soldiers coming.'

'Mrs. M.: "He certainly was a very brave man." '

The same year that the 'Mechanics' published their factual account of his life, the town of Acton completed their battle monument and the Reverend John Pierpont delivered a six-page poem. This ran in part,

> '... The foremost Paul Revere
> At Warrens bidding, has the gauntlet run,
> Unscathed, and dashing into Lexington,
> While midnight wraps him in her mantle dark
> Halts at the house of Reverent Mr. Clark.'

It would seem that Paul Revere's ride had already taken a legendary form — a poem in search of a poet. If Longfellow had followed Revere's own account (already published at least twice), it is unlikely he would have made the mistake of placing Revere on the wrong side of the Charles and bringing him all the way to Concord, although this was a mistake already made by 'Eb. Stiles.' He may have vaguely known all his life something of this story, for it was already being simplified and put into romantic form. His diary for 1860 suggests (at least) that he got it from a mysterious 'Mr. H.': 'April 5, Go with Sumner to Mr H. of the North End who acts as guide,' showing the sights of the North End — Copp's Hill, etc., and then 'Old North.' 'We climb the tower to the chime of bells, now the home of innumerable pigeons. From this tower [as the 'guide' probably told him] were hung the lanterns as a signal that the British troops had left Boston for Concord.' 'Mr H.' probably also told him how Revere waited 'on the opposite side.' 'April 6.... Paul Revere's ride begun on this day.' (Nor had he done much research.) 'April 19. I wrote a few lines in "Paul Revere's Ride," this being the day of his achievement.'

Dixon Wecter, in commenting on the sudden burst of Paul Revere's fame, says: 'Silver made by Revere grew rapidly in value, until a good piece fetched $5,000; it was rumored that the late J. P. Morgan offered Mrs. Marston Perry $100,000 for Revere's famous "Sons of Liberty" punch bowl. His engravings and caricatures were cherished. The folk mind, upon learning that Paul Revere made false teeth and that George Washington wore false teeth, invented the well-known statement that Revere made a set of dentures for the master of Mt. Vernon.'

On the hundredth anniversary of the Battle of Lexington, lanterns were hung in the steeple of Christ's Church. Paul Revere's fame had, in twelve years, swept the country. Samuel H. Newman, the son of Robert Newman, 'walked out of the vestry with his lighted lanterns, and down the crowded aisle, and up into the tower . . . the excited people made the house rock with their response as if the cannons of Concord and Lexington were even then rending the air.'

But Longfellow, so responsible for the excitement, wrote of that day: 'Bad day for me; neuralgia raging. In the evening my girls drive over to Prospect Hill to see the lighting of Paul Revere's lanterns in the belfry of Old North Church.'

# GENEALOGICAL DATA

Paul Revere
>Baptized January 1, 1735.
>Married (1) August 4, 1757, Sara Orne.
>>(2) September 23, 1773, Rachel Walker.
>Died May 10, 1818.

Sara Orne
>Born in Boston April 2, 1736.   (Family Bible.)
>Married August 4, 1757, Paul Revere.
>Died May 3, 1773.

The above dates are all we know definitely about Sara Orne. There was at the time of her birth and for some years afterward only one Orne family in Boston. The marriage of John Orne and Martha Lackey is recorded in the files of Christ's Church and also in the vital statistics of Boston.

Their children were baptized in the First Church as follows:

Elizabeth, daughter of John and Martha, bapt. October 25, 1730.
John, son of            "     "     "     "   December 10, 1732.
James, son of           "     "     "     "     April 21, 1736.
Martha, daughter of     "     "     "   dec'd November 7, 1736.

There the record ends. Sara may have been a twin with Martha or Martha may have been a child born earlier.

The father of these children, John Orne, was a son of John and Elizabeth (Williams) Orne, born February 16, 1709. His father, John, a cordwainer, died at the time of the terrible smallpox epidemic in Boston. He is buried in the Granary with two little daughters who died at the same time. His wife, Elizabeth, was a woman of property and social standing. She was sister of Jonathan Williams, an important man in the Boston of his day. They were the children of Robert Williams, a founder of Roxbury. A third

John was the father of this second John, a cordwainer of Salem,
who moved to Boston. He married Mary Clark of Westfield. He
was a son of the original John Horne.    Another son of John Horne
was Joseph, who was a great-grandfather of the Lois Orne of
Salem who married Doctor William Paine of Worcester in 1773.
Sara's probable father would have been a second cousin of the
father of Lois Orne. The Boston Ornes seemed to keep in touch
with their cousins in Salem. When Doctor Paine wished to make a
very extraordinary and beautiful bridal gift to his fiancée he gave
an order to Paul Revere for many pieces of silver to be marked
'L.O.' for Lois Paine, several of which bore the Orne arms. The
bill for these pieces of silver was one hundred and eight pounds.
A large proportion of them is owned by the Worcester Art Museum.

Children of Sara Orne Revere:

(1) Deborah  Born April 8, 1758.
             Married January 14, 1781, Amos Lincoln.
             Died January 8, 1797.

(2) Paul     Born January 6, 1760.
             Married July 25, 1782, Sally Edwards.
             Died January 16, 1813.

(3) Sara     Born January 3, 1763.
             Married March 20, 1778, John Bradford.
             Died July 5, 1791.

(4) Mary     Born March 31, 1764.
             Died April 20, 1768.

(5) Frances  Born February 19, 1766.
             Married May 27, 1788, Thomas Stevens Eayres.
             Died June 9, 1799.

(6) Mary     Born March 19, 1768.
             Married June 15, 1797, Jedediah Lincoln.
             Died August 12, 1853.

(7) Elizabeth Born December 5, 1770.
             Married May 24, 1797, Amos Lincoln.
             Died April 10, 1805.

(8) Isanna   Born December 15, 1772.
             Died September 19, 1773.

Rachel (Walker) Revere
   Daughter of Richard and Rachel (Carlile) Walker.
   Born in Boston December 29, 1745 (Family Record).
   Married September 23, 1773, Paul Revere.
   Died June 26, 1813.

Her parents:

Richard Walker. It has not been possible to trace this Richard Walker. Richard was a favorite name among the Walkers and there were several in Boston who might have been the husband of Rachel Carlile. We only know that he died December 28, 1777.

Rachel Carlile was the daughter of John and Hannah (Moore) Carlile.

> Born March 25, 1705.
> Died May 18, 1782.

Her grandparents:

John Carlile. Without doubt of the Carlile family of York, Maine. Married Hannah Moore.

Hannah Moore, the daughter of Captain Thomas Moore and his wife Sarah.

> Born in Boston April 26, 1662.
> Married John Carlile.
> Died before July 1, 1740.

Her mother, Sarah Moore, died November, 1712, aged eighty years. She was buried in King's Chapel Yard.

Children of Rachel (Walker) Revere:

| | | |
|---|---|---|
| (1) Joshua | Born December 7, 1774. | |
| | Died August, 1801. | |
| (2) John | Born June 10, 1776. | |
| | Died June 27, 1776. | |
| (3) Joseph Warren | Born April 30, 1777. | |
| | Married April 16, 1821, Mary Robbins. | |
| | Died October 12, 1868. | |
| (4) Lucy | Born May 15, 1780. | |
| | Died July 9, 1780. | |
| (5) Harriet | Born July 21, 1783. | |
| | Died June 27, 1860. | |
| (6) John | Born December 25, 1784. | |
| | Died March 13, 1786. | |
| (7) Maria | Born July 14, 1785. | |
| | Married May 8, 1814, Joseph Balastier. | |
| | Died at Singapore August 22, 1847. | |
| (8) John | Born March 27, 1787. | |
| | Married Lydia LeBaron Goodwin. | |
| | Died April 30, 1847. | |

Paul Revere's brothers and sisters:

Deborah Baptized February 22, 1731/2.
         Married February 22, 1759, Thomas Metcalf.
Frances  Baptized July 18, 1736.
         Married June 7, 1759, Edward Calleteau.
John     Baptized August 27, 1738.
         Died young.
Thomas   Baptized January 13, 1739/40.
         Married Mary (perhaps Churchill).
         Estate settled in 1818.
John     Baptized October 11, 1741.
         Married June 26, 1764, Anna Clemens.
         Died August, 1775 (John Boyle).
Mary     Baptized July 17, 1743.
         Married (1) March 21, 1765, Edward Rosé.
                 (2) March 6, 1791, Alexander Baker.
         Died December 27, 1801.  Buried at Copp's Hill.
Elizabeth twin with Mary.
         Baptized July 18, 1743.
Elizabeth Baptized January 20, 1744/5.
         Married David Moseley.

His parents:

Apollos Rivoire, afterward called Paul Revere.
    Born November 30, 1702.
    Married June 19, 1729, Deborah Hitchbourn.
    Died in Boston July 22, 1754.
Deborah Hitchbourn
    Born January 25, 1703/4.
    Died May 23, 1777.

His uncles and aunts:

Thomas Hitchbourn
    Born June 30, 1703.
    Married January 4, 1734, Isannah Fadrée.
    Died June 16, 1777.  Buried in the Granary.
Nathaniel Hitchbourn
    Born October 28, 1709.
    Probably died young.
Richard Hitchbourn
    Born March 10, 1710/11.
    Probably died young.

Mary
  Born November 30, 1713.
  Married August 12, 1736, Captain Philip Marrett.
  Died September 25, 1778.
Frances
  Born May 16, 1706.
  Married (1) April 6, 1727, John Montgomery.
           (2) April 16, 1731, Joseph Douglass.

His grandparents:

Isaac Rivoire, of Riaucaud, France.
  Married, in 1694, Serenne Lambert.
Thomas Hitchbourn, joiner.
  Born in Boston March 2, 1676.
  Married Frances Pattishall April 1, 1703.
  Died November 6, 1731, aet. 56. Is buried in the Granary.
Thomas Hitchbourn was probably a son of Thomas Hitchbourn and
  his wife Ruth. It was this older Thomas who beat his drum
  through the streets of Boston with a Challenger carrying a naked
  sword.
A still older generation was Davy and his wife Ruth — Davy who
  was sentenced in 1641 to wear an iron collar 'till the Court please
  and serve his master.'
Frances Pattishall
  Born in Boston in 1676.
  Died September 14, 1749, aged 73. Buried in the Granary.

His great-grandparents with a few older generations:

Jean Rivoire, of Riaucaud, France.
His wife, Magdalena Malapongue.
Richard Pattishall, of Boston, New York and Maine.
  He was the son of Edmund Pattishall of St. Mary Strand and his
  wife, Martha Denham. They were married in England about
  1634. Richard, their oldest son, was baptized May 26, 1636.
  He came to this country with his father and one or more brothers
  and sisters. His first wife was Abigail. The second, from whom
  Paul Revere was descended, was Martha Woody.
Captain Pattishall was killed by the Indians on board his sloop at
  Pemaquid, in 1689.
Martha Woody, the daughter of Captain Richard Woody and his
  wife, Frances Dexter, was born the 25th day of the 11th month,
  1651. She died April 21, 1718. She and her sister both seem to

have been good friends of the Sewalls. The Judge attended her
funeral with purple gloves and a mourning scarf, supplied by her
family. She was buried in the King's Chapel Burying Ground.

Richard Woody was an important citizen of Roxbury. In 1678 he
was ensign to Captain John Hull, who was lieutenant. He was
son of an older Richard Woody and his wife, Ann. He was born
about 1615. Married December 29, 1646, to Frances Dexter, a
daughter of the famous Thomas Dexter of Lynn and other places.

In 1673 the whole Woody family were dismissed to the Third Church
in Boston. They lived near Fort Hill in the south part of Boston.
Later they deeded this home to Richard Pattishall. Frances
seems to have had two brothers, but only one sister, Mary, who
married Captain James Oliver, and so it came about that Thomas
Dexter, her father, was buried in the Oliver tomb in the King's
Chapel Yard.

April, 1681, Sewall writes, 'Goodwife Everitt, Winthrop and Capt.
Richard Woode dye suddenly.'

Frances Dexter was born in England.

# BIBLIOGRAPHY

## *Manuscripts*

Account Book of Dr. John Clarke of Boston and later of his son Dr. William. 1732–1768. Massachusetts Historical Society.

Christ-Church Records. Deposited in the Athenaeum.

Crocker, Hannah Mather. Reminiscences. Owned by N. E. Hist. Geneal. Society.

Dolbear Papers. Owned by Mass. Hist. Society.

First Church Records. In City Registry, Boston.

Greenough Papers. Owned by Mass. Hist. Society.

Hancock Papers. Copies made by Henry A. Phillips. Owned by Amer. Antiq. Society.

Isaiah Thomas Papers. Owned by the Amer. Antiq. Society.

King's Chapel Records. In City Registry, Boston.

Massachusetts State Archives. State House.

Papers of the Supreme Judicial Court. Boston Court House.

Registry of Deeds and Probate Court of Suffolk County. Boston Court House.

Revere Manuscripts. 16 vols. Owned by the Mass. Hist. Society.

Salisbury Letters. Owned by Amer. Antiq. Society.

Second Church Records. In City Registry, Boston.

Story of the Battle of Lexington and Concord. Poem by Eb. Stiles. Owned by Mass. Hist. Society.

## *Newspapers of the Period*

Boston, Columbian Centinel.

Boston Evening Post.

Boston Gazette.

Boston Independent Chronicle.

Boston and Worcester Massachusetts Spy.

Boston News Letter.

Boston Weekly Post-Boy.

## *Periodicals and Magazines*

Adams, Randolph G. New Light on the Boston Massacre. In Amer. Antiq. Society Proc., 1937, vol. 47, pp. 259–354.

Andrews, John. Letters 1772–1776. In Mass. Hist. Soc. Proc., vol. 8, pp. 316–412.

Belknap, Jeremy. Diaries in Mass. Hist. Soc. Proc., vol. 1, p. 85; vol. 3, pp. 295–311; vol. 19, pp. 393–423.

Boyle, John. Journal of Occurrences in Boston, 1759–1778. In N. E. Hist. Geneal. Register, vol. 84, pp. 142, 248, 357; vol. 85, pp. 5, 117.

Bumstead, Jeremiah. Diary, 1722–27. In N. E. Hist. Geneal. Register, vol. 15, pp. 193–204, 305–315.

Cooper, Samuel. Diary, 1775–1776. In Amer. Hist. Review, vol. 6, pp. 301–341.

Early American Artists and Mechanics — Paul Revere. In New England Magazine, 1832, vol. 3, pp. 305–314.

Goodell, Abner C. Execution of Mark and Phillis. In Mass. Hist. Soc. Proc., vol. 20, pp. 122–157.

Graham, Rev. John. Diary, 1756. In Magazine of American History, 1882, vol. 8, p. 206.

Hart, Charles H. Paul Revere's Portrait of Washington. In Mass. Hist. Soc. Proc., ser. 2, vol. 18, pp. 83–85.

Lee, Henry. Account of visit to North End about 1830. In Mass. Hist. Soc. Proc., vol. 18, pp. 344–351.

Matthews, Albert, Joyce, Junior. In Publications of Colonial Society of Mass., vol. 8, pp. 90–104.

New Brick Church. Boston Records, 1722–1775. In N. E. Hist. Geneal. Register, vol. 18, pp. 237, 337.

Price, Ezekiel. Diary of, 1775–1776, in Mass. Hist. Soc. Proc., Nov. 1863; 1777–1778, in N. E. Hist. Geneal. Register, Oct. 1865.

Royal American Magazine. Boston, 1774–1775.

Schuller, Dr. Rudolf, translated from Spanish. Francisco de Miranda. In Old-Time New England, vol. 26, pp. 3, 41.

Smith, Ballard. Gunpowder for Bunker Hill. In Harper's Magazine, vol. 73, 1886, pp. 236–243.

Smith, Fitz-Henry, Jr. French at Boston during the Revolution. In Bostonian Society Publications, vol. 10, pp. 9–75.

Sons of Liberty of Boston, List of. In Mass. Hist. Soc. Proc., ser. 2, vol. 12, pp. 139–142.

Sumner, W. H. Memoir of Gov. Increase Sumner. In N. E. Hist. Geneal. Register, vol. 8, pp. 105–128.

Tarring and Feathering in New England, 1770. In Old-Time New England, vol. 20, pp. 30–43.

Watson, John Lee. Revere's Signal. In Mass. Hist. Soc. Proc., 1876, vol. 15, pp. 164–177.

### Books

Adams, John. Works of John Adams. 10 vols. Boston, 1856.

Adams, John and Abigail. Familiar Letters of John Adams and his Wife, Abigail Adams during Revolution. New York, 1876.

Anburey, Thomas. Travels Through Interior Parts of America. 2 vols. Boston and New York, 1923.

Andrews, William Loring. Paul Revere and his Engravings. New York, 1901.

Avery, Clara Louise. Early American Silver. New York, 1930.

Bacon, Capt. William. Journal of our March from Dedham to Albany. (Printed in Dedication of Monument to Memory of Men of Walpole, 1901.)

Barker, John. British in Boston, being diary of Lieut. John Barker. Cambridge, 1924.

Baxter, James Phinney, ed. Documentary History of the State of Maine, 2d series, vol. 17. Portland, 1913.

Belcher, Henry. First American Civil War. London, 1911.

Belknap, Jeremy. Belknap Papers. Mass. Hist. Soc. Coll., 5th series, vols. 1–2. Boston, 1877.

Benson, Adolph B., ed. Peter Kalm's Travels in North America. 2 vols. New York, 1937.

Bentley, William. Diary. 4 vols. Salem, 1905–14.

Bigelow, Francis H. Historic Silver of Colonies and its Makers. New York, 1917.

Bishop, James L. History of American Manufactures. 2 vols. Philadelphia, 1864.

Boardman, Samuel L. Peter Edes, biography. Bangor, 1901.

Bolton, Charles K. Founders. Portraits of persons born abroad who came to Colonies before 1701. 3 vols. 1919–26.

Boston Directories, 1789–1840.

Boston, Museum of Fine Arts. American Church Silver of 17th and 18th Centuries. Boston, 1911.

Boston, Record Commercial Reports. Boston, 1876–1909.

Bradley, Arthur G. Colonial Americans in Exile. New York [1932].

Breck, Samuel. Recollections of. London, 1877.

Bridgman, Thomas. Memorials of the Dead in Boston. Copp's Hill Burying Ground. Boston, 1852.

Bridgman, Thomas. Memorials of the Dead in Boston. (King's Chapel Burying Ground.) Boston, 1853.

Bridgman, Thomas. Epitaphs from Copp's Hill Burying Ground. Boston, 1851.

Buckingham, Joseph T. Address delivered before Massachusetts Charitable Mechanic Association. Boston, 1830.

Chamberlain, Allen. Beacon Hill. Boston and New York, 1925.

Chandler, Peleg W. American Criminal Trials. 2 vols. Boston, London, 1841–44.

Chapin, Henry. Address, Unitarian Church, Uxbridge, Mass., 1864. Worcester, 1881.

Checkley, Samuel. Diary, 1735. Reprint, pub. in Colonial Society of Mass., vol. 12. Cambridge, 1909.

Chinard, Gilbert. Honest John Adams. Boston, 1933.

Clark, Jonas. Fate of Blood-thirsty Oppressors. Boston, 1776.

Clark, Victor S. History of Manufactures in U. S. Washington, 1916.

Clarke, Hermann F. John Coney, Silversmith. Boston and New York, 1932.

Copley, John S., and Henry Pelham. Letters and Papers. Mass. Hist. Soc. Coll., vol. 71, 1914.

Curwen, Samuel. Journal and Letters of Late Samuel Curwen. New York and Boston, 1842.

Dankers, Jasper. Journal of a Voyage to New York, 1679–1680. In L. I. Hist. Soc., vol. 1, 1867.

De Berniere, Henry. General Gage's Instructions, etc. Boston, 1779.

Dexter, Mrs. Elisabeth W. Colonial Women of Affairs. Boston and New York, 1924.

Dow, George Francis. Arts and Crafts in New England. Topsfield, 1927.

Dow, George Francis. Every Day Life in Massachusetts Bay Colony. Boston, 1935.

Drake, Samuel A. Historic Fields and Mansions of Middlesex. Boston, 1874.

Drake, Samuel A., ed. History of Middlesex County Mass. Boston, 1880.

Drake, Samuel A. Old Boston Taverns and Tavern Clubs. Boston, 1917.

Drake, Samuel A. Old Landmarks and Historic Personages of Boston. Boston, 1873.

Drake, Samuel G. History and Antiquities of Boston. Boston, 1856.

Dresser, Louisa. Seventeenth Century Painting in New England. Worcester, 1935.

Dunlap, William. History of Rise and Progress of Arts of Design in U. S. 3 vols. Boston, 1918.

Earle, Mrs. Alice Morse. Customs and Fashions in Old New England. New York, 1893.

Eaton, Arthur W. H. Famous Mather Byles. Boston, 1914.

Flagg, Josiah Foster. Family Dentist. Boston, 1822.

Forbes, Mrs. Harriette Merrifield. New England Diaries. [Topsfield] 1923.

Ford, Worthington C. Broadsides, Ballads, etc. printed in Massachusetts, 1639–1800. (Mass. Hist. Soc. Coll., vol. 75. Boston, 1922.)

Franklin, Benjamin. Autobiography, 1915.

French, Allen. General Gage's Informers. Ann Arbor, 1932.

French, Allen. Day of Concord and Lexington. Boston, 1925.

French, Hollis. List of Early American Silversmiths and their Marks. (Walpole Society.) New York, 1917.

Frothingham, Richard. Life and Times of Joseph Warren. Boston, 1865.

Frothingham, Richard. History of Siege of Boston, and Battles of Lexington, Concord and Bunker Hill. Boston, 1849.

Gettemy, Charles F. True Story of Paul Revere. Boston, 1905.

Goss, Elbridge H. Life of Colonel Paul Revere. 2 vols. Boston, 1891.

Gravestone Inscriptions in the Granary Burying Ground, Boston. Salem, 1918.

Greenwood, Isaac J. Greenwood Family. [Concord] 1934.

Haggard, Howard W. Devils, Drugs, and Doctors. New York and London, 1929.

Hart, Albert Bushnell, ed. Commonwealth History of Massachusetts. 5 vols. New York, 1927–1930.

Hazen, Edward. Panorama of Professions and Trades. Philadelphia, 1836.

Howe, John. Journal Kept by John Howe, as a British Spy. Concord, N.H., 1827.

Holland, Henry W. William Dawes and his Ride with Paul Revere. Boston, 1878.

Hosmer, James K. Life of Thomas Hutchinson. Boston and New York, 1896.

Hulton, Ann. Letters of a Loyalist Lady. Cambridge, 1927.

Huntoon, Daniel T. V. History of Town of Canton. Cambridge, 1893.

Hutchinson, Thomas. Diary and Letters of. 2 vols. London, 1883–1886.

Hutchinson, Thomas. History of the Colony of Massachusetts Bay. 3 vols. Boston, 1764–1828.

Jenkins, Stephen. Old Boston Post Road. New York and London, 1913.

Jones, E. Alfred. Loyalists of Massachusetts. London, 1930.

Keir, Malcolm. Epic of Industry. New Haven, 1926.

Knight, Mrs. Sarah Kemble. Journal of Madam Knight. Boston, 1920.

Late News of the Excursion and Ravages of the King's Troops on the Nineteenth of April 1775 ... Narratives by Lt. William Sutherland and Richard Pope (Club of Odd Volumes). Cambridge, 1927.

Lewis, Alonzo, and James R. Newhall. History of Lynn, Mass. Boston, 1865.

Loring, James S. Hundred Boston Orators. Boston, 1852.

Lossing, Benson J. Pictorial Field-Book of Revolution. 2 vols. New York, 1851.

Lufkin, Arthur W. History of Dentistry. Philadelphia, 1938.

Mackenzie, Frederick. British Fusilier in Revolutionary Boston. Ed., Allen French. Cambridge, 1926.

Mann, Herman. Female Review: or Memoirs of an American Young Lady [Deborah Sampson]. Dedham, 1722–1833.

Marble, Mrs. Annie Russell. From 'Prentice to Patron. New York and London, 1935.

Massachusetts Soldiers and Sailors of the Revolutionary War. 17 vols. Boston, 1896–1908.

Miller, John C. Sam Adams. Boston, 1936.

Morison, Samuel Eliot. Builders of Bay Colony. Cambridge, 1930.

Morison, Samuel Eliot. Life and Letters of Harrison Gray Otis. Boston and New York, 1913.

Morison, Samuel Eliot. Maritime History of Massachusetts. Boston and New York, 1921.

Murdock, Harold. Nineteenth of April, 1775. Boston, 1923.

Murray, James. Impartial History of the War in America. 2 vols. Boston, 1781, 1782.

Nichols, Arthur H. Bells of Paul and Joseph Revere. Boston, 1911. (Hist. Coll. Essex Inst. Jan., 1912.)

Palfrey, John G. History of New England. 5 vols. Boston, 1858–1890.

Parker, Mrs. Barbara N. John Singleton Copley. Biographical Sketches by Anne Bolling Wheeler. Boston, 1938.

Parkman, Francis. Montcalm and Wolfe. 2 vols. Boston, 1884.

Parrington, Vernon L. The Colonial Mind, 1620–1800. New York [1927].

Phillips, James Duncan. Salem in the Eighteenth Century. Boston and New York, 1937.

Place, Charles A. Charles Bulfinch Architect and Citizen. Cambridge, 1925.

Porter, Edward G. Rambles in Old Boston. Boston, 1887.

Quincy, Josiah. Memoir of Josiah Quincy, Junior. Boston, 1875.

Riedesel, Friederike Charlotte Luise. Letters and Memoirs. New York, 1827.

Robbins, Chandler. History of the Second Church in Boston. Boston, 1852.

Roberts, Oliver A. History of Ancient and Honorable Artillery Company. 4 vols. Boston, 1895–1901.

Rowe, John. Letters and Diary of. Boston, 1903.

Sabine, Lorenzo. American Loyalists. Boston, 1847.

Sargent, Lucius Manlius. Dealings with the Dead. Boston, 1856.

Schlesinger, Arthur M. Colonial Merchants and American Revolution. New York, 1918.

Sewall, Samuel. Diary of, 1674–1729. (In Mass. Hist. Soc. Collections, ser. 3, vols. 5–7, 1878–1882.)

Short Narrative of the Horrid Massacre in Boston. Boston, 1770.

Small, Isaac M. Shipwrecks on Cape Cod. North Truro, 1925.

Stark, James H. Loyalists of Massachusetts. Boston, 1910.

Stauffer, David M. American Engravers upon Copper and Steel. 2 vols. New York, 1907.

Stiles, Ezra. Literary Diary of. 3 vols. New York, 1901.

Taylor, Emerson G. Paul Revere. New York, 1930.

Thacher, James. American Medical Biography. Boston, 1828.

Thatcher, Benjamin B. Traits of the Tea Party, being a memoir of George R. T. Hewes. New York, 1835.

Thwing, Annie Haven. Crooked and Narrow Streets of Town of Boston. Boston, 1920.

Tudor, William, ed. John Tudor Diary. Boston, 1896.

Tudor, William. Life of James Otis. Boston, 1823.

Tupper, Frederick, and Helen T. Brown. Grandmother Tyler's Book. New York, 1925.

Van Tyne, Claude H. Causes of War of Independence. Boston and New York, 1922.

Watson, John L. Paul Revere's Signal. Cambridge, 1877.

Wecter, Dixon. Hero in America. New York, 1941.

Weeden, William B. Economic and Social History of New England. Boston and New York, 1890.

Wehle, Harry B. American Miniatures, 1730–1850. Garden City, 1927.

Wells, William V. Life and Public Services of Samuel Adams. Boston, 1886.

Wheildon, William W. History of Paul Revere's Signal Lanterns. Boston, 1878.

Wilson, Daniel M. Three Hundred Years of Quincy. Boston, 1926.

Winslow, Anna Green. Diary of. Boston and New York, 1894.

Winslow, Ola E. American Broadside Verse. New Haven, 1930.

Winsor, Justin. Memorial History of Boston. 4 vols. Boston, 1880–1881.

Winsor, Justin. Narrative and Critical History of America. 8 vols. Boston and New York, 1884–1889.

Wood, William, and Ralph H. Gabriel. The Winning of Freedom (Pageant of America, vol. 6). New Haven, 1927.

Wyman, Thomas Bellows. Genealogies and Estates of Charlestown, Mass. 2 vols. Boston, 1879.

Yale University, Gallery of Fine Arts. Masterpieces of New England Silver. Cambridge, 1939.

# INDEX

Adams, Abigail, quotation from letter to John, 281; quoted on Church trial, 296; quoted on Boston fortifications, 319; letter on Joyce Jr., 327; on Continental Army, 355

Adams, 'merchant,' 172

Adams, John, 23; quoted, 24; personal characteristics, 56, 86–87; on James Otis, 64, 66; inoculated by Joseph Warren, 78; quoted on John Hancock, 84; in caucus, 119; dislike of Otis, 123; counsel for Hancock on *Liberty* case, 137–138; quoted on baiting the British soldiers, 152, 156; on the night of the Boston Massacre, 158; defense of British regulars, 165–166, 178; elected to General Court, 178; receipt for a patriot, 187; liked his horse, 195; ride to Philadelphia, 206; impressions of New York and Philadelphia, 207; foresaw reprisal for Tea Party, 208; faith in Revere, 216; at first Continental Congress, 227; at second Continental Congress, 288; praises Thomas Crafts, 318; despair before Burgoyne surrender, 336; nominated George Washington, Commander-in-chief, 337; mentioned, 413; at home in Quincy, 431; on Thomas Hutchinson, 431

Adams, John Quincy, 423

Adams, Deacon Samuel, 25, 85, 119

Adams, Samuel, at Harvard, 23, 25–26; frees wife's slave, 37; mentioned, 56, 73; summary of career of, 85–86; enlists support of John Hancock, 87, 88, 89; connection with Pope's Day mobs, 96, 97; learns control of mob actions, 107–108; portrait by Copley, 113; member of caucuses, 119; leader of Long Room Club, 122; complaints against British regulars, 142; strategy in promoting Boston Massacre, 152; got British troops removed to Castle Island, 163; makes political capital of Massacre, 166–167; suspected after Boston Massacre, 168; almost lost Whig Party, 187, 188; wouldn't ride a horse, 195; organizes public against tea, 195, 196, 197, 198;

ride to Philadelphia, 206; sees the political capital in Boston Tea Party, 208; arrest demanded, 225; at first Continental Congress, 227; moderator at Boston Massacre commemoration, 75, 239–240; Gage decides to arrest, 244; in Lexington, 247; warned by Revere, 261; comment on battle of Lexington, 269; help to Revere on powder manufacturing, 303–304; at Second Continental Congress, 337; disappointed with result of Revolution, 366–367; de Miranda's comment on, 368; hatred of British commerce, 367, 370, 371, 372; harshness in Shays' Rebellion, 381; votes to ratify Constitution, 383; lays State House corner stone, 398; approves of French Revolution, 421; grave of, 453; huge dog belonging to, 469; interpretations of, 471

Adams, Mrs. Sam, on Tories in Boston, 225

Admiralty courts, 63, 137–138

Albany, 45

*Albatross*, 394

Alexander, Giles, 212

Algerian pirates, 392–393

Allen, Colonel Ethan, 289

American Revolution. *See* Revolution, American

Amherst, Lord Jeffrey, 59, 141

Amory, Thomas, 316

Anburey, Lieut. Thomas, 335

Andrews, Benjamin, 347–348

Andros, Sir Edmund, 14, 98

Anne Street, 8, 49, 385, 456, 470

Ansart, Lewis, 321, 344, 386

Apprentices, 8–10, 11, 28, 396

Arms, owned by Boston citizens, 140; turned in to Gage, 281

Army, in French and Indian wars, 43–44; diseases in camps, 46. *See also* Continental Army, British Army

Arnold, Benedict, 323

Artisans, working conditions of, 117; check on mobs, 103, 107; dependent on commerce, 384; association of, 395–398

Atheists, 120, 121

Atkins, Captain, 172–173, 307

Atlantic Avenue, 49

Breed's Hill. *See* Bunker Hill
Brickley, Nat., 316
Brigham, Clarence S., 134
Brimmer, Martin, 126
British Army in America, arrival of, 138, 139, 140; characteristics of the men, 141–143, 144; effect on Boston business, 144; Revere engraving of the landing of, 144–145; social position in Boston, 145–146; tar-and-feathering in spite of presence of, 209; to enforce the Boston Port Bill, 221–222; winter quarters, 229; pass regulations, 231; desertions from, 233–234; no taking of hostages, 276, 281, 294; takes New York and Newport, 323; at Castine, Me., 353
Brown, John, Jr., 32
Brown, Solomon, 475
Bruce, Stephen. 200
Brush, Crean, 312, 316
Buckman Tavern, 260
Bulfinch, Charles, 398, 423
Bulfinch, Mrs., 368
Bumstead, Jeremiah, 481
'Bunch of Grapes,' 143
Bunker Hill, battle of, 290–293
Burgoyne, Gen. John, 241, 314, 333; surrender of, 336
Burr, Aaron, 275, 455
Burt, Benjamin, 121, 171, 331, 398
Bute, Lord John Stuart, 101
Butts, Sam, 68
'Byles Girls,' 306, 311, 330, 444–445, 482
Byles, Rev. Mather, Tory, 116, 305–306, 311, 326; puns, 329–330; death of, 462–463

Cabot family, 361
Caldwell, James, 156, 159, 452
Calef, Dr. John, 135, 355
Calleteau, Edward, 488
Campbell, William, 119, 121
Candy, Foster, 200
Cannon, shortage of, 320
Canton, China, 379, 382
Canton, Mass., 424, 429
'Canton Dale,' 429
Card-playing, 423
Carlile, Hannah (Moore), 487
Carlile, John, 487
Carnes, Capt. Thomas Jenness, 359
Carr, Col., 141
Carr, Patrick, 156, 166. 452
Cary, Nathaniel, 316, 327, 328
Castine, Maine, 353, 355
Castle,' 'The, 18
Castle Island, 3, 49, 103, 136, 236, 308, 345, 346–347
Catholic Church in New England, 5, 340, 413, 440
Caucuses, Whig, 119–125
Chamberlain, Mellen, 472
Chandler, Lucretia, 71, 310, 331

Chaperonage, 378
Charles Street, 454
Charlestown, 258, 290
Charter Street, 49, 393, 416, 417
Chase, Thomas, 237
Chatham, William Pitt, Earl of, 225
Checkley, Rev. Samuel, diary of, 471
*Chesapeake*, 439
Cheverus, John, 440–441
China trade, 379–380, 382
Christmas, 31
Christ's Church, 31, 32, 248, 387, 391, 457, 474
Church, Capt. Benjamin, 111
Church, Dr. Benjamin, mentioned, 78, 111; member Whig Party, 97, 120, 124; described as Son of Liberty, 126; verse by, 135; double dealing of, 135; at Boston Massacre, 158; traitor to Revolution, 235, 295–297; after Battle of Lexington, 275; goes to Boston ostensibly for Committee, 278, 279; signs permit for Lady Frankland, 282; exchanged, 316; Revere's memories of, 447, 449
Church, importance of, in colonial Boston, 12–13
Church bells, 50
Churches, New North, 8, 13; 'New Brick' ('Revenge'), 13; *See also* Christ's, Cockerel, King's Chapel, Old North, Old South
Clark, Dr. John, 29–30, 36, 78, 469
Clark, John, Revere's London agent, 371
Clark, Rev. Jonas, 246, 260, 448
Clark, William, 23
Clark house, 23–24, 30, 173, 246, 256–257, 260, 456
Clark's Wharf, 34, 35, 36, 48, 72
'Clay Pounds' of Cape Cod, 345, 348–349, 350
Clemens, Anna, 477
Clemens, Isaac, 245, 283, 307, 477
Clergy, attitude toward American Revolution, 97
Clinton, Sir Henry, 241, 307
Cobbler's Court, 456
Cochran, Capt., 57, 68
Cochrane, Capt., 252
Cockerel,' 'The, 13, 17, 31, 385
Codman, John, 37–38
Collins, Ezra, 285, 469
Colonies, troops of, 45; divided, 45; attitude toward England, 60, 61–62; united in protest against Stamp Act, 101; reaction to Mass. circular letter on Townshend Acts, 133, 134; union temporarily broken, 187; reaction to Boston Port Bill, 216, 217, 224; reaction to prospect of revolution, 227, 228; support of Mass., 287, 288
*Columbian Centinel*, 438, 479